FUNDAMENTALS of

INTERNATIONAL BUSINESS

D0731273

FUNDAMENTALS of
INTERNATIONAL BUSINESS

SECOND EDITION

MICHAEL R. CZINKOTA
Georgetown University

ILKKA A. RONKAINEN
Georgetown University

MICHAEL H. MOFFETT
*The American Graduate School of
International Business (Thunderbird)*

BRONXVILLE, NEW YORK
http://www.wessex21c.com

Fundamentals of International Business
Michael R. Czinkota, Ilkka A. Ronkainen, Michael H. Moffett

Editor
Susan Petty

Copy Editor
Margaret Allyson

Designer
Anna Botelho

Cover Designer
Fusion 29

Permissions Editor
Linda Blundell

Indexer
Judith Gibbs

Production Assistant
David Crowell

Library of Congress Cataloging-in-Publication Data

Czinkota, Michael R., Ronkainen, Ilkka A., Moffett, Michael H.
  Fundamentals of international business / Michael R. Czinkota, Ilkka Ronkainen, Michael H. Moffett—2nd ed.
    p. cm.
ISBN 978-0-97973-442-7

Cataloging information is on file with the Library of Congress.

About WESSEX

Wessex publishes college- and graduate-level textbooks at significantly reduced prices compared to traditional publications. Wessex textbooks are also available for reading online at even lower prices. For information on *Fundamentals of International Business*, see **http://www.fib21c.com**. For information on *Managing Marketing in the 21st Century* and *The Virgin Marketer*, see **http://www.mm21c.com**.

Wessex also publishes trade books like *Managing Global Accounts*,
see **http://www.wessex21c.com**.

You can learn more about activities related to Wessex at **http://www.axcesscapon.com**.

AXCESS CAPON

About the typeface

This book was set in 10 point ITC Berkeley Oldstyle from Bitstream. ITC Berkeley Oldstyle was created by Frederic W. Goudy of Bloomington, Illinois. Frederic W. Goudy was a prolific American book and type designer active 1896–1946, and whose consciously archaic style is readily recognizable.

TO MY PERSONAL FUNDAMENTALS:
ILONA AND MARGARET
—MRC

TO MY FAMILY:
SANNA, SIRKKA, SUSAN,
ALEX, AND ALPO
—IAR

TO CAITLIN KELLY
AND SEAN MICHAEL
—MHM

PREFACE

Fundamentals of International Business is an introductory international business text for use at the undergraduate level. Its comprehensive coverage of the subject also makes it appropriate for use in MBA programs.

The book's content is streamlined when compared to the array of international business texts now available, but sufficiently rigorous and demanding to satisfy the professional integrity of the instructor.

The ever-growing cultural diversity of students attending U.S. colleges and universities has influenced the development of this text. These students bring a wide range of learning experiences and a richness of cultural backgrounds to the classroom. We are sensitive to these conditions and to the educational opportunities they present to instructors and reflect them in our approach to the field and to learning.

Coverage

Here is what makes this book special:

Individuals, business, and government are mutually interdependent. Therefore, we work hard to highlight the interrelationships and linkages among these three pillars of international business. In the chapters, the questions, and the vignettes, the reader will discern this nexus of personal needs, policy requirements, and business activities.

As there is more than one point of view regarding globalization, both the instructor and the student are provided with the insights and the materials to obtain an overview of the different perspectives and gain the ability to formulate their own personal views. We do so by providing not only the different arguments, but also by the facts and insights that allow for a scrutiny of these arguments.

As a result of our work with companies, we know that international business is the realm of small and medium-sized firms as well as large, multinational corporations. This text presents a balanced coverage of the subject matter, analyzing decision-making in the context of their corporate conditions. We have incorporated cutting-edge primary source research, such as the 2008 Georgetown Delphi Study, which provides students with invaluable insights into the worldview of contemporary real-life practitioners. Also addressed are important topics that are only marginally discussed in other international business texts, such as supply-chain management (logistics), countertrade, north—south economic integration, and the development of global management talent.

Conscience

We place major emphasis on international business in the context of the environment and sustainability. Both in the text itself as well as in the different vignettes of the chapters, we stimulate thinking about the way we affect the world and how the world affects us.

The roles of culture, policies, and politics, both domestic and international, are given in-depth exploration as well. The dimensions of ethics, social responsibility, diversity, and demographics are addressed through examples and vignettes. We appreciate the role, present and future, of corporate transparency, veracity, and vision. For example, the issues of grassroots consumer pressure and sweatshops is explored, highlighting the need for acceptable working conditions and internationally enforced standards, as well as the rise of a new type of socially-conscious, organized consumer base.

Commitment

Our work in international business has also taught us that commitment and trust are key to global success. We are firmly committed to our work and personally stand fully behind it. If you have questions or concerns about this book, feedback of praise or complaint, please contact us at any time. Here is our contact information:

Prof. Michael R. Czinkota	**czinkotm@georgetown.edu**
Prof. Ilkka A. Ronkainen	**ronkaii@georgetown.edu**
Prof. Michael H. Moffett	**moffettm@t-bird.edu**

USE OF WORLD WIDE EXAMPLES The global orientation of this book is reinforced by drawing on worldwide examples, trends, and data, rather than relying only on U.S.-based information. The reality and pragmatism of our content is ensured by always addressing the issue of "What does all this mean for firms in terms of implementing international business activities?"

Organization

Fundamentals of International Business contains 14 streamlined chapters, which translates into approximately one chapter per week for the traditional 15-week semester. Five parts of two to four chapters each organize the text to flow logically from introductory material, to the global environment, to marketing and financial considerations in the global marketplace.

Part One provides an overview of the key issues facing international business today and touches on how these topics will be dealt with in the text.

Part Two focuses on the similarities and differences between cultures, and how global politics both influences and is influenced by cultural factors.

Part Three shifts to the theoretical foundations surrounding global trade and investments, explaining the environment in which these occur.

Part Four explores the international monetary system, including the discussion of global financial management.

Part Five is devoted to global operations, investigating strategic management issues.

Part Six describes the future of global business and the future for students of the field.

Distinguishing Pedagogical Features

A number of unique features in this text make substantial contributions to the learning process. These features deliver hands-on learning that captures student interest and leads to practical knowledge.

- **Integrated Learning System:** This text uses the integrated learning system to structure the text and the teaching supplements around learning objectives. The numbered objectives are identified in the chapter introduction, and each is precisely addressed in the summary section at the end of the chapter. Numbered icons within the chapter margins mark where each objective is covered within the text.

The integrated learning system also makes lecture and test preparation easier. All of the text's major supplements are organized around the learning objectives, helping students and instructors focus on the key points of each chapter.

- **Opening Vignette:** An opening vignette sets the stage for the chapter, including one or two questions for students to consider and debate as they read the chapter.

- **World View:** This box offers concrete examples of the issues confronting global business decision-makers in the classroom.

- **Quick Take:** A "Quick Take" vignette is a real-world example to provide context for concepts presented in the text.

- **Culture Clues:** Interspersed throughout the text are "Culture Clues" that provide practical tips and insights to different cultures.

Culture Clues

- **Fast Facts:** Throughout the text, these facts are presented in a Q and A format. They focus mainly on geography-oriented topics and are meant to provide immediate feedback to the student about the absorption of the text material at hand.

Fast Facts

- **Marginal Glossary:** An extensive marginal glossary makes it easier for students to define and understand key terms. An end-of-the-book glossary contains all key terms and definitions in a convenient alphabetical form.

SOCIAL STRATIFICATION

The division of a particular population into classes.

- **Maps:** To increase the geographic literacy of students, the text contains excellent maps that provide the instructor with the means to demonstrate concepts visually, such as political blocs, socioeconomic variables, and transportation routes. The maps are integrated throughout the text.

- **Chapter Summary, Review Questions, and Critical Skill Builders:** Each chapter closes with a summary of key points that students should retain, organized by learning objective. The review questions and critical skill builder questions are complementary learning tools that will enable students to check their understanding of key issues, to think beyond basic concepts, and to determine areas that require further study. All these tools help students discriminate between main and supporting points and provide mechanisms for self-teaching.

- **On the Web:** Each chapter contains two to three Internet exercises to involve students in the high-tech world of cyberspace. Students are asked to explore the web for research into topics related to each chapter. This hands-on experience helps to develop Internet, research, and business skills.

- **Brief Format:** This text focuses on the essentials to provide a practical and inexpensive alternative to the standard texts on the market.

- **Up-to-Date Research:** Extra effort has been made to provide extensive current research information. The endnote resources enable the instructor and the student to incorporate additional information where it is useful and desirable.

- **In-Depth Tables and Figures:** Many of the tables and figures have been specifically designed and developed to enhance student understanding of the text material.

- **Critical Presentation and Explanation:** The complex nature of topics and theories in international business are presented with their pros and cons. The goal is to allow students an in-depth exploration of the struggles among various theories, policies, strategies, and structures.

Supplementary Material

Instructor's Manual with Test Bank: Designed to provide support for instructors new to the course, as well as innovative materials for experienced professors, the Instructor's Manual includes suggested course outlines, chapter objectives, annotated learning objectives, suggestions for teaching, and further questions for discussion. Additionally, the Instructor's Manual includes answers and teaching notes to end-of-chapter materials. The Test Bank includes true/false, multiple choice, and short-answer questions.

PowerPoint Lecture Presentation: Also available on the web site, the PowerPoint Lecture Presentation enables instructors to customize their own multimedia classroom presentation. Containing approximately 200 slides, the package includes figures and tables from the text, as well as outside material to supplement chapter concepts. Material is organized by chapter, and can be modified or expanded for individual classroom use. PowerPoints are also easily printed to create customized transparency masters.

Web site (*http://www.fib21c.com*): The web site is a comprehensive resource-rich location for both instructors and students to find pertinent information. It includes the On the Web feature as well as additional resources. The Instructor Resources contain a download of the Instructor's Manual and Test Bank, and PowerPoint Lecture Presentation.

Student Study Guide: The purpose of the Student Study Guide is to provide students with a quick and easy way to access the main points in each chapter. The guide is available on the web site (*http://www.fib21c.com*). Students can download and print each chapter for a small fee.

Acknowledgments

We are grateful to many reviewers for their imaginative comments and criticisms and for showing us how to get it even more right:

Larry Colfer
Drexel University

Dharma DeSilva
Wichita State University

Robert Edwards
County College of Morris

Philip Kearney
Niagara Community College

Steve Kober
Pierce College

Anthony Koh
University of Toledo

Behnam Nakhai
Millersville University

Scott Norwood
San Jose State University

Brian Peach
University of West Florida

Harold Purdue
Urbana University

Pollis Robertson
Kellogg Community College

Cory Simek
Webster University

Nini Yang
San Francisco State University

A key role was played by Dafina Nikolova Doran, PhD Candidate at Georgetown University, who served as editorial and research contributor.

Foremost, we are grateful to our families, who have had to tolerate late-night computer noises, weekend library absences, and curtailed vacations. The support and love of Ilona Vigh-Czinkota and Margaret Victoria Czinkota, Susan, Sanna, and Alex Ronkainen, Megan

Murphy, Caitlin Kelly, and Sean Michael Moffett gave us the energy, stamina, and inspiration to write this book.

Michael R. Czinkota
Ilkka A. Ronkainen
Michael H. Moffett
June 2008

ABOUT THE AUTHORS

Michael R. Czinkota teaches international marketing and business at the Graduate School and the Robert Emmett McDonough School of Business at Georgetown University, USA, and at the University of Birmingham in the United Kingdom. He has held professorial appointments at universities in Asia, Australia, Europe, South Africa, and the Americas.

Dr. Czinkota served in the U.S. government as Deputy Assistant Secretary of Commerce. He also served as head of the U.S. Delegation to the OECD Industry Committee in Paris and as senior advisor for Export Controls.

Dr. Czinkota's background includes eight years of private-sector business experience as a partner in a fur-trading firm and in an advertising agency. His research has been supported by the U.S. government, the National Science Foundation, the Organization of American States, and the American Management Association. He was listed as one of the three most published contributors to international business research in the *Journal of International Business Studies*, and has written several books, including *Best Practices in International Marketing* and *Mastering Global Markets*.

Dr. Czinkota served on the Global Advisory Board of the American Marketing Association, the Global Council of the American Management Association, and the Board of Governors of the Academy of Marketing Science. He is on the editorial board of *Journal of the Academy of Marketing Science*, *Journal of International Marketing*, and *Asian Journal of Marketing*. For his work in international business and trade policy, he received the Lifetime Research Achievement Award in International Marketing from the American Marketing Association. He was named a Distinguished Fellow of the Academy of Marketing Science, a Fellow of the Chartered Institute of Marketing, and a Fellow of the Royal Society of Arts in the United Kingdom. He has been awarded honorary degrees from the Universidad Pontifica Madre y Maestra in the Dominican Republic and the Universidad del Pacifico in Lima, Peru.

Dr. Czinkota serves on several corporate boards and has worked with corporations, such as AT&T, IBM, GE, Nestlé, and US WEST. He advises the Executive Office of the President of the United States, the United Nations, and the World Trade Organization. Dr. Czinkota is often asked to testify before the United States Congress.

Dr. Czinkota was born and raised in Germany and educated in Austria, Scotland, Spain, and the United States. He studied law and business administration at the University of Erlangen-Nürnberg and was awarded a two-year Fulbright Scholarship. He holds an MBA in international business and a PhD in logistics from The Ohio State University.

Ilkka A. Ronkainen is a member of the faculty of marketing and international business at the McDonough School of Business at Georgetown University. He also serves as a docent of international marketing at the Helsinki School of Economics. He teaches in both schools' undergraduate, graduate, and executive programs. He is the founder and program director of Georgetown's summer program in Hong Kong.

Dr. Ronkainen holds a PhD and MBA from the University of South Carolina as well as an MS (Economics) degree from the Helsinki School of Economics. He has received the award in undergraduate teaching excellence twice and the International Executive MBA best teacher award twice at Georgetown University.

Ilkka Ronkainen has published extensively in both academic journals and the trade press. He is co-author of *International Marketing* (8ᵗʰ edition) and *International Business* (7ᵗʰ edition). His trade books include *The International Marketing Imperative* and *Mastering Global Markets*. He serves on the editorial review boards of *Journal of Business Research*, *International Marketing Review*, and *Multinational Business Review*. He has served as the North American coordinator for the European Marketing Academy and as a board member of the Washington International Trade Association during which time he started the association's newsletter, *Trade Trends*.

Dr. Ronkainen serves as a consultant to a wide variety of U.S. and international institutions. He has worked with entities such as IBM, the Rank Organization, and the Organization of American States. He maintains close relations with a number of Finnish companies in support of their internationalization and educational efforts.

Michael H. Moffett is the Continental Grain Professor of Finance at the Thunderbird School of Global Management in Glendale, Arizona (USA). Formerly Associate Professor of Finance at Oregon State University (USA), he has held teaching or research appointments at the University of Michigan, Ann Arbor (USA), the Brookings Institution, Washington, D.C. (USA), the University of Hawaii at Manoa, the Aarhus School of Business (Denmark), the Helsinki School of Economics and Business Administration (Finland), the International Centre for Public Enterprises (Yugoslavia), and the University of Colorado, Boulder (USA).

Professor Moffett's primary areas of teaching and research expertise are in multinational financial management, focusing on the multitude of strategic and organizational decisions directly related to the commitment and management of cash flow and investment capital in creating and managing value formation. Professor Moffett received a BA (Economics) from the University of Texas at Austin (1977), an MS (Resource Economics) from Colorado State University (1979), an MA (Economics) from the University of Colorado, Boulder (1983), and PhD (Economics) from the University of Colorado, Boulder (1985).

Dr. Moffett has authored, co-authored, or contributed to a multitude of journal articles, books and other publications. He is co-author of several books in multinational business and finance, as well as the author of more than 50 case studies in international business, strategy, and financial management. Professor Moffett has acted as a consultant and educator for many global businesses.

BRIEF CONTENTS

CONTENTS

PART 1

GLOBALIZATION

While the globalization of business opens new opportunities for governments, firms, and individuals, it also brings challenges. Part 1 describes a global business and political environment in constant flux and explains the benefits as well as the criticisms of the move toward globalization. By exploring factors such as intense competition, production on a global scale, and rapid dissemination of technology, Part 1 demonstrates the need for firms to participate in international business if they are to survive and grow.

CHAPTER 1

It's Not Just Money Anymore

The sole purpose of international business used to be the maximization of profit, but today's executives have new questions to answer: Who pays the environmental and social costs of bringing a product to the global marketplace? When loggers take more timber than nature replaces, or fishermen deplete a fishery, it's society that foots the bill. The prices resulting from clear-cutting and overfishing do not take into account the societal costs of losing a forest or the catch of fish for future generations. Who protects farmers whose sales and incomes are at the mercy of big customers such as Wal-Mart or Tesco?

Increasingly, product labeling and branding are proving an effective means of bringing the environmental and social costs of a product's production into the marketplace. Product labels inform consumers about the environmental background of a product and often include the processes and production methods used. The Forest Stewardship Council's "FSC" label, the Marine Stewardship Council's "MSC" label, and Fair Trade label have proven particularly successful.

The idea of a sustainable fish label started in 1997, when Unilever, the world's largest buyer of seafood, and the World Wide Fund for Nature formed the MSC. Unilever made this move after realizing that the future of its fish-finger and cod-fillet businesses relied on a sustainable source of white fish. Today there are 1,123 products around the world with an MSC label. New commitments to MSC from Sainsbury's, Tesco, and Wal-Mart show that the demand for sustainably sourced fish is growing fast.

Though environmental labels are becoming more popular with manufactured goods, retailers have been reluctant to brand products as "green" because of lackluster sales. Though products might not sell as quickly as retailers would like, environmental leaders suggest that their presence on the shelves will teach millions of shoppers about the impact of a wide variety of products. Labels are not the solution to every negative environmental externality, in the absence of established governance, but good labels do provide an incentive for change.

SOURCES: "Ecological labelling takes off," *The Economist*, January 28, 2008, **www.economist.com**, accessed February 14, 2008; "Ecological Labelling," *Natural Capital*, August 8, 2006, **www.envecon.wordpress.com**, accessed February 14, 2008; Michael Barbaro, "Home Depot to Display an Environmental Label," *The New York Times*, April 17, 2007.

LEARNING OBJECTIVES

1. To learn the definition of international business

2. To recognize today's global linkages that drive nations and firms to operate across borders

3. To understand the U.S. position in world trade and the impact international business has on the nation

4. To appreciate the opportunities and challenges offered by international business

5. To consider the effects of global concerns about uncertainty, risk, and terrorism on international business

As You Read This Chapter

1. Think of the ways in which globalization creates links between nations. How beneficial are such linkages?
2. Considering the criticisms of globalization, is it possible for nations to now turn their backs on its principles?

WELCOME TO THE WORLD OF GLOBAL BUSINESS

You are about to set out on an exciting journey in which you will explore the world through new eyes: from the unique perspective of international business. While you will learn much about why and how businesses operate on a global scale, you will also encounter many other disciplines, including economics, politics, geography, history, language, anthropology, demography, jurisprudence, and statistics. You will discover why it is imperative for nations to participate in the global marketplace, for failure to do so leads inexorably to declining economic influence and deteriorating standards of living. **Globalization**—defined as awareness, understanding, and response to global developments and linkages—holds the promise of improved quality of life and a better society, even leading, some believe, to a more peaceful world.

On an individual level, as a student of international business, you are likely to work at some point in your career either for a multinational organization or a smaller firm that engages in international activities. Manufacturing and service companies across the entire spectrum of industry are going global. In an era of open borders, global supply chains, and burgeoning technology that enables instant communication and virtually free ways of reaching millions of people, there emerges an unprecedented opportunity for individuals to enter the international business arena. It has become easier for start-up firms to challenge even giant competitors.

As hundreds of examples in this book will reveal, speed, flexibility, creativity, and innovation—all enabled by advances in technology—are as important to international success as size. Understanding international business is a crucial part of career development, not just for future business managers but for budding entrepreneurs as well.

International business offers companies new markets. For the last five decades, international trade and investment have grown at a faster rate than domestic economies. Today and in the future, only a combination of domestic and international activities will allow for expansion, growth, and increased income. International business enables the flow of ideas, services, and capital across the world. The result is higher levels of innovation, faster dissemination of goods and information worldwide, more efficient use of human capital, and improved access to financing. International business facilitates the mobility of factors of production—except land—and provides challenging employment opportunities.[1]

International business benefits consumers by offering new choices. Consumers not only have a wider variety of goods to choose from, but international competition leads to improved quality and reduced prices. The car you drive is likely made by Germany's Daimler or by one of several Japanese automakers. The Amoco station where you fill up with gas belongs to British oil company BP, while Shell is a Dutch company. Burger King and Seagram's Seven Crown are owned by Britain's beverage giant Diageo, while Snapple and 7 UP belong to Cadbury Schweppes, another British company. Retail chains Brooks Brothers and Casual Corner are part of an Italian conglomerate. Universal Studios is a subsidiary of the French media company, Vivendi, which is also a major operator of pay-per-view television in the United States. Even the quintessential American coffee, Taster's Choice, is owned by Nestlé SA of Switzerland.[2]

International business is not without its challenges. Since it opens up markets to competition, it can—just like Janus, the two-faced Roman god—deliver benefits and opportunity to some, while causing others to falter. Because of its ability to impact citizens, firms, and economies negatively as well as positively, international business and the ways in which it is conducted are of vital concern to countries, companies, and individuals.

GLOBALIZATION

Awareness, understanding, and response to global developments and linkages.

WHAT IS GLOBAL BUSINESS?

IMPORT-EXPORT TRADE

The sale and purchase of tangible goods and services to and from another country.

FOREIGN DIRECT INVESTMENT (FDI)

The establishment or expansion of operations of a firm in a foreign country. Like all investments, it assumes a transfer of capital.

Global business consists of transactions that are devised and carried out across national borders to satisfy the objectives of individuals, companies, and organizations. These transactions take on various forms, which are often interrelated. Primary types of international business are **import-export trade** and **foreign direct investment (FDI)**. The latter is carried out in varied forms, including wholly owned subsidiaries and joint ventures. Additional types of international business are licensing, franchising, and management contracts.

As the definition indicates, and as for any kind of domestic business, "satisfaction" remains a key tenet of global business. Beyond this, because transactions are across national borders, participating firms are subject to a new set of macroenvironmental factors, to different constraints, and to quite frequent conflicts resulting from different laws, cultures, and societies. The basic principles of business still apply, but their application, complexity, and intensity

Quick Take *Controlling the Dark Side of Globalization*

Labor abuse is one of the most public drawbacks of globalization. Over the past 15 years, the U.S. media has publicized numerous stories of unhealthy working conditions, 20-hour shifts, and minimal pay. From Nike in Vietnam to Kathy Lee Gifford in Honduras, plenty of companies have found themselves in the midst of sweatshop scandals.

What is a conscientious consumer to do? Students at campuses around the U.S. have banded together in the search for a solution. What began as largely disjointed protests, letter-writing campaigns, and various other forms of student activism centered around individual cases has gradually evolved into a coordinated large-scale effort called United Students Against Sweatshops. It is active at about 50 to 60 campuses around the country. The organization has successfully advocated a "designated suppliers program" that requires companies producing the apparel sold on campuses to establish long-term relationships with garment factories so workers can be guaranteed a "living wage." The consolidated power of student consumers is ensuring manufacturing accountability on a national scale. Industry leaders have responded with the Fair Labor Association

(FLA)—a nonprofit organization dedicated to ending sweatshop conditions in factories worldwide and eradicating abusive labor conditions. The power of unified consumer action is not to be underestimated.

So putting an end to labor abuses around the world is good, right? "Wrong" says Harvard economist Jeffrey Sachs. He is not concerned that there are too many sweatshops, but that there are too few. Sachs' opinion is based on the theory of comparative advantage, which states that international trade will, in the long run, make most parties better off. According to this theory, poor countries can develop by doing something that they do "better" than rich countries (in this case, provide cheap labor). Eventually, as the developing country becomes wealthier, its people come to enjoy higher living standards. Does that mean that the "dark" side of globalization is a blessing in disguise?

SOURCE: Allen Meyerson, "In Principle, A Case for More Sweatshops," *The New York Times*, June 22, 1997; [**http://en.wikipedia.org/wiki/Sweatshop#accessed 5/31/2007**].

vary substantially. To operate outside national borders, firms must be ready to incorporate international considerations into their thinking and planning, making decisions related to questions such as these:

- How will our idea, good, or service fit into the international market?
- Should we enter the market through trade or through investment?
- Should I obtain my supplies domestically or from abroad?
- What product adjustments are necessary to be responsive to local conditions?
- What threats from global competition should be expected, and how can these threats be counteracted?

When management integrates these issues into each decision, international markets can provide growth, profit, and needs satisfaction not available to those that limit their activities to the domestic marketplace. The aim of this book is to prepare you, as a student of international business, to participate in this often-complex decision process.

GLOBAL LINKS TODAY

Today, world trade and investment are central to the well-being of the global community. In centuries past, trade was conducted internationally, but not at the level or with the impact on nations, firms, and individuals that it has recently achieved. In the past 30 years alone, the volume of international trade in goods and services has expanded from $200 billion to more than $14 trillion.[3] As Figure 1.1 shows, the growth in the value of trade has greatly exceeded the level of overall world output. During the same period, foreign direct investment (FDI) mushroomed to more than $10.1 trillion. The sales of foreign affiliates of **multinational corporations** are now twice as high as global exports.[4]

MULTINATIONAL CORPORATIONS

Companies that invest in countries around the globe.

The sheer volume and value of international trade has led to the forging of a network of global links around the world that binds us all—countries, institutions, and individuals— much closer than ever before. These links tie together trade, financial markets, technology, and living standards in unprecedented ways. The collapse of Argentina's currency following its divorce from the U.S. dollar resonated throughout South America and affected trade in the United States, Europe, and the Far East. The economic turmoil in Asia influenced stock markets, investments, and trade flows around the world. A 2007 announcement by the U.S. Federal Reserve, lowering a key interest rate, reverberated throughout the world stock markets, pushing the Japanese NIKKEI into bear-market territory (defined as a fall of 20 percent from its high). Terrorist attacks and the resulting wars in Afghanistan and Iraq affected stock markets, investments, and trade flows in all corners of the globe. Corrupt accounting practices by U.S.-based multinationals sent world stock markets into shock.[5]

Global linkages have also become more intense on an individual level. Communication has built new international bridges, be it through music or through international programming transmitted by CNN or MTV. New products have attained international appeal and encouraged similar activities around the world: We carry colorful cell phones; we dance the same dances; we eat hamburgers and drink double lattes. Transportation links and Internet access allow individuals from different countries to meet or otherwise interact with unprecedented ease.

Culture Clues   When attending your first meeting with a prospective business partner in Russia, especially one with whom you hope to establish a long-term relationship, it is perfectly acceptable and even expected to bring a gift, such as a nice bottle of wine or other alcohol (try to select something other than vodka, which is widely available).

FIGURE 1.1   Growth of World Output and Trade, 1992–2006

Annual percentage change

[Bar chart showing Annual percentage change from 1992 to 2006, comparing Trade Volume and Output]

Legend:
■ Trade Volume
■ Output

SOURCE: IMF, *World Economic Outlook*, September 2006

Large firms are expanding around the globe. They may become so well entrenched that they are thought of as local firms.

Common cultural pressures result in similar social phenomena and behavior—for example, more dual-income families are emerging around the world, which leads to higher levels of spending.

International business has also brought a global reorientation in production strategies. Only a few decades ago, for example, it would have been thought impossible to produce parts for a car in more than one country, assemble it in another, and sell it in yet other countries around the world. Today, such global strategies, coupled with production and distribution sharing, are common. Consumers, union leaders, policymakers, and sometimes even the firms themselves are finding it increasingly difficult to define where a particular product was made, since subcomponents may come from many different nations. Firms are also linked to each other through global supply agreements and joint undertakings in research and development.

Figure 1.2 gives an example of how such links result in a final consumer product.

Firms and governments are recognizing production's worldwide effects on the environment common to all. For example, high sulfur emissions in one area may cause acid rain in another. Pollution in one country may result in water contamination in another.

It is not just the production of goods that has become global. Increasingly, service firms are part of the global scene. Consulting firms, insurance companies, software firms, and universities are participating to a growing degree in the international marketplace.

Service activities can have cross-national impacts as well. For example, weaknesses in some currencies, due to problems in a country's banking sector, can quickly spill over and affect the

FIGURE 1.2 Global Components of a Bic Mac®

THE GLOBAL COMPONENTS OF A BIG MAC® IN UKRAINE

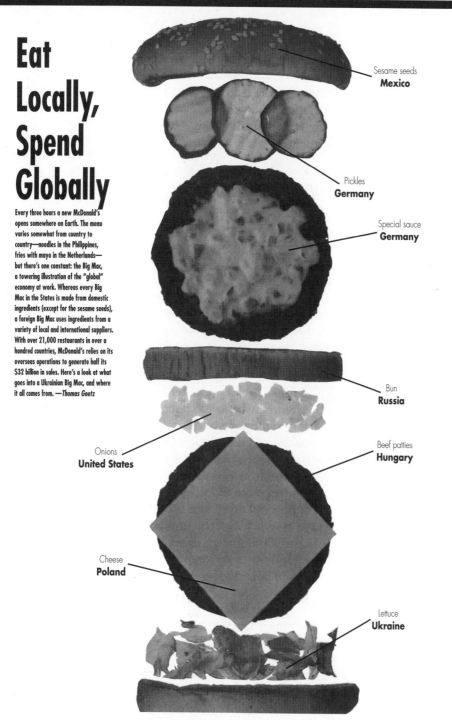

Eat Locally, Spend Globally

Every three hours a new McDonald's opens somewhere on Earth. The menu varies somewhat from country to country—noodles in the Philippines, fries with mayo in the Netherlands—but there's one constant: the Big Mac, a towering illustration of the "global" economy at work. Whereas every Big Mac in the States is made from domestic ingredients (except for the sesame seeds), a foreign Big Mac uses ingredients from a variety of local and international suppliers. With over 21,000 restaurants in over a hundred countries, McDonald's relies on its overseas operations to generate half its $32 billion in sales. Here's a look at what goes into a Ukrainian Big Mac, and where it all comes from. —*Thomas Goetz*

Sesame seeds
Mexico

Pickles
Germany

Special sauce
Germany

Bun
Russia

Onions
United States

Beef patties
Hungary

Cheese
Poland

Lettuce
Ukraine

Source: Used with permission from McDonald's Corporation.

COMPOSITION OF TRADE

The ratio of primary commodities to manufactured goods and services in a country's trade.

currency values of other nations. The deregulation of some service industries, such as air transport or telephony, can have a ripple effect on the structure of these industries around the world.

All these changes have affected the international financial position of countries and the ownership of economic activities. For example, the United States, after having been a net creditor to the world for many decades, has been a world debtor since 1985. This means that the nation owes more to foreign institutions and individuals than to U.S. entities. The shifts in financial flows have had major effects on international direct investment into plants as well. U.S. direct investment abroad in 2006 had a market value of more than $4.37 billion; foreign direct investment in the United States had grown to $3.22 billion.[6] The U.S. holds the world's largest individual gold reserves (8,134 tons, as of December 2007).[7] In today's era of multinational corporations, countless people around the world toil for foreign bosses. All of these developments make nations more dependent on one another than ever before.

This interdependence, however, is not static. On an ongoing basis, realignments take place on both micro and macro levels that make past orientations at least partially obsolete. For example, for its first 200 years, the United States looked to Europe for markets and sources of supply. But today, the picture has shifted: In 2007, merchandise trade across the Pacific totaled $930 billion, $236 billion more than trade across the Atlantic.[8] Furthermore, the relative participation of countries in world trade is shifting. The market share of Western Europe in trade, for example, has been on the decline. Concurrent with this shift, the global market shares of Japan, Southeast Asian countries, and China have increased dramatically.

The **composition of trade** has also been changing. For example, from the 1960s to the 1990s, the trade role of primary commodities has declined precipitously while the importance of manufactured goods has increased. This has meant that those countries and workers who had specialized in commodities such as caoutchouc (rubber plantations) or mining were likely to fall behind those who had embarked on strengthening their manufacturing sector. With sharply declining world market prices for their commodities and rising prices for manufactured goods, commodity producers were increasingly unable to catch up. More recently, there has been a shift from manufacturing to services—perhaps presaging a similar shift of trade composition for the future.

Not only are the environment and composition of trade changing, but the pace of that change is accelerating. Atari's Pong was first introduced in the early 1980s; today, action games and movies are amazingly sophisticated. The first office computers emerged in the mid-1980s; today, home computers have become commonplace. E-mail was introduced to a mass market only in the 1990s; today, many college students hardly ever send personal notes using a stamp and an envelope.[9]

As we shall see in coming chapters, all these changes and the speed with which they come about significantly affect countries, companies, and individuals, altering almost every aspect of the global marketplace.

U.S. INTERNATIONAL TRADE POSITION

3 LEARNING OBJECTIVE

From a global perspective, the United States has gained in prominence as a market for the world but has lost some of its importance as a supplier. In spite of the decline in the global market share of U.S. exports, the nation's international activities have not been reduced. On the contrary, exports have grown rapidly and successfully. However, many new participants have entered the international market. Competitors from both Europe and Asia have aggressively won a share of the growing world trade, with the result that U.S. export growth has not kept pace with total growth of world exports.

WORLD VIEW

LENDERS TARGET WOMEN IN THE DEVELOPING WORLD

The women of the developing world are gaining a measure of economic autonomy as perceptions of their role in emerging economies change. Recently, international organizations and banks have moved to increase funding to women-led small businesses and farming projects. The motivation to target women has less to do with sexual politics than with the economic reality that women do much of the work in developing countries. A recent World Bank study found that women head half the households in sub-Saharan Africa, while women in the villages of Cameroon work twice as many hours per week as men. Their earnings are more likely than men's to be used for the health and education of the next generation. Women are more likely to repay loans, as well, and are less prone to waste development money.

In the developing world's vast "informal sector," many so-called microenterprises, ranging from street vendors to one-person apparel makers, are run by women. Though statistics are shaky, informal-sector businesses make up as much as half of all economic activity in many developing countries.

Microcredit to poor borrowers works because repaying loans fosters enterprise rather than dependency. The schemes also are self-sustaining. According to the World Bank, the number of people borrowing from an estimated 7,000 microfinance institutions has grown to 16 million—a more than fourfold increase since 1999.

Because of the high repayment rate, microfinance has become profitable. The largest microlenders no longer need subsidies or even commercial loans from international financial institutions or philanthropists. ProCredit, representing 19 microfinance banks in countries from Moldova to Ecuador, was established in 1998. It now boasts over 2.2 million customer accounts and arrears by volume of a minuscule 1.2 percent.

In Niger, CARE is helping establish women's savings groups in about 45 villages. Around 35 women contribute 50 cents per week. Two-week loans are made, with an interest rate of approximately 10 percent. Periodically the women liquidate their banks and distribute the money for certain needs. But the banks always start up again. Once they have had a bank, the women don't want to go without one.

Microlenders in rural areas encourage poor women in villages to cross-guarantee each others' loans, with the resulting peer pressure keeping default rates to a minimum.

In Bangladesh, the Grameen Bank grants a loan to only one member of a group of borrowers at a time; the next borrower is granted a loan only when the outstanding loan is repaid. In urban areas, a stepped lending scheme is more effective at keeping default rates low. In these schemes, the borrower puts up a little money and the microlender lends her about the same amount. A larger loan can then be granted if she repays the original loan promptly, providing an incentive.

SOURCE: "Africa's Women Go to Work," *The Economist,* January 13, 2001, pp. 43–44; Tim Carrington, "Gender Economics: In Developing World, International Lenders Are Targeting Women," *The Wall Street Journal,* June 22, 1994, A1; *The Economist,* "Time to Take the Credit," March 15, 2007.

U.S. exports, as a share of the **gross domestic product (GDP)**, have grown substantially in recent years. However, this increase pales in comparison to the international trade performance of other nations. Since 1999, about 8 percent of Germany's real GDP growth was generated from net exports, with real exports growing by more than 7 percent annually since 2000.[10] Japan, in turn, which so often is maligned as the export problem child in the international trade arena, exports less than 10 percent of its GDP.[11] Table 1.1 on page 10 shows the degree to which the U.S. comparatively "underparticipates" in international business on a per capita basis, particularly on the export side.

GROSS DOMESTIC PRODUCT (GDP)

Total monetary value of goods produced and services provided by a country over a one-year period.

Culture Clues   When going to a business meeting in India, bring family photos. Indians enjoy talking about each other's families, which is seen as building trust and rapport before doing business.

TABLE 1.1 Exports and Imports per Capita for Selected Countries (US$) (2008)

COUNTRY	EXPORTS PER CAPITA	IMPORTS PER CAPITA
Canada	$13,251	$11,875
China	920	690
Germany	16,520	13,610
India	120	200
Japan	5,230	4,490
Mexico	2,436	2,536
United Kingdom	6,810	8,771
United States	3,750	6,536

SOURCES: CIA, *The World Factbook*, 2008

Global Business Imperative

MACROECONOMIC LEVEL

Level at which trading relationships affect individual markets.

MICROECONOMIC LEVEL

Level of business concerns that affect an individual firm or industry.

Why should we worry about this underparticipation in trade? Why not simply concentrate on the large domestic market and get on with it? Why should it bother us that the largest portion of U.S. exports is attributed to only 2,500 companies?[12]

U.S. international business outflows are important on the **macroeconomic level** in terms of balancing the trade account. Lack of export growth has resulted in long-term trade deficits. In 1983, imports of products exceeded exports by more than $70 billion. While in ensuing years exports increased at a rapid rate, import growth also continued. As a result, in 2007, the U.S. merchandise trade deficit was estimated to be at $458 billion.[13] Ongoing annual trade deficits in this range are not sustainable in the long run. Such deficits add to the U.S. international debt, which must be serviced and eventually repaid.[14] Exporting is not only good for the international trade picture but also a key factor in increasing employment. It has been estimated that $1 billion of exports supports the creation, on average, of 11,500 jobs.[15] Imports, in turn, bring a wider variety of products and services into a country. They exert competitive pressure for domestic firms to improve. Imports, therefore, expand the choices of consumers and improve their standard of living.

On the **microeconomic level**, participation in international business allows firms to achieve economies of scale that cannot be achieved in domestic markets. Addressing a global market greatly adds to the number of potential customers. Increasing production lets firms climb the learning curve more quickly and therefore makes goods available more cheaply at home. Finally, and perhaps most importantly, international business permits firms to hone their competitive skills abroad by meeting the challenge of foreign products. By going abroad, firms can learn from their foreign competitors, challenge them on their ground, and translate the absorbed knowledge into productivity improvements back home. Research has shown that U.S. multinationals of all sizes and in all industries outperformed their strictly domestic counterparts—growing more than twice as fast in sales and earning significantly higher returns on equity and assets. Workers also benefit, since exporting firms of all sizes typically pay significantly higher wages than nonexporters. As Table 1.2 on page 11 shows, all five of the top ten most admired corporations worldwide are substantial exporters and international investors.

While there are distinct benefits of going global, there are also clear risks for those firms that opt not to do so. Firms that operate only in the domestic market can no longer ignore the onslaught of foreign competition that diminishes their domestic market share. Firms in the

Quick Take   *Price Wars in China*

December 11, 2001, marked China's entry into the World Trade Organization. The country's sheer size (20 percent of the world's population) and spectacular economic growth of over 10 percent per year, have made it an economic force to be reckoned with. In 2006, China had the largest current account surplus in the world—nearly $180 billion. Those who hoped that the People's Republic's entry into the WTO would pave the way for harmonious relations with the United States and the European Union might be disappointed. China has been involved in highly publicized clashes with both the EU and US on many issues, ranging from intellectual property rights to wheat gluten. An interesting attitude marker can be derived through the public statements, made by Chinese public officials in these conflict situations. For example, at the December 11, 2007, broad bilateral trade talks between the United States and China, the Chinese Vice Premier Wu Yu addressed the string of scandals with hazardous imports from her country (ranging from harmful lead paint on children's toys to poisonous wheat gluten), by accusing the US of protectionism.

"There have been some disharmonious notes in China-US relations this year. The inclination to politicize (trade) issues has increased. . . . The U.S. media hyped the quality of Chinese exports, causing serious damage to China's national image," she said. It would appear that China will continue to pursue its economic agenda within the confines of WTO institutional rules, accusing rivals of protectionism, when it feels that its interest is threatened.

SOURCES: "US and China in Clash Over Trade," BBC News, "U.S. and China in Clash over Trade, December 11, 2007 [**http://news.bbc.co.uk/2/hi/business/7136915.stm**]; Matt Moore, "Meeting Aims to Boost EU-China Business," *Washington Post*, November 5, 2007.

technology sector, for instance, have seen the prices of their products and their sales volumes drop sharply because of global competition. The steel, automotive, and textile sectors of the global economy experience fierce pressure from abroad. Farmers, too, because of increased

TABLE 1.2 Global Most-Admired Companies

2008 RANK	COMPANY
1	Apple
2	General Electric
3	Toyota Motor
4	Berkshire Hathaway
5	Procter & Gamble
6	FedEx
7	Johnson & Johnson
8	Target
9	BMW
10	Microsoft

Source: **http://money.cnn.com/magazines/fortune/globalmostadmired/2008/top50/index.html**

International Trade as a Percentage of Gross Domestic Product

Total Gross Domestic Product by Region
(in millions of US $)

United States
$13,163,870

Europe Area
$10,636,418

Japan
$4,368,435

China and India
$3,556,494

Latin America and Caribbean
$2,964,189

East Asia & Pacific
$3,616,708

Eastern Europe and Central Asia
$2,499,359

Middle East and North Africa
$734,423

Canada
$1,271,593

Sub-Saharan Africa
$712,731

South Asia
$1,146,716

SOURCE: *2006 World Development Indicators*, The World Bank.

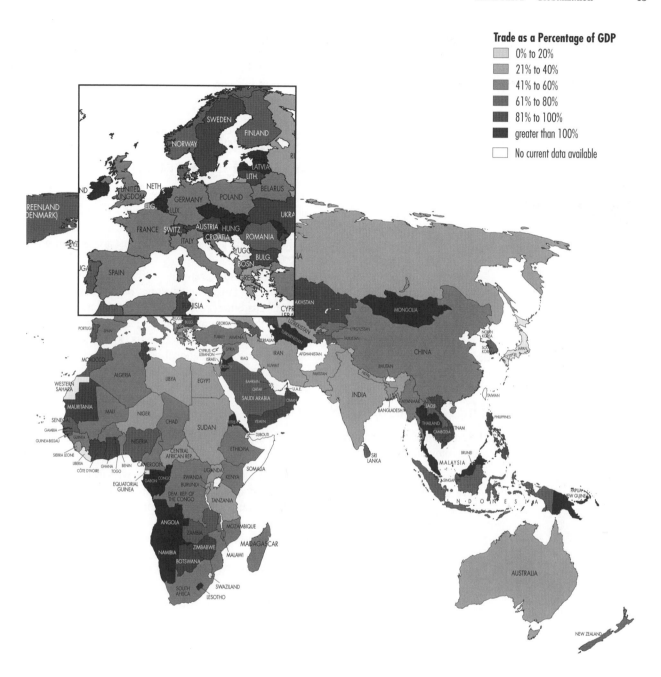

Trade as a Percentage of GDP
- 0% to 20%
- 21% to 40%
- 41% to 60%
- 61% to 80%
- 81% to 100%
- greater than 100%
- No current data available

competition, trade restricting government actions, and unfair foreign trade practices, have been under siege.

These developments demonstrate that it has become virtually impossible to disregard the impact of international business. You can run, but you cannot hide, for participation in the world market has become an unavoidable imperative.

INTERNATIONAL BUSINESS IN A NEW ERA OF RISK AND UNCERTAINTY[16]

5   LEARNING OBJECTIVE

The terrorist attacks of September 11, 2001, against the United States created a fissure in American life. The nation's sense of stability, feeling of security, and attitudes toward the world were profoundly changed by the events of a few hours. The emotional reaction was immediate and felt throughout the world, and the economic impact of the terrorist attacks continue, expressed by new views of risk and uncertainty.

Directly or indirectly, virtually all business activities were affected by the events. Overall consumer demand went into shock worldwide, and in some industries, particularly for luxury goods, it declined precipitously. The marginal customers who had gradually become important to many industries dropped out in droves as they hunkered down to observe everyone else's reactions. Airlines, airports, concession stands, hotels, and travel agents experienced massive dislocations. Some reactions to the events spanned international boundaries and resulted in changed approaches to business and to policy decisions around the world.

The International Reaction

The attacks have led to a changed global environment best characterized on five key dimensions: vulnerability, outrage, collaboration, politics, and connection.

1. *Vulnerability*   We now know that terrorism can affect not only those who fly or those who live and work beneath aviation routes—anyone who is present or participates in any activity within any country is at risk. Protection is difficult, if not impossible, and there are ample and varied tools that might be used for another attack.
2. *Outrage*   The attacks do not represent a condition of moral ambivalence, where differing viewpoints lead to interpretations favoring one perspective over another. The self-righteous cruelty of the attacks repels almost all nations and touches individuals like a cold wind that makes sweat-beaded skin shiver.
3. *Collaboration*   Ever since the demise of the Soviet Union as a competing superpower, even the closest U.S. allies have been reluctant to embrace a joint direction or a common interest. The rapid formation of a coalition on the political level in support of the hunt for terrorists is only one indication of this sense of collaboration. Equally indicative on the policy side are agreements on implementation, such as how to identify bank accounts held by terrorist organizations and how to freeze them. Some argue that the subsequent U.S. intervention in Iraq depleted the international reserve of goodwill. However, the newly

Culture Clues   Shoes are forbidden within Muslim mosques and Buddhist temples. Never wear them into Japanese homes or restaurants unless the owner insists. In Indian and Indonesian homes, if the host goes shoeless, do likewise.

WORLD VIEW

TRADE-OFFS IN TRADE POLICY

The whole notion of reducing trade barriers is in serious trouble. Some of the sources of this trouble include the slow growth of most of the world's economies, increased competition from developing countries, global excess capacity in most industries, and, as a result of all of these forces, the politically disruptive weakness of job markets around the world. A heightened perception of risk connected to operating across national borders exacerbates these problems.

In the face of risk, the desire of nations to unite on a political front forces an uneasy alliance between economic policy and international politics. Recently, Pakistan, a crucial U.S. ally, pressed for the reduction of tariffs on its textiles to allow clothing made in Pakistan to enter the United States at below-market prices. U.S. manufacturers immediately protested that any change in tariffs would severely damage the already-beleaguered textile industry of South Carolina. Around the same time, under constant pressure from U.S. steelmakers, the government raised tariffs to effectively block imported steel. The tariffs went into effect despite strenuous

objections from political advisors that the move would adversely affect relationships with such countries as Kazakhstan, another key partner on the Afghan border, and Russia, which may prove the most important U.S. ally in the war against terror.

Different perspectives require different trade-offs. While Senator Ernest "Fritz" Hollings (D-South Carolina) believes in the need for full protection of the textile manufacturers in his state, U.S. trade representative Robert Zoellick favors the use of trade to ease political frictions. "If we want to support countries over the long term in a conflict with terror," he says, "we'll have to pay attention to the economic problems they have."

SOURCES: Helene Cooper, "Pakistan's Textile Bind Presents Bush Team with a Tough Choice" and "Trade Craft Is Employed on War's Economic Front," *The Wall Street Journal*, October 29, 2001; "At Daggers Drawn," *The Economist*, May 8, 1999, **http://www. economist.com**.

---

established networks of collaboration in intelligence-gathering and financial oversight demonstrate that the international community collaborates in the face of the terrorist threat.

4. *Politics*   For more than 40 years after World War II, the Coordinating Committee for Multilateral Export Controls (COCOM), an organization of 16 Western nations, had largely denied or at least delayed the transfer of Western technology to unfriendly countries. During the 1990s, however, disagreement about what items required international export control was rampant in policy forums. The fact that an item or a technology was available in neutral countries or could be used for civilian as well as military purposes became an excuse for relinquishing control altogether rather than designing more effective controls. Increased risk has led to questioning of the easing of export control in light of the dangers of nuclear proliferation and international terrorism. As far as technology is concerned, closer collaboration among partner countries has actually resulted in an easing of export-control policies. A tightening of the restrictions of questionable exports to dubious customers seems to have eased the way for exports to friendly countries.

5. *Connection*   Finally, there is a new sense of what nations have in common. For quite some time, when global issues were addressed, local concerns were emphasized. Countries focused on the customs and products that make them different from one another and possibly separate them. Now we think more of the issues that make us behave alike and strengthen the bonds between us.

Fast Facts

Which Eastern nation relies on a self-defense force rather than on a military force for its defenses?

Japan. At the end of World War II, Japan's armed forces were demobilized, and the nation renounced its right to use military force as a means of settling international disputes.

These five features of common sense bode well for a future of international negotiations, policy directives, and formulation of joint approaches to the progress of globalization.

 ## STRUCTURE OF THE BOOK

This book is intended to enable you to become a better, more successful participant in the global business arena. It is written both for those who simply want to know more about what is going on in international markets and for those who want to translate their knowledge into successful business transactions. The text melds theory and practice to balance conceptual understanding with knowledge of day-to-day realities. To do so effectively, it addresses the interests of both beginning internationalists and multinational corporations.

The beginning international manager will need to know the answers to basic, yet important questions: How can I find out whether demand for my product exists abroad? What must I do to get ready to market internationally? These issues are also relevant for managers in multinational corporations, but the questions they consider are often much more sophisticated. Of course, the resources available to address them are also much greater.

Throughout the book, public policy concerns are included in discussions of business activities. In this way, you are exposed to both macro and micro issues. Part 1 introduces the concept of globalization and underlines the critical importance of international activities to the future survival and growth of firms.

Part 2 describes the macroenvironment for international business and explores the cultural, political, legal, and economic forces that drive globalization. Part 3 presents the theoretical dimensions of international trade and investment, exploring the effect of international economic activities on a nation. Part 4 explains the role of the international monetary system, showing how fluctuations in foreign exchange impact the conduct of business. It also presents strategies for international financial management. Part 5 helps firms initiate and develop a global business strategy and lay out the options for market entry and the steps essential to success—from planning to research to marketing to logistics and operations management.

Part 6 looks to the future, anticipating changes that will continue to affect the dynamics of the international business environment as it exists today and as it develops tomorrow.

We hope that upon finishing the book, you will not only have completed another academic subject but also will be well-versed in the theoretical, policy, and strategic aspects of international business and therefore will be able to contribute to improved international competitiveness and a better global standard of living.

Fast Facts

This, the world's fourth-largest continent, with an area of 6,883,000 square miles, is home to 380 million people. (Hint: Virtually the whole continent lies east of Savannah, Georgia.) SOURCE: "The World Factbook 2006-2007," CIA.

South America

Migration Flow and Population

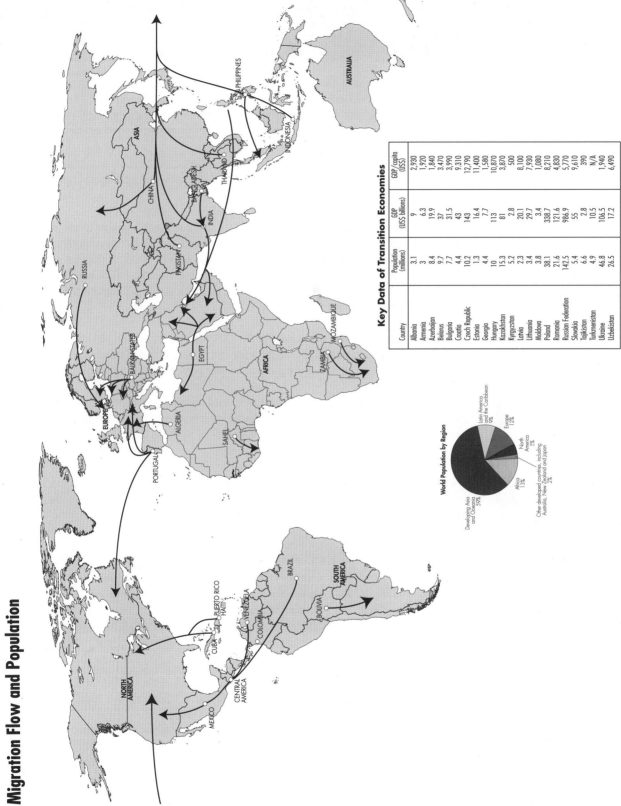

Key Data of Transition Economies

Country	Population (millions)	GDP (US$ billions)	GDP/capita (US$)
Albania	3.1	9	2,930
Armenia	3	6.3	1,920
Azerbaijan	8.4	19.9	1,840
Belarus	9.7	37	3,470
Bulgaria	7.7	31.5	3,990
Croatia	4.4	43	9,310
Czech Republic	10.2	143	12,790
Estonia	1.3	16.4	11,400
Georgia	4.4	7.7	1,580
Hungary	10	113	10,870
Kazakhstan	15.3	81	3,870
Kyrgyzstan	5.2	2.8	500
Latvia	2.3	20.1	8,100
Lithuania	3.4	29.7	7,930
Moldova	3.8	3.4	1,080
Poland	38.1	338.7	8,210
Romania	21.6	121.6	4,830
Russian Federation	142.5	986.9	5,770
Slovakia	5.4	55	9,610
Tajikistan	6.6	2.8	390
Turkmenistan	4.9	10.5	N/A
Ukraine	46.8	106.5	1,940
Uzbekistan	26.5	17.2	6,490

World Population by Region

Latin America and the Caribbean 9%
Europe 12%
North America 5%
Other developed countries, including Australia, New Zealand and Japan 2%
Developing Asia and Oceania 59%
Africa 13%

SUMMARY

International business has been conducted ever since national borders were formed and has played a major role in shaping world history. Growing in importance over the past three decades, it has shaped an environment which, due to economic linkages, today presents us with a global marketplace.

 Global business involves transactions across borders, primarily through export-import trade and foreign direct investment (FDI).

 In the past three decades, world trade has expanded from $200 billion to more than $14 trillion, while international direct investment has grown to $10.1 trillion. Both outpace the growth of most domestic economies, increasing the importance of international business. Global links have made possible investment strategies and business alternatives that offer tremendous opportunities. Yet these changes and the speed of change can also represent threats to nations, firms, and individuals.

 Over the past 30 years, the dominance of the U.S. international trade position has gradually eroded. It has gained in prominence as a market and has decreased in importance as a producer of goods. New participants in international business compete fiercely for world market share.

 Individuals, corporations, and policymakers around the globe have awakened to the fact that international business is a major imperative and offers opportunities for future growth and prosperity. International business provides access to new customers, affords economies of scale, and permits the honing of competitive skills.

 A heightened awareness of the risks—both to firms and individuals—connected to business across borders has led to a changed global environment best characterized on five key dimensions: vulnerability, outrage, collaboration, politics, and connection.

KEY TERMS AND CONCEPTS

globalization	multinational corporation	macroeconomic level
import-export trade	composition of trade	microeconomic level
foreign direct investment (FDI)	gross domestic product (GDP)	

REVIEW QUESTIONS

1. Will future expansion of international business be similar to that in the past?
2. Does increased international business mean increased risk?
3. What areas of business decision-making are affected by changes in the global business environment?
4. Explain the decline in U.S. exports and the effects of that decline.
5. With wages in some countries at one-tenth of U.S. wages, how can America compete?
6. Compare and contrast domestic and international business.
7. Why do more firms in other countries enter international markets than do firms in the United States?
8. What is your view of post–September 11 risk and uncertainty on the conduct of cross-border transactions?

CRITICAL SKILL BUILDERS

1. Is it beneficial for nations to become dependent on one another? Why or why not? Prepare your arguments for and against and participate in a class debate on this topic.

2. China joined the World Trade Organization in 2001. How has membership affected the Chinese world trade market share? How has it affected the Chinese domestic market? Research and discuss.

3. Select a business in your area. Find out how the company is currently involved in international activities, either in the procurement of supplies or the marketing of finished products. How might this firm take further advantage of ongoing shifts in the global business environment? Prepare a report on past activities and future opportunities.

4. Using your library and Internet resources, research such issues as global equity, sustainable development, and the forgiving of debt of the poorest countries. What are the arguments for and against forgiving the debt of countries that borrow money and then can't afford to repay it?

5. Do you believe that terrorism furthers the cause of globalization or drives a wedge between nations? Prepare your arguments and discuss in small groups.

ON THE WEB

1. Using World Trade Organization data (shown on the International Trade page of its web site, http://www.wto.org), determine the following information: (a) the fastest-growing traders; (b) the top ten exporters and importers in world merchandise trade; and (c) the top ten exporters or importers of commercial services.

2. Foreign factories to which U.S. companies outsource manufacturing are under continued criticism for poor working conditions and unfair wages. Using the case studies available on Nike's web site (see http://www.nikebiz.com) and other Internet sources you find, assess the criticisms and the ability of a company to address them.

3. Visit **http://www.worldbank.org** to review the discussion of the reconstruction of Afghanistan. Discuss the responsibility of developed nations to provide funding for the reconstruction.

ENDNOTES

1. Louise Blouin MacBain, "Doha: No Hostage to American Politics," *Forbes*, January 3, 2008.
2. Elizabeth Weise, "Buying American? It's not in the bag." *USAToday*, **http://www.usatoday.com/news/health/2007-07-10-buying-american_N.htm** Accessed December 27, 2008.
3. World Trade Organization, International Trade and tariff Data 2007, [**http://www.wto.org/**] [accessed December 14, 2007.
4. World Investment Report 2007, United Nations Conference on Trade and Development, New York, 2007, and online at **http://www.unctad.org/Templates/WebFlyer.asp?intItemID=4361&lang=1**.
5. Michael R. Czinkota, Illka Ronkainen, and Bob Donath, *The New Trade Globalist* (Cincinnati: Thomson, 2003); "Nikkei hits a 19-month low as nervous investors worry about U.S. slowdown," *International Herald Tribune*, January 11, 2008.
6. U.S. Department of Commerce, BEA: Survey of Current Business, Vol. 87, No. 12, December 2007, **http://www.bea.gov/scb/index.htm**.
7. "Official Reserves," Economic and Financial Indicators, Markets and Data, *The Economist*, January 3, 2008, online at **http://www.economist.com/markets/indicators/**.
8. "2007 Foreign Trade Statistics," U.S. Census Bureau, **www.census.gov/foreign-trade/balance/** [accessed March 2, 2008].
9. Michael R. Czinkota and Sarah McCue, *The STAT-USA Companion to International Business, Economics and Statistics Administration* (Washington, D.C.: U.S. Department of Commerce, 2007).
10. Stephan Danninger and Fred Joutz, "What Explains Germany's Rebounding Export Market Share?" *IMF Working Paper*, February 2007.
11. Quarterly National Accounts, 2007, OECD, Paris, online at **http://www.oecd.org/statsportal/0,3352,en_2825_293564_1_1_1_1_1,00.html**,

12. "2007 Foreign Trade Statistics," U.S. Census Bureau, **http://www.census.gov/foreign-trade/Press-Release/edb/2006/edb-2a.pdf** [accessed February 21, 2008].

13. "2007 Foreign Trade Statistics," U.S. Census Bureau, **http://www.census.gov/foreign-trade/historical/gands.pdf** [accessed March 3, 2008].

14. "Accelerating the Globalization of America: The Role of Information Technology," Catherine L. Mann, June 2006, *Institute for International Economics*.

15. Howard Lewis III and J. David Richardson, *Why Global Commitment Really Matters*, Institute for International Economics, Washington, D.C., 2001; "Accelerating the Globalization of America: The Role of Information Technology," Catherine L. Mann, June 2006, Institute for International Economics.

16. This section is based on Michael Czinkota, "Managing Internationally in the Face of Terrorism Induced Uncertainty," (with P. Liesch, J. Stern, and G. Knight) in *Handbook of 21st Century Management*, Los Angeles: Sage, 2008.

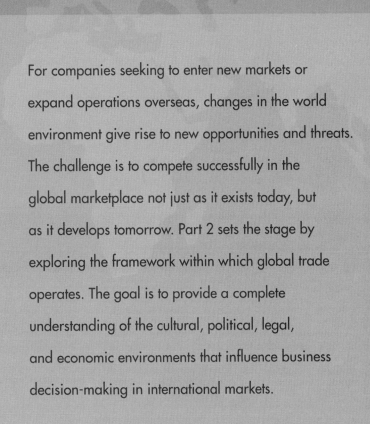

PART 2

GLOBALIZATION DRIVERS

For companies seeking to enter new markets or expand operations overseas, changes in the world environment give rise to new opportunities and threats. The challenge is to compete successfully in the global marketplace not just as it exists today, but as it develops tomorrow. Part 2 sets the stage by exploring the framework within which global trade operates. The goal is to provide a complete understanding of the cultural, political, legal, and economic environments that influence business decision-making in international markets.

CHAPTER 2

Romancing the Globe

Of all the brands in the world, there is none more consistent than Disney, which stands for "family magic" whether in Penang, Pisa, or Peoria. This does not mean, however, that a cookie-cutter approach of transplanted products from the United States works in key markets such as China, India, Latin America, Russia, and South Korea. Global markets want more than homogeneous, plain-vanilla products and services, and prefer those that are in tune with local and regional preferences.

For the last ten years, the Walt Disney Company has made it a priority to build its international business in television, movies, retail, and theme parks with the goal of half of profits to come from overseas by 2010 (in 2006, one-quarter came from overseas). The main approach of getting to the goal is by **embracing local culture**.

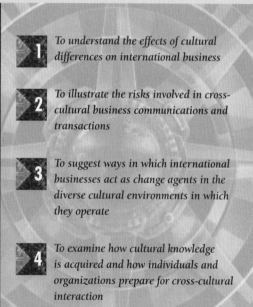

LEARNING OBJECTIVES

1. *To understand the effects of cultural differences on international business*

2. *To illustrate the risks involved in cross-cultural business communications and transactions*

3. *To suggest ways in which international businesses act as change agents in the diverse cultural environments in which they operate*

4. *To examine how cultural knowledge is acquired and how individuals and organizations prepare for cross-cultural interaction*

Disney's theme park in Hong Kong, which opened in 2005, suffered a 30 percent drop in attendance in its second year, largely due to its lack of appeal to mainland Chinese audiences. The first big opportunity to reverse the trend is a stroke of astrological fortune: The year 2008 is the year of the rat — allowing Disney to proclaim it the Year of the Mouse. The Disneyland Chinese New Year campaign featured a logo with the Chinese character for luck flipped upside down (a New Year tradition), with mouse ears added on top. Inside the park, dumplings and turnip cakes are featured on the menus. The parade down Main Street, USA, is being joined by the "Rhythm of Life Procession," featuring a dragon dance and puppets of birds, flowers, and fish, set to traditional Chinese music.

© AP/WIDE WORLD PHOTOS/ANAT GIVON

Disney's efforts to give its Hong Kong park a more Chinese character reflect a broader effort by the company to **understand local culture**. Research is conducted in the homes of Chinese consumers, asking about their knowledge of the Disney brand and their lifestyles as busy families. One result of such research is that Disneyland ads feature one child (the Chinese government limits most couples to just one child), two parents, and two grandparents (many households are extended ones) sharing branded Disney activities, such as watching a movie or giving a plush version of the mouse as a gift.

Adapting products and processes to local markets is a key ingredient of successful global strategy. The gods of wealth, longevity, and happiness have been added to the Hong Kong Disneyland gang. To support the marketing efforts of the theme park, Disney has expanded its TV, on-line, and film businesses in China. *The Secret of the Magic Gourd* was the first-ever Disney movie made just for Chinese audiences. The movie also meant a departure from Disney's obsession with going it alone in that it joined local experts (including the state-run China Film Group) to produce the culturally customized product.

The role of **local employees** is critical in gaining cultural knowledge. Disney has given more power to local managers to develop completely local approaches, to adapt U.S. franchises by making local versions of them, or to build interest in U.S. shows like "Hannah Montana" and "Kim Possible." It is also important to help employees understand the overall structure. Chinese executives and staff benefit from visits to Burbank, California, and interaction with Disney executives from around the world to combine Disney and Chinese values.

The same processes are being replicated in the other emerging markets targeted by Disney. Local versions of *High School Musical* for India, Latin America, and Russia are part of Disney's plan to invest $100 million in movies outside of the United States by 2010. The *High School Musical* cast for the Indian version was chosen in an *American Idol*-style competition. To create interest, Disney aired a dubbed version of the American movie and launched "My School Rocks," a dance competition featuring *High School Musical* songs. A CD of the movie soundtrack with Hindi lyrics and Indian instruments has been successful due to the low cost at retail.

SOURCES: "Main Street, H.K.," *The Wall Street Journal*, January 23, 2008, B1-B2; "Disney Rewrites Script to Win Fans in India," *The Wall Street Journal*, June 11, 2007, A1, A10; Ibsen Martinez, "Romancing the Globe," *Foreign Policy*, November/December 2005, 48-56.

As You Read This Chapter

1. Consider whether the following statement is accurate: "The more the world becomes global, the more people want their own culture."
2. Assess the degree to which international business is a cultural change agent both for the good and the bad.

As new markets open up for world trade and global competition intensifies, businesses of all sizes and in all sectors are expanding their operations overseas at unprecedented rates. In fact, business across borders has become so much the norm that distinctions between domestic and international markets and operations have blurred. Yet while advances in communications and transportation have made the business world a smaller place, the cultural differences that divide nations and govern international interactions are as complex as ever.[1] A key success factor in operating smoothly across borders is understanding the diverse behaviors, attitudes, and values that drive human interaction.

This chapter explores how cultural differences manifest themselves in business situations. Success in new markets requires smooth adaptation to unfamiliar cultural environments, best achieved through patience, flexibility, and appreciation of the values and beliefs of potential business partners. This means recognizing cultural competence as a key management skill that directly affects both revenues and profitability in new markets. The chapter also determines similarities across cultures, showing how these can be exploited in strategy formulation.

WHAT IS CULTURE?

Culture is the unique combination of learning and experience that gives an individual an anchoring point, an identity, as well as codes of conduct. Scholars have defined culture in more than 160 ways, but all of the definitions share some key common elements.[2] Culture is learned, shared, and transmitted from one generation to the next. It is primarily passed on from parents to their children but also transmitted by social organizations, special-interest groups, governments, schools, and churches. Culture affects not only the way people behave but the ways they think. For this reason, it has been termed "the collective programming of the mind."[3] Through cultural influences, common ways of thinking and behaving are developed, then reinforced through social pressure. Within the same national borders, intercultural

LEARNING OBJECTIVE

differences based on religion, race, or geographic region have resulted in the emergence of distinct subcultures, such as the Hispanic subculture in the United States.

For the purposes of this text, **culture** is defined as an integrated system of learned behavior patterns that are characteristic of the members of any given society. It includes not just everything a group thinks, says, does, and makes — its customs, language, and material artifacts — but the group's shared systems of attitudes and feelings, too. The definition, therefore, encompasses a wide variety of elements from the materialistic to the spiritual. Culture is inherently conservative, resisting change and fostering continuity. Every person is brought up in a particular culture, learning the "right way" of doing things. Problems may arise when a person from one culture has to adjust to another one. The process of **acculturation** — adjusting and adapting to a specific culture other than one's own — is one of the keys to success in international business operations.

Figure 2.1 distinguishes between high- and low-context cultures. In **high-context cultures**, such as Japan and Saudi Arabia, the context of a communication is at least as important as what is actually said. The speaker and the listener rely on a common understanding of the context. In **low-context cultures**, however, most of the information is contained explicitly in the words. North American cultures engage in low-context communications. Unless one is aware of this basic difference, messages and intentions can easily be misunderstood. Consider, for instance, the different approaches in as simple a business communication as the exchange of business cards. A Chinese or Japanese businessperson carefully presents the card with both hands. Etiquette requires that foreigners study the card when it is handed to them and place it on the table before them. The behavior of an American executive who proffers a travel-worn card

CULTURE

An integrated system of learned behavior patterns that are characteristic of the members of any given society.

ACCULTURATION

The process of adjusting and adapting to a specific culture other than one's own.

HIGH-CONTEXT CULTURE

Culture in which behavioral and environmental nuances are an important means of conveying information.

LOW-CONTEXT CULTURE

Culture in which most information is conveyed explicitly rather than through behavioral and environmental nuances.

FIGURE 2.1   Context Orientation in Major Cultures

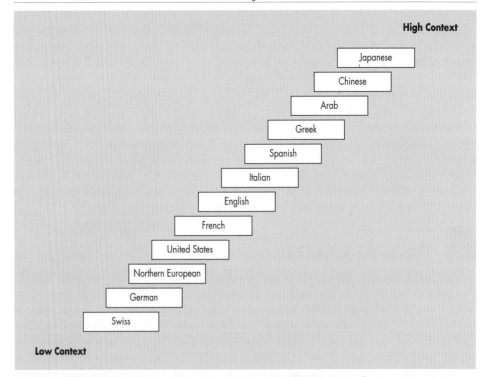

SOURCEs: Adapted from E. T. Hall, and Mildred Reed Hall, *Understanding Cultural Differences* (Yarmouth, ME: Intercultural Press, 1990).

or — worse still — makes notes on a card he or she is given is considered offensive, even insulting.[4]

Borrowing and interaction among cultures often serve to narrow the gaps between them. It is not uncommon, for instance, for products or brands to act as **change agents**, able to alter commonly held values or behavior patterns that eventually result in the blurring of cultural distinctions. In China and Hong Kong, for example, McDonald's has altered some age-old eating habits and preferences, particularly among the younger generation. While there are some concessions to local cuisine, the most popular menu items are burgers and French fries. The fast-food chain has disciplined its Chinese customers to an entirely new dining routine — as in the United States, they wait in an orderly line, serve and seat themselves, and even clear away their trays afterward. McDonald's has 30,000 outlets in 119 countries, and most of its revenues now come from operations outside the United States.

CHANGE AGENT

A institution or person who facilitates change in a firm or in a host country.

WORLD VIEW

CULTURAL SUSTAINABILITY

In a vote cast as a battle of global conformity vs. cultural diversity, delegates to a U.N. agency turned aside strong U.S. objections in 2005 and overwhelmingly approved the first international treaty designed to protect movies, music, and other cultural treasures from foreign competition. The 148-2 vote at the U.N. Educational, Scientific, and Cultural Organization emerged as a referendum on the world's love-hate relationship with Hollywood, Big Macs, and Coca-Cola.

"The American delegate doesn't like to hear the word 'protection,'" Joseph Yai Olabiyi Babalola, clad in the ornate gold robes of his tiny country, Benin, told UNESCO delegates. "Not all countries are equal — some need to be protected." U.S. officials say the measure could be used to unfairly obstruct the flow of ideas, goods, and services across borders. Films and music are among the United States' largest exports — the foreign box-office take for American movies was $16 billion in 2004. Assuring access to overseas markets for these products has been a prime U.S. goal at the World Trade Organization. Louise Oliver, U.S. ambassador to UNESCO, told delegates at the organization's headquarters near the Eiffel Tower that the measure was "too flawed, too prone to abuse for us to support." She contended that dictators could potentially use it to control what their citizens read.

The measure passed at a time of growing fear in many countries that the world's increasing economic interdependence, known as globalization, is bringing a surge of foreign products across their borders that could wipe out local cultural heritage. France, for instance, has long kept measures in place to protect its film industry against imports, notably Hollywood productions. Called the Convention on the Protection and Promotion of Diversity of Cultural Expressions, the document declares the rights of countries to "maintain, adopt, and implement policies and measures that they deem appropriate for the protection and promotion of the diversity of cultural expressions on their territory." Cultural expressions are defined as including music, art, language, and ideas as well as "cultural activities, goods, and services." Advocates say it could help small nations promote and distribute their cultural products on the world market. The convention would go into effect if 30 countries ratify it, a step that U.S. officials say is inevitable.

What its practical effect would be remains unclear. But proponents and dissenting U.S. officials agree that it would at least allow countries to require that imported movies have subtitles or dubbing in native languages. Supporters included some of America's closest allies, such as Canada and Britain. British delegate Timothy Craddock called the document "clear, carefully balanced, and consistent with the principles of international law and fundamental human rights." In the vote, only Israel sided with the United States. Four countries abstained.

The showdown came two years after the United States rejoined UNESCO following a two-decade boycott that began over objections to the organization's media policy. Many American officials said UNESCO was inherently anti-American. "Everyone would love to make this into some big U.S.-against-the-world routine," U.S. delegate Oliver said in an interview, insisting that the vote was not a sign of anti-Americanism. "It's the U.S. standing for principles, the U.S. standing for freedom, the U.S. saying things that should be said." She and other U.S. officials have not suggested that the United States might withdraw from UNESCO again over this issue.

SOURCES: Molly Moore, "U.N. Body Endorses Cultural Protection: U.S. Objections Are Turned Aside," *Washington Post*, October 21, 2005; A14. See also **www.cptech.org/unesco/**.

In bringing about change or in encouraging increasingly homogeneous demand across markets, global businesses open themselves to charges of "cultural imperialism." They are sometimes accused of pushing Western behaviors and values — along with products and promotions — into other cultures. McDonald's, KFC, Coca-Cola, Disney, and Pepsi, for example, have all drawn the ire of anti-American demonstrators. Some countries, such as Brazil, Canada, France, and Indonesia, use restrictive rules and subsidies to protect their "cultural industries," including music and movies. France's measures include, for example, "prix unique du livre," a limitation on the percentage of discount on books (to support small publishing houses and help maintain small bookstores); quotas on non-French movies on French national TV channels, and mandatory financing of films by TV channels (as a provision in their license) as well as for French music on radio channels; and "avance sur recettes" or "fonds de soutien," a financial state advance on all French films.[5] Such subsidies have allowed the French to make 200 films a year, twice as many as the United Kingdom. Worldview: Cultural Sustainability illustrates how widespread these concerns are.

 # ELEMENTS OF CULTURE

2 LEARNING OBJECTIVE

Attempts to understand culture have led to the development of many generalizations intended to provide insight into the way of life of any group of people. Cultures are typically described and compared according to such concrete elements as language, infrastructure, social institutions, education, or such abstract elements as religion, values and attitudes, manners and customs, and aesthetics. These characteristics, summarized in Table 2.1, which occur across all cultures, may be uniquely manifested in a particular society, bringing about cultural diversity. The ease with which an international firm adapts to cultural characteristics and the sensitivity with which it approaches cultural differences factors into its success in new markets. Naturally, while some goods and services or management practices require very little adjustment, others have to be adapted dramatically to suit the new environment.

Language

Language has been described as the mirror of culture. Language itself is multidimensional. This is true not only of the spoken word but also of the nonverbal language of international business. Messages are conveyed not just by the words used but by how those words are spoken and through such nonverbal means as gestures, body position, and eye contact.

Very often, mastery of the language is required before a person is acculturated. Language mastery must go beyond technical competency, because every language has words and phrases that can be readily understood only in context. Such phrases are carriers of culture; they represent special ways a culture has developed to view some aspect of human existence.

TABLE 2.1 Elements of Culture

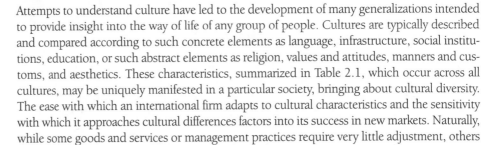

CONCRETE ELEMENTS	ABSTRACT ELEMENTS

• Language
  Verbal
  Nonverbal
	• Religion

	• Values and attitudes
• Infrastructure	• Manners and customs
• Education	• Aesthetics
• Social institutions	

Language capability serves four distinct roles in international business:

1. Language aids information-gathering and evaluation. Fluency in the language diminishes the manager's dependence on the perceptions and opinions of others. The best intelligence on a market is gathered by becoming part of that market rather than by observing it from the outside. This is why local managers of a multinational corporation should be the firm's primary source of political information — they are in the best position to assess potential risk and opportunity.
2. Language provides access to local society. People are far more comfortable speaking their own language, and this should be treated as an advantage. Although English may be widely spoken and may even be the official company language, conversing in the local language can make a dramatic difference.
3. Language reduces the risk of errors. The ability to speak fluently without the use of an interpreter ensures accuracy of communication.
4. Language extends beyond the mechanics of communication into the accurate interpretation of cultural contexts that may influence business operations.

The manager's command of the national language(s) in a market must go beyond simple word recognition. Consider, for example, how dramatically different English terms can be when used in the United Kingdom or the United States. In negotiations, for example, when U.S. delegates speak of "tabling a proposal," it means that they want to delay a decision, but their British counterparts understand the expression to mean that immediate action is to be taken. Other languages are not immune to this phenomenon either. Goodyear has identified five different terms for the word "tire" in the Spanish-speaking Americas, influencing the localization of its communications. Another example is the adaptation of advertising into Arabic. When this is carried out without considering that Arabic reads from right to left, the creative concept can be destroyed.

Table 2.2 lists the populations who speak the world's top ten languages. While some 514 million people speak English as their first language and about a billion speak it as their second, English as an international language has met much resistance. The French have sought to banish English expressions from such documents as legal contracts and to restrict their use in public signage. Following in French footsteps, the Germans have founded a society for the protection of the German language from the spread of "Denglish." Poland recently directed that all companies selling or advertising foreign products use Polish in their advertisements. In Hong Kong, the Chinese government is promoting the use of Mandarin and Cantonese rather than English as the language of commerce, while some people in India — with its 800 dialects — scorn the use of English as a lingua franca because it is a reminder of British colonialism.[6]

Despite the fact that English is encountered daily by anyone who surfs the Web, the "e" in e-business does not stand for English. In a recent survey, one-third of senior managers in Europe stated that they prefer not to communicate in English online. Only half of French middle managers and one in five of their German counterparts consider themselves fluent enough to communicate well in English. Fully three-quarters of those surveyed considered that being forced to use nonlocalized content on the Internet had a negative impact on productivity.[7] The conclusion? A truly global portal works only if online functions are provided in a multilingual and multicultural format.

Culture Clues   Starting in late 2007, Internet users have been able to use addresses in 11 languages that do not use the Roman alphabet. Russians, for example, are able to type in Web addresses entirely in the Cyrillic characters instead of having to revert to English. The change has also involved languages such as Chinese, Arabic, and Korean. There are a billion people on the Internet; this move will accelerate the incorporation of the next billion.

TABLE 2.2 Top Ten World Languages

LANGUAGE	APPROX. NUMBER OF SPEAKERS
1. Chinese (Mandarin)	1,075,000,000
2. English	514,000,000
3. Hindustani*	496,000,000
4. Spanish	425,000,000
5. Russian	275,000,000
6. Arabic	256,000,000
7. Bengali	215,000,000
8. Portuguese	194,000,000
9. Malay-Indonesian	176,000,000
10. French	129,000,000

*Encompasses multiple dialects, including Hindi and Urdu.

Sources: Adapted from Raymond G. Gordon, *Ethnologue*, 13th ed. (Summer Institute of Linguistics, Inc.: 1996), accessed from **http://www.infoplease.com/ipa/A0775272.html** (downloaded January 30, 2008).

BACKTRANSLATION

The retranslation of text to the original language by a different person from the one who made the first translation. Useful to find translation errors.

Dealing with language invariably requires local assistance. A good local advertising agency and market research firm can prevent many problems. To make sure an ad travels smoothly into new cultures, the simplest method of control is **backtranslation** — translating a foreign-language version back to the original language by a different person than the one who made the first translation. Backtranslation might, for instance, have helped in KFC's attempts to translate its "Finger-Licking Good" campaign around the world. Instead, viewers were aghast at local billboards suggesting that KFC is "So Good It Makes You Want to Eat Your Fingers."[8] Translation software, considered 85 percent accurate, can help take care of obvious blunders like this. In addition, to assess the quality of any translation, whether made by software, over the Internet, or by local ad agencies, it is advisable to test any new message in local markets to completely evaluate its impact.[9]

Translation of advertising from one culture to another involves a good deal more than finding the right words. Messages conveyed in advertising are fundamentally linked to culture, and that means communicating in ways that are meaningful to each particular market. For example, MasterCard adapted its clever "Priceless" campaign — "intangible moments that transcend price-tags" — for the Hispanic market. The key was to create a situation that was culturally attuned to the target audience. With a focus on family, the pillar of Hispanic culture, the ad features a grandmother and granddaughter shopping for a meal. As the grandmother selects onions, an announcer lists the price in Spanish, "Cebollas, 4 dolares, " followed by "El tiempo que toma en cocinarse: no tiene precio." (The time it takes to simmer: priceless). The ad ends with a translation of MasterCard's central message: "There are some things that money can't buy; for everything else there is MasterCard. Accepted everywhere, even at small shops."[10]

Finally, keep in mind that language has a historic as well as a local context. Nokia launched an advertising campaign in Germany for the interchangeable covers for its portable phones using a theme "Jedem das Seine" ("to each his own"). The campaign was withdrawn after the American Jewish Congress pointed out that the same slogan was found on the entry portal to Buchenwald, a Nazi-era concentration camp. Similarly, a recent rendition of the prelude to *Tristan and Isolde* by world-renowned conductor Daniel Barenboim broke Israel's longtime ban on the music of the German composer Wagner. The performance drew the fury of Israel's leaders.[11]

Quick Take   *Lost in Translation*

Most people realize how difficult English can be only when seen through the eyes of non-native speakers. The Chinese have been extraordinarily adept at unintentionally hilarious translations, but the government is not amused, particularly with the 2008 Beijing Olympics as a national showcase. As a result, China launched a drive to clamp down on bad English in 2006. New translation guides were handed out at hotels and shopping malls, on buses, and at tourist attractions. Ten teams of linguistic monitors patrolled the city's parks, museums, subway stations, and other public places searching for gaffes to fix.

For years, foreigners in China have delighted in the loopy English translations that appeared on the nation's signs. They have ranged from the offensive ("Deformed Man," outside toilets for the handicapped) to the sublime (on park lawns, "Show Mercy to the Slender Grass"). Signs for emergency exits at the Beijing airport read "No entry at peacetime."

The city has replaced 6,300 road signs that carried bewildering admonitions such as: "To take notice of safe: The slippery are very crafty." (Translation: Be careful, slippery.) Replacing signs will cost the city a substantial amount of money, although it is not clear how much. Some of the faulty ones are decades old and are carved in marble.

Some of the many Westerners living in Beijing view the disappearance of China's lost-in-translation signs as part of a broader modernization drive that is causing Beijing to lose some of its character. Other foreigners lament the loss of a source of amusement.

SOURCES: "Tired of Laughter, Beijing Gets Rid of Bad Translations," *Wall Street Journal*, February 5, 2007, A1, A13; "China Clamping Down on Bad English Translations," *Pittsburgh Post-Gazette*, October 17, 2006, A1; and "Beijing Stamps Out Bad English," *BBC News*, October 15, 2006, available at *news.bbc.co.uk*.

Nonverbal Language

Language goes beyond the spoken word, encompassing nonverbal actions and behaviors that reveal hidden clues to culture. Four key topics — time, space, body language, and friendship patterns — offer a starting point from which managers can begin to acquire the understanding necessary to do business in foreign countries.

Understanding national and cultural differences in the concept of time is critical for an international business manager. In many parts of the world, time is flexible and is not seen as a limited commodity; people come late to appointments or may not come at all. In Mexico, for instance, it's not unusual to show up at 1:45 P.M. for a 1:00 P.M. appointment. While a late-afternoon siesta cuts apart the business day, businesspeople will often be at their desks until 10:00 at night. In Hong Kong, too, it is futile to set exact meeting times, because getting from one place to another may take minutes or hours, depending on traffic. Showing indignation or impatience at such behavior would astonish an Arab, Latin American, or Asian. Perception of time also affects business negotiations. Asians and Europeans tend to be more interested in long-term partnerships while Americans are eager for deals that will be profitable in the short term, meaning less than a year.

Individuals vary in their preferences for personal space. Arabs and Latin Americans like to stand close to people when they talk. If an American, who may not be comfortable at such close range, backs away from an Arab, this might incorrectly be perceived as a negative reaction.

Also, Westerners are often taken aback by the physical nature of affection between Slavs — for example, being kissed squarely on the lips by a business partner, regardless of sex.

International body language, too, can befuddle international business relations.

For example, an American manager may, after successful completion of negotiations, impulsively give a finger-and-thumb "OK" sign. In southern France, this would signify that the deal was worthless, and in Japan that a little bribe had been requested; the gesture would be grossly insulting to Brazilians.

In some countries, extended social acquaintance and the establishment of appropriate personal rapport are essential to conducting business. The feeling is that one should know one's business partner on a personal level before transactions can occur.

Therefore, rushing straight to business will not be rewarded, because deals are made on the basis of not only the best product or price, but also the entity or person deemed most trustworthy. Contracts may be bound on handshakes, not lengthy and complex agreements — a fact that makes some, especially Western, businesspeople uneasy.

Infrastructure

ECONOMIC INFRASTRUCTURE

The transportation, energy, and communication systems in a country.

SOCIAL INFRASTRUCTURE

The housing, health, educational, and other social systems in a country.

FINANCIAL INFRASTRUCTURE

Facilitating financial agencies in a country; for example, banks.

MARKETING INFRASTRUCTURE

Facilitating marketing agencies in a country; for example, market research firms, channel members.

CULTURAL CONVERGENCE

Increasing similarity among cultures accelerated by technological advances.

A culture's infrastructure is directly related to how society organizes its economic activity. The basic **economic infrastructure** consists of transportation, energy, and communications systems. **Social infrastructure** refers to housing, health, and educational systems. **Financial and marketing infrastructures** provide the facilitating agencies for the international firm's operation in a given market — for example, banks and research firms. In some parts of the world, the international firm may have to be a partner in developing the various infrastructures before it can operate, whereas in others it may greatly benefit from their high level of sophistication.

The level of infrastructure development can be used to aid segmentation in international markets. Companies like General Electric, for example, may see a demand for basic energy-generating products in developing countries, while markets with sophisticated infrastructures are ripe for such goods as time-saving home appliances.

While infrastructure is often a good indicator of potential demand, goods sometimes discover unexpectedly rich markets due to the informal economy at work in developing nations. In Kenya, for example, where most of the country's 30 million population live on less than a dollar a day, more than 770,000 people have signed up for mobile phone service during the last few years; wireless providers are scrambling to keep up with demand. Leapfrogging older technologies, mobile phones are especially attractive to Kenya's thousands of small-time entrepreneurs — market-stall owners, taxi drivers, and even hustlers who sell on the sidewalks. For most, income goes unreported, creating an invisible wealth on the streets. Mobile phones outnumber fixed lines in Kenya as well as in Uganda, Venezuela, Cambodia, South Korea, and Chile.[12]

Technological advances often influence the pace of cultural change. Color television, for example, spreads words and images of Western cultures around the world, showing developing nations another way of life. Compact discs and MTV via satellite do the same. When exposure to foreign cultures is accelerated by technological advances, the result is **cultural convergence**. Due to such influences, consumers seek more diverse products as a way of satisfying their demand for a higher quality of life and more leisure time. Consider, for example, the power of the Internet. Far more than a way to communicate, the Internet has become a market for goods, an information system, and a virtual meeting place. In its ability to change ways of life, the Internet is more pervasive than television or even electricity.[13] World View: Wired into the Future explores the impact of the Internet in cultures that lack core infrastructure elements.

The degree to which infrastructure is developed affects multiple decisions related to the introduction of products into new markets. Kenya's new mobile phone owners, for example, use prepaid calling cards to make calls, because there is no secure system in place for bill collection. American consumers demand slick, attractive packaging on most goods, but some foreign markets find it impossible to match the same standards. While TV advertising may be the medium of choice for top brands in the home market, low ownership levels of television sets, radios, or PCs may lead to alternative advertising strategies overseas.

Education

Education, either formal or informal, plays a major role in the passing on and sharing of culture. Educational levels of a culture can be assessed using literacy rates, enrollment in secondary education, or enrollment in higher education available from secondary data sources. International firms also need to know about the qualitative aspects of education, namely varying emphasis on particular skills and the overall level of the education provided. Japan and South Korea, for example, emphasize the sciences, especially engineering, to a greater degree than Western countries.

Educational levels also affect the types of new products introduced and the manner in which they are sold and marketed. For instance, a high level of illiteracy suggests the use of visual aids rather than printed manuals. Successful marketing of sophisticated technologies depends greatly upon the educational level of prospective users. Product adaptation decisions are often influenced by the extent to which targeted customers are able to — or can be educated to — use the good or service properly.

Education also affects other business functions. Recruitment of local sales personnel, for example, depends on the availability of adequately educated people. In some cases, international firms routinely send locally recruited personnel to headquarters for training. In recent years, U.S. manufacturing companies have outsourced multiple operational tasks, from customer service to software design, to India. The highly educated Indian population, with fluency in English, is sought after for its skills as well as its comparatively low costs.

In some instances, recruitment of local personnel by international firms is stifled by cultural pressures. In Japan, the culture has traditionally placed a premium on loyalty, and employees are encouraged to consider themselves lifelong members of the corporate family. A talented Japanese graduate is taking a risk by accepting a position with an international firm rather than a Japanese company. If the foreign employer decides to leave Japan, employees may find themselves stranded in mid-career, unable to find their place in the Japanese business system.

As testimony to the value of educational systems overseas, the number of U.S. students seeking to attend colleges abroad is at an all-time high. The rapid rise in applications to top-ranked schools in the United Kingdom, France, Spain, Japan, and China reveals a desire for international experience that schools at home fall short in providing.[14]

> ### Fast Facts
> Students in which country go to school the longest, at 20 years on the average?
>
> Australia; from primary school to college.

Social Institutions

Social institutions affect the ways people relate to one another. The family unit, which in Western industrialized countries consists of parents and children, in a number of cultures is extended to include grandparents and other relatives. This affects consumption patterns and must be taken into account, for example, when conducting market research.

The concept of kinship, or blood relations between individuals, is defined in a very broad way in societies such as those in sub-Saharan Africa. Family relations and a strong obligation to family are important factors to consider in human resource management in those regions. Understanding tribal politics in countries such as Nigeria may help the manager avoid unnecessary complications in executing business transactions.

The division of a particular population into classes is termed **social stratification**.

SOCIAL STRATIFICATION

The division of a particular population into classes.

WORLD VIEW

WIRED INTO THE FUTURE

The Internet has proven to be an agent of change in the most unlikely of situations. The tiny farming village of Rovieng, deep in Cambodia's northern hinterland, has no telephones and no electricity. Yet lately, with the help of an American aid organization, young women in this far-flung community are weaving silk scarves that will find their way to customers a world away.

Portable web technology, satellite dishes, and solar panels create a link through which this desolate, impoverished region hopes to gain a foothold in the modern world.

Handwoven accessories sold over the Internet are just a part of the picture. The Rovieng community has set up a small but profitable pig farm — new piglets are sold at market prices negotiated online, and the proceeds go into the village's health-care fund. Children, too, have the opportunity to explore the world through the web. While their parents are intimidated by language barriers — there is no web content written in their native tongue — children show no such reservations and click with ease through sites that captivate them. The experience not only makes them familiar with computers and the mechanics of the Internet, but motivates them to learn about cultures they barely knew existed. It remains to be seen whether the web will change the futures of Rovieng children. For one thing, the funding that makes their online connections possible may evaporate as quickly as it appeared. But as a sign of their eagerness for social transformation, the villagers have already changed the name of their hamlet to Robib, to "make it easier for Americans to pronounce."

Children in the far reaches of Malaysia, too, have been given an opportunity to hook up to the Internet. Under the auspices of the United Nations Development Program, a bus loaded with 20 personal computers is helping to bridge the digital divide by delivering technology to the region's most remote schools. The bus goes to areas where educational infrastructure is virtually nonexistent. Then, a diesel-powered generator onboard fires up the PCs. If a telephone jack is not available for Internet access, the computers are linked up to a server on the bus. In teacher-directed sessions, children learn the basics of navigating the web, sending e-mails, and creating simple documents.

In time, the experience may equip children from poverty-stricken agrarian regions with the skills that will help them find opportunities outside the village setting.

While online access has quickly become a way of life in developed nations, less than one in a thousand people in the world's poorest communities have experienced the power of the Internet to change their societies. Even though wiring these regions cannot solve the immense problems of feeding and educating the world's poorest people, it does offer a hope for future self-sufficiency. Says Vinos Thomas, a vice president of the World Bank, "The idea is to be able to give people the information and the means they need to grow out of poverty themselves."

The Global Alliance for Information and Communication Technologies and Development (GAID), an initiative approved by the United Nations Secretary-General in 2006, was launched after comprehensive worldwide consultations with governments, the private sector, civil society, the technical and Internet communities, and academia. With its multi-stakeholder approach, the Alliance, headed by the chairman of Intel, reaffirms the belief that a people-centered and knowledge-based information society is essential for achieving better life for all.

SOURCES: Marguerite Reardon, "For Intel, the Business Side of Doing Good," www.news.com, October 22, 2007; Rajiv Chandbasekaran, "Cambodian Village Wired to the Future," *The Washington Post*, May 13, 2001, p. A1; Wayne Arnold, "Malaysia's Internet Road Show," *The New York Times*, August 23, 2001, G1; see also www.un-gaid.org.

Stratification ranges from the situation in northern Europe, where most people are members of the middle class, to highly stratified societies in which the higher strata control most of the buying power and decision-making positions.

Reference groups are an important part of the socialization process of consumers worldwide. These groups provide the values and attitudes that influence behavior. Primary reference groups include the family and co-workers and other intimate acquaintances. Secondary reference groups are social organizations where less-continuous interaction takes place, such as professional associations and trade organizations. In addition to providing socialization, reference groups develop a person's concept of self, which is manifested, for example, through the choice of products used. Reference groups also provide a baseline for compliance with group norms, giving the individual the option of conforming to or avoiding certain behaviors.

REFERENCE GROUP

A group, such as the family, co-workers, and professional and trade associations, that provides the values and attitudes that influence and shape behavior, including consumer behavior.

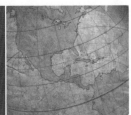

Culture Clues   Gifts should always be chosen with great care. An ideal gift is one that represents the giver's own culture while being sensitive to the recipient's. For example, a Finn may give a Suunto compass to a Saudi business partner (to help him determine the direction for daily prayers). Giving gifts that are easily available in that country (e.g., chocolates to a Swiss) is not advisable. Some gifts are not suitable: Clocks or other timepieces are symbols of death in China, while handkerchiefs symbolize tears in Latin America and Korea. Many companies in the United States have policies that do not allow the giving and receiving of gifts.

Social organization also determines the roles of managers and subordinates and how they relate to one another. In some cultures, managers and subordinates are separated explicitly and implicitly by various boundaries ranging from social class status to separate office facilities. In others, cooperation is elicited through equality. For example, Nissan USA has no privileged parking spaces and no private dining rooms. Everyone wears the same type of white coveralls, and the president sits in the same room with a hundred other white-collar workers. Fitting an organizational culture to the larger context of a national culture has to be executed with care. Changes that are too dramatic may disrupt productivity or, at the minimum, arouse suspicion.

Although Western business has impersonal structures for channeling power and influence — primarily through reliance on laws and contracts — the Chinese emphasize *guanxi*, or personal relationships. For instance, while legal contracts form a useful agenda and are a symbol of progress, business obligations come from relationships, not formalized agreements. McDonald's found this out in Beijing, where it was evicted from a central building after only two years despite a 20-year contract. The incomer had a strong *guanxi*, whereas McDonald's had not kept its personal relationships in good repair. Note, too, that although technology has speeded the course of business, the Chinese are used to thinking in terms of hundreds of years rather than days or even months. It takes patience and tenacity to develop good *guanxi*.[15]

Religion

In cultures the world over, people turn to religion in search of a reason for being and legitimacy in the belief that they are part of a larger context. Religion both acknowledges the existence of a higher power and defines certain ideals for life, which in turn are reflected in the values, attitudes, and behaviors of societies and individuals. As well as providing insight into the differences between cultures, religion provides a basis for transcultural similarities as peoples from different nations share similar beliefs and behaviors.

Religion provides the basis for transcultural similarities under shared beliefs and behavior. The impact will vary depending on the strength of the dominant religious tenets. While religion's impact may be quite indirect in Protestant Northern Europe, its impact in countries where Islamic fundamentalism is on the rise may be profound. The influence of these similarities will be assessed in terms of the dominant religions of the world. Other religions may have smaller numbers of followers, such as Judaism with 14 million followers around the world, but their impact is still significant due to the many centuries during which they have influenced world history. While some countries may officially have secularism, such as Marxism-Leninism, as a state belief (e.g., Vietnam and Cuba), traditional religious beliefs still remain a powerful force in shaping behavior.

Within the context of international business, the influence of religion is evident, for example, in attitudes toward entrepreneurship, consumption, and social organization.

International managers must be aware of the differences not only *among* the major religions but also *within* them. In Hinduism, for example, people are divided into subgroups that determine their status and to a large extent their ability to consume.

Fast Facts

What city has Europe's largest Muslim population?

Moscow with 2.5 million Muslims. London and Paris have 607,000 and 1.7 million, respectively.

CHRISTIANITY. With more than 2 billion people in diverse nations, Christianity is the world's largest religion. While there are many subgroups, the major division is between Catholicism and Protestantism. A prominent difference is attitudes toward making money. While Catholicism questions the value of personal gain, the Protestant ethic emphasizes the importance of work and the accumulation of wealth for the glory of God. At the same time, Protestantism encourages frugality — hard work leads to accumulation of wealth, which, in turn, forms the basis for investment. Some scholars, in fact, believe that the Protestant work ethic is responsible for the development of capitalism in the Western world and the rise of predominantly Protestant countries into world economic leadership.[16]

Major holidays are often tied to religion and are observed differently from one culture to the next. Firms operating in foreign cultures are advised to keep this in mind when planning marketing events or in operating local offices. Christian cultures observe Christmas and exchange gifts on either December 24 or December 25, with the exception of the Dutch, who exchange gifts on St. Nicholas Day, December 6. Tandy Corporation, in its first year in the Netherlands, targeted its major Christmas promotion for the third week of December with less than satisfactory results. During Mexico's *Día de los Muertos* (Day of the Dead) festivities from October 31 to November 2, it is pointless to attempt to keep local offices open, since the culture gives priority to observing the holiday.

ISLAM. Islam, which reaches from the west coast of Africa to the Philippines and across a broad band that includes Tanzania, central Asia, western China, India, and Malaysia, has more than 1.2 billion followers. Islam is also a significant minority religion in many parts of the world, including Europe. Islam has a pervasive role in the life of Muslims, its followers. *Sharia*, the law of Islam, for example, requires five daily periods of prayer, fasting during the holy month of Ramadan, and that each Muslim make a pilgrimage to Mecca, Islam's holy city.

Some people believe that Islam's basic fatalism (that is, nothing happens without the will of Allah) and traditionalism have deterred economic development in countries observing the religion. While Islam has proven supportive of entrepreneurship, it nevertheless strongly discourages acts that may be interpreted as exploitation. Consider the violent protests that erupted in Karachi, Jakarta, and other Muslim cities following the entry of American troops into Afghanistan. A bomb explosion at a Coca-Coca bottling plant in Guntar, India, is one of many attacks against companies that are seen to symbolize the exploitation of Muslim countries by American business interests. Quick Take: Coping with Culture Clashes explains how one local businessman took steps to avoid charges of cultural exploitation.

Religion impacts the types of goods and services it is possible to bring into new markets. When beef or poultry is exported to an Islamic country, the animal must be killed in the *halal* method and certified appropriately. Religious restrictions on products (for example, alcoholic beverages) can reveal opportunities, as evidenced by successful launches of several nonalcoholic beverages in the Middle East. Other restrictions may call for innovative solutions — like the use of video cameras to monitor building projects inside the city of Mecca, where non-Muslims are not allowed access.

The role of women in society is tied to religion, especially in the Middle East, and this affects the conduct of business in various ways. Religion influences women's roles not only as consumers, but as influencers of consumption. Companies seeking to do business in Muslim countries may not be able to use female managers. In other cases, in order to communicate directly with Muslim women, companies may have to use female sales personnel only.

Religions of the World: A Part of Culture

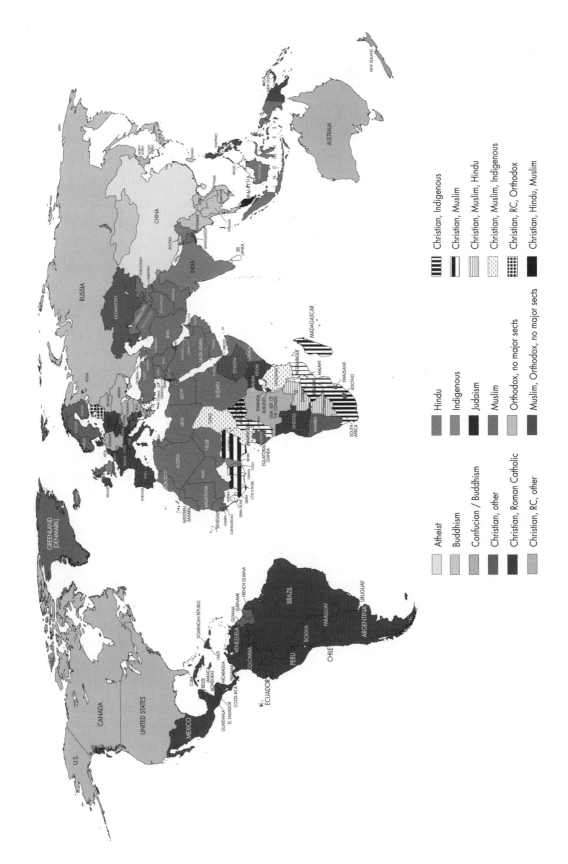

Atheist

Buddhism

Confucian / Buddhism

Christian, other

Christian, Roman Catholic

Christian, RC, other

Hindu

Indigenous

Judaism

Muslim

Orthodox, no major sects

Muslim, Orthodox, no major sects

Christian, Indigenous

Christian, Muslim

Christian, Muslim, Hindu

Christian, Muslim, Indigenous

Christian, RC, Orthodox

Christian, Hindu, Muslim

Data from the *World Fact Book*, January 24, 2007.

Quick Take *Coping with Culture Clashes*

When cultures clash between nations, businesses have to adjust their strategies to new realities. Two examples, one of a global entity and the other of a local business, highlight the creativity individuals have used to keep things going.

Hardliners in Iran would rather have Iranian consumers drink Zamzam Cola, named after a blessed well in Mecca, or other local brands. Some theocrats have even launched attacks on Coke as a "Great Satan" brand whose profits may eventually benefit Iran's enemies. At the same time, most of corporate America is prohibited by the U.S. government's sanctions from doing business in Iran. How is it then that Coca-Cola trucks make their rounds in the Iranian market? Iran's trendy young consumers are not engaged in the Palestinian conflict to the same degree as their elders, and opinion polls suggest that they are tired of their government's standoff with Washington over uranium enrichment. Teheran shopkeepers joke with their customers not to buy Coca-Cola because it is American, seemingly making them want to buy even more. The U.S. government, on its part, has bent its rules for foodstuffs, a loophole through which the Coca-Cola Company is able to get its concentrate into Iran via Irish subsidiaries.

Occasionally in some parts of the world, anti-U.S. sentiments have become extreme. Business owners with ties to U.S. corporations have had to barricade their doors as demonstrators have defaced billboards for Nike and Pepsi, set fire to a KFC restaurant, and poured bottles of Coca-Cola into the streets. Finding himself on the receiving end of anti-American attacks, Bambang Rachmadi, the owner of an 85-outlet chain of McDonald's restaurants in Indonesia, took action. He quickly repositioned his franchise, allying it as closely as possible with Islamic culture and beliefs.

Signs in Arabic announced that McDonald's Indonesia was Muslim-owned and that all sandwiches were certified *halal*, prepared according to Muslim laws.

Menu choices — mostly chicken and rice — were touted as home-grown, and the chain's 8,000 employees — all Indonesians — were encouraged to wear Muslim dress. Bambang's message was clear: "If you destroy it [McDonald's Indonesia], you'll only destroy a job for a Muslim."

SOURCES: Eric Ellis, "Iran's Cola War," *Fortune*, March 5, 2007, 35-38; Conor Dignam, "Brand Builders vs. Flag Burners," *Ad Age Global*, December 2001, p. 4; Jay Solomon, "How Mr. Bambang Markets Big Macs in Muslim Indonesia," *The Wall Street Journal*, October 26, 2001, A1.

HINDUISM. Hinduism has 860 million followers, mainly in India, Nepal, Malaysia, Guyana, Suriname, and Sri Lanka. As well as a religion, Hinduism is a way of life predicated on the caste, or class, to which one is born. While the caste system has produced social stability, it has negative influences on business. For example, because it is difficult for individuals to rise above their caste, there is limited incentive for individual effort. The caste system also limits integration and coordination in a mixed-caste workforce, raising severe problems. Since Hinduism places value on spiritual rather than materialistic achievement, it may hamper individual drive for business success.

The family is an important element of Hindu society, with extended families being the norm. The extended family structure affects the purchasing power and consumption of Hindu families, and market researchers, in particular, must take this into account in assessing market potential and consumption patterns.

Even in their home markets, companies must be careful to take religious sensitivities into consideration. Recently, British food company Van Den Berg Foods was forced to take ads for its Chicken Tonight meat sauce off the air following complaints that the commercial ridiculed the Hindu religion.[17]

BUDDHISM. Buddhism, which extends its influence throughout Asia from Sri Lanka to Japan, has 360 million followers. Although it is an offspring of Hinduism, it has no caste system. Life is seen as filled with suffering, and the solution is to achieve nirvana — a spiritual state marked by an absence of desire. The central theme of Buddhism is spiritual achievement rather than accumulation of worldly goods.

CONFUCIANISM. Confucianism has over 150 million followers throughout Asia, especially among the Chinese, and has been characterized as a code of conduct rather than a religion. Its teachings, however, which stress loyalty and relationships, have been broadly adopted. Loyalty to central authority and placing the good of a group before that of the individual may explain the economic success of Japan, South Korea, Singapore, and the Republic of China. It also has led to cultural misunderstandings: Western societies often perceive the subordination of the individual to the common good as a violation of human rights. The emphasis on relationships is very evident in developing business ties in Asia. Preparation may take years before understanding is reached and actual business transactions can take place.

Values and Attitudes

Values are shared beliefs or group norms that have been internalized by individuals.[18] **Attitudes** are evaluations of alternatives based on these values. Differences in cultural values affect the way business planning is executed, decisions are made, strategy is implemented, and personnel are evaluated.

The more rooted values and attitudes are in central beliefs (such as religion), the more cautious international companies have to be. While Western nations tend to view change as basically positive, tradition-bound societies treat it with an attitude of suspicion — especially when change is driven by a foreign entity. The Japanese culture, for instance, raises an almost invisible — and often unscalable — wall against all *gaijin* (foreigners). Many middle-aged bureaucrats and company officials believe that buying foreign products is downright unpatriotic. The resistance is not so much to foreign products as to those who produce and market them.

To counter the perceived influence of Mattel's Barbie and Ken dolls on Iranian values, a government agency affiliated with Iran's Ministry of Education is marketing its own Dara and Sara dolls. The new products, a brother and sister, are modeled on Iranian schoolbook characters. Sara is dressed in a white headscarf covering black or brown curls. A popular outfit is a full-length, flower-dotted chador, which covers the doll from head to toe. One toy seller explained that playing with Mattel's golden-haired, skimpily dressed Barbie may lead girls to grow up into women who reject Iranian values.[19]

Cultural attitudes are not always a deterrent to foreign business practices or foreign goods. Japanese youth, for instance, display extremely positive attitudes toward Western goods, from popular music to Nike sneakers to Louis Vuitton haute couture to Starbucks lattes. Even in Japan's faltering economy, global brands are able to charge premium prices if they can tap into cultural attitudes that revere imported goods. Similarly, attitudes of U.S. youth toward Japanese "cool" have increased the popularity of authentic Japanese "manga" comics and animated cartoons. Pokémon cards, Hello Kitty, and Sony's tiny minidisc players are examples of Japanese products that caught on in the United States almost as quickly as in Japan.[20]

While products that hit the right cultural buttons can be huge successes in foreign markets, not all top brands will translate easily from one culture to another. For example, while the

VALUES

Shared beliefs or group norms internalized by individuals.

ATTITUDES

Evaluation of alternatives based on values.

Disneyland concept worked well in Tokyo, it had a tougher time in Paris. One of the main reasons was that, while the Japanese have positive attitudes toward American pop culture, the Europeans are quite content with their own cultural values and traditions. To fix its mistakes, Euro Disney, the Euro-centric resort now features restaurants, rides, and theaters targeted to appeal to the indigenous cultures throughout Europe.[21]

Manners and Customs

Manners and customs provide clues to culture and are influenced by religion, values, and attitudes. While the pervasive success of global brands like McDonald's and Coke may seem to indicate a narrowing of differences, this does not mean that cultural distinctions are blurring or that other nations are becoming "Westernized." Saudi Arabia, for example, is modern and is a market for U.S. and European goods, but it still resists Western influences.

Manners and customs influence the ways in which different cultures use products. While style-conscious consumers in Shanghai, for example, use their mobile phones as fashion accessories, proudly displaying them wherever they go, the opposite happens among teen boys in London.[22] They are far more likely to hide their phones, particularly if the design is flashy. Procter & Gamble recently launched an international advertising campaign for Tampax tampons, a product that is generally not used outside the United States, Canada, and Western Europe. In addition to overcoming religious and sensitivity obstacles, a primary objective of the campaign was to educate consumers on the benefits and use of the product. In Mexico, P&G used intimate in-the-home sessions through which salespeople advised groups of consumers about the health benefits of tampons and dispelled myths associated with the product.[23] The lesson in both the mobile phone and P&G examples is not to assume cross-border similarities, even if many indicators converge. The questions to ask are the same central issues that inform domestic business strategies: "What are we selling?" "What are the benefits we are providing?" and "Who or what are we competing against?" In addition, sound research techniques — including such methods as focus-group research that test the potential acceptance of new products, along with consumer usage and attitude studies — must precede market entry.

Understanding manners and customs is especially important in business negotiations, because interpretations based on one's own frame of reference may lead to incorrect conclusions. Americans, for instance, tend to interpret inaction or silence as negative signs, while the Japanese use silence to get business partners to sweeten a deal. Even a simple agreement may take days to negotiate in the Middle East because the Arab party may want to talk about unrelated issues or do something else for a while. The aggressive style of Russian negotiators, who often make requests for last-minute changes, astonishes ill-prepared negotiators. Even within Europe, there are stark differences. While an Italian might open negotiations with detailed background information on the company, German counterparts — who typically do extensive research before approaching the negotiating table — may interpret this as idle boasting and a waste of their time. Southern Europe, with its Catholic background and open-air lifestyle, tends to favor personal networks and social context. In contrast, the Protestant tradition of Northern Europe emphasizes numerical and technical detail.

 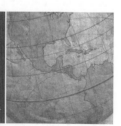

Culture Clues The Shanghai World Financial Center (developed largely by the Japanese Mori Building Corporation) became the tallest structure in China in 2008 at 492 meters/1,641 feet. The most distinctive feature in the design of the building is an opening at the peak (the functional reason of which is to allow airflow). The opening originally was meant to be a circular moon gate, but the intended design met with opposition from the Chinese who saw it resemble the rising sun design of the Japanese flag. It was replaced by a trapezoidal hole featuring an observation deck on the 100th floor.

Common stumbling blocks that derail international negotiations include insufficient preparation on the part of the host country, its history, culture, government, and image of foreigners; lack of sensitivity toward different ways of thinking; lack of familiarity with the decision-making process, the role of personal relationships, and the time it takes to complete negotiations successfully. Another factor, particularly with high-context cultures as in Japan and China, is failure to recognize the importance of allowing negotiating partners to "save face" by accepting compromises.

Aesthetics

Each culture makes a clear statement concerning good taste, as expressed in the arts and in the particular symbolism of colors, form, and music. What is and what is not acceptable may vary dramatically even in otherwise highly similar markets. Sex, for example, is a big selling point in many countries. In an apparent attempt to preserve the purity of Japanese womanhood, advertisers frequently turn to blonde, blue-eyed foreign models to make the point. In introducing the shower soap Fa to the North American market from the European market, Henkel extended its European advertising campaign to the new market. The main creative difference was to have the young woman in the waves don a bathing suit rather than be naked as in the German original.

Color is often used as a mechanism for brand identification, feature reinforcement, and differentiation. In international markets, colors have more symbolic value than in domestic markets. Black, for instance, is considered the color of mourning in the United States and Europe, whereas white has the same symbolic meaning in Japan and in most of the Far East. In Singapore, green is associated with death and is to be avoided in most product advertising.

With the global reach of the Internet, symbols as well as colors must be tested for universal appropriateness. The e-mailbox with its red flag is baffling to users outside of the United States and Canada. Similarly, the trash can on the e-mail interface may look to some like the British-styled mailbox. A British software application used the owl as a help icon only to find that in some countries it was not a symbol of wisdom but of evil and insanity.[24]

International firms such as McDonald's have to take into consideration local tastes and concerns in designing their outlets. They may have a general policy of uniformity in building or office space design, but local tastes often warrant modifications.

Respecting local cultural traditions may also generate goodwill toward the international marketer. For example, McDonald's painstakingly renovated a 17th-century building for their third outlet in Moscow.

UNDERSTANDING CULTURAL DIFFERENCES

Any analysis of culture is incomplete without the basic recognition of cultural differences. Adjusting to differences requires putting one's own cultural values aside. It has been suggested that natural **self-reference criterion** — the unconscious reference to one's own cultural values — is the root of most international business problems.[25]

However, recognizing and admitting this are often quite difficult. The following analytical approach is recommended to reduce the influence of cultural bias:

1. Define the problem or goal in terms of the domestic cultural traits, habits, or norms.
2. Define the problem or goal in terms of the foreign cultural traits, habits, or norms. Make no value judgments.
3. Isolate the self-reference criterion influence in the problem and examine it carefully to see how it complicates the problem.
4. Redefine the problem without the self-reference criterion influence.

LEARNING OBJECTIVE 3

SELF-REFERENCE CRITERION

The unconscious reference to one's own cultural values.

Let's see how this approach is applied to a product introduction. Kellogg's, for instance, wanted to introduce breakfast cereals into markets where breakfast is traditionally not eaten or where consumers drink very little milk. This involved deciding how best to instill a new habit. In France and Brazil, Kellogg's discovered that the traits, habits, and norms concerning the importance of breakfast are quite different from those in the United States. The company needed to address these differences before the product could be introduced. In France, Kellogg's aimed its commercials as much at providing nutrition lessons as at promoting the product. To gain entry into the Brazilian market, the company decided to advertise during a soap opera, knowing that consumers often emulated the characters on popular television shows.

Understanding cultural differences requires constant monitoring of changes caused by outside events as well as changes caused by the business entity itself. Controlling **ethnocentrism** — the tendency to consider one's own culture superior to others — can be achieved only by acknowledging it and properly adjusting to its possible effects in managerial decision-making. For decades, accusations of ethnocentrism — as well as charges of outright racism — scuttled attempts of South African companies to introduce much-needed technologies and infrastructure improvements into struggling African nations from Uganda to Nigeria to Cameroon. In recent years, South Africans have been able to rebuild decrepit railway systems, revitalize

ETHNOCENTRISM

The regarding of one's own culture as superior to others'.

FIGURE 2.2   Culture Dimension Scores for 12 Countries (0=low; 100=high)

SOURCE: Data derived from Geert Hofstede, "Management Scientists Are Human," *Management Science* 40, no. 1 (1994): 4–13.

banking, and bring cell phones, cash machines, and computer technology to the impoverished continent. Despite their successes, executives constantly face criticisms that they enter African markets with a sense of superiority and little sensitivity.[26] This example serves to illustrate that international managers need not only be armed with knowledge and experience of host cultures, but also must be aware of how their own cultures are perceived in the markets they wish to enter. They must resist the urge to measure other cultures with their own cultural barometers.

It has been argued that differences among cultures can be explained according to four dimensions of culture[27]:

1. *Individualism* —"I" consciousness versus "we" consciousness
2. *Power distance* —levels of equality in society
3. *Uncertainty avoidance* —need for formal rules and regulations
4. *Masculinity* —attitude toward achievement, roles of men and women

Figure 2.2 presents a summary of 12 countries' positions along these dimensions. Japan, for example, displays the highest uncertainty avoidance and might therefore be receptive to such risk-reducing marketing programs as return privileges and extended warranties. Since individualism is highly regarded in the United States, promotional appeals that promise empowerment are likely to be effective. In Arab countries, power distance scores high, indicating that consumers may respond well to promotions that imply status in society.

In addition to the four cultural dimensions in Figure 2.2, a fifth — long-term versus short-term orientation — has also been considered. Asian countries — China, Hong Kong, Taiwan, Japan, and South Korea — score high on this dimension, while most Western countries do not. This may help explain why the Japanese tend to evaluate marketing decisions based on long-term market share rather than on short-term profit motivations.

Companies such as Intertrend Communications provide expertise that can help companies avoid cultural mistakes in their advertising. For example, Intertrend created ads for the Southern Gas Company that promoted a product to three distinct subcultural groups in Asia: the Chinese, Korean, and Vietnamese markets.

GAINING CULTURAL KNOWLEDGE

Knowledge of a culture is generally acquired in one of two ways, and both are essential for developing the level of cultural competence required for doing business in foreign markets. Objective or factual information is obtained from others through communication, research, and education. **Experiential knowledge**, on the other hand, can be acquired only by being involved in a culture other than one's own. Global capability is developed through foreign assignments, networking across borders, and the use of multicountry, multicultural teams to develop strategies and programs.

A variety of sources and methods is available to managers to extend both their factual and experiential knowledge of cultures other than their own. Specific-country studies, for example, are published by the U.S. government, private companies, and universities. The U.S. Department of Commerce's Country Commercial Guides cover more than 133 countries, while the Economist Intelligence Unit's Country Reports offer intelligence on 180 countries. Culture-grams, published by the Center for International Area Studies at Brigham Young University, detail the customs of people of 187 countries. Organizations such as advertising agencies, banks, consulting firms, and transportation companies often offer clients background information on the markets they serve. Runzheimer International, for instance, reports on employee relocation and site selection for 44 countries, *World Trade* magazine's "Put Your Best Foot Forward" series covers Europe, Asia, Mexico, Canada, and Russia.[28]

4 LEARNING OBJECTIVE

EXPERIENTIAL KNOWLEDGE

Acquisition of cultural competence through personal involvement.

Developing Cultural Competence

A dilemma for companies entering global markets is the lack of adequately trained international managers. Inadequate foreign-language and international business skills have cost U.S. firms contracts and have resulted in weak negotiations and ineffectual management. The terrorist attacks of September 11, 2001, for instance, alerted the U.S. government not only to the national lack of competence in foreign-language skills, but also to the nation's failure to educate its population to cultural sensibilities at home and around the world.[29] Because more firms than ever before are operating in international environments, the need for cultural sensitivity training at all levels of the organization has never been greater. Even when cultural awareness is high, there is room for improvement. Further, today's training must encompass not only outsiders to the firm but also interaction within the corporate family as well. However inconsequential the degree of interaction may seem, it can still cause problems if proper understanding is lacking.

Some companies try to avoid the training problem by hiring only nationals or well-traveled Americans for their international operations. This makes sense for the short-term management of overseas operations but will not solve long-term training needs, especially if transfers to a culture unfamiliar to the manager are likely. International experience may not necessarily transfer from one market to another.

FIGURE 2.3   Cross-Cultural Training Methods

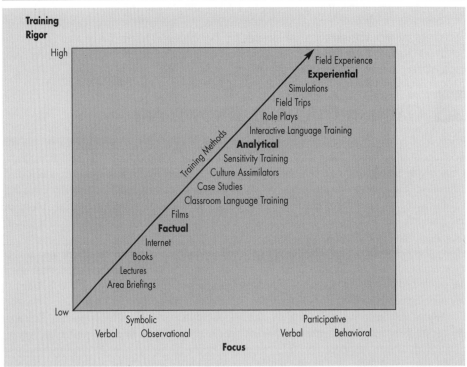

SOURCE: Adapted from J. Stewart Black and Mark Mendenhall, "A Practical but Theory-Based Framework for Selecting Cross-Cultural Training Methods," in *International Human Resource Management*, eds. Mark Mendenhall and Gary Oddou. Copyright © 1991, p. 188. By permission of South-Western College Publishing, a division of International Thomson Publishing, Inc., Mason, OH.

Formal Training Programs

The most effective way to foster cultural sensitivity and acceptance of new ways of doing things within the organization is through internal education programs. The objective of formal training programs is to foster the four critical characteristics of preparedness, sensitivity, patience, and flexibility in managers and other personnel. Of course, such programs vary dramatically in terms of their rigor, involvement, and cost. Figure 2.3 summarizes their scope.

Area briefings are the simplest and least expensive form of cultural training, providing factual preparation on specific countries prior to an overseas assignment. However, their practical purpose is limited because, alone, they provide little context in which factual information can be understood or applied; i.e., action learning is key.[30] Far more effective are training programs that also include general cultural information (values, practices, and assumptions of countries other than one's own) and self-specific information (training that allows managers to identify their own cultural paradigms, including their values, assumptions, and perceptions about others).

As well as area briefings and factual information gained through such methods as reading, research, case studies, and — time permitting — classroom language training, comprehensive programs include cultural assimilation training. For instance, by using a **cultural assimilator** — a program in which trainees respond to scenarios of specific situations in particular countries — trainers are able to evaluate a manager's preparedness for an overseas assignment. Programs like these are particularly useful in cases of transfers abroad at short notice. Programs have been developed for the Arab countries, Japan, Iran, Thailand, Central America, and Greece.

Sensitivity training focuses on enhancing a manager's flexibility in situations that are quite different from those at home. It assumes that understanding and accepting oneself is critical to understanding people from other cultures. Role-playing and other face-to-face settings are particularly effective for sensitivity training, but Web-based methods are also gaining popularity, particularly in time-strapped situations.

The most comprehensive training model includes **field experience**, which exposes a manager to a different cultural environment for a limited amount of time.

Since the expense of placing and maintaining an expatriate within a foreign culture is high and success is not guaranteed, field experience is rarely used in training. As a halfway measure, some companies have experimented by placing trainees — and sometimes their families — within a domestically located host family from the culture to which the trainee is to be assigned.

Regardless of language ability or the degree of training, preparation, and positive personal characteristics, remember that in a culture that is not his or her own, a manager will always be a foreigner. This means that a manager should never rely on his or her own judgment alone when local managers can be consulted. In many instances, a manager should have an interpreter present at negotiations, especially if the manager is not completely bilingual.

Culture Shock

The effectiveness of orientation training can be measured only after managers begin their assignments overseas. Once there, a unique phenomenon they face is **culture shock**, a pronounced reaction to the psychological disorientation people feel when they move for an extended time in a markedly different culture. Although they all experience it, individuals differ widely in how they allow themselves to be affected by culture shock.

While the severity of culture shock may be a function of the individual's lack of adaptability, it may equally be a result of the firm's lack of understanding of the situation into which the manager was sent. Often, goals set for a subsidiary or a project may be unrealistic, or the means

AREA BRIEFINGS

Training programs that provide factual preparation prior to an overseas assignment.

CULTURAL ASSIMILATOR

Training program in which trainees for overseas assignments must respond to scenarios of specific situations in a particular country.

SENSITIVITY TRAINING

Human relations training that focuses on personal and interpersonal interactions; training that focuses on enhancing an expatriate's flexibility in situations quite different from those at home.

FIELD EXPERIENCE

Experience acquired in actual rather than laboratory settings; training that exposes a corporate manager to a cultural environment.

CULTURE SHOCK

Pronounced reactions to the psychological disorientation that most people feel when they move for an extended period of time into a markedly different culture.

Quick Take *Online Cultural Training*

Managers heading abroad to negotiate a deal or relocating to a foreign environment or multicultural teams working within large organizations are just some of the scenarios that benefit from cross-cultural training. Skimping on training in this area can be potentially hazardous. For example, those going to Japan unprepared for high levels of etiquette and ceremony risk offending valuable clients. Employees who move to Hong Kong are often responsible for working with multiple countries and therefore require the know-how to work in a variety of cultural settings.

However, it is nearly impossible to cover such complex cross-cultural training in one- or two-day training periods. Furthermore, such training costs in excess of $1,000 per head per day. Therefore, many organizations are adding online training following the face-to-face classroom training in order to gain continuous and additional training. Many of the programs used the following elements:

1. *Detailed scenarios.* Training materials feature realistic business situations and events tied to elements in the learner's background. More than a briefing, sessions become a guided, narrated experience full of custom-created learning opportunities.

2. *Gradual delivery.* The ability to control the flow of information to the participant supports the learning process. Not only is training flexible enough to fit into a busy schedule, but it effectively mimics the real-life flow of data that informs decision-making.

3. *Support.* Participants have instant access to detailed materials at any time of day and from any location. They can check their perceptions against training materials or complete tailor-made exercises, reinforcing learning. They can also seek feedback on key issues.

4. *Online discussions.* Sessions can be simulcast to hundreds of participants around the world. Participants benefit from the pooled learning experience, which mimics real-life decision-making.

SOURCES: Ross Bentley, "It Pays to Be a Cross-Culture Vulture," *Personnel Today*, January 23, 2007, 8; Jessica Caplan, "Innovations in intercultural training," *China Staff*, November 2004, 1, 4; and Peter T. Burgi and Brant R. Dykehouse, "On-Line Cultural Training: The Next Phase," *International Insight*, Winter 2000, pp. 7-10.

by which they are to be reached may be inadequate. Situations like these can lead to the external manifestations of culture shock, such as bitterness and even physical illness. In extreme cases, they can lead to hostility toward anything in the host environment.

Managers typically go through four distinct stages when adapting to a new culture. The duration of each stage is highly individual.

1. *Initial euphoria* — enjoying the novelty of living in the host culture, largely from the perspective of a spectator
2. *Irritation and hostility* — experiencing cultural differences as participation in the culture increases
3. *Adjustment* — adapting to the situation, which in some cases leads to biculturalism and even accusations from corporate headquarters of "going native"
4. *Re-entry* — returning home

SUMMARY

Some companies approach overseas markets with the attitude that business is business the world around, following the model of Pepsi and McDonald's. But while globalization is a fact of life, cultural convergence is not. Most companies, recognizing cultural differences, tailor their business approaches to individual cultures. Those that are successful in international markets share an important quality: patience. They do not rush into new situations but rather build their operations carefully by following the most basic business principles. These principles are to know your adversary, know your audience, and know your customer.

 Culture is a system of learned behavior patterns characteristic of the members of a given society. It is constantly shaped by a set of dynamic variables, both concrete and abstract.

 Concrete influences on culture include language, infrastructure, education, and social institutions. Abstract or spiritual influences encompass religion, values, and attitudes, manners and customs, and aesthetics.

 The tendency to view other cultures from the perspective of the individual's own cultural influences is known as the self-reference criterion. International managers can reduce this cultural bias — as well as ethnocentrism — with a thorough understanding of and sensitivity toward cultural differences.

 To cope in new cultural environments, an international manager needs both factual and interpretive knowledge of culture. To some extent, the factual knowledge can be learned; its interpretation comes only through experience.

It is possible to compare cultures along four key dimensions: individualism, power distance, uncertainty avoidance, and masculinity. Recent studies have also suggested a fifth dimension: long-term versus short-term orientation.

The most complicated problems in dealing with the cultural environment stem from the fact that one cannot learn culture — one has to live it. Training that includes experiential knowledge as well as factual knowledge is essential for managers assigned overseas.

KEY TERMS AND CONCEPTS

culture	financial infrastructure	ethnocentrism
acculturation	marketing infrastructure	experiential knowledge
high-context culture	cultural convergence	area briefings
low-context culture	social stratification	cultural assimilator
change agent	reference group	sensitivity training
backtranslation	values	field experience
economic infrastructure	attitudes	culture shock
social infrastructure	self-reference criterion	

REVIEW QUESTIONS

1. What is culture? Suggest some of the ways in which it influences the conduct of international business.
2. List the core elements of culture.
3. What kinds of business decisions are influenced by spiritual or abstract elements of culture? Give examples.
4. What is the self-reference criterion?
5. List five dimensions through which comparisons of cultures are possible.
6. What is the difference between factual cultural knowledge and experiential cultural knowledge?
7. What are the requirements of an effective cross-cultural training program?
8. Describe culture shock and explain why it occurs.

CRITICAL SKILL BUILDERS

1. Comment on the assumption, "If people are serious about doing business with you, they will speak English."

2. You are on your first business visit to Germany. You feel confident about your ability to speak the language (you studied German in school and have taken a refresher course), and you decide to use it. During introductions, you want to break the ice by asking "Wie geht's?" and insisting that everyone call you by your first name. Speculate as to the reaction.

3. Q: "What do you call a person who can speak two languages?"
A: "Bilingual."

Q: "How about three?"
A: "Trilingual."

Q: "Excellent. How about one?"
A: "Hmmmm. . . . American!"

Is this joke malicious, or is there something to be learned from it?

4. What can be learned about a culture from reading and attending to factual materials?

5. Provide examples of how the self-reference criterion might manifest itself.

6. Is any international business entity not a cultural imperialist? How else could one explain the phenomenon of multinational corporations?

ON THE WEB

1. Many companies, such as Cultural Savvy, provide cross-cultural consulting, coaching, and training. Using the company's Web site (**www.culturalsavvy.com**), assess the different ways such consultants can play an important role in mastering cultural competency.

2. Compare and contrast a global company's home pages for cultural influences. For example, **www.coca-cola.com/glp/d/index.html** will allow you to enter six regions of the world where the Coca-Cola Company has operations.

ENDNOTES

1. Pankaj Ghemawat, "Distance Still Matters," *Harvard Business Review*, 79, September 2001, pp. 137-47.
2. Alfred Kroeber and Clyde Kluckhohn, *Culture: A Critical Review of Concepts and Definitions* (New York: Random House, 1985), p. 11.
3. Geert Hofstede, "National Cultures Revisited," *Asia-Pacific Journal of Management* 1, September 1984, pp. 22–24.
4. Helen Brower, "Tips for Business Travelers," *Travel Weekly*, November 13, 2000, p. 90.
5. **www.understandfrance.org/France/FrenchMovies.html**; "Subsidy Wars," *The Economist*, February 24, 2005, 76.
6. "A World Empire by Other Means," *The Economist*, December 22, 2001, p. 65.
7. Keith B. Richburg, "French Snared in Web of English," *The Washington Post*, September 27, 2000, p. A19; Rory Cowan, "The e Does Not Stand for English," *Global Business*, March 2000, p. L22.

8. Allyson L. Stewart-Allen, "Don't Lose Advertising in the Translation," *Marketing News*,June 5, 2000, p. 16.

9. Stephen P. Iverson, "The Art of Translation," *World Trade*, April 2000, pp. 90–92.

10. Isis Artze, "Marketing to Show Empathy," *Hispanic*, January/February 2001, p. 70.

11. Anthony Tommasini, "A Cultural Disconnect on Wagner," *The New York Times*, August 5, 2001, Arts and Leisure, p. 2; "Nokia Veti Pois Mainoskampanjansa," *Uutislehti* 100, June 15, 1998, p. 5.

12. Chris Tomlinson, "Africa's Wireless Usage Surges," *The Chicago Tribune*, July 11, 2002, S4, p. 6.

13. "Inside the Machine," *The Economist*, November 9, 2000, p. 5.

14. Amy Argetsinger, "More U.S. Students Heed Canada's Call," *The Washington Post*, April 29, 2001, pp. C1, C9.

15. Brower, "Tips for Business Travelers"; Y. H. Wong and Ricky Yee-kwong, "Relationship Marketing in China: Guanxi, Favoritism, and Adaptation," *Journal of Business Ethics* 22, no. 2, 1999, pp. 107–18.

16. David McClelland, *The Achieving Society* (New York: Irvington, 1961), p. 90.

17. "Chicken Tonight TV Ads Banned for 'Ridiculing' Hindu Religion," *Marketing Week*, March 8, 2001, p. 6.

18. Roger D. Blackwell, James F. Engel, and Paul W. Miniard, *Consumer Behavior*, 9th ed. (Mason, OH: South-Western, 2001), p. 381.

19. "Iran Unveils Islamic Twin Dolls to Fight Culture War," AP Worldstream, March 5, 2002.

20. Douglas McGray, "Japan's Gross National Cool," *Foreign Policy*, May/June 2002, p. 44.

21. John Tagliabue, "Disney's New Park Has a European Accent," *The New York Times*, June 9, 2002, Travel Advisory, p. 5.

22. Rob Kaiser, "Motorola Heeds Style Call," *The Chicago Tribune*, February 11, 2002, p. 1.

23. Emily Nelson and Miriam Jordan, "Seeking New Markets for Tampons," *The Wall Street Journal*, December 8, 2001, A1.

24. Greg Bathon, "Eat the Way Your Mama Taught You," *World Trade*, December 2000, pp. 76–77.

25. James A. Lee, "Cultural Analysis in Overseas Operations," *Harvard Business Review*, 44, March/April 1966, pp. 106–14.

26. Rachel L. Swarns, "Awe and Unease As South Africa Stretches Out," *The New York Times*, February 17, 2002, Section 1, p. 1.

27. Geert Hofstede, *Culture's Consequences: International Differences in Work-Related Values* (Beverly Hills, CA: Sage Publications, 1984), Chap. 1; Geert Hofstede and Michael H. Bond, "The Confucius Connection: From Cultural Roots to Economic Growth," *Organizational Dynamics* 16, Spring 1988, pp. 4–21.

28. U.S. Department of Commerce, **http://www.ita.doc.gov**; Economist Intelligence Unit, **http://www.eiu.com**; Culturegrams, **http://www.culturegrams.com**; Runzheimer International, **http://www.runzheimer.com**; *World Trade* (**http://www.worldtrademag.com**).

29. David Maxwell and Nina Garrett, "Meeting National Needs, *Change*, May/June 2002, pp. 22–28.

30. Maureen Lewis, "Why Cross-Cultural Training Simulations Work," *Journal of European Industrial Training* 29 (number 7, 2005): pp. 593-98.

CHAPTER 3

Trade Tug-of-War

Situated in the plains of Shandong Province near the Yellow Sea coastline, Weifang was once an agrarian region famous for its vegetables. During the Cultural Revolution of the

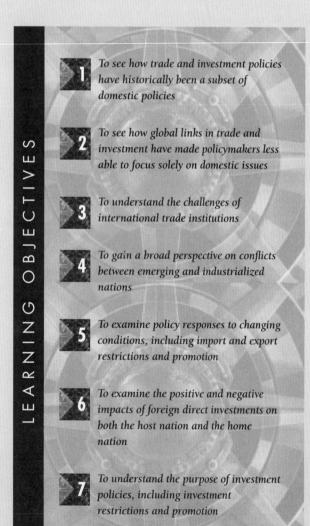

1970s, however, it became an industrial center producing chemicals, electronics, textiles, and diesel engines.

Seven years ago, the aging state-owned Weifang East Steel Pipe factory experienced major financial difficulties. Strangled by debt, it was unable to pay its workers. After realizing that blocking the factory's gates and protesting in front of local municipal buildings did little to produce a paycheck, workers changed their approach. Inspired by the spirit of capitalism that consumes modern China, more than 50 employees borrowed from banks against their homes to buy the Weifang factory, install new equipment, and produce higher quality steel pipe.

Today, the factory faces a new crisis, but this time the workers' anger is aimed at the United States, which is set to impose punishing tariffs on Chinese steel pipe imports at the request of struggling American steel makers.

China has recently become not only the world's largest producer, but also the world's largest consumer of steel and steel products. In 2001 China started to export some of its steel, pumping cheaper goods into the international market and threatening the ability of U.S. companies to compete. Though steel pipe exports accounted for less than $1 billion of the huge trade deficit between the U.S. and China in 2006, China has more than doubled its share of pipe sold in the United States in two years. China now captures more than a quarter of the U.S. steel pipe market. Due to this steel influx, several U.S. steel pipe factories have recently shut down, putting hundreds of Americans out of work.

U.S. producers of steel pipe argue that, though the Weifang factory is now private, it continues to reap the benefits of past subsidies for land, utilities, and other costs as well as from current subsidies for raw steel. A recent study by the Alliance for American Manufacturing estimates that subsidies, as large as $27.11 billion, were provided to Chinese iron and steel companies between 2000 and 2007. The U.S. government insists that China unfairly and illegally supports exports to undercut U.S. producers. China denies subsidizing its steel industry. Instead, it perceives possible American tariffs to be an unfair assault on China's use of Western business models to modernize, provide jobs, and improve its standing among the world's economic powers.

SOURCES: "Huge Energy Subsidies Bolster China's Steel Export, *Comtex News Network, Inc.*, January 11, 2008, **http://www.lexisnexis. com/clients/senate/**, January 14, 2008; Robert J. Samuelson, "Goodbye, Free Trade; Hello, Mercantilism; As countries grow more interdependent, they're also becoming more nationalistic," *Newsweek*, January 7, 2008; Steven R. Weisman, "Trade war thwarts China's burgeoning capitalist U.S. tariffs idle a worker-owned plant," *International Herald Tribune*, December 11, 2007.

As You Read This Chapter

1. The concepts of opportunity cost and competitive advantage suggest that Chinese subsidies for steel pipe exports are beneficial to the American economy, since they are passed on as savings to US consumers and encourage the relocation of American resources to more competitive industries. If that is the case, what could explain the imposition of tariffs?
2. If the subsidy estimate from the Alliance for American Manufacturing is accurate, what are some reasons that the Chinese government would choose to spend such a large amount on the domestic steel industry?

Every nation has its own international trade and investment policies. The policies may be publicly pronounced or kept secret; they may be disjointed or coordinated. They may be applied consciously or determined by a *laissez-faire* attitude, which means that government does not intervene in market activities. Whatever form they take, trade policy actions come into play when measures taken by governments affect the flow of trade and investment across national borders. This chapter explores trade and investment issues from both the host country and the home country perspectives, with a focus on what happens when the interests of multiple nations come into conflict.

WHAT ARE TRADE AND INVESTMENT POLICIES?

Government policies are designed to regulate, stimulate, direct, and protect national activities. The exercise of these policies is the result of **national sovereignty**, which provides a government with the right and responsibility to shape the environment of the country and its citizens. Because they are border-bound, governments focus mainly on domestic policies. Nevertheless, many policy actions have repercussions on other nations, firms, and individuals abroad and are therefore a component of a nation's trade and investment policy.

Influence of Domestic Policy

Domestic policy can be subdivided into two groups of actions that affect trade and investment. The first affects trade and investment indirectly, the second directly.

The **domestic policy** actions of most governments aim to increase the standard of living of the country's citizens, to improve the quality of life, to stimulate national development, and to achieve full employment. Clearly, all of these goals are closely intertwined. For example, an improved standard of living is likely to contribute to national development. Similarly, **quality of life** and **standard of living** are interlinked. Also, a high level of employment plays a major role

NATIONAL SOVEREIGNTY

The supreme right of nations to determine national policies; freedom from external control.

DOMESTIC POLICY

Public policy concerned with national issues but that may have direct or indirect bearing on foreign trade and investment.

QUALITY OF LIFE

The standard of living combined with environmental and cultural factors; it determines the level of well-being of individuals.

STANDARD OF LIVING

The level of material affluence of a group or nation, measured as a composite of quantities and qualities of goods.

in determining standard of living. Yet all of these policy goals also indirectly affect international trade and investment. For example, if foreign industries become more competitive and rapidly increase their exports, employment in importing countries may suffer. Likewise, if a country accumulates large quantities of debt, which at some time must be repaid, present and future standards of living may be threatened.

Policy affects trade and investment in more direct ways, too. A country may pursue policies of increased development that mandate either technology transfer from abroad or the exclusion of foreign industries to the benefit of domestic firms. Also, government officials may believe that imports threaten the culture, health, or standards of living of the country's citizens and thus the quality of life. As a result, nations develop regulations aimed at protecting their citizens.

Influence of Foreign Policy

FOREIGN POLICY

The area of public policy concerned with relationships with other countries.

Nations also institute **foreign policy** measures that, while designed with domestic concerns in mind, are explicitly aimed at exercising influence abroad. One major goal of foreign policy is national security. For example, nations may develop alliances, coalitions, and agreements to protect their borders or their spheres of interest.

Similarly, nations may take measures to enhance their national security preparedness in case of international conflict. They may even take action to restrict or encourage trade and investment flows in order to preserve or enhance the capability of industries that are important to national security.

Another goal of foreign policy may be to improve trade and investment opportunities. To develop new markets abroad and increase their sphere of influence, for instance, nations may give foreign aid to other countries. Such aid may be long-term, such as the generous Marshall Plan funds awarded by the United States for the reconstruction of Europe, or may serve as emergency measures.

The United States is the world's largest single-country donor of foreign aid, providing $23.5 billion in 2006. In recent years, debt forgiveness has played a major role in helping developing countries make advanced repayment of external public debt. For the heavily indebted poor countries, the debt levels of 2006 are estimated to have come down to half the level of five years ago.[1]

Conflicting Policies

Each country develops its own domestic and foreign policies, and therefore policy aims vary from nation to nation. Inevitably, conflicts arise. For example, full employment policies in one country may directly affect employment policies in another. Similarly, the development aims of one country may reduce the development capability of another. Even when health issues are concerned, disputes arise. One nation may argue that its regulations are in place to protect its citizens, while other nations interpret domestic regulations as market barriers. As described in the case that opens this chapter, U.S. tariffs on Chinese steel imports aim to protect American steel producers by limiting a multi-billion dollar industry in China.[2]

Ongoing disagreement between the U.S., Europe, and China over the safety of Chinese-produced toys is another example. While the U.S. claims that levels of lead found in toys make them too dangerous for children to play with, China counters that the U.S. uses overly stringent safety standards to restrict imports.[3]

Conflicts among national policies have always existed but have come into prominence only in recent decades. The reason lies in the changes that have taken place in the world trade and investment climate. These changes are discussed next.

Quick Take   *Does Use Matter?*

Recently, the South African Court of Appeals convened to settle a dispute between The Baking Tin, an importer of kitchen containers, and the South African Revenue Service (SARS). The appeals court set out to determine whether aluminum foil containers imported by the company were subject to anti-dumping duties.

The Baking Tin claimed that the containers it imported are consumables and that its goods do not constitute hollow-ware. In addition, it argued that its containers were supplied to food manufacturers for the purpose of preparing food for the consumer. A South African pie company, for example, might buy these tins to package its pies. The consumer, after eating the pie, is then expected to dispose of the containers. For this reason, The Baking Tim declared that the containers could not be classified as kitchen or household articles.

SARS, on the other hand, argued that the containers were hollow-ware for table or kitchen use and, therefore, subject to duties at the rate of 30 percent and liable to anti-dumping duties, which would shut The Baking Tin out of the South African market.

Siding with SARS, the appeals court followed an internationally recognized principle of tariff classification stating that the purpose for which containers are manufactured is not to be taken into account during customs classification. Accordingly, the decisive criteria for customs classification of a particular good are its objective characteristics and properties. In the end, the court held that The Baking Tin's aluminum containers were hollow-ware and were thus subject to duties.

Since this case, however, the South African International Trade Administration Commission has published a notice suggesting that tariffs and duties may be lifted on 31 products, including aluminum hollow-ware. This would allow companies like The Baking Tin access to the South African market and would lower costs to domestic producers using imported goods in their production.

SOURCES: Sanchia Temkin, "Decision on food containers may affect many importers," *Business Day*, October 8, 2007; David Christianson, "South Africa: Industries in Revolt Over Tariff Threat," *Business Day*, January 15, 2008.

POST-WAR GLOBAL TRADE REGULATION

The **General Agreement on Tariffs and Trade (GATT)** started out in 1947 as a set of rules to ensure nondiscrimination, transparent procedures, the settlement of disputes, and the participation of the lesser-developed countries in international trade. To increase trade, GATT used tariff concessions, through which member countries agreed to limit the level of tariffs they would impose on imports from other GATT members. An important tool is the **most-favored nation (MFN)** clause, recently renamed as "normal trade relations." It called for member countries to grant each other the same treatment accorded any other nation with respect to imports and exports. MFN is, in effect, an equal-opportunity clause.

In time, GATT became the governing set of regulations for settling international trade disputes. It evolved into an institution that sponsored various successful rounds of international trade negotiations with an initial focus on the reduction of high tariffs that restricted cross-border trade. Headquartered in Geneva, Switzerland, the GATT Secretariat conducted its work as instructed by the representatives of its member nations. Even though the GATT had no

LEARNING OBJECTIVE 1

GENERAL AGREEMENT ON TARIFFS AND TRADE (GATT)

An international code of tariffs and trade rules signed by 23 nations in 1947; headquartered in Geneva, Switzerland; 151 members currently; now part of the World Trade Organization.

MOST-FAVORED NATION (MFN)

A term describing a GATT clause that calls for member countries to grant other member countries the same most favorable treatment they accord any country concerning imports and exports, now also known as *normal trade relations*.

WORLD TRADE ORGANIZATION (WTO)

The institution that supplanted GATT in 1995 to administer international trade and investment accords (see **http://www.wto.org**)

GENERAL AGREEMENT ON TRADE IN SERVICES (GATS)

A legally enforceable pact among GATT participants that covers trade and investments in the services sector.

independent enforcement mechanism and relied entirely on moral suasion and on frequently wavering membership adherence to its rules, it achieved major progress for world trade.

Early in its history, the GATT accomplished the reduction of duties for trade in 50,000 products, amounting to two-thirds of the value of the trade among its participants.

In subsequent years, special GATT negotiations, such as the Kennedy Round — named after John F. Kennedy — and the Tokyo Round, further reduced trade barriers and improved dispute-settlement mechanisms. The GATT also developed better provisions for dealing with subsidies and more explicit definitions of roles for import controls.

In early 1995, the GATT was supplanted by a new institution, the **World Trade Organization (WTO)**, which now administers international trade and investment accords. Through the **General Agreement on Trade in Services (GATS)**, an entire new set of rules was designed to govern the service area. Agreement also was reached on new rules to encourage international investment flows.

In 2001, a new round of international trade negotiations was initiated. Since the agreement to embark on a new round was reached in the city of Doha (Qattar), the negotiations are known as the Doha Round. The aim was to further hasten implementation of liberalization to help developing and impoverished nations in particular. Another goal was to expand the role of the WTO to encompass more trade activities where rules were deemed insufficient, due either to purposeful exclusion by governments in earlier negotiations or to new technology changing the global marketplace. Regulations covering trade in agricultural goods, anti-dumping, and electronic commerce are all examples. In the agriculture sector, there have not been any signs of compromise on major issues such as the reduction of customs duties, the handling of sensitive products, and the reduction of domestic subsidies, although substantial progress has been made in the levels of communication among participating nations.

The Doha negotiations have been quite slow. Launched in 1999, they have not yet concluded. Suspended during the summer of 2006 due to significant disagreements, the talks were resumed in late fall 2006. Claims by developing countries that wealthy nations unfairly subsidize domestic agriculture and impose import taxes were a major cause of conflict. Until early summer 2007, the core negotiations mainly took place between India, Brazil, the EU, and the USA. With the parties unable to agree on a common position on agriculture and non-agriculture market access, the negotiations continue.[4]

The World Trade Organization

The World Trade Organization is the only international body dealing with the rules of trade between and among nations. At the heart of the WTO are agreements, negotiated and signed by most of the world's trading nations. These documents provide the legal ground rules for international commerce. Their goal is to help producers of goods and services, exporters, and importers conduct business in the global marketplace.

The WTO has three main purposes:

1. To help trade flow as freely as possibly as long as there are no undesirable side-effects. In part, this means removing obstacles to trade. It also means making rules transparent and predictable so that individuals, companies, and governments know their scope of influence.
2. To serve as a forum for trade negotiations among the community of trading nations.
3. To settle trade disputes among member nations. Recent cases have included heated disputes over steel tariffs. Other contentious issues include trade in U.S. cotton and South Korean-made semiconductors.

The GATT and now the WTO have made major contributions to improved trade and investment flows around the world. Their successes have resulted in improvements in the economic well-being of nations around the world.

© GETTY IMAGES/PHOTODISC

Cattle in Europe are raised without hormones. Since 1989 hormone-fed beef has been banned in European countries, effectively restricting imports of U.S. beef. A WTO review of the hormones found the ban was not based on scientific evidence. Despite threats of sanctions, the ban has not been lifted.

To understand both the benefits and the challenges of entering the WTO, consider the case of China, one of its most recent members. WTO accession provided China not only with easier access to global markets, but with the opportunity to reform its inefficient industries and farms. By 2007, it had become the world's second largest trader. China's limited economic reform over the last 20 years has allowed its businesses to flourish and the standard of living for millions of people to rise slowly but steadily. Since joining the WTO in 2001, China has shown major economic growth. Due to increased opening and reform, its political and social stability has increased, and labor productivity has improved. Ever since joining the WTO, the country's economy has grown between 8 and 9 percent annually.[5]

CHANGES IN THE GLOBAL POLICY ENVIRONMENT

Three major changes have occurred over time in the global policy environment: a reduction of domestic policy influence, a weakening of traditional international institutions, and a sharpening of the conflict between industrialized and developing nations. These three changes in turn have had a major effect on policy responses in the international trade and investment field.

Reduction of Domestic Policy Influences

The effects of growing global influences on domestic economies have been significant. Policy-makers have increasingly come to recognize that it is very difficult to isolate domestic economic activity from international market events. Again and again, domestic policy measures are vetoed or counteracted by the activities of global market forces. Decisions that were once clearly in the domestic purview now have to be revised due to influences from abroad. At the same time, the clash between the fixed geography of nations and the nonterritorial nature of many of today's problems and solutions continues to escalate. Nation-states may simply no longer be the natural problem-solving unit. Local government may be most appropriate to address some of the problems of individuals, while transnational or even global entities are required to deal with larger issues such as economics, resources, or the environment.

Agricultural policies, for example—historically a domestic issue—have been thrust into the international realm. Any time a country or a group of nations such as the European Union contemplates changes in agricultural subsidies, quantity restrictions, or even quality regulations, international trade partners are quick to speak up against the resulting global effects of such changes. Quick Take: Pineapples of Change, on page 54, demonstrates how product safety and quality measures are influenced by global concerns.

When countries contemplate specific industrial policies that encourage, for example, industrial innovation or collaboration, they often encounter major opposition from trading partners who believe that their own industries are jeopardized by such policies. Those reactions and the resulting constraints are the result of growing interdependencies among nations and closer links between industries around the world. The following examples highlight the global benefits of trade.

- In 2007, U.S. exports have grown at more than twice the rate of U.S. imports.
- U.S. jobs supported by goods exported pay 13 to 18 percent more than other jobs.
- A company that exports is almost ten times more likely to succeed than a competitor who does not.
- Increased international trade has raised real incomes, restrained prices, introduced greater product variety, spurred technological advances and innovation, and raised real living standards.
- Wages paid by manufacturing plants that export are 9 percent higher on average than wages paid by non-exporting plants of the same size.

Quick Take   *Pineapples of Change*

Though native to South and Central America, pineapples sold in the United States have primarily been grown in Hawaii. For many Americans, Hawaii has been equated with pineapple exports. A new variety of pineapple, however, has changed all that.

In 1996, the first "Gold" or MD2 strain of pineapple hit the retail market. Since then, Del Monte, one of the world's leading pineapple producers, has seen a 174 percent gain in pineapple sales. The success of this new variety of pineapple is attributed to its sweetness, lower level of acidity, and uniformity. The Hawaiian Champaka, previously the primary pineapple sold in the U.S., was sometimes sour or hard; customers never knew what they were getting.

With the development of this new product, the pineapple industry has changed. Almost all the major producers now grow a version of MD2 and are tailoring their production to fit the needs of this new strain. Since Hawaii's climate and soil are not very conducive to growing this new, sweeter variety, many producers are moving to plantations in South and Central America. Del Monte, for example, will plant its last commercial crop in Hawaii in 2008. This change provides an example of how environmental changes can alter the competitive picture around the world, with no fault by workers, producers, or consumers. Change is what often promotes progress. The shift in consumer preferences from tuna fish packaged in oil to tuna packaged in water led to a weeding out of competitors some decades ago.

Those affected, however, do not need to stand still. Hawaiian farmers now grow specialized crops such as noni, papaya, and macadamia nuts to fill the void. The revenue drop from pineapple from 1984 to 2004 has been restored by revenue from products such as coffee, flowers, mangoes, and other tropical fruits. Product decisions by companies like Del Monte free large numbers of workers and vast expanses of land and have accelerated growth in the specialized crop industry. Former pineapple plantations and those working on them have been quickly absorbed in Hawaii's ever-growing specialty foods market.

SOURCES: Mark Niesse, "Pineapple Ends Reign in Hawaii," *The Washington Post*, May 21, 2006; Stephanie Witt Sedgwick, "The Pineapple's Sweet Spot," *The Washington Post*, January 2, 2008.

- International trade in goods and services exposes firms to foreign competition and reduces their ability to charge high markups above production costs.
- Increased imports by China, of both manufactured goods and raw materials, has boosted exports and growth in many economies, especially in China's Asian neighbors and commodity exporters (such as Brazil and Chile).[6]

Consider, too, that some of today's products would be nearly impossible to build if manufacturers were unable to source supplies from and sell resulting goods into multiple global markets. Figure 3.1, for instance, shows how essential multinational links are to the aircraft industry. Further, with so many product components being sourced from so many countries around the world, it becomes increasingly difficult to decide what constitutes a domestic product. In light of this uncertainty, policy actions against foreign products become more difficult as well.

CURRENCY FLOWS

The flow of currency from nation to nation, which in turn determines exchange rates.

To some extent, the complex links that trade fosters between nations have turned the economic world inside-out. For example, trade flows once determined **currency flow**s and therefore exchange rates. In the more recent past, currency flows have taken on a life of their own, increasing from an average daily trading volume of $18 billion in 1980 to almost $3 trillion in 2007.[7] As a result, currency flows have begun to set the value of exchange rates, independent of trade. These exchange rates, in turn, have now begun to determine the level of trade. Governments that want to counteract these developments with monetary policies find that currency flows vastly outnumber the financial flows that can be marshaled by governments, even when acting in concert. The interactions between global and domestic financial flows have severely limited the freedom for governmental action. For example, if the European Central Bank or the U.S. Federal Reserve changes interest-rate levels, these changes not only influence domestic activities but also trigger international flows of capital that may reduce, enhance, or even negate the domestic effects. Similarly, rapid technological change and vast advances in communication permit firms and countries to quickly emulate innovation and counteract carefully designed plans. As a result, governments are often powerless to implement effective policy measures, even when they know what to do.

Governments also find that domestic regulations often have major international repercussions. Consider, for example, the impact of U.S. legislation that restricts foreign ownership

Fast Facts

Where is the world's largest rain forest?

The Amazon in South America is the world's largest rain forest. It is an area almost as big as 48 of the 50 states of the United States and contains more plant and animal species than any other place on Earth. It is being burned and cleared at a rate of about 4 percent each year, contributing to global warming.

FIGURE 3.1 Who Builds the Boeing 777?

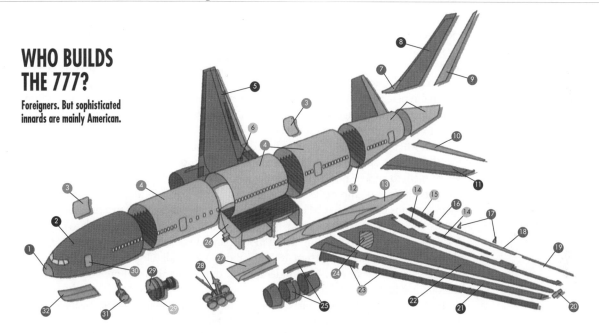

WHO BUILDS THE 777?

Foreigners. But sophisticated innards are mainly American.

BOEING	INTERNATIONAL SUPPLIERS	JAPANESE SUPPLIERS	JAPANESE SUPPLIERS
2 Nose section	1 Radome	3 Cargo doors	6 Fixed trailing edge
5 Trailing edge panels	7 Dorsal fin	4 Fuselage panels	12 Floor beams
8 Vertical fin	9 Rudder	13 Wing-to-body fairing	14 Spoilers
11 Horizontal stabilizer	10 Elevator	24 In-spar ribs	15 Inboard flaps
21 Fixed leading edge	16 Flaperon	26 Wing center section	23 Leading edge slats
22 Wing box	17 Flap support fairings	27 Main landing gear doors	29 Engine
25 Nocelles, struts, and fairings	18 Outboard flap	30 Passenger doors	
	19 Aileron		
	20 Wing tip assembly		
	28 Main landing gear		
	29 Engine		
	31 Nose landing gear		
	32 Nose landing gear doors		

SOURCE: Boeing ad, **http://www.boeing.com**.

of telecommunications equipment and technology. Because these industries are considered sensitive in terms of national security, proposed purchases or mergers with non-U.S. companies are subject to review by the **Committee on Foreign Investments (CFIUS)**. The scrutiny extends beyond telephone networks to the supposed boundary-free Internet. Nippon Telegraph & Telephone's acquisition of Verio Inc., which hosts 400,000 Web sites for small- and mid-sized businesses, marked the first time that legislation allowing law enforcement agencies access to telephone networks — or wiretapping — was applied to an Internet company. NTT is partly owned by the Japanese government. In direct conflict with FCC regulations, which bans the granting of licenses to companies with more than 25 percent ownership by a foreign government, WTO rules allow multinational telecom mergers. The NTT acquisition of Verio threw the doors open to other suitors of U.S. communications companies. In 2006, CFIUS investigated the acquisition of the London-based Peninsular and Oriental (P&O), a stream navigation company, by state-owned Dubai Ports World. Since P&O controlled the cargo operations of various U.S. ports, the purpose of the investigation was to ensure that port security of the United States would not be compromised. Since DP World only hoped to take on the functions previously performed by P&O, namely the off- and on-loading of cargo, and did not plan to manage port security, nor to own any ports, CFIUS allowed the transaction to move forward. However, a major public outrage focused on foreign control of U.S. facilities.[8]

Legislators around the world are continuously confronted with such international links. In some countries, the implications are understood, and new legislation is devised with an understanding of its international consequences. In other nations, legislators often ignore the international repercussions. Given the ties between economies, this threatens to place firms at a competitive disadvantage in the international marketplace, or it may make it easier for foreign firms to compete in the domestic market.

Even when policymakers want to take decisive steps, they are often unable to do so. Japanese electronics companies, led by Hitachi, Toshiba, and Mitsubishi, convinced the Japanese government to impose **punitive tariffs** on imported DRAM chips. The targets of the complaints were South Korean chip makers, Samsung and Hynix Semiconductor Inc., accused of selling memory chips into Japan at below the cost of producing them. Due to a dramatic falloff in the semiconductor industry worldwide, however, the dumping charges are tough to prove—prices for chips across the board plummeted more than 90 percent in a one-year period, including those of Japanese manufacturers. In 2007 the World Trade Organization ruled that Japan's countervailing duties were illegal under international trade rules and ordered Tokyo to remove the punitive trade barrier.[9]

In situations like this, policymakers find themselves with increasing responsibilities, yet with fewer and less effective tools to carry them out. More segments of the domestic economy are vulnerable to international shifts at the same time that they are becoming less controllable. To regain some power to influence policies, some governments have sought to restrict the influence of world trade by erecting barriers, charging tariffs, and implementing import regulations. However, these measures too have been restrained by the existence of international agreements forged through institutions such as the WTO or bilateral negotiations. World trade has therefore changed many previously held notions about the sovereignty of nation-states and extraterritoriality. The same interdependence that made us all more affluent has also left us more vulnerable.

WEAKENING INTERNATIONAL INSTITUTIONS

The intense links among nations and the new economic environment resulting from new market entrants with different economic systems are weakening the traditional international institutions and are therefore affecting their roles.

The formation of the WTO has provided the former GATT with new impetus. However, the organization is confronted with many difficulties. One of them is the result of the organization's success. Historically, a key focus of the WTO's predecessor was on reducing tariffs. With tariff levels at an unprecedented low level, however, attention now has to rest with areas such as **nontariff barriers**, which are much more complex and indigenous to nations. As a consequence, any emerging dispute is likely to be more heatedly contested and more difficult to resolve. A second traditional focus rested with the right to establishment in countries. Given today's technology, however, the issue has changed. Increasingly, firms will clamor for the right to operations in a country without seeking to establish themselves there. For example, given the opportunities offered by telecommunications, one can envision a bank becoming active in a country without establishing a single office or branch.

Another key problem results from the fact that many disagreements were set aside for the sake of concluding negotiations. Disputes in such areas as agriculture or intellectual property rights protection continue to cause a series of trade conflicts among nations. If the WTO's dispute settlement mechanism is then applied to resolve the conflict, outcries in favor of national sovereignty may cause nations to withdraw from the agreement whenever a country loses in a dispute.

A final major weakness of the WTO may result from the desire of some of its members to introduce "social causes" into trade decisions. It is debatable, for example, whether the WTO should also deal with issues such as labor laws, competition, and emigration freedoms. Other issues, such as freedom of religion, provision of health care, and the safety of animals have been raised as well. It will be difficult for the WTO to remain a viable organization if too many non-trade-related issues are loaded onto its trade and investment mission. The 151 governments participating in the WTO have diverse perspectives, histories, relations, economies, and ambitions. Many of them fear that social causes can be used to devise new rules of protectionism against their exports. Then there is also the question of how much companies—which, after all, are the ones doing the trading and investing—should be burdened with concerns outside of their scope.

Similar problems have befallen international financial institutions. For example, although the **International Monetary Fund (IMF)** functions effectively, it is currently under severe challenge by new substantial financial requirements. So far, the IMF has been able to smooth over the most difficult problems but has not found ways to solve them. For example, the IMF promised Turkey a gradual disbursement of $10 billion in loans to avert economic crisis and promote economic growth.[10] Yet, given the financial needs of many other nations, the IMF simply may not have enough funds to satisfy the needs of all. In cases of multiple financial crises, it then is unable to provide its traditional function of calming financial markets in turmoil.

Apart from its ability to provide funds, the IMF must also rethink its traditional rules of operations. For example, it is quite unclear whether stringent economic rules and benchmark performance measures are equally applicable to all countries seeking IMF assistance. New economic conditions that have not been experienced to date may require different types of approaches. The link between economic and political stability also may require different considerations, possibly substantially changing the IMF's mission.

World Bank president Robert Zoellick has set out a vision for the bank to act as a "catalyst" for private and public action, extending the benefits of global integration to the poor and making globalization more "inclusive and sustainable. The World Bank successfully met its goal of aiding the reconstruction of Europe but has been less successful in furthering the economic goals of the developing world. Some even claim that instead of alleviating poverty, misguided bank policies may have *created* poverty.[11]

The pressures upon the WTO, the IMF, and the World Bank demonstrate that at a time when domestic policy measures are becoming less effective, international institutions that could help to develop substitute international policy measures have been weakened by new challenges to their traditional missions and insufficient resources to meet such challenges.

NONTARIFF BARRIERS

Barriers to trade, other than tariffs. Examples include buy-domestic campaigns, preferential treatment for domestic bidders, and restrictions on market entry of foreign products, such as involved inspection procedures.

INTERNATIONAL MONETARY FUND (IMF)

A specialized agency of the United Nations established in 1944. An international financial institution for dealing with Balance of Payment problems; the first international monetary authority with at least some degree of power over national authorities (see **http://www.imf.org**).

WORLD BANK

An international financial institution created to facilitate trade (see **http://www.worldbank.org**).

WORLD VIEW

COOLING OFF ON GLOBAL WARMING

Ozone depletion, acid rain, global warming, and the melting of the polar ice caps make headlines daily. But while economically advanced nations view environmental threats as a common responsibility of humanity, emerging nations consider them too much of a burden to handle — unless, that is, there are financial incentives to do so. In essence, developing countries suggest a straightforward bargain: If we get money, they say to wealthy nations, we will protect the environmental resources you claim to value so highly.

Conflicting opinions on the obligations of developing nations threaten to scuttle even the Kyoto Protocol, a massive plan involving hundreds of nations that was devised to reduce the gas emissions blamed for global warming. The United States refused to ratify the agreement, claiming that it fails to mandate emissions quotas from developing countries while unfairly committing industrialized nations to cut emissions by 5 percent between 2008 and 2012. The decision sparked the fury of European environmentalists. "If one wants to be a world leader," European Commission President, Romano Prodi, fired back, "one must know how to look after the entire earth, and not only American industry."

Tempers run high, too, in battles over preservation. The rosy periwinkle, for instance, a pink shrub found only in Madagascar, has proven effective in fighting childhood leukemia and Hodgkin's disease. Without efforts to protect its habitat, the plant's scientific potential cannot be exploited. Similarly, plant genes found only in Africa can be used to improve varieties of wheat, corn, rice, and tomatoes. Some countries have stepped in to preserve biodiversity. The United States, for instance, recently forgave $26 million in outstanding loans to Costa Rica in exchange for Costa Rica's promise to conserve ecologically critical rain forests. In spite of wide praise for debt-for-nature swaps, many developing nations see them as a dangerous attempt to somehow put areas of sovereign territory off-limits to domestic control.

SOURCES: "Costa Rica gets $26 million in debt relief in return for forest conservation," *The Associated Press*, October 17, 2007, **http://www. iht.com**, accessed January 20, 2008; "Kyoto Protocol," United Nations Convention on Climate Change, **http://unfccc.int/kyoto_protocol/ items/2830.php**, accessed January 20, 2008; "Europe Backs Kyoto Accord," BBC News, March 31, 2001, **http://news.bbc.co.uk**, accessed January 19, 2008; UN Division for Sustainable Development, **http://www.un.org/esa**.

CONFLICT BETWEEN INDUSTRIALIZED AND DEVELOPING NATIONS

4 LEARNING OBJECTIVE

In the 1960s and 1970s, it was hoped that the developmental gap between industrialized nations and many countries in the less-developed world could gradually be closed. This goal was to be achieved with the transfer of technology and the infusion of major funds. Even though the 1970s saw vast quantities of petrodollars available for recycling and major growth in borrowing by some developing nations, the results have not been as expected. Although several less-developed nations have gradually emerged as newly industrialized countries (NICs), even more nations are facing grim economic futures.

In Latin America, many nations are still saddled with enormous amounts of debt, rapidly increasing populations, and very fragile economies. The developing countries of Africa also face major debt and employment problems. In view of their shattered dreams, policymakers in these nations have become increasingly aggressive in their attempts to reshape the ground rules of the world trade and investment flows. Although many policymakers share the view that major changes are necessary to resolve the difficulties that exist, no clear-cut solutions have emerged.[12]

Culture Clues   *Connections* is a key word in conducting business in Saudi Arabia. Well-connected people find that progress is made much faster. Connections in the Middle East are vital to gain access to public and private decision-makers.

Lately, an increase in environmental awareness has contributed to a further sharpening of the conflict. World View: Cooling Off on Global Warming demonstrates that developing countries place different emphasis on environmental protection. If they are to take measures that will assist industrialized nations in their environmental goals, they expect to be assisted and rewarded. Yet many in the industrialized world view environmental issues as a global obligation, rather than as a matter of choice, and are reluctant to pay. Companies like petroleum giant BP develop advertising campaigns to demonstrate their commitment to the global environment by developing technologies to reduce ozone pollution.

Policy Responses to Changing Conditions

The word *policy* conjures up an image of a well-coordinated set of governmental activities. Unfortunately, in the trade and investment sector, as in most of the domestic policy areas, this is rarely the case. Policymakers too often need to respond to short-term problems; they need to worry too much about what is politically salable to multiple constituencies; and, in some countries, they are in office too short a time to formulate a guiding set of long-term strategies. Because of public and media pressures, policymakers must also be concerned with current events—such as monthly trade deficit numbers and investment flow figures—that may not be very meaningful in the larger picture. In such an environment, actions may lead to extraordinarily good tactical measures but fail to achieve long-term success.

IMPORT RESTRICTIONS

Worldwide, most countries maintain at least a surface-level conformity with international principles. However, many exert substantial restraints on free trade through import controls and barriers. Some of the more frequently encountered barriers are listed in Table 3.1. They are particularly common in countries that suffer from major trade deficits or major infrastructure problems, causing them to enter into voluntary restraint agreements with trading partners or to selectively apply trade-restricting measures such as tariffs, quotas, or nontariff barriers against trading partners.

Tariffs are taxes on imports based primarily on the value of imported goods and services. **Quotas** are restrictions on the number of foreign products that can be imported. Nontariff barriers consist of a variety of measures such as testing, certification, or simply bureaucratic

TARIFFS

Taxes on imported goods and services, instituted by governments as a means to raise revenue and as barriers to trade.

QUOTAS

Legal restrictions on the import quantity of particular goods, imposed by governments as barriers to trade.

TABLE 3.1 Trade Barriers

How many ways are there to raise a barrier? The likely answer is hundreds. Here are just a few of the obstacles that exporters encounter.

• Advance import deposits	• Global quotas	• Selected purchases licenses
• Barter and countertrade licenses	• Health and sanitary prohibitions	• Service charges
• Consular invoice fees	• Industry group fees	• Special import authorization
• Consumption taxes	• Licensing fees	• Stamp taxes
• Country quotas	• Local content rules	• Transportation taxes
• Customs surcharges	• Re-expat requirements	• Turnover taxes
• Excise duties	• Re-expat requirements	• Value-added taxes
• Foreign exchange licensing	• Restrictive licensing	• Voluntary export restraints
• Foreign exchange trade taxes	• Seasonal prohibitions	

SOURCE: Adapted and updated 2008 by Michael Czinkota from original list by Mark Magnier.

The Global Environment: A Source of Conflict between Developed and Less-Developed Nations

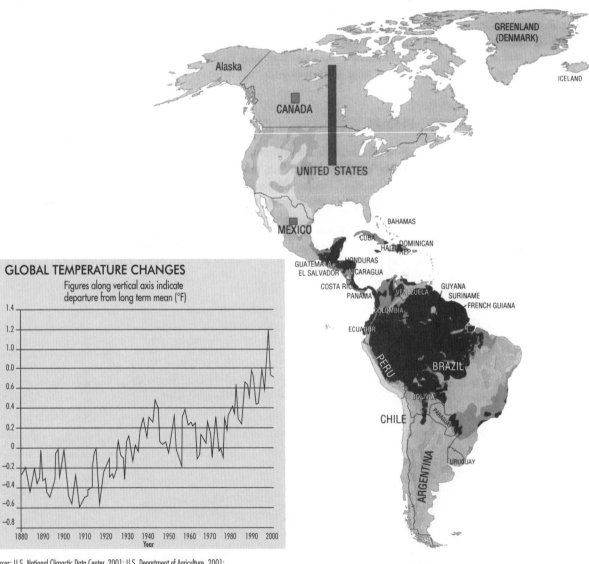

DESERTIFICATION
Areas with risk of desertification
Existing deserts

GLOBAL TEMPERATURE CHANGES
Figures along vertical axis indicate departure from long term mean (°F)

Sources: U.S. National Climactic Data Center, 2001; U.S. Department of Agriculture, 2001;
    National Geographic Society, Biodiversity map supplement, Feb. 1999;
    AAAS Atlas of Population and Environment, 2000; United Nations Environment Programme, 2001;
    World Resources Institute, World Resources, 1998–1999;
    Energy Information Administration, International Energy Annual, 1999.

RAINFOREST DESTRUCTION

- Present distribution of forest area
- Area originally forested

GREENHOUSE GAS EMISSIONS

Million metric tons of carbon equivalent

- 100–200
- 200–400
- over 400

Color of bar indicates total emissions;
height of bar per capita level of emissions

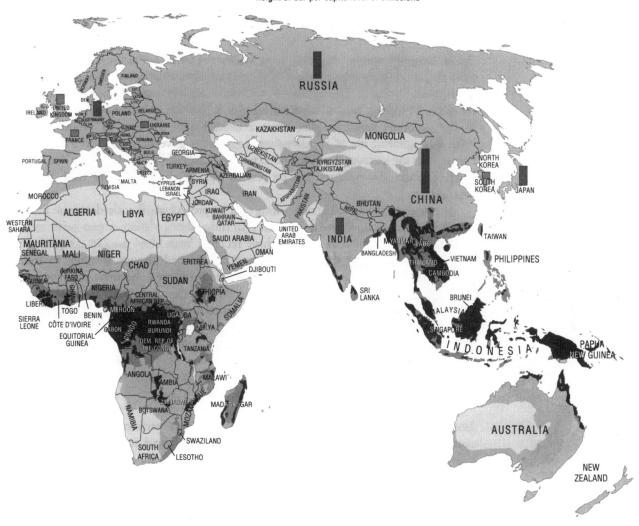

hurdles that have the effect of restricting imports. All of these measures tend to raise the price of imported goods. They therefore constitute a transfer of funds from the buyers (or, if absorbed by them, the sellers) of imports to the government, and—if accompanied by price increases of competing domestic products—to the domestic producers of such products.

VOLUNTARY RESTRAINT AGREEMENTS

Trade-restraint agreements resulting in self-imposed restrictions that are used to manage or distort trade flows, but do not violate existing international trade rules.

Voluntary restraint agreements are designed to help domestic industries reorganize, re-structure, and recapture production prominence. Even though officially voluntary, these agreements are usually implemented through severe threats against trading partners. Due to their "voluntary" nature, the agreements are not subject to any previously negotiated bilateral or multilateral trade accords.

Tariffs and Quotas

Many countries use anti-dumping laws to impose tariffs on imports. Anti-dumping laws, discussed further in Chapter 4, are designed to help domestic industries that are injured by unfair competition from abroad due to products being "dumped" on them. Dumping may involve selling goods overseas at prices lower than those in the exporter's home market or at a price below the cost of production or both. The growing use of anti-dumping measures by governments around the world complicates the pricing decisions of exporters. Large domestic firms, on the other hand, can use the anti-dumping process to obtain strategic shelter from foreign competitors.

In emerging markets, barriers often exist to protect small-scale domestic industries from larger-scale overseas producers. In India, for example, a stiff import tariff of 150 percent exists on foreign brands of wine. Though wine production jumped from two million liters and four producers in 2001 to 13 million liters and 51 wineries in 2007, the industry is still in its infancy. Until the nation develops and implements technology needed to produce on a larger scale, industrialized producers from around the world are seen to pose a threat to India's wine industry. As soon as the wine industry becomes competitive enough to compete on the world market, India promises that these tariffs will be lifted. Given past experiences, however, many doubt that the Indian government will do so voluntarily.[13]

Nontariff Barriers

Nontariff barriers include buy-domestic campaigns, preferential treatment for domestic bidders compared with foreign bidders, national standards that are not comparable to international standards, and an emphasis on the design rather than the performance of products. In India, for example, major exports from neighboring Bangladesh such as leather goods, melamine products, and cosmetics are restricted from entering the Indian market because of stringent requirements on packaging, biosecurity, laboratory testing, sanitary-phytosanitary permits, and mandatory labeling.[14] Such nontariff barriers are often the most insidious obstacles to free trade, because they are difficult to detect and hard to quantify, and demands for their removal are often stifled by the lack of economic resources to do so. Frequently, they are also blocked by resistance that results from a nation's cultural and historic heritage.

Fast Facts

Fast Facts What is the distance around the Earth at the equator?

The circumference of the Earth at the equator is 24,901.45 miles (40,074.89 km). The Earth rotates counterclockwise on its axis at approximately 1,000 miles per hour (1,609 km per hour), making one complete revolution each day.

Effects of Import Restrictions

Policymakers are faced with several problems when trying to administer import controls. First, most of the time such controls exact a huge price from domestic consumers. Import controls may mean that the most efficient sources of supply are not available. The result is either second-best products or higher costs for restricted supplies, which in turn cause customer service standards to drop and consumers to pay significantly higher prices. Even though these costs may be widely distributed among many consumers and are not very obvious, the social cost of these controls may be quite damaging to the economy. For example, while citizens of the European Union may be forced by import controls to pay an elevated price for all the agricultural products they consume, agricultural producers in the region benefit from higher incomes. Achieving a proper trade-off is often difficult, if not impossible, for the policymaker.

A second major problem resulting from import controls is the downstream change in the composition of imports that may result. For example, if the importation of copper ore is restricted, through either voluntary restraints or quotas, producing countries may opt to shift their production systems and produce copper wire instead, which they can export. As a result, initially narrowly defined protectionist measures may snowball in order to protect one downstream industry after another. Downstream effects can hurt domestic industries, too. Recently, the Philippines reduced tariffs on oil imports to lessen the downstream effect of high oil prices on all the industries that rely on oil.

Another major problem that confronts the policymaker is that of efficiency. Import controls designed to provide breathing room to a domestic industry so it can either grow or recapture its competitive position often do not work. Rather than improve the productivity of an industry, such controls may provide it with a level of safety and a cushion of increased income, which cause it to lag even further behind in technological advancements.

It is also important to consider the corporate response to import restrictions. Corporations faced with restrictions often enlist the support of their home governments to knock down barriers to trade or to erect similar barriers to protect them in their home markets. The result of corporate influences over regulations can be a gradually escalating set of trade obstacles.

Finally, corporations can circumvent import restrictions by shifting to foreign direct investment. For example, instead of conducting trade, corporations can shift to foreign direct investment. The result may be a drop in trade inflow, yet the domestic industry may still be under strong pressure from foreign firms. The Japanese automobile manufacturer, Honda, for instance, invests over $9 billion a year in the United States and employs more than 120,000 Americans. Six major assembly plants churn out more than 1 million cars, motorcycles, and all-terrain vehicles, infusing local economies with jobs as well as spurring development in the states in which those plants are located.[15] Despite increased competition in the home market due to the job-creation effects that result from shifting operations from the home country, policymakers who implement import controls achieve a favorable economic objective. Investments often have a variety of effects.

Export Restrictions

In addition to imposing restraints on imports, nations also control their exports. The reasons include national security concerns. As explained in Chapter 4, for example, U.S. export legislation focuses on the control of weapons or high-technology exports that might adversely affect the safety of the nation. Exports are also controlled for reasons of foreign policy (a government's desire to send a political message to another country), short supply, or the desire to retain capital.

Export restrictions are almost never in the best interests of firms. Moreover, as explained further in Chapter 4, they rarely achieve their stated purpose. If, for example, exports from the United States are restricted, the targeted government simply obtains similar products from companies in other nations. Although perhaps valuable as a tool of international relations, such policies too often end up giving a country's firms a reputation for unreliability, with the result that orders are diverted elsewhere.

Export Promotion

The desire to increase participation in international trade and investment flows has led nations to implement export promotion programs. These programs are designed primarily to help domestic firms enter and maintain their position in international markets and to match or counteract similar export promotion efforts by other nations.

Most governments supply some support to firms participating or planning to participate in international trade. Typically, support falls into one of four categories: export information and advice, production support, marketing support, or finance and guarantees. While such support is widespread and growing, its intensity varies by country. To help improve the international performance of U.S. firms, the Department of Commerce offers information services that provide data on foreign trade and market developments. Its **Commercial Service** posts hundreds of professionals around the world to assist business executives. In addition, a national network of export assistance centers has been created, capable of providing one-stop shops for exporters in search of export counseling and financial assistance. Also, an advocacy network helps U.S. companies win overseas contracts for large government purchases abroad. Other countries try to help their firms through international support programs.

To assist in export financing, the Export-Import Bank of the United States provides U.S. firms with long-term loans and loan guarantees so that they can bid on contracts where financing is a key issue. In response to actions by foreign competitors, the bank has, on occasion, also offered **mixed aid credits**. These credits, which take the form of loans composed partially of commercial interest rates and partially of highly subsidized developmental aid interest rates, result in very low-interest loans to exporters.

Tax legislation also encourages exports by making the high cost of living of employees posted overseas easier to bear. A revision in the tax code now allows a substantial portion of income earned abroad to remain tax-free (up to $85,700 in 2008).

Any export promotion raises several questions. One concerns the justification of the expenditure of public funds for what is essentially a for-profit activity. Companies argue that, especially for smaller firms, the start-up cost for international operations is sufficiently high to warrant some kind of government support. A second question focuses on the capability of government to provide support. Both for the selection and reach of firms as well as the distribution of support, government is not necessarily better equipped than the private sector to do a good job. A third issue concerns competitive export promotion. Countries that provide export support may well distort the flow of trade. If other countries then increase their support to counteract the effects, all that results is the same volume of trade activity, but at subsidized rates. It is therefore important to carefully evaluate export promotion activities as to their effectiveness and competitive impact. Perhaps such promotion is beneficial only when it addresses existing market gaps.

Import Promotion

Some countries have also developed import promotion measures. The measures are implemented primarily by nations that have accumulated and maintained large balance-of-trade surpluses. They hope to allay other nations' fears of continued imbalances and to gradually redirect trade flows.

Japan, for example, has completely refurbished the operations of the Japan External Trade Organization (JETRO) (**http://www.jetro.org**). This organization, which initially was formed to encourage Japanese exports, has now begun to focus on the promotion of imports to Japan. It organizes trade missions of foreign firms coming to Japan, hosts special exhibits and fairs within Japan, and provides assistance and encouragement to potential importers.

COMMERCIAL SERVICE

A department of the U.S. Department of Commerce that gathers information and assists business executives in business abroad (see **http://www.usatradeonline.gov**).

MIXED AID CREDITS

Credits at rates composed partially of commercial interest rates and partially of highly subsidized developmental aid interest rates.

Culture Clues   To the Japanese there is almost no distinction between the business day and the business night. They consider it part of both their personal and professional lives to spend virtually every evening with business associates. "You get through to a man's soul at night," is a popular saying among Japanese businesspeople.

INVESTMENT POLICIES

6 LEARNING OBJECTIVE

The discussion of policy actions has focused thus far on merchandise trade. Similar actions are applicable to investment flows and, by extension, to international trade in services. In order to protect ownership, control, and development of domestic industries, many countries attempt to influence investment capital flows. Most frequently, investment-screening agencies decide on the merits of any particular foreign investment project. Investment in Canada, for example, is a government agency that scrutinizes foreign investments. Most developing nations similarly require special government permission for investment projects. This permission frequently carries with it certain conditions, such as levels of ownership permitted, levels of dividends that can be repatriated, numbers of jobs that must be created, or the extent to which management can be carried out by individuals from abroad. As noted earlier in the chapter, the United States restricts foreign investment only in instances where national security or related concerns are at stake.

Host-Country Perspective on Investment Policies

The host government is caught in a love-hate relationship with foreign direct investment. On the one hand, the host country has to appreciate the various contributions, especially economic, that foreign direct investment can make. On the other, allowing investment from abroad gives rise to fears of dominance, interference, and dependence. The major positive and negative impacts of foreign investment policies are summarized in Table 3.2 and are discussed below.

Positive Effects

Capital inflows that result from foreign direct investment benefit all countries by making more resources available, but particularly those nations with limited domestic sources and restricted opportunities to raise funds in the world's capital markets. Another benefit of foreign direct investment is the transfer of technology from developed to developing nations. **Technology transfer** includes not only the introduction of new technologies, but also of the knowledge and skills to operate those technologies. In industries where the role of intellectual property is substantial, such as pharmaceuticals or software development, access to parent companies' research and development provides benefits that may be far greater than those gained through infusion of capital. Technology transfer explains in part the eagerness of many governments to invite multinational corporations to establish R&D facilities in their countries.

TECHNOLOGY TRANSFER

The transfer of systematic knowledge for the manufacture of a product, the application of a process, or the rendering of a service.

    Foreign direct investment can help develop particular industry sectors or particular geographical regions, lowering unemployment levels. Furthermore, the costs of establishing an

TABLE 3.2 Pros and Cons of Foreign Direct Investment in Host-Country Economies

PROS	CONS
• Improved capital flows	• Low levels of research and development
• Technology transfer	• Risk of increased capital outflows
• Regional development	• Stifling of domestic competition and
• Increased competition, benefiting economy	entrepreneurship
	• Erosion of host culture
• Favorable balance of payments	• Disruption of domestic business practices
• Increased employment opportunities	• Risk of interference by foreign governments

industry are often prohibitive and the time needed excessive for the domestic industry, even with governmental help, to try it on its own. In many developing countries, foreign direct investment may be a way to diversify the industrial base and thereby reduce the country's dependence on one or a few sectors.

At the company level, foreign direct investment may intensify competition and result in benefits to the economy as a whole, as well as to consumers, through increased productivity and, possibly, lower prices. Competition typically introduces new techniques, goods and services, and ideas. It also often improves existing patterns of how business is done.

Foreign direct investment has a long-term positive impact on the balance of payments of the host country. Import substitution, export earnings, and subsidized imports of technology and management all assist the host nation on the trade account side of the balance of payments. Not only may a new production facility substantially decrease the need to import the type of products manufactured, but it may start earning export revenue as well. Several countries, such as Brazil, have imposed export requirements as a precondition for foreign direct investment. On the capital account side, foreign direct investment may have short-term impact in lowering a deficit as well as long-term impact in keeping capital at home that otherwise could have been invested or transferred abroad. However, measurement is difficult because significant portions of capital flows may miss—or evade—the usual government reporting channels.

Jobs are often the most obvious reason to cheer about foreign direct investment. Foreign companies directly employ three million Americans—about 3 percent of the workforce—and indirectly create opportunities for millions more. The benefits reach far beyond mere employment. Salaries paid by multinational corporations are usually higher than those paid by domestic firms. The creation of jobs translates also into the training and development of a skilled work force. Consider, for example, the situation of Egypt, whose economy is largely dependent on tourism. Fears of international terrorism, following the events of September 11, 2001, combined with a global economic downturn, have resulted in increased unemployment. Were foreign investors to withdraw from Egypt's shaky tourism industry, the impact on the country's economy could have spelled disaster. To diversify its industries, Egypt has turned to attract foreign investment into property development, banking, and telecommunications. In 2006, foreign direct investment increased to over $8 billion, up from $2 billion in 2003.[16]

The combined effects of all the benefits accruing from foreign direct investment can lead to overall improvements in the standard of living in the host country, as well as increasing its access to and competitiveness in world markets.

World View: Bringing in the Money describes some of the incentives offered by nations to compete for foreign direct investment.

Negative Effects

Since foreign direct investment is most often concentrated in technology-intensive industries, research and development issues are often an area of tension. Rather than support R&D centers in all countries in which they operate, multinational corporations usually concentrate this function in just a few markets. This means that not all host countries benefit from technology transfer. Worse still, in some cases, multinational firms have withdrawn R&D from certain markets, blunting their ability to acquire technological know-how. Furthermore, the multinational firm may contribute to the brain drain by attracting scientists from host countries to its central research facility. Many countries have demanded and received research facilities on their soil, where they can better control results. They do so because they are weary of the technological dominance of such countries as the United States and Japan, seeing it as a long-term threat.

From an economic perspective, capital inflows resulting from foreign direct investment are often accompanied by higher, longer-term outflows that do not benefit the host government. For example, when multinational chains built hotels in the Caribbean, the shortage of local

Fast Facts

If you order "Mountain Chicken" in Montserrat or Dominica (both in the West Indies), what do you get?

Frog's legs that are the size of chicken's legs.

WORLD VIEW

BRINGING IN THE MONEY

Vietnam hopes to greatly increase Foreign Direct Investment (FDI) and expects continued growth through 2010. To accomplish this, Vietnam removed trade barriers, which prevent foreign investors from entering the Vietnamese market. In addition, the country is strengthening its infrastructure, increasing the number of skilled workers, improving its investment framework, and establishing overseas investment offices.

Using the country's Southern Key Economic Zone as an example (a zone that attracts the majority of the country's FDI and contributes 40 percent to annual GDP), the Vietnamese Ministry of Planning and Investment also intends to establish or expand 22 industrial parks throughout Vietnam, which should grow to 109 by 2015.

Vietnam has already attracted companies from Thailand, China, Australia, and the United Kingdom to build a multi-billion-dollar crude oil refining and petrochemical complex. This Thai-led alliance also plans to build four new chemical plants in the coming years.

Countries once isolated from international trade are now trying to attract FDI since they understand that such investment creates jobs, increased tax revenues, research and development, and an improved standard of living.

SOURCES: "Vietnam to build more industrial parks," *Xinhua News Agency—CEIS*, December 10, 2007; "Vietnam's economic zone eyes more foreign investment," *Xinhua News Agency—CEIS*, October 31, 2007; "Foreign firms to build Vietnam's second oil refinery," *Xinhua News Agency—CEIS*, January 7, 2008; "Vietnam eyes bigger realized foreign capital in 2008", *Xinhua News Agency—CEIS*, January 7, 2008.

suppliers meant that much-needed foreign currency was spent on imported supplies. In other cases, multinationals simply prefer to use existing suppliers in their own countries rather than develop local supplier networks. Host countries do not look favorably on multinationals that keep the import content of a product high, especially when local suppliers are available.

Another frequent complaint is that investors fail to follow through on their promises. Rather than training local personnel for management roles, staff are hired from overseas. Rather than stimulate local competition and encourage entrepreneurship, multinationals, with their often-superior product offerings and marketing skills, can reduce competition.

Multinational companies are, by definition, change agents. That is, welcome or not, the products and services they generate and market bring about change in the lifestyles of consumers in the host country. For example, the introduction of fast-food restaurants to Taiwan dramatically altered eating patterns, especially of teenagers, who make these outlets extremely popular and profitable. Concern has been expressed about the impact on family life and the higher relative cost of eating in such establishments.

Multinational corporations also influence business practices in the host nation. Higher salaries and flexible work schedules, for example, may disrupt local practices. Some company practices may not be exportable. For instance, taking older employees off production lines to make room for more productive workers—a common-enough practice in Japan—may go against the grain of local workplace ethics, not to mention trade union rules and antidiscrimination laws

Some host nations express concerns over the possibility of interference, economically and politically, by the home government of the multinational corporation; that is, they fear that the presence of a multinational may be used as an instrument of influence, affecting their economies in ways they cannot control.

HOME-COUNTRY PERSPECTIVE ON INVESTMENT POLICIES

Most of the aspects of foreign direct investment that concern host countries apply to the home country as well. Foreign direct investment means addition to the home country's gross domestic product from profits, royalties, and fees remitted by affiliates. In many cases, intracompany transfers bring about additional export possibilities. Many countries promote foreign direct investment as a means to stimulate economic growth—an end that would expand export markets and possibly serve political motives, as well. Japan and China, for example, have attempted to gain preferential access to raw materials by purchasing firms that own the deposits. China is also aggressively pursuing investments in the oil industries of developing countries, such as Sudan, in an effort to ensure future supply security. Other factors of production can be obtained through foreign direct investment as well. Companies today may not have the luxury of establishing R&D facilities wherever they choose but must locate them where human resources are available. Telecommunications giant Nortel Networks, for example, employs 17,400 engineers, designers, scientists, and other R&D employees at 31 sites around the world. Technology giant DuPont, for example, will open a global knowledge center in Hyderabad, India, which will start by employing 600 R&D scientists.[17]

The biggest negative against foreign investment from the home-country perspective centers on employment. Many unions point not only to outright job loss but also to ripple effects on imports and exports. For instance, when manufacturing plants are developed overseas, products often find their way back to the domestic market as low-priced imports. The result is more job losses from local companies that can no longer compete. Electronics manufacturers who have moved plants to Southeast Asia and Mexico have justified their decisions as cost-cutting competitive measures.

Another critical issue is that of technological advantage. Some critics claim that, by establishing plants abroad or forming joint ventures with foreign entities, the country may in time risk its competitive lead in the world marketplace. The argument is that developing nations, that have saved the time and expense involved in developing new technologies, are then able to leapfrog over companies that brought the technologies to them.

Restrictions on Investment

Many nations restrict exports of capital, because outward capital flows can severely damage their economies. Particularly in situations where countries lack necessary foreign exchange reserves, governments are likely to place restrictions on capital outflow. In essence, government claims to have higher priorities for capital than its citizens. They, in turn, often believe that the return on investment or the safety of the capital is not sufficiently ensured in their own countries. The reason may be governmental measures or domestic economic factors, such as inflation. These holders of capital want to invest abroad. By doing so, however, they deprive their domestic economy of much-needed investment funds.

Once governments impose restrictions on the export of funds, the desire to transfer capital abroad only increases. Because companies and individuals are ingenious in their efforts to achieve **capital flight**, governments, particularly in developing countries, continue to suffer. In addition, few new outside investors will enter the country because they fear that dividends and profits will not be remitted easily.

Investment Promotion

Many countries implement policy measures to attract foreign direct investment. These policies can result from the need of poorer nations to bring in foreign capital without taking out more

LEARNING OBJECTIVE **7**

CAPITAL FLIGHT

The flow of private funds abroad, because investors believe that the return on investment or the safety of capital is not sufficiently ensured in their own countries.

loans that call for fixed schedules of repayment. In industrialized nations, investment promotion usually arises from the pressure to provide jobs: Foreign direct investment can serve to increase employment and income. Increasingly, even state and local governments are participating in investment promotion. Some U.S. states, for example, are sending out Invest in the USA missions on a regular basis. Others have opened offices abroad to inform local businesses about the beneficial investment climate. UK Trade &Investment (**http://www.ukinvest.gov.uk**) is another example.

Incentives offered by policymakers to facilitate foreign investments are mainly of three types: fiscal, financial, and nonfinancial. **Fiscal incentives** are specific tax measures designed to attract foreign investors. They typically consist of special depreciation allowances, tax credits or rebates, special deductions for capital expenditures, tax holidays, and the reduction of tax burdens. **Financial incentives** offer special funding for the investor by providing, for example, land or buildings, loans, and loan guarantees. **Nonfinancial incentives** include guaranteed government purchases; special protection from competition through tariffs, import quotas, and local content requirements; and investments in infrastructure facilities.

FISCAL INCENTIVES

Incentives used to attract foreign direct investment that provide specific tax measures to attract the investor.

FINANCIAL INCENTIVES

Monetary offers intended to motivate; special funding designed to attract foreign direct investors that may take the form of land or building, loans, or loan guarantees.

NONFINANCIAL INCENTIVES

Nonmonetary offers designed to attract foreign direct investors that may take the form of guaranteed government purchased, special protection from competition, or improved infrastructure facilities.

Quick Take *Strong Name to Combat Weakness*

Once among the world's most stable currencies, the Venezuelan Bolivar—which for decades traded at 3.3 to the U.S. dollar—has seen a steady decline in value. Economic mismanagement paired with a turbulent cycle of oil booms and busts has caused nationwide inflation. At 20 percent through most of 2007, inflation has eroded support for the Venezuelan government by causing shortages in basic food items like chicken, beans, and milk. The poor and working-class Venezuelans, who have long backed President Hugo Chavez based on his spending on clinics, schools, and food subsidies, are now looking for change. The country's poor have been hit hard by rising prices. Increased inflation has also greatly affected levels of foreign direct investment (FDI). In 2006 the country experienced an outflow of $500 million. Though this number jumped to an inflow of $400 million in 2007, the country has the lowest FDI levels of Latin America's top six economies.

In order to boost consumer confidence, bring down inflation, and increase FDI, the Venezuelan government has started to issue a new currency called the Strong Bolivar. By setting the new currency to equal 1,000 (old) Bolivar, the face value of the new currency will be similar to those of surrounding countries. With this move, the Chavez administration hopes to shape people's perceptions. Price tags of single- and double-digit prices should have a positive psychological impact on consumers and investors.

In the past, several other Latin American countries changed their currency in an effort to stabilize their economies and battle inflation. In the 1990s, Peru replaced the *inti* for the new *sol*, Brazil exchanged its *cruzeiro* real for the *real*, and Mexico cut three zeros off its peso.

Though Venezuela's new currency may improve confidence in the country in the short term, it will have little long-term advantage unless new economic policies, like reduced government spending, are adopted to reduce inflation.

SOURCES: John Otis, Jose Orozco, "Venezuela works on confidence as currency loses some zeroes / Circulation of the strong Bolivar also aimed at collaring inflation," *Houston Chronicle*, December 23, 2007; "Latin America: Record FDI," *Chronicle*, January 14, 2007, **http://www.latinbusinesschronicle.com/app/article.aspx?id=1978**, accessed January 19, 2008.

SUMMARY

All countries have international trade and investment policies. The importance and visibility of these policies have grown dramatically as international trade and investment flows have become more relevant to the well-being of most nations. Given the growing links among nations, it will be increasingly difficult to consider domestic policy without looking at international repercussions. To enhance international trade and investment in the future, nations must cooperate closely and view domestic policymaking in a global context.

 International trade and investment policies have evolved as a subset of domestic policies. Increasingly, however, the ability of policymakers to focus primarily on domestic issues is reduced because of global links in trade and investment. First the GATT and now the WTO seek to improve trade investment flows around the world by establishing rules that ensure nondiscrimination, transparent procedures, and a forum for the settlement of trade disputes.

 Policymakers have shifted their focus from domestic issues to broader international issues due to a general reduction of domestic policy influence, the weakening of traditional global institutions, and the accelerated conflict between industrialized and developing nations.

 International trade institutions face many challenges stemming from strengthening links and interdependence among nations' policies, economics, and legal systems. Several international agencies facilitate mediation and negotiation.

 Efforts continue to close the gap between industrialized and emerging nations. These efforts include technology, financial resources, and policy changes in international interactions. The motives behind equalizing a nation's status are not always pure, and arguments have been made that industrialized nations ultimately act in their own self-interest.

 Many nations seek to restrict imports, and thereby protect domestic industries, by creating tariff barriers, such as quotas on imports, voluntary restraint agreements, and anti-dumping laws. In addition, a variety of nontariff barriers include buy domestic campaigns, preferential treatment for domestic bidders, and the imposition of national rather than international standards. All these restrictions have repercussions that negatively affect industries and consumers.

Several nations seek to restrict exports, often for reasons of foreign policy, national security, short supply, or the desire to retain capital.

Nations attempt to promote exports though dissemination of information, production and marketing support, and financial assistance.

 Through foreign direct investment, governments are able to receive needed products or to attract economic activity. While restricting such investments may permit more domestic control over industries, it also denies access to foreign capital. This, in turn, can result in a tightening up of credit markets, higher interest rates, and a decreased impetus for innovation.

 Investment policies aim to benefit both parties, while at the same time protecting each country's interests. Restrictions on outflow of foreign investment aim to protect a country's economy, primarily in the employment sector, while promotions to increase FDI are the result of poorer nations' desire to garner capital without potentially incurring further debt.

KEY TERMS AND CONCEPTS

national sovereignty	General Agreement on	quotas
domestic policy	Trade in Services (GATS)	voluntary restraint agreements
quality of life	currency flows	commercial service
standard of living	Committee on Foreign Investments	mixed aid credits
foreign policy	in the United States (CFIUS)	technology transfer
General Agreement on Tariffs	punitive tariffs	capital flight
and Trade (GATT)	nontariff barriers	fiscal incentives
most-favored nation (MFN)	International Monetary Fund (IMF)	financial incentives
World Trade Organization	World Bank	nonfinancial incentives
(WTO)	tariffs	

REVIEW QUESTIONS

1. Explain the relationship between domestic and international trade policies.
2. Summarize the role of the GATT and WTO in international trade regulation.
3. Explain changes that have occurred in the global policy environment due to increased international trade.
4. Outline the major benefits and drawbacks of trade restrictions.
5. What methods do nations use to discourage imports?
6. What methods can nations use to promote exports?
7. Summarize the positive and negative effects of foreign direct investment on trade from the host-country perspective.
8. How does foreign investment impact the home-country's economy?

CRITICAL SKILL BUILDERS

1. Why would policymakers sacrifice major international progress for minor domestic policy gains? In teams, prepare arguments for and against protecting domestic industries. Present your arguments in a class debate.
2. Discuss the impact of import restrictions on consumers in both the home country and international markets.
3. Consider the conflict between industrialized and developing nations. What are its root causes and how might international trade policies alleviate them?
4. Do investment promotion programs of state (or provincial) governments make sense from a national perspective? Why or why not? Discuss in groups.
5. Consider why Japanese carmakers have set up manufacturing plants in the United States. How do their U.S. operations enhance their performance in both the home country and the host nation? Research specific examples to support your arguments.

ON THE WEB

1. The Bureau of Economic Analysis (**http://www.bea.gov**) and Stat-USA (**http://www.stat-usa.gov**) provide a multitude of information about the current state of the U.S. economy. Look under the International subtitle on the Bureau of Economic Analysis main page and click on Operations of Multinational Companies. Go to the International Investment Tables (D-57) to find the current market value of direct investment abroad as well as the value of direct investment in the United States.

2. Check the U.S. Department of Commerce web site (**http://www.doc.gov**) to determine the assistance available to exporters. Which programs do you find most helpful to firms?

3. Go to the World Bank web site (**http://www.worldbank.org**) to obtain an overview of the bank's purpose and programs. Search for criticism of bank programs on other web sites and prepare a two-page report on key issues.

ENDNOTES

1. "Risks lie ahead following stronger trade in 2006, WTO reports," *WTO: 2007 Press Releases*, **http://www.wto.org/english/news_e/pres07_e/pr472_e.htm**, accessed January 8, 2008. —

2. Steven R. Weisman, "Trade war thwarts China's burgeoning capitalist U.S. tariffs idle a worker-owned plant," *International Herald Tribune*, December 11, 2007.

3. Michael Sasso, "China Says It's Cleaning Up Products, Pollution," *Tampa Tribune*, Tampa, Florida: December 7, 2007; "Huge Energy Subsidies Bolster China's Steel Export, *Comtex News Network, Inc.*, January 11, 2008, **http://www.lexisnexis.com/clients/senate**/, January 14, 2008.

4. "Doha Round: Summary," *Schweizerische Eidgenossenschaft*, **http://www.seco.admin.ch/themen/00513/01238/01241/index.html?lang=en**, accessed on January 16, 2008.

5. Xu Dashan, "China's economy to grow 8% annually from 2006 to 2010," *China Daily*, March 21, 2005, **http://www. chinadaily.com.cn/english/doc/2005-03/21/content_426718.htm**, accessed January 16, 2008.

6. "Benefits of Trade with China," *International Trade News*, May 24, 2007; "Statement of Ambassador John K. Veroneau, Deputy U.S. Trade Representative Office of the United States Trade Representative Before the Committee on Small Business," November 1, 2007, **http://www.ustr.gov/assets/Document_Library/USTR_Testimony/2007/asset_upload_file713_13485.pdf**, accessed January 19, 2008.

7. Bank for International Settlements, **http://www.bis.org/publ/rpfxf07t.htm**, Accessed March 28, 2008.

8. "Fact Sheet: The CFIUS Process and the DP World Transaction," The White House Press Releases, February, 2006, **www.whitehouse.gov**, accessed January 4, 2008.

9. "Briefing – Asia information technology," November 29, 2007, **www.zibb.com**, accessed January 4, 2008.

10. "Turkey, IMF complete talks, agrees to join two upcoming reviews," *The New Anatolian*, December 24, 2007.

11. Anup Shah, "Structural Adjustment—a Major Cause of Poverty, July 2, 2007, **http://www.globalissues.org/TradeRelated/SAP.asp**, accessed January 18, 2008; Krishna Guha, "Tackling Poverty A Priority for Zoellick," *Financial Times*, October 11, 2007.

12. Gumisai Mutume, "Wanted: jobs for Africa's young people," Africa Renewal, United Nations, **http://www.un.org/ecosocdev/geninfo/afrec/newrels/203-jobs.html**, accessed January 18, 2008.

13. Shyam Pandharipande, "Wine industry is fastest growing in India," *Indo-Asian News Service*, January 18, 2008, **http://www.hindustantimes.com**, accessed January 22, 2008.

14. Jasim Uddin Khan, "Dhaka lists products as Safta meet on non-tariff barriers begins Monday," *The Daily Star*, January 26, 2008.

15. **http://www.hondacorporate.com**, accessed January 2, 2003; "Philippines trims oil import tariff," *AFP*, January 8, 2008; **www.hondacorporate.com**, accessed January 25, 2008.

16. "Noted … ," *The Wall Street Journal*, October 17, 2001, p. B7; "Lonely as a Pyramid, without Tourists," *The Economist*, January 3, 2002; William Wallis, "A break from the past? The Economy: William Wallis reports on levels of growth not seen since the late 1980s," *Financial Times*, December 13, 2006.

17. Gaurav Choudhury, "DuPont to set up global knowledge centre," *The Hindustan Times*, December 4, 2007; Dana Harman, "In Sudan, China focuses on oil wells, not local needs," *The Christian Science Monitor*, June 25, 2007.

CHAPTER 4

Guns, Corruption, and Terrorism

In a global economy, companies transact business in emerging nations where the political and legal climates are unfamiliar and often unstable. When corruption, lawlessness, and political turmoil reign, productive trade relationships are under constant threat and yet continue in the face of adversity.

Before the September 11 terrorist attacks on the United States, a brisk trade of contraband goods across borders played a critical role in the fragile economies of Afghanistan and Pakistan. Electronics from Dubai, televisions from Japan, and cosmetics from Iran all moved swiftly through Taliban-controlled checkpoints, selling in Pakistan at far lower prices than legally imported items. Millions of dollars in "Islamic levies" imposed by the Taliban, along with protection money paid to powerful people in Pakistan, also facilitated the trafficking of drugs across borders, headed for black-market bazaars in Pakistan. Together, drugs and illegal contraband were valued at $30 billion a year—half of Pakistan's official gross domestic product. Following the attacks, Afghan warlords quickly took control of border cities, such as Herat on the Afghan-Iran border, sustaining the underground economy even in the midst of political chaos.

Some analysts are concerned that this unimpeded flow of goods across the border could prove dangerous from a security standpoint. More than half a decade after the NATO intervention, there is talk of a possible Taliban resurgence, especially along the border with Pakistan, as exemplified by continued fighting between rival tribal groups in places like South Waziristan. Opium production in the country has soared, and about 70 percent is smuggled through Pakistan and Iran. As drugs are leaving Afghanistan, guns are coming in. More stringent supervision and control are necessary, in order to make sure that no weapons and narcotics are making their way across the border alongside the crates of Sony flat-screens.

A world away, in war-torn Sierra Leone, bribery and violence have long been a part of doing business. At the core of the troubles is Sierra Leone's black-market diamond trade, estimated to be worth as much as $100 million a year. During the country's decade-long civil war, rebel forces grew from a small, loose band to 20,000 well-armed troops, financed by "conflict diamonds." Soldiers armed with assault rifles controlled "checkpoints," demanding "tolls" in return for safe conduct. A United Nations-guaranteed peace now exists in Sierra Leone, and embattled UN peacekeepers struggle to stabilize the region and reintegrate ex-militiamen into society.

Key to these efforts is halting the illegal diamond trade. There is a need for uniform standards in tracking the origin,

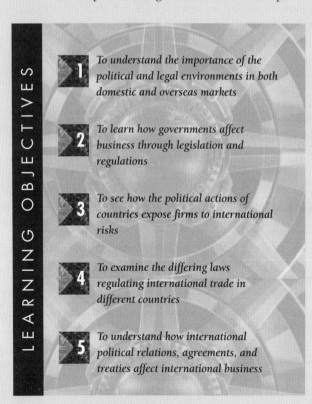

1 To understand the importance of the political and legal environments in both domestic and overseas markets

2 To learn how governments affect business through legislation and regulations

3 To see how the political actions of countries expose firms to international risks

4 To examine the differing laws regulating international trade in different countries

5 To understand how international political relations, agreements, and treaties affect international business

or provenance, of the sparkly stones. The Kimberly process is a certification scheme to ensure that diamonds are not financing bloodshed. The world's largest diamond trader—De Beers, has introduced the Forevermark, a microscopic engraving that guarantees a stone's origin. The Canadian government has introduced its own certification project. However, according to the advocacy group Global Witness, the diamond industry is still not sufficiently transparent, and large-scale smuggling persists in Sierra Leone, as well as in other conflict-prone countries, such as Angola and the Democratic Republic of Congo.[1]

As You Read This Chapter

1. Risk is the price of opportunity. Do you agree?
2. Should multinational firms do business in potentially unstable environments if it means they are fueling an invisible, illegal economy?

Politics and laws play a critical role in international business. Unexpected political or legal influences can send the best-laid plans awry. Failure to anticipate or factor in these elements frequently proves the undoing of otherwise-successful business ventures.

Of course, a single international political and legal environment does not exist. This means that business executives must be aware of political and legal factors on several, often conflicting, dimensions. While it is useful, for instance, to understand the complexities of the host country's legal system, such knowledge may not protect against sanctions imposed by the firm's home country.

This chapter will examine politics and laws from the manager's point of view. The two subjects are considered together because laws generally are the result of political decisions. The chapter explores the international political and legal environment in three segments: the politics and laws of the home country, those of the host country, and the bilateral and multilateral agreements, treaties, and laws governing the relations among host and home countries.

 ## HOME-COUNTRY PERSPECTIVE

No manager can afford to ignore the rules and regulations of the country from which he or she conducts international business transactions. Many of these regulations do not specifically address international business issues, but they can have a major impact on a firm's opportunities abroad. Consider, for example, how minimum-wage legislation in the home country affects international competitiveness. If the cost of adhering to domestic safety regulations forces a firm to price its goods higher than those of overseas competitors, the firm risks losing international market share. Moving manufacturing to regions of the world where labor costs are lower may be the solution. In the trade of commodity-type products such as steel or chemicals, where there are few significant differences between one firm's output and another's, competitiveness is an even greater factor. For example, U.S. legislation requires chemical manufacturers to pay into the Environmental Superfund, thereby increasing costs. Overseas competitors are not required to make similar payments in their home countries. As a result, U.S. chemical firms are at a cost disadvantage when competing in international markets.

Other legal and regulatory measures single out international operations. In the United States, following a widely publicized scandal involving the testing of an experimental meningitis medication on Nigerian children by U.S.-based Pfizer, an amendment to the Export Administration Act was passed, restricting the export of potentially dangerous experimental drugs to developing countries. There is some debate about the effectiveness of this measure, considering that companies are still able to conduct such trials through foreign-based subsidiaries. Currently, the majority of clinical tests are conducted outside of highly developed nations, which might be explained with a simple issue of supply. Even though the average American buys 10 prescriptions per year, fewer than one in 20 is willing to take part in a drug trial.[2] Other laws address standards by regulating product content and quality. Frequently, such standards favor national firms and exclude imports that fail to satisfy them. Still other regulations aim to protect a citizenry from outside influences that its culture deems unacceptable. Quick Take: Caught in the Web explains how governments attempt to control Internet content considered offensive or illegal.

In most countries, the political environment tends to support the international business efforts of firms headquartered there. For example, a government may work to reduce trade barriers and thereby increase trade opportunities through bilateral and multilateral negotiations. Sometimes, however, political decisions can restrict the practice of international business. The failure of the United States to ratify the World Trade Organization's Kyoto Protocol on greenhouse-gas reduction, for example, may deny its firms access to emerging markets.

Three main areas of governmental activity are of concern to the international business manager. They are embargoes and trade sanctions, export controls, and the regulation of international business behavior.

Quick Take   *Caught in the Web*

Governmental efforts to regulate Internet content have intensified in recent years. From China's attempts to block Google searches to France's fight to stop Yahoo! from selling Nazi memorabilia, governments increasingly control their citizens' web-surfing. In the French case, a ruling by the Tribunal de Grande Instance invoked the nation's hate-speech laws to bar Yahoo! from providing French citizens access to auctions of Nazi paraphernalia on its U.S. web site. The case resulted in nearly six years of litigation. Yahoo! had voluntarily blocked access to content on its local French site—**yahoo.fr**—prior to the Tribunal's decision. The question was whether the French government had the authority to pull the memorabilia

from the main Yahoo! U.S. site. The latest development—in 2006, by the U.S. 9th Circuit Court of Appeals—issued a 99-page split decision that asserted jurisdiction over the dispute but declined to issue a conclusive ruling. This case demonstrates that in many ways the Internet remains the Wild West of governmental regulation, as lawmakers, technology providers, and users jostle to establish acceptable use boundaries.

SOURCES: "The Law, Borders, and the Internet" Michael Geist, BBC News, January 24, 2006. "Google's China Problem (and China's Google Problem)" Clive Thompson, *The New York Times*, April 23, 2006.

Embargoes and Sanctions

SANCTION

A governmental action, usually consisting of a specific coercive trade measure, which distorts the free flow of trade for an adversarial or political purpose rather than an economic one.

EMBARGO

A governmental action, usually prohibiting trade entirely, for a decidedly adversarial or political rather than economic purpose.

The terms **sanction** and **embargo** refer to governmental actions that distort free flow of trade in goods, services, or ideas for decidedly adversarial and political (rather than economic) purposes. Sanctions tend to consist of specific coercive trade measures, such as the cancellation of trade financing or the prohibition of high-technology trade. Embargoes are usually much broader in that they prohibit trade entirely. For example, the United States imposes sanctions against some countries by prohibiting the export of weapons to them, but the decades-long embargo against Cuba bans all but humanitarian trade. To better understand sanctions and embargoes, it is useful to examine the auspices and legal justifications under which they are imposed.

Trade embargoes have been used quite frequently and successfully in times of war or to address specific grievances. In 1284, when a German ship was pillaged by the Norwegians, the Hansa, an association of north German merchants, instigated an economic blockade against Norway. The export of grain, flour, vegetables, and beer was prohibited on pain of fines and confiscation of goods. The blockade was a complete success. Deprived of grain from Germany, the Norwegians were unable to obtain it from England or elsewhere. As a contemporary chronicler reports: "Then there broke out a famine so great that they were forced to make atonement." Norway was made to pay indemnities for the financial losses caused and to grant the Hansa extensive trade privileges.[3]

Over time, economic sanctions and embargoes have become a principal tool of foreign policy. They are often imposed unilaterally in the hope of changing a country's government or at least changing its policies. Reasons for imposing sanctions and embargoes have varied: They range from upholding human rights to attempts to promote nuclear nonproliferation or anti-terrorism.

A fundamental problem with sanctions is that their unilateral imposition frequently fails to produce the desired results. Sanctions may make obtaining goods more difficult or expensive for the sanctioned country, yet their purported objective is almost never achieved.

However, such unilateral measures often fall short. For example, U.S. agencies have implemented multiple sanctions against Iran for more than two decades. Since those sanctions were typically imposed only by the U.S., Iran has signed contracts with foreign firms within the last five years reported at about $20 billion to support the development of its oil resources. Iranian banks also are able to fund their activities in currencies other than the dollar. Overall, Iran's trade with the world has grown since the U.S. imposed sanctions.[4]

In order to work, sanctions need to be imposed multilaterally and affect goods that are vital to the sanctioned country—goals that are clear, yet difficult to implement. Consider, for instance, the dependence of countries like Japan, Korea, and the United States on imported oil. Of the ten countries that export the most oil to the United States, only Canada and Mexico are politically stable. Among the others, Iraq in particular is still undergoing reconstruction. After more than a decade of sanctions, Iraq's oil infrastructure is in desperate need of modernization and investment. It will be quite some time before production returns to pre-war levels, a fact that has already led to some instability in the price of oil, negatively affecting the U.S. economy as well as others around the world.[5]

Sanctions usually mean significant loss of business. A study by the Institute of International Economics determined that in 2005 the U.S. had imposed sanctions on 26 countries, accounting for more than half the world's population, which cost America between $15 billion and $19 billion in lost exports annually.[6] Due to these costs, sanctions almost always raise the issue of compensation to firms and industries most adversely affected by them. For example, during the embargo against Iraq, which was imposed following its invasion of Kuwait in 1990, agreements were made for financial compensation to Iraq's trading partners. Yet, trying to impose sanctions slowly or making them less expensive to ease the burden on the commercial sector undercuts their ultimate chance for success.

The international business manager is often caught in this political web and loses business as a result. Frequently, firms try to anticipate sanctions based on their evaluations of the international political climate. Nevertheless, even when all reasonable precautions are taken, firms still suffer substantial losses due to contract cancellations once sanctions or embargoes are put in place.

Export Controls

Many nations have **export-control systems** designed to deny or at least delay the acquisition of strategically important goods by political adversaries. The legal basis for export controls varies from nation to nation. For example, in Germany, armament exports are governed by the War Weapons Control Law. The exports of other goods are covered by the German Export List. **Dual-use items**, which are goods useful for both military and civilian purposes, are then controlled by the Joint List of the European Union. The U.S. export-control system is based on the Export Administration Act and the Munitions Control Act. These laws control all export of goods, services, and ideas. The determinants for controls are national security, foreign policy, short supply, and nuclear nonproliferation. World View: Bullets, Bugs, and Bytes explores how the U.S. makes decisions regarding export controls.

Export licenses are issued by the Department of Commerce, which administers the Export Administration Act. In consultation with other government agencies—particularly the departments of State, Defense, and Energy—the Commerce Department has drawn up a list of commodities whose export is considered particularly sensitive. In addition, a list of countries differentiates nations according to their political relationship with the U.S. Finally, there is a list of individual firms in each country that are considered to be unreliable trading partners because of past trade-diversion activities.

After an export license application has been filed, specialists in the Department of Commerce match the commodity to be exported with the **critical commodities list**, a file containing information about products that are either particularly sensitive to national security or controlled for other purposes. The product is then matched with the country of destination and the recipient company. If no concerns regarding any of the three steps exist, an export license is issued. Control determinants and the steps in the decision process are summarized in Figure 4.1.

This process may sound overly cumbersome, but it does not apply in equal measure to all exports. Most international business activities can be carried out under "no license required"

EXPORT-CONTROL SYSTEM

A system designed to deny or at least delay the acquisition of strategically important goods to adversaries; in the U.S., based on the Export Administration Act and the Munitions Control Act.

DUAL-USE ITEM

Good or service that is useful for both military and civilian purposes.

EXPORT LICENSE

A license obtainable from the U.S. Department of Commerce Bureau of Industry and Security, which is responsible for administering the Export Administration Act.

CRITICAL COMMODITIES LIST

A U.S. Department of Commerce file containing information about products that are either particularly sensitive to national security or controlled for other purposes.

FIGURE 4.1   U.S. Export-Control System

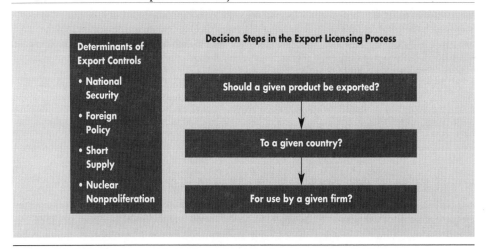

WORLD VIEW

BULLETS, BUGS, AND BYTES

To keep the world a safe place, nations must ensure that the promotion of trade is carefully balanced with responsible foreign policy. Clearly, arms embargoes that keep advanced weaponry out of countries like Iran and Libya that support worldwide terrorism are necessary export controls. But what about supercomputer exports to India or Pakistan? Will they be used to advance the nations' economies or to speed development of nuclear weapons? In a delicate balancing act, U.S. export policy is swayed by manufacturers, the national political climate, shifts in the geopolitical map, and rapid technology advances.

Across a range of industries, companies that trade internationally are subject to scrutiny by the Commerce Department's Bureau of Industry and Security (BIS). Penalties imposed include judgments against Northrop Grumman for illegal exports of navigation equipment to Singapore; a California technology company for unlicensed exports of export controlled technology to China; and a Texas company for exports of telecommunications equipment to Cuba.

In 2007, ITT Corporation, the leading manufacturer of military night-vision equipment for the U.S. Armed Forces, admitted to illegally exporting restricted night-vision data to China, Singapore, and the United Kingdom. The company also pleaded guilty to charges that it omitted statements of material fact in required arms exports reports. The $100 million penalty is believed to be one of the largest ever in a criminal export-control case.

Fears of biological warfare following anthrax attacks in the U.S. mail have increased the urgency of developing international inspection protocols to monitor the development of technologies behind biological weaponry.

Even more difficult to control is how foreign governments use powerful computer technologies, a key ingredient in sophisticated armaments. The Bush administration, in a move to help U.S. companies gain competitive ground in fast-growing information technology markets, recently eased regulations covering export of high-performance computers to India, Pakistan, Israel, China, and Russia. The new rulings allow these nations to import U.S. computers capable of processing information at the speed of 190,000 million theoretical operations per second (MTOPS). The previous limit was 85,000. Additionally, the Bush administration made a significant revision in computer controls and implemented a major change in controls on general-purpose semiconductors for civilian uses. It is currently working on changes to controls on thermal imaging technology and encryption controls. A new Office of Technology Evaluation has been established to help the government understand not only what is coming over the horizon, but also what is already widely available on world markets.

To balance the interests of U.S. computer and chip manufacturers against national security concerns, the U.S. government has grouped countries into four tiers. Each tier has different specifications for which computers may be exported under what conditions. In tier four, with countries such as Iraq and Libya, an embargo is in effect, and no computers can be exported at all. At the other extreme, tier one companies in Canada, Western Europe, and Mexico, for example, can purchase any computer without U.S. federal review—as long as it is not diverted to unfriendly nations through re-export.

Export controls extend beyond sensitive products to encompass technological know-how. U.S. companies must obtain an export license before a non-U.S. individual can work on a technology that would require one. The reach of the so-called **deemed export** regulation even affects foreign nationals attending universities or conferences in the U.S. In effect, foreign engineers, scientists, and students are treated as though they are foreign countries.

While high-tech firms claim that this measure constitutes "bureaucratic overkill" and stalls the hiring of high-demand specialists, the BIS insists that it helps keep sensitive information out of dangerous hands.

SOURCES: BXA Press Page, Bureau of Export Administration, **http://www.bxa.doc.gov/press**, accessed January 2, 2003; Robert McMillan, "Bush Relaxes Computer Exports to Some Countries," *Newsbytes*, January 3, 2002, **http://www.newsbytes.com**; "A Viral Bust-Up," *The Economist*, December 6, 2001, p. 46; Vernon Loeb, "Lockheed Aided China on Rocket Motor, U.S. Says," *The Washington Post*, April 6, 2000, p. A1; Gary Milhollin, "With Looser Computer Controls, We're Selling Our Safety Short," *The Washington Post*, March 12, 2000, p. B3; Jennifer Weeks, "When Too Much Is Classified, Too Little Is Secure," *The Washington Post*, June 15, 2000, p. B3; (U.S. Department of Justice, "Major U.S. Export Enforcement Actions in the Past Year," **http://www.bis.doc.gov/news/2007/doj10_11_07factsheet.html**; "Bush Wants Export Controls Updated," *USA Today*, (January 22, 2008); U.S. Department of Justice, "Major U.S. Export Enforcement Actions in the Past Year," **http://www.bis.doc.gov/news/2007/doj10_11_07factsheet.html**.

DEEMED EXPORT

Addresses people rather than products where knowledge transfer could lead to a breach of export restrictions.

(NLR) conditions. NLR provides blanket permission to export to most trading partners, provided that neither the end user nor the end use is considered sensitive. It therefore pays to check out the denied persons list published by the U.S. government (**http://www.bis.doc.gov/DPL**) to ensure that one's trading partner is not a prohibited one. However, the process becomes more complicated when it involves products incorporating high-level technologies and unfriendly nations. The exporter must then apply for an export license, which consists of written authorization to send a product abroad. In most cases, license applications can be downloaded and submitted via the Internet.

Export controls are increasingly difficult to implement and enforce for several reasons. First, the number of countries able to manufacture products of strategic importance, such as advanced weaponry, has increased. Industrializing nations, which only a decade ago were seen as poor imitators at best, are now at the forefront of cutting-edge technology. Second, products that are in need of control are developed and disseminated very quickly. Product life cycles are so short that even temporary delays in distribution may result in a significant setback for a firm. Third, because of advances in miniaturization, products that are in need of control are shrinking in size. The smuggling and diversion of such products have become easier because they are easier to conceal. Finally, the transfer of technology and know-how has increasingly taken on major strategic significance. Because such services are often invisible, performed by individuals, and highly personalized, they are easy to transship and therefore difficult to trace and control.

Regulating International Business Behavior

Home countries may implement special laws and regulations to ensure that the international business behavior of firms headquartered there is conducted within appropriate moral and ethical boundaries. The definition of appropriateness shifts from country to country and from government to government. Therefore, the content, enforcement, and impact of such regulations on firms may vary substantially. As a result, the international manager must walk a careful line, balancing the expectations held in different countries.

BOYCOTTS One method nations and sometimes localities or individuals use in an attempt to affect international business activities is **boycotts**. A boycott is a collaboration to prevent a country from carrying on international trade by deterring or obstructing other countries from dealing with it. The ongoing boycott by Arab nations who blacklist firms that deal with Israel is just one example. It has led to anti-boycott laws in the United States through which the government denies foreign income tax benefits to companies that comply with the boycott.

Caught in a web of governmental activity, firms may be forced either to lose business or to pay substantial fines. This is especially true if the firm's products are competitive but not unique, so that the supplier can opt to purchase them elsewhere. The heightening of such conflict can sometimes force companies to search for new, and possibly risky, ways to circumvent the law or to totally withdraw operations from a country.

ANTITRUST LEGISLATION **Antitrust laws** are another area of regulatory activity that affects international business. Antitrust laws prohibit monopolies, restraint of trade, and conspiracies that inhibit competition. In reviewing plans to sell off the nation's two major airlines that account for 80 percent of domestic air traffic, Mexico's antitrust watchdog agency ruled that the two must be sold separately in order to preserve competition.[7] While antitrust laws apply to international operations as well as domestic firms, the United States has taken steps to protect from antitrust legislation any firm cooperating in the development of foreign markets. For example, the Webb-Pomerene Act of 1918 and the Export Trading Company Act of 1982 both sought to aid export efforts by limiting the international scope of antitrust laws. However, this legislation does not help the firm battle charges of antitrust actions overseas. When Wal-Mart, the world's largest retailer, attempted to attract German shoppers by selling basic staples like milk and bread at below-market price, it fell victim to Germany's strict antitrust laws and was forced to raise its prices.[8]

BOYCOTT

An organized effort to refrain from conducting business with a particular seller of goods or services; used in the international arena for political or economic reasons.

ANTITRUST LAWS

Laws that prohibit monopolies, restraint of trade, and conspiracies to inhibit competition.

BRIBERY AND CORRUPTION In many countries, payments or favors to grease the wheels of business or government are a way of life, forcing international companies to make payments to foreign officials in order to conduct business. While most countries forbid the exchange of money or other favors in order to gain competitive contracts, some—like the United States—allow what are known as "facilitation payments" or payments made to expedite routine needs such as processing paperwork, obtaining permits, or gaining customs clearance. In some countries, facilitation payments are even tax-deductible.

A recent survey in Mexico reports that a quarter of government services hinge on the payment of bribes, which speed the pace of Mexico's cumbersome bureaucracies.[9] The Organization for Economic Cooperation and Development (OECD) took steps to stamp out corruption by adopting a treaty that criminalizes the bribery of foreign public officials. Working industry-by-industry and enlisting the voluntary participation of top corporations, the OECD seeks to crack down on the world's worst offenders. Figure 4.2 shows the corruption perceptions index of 2007. Backing OECD efforts, the World Bank is compiling a blacklist of bribers and encourages even poorer states to prosecute the offenders. In a recent precedent-setting trial in the African nation of Lesotho, 12 Western contractors were hauled into court, accused of paying $1.1 million in bribes to a government official. On June 19, 2007, South Africa became the 37th signatory and first African country to join the OECD's Anti-Bribery Convention.[10]

Regulations governing bribery and corruption leave managers operating in international environments with the tough choice of either adhering to home-country laws or following foreign business practices. To compete internationally, executives argue, they must be free to use the most common methods of competition in host countries. In time, the emerging consensus among international organizations that bribery should be outlawed may level the playing field.

FIGURE 4.2   Corruption Perception Index 2007

SOURCES: **http://www.transparency.org/policy_research/surveys_indices/cpi/2007**

INTERNATIONAL BUSINESS ETHICS Differences in ethical standards around the world divide nations on such issues as environmental protection, global warming, pollution, and moral behavior. What may be frowned upon or even illegal in one country is often customary or at least acceptable in others. China, for example, may use prison labor in producing products for export, but U.S. law prohibits their import. Similarly, low safety standards are accepted in the sweatshops of Malaysia, but they may outrage potential buyers of low-cost apparel in foreign markets. While other nations push for a moratorium on commercial whaling, Japan and Norway—whose people consider whaling a tradition and whale blubber a delicacy—have fought for exemptions from International Whaling Commission rulings to allow them to kill and sell whales.[11] As a truly global example, cutting down the Brazilian rain forest may be acceptable to the government of Brazil, but scientists and consumers the world over vehemently object because it factors in to climate changes and global warming.

When it comes to ethical issues like these, international managers have an opportunity to act as change agents, asserting leadership in implementing change. Keep in mind that not everything should be exploited for profit, even if such exploitation is legal in the country of operation. If they choose to adhere to ethical standards, firms not only benefit in the long term from consumer goodwill, but avoid the possibility of later recrimination.

 # HOST-COUNTRY PERSPECTIVE

The political and legal environment at work in the host country affects the conduct of international business in a variety of ways. To be effective, the international manager needs to work within the scope of local laws and policies, anticipating and planning for changes that may affect operations today and in the future.

Political Action and Risk

Ideally, business is best conducted in countries with stable and friendly governments. But this does not describe the reality of today's global business environment. Particularly in nations where government stability is in question, it is critical to monitor policies, practices, and current events that could adversely affect corporate operations.

There is **political risk** in every nation, but the range of risks varies widely from country to country. In general, political risk is highest in countries that do not have a history of stability and consistency. Even in countries that seem stable, however, popular movements arising from civil unrest have been known to sweep away ruling parties and cause major setbacks in the operation of business. There are three major types of political risk:

1. **Ownership risk.** Companies with foreign subsidiaries, for example, are exposed to the risk of losing properties. In some political situations, loss of life is also a serious possibility.
2. **Operating risk.** Any company dealing with partners in politically unstable environments risk interference or setbacks to ongoing operations, including loss of contracts or disruption of local manufacturing facilities.
3. **Transfer risk.** The difficulty of shifting funds from troubled countries leads to potential losses.

Firms can be exposed to political risk not only because of government actions but due to actions outside the control of governments. Figure 4.3 summarizes some of these risks.

 **3 LEARNING OBJECTIVE**

POLITICAL RISK

The risk of loss by an international corporation of assets, earning power, or managerial control as a result of political actions by the host country.

OWNERSHIP RISK

The risk inherent in maintaining ownership of property.

OPERATING RISK

The danger of interference by governments or other groups in one's corporate operations abroad.

TRANSFER RISK

The danger of having one's ability to transfer profits or products in and out of a country inhibited by governmental rules and regulations.

Culture Clues   Confucianism and the importance it places on status differences remain influential in Korea. Acknowledging differences in rank and showing respect for symbols of authority are important to Koreans. Most foreign business executives are perceived as belonging to the upper-middle or higher class.

FIGURE 4.3   Exposure to Political Risk

Contingencies may include:	Loss May Be the Result of:	
	The actions of legitimate government authorities	Events caused by factors outside the control of government
The involuntary loss of control over specific assets without adequate compensation	• Total or partial expropriation • Forced divestiture • Confiscation • Cancellation or unfair calling of performance bonds	• War • Revolution • Terrorism • Strikes • Extortion
A reduction in the value of a stream of benefits expected from the foreign-controlled affilate	• Nonapplicability of "national treatment" • Restriction in access to financial, labor, or material markets • Controls on prices, outputs, or activities • Currency and remittance restrictions • Value-added and export performance requirements	• Nationalistic buyers or suppliers • Threats and disruption to operations by hostile groups • Externally induced financial constraints • Externally imposed limits on imports or exports

SOURCE: José de la Torre and David H. Neckar, "Forecasting Political Risks for International Operations," in H. Vernon-Wortzel and L. Wortzel, *Global Strategic Management: The Essentials*, 2nd ed, p. 195. Copyright © 1990. This material is used by permission of John Wiley & Sons, Inc.

McDonald's franchises, both within and outside the United States, have been the targets of international terrorists around the world, from Canada to France to Moscow to Seattle.

VIOLENCE AND CONFLICT Violence and conflict—often directed at overseas interests—pose the most dangerous of political risks to international businesses. Guerrilla warfare, civil disturbances, and terrorism all expose global corporations as potential targets. International terrorists have frequently targeted U.S. corporate facilities, operations, and personnel abroad. Following U.S. military strikes in Afghanistan, for instance, a group of suspected Muslim militants in Pakistan kidnapped and murdered journalist Daniel Pearl, a reporter with *The Wall Street Journal*, a newspaper perceived by many as the flagship of U.S. business journalism.

International terrorists have frequently targeted U.S. corporate facilities, operations, and personnel abroad. Since the September 11 attacks on the World Trade Center and the Pentagon, it is realistic to expect that future attacks can take place anywhere. American companies, which account for nine out of ten of the world's most powerful brands, have proven particularly vulnerable. Bombings, arson, hijacking, and sabotage, as well as extortion of funds through the kidnapping of business executives, are all a reality of international business. A cruel irony, however, is that many of the businesses on the receiving end of anti-American attacks are locally owned franchises of U.S. business concepts. Therefore, the ones suffering most from such attacks are the local owners and local employees.[12] The horrors of 9/11 have shown the omnipresence of terrorism to the world. Given the symbolism attributed to the United States, U.S. firms have to be particularly aware of some of the risks incurred when doing business abroad.

In many countries, particularly in the developing world, coups d'état can result in drastic changes in government. The new government often will attack foreign firms as remnants of a Western-dominated colonial past, as has happened in Cuba, Nicaragua, and Iran. Even if such changes do not represent an immediate physical threat, they can lead to drastic policy changes that threaten the survival of foreign businesses in those regions. In the past few decades we

Quick Take   *Baby Backs off the Menu*

During Europe's foot and mouth disease scare, hundreds of thousands of pounds of frozen Danish pork ribs sat in American ports from Puerto Rico to Baltimore. Even though Denmark had no reported cases of the disease, it quickly became a casualty of a U.S. Department of Agriculture blanket ban on all fresh meat imports from the European Union. Denmark insisted that its pork products posed no risk whatsoever, since the time it took to ship them to the United States exceeded the two-week incubation period for foot and mouth. Since there is virtually no market in Europe for pork ribs—Danes consider them a waste product—Denmark depends on the United States for more than 50 percent of all sales. And since Denmark is the primary source of a favorite American dish—barbecued baby back ribs—customers at restaurants like Outback Steakhouse and Chili's either went hungry or paid more for home-raised substitutes. After several weeks during which prices skyrocketed, with restaurants paying twice the norm for dwindling supplies, Denmark was finally exempted from the ban.

SOURCES: "U.S. Eases Ban on European Meat," Associated Press Worldstream, May 25, 2001; Judith Weinraub, "Boatloads of Baby Backs," *The Washington Post*, April 11, 2001, pp. F1, F5.

---

have seen coups in Venezuela, Ghana, Ethiopia, Iraq, and Iran, for example, that have seriously impeded the conduct of international business.

Not as drastic, but still worrisome, are changes in government policies that are not caused by changes in the government itself. These occur when, for one reason or another, a government feels pressured to change its policies toward foreign businesses. The pressure may be the result of nationalist or religious factions or widespread anti-Western feeling. Consider, for instance, Russia's ban on U.S. poultry products, believed to have been exposed to salmonella caused by the infusion of antibiotics and feed additives. Chicken is the number-one American export to Russia, valued at more than $600 million a year. When the United States agreed to exclude 14 American poultry producers from the list of approved exporters, critics suspected a political motivation for the ban. Many believed it was a protectionist measure, put in place to retaliate against recent U.S. sanctions on foreign steel, of which Russia is a major exporter.[13]

EXPROPRIATION, CONFISCATION, AND DOMESTICATION Less extreme than the risk of violence or conflict, political unrest can lead to changes that nevertheless damage business operations. Through **expropriation**, for example, a host government may transfer ownership of an international business to a domestic entity. While compensation is payable under expropriation, the settlements are usually far from satisfactory to the foreign companies who have lost ownership. In recent years, the use of expropriation as a policy tool has declined sharply, suggesting that governments have come to recognize that the damage they inflict on themselves through expropriation exceeds the benefits they receive. When Canada signed the North American Free Trade Agreement, for example, one of the clauses exposed its government to lawsuits from foreign investors who objected to some of Canada's controversial environmental regulations, including bans on gasoline additives and restrictions on the cross-border trade of toxic waste. Objectors claimed that these constituted expropriations unfairly restricted free trade.[14]

Fast Facts

What would happen if the Earth's polar ice caps were to melt, let's say as a result of extreme global warming?

If they melt, the average sea level would rise by about 60 feet, a catastrophe that would submerge half of the world's most-populated areas.

EXPROPRIATION

The government takeover of a company with compensation frequently at a level lower than the investment value of the company's assets.

Terrorist Activity Outside the U.S.: A Factor in International Business Decisions

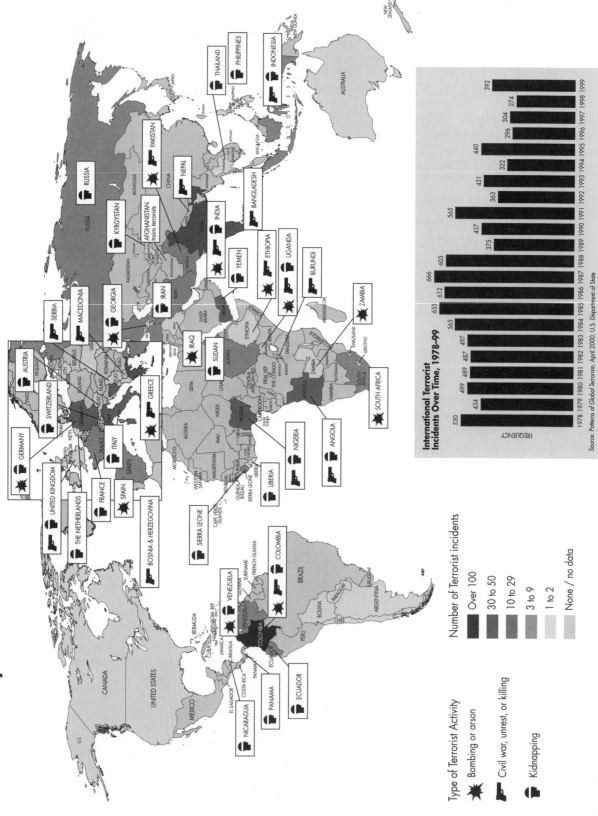

International Terrorist Incidents Over Time, 1978–99

FREQUENCY

1978: 530
1979: 434
1980: 499
1981: 489
1982: 487
1983: 497
1984: 565
1985: 635
1986: 612
1987: 666
1988: 605
1989: 375
1990: 437
1991: 565
1992: 363
1993: 431
1994: 322
1995: 440
1996: 296
1997: 304
1998: 274
1999: 392

Source: *Patterns of Global Terrorism*, April 2000; U.S. Department of State

Number of Terrorist incidents
- Over 100
- 30 to 50
- 10 to 29
- 3 to 9
- 1 to 2
- None / no data

Type of Terrorist Activity
- Bombing or arson
- Civil war, unrest, or killing
- Kidnapping

Similar to expropriation, **confiscation** also results in a transfer of ownership from the firm to the host country. It differs in that it does not involve compensation for the firm. Some industries are more vulnerable than others to confiscation and expropriation because of their importance to the host country's economy and their lack of ability to shift operations. For this reason, such sectors as mining, energy, public utilities, and banking have frequently been targets of such government actions.

More subtle in approach than either confiscation and expropriation but equally devastating for international businesses is the attempt to gain control over foreign investment though **domestication**. In these cases, the local government demands transfer of ownership and management responsibilities. It can impose **local content regulations** to ensure that a large share of the product is locally produced or demand that a larger share of profits is retained in the country. Changes in labor laws, patent protection, and tax regulations are also used for purposes of domestication.

Domestication can have profound effects on an international business operation for a number of reasons. If a firm is forced to hire nationals as managers, poor cooperation and communication can result. If domestication is imposed within a very short time span, corporate operations overseas may have to be headed by poorly trained and inexperienced local managers. Domestic content requirements may force a firm to purchase its supplies and parts locally, resulting in increased costs, decreased efficiency, and lower-quality products. Export requirements imposed on companies may create havoc for their international distribution plans and force them to change or even shut down operations in third countries.

INTELLECTUAL PROPERTY RIGHTS A potentially damaging outcome of local government action is the lack of enforcement or weakening of **intellectual property rights (IPR)**. Without protection, companies run the risk of losing their core competitive edge, since domestic firms are able to imitate their products and offer them for sale at lower prices.

A World Trade Organization agreement sets minimum standards of protection to be provided for copyrights, trademarks, geographical indications, industrial designs, patents, layout designs of integrated circuits, and undisclosed information, such as trade secrets and test data.[15] While not all-encompassing, these standards provide substantial assurances of protection, which—after an implementation delay for the poorest countries—will apply to virtually all parts of the world.

Poor IPR legislation and enforcement in the otherwise-lucrative markets of Asia illustrate a clash between international business interests and developing nations' political and legal environments. China, Indonesia, Malaysia, Singapore, Taiwan, Thailand, and the Philippines have the world's worst records for copyright piracy and intellectual property infringements. In an attempt to reduce piracy in Ukraine, where record industry estimates put the cost of pirated CDs at $20 million a year, the United States imposed trade sanctions on Ukrainian textile and metal exports. The following week, a major police raid on a compact disc market in Kiev led to the seizure of 13,000 CDs and video tapes. Similarly, during a crackdown in China, five illegal DVD disc production lines, with an estimated value of $2 million, were seized in the remote province of Guangdong.[16]

To counter accusations of IPR violations, newly industrialized countries argue that the laws discriminate against them because they impede the diffusion of technology and artificially inflate prices. Furthermore, although these nations are becoming increasingly aware that strong

CONFISCATION

The forceful government seizure of a company without compensation for the assets seized.

DOMESTICATION

Government demand for partial transfer of ownership and management responsibility from a foreign company to local entities, with or without compensation.

LOCAL CONTENT REGULATION

Regulation to gain control over foreign investment by ensuring that a large share of the product is locally produced or a larger share of the profit is retained in the country.

4   LEARNING OBJECTIVE

INTELLECTUAL PROPERTY RIGHTS (IPR)

Legal right resulting from industrial, scientific, literary, or artistic activity.

Culture Clues   Russians are renowned for their negotiating ability. They will stall for time if they do not think they can win. They are famous for unnerving negotiators by continuously delaying the proceedings and trying for a better deal.

IPR protection will encourage technology transfer and foreign investment, their legislative structures often fail to keep pace with the needs of their rapidly transforming economies. For IPR to act as a catalyst for innovation rather than as a barrier to trade, developing nations need to be vigilant against new forms of piracy, particularly those that arise via the Internet.[17] The Web is a key tool in disseminating knowledge and information. Its use already has raised many intellectual property rights issues.

Economic Risk

Most businesses operating abroad face a number of other risks that are less dangerous but probably more common than those explored so far. A host government's political situation or desires may lead it to impose economic regulations or laws that restrict or control international business activities.

EXCHANGE CONTROLS

Controls on the movement of capital in and out of a country, sometimes imposed when the country faces a shortage of foreign currency.

EXCHANGE CONTROLS Nations facing foreign currency shortages, for instance, sometimes impose **exchange controls** that restrict the movement of capital into and out of the country, making it difficult to remove business profits from or make investments in the host country. Sometimes exchange controls are levied selectively against certain products or companies in an effort to reduce the importation of goods that are either sufficiently available through domestic production or that are considered to be luxuries and therefore not considered valid expenditure of foreign currency resources. Exchange controls often affect the importation of parts, components, or supplies that are vital to production operations in the country. They may force a firm either to alter its production program or shut down its entire plant.

In the wake of a severe devaluation of its currency, consumers in Argentina have had to adjust to a sharp drop in their standard of living. For decades, Argentina was an affluent, stable marketplace, and its consumers were used to ready availability of imported goods. A major decline in its currency now makes many imports far too expensive. As a result, Argentina is battling factory closings, severe unemployment, bankruptcies, and extreme shortages of basic goods.

TAX POLICY

A means by which countries may control foreign investors.

TAX POLICY Countries may also use **tax policy** in their efforts both to invite foreign investment and to control multinational corporations and their capital. For example, Hong Kong cites low taxes as the number-one reason why foreign companies have set up regional operations in its city. Beyond inviting investors, tax policies may raise much-needed revenue for the host country. However, tax increases can severely damage the operations of foreign investors. This damage, in turn, frequently results in decreased income for the host country in the long run. The raising of tax rates needs to be carefully differentiated from increased tax scrutiny of foreign investors. Many governments believe that multinational firms may be tempted to shift tax burdens to lower-tax countries by using artificial pricing schemes between subsidiaries. In such instances, governments are likely to take measures to obtain their fair contribution from multinational operations. World View: Tax Codes Bring Conflicts—and Flexibility, Too looks at differences between tax codes that threaten to disrupt trade relations between the United States and the European Union.

PRICE CONTROL

Government regulation of the prices of goods and services; control of the prices of imported goods or services as a result of domestic political pressures.

PRICE CONTROLS In many countries, domestic political pressures can force governments to control the prices of imported products or services, particularly in sectors considered highly sensitive from a political perspective, such as food or health care. A foreign firm involved in these areas is vulnerable to **price controls** because the government can play on citizens' nationalistic tendencies to enforce the controls. Particularly in countries that suffer from high inflation, frequent devaluations, or sharply rising costs, the international executive may be forced to choose between shutting down operations or continuing production at a loss in the hope of recouping profits when the government loosens or removes its price restrictions.

Price controls can also be administered to prevent prices from being too low. As explained in more detail in Chapters 3 and 11, governments have enacted **anti-dumping laws**, which prevent foreign competitors from pricing their imports unfairly low in order to drive domestic competitors out of the market. Since dumping charges depend heavily on the definition of "fair" price, a firm can sometimes become the target of accusations quite unexpectedly. Proving that no dumping took place can become quite onerous in terms of time, money, and information disclosure.

Managing Risk

Considering the many types of risks discussed so far, one might ask why companies choose to do business in risky markets. The answer lies in the connection between risk and reward. If the returns are high, risk becomes acceptable. The poorest and most war-torn of African nations, for example, pose extremely high levels of risk. In some, the risks are so great that firms tend to invest only in projects that promise quick returns. Yet, historically, average return on foreign

ANTI-DUMPING LAW

Legislation that allows the imposition of tariffs on foreign imports, designed to help domestic industries injured by unfair competition from abroad in cases where imported products are sold at less than fair market value.

WORLD VIEW

TAX CODES BRING CONFLICTS— AND FLEXIBILITY, TOO

A ruling by the World Trade Organization in January 2002 set the United States and the European Union at loggerheads. Contrary to the U.S. tax code, the ruling forbids corporations from claiming tax exclusions on profits earned from overseas operations. Europe's goal is to force Washington to eliminate offshore tax shelters through which revenues from export sales are channeled, thus increasing the profitability of U.S. exports. If the United States refuses to amend its tax code to comply, the EU is entitled to impose countermeasures, such as raising barriers against U.S. goods.

There is a lot at stake. The EU and the U.S. are each other's main trading partners, accounting for the largest bilateral trade relationship in the world. Their economies combined are 58 percent of global GDP. They account for 37 percent of world trade. EU-U.S. trade in goods and services is worth around EUR 420 billion a year or approx. EUR 1.15 billion a day. The total EU and U.S. Foreign Direct Investment in each other's economy is valued at approximately EUR 1.5 trillion. This has created close to 14 million jobs on both sides of the Atlantic combined.

But tax policy differences also exist at the local level. In 2008, for example, Germany divulged that the BND—its Secret Service—had purchased customer data from a bank employee in the Principality of Liechtenstein. The information was then used to arrest German citizens (among them prominent leaders such as the head of the Postal Service) who had deposited funds in Liechtenstein in order to

avoid German taxes. Liechtenstein does not recognize tax evasion as a crime and therefore limits its collaboration with other governments in reporting deposits or dividend and interest payments. Once the customer data showed the magnitude of the sums deposited but not taxed (hundreds of millions of dollars), the German government was adamant in pressuring Liechtenstein and other small countries such as Monaco and Luxembourg to introduce a more transparent banking system. However, a strong counterargument claimed that all such measures would achieve was to have tax evaders transfer their funds to Singapore, Hong Kong or Dubai.

SOURCES: Geoff Winestock, "How One Trade Dispute Fuels Another," *The Wall Street Journal*, March 12, 2002, p. A18; "Taiwan: Lots of Pain, Not Much Gain," January 28, 2002, and "Taiwan's Misplaced Dread over China," January 29, 2002, BusinessWeek Online, **http://www.businessweek.com**; "Testing Times," *The Economist*, January 17, 2002; Joseph Kahn, "As Vote Nears, Bush Presses for New Trade Powers," *The New York Times*, December 5, 2001; Charlene Barshefsky, "The Transatlantic Alliance," occasional paper, American Council on Germany, June 15, 2001; Daniel Schoenwitz, "Asiens Steuerparadiese locken," *Handelsblatt*, January 15, 2008; "Steuerfrei in Dubai, *Handelsblatt*, January 15, 2008; European Commission, Report on U.S. Trade Barriers, February 15, 2007, **http://ec.europa.eu/trade/issues/sectoral/mk_access/pr150207_en.htm**.

direct investment in Africa has been higher than in any other region of the world. This goes to show that along with risk comes opportunity—and along with opportunity come potentially rich rewards.[18]

To make risk acceptable, companies that trade overseas can take various approaches to manage it. Obviously, in situations where a newly empowered government is dedicated to the removal of all foreign influences, there is little a firm can do. In less extreme cases, however, managers can take actions to reduce risk, provided they understand the root causes of the host country's policies.

Adverse governmental actions are usually the result of nationalism, the deterioration of political relations between home and host country, the desire for independence, or opposition to colonial remnants. If a host country's citizens feel exploited by foreign investors, government officials are more likely to take anti-foreign action. To reduce the risk of government intervention, the international firm needs to demonstrate that it is an integral part of the host country, rather than an exploitative foreign corporation. Achieving this involves intensive local hiring and training practices, better pay, contributions to charity, and societally useful investments. In addition, the company can form joint ventures with local partners to demonstrate that it is willing to share its gains with nationals. Although such actions will not guarantee freedom from political risk, they will certainly lessen the exposure.

Close monitoring of political development also reduces vulnerability to political risk. Increasingly, private-sector firms offer monitoring assistance, permitting the overseas corporation to discover potential trouble spots as early as possible and to react quickly to prevent major losses.

Firms can take out insurance to cover losses due to political and economic risk. In Germany, for example, Hermes Kreditanstalt (**http://www.hermes.de**) offers insurance services to exporters. Its web site promises products adapted to the special requirements of every country it covers. In the United States, the Overseas Private Investment Corporation (OPIC) (**http://www.opic.gov**) covers three types of risk insurance: currency inconvertibility insurance, debt service, and other remittances from local currency into U.S. dollars; expropriation insurance, which covers the loss of an investment due to expropriation, nationalization, or confiscation by a foreign government; and political violence insurance, which covers the loss of assets or income due to war, revolution, insurrection, or politically motivated civil strife, terrorism, and sabotage. Usually policies do not cover commercial risks. Moreover, they cover only actual losses—not lost profits. In the event of a major political upheaval, however, risk insurance can be critical to a firm's survival.

The discussion to this point has focused primarily on the political environment. Laws have been mentioned only as they appear to be the direct result of political change. However, the laws of host countries need to be considered on their own to some extent, for the basic system of law is important to the conduct of international business.

Legal Differences and Restraints

Countries differ in their laws as well as in their use of the law. While in most Western cultures law is a function of society, in theocratic cultures it is usually a mix of societal and spiritual guidance. Hebrew law and Islamic law (the Sharia) are the result of the dictates of God, scripture, and prophetic utterances and practices.

Yet even in nations where the legal systems are similar, attitudes toward the law differ greatly. For example, in recent decades, the United States has become an increasingly litigious society in which institutions and individuals are quick to initiate lawsuits. Court battles are often protracted and costly, and even the threat of a court case can reduce business opportunities. In contrast, Japan, with a fraction of the number of lawyers who practice in the United States, tends to minimize the role of the law. Litigation in Japan means that the parties have failed to compromise, which is contrary to Japanese tradition and results in loss of face. Consider the international brouhaha that ensued when the USS *Greenville*, an American submarine, sank the *Ehime Maru*, a Japanese fishing vessel, causing nine fatalities. The accident occurred while U.S. officers were demonstrating emergency surfacing procedures to on-board visitors. On the advice of his attorney, the U.S. commander made no public comments—not even an apology— since this may been interpreted as an admission of guilt, leading to a court-martial. In the months that followed, U.S. lawyers considered that the commander handled the situation well, allowing the courts to find a resolution. Yet, from a Japanese perspective, his actions were deemed disrespectful to Japanese culture.[19]

BASIC SYSTEMS OF LAW From an international business perspective, the two major legal systems worldwide can be categorized into common law and code law. **Common law** is based on tradition and depends less on written statutes and codes than on precedent and custom. Common law originated in England and is the system of law in the United States. **Code law** is based on a comprehensive set of written statutes. Countries with code law try to spell out all possible legal rules explicitly. Code law is based on Roman law and is found in the majority of the nations of the world.

While, in general, common law tends to be less rigid than code law, the differences do not, in practice, have a major influence on international business. The reason is that many common-law countries, including the United States, have adopted commercial codes to govern the conduct of business.

Host-country laws that may affect the firm's ability to do business are many and various. Tariffs and quotas, for example, influence the entry of foreign goods. Some goods may require special licenses. Other laws restrict entrepreneurial activities. In Argentina, for example, pharmacies must be owned by pharmacists. The law also prevents the addition of a drug counter to an existing business such as a supermarket. Laws also regulate the ability of foreign enterprises to buy property on which to build manufacturing plants or overseas offices.

Local regulations that have a major impact on the international firm's success are often overlooked—for example, a set of intricate regulations designed to protect local merchants used to hamper the opening of new department stores and supermarkets in Japan. The lack of large stores as conduits for the sale of imported consumer products severely restricted opportunities for market penetration of imported merchandise. Only after intense pressure from the outside did the Japanese government reconsider the regulations. Similarly, with the intent of protecting local products, seemingly innocuous laws in Switzerland decide what can be labeled as a "Swiss Army Knife," while in Europe the debate over what constitutes "French" wine has been going on for years.

Often, laws are specifically designed to protect domestic industries by reducing imports. Russia, for instance, charges a 20 percent value-added tax on most imported goods; assesses high excise taxes on goods such as cigarettes, automobiles, and alcoholic beverages; and provides a burdensome import licensing regime for alcohol to depress Russian demand for imports.[20]

Specific legislation may regulate what does and does not constitute deceptive advertising. Many countries prohibit claims that compare products to the competition, or they restrict the use of promotional devices. Even when no laws exist, regulations may hamper business operations. For example, in some countries, firms are required to join the local chamber of commerce or become a member of the national trade association. These institutions in turn may have internal sets of rules that specify standards for the conduct of business.

COMMON LAW

Law based on tradition and depending less on written statutes and codes than on precedent and custom— used in the United States.

CODE LAW

Law based on a comprehensive set of written statutes.

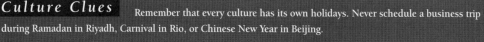

Culture Clues   Remember that every culture has its own holidays. Never schedule a business trip during Ramadan in Riyadh, Carnival in Rio, or Chinese New Year in Beijing.

Quick Take   *The Archbishop and the Law*

Rowan Williams is the archbishop of Canterbury and the spiritual leader of the approximately 80 million-member global Anglican Church. He stirred up some controversy when he examined the role of Sharia in British life. Sharia is the body of Islamic religious law that is based on the Koran, the words and actions of the Prophet Mohammad and the rulings of Islamic scholars. It typically finds its application mainly in Muslim countries.

The archbishop suggested that, with a population of more than 2 million Muslims in Great Britain, Sharia already figures prominently in the lives of many. For example informal neighborhood councils provide rulings on family issues such as divorce; banks, such as HSBC, already market mortgages that comply with Sharia rules of lending. Perhaps Muslims in Britain would be more comfortable and willing to build a more constructive relationship with their fellow citizens if they could choose Sharia law for the settling of civil disputes.

Many commentators, which included the British Prime Minister Gordon Brown strongly opposed such thinking. There was the feeling that such a move would undermine British values and laws and substantially weaken the position of women. Perhaps not since Thomas Becket ran afoul of King Henry II in 1170 was there such controversy surrounding the archbishop and the law.

SOURCES: Karla Adam, "Archbishop Defends Remarks on Islamic Law in Britain," *The Washington Post*, February 12, 2008, p. A11; "Archbishop of Canterbury: Sharia law unavoidable in Britain," *Christian Today*, February 7, 2008; Matthew Lynn, "Archbishop Williams is Wrong to Back Sharia Law," *Bloomberg.com*, February 28, 2008.

Influencing Politics and Laws

Many areas of politics and law are not immutable. Viewpoints can be modified or even reversed, and new laws can supersede old ones. To achieve change, however, some impetus for it—such as the clamors of a constituency—must occur.

The international manager has various options. One high-risk option is to simply ignore prevailing rules and expect to get away with doing so. A second option is to provide input to trade negotiators and expect any problem areas to be resolved in multilateral negotiations. The drawbacks are that this is a time-consuming process, and issues remain outside the control of the firm.

A third option involves the development of coalitions and constituencies that can motivate legislators and politicians to implement change. Even simple changes, such as the way key terms are defined, can positively influence the business environment. Consider, for example, the change in terminology used in the United States to describe trade relations between two nations. For years, attempts to normalize relations with China by granting "most-favored nation" (MFN) status drew the ire of objectors who questioned why China deserved to be treated in a "most-favored" way. Lost in the debate was the fact that the term "most-favored nation" was taken from WTO terminology and indicated only that China would be treated like any other nation for the purposes of trade. When the term was changed to "normal trade relations," tensions eased.

Beyond the recasting of definitions, firms can effect change in other ways. A manager may, for example, explain the employment and economic effects of certain laws and regulations

Fast Facts

One of the smallest nations in the world is also the oldest country in Europe and the oldest republic in the world. Most of its citizens earn their living making and selling postage stamps. Name it.

San Marino, on the slopes of the Apennines, entirely within Italy, has been an independent Republic since 1631. It covers 24 square miles.

and demonstrate the benefits of change. The firm might also enlist the help of local suppliers, customers, and distributors to influence decision-makers. The public at large can even be involved through public statements or advertisements.

Developing coalitions is no easy task. Companies often turn to **lobbyists** for help, particularly when addressing narrow economic objectives or single-issue campaigns. Lobbyists are usually well-connected individuals and firms that can provide access to policymakers and legislators in order to communicate new and pertinent information. Brazilian citrus exporters and computer manufacturers, for example, use U.S. legal and public relations firms to provide them with information about relevant U.S. legislative activity. The Banco do Brasil has used lobbyists to successfully restructure Brazilian debt and establish U.S. banking regulations favorable to Brazil.

Although representation of the firm's interests to government decision-makers and legislators is entirely appropriate, the international manager must also consider any potential side-effects. Major questions can be raised if such representation becomes very overt. Short-term gains may be far outweighed by long-term negative repercussions if the international firm is perceived as exerting too much political influence. (See Pfizer case.)

INTERNATIONAL RELATIONS AND LAWS

In addition to understanding the politics and laws of both home and host countries, the international manager must consider the overall international political and legal environment. This is important because policies and events occurring among countries can have a profound impact on firms trying to do business internationally.

International Politics

The effect of politics on international business is determined by both the **bilateral agreements** between home and host countries and by **multilateral agreements** governing relations among groups of countries.

The government-to-government relationship can have a profound influence in a number of ways, particularly if it becomes hostile. For example, political tensions in the bilateral U.S.-China relationship, due to China's growing bilateral trade surplus, possible currency manipulation, and violations of intellectual property rights, could potentially jeopardize the interests of U.S. companies in that country.[21]

International political relations do not always have harmful effects. If bilateral political relations between countries improve, business can benefit. One example is the improvement in Western relations with Central Europe following the official end of the Cold War. The political warming opened the potentially lucrative former Eastern bloc markets to Western firms.

The overall international political environment has effects, whether good or bad, on international business. For this reason, the good manager will strive to remain aware of political currents and relations worldwide and attempt to anticipate and plan for changes.

International Law

International law plays an important role in the conduct of international business. Although no enforceable body of international law exists, certain treaties and agreements are respected by a number of countries and profoundly influence international business operations. For example, the World Trade Organization (WTO) defines internationally acceptable economic practices for its member nations. Although it does not directly deal with individual firms, it does affect them indirectly by providing some predictability in the international environment.

LOBBYISTS

Well-connected individuals or firms that can provide access to policymakers and legislators to communicate new and pertinent information.

5 LEARNING OBJECTIVE

BILATERAL AGREEMENT

Agreement or treaty between two nations focusing only on their interests.

MULTILATERAL AGREEMENT

Trade agreement or treaty among more than two parties; the intricate relationships among trading countries.

INTERNATIONAL LAW

The body of rules governing relationships between sovereign states; also certain treaties and agreements respected by a number of countries.

The Patent Cooperation Treaty (PCT) provides procedures for filing one international application designating countries in which a patent is sought, which has the same effect as filing national applications in each of those countries. Similarly, the European Patent Office examines applications and issues national patents in any of its member countries. Other regional offices include the African Industrial Property Office (ARIPO), the French-speaking African Intellectual Property Organization (OAPI), and one in Saudi Arabia for six countries in the Gulf region.

International organizations, such as the United Nations and the Organization for Economic Cooperation and Development, provide multilateral agreements that affect international business. These codes and guidelines, such as the UN Code of Conduct for Transnational Corporations, are general in scope. They can also be very specific, such as the Code on International Marketing of Breast-milk Substitutes, developed by the World Health Organization. Even though there are 34 such codes in existence, the lack of enforcement ability hampers their full implementation.

In addition to multilateral agreements, firms are affected by bilateral treaties and conventions between the countries in which they do business. For example, a number of countries have signed bilateral Treaties of Friendship, Commerce, and Navigation (FCN). The agreements generally define the rights of firms doing business in the host country. They normally guarantee that firms will be treated by the host country in the same manner in which domestic firms are treated. While these treaties provide for some sort of stability, they can also be canceled if relations worsen.

The international legal environment also affects the manager to the extent that firms must concern themselves with jurisdictional disputes. Because no single body of international law exists, firms usually are restricted by both home- and host-country laws. If a conflict occurs between contracting parties in two different countries, a question arises concerning which country's laws are to be used and in which court the dispute is to be settled. Sometimes the contract will contain a jurisdictional clause, which settles the matter with little problem. If the contract does not contain such a clause, however, the parties to the dispute have a few choices. They can settle the dispute by following the laws of the country in which the agreement was made, or they can resolve it by obeying the laws of the country in which the contract will have to be fulfilled. Which laws to use and in which location to settle the dispute are two different decisions. As a result, a dispute between a U.S. exporter and a French importer could be resolved in Paris but be based on New York State law. The importance of such provisions was highlighted by the lengthy jurisdictional disputes surrounding the explosion of a chemical factory in Bhopal, India.

In cases of disagreement, the parties can choose either litigation or arbitration. Litigation is usually avoided for several reasons. It often involves extensive delays and is very costly. In addition, firms may fear discrimination in foreign countries. **Arbitration** generally brings quicker, less costly results. The procedures are often spelled out in the original contract and usually provide for an intermediary who is judged to be impartial by both parties.

ARBITRATION

The procedure for settling a dispute in which an objective third party hears both sides and makes a decision; a procedure for resolving conflict in the international business arena through the use of intermediaries such as representatives of chambers of commerce, trade associations, or third country institutions.

SUMMARY

The political and legal environment in the home and host countries and the laws and agreements governing relationships among nations are important to the international business executive. Compliance is mandatory in order to successfully do business abroad. To avoid the problems that can result from changes in the political and legal environment, it is essential to anticipate changes and to develop strategies for coping with them. Whenever possible, the manager must avoid being taken by surprise and letting events control business decisions.

Governments affect international business through legislation and regulations, which can support or hinder business transactions. Export sanctions, embargoes, and export controls are used both to preserve national security and improve economic conditions for domestic firms.

Governments regulate the conduct of international firms through such means as boycotts that limit its trade partners. Other methods of regulation include the setting of standards that relate to bribery and corruption and laws governing the restraint of competition. The firm's and the individual's ethical codes and beliefs influence the conduct of business overseas.

Political instability as well as such government actions as expropriation, confiscation, or domestication expose firms to international risk. In the event of a loss, firms may rely on insurance for political risk, or they may seek redress in court.

Different countries have different laws. One clearly pronounced difference is between code-law countries, where all possible legal rules are spelled out, and common-law countries such as the United States, where the law is based on tradition, precedent, and custom.

International political relations, agreements, and treaties influence international business. Arbitration, rather than litigation, is often the quickest and most effective way to resolve disagreements.

KEY TERMS AND CONCEPTS

sanction	ownership risk	price control
embargo	operating risk	anti-dumping law
export-control system	transfer risk	common law
dual-use item	expropriation	code law
export license	confiscation	lobbyists
critical commodities list	domestication	bilateral agreement
deemed export	local content regulation	multilateral agreement
boycott	intellectual property rights (IPR)	international law
antitrust laws	exchange controls	arbitration
political risk	tax policy	

REVIEW QUESTIONS

1. What are the differences between embargoes and sanctions? Give an example of each.
2. What types of products or services are typically not granted export licenses? Why are they prohibited?
3. What happens in a boycott? Are boycotts effective?
4. Describe the three types of political risk.
5. What are the differences between expropriation, confiscation, and domestication? How might each be applied?
6. What is the purpose of anti-dumping laws?
7. What is the difference between common law and code law?
8. What is arbitration and when is it useful?

CRITICAL SKILL BUILDERS

1. Discuss this potential dilemma: "High political risk requires companies to seek a quick payback on their investments. Striving for a quick payback, however, exposes firms to charges of exploitation and results in increased political risk."

2. In teams, debate this statement: "The national security that our export control laws seek to protect may be threatened by the resulting lack of international competitiveness of our nation's firms."

3. Discuss the advantages and disadvantages of common law and code law.

4. The United States has been described as a litigious society. How does frequent litigation affect international business?

5. After you hand your passport to the immigration officer in country X, he misplaces it. A small "donation" would certainly help him find it again. Should you give him the money? Is this a business expense to be charged to your company? Should it be tax-deductible? Many business executives believe that a nation has no right to apply its moral principles to other societies and cultures. Do you agree?

ON THE WEB

1. What are some of the countries suspected of nuclear proliferation? What types of exports might be barred from going to these countries? If your product is classified as a dual-use item, how would you go about obtaining a export license? What are some of the penalties that the U.S. government can impose on noncompliant exporters? See **http://www.bis.doc.gov**.

2. According to the anticorruption monitoring organization Transparency International, which countries have the highest levels of corruption? Which have the lowest levels? Use the Corruption Perceptions Index found at **http://www.transparency.org** to form your conclusions. What problems might an exporter have in doing business in a country with high levels of corruption?

3. Due to successful international negotiations in the Uruguay Round, the World Trade Organization now has agreement on significant dimensions of the trade-related aspects of intellectual property rights (TRIPS). Referring to **http://www.wto.org**, summarize these.

ENDNOTES

1. "The Great Game revisited," *The Economist*, March 22, 2007; Paul Anderson, "Pakistan seeks more anti-drug aid," BBC News, March 2, 2005; "If You Want a Mercedes, Try Herat," *The Economist*, January 24, 2002, p. 37; "Changing Facets," *The Economist*, Feb 22, 2007; Global Witness, **http://www.globalwitness.org/pages/en/conflict_diamonds.html**.
2. Sonia Shah, "Body Hunting: The Outsourcing of Drug Trials," *The Globalist*, January 31, 2007.
3. Philippe Dollinger, *The German Hansa* (Stanford, CA: Stanford University Press, 1970), p. 49.
4. Iran Sanctions: Impact in Furthering U.S. Objectives is Unclear and Should be Reviewed, Report 08-58, U.S. General Accountability Office, Washington D.C., December 18, 2007.
5. Energy Information Administration, "Iraq Country Analysis Brief," August 2007, **http://www.eia.doe.gov/emeu/cabs/Iraq/pdf.pdf**; Energy Information Administration, "Crude Oil and Total Petroleum Imports," accessed January 15, 2008, **http://www.eia.doe.gov/pub/oil_gas/petroleum/data_publications/company_level_imports/current/import.html**; accessed January 21, 2008.
6. Kimberly Ann Elliott, Gary Clyde Hufbauer, Jeffrey J. Schott and Barbara Oegg, *Economic Sanctions Reconsidered*, 3rd ed., Peterson Institute for International Economics, Washington D.C., November 2007.
7. "Mexico to Auction Two Airlines," *Associated Press Online*, July 14, 2002.
8. "Springtime for Wal-Mart and Germany," *VisualStore*, April 5, 2002, **http://www.visualstore.com**.
9. Kevin Sullivan, "For Many in Mexico, Bribes a Way of Life," *The Washington Post*, October 31, 2001, p. A23.
10. "The Short Arm of the Law," *The Economist*, February 28, 2002, p. 14; **http://www.oecd.org/department/0,3355,en_2649_34855_1_1_1_1_1,00.html**, Retrieved Jan. 15, 2008.
11. "For Watching or Eating?" *The Economist*, July 28, 2001, p. 48.
12. Conor Digman, "Brand Builders vs. Flag Burners," *Ad Age Global*, December 2001, p. 4.
13. "Russians Agree to Lift Embargo on U.S. Poultry," *Associated Press*, April 1, 2002, **http://www.iht.com**.

14. Luke Eric Peterson, "Investor Right and Wrongs," *Toronto Star*, June 14, 2002.

15. See Trade Related Aspects of International Property Rights (TRIPS), **http://www.wto.org**.

16. "Thousands of Pirated Tapes Seized During Police Raid in Ukraine," *Associated Press Worldstream*, January 28, 2002; "Five Pirated Production Lines Seized," *Xinhau News Agency*, July 18, 2002.

17. "WTO Members Warned Not to Let IP Rights Become Trade Barriers," *Asia Pulse*, July 10, 2002.

18. "Risky Returns," *The Economist*, May 25, 2000, p. 85.

19. "Aggressive PR Saves Waddle," *O'Dwýer's PR Daily*, April 23, 2001; Joseph Coleman, "Japanese Demand Traditional Apology from Sub Commander," **http://www.nctimes.net**, February 23, 2001.

20. National Trade Estimate Report on Foreign Trade Barriers, Office of the United States Trade Representative, Washington, DC, 2000, **http://www.ustr.gov**; Michael R. Czinkota, "The Policy Gap in International Marketing," *Journal of International Marketing*, 8, 1, 2000: pp. 99–111.

21. "Bush Wants Export Controls Updated," *USA Today*, January 22, 2008; "Keeping Their Balance," *The Economist*, Feb. 24, 2005; "America's Fear of China," *The Economist*, May 17, 2007.

CHAPTER5

ECONOMIC INTEGRATION

Building Blocks toward Worldwide Free Trade

As businesses have become increasingly dependent on exports and overseas trade, regional groupings based on economics rather than geography alone have gained in importance. There are at least 32 such groupings in existence: three in Europe, four in the Middle East, five in Asia, and ten each in Africa and the Americas. Trade within the three major blocs—American, European, and Asian—has grown rapidly, while trading with outsiders is either declining or growing at a far more moderate rate.

Some of the world's regional groupings have the super-structure of nation-states. The European Union is the best example. Some, such as the ASEAN Free Trade Area (AFTA), are multinational agreements that may, at least at present, be more political arrangements than cohesive trading blocs. Still other groupings are not trading blocs per se, but work to further them. The Free Trade Area of the Americas (FTAA) is a policy initiative to bring together five major blocs in the Western hemisphere to compete more effectively against Europe and Asia. It was supposed to be in effect in 2005, but due to political changes in South America and disputes over agriculture and intellectual property rights, there is little chance for a comprehensive trade agreement in the fore-seeable future. As a matter of fact, an alternative has arisen in opposition to the U.S.-led FTAA. The Bolivarian Alternative for the People of Our America (led by Venezuela) focuses more on social welfare and economic aid than trade liberalization. Regional economic integration in Asia has been driven more by market forces than by treaties and also by a need to maintain balance in negotiations with Europe and North America. Broader formal agreements are in formative stages; for example, the Asia Pacific Economic Cooperation (APEC) proposes to bring together partners from multiple continents and blocs, linking AFTA members with such economic powerhouses as China, South Korea, Taiwan, and the United States.

Regional groupings are constantly being developed in multiple ways: either internally, by adding new dimensions to the existing ones, or by creating new blocs. In 1995, in-formal proposals were made to create a new bloc between NAFTA and EU members called TAFTA, the Transatlantic Free Trade Area. Since the elimination of the Soviet Union in 1991, 12 former republics have tried to forge common economic policies—most recently through an arrangement called the Eurasian Economic Community, but thus far the customs union consists only of Belarus, Kazakhstan, and Russia. In 2002, the first common currency for a bloc was introduced when 12 member countries adopted the euro. The number of users has since risen to 15.

Trading difficulties both within and between blocs present challenges for companies that already face ever-intensifying competition. While firms remain under pressure to globalize, protectionist measures at home and within the blocs with whom they wish to trade can interfere with the development of overseas markets. Economic nationalism is effectively eroding some of the corporate benefits achieved through the formation of trading blocs.[1]

As You Read This Chapter

1. What happens when the interests of one trading bloc conflict with those of another?
2. Should firms be able to trade with whomever they choose, regardless of the bloc potential customers belong to?

As discussed in the last two chapters, the benefits of free trade are available only if nation-states are willing to give up some measure of independence and autonomy. Agreements among countries to establish links through movement of goods, services, capital, and labor across borders have resulted in increased economic integration. Some predict, however, that the regional trading blocs of the new economic world order will allow the rise of a handful of protectionist superstates that, although liberalizing trade among members, may raise barriers to external trade.

Economic integration is best viewed as a spectrum. At one extreme we might envision a truly global economy in which all countries share a common currency and agree to a free flow of goods, services, and factors of production. At the other extreme would be a number of closed economies, each independent and self-sufficient. The various integrative agreements in effect today lie along the middle of this spectrum and are the subject of this chapter.

The chapter begins with an explanation of the various levels of economic integration that define the nature and degree of economic links among countries. Here, we review the arguments for and against economic integration. Next, the European Union, the North American Free Trade Agreement, the Asia Pacific Economic Cooperation, and other economic alliances are discussed. The chapter concludes with a summary of strategic challenges for international companies that arise from economic integration.

LEVELS OF ECONOMIC INTEGRATION

A **trading bloc** is a preferential economic arrangement among a group of countries. The forms it may take are shown in Figure 5.1. From least to most integrative, they are the free trade area, the customs union, the common market, and the economic union.[2] The success of these blocs, from their establishment to future expansion institutionally and geographically, will depend (1) on leadership of selected countries (i.e., every bloc needs an "engine"); (2) their proximity in terms of geography, culture, administrative dimensions, and basic economic factors; and (3) their commitment to regional cooperation. For example, the biggest trading partners for any of the European Union member nations are other EU countries. Countries that have traditionally not traded with each other and/or have relations driven by animosities (e.g., in South Asia) have a more challenging time in implementing economic integration.

LEARNING OBJECTIVE

TRADING BLOC

Formed by agreements among countries to establish links through movement of goods, services, capital, and labor across borders.

FIGURE 5.1   Forms of Economic Integration in Regional Markets

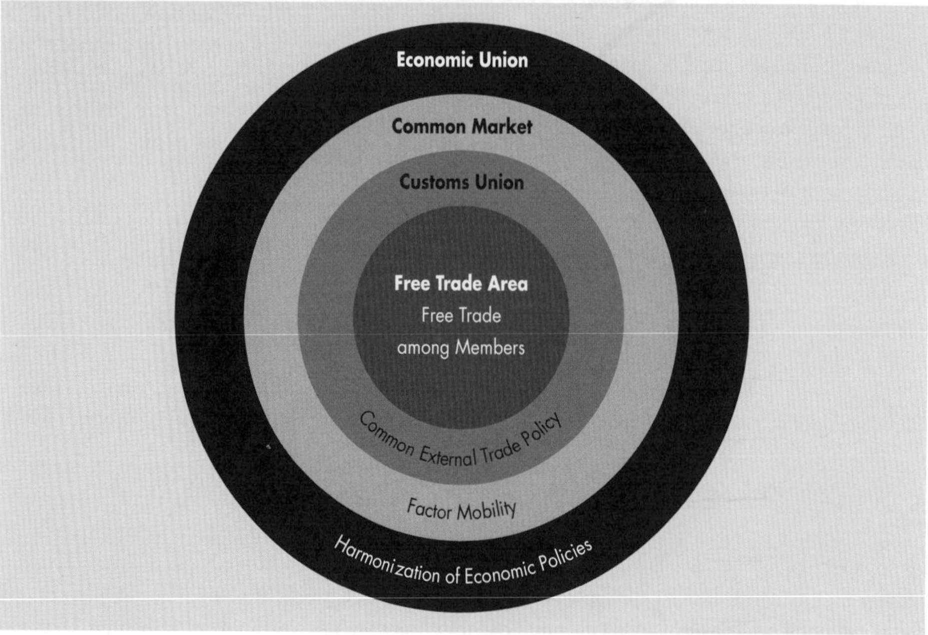

The Free Trade Area

FREE TRADE AREA

An area in which all barriers to trade among member countries are removed, although sometimes only for certain goods or services.

The **free trade area** is the least restrictive form of economic integration among countries. The European Free Trade Area (EFTA) and the North American Free Trade Agreement (NAFTA) are two notable examples. In a free trade area, all barriers to trade among member countries are removed. Therefore, goods and services are freely traded among member countries in much the same way that they flow freely between, for example, South Carolina and New York. No discriminatory taxes, quotas, tariffs, or other trade barriers are allowed. Sometimes a free trade area is formed only for certain classes of goods and services. An agricultural free trade area, for example, implies the absence of restrictions on the trade of agricultural products only. The most notable feature of a free trade area is that each country continues to set its own policies in relation to nonmembers. In other words, each member is free to set any tariffs, quotas, or other restrictions that it chooses on trade with countries outside the free trade area. Members are also able to exempt other nations or groups of nations from such restrictions. NAFTA member Mexico, for instance, has a number of bilateral free trade agreements with other blocs (the European Union) and nations (Chile) to improve trade and to attract foreign direct investment.

The Customs Union

CUSTOMS UNION

Collaboration among trading countries in which members dismantle barriers to trade in goods and services and also establish a common trade policy with respect to nonmembers.

The **customs union** is one step further along the spectrum of economic integration. Like members of a free trade area, members of a customs union dismantle barriers to trade in goods and services among themselves. In addition, the customs union establishes a common trade policy with respect to nonmembers. Typically, this takes the form of a common external tariff; imports from nonmembers are subject to the same tariff when sold to any member country. Tariff revenues are then shared among members according to a prespecified formula. The Southern African Customs Union is the oldest and most successful example of economic integration in Africa.

The Common Market

Still further along the spectrum of economic integration is the **common market**. Like the customs union, a common market has no barriers to trade among members and has a common external trade policy. In addition, factors of production are mobile among members. **Factors of production** include labor, capital, and technology. Thus restrictions on immigration, emigration, and cross-border investment are abolished. The importance of **factor mobility** for economic growth cannot be overstated. When factors of production are freely mobile, then capital, labor, and technology may be employed most productively. To see the importance of factor mobility, imagine the state of the U.S. economy if unemployed steelworkers in Pittsburgh were prevented from migrating to the growing Sunbelt in search of better opportunities. Alternatively, imagine that savings in New York banks could not be invested in profitable opportunities in Chicago.

Despite the obvious benefits, members of a common market must be prepared to cooperate closely in monetary, fiscal, and employment policies. Further, while a common market will enhance the productivity of members in the aggregate, it is by no means clear that individual member countries always benefit. Because of these difficulties, the goals of common markets have proved to be elusive in many areas of the world, notably Central America and Asia.

The Economic Union

The creation of a true **economic union** requires integration of economic policies in addition to the free movement of goods, services, and factors of production across borders. Under an economic union, members would harmonize monetary policies, taxation, and government spending. In addition, a common currency would be used by all members. This could be accomplished de facto, or in effect by a system of fixed exchange rates. Clearly, the formation of an economic union requires nations to surrender a large measure of their national sovereignty to supranational authorities in community-wide institutions such as the European Parliament. The ratification of the Maastricht Treaty by all member countries created the European Union, effective January 1, 1994. The treaty (jointly with the Treaty of Amsterdam, 1999 and the Nice Treaty, 2001) set the foundation for economic and monetary union (EMU) with the establishment of the euro as the common currency. A total of 27 countries are currently part of the European Union. In addition, the treaties set the foundation for moves toward a **political union** with common foreign and security policies, as well as judicial cooperation. Efforts to tie the members closer together through a Constitution for Europe have, however, failed.

COSTS AND BENEFITS OF ECONOMIC INTEGRATION

There are a number of arguments for and against economic integration. They center on (1) trade creation and diversion; (2) the effects of integration on import prices, competition, economies of scale, and factor productivity; and (3) the benefits of regionalism versus nationalism.

2 LEARNING OBJECTIVE

COMMON MARKET

A group of countries that agree to remove all barriers to trade among members, to establish a common trade policy with respect to nonmembers, and also to allow mobility for factors of production—labor, capital, and technology.

FACTORS OF PRODUCTION

All inputs into the production process, including capital, labor, land, and technology.

FACTOR MOBILITY

The ability to freely move factors of production across borders, as among common market countries.

ECONOMIC UNION

A union among trading countries that has the characteristics of a common market and also harmonizes monetary policies, taxation, and government spending and uses a common currency.

POLITICAL UNION

A group of countries that have common foreign policy and security policy and that share judicial cooperation.

Trade Creation and Trade Diversion

Chapter 3 illustrated that when trade barriers between two nations are removed, the countries and their industries are able to maximize efficient use of resources and trade for goods. The result is that both countries gain from trade—a win-win situation. But are such gains possible when free trade is limited to a single group of countries? The classic example of the entry of Spain into the European Union demonstrates not just the benefits of trade creation, but the resulting drawback of trade diversion.

In 1986, Spain formally entered the European Union. Prior to membership, Spain's trade with EU countries was restricted by the common external tariff, imposed on all nonmembers, including the United States, Canada, and Japan. A 20 percent tariff, for example, was applied to exports of agricultural products to the EU. This meant that low-cost U.S. wheat at $3.00 a bushel and Spanish wheat at $3.20 were both hurt by the tariff, boosting their costs to $3.60 and $3.84 respectively. When Spain joined the EU, tariffs were lifted, allowing Spain to win out on price over U.S. wheat producers by $.40 a bushel. As a result, trade flows changed. The increased export of wheat and other products by Spain to the EU as a result of its membership is termed **trade creation**. The elimination of the tariff literally created more trade between Spain and the EU. At the same time, because the United States is outside the EU, its products suffered the higher price as a result of tariff application. U.S. exports to the EU fell. When the source of trading competitiveness is shifted in this manner from one country to another, it is termed **trade diversion**. The recent debacle between the United States and the EU over tariffs on steel imported into the United States is another example. Hit with 30 percent tariffs, steel producers from Europe—as well as Japan, South Korea, China, Brazil, Australia, and New Zealand—are unable to compete, and trade is diverted to domestic suppliers and to U.S. partners in NAFTA, Mexico, and Canada.[3]

Whereas trade creation is a distinct positive of free trade for member nations, usually resulting in lower prices, trade diversion is inherently negative. This is because it shifts competitive advantage away from lower-cost producers to the higher-cost producers. The benefits of Spain's membership are enjoyed by Spanish farmers (greater export sales) and EU consumers (lower prices). The two major costs are reduced tariff revenues (borne by the EU) and lost sales (suffered by the United States).

From the perspective of nonmembers, the formation or expansion of a customs union is obviously negative. It is particularly damaging for emerging economies that need to build overseas trade. From the perspective of members of the customs union, the formation or expansion is beneficial only if trade-creation benefits exceed trade-diversion costs. When Finland and Sweden joined the EU, the cost of an average food basket decreased by 10 percent.

Reduced Import Prices

When a small country imposes a tariff on imports, the price of goods typically rises because sellers increase prices to cover the cost of tariffs. In turn, such prices lead to lower demand for imports. If a bloc of countries, as opposed to a single nation, imposes tariffs, the fall in demand can be substantial, forcing exporting countries to reduce their prices. Because of its greater market power relative to that of a single country, the trading bloc is able to improve its trading position and garner such low-price benefits. Any gain in the trade position of bloc members, however, is offset by a deteriorating trade position for exporting countries. Again, unlike the win-win situation resulting from free trade, the scenario involving a trade bloc is instead win-lose.

TRADE CREATION

A benefit of economic integration; the benefit to a particular country when a group of countries trades a product freely among themselves but maintains common barriers to trade with nonmembers.

TRADE DIVERSION

A cost of economic integration; the cost to a particular country when a group of countries trades a product freely among themselves but maintains common barriers to trade with nonmembers.

Increased Competition and Economies of Scale

Integration increases market size and therefore may result in a lower degree of monopoly in the production of certain goods and services. This is because a larger market will tend to increase the number of competing firms, resulting in greater efficiency and lower prices for consumers. Moreover, less-energetic and -productive economies may be spurred into action by competition from the more industrious bloc members.

Many industries, such as steel and automobiles, require large-scale production in order to obtain economies of scale. This is why certain industries are simply not economically viable in smaller, trade-protected countries. However, the formation of a trading bloc enlarges the market so that large-scale production by a firm—and lower per-unit costs that result from it— is justified. Lower costs resulting from greater production for an enlarged market are called **internal economies of scale**. Sometimes increased production is possible as a result of adopting common standards. Ericsson and Nokia, now global powerhouses, both benefited when the EU adopted the GSM standard for wireless communication, allowing companies like these to build scale beyond their small domestic markets.

In a common market, **external economies of scale** may also be present at the industry level. Because a common market allows factors of production to flow freely across borders, firms may now have access to cheaper capital, more highly skilled labor, or superior technology. These factors will improve the quality of the firms' goods or services or will lower costs or both.

INTERNAL ECONOMIES OF SCALE

Lower production costs resulting from greater production within one firm for an enlarged market.

EXTERNAL ECONOMIES OF SCALE

Lower production costs resulting from the inter-action of many firms.

Higher Factor Productivity

When factors of production are freely mobile, the wealth of common market countries, in aggregate, will likely increase. This is because factor mobility leads to the movement of labor and capital from areas of low productivity to areas of high productivity. In addition to the economic gains from factor mobility, there are other benefits not so easily quantified. The free movement of labor fosters a higher level of communication across cultures. This, in turn, leads to a higher degree of cross-cultural understanding: As people move, their ideas, skills, and ethnicity move with them.

Again, however, factor mobility will not necessarily benefit each country in the common market. A poorer country, for example, may lose badly needed investment capital to a richer country, where opportunities are perceived to be more profitable. Another disadvantage of factor mobility that is often cited is the brain-drain phenomenon. A poorer country may lose its most talented workers when they are free to search out better opportunities. More-developed member countries worry that companies may leave for other member countries where costs of operation, such as social costs, are lower. Many multinationals, such as Philips and Goodyear, have shifted their MERCOSUR production to Brazil from Argentina to take advantage of lower costs and incentives provided by the Brazilian government.[4]

Regionalism versus Nationalism

Economists have composed elegant and compelling arguments in favor of the various levels of economic integration. It is difficult, however, to turn these arguments into reality in the face of intense nationalism. Integration, by its very nature, requires the surrender of national power and self-determinism. As demonstrated in World View: Integration and Sustainability, the biggest impediment is the reluctance of nations to surrender a measure of their autonomy.

A listing of the world's major regional trade organizations is provided in Table 5.1.

(C) ZEFA VISUAL MEDIA—GERMANY

The European Union has several governing bodies, one of which is the EU Parliament. The Parliament has 785 members elected every five years by popular vote in their home nations. The Parliament has power to veto membership applications and trade agreements with non-EU countries.

TABLE 5.1 Major Regional Trade Organizations

AFTA	ASEAN Free Trade Area	Brunei, Cambodia, Indonesia, Laos, Malaysia, Myanmar, Philippines, Singapore, Thailand, Vietnam
ANCOM	Andean Common Market	Bolivia, Colombia, Ecuador, Peru
APEC	Asia Pacific Economic Cooperation	Australia, Brunei, Canada, Chile, China, Hong Kong, Indonesia, Japan, Malaysia, Mexico, New Zealand, Papua New Guinea, Peru, Philippines, Russia, Singapore, South Korea, Taiwan, Thailand, United States, Vietnam
CACM	Central American Common Market	Costa Rica, El Salvador, Guatemala, Honduras, Nicaragua
CARICOM	Caribbean Community	Antigua and Barbuda, Bahamas, Barbados, Belize, Dominica, Grenada, Guyana, Jamaica, Montserrat, St. Kitts-Nevis, St. Lucia, St. Vincent and the Grenadines, Suriname, Trinidad-Tobago
ECOWAS	Economic Community of West African States	Benin, Berkina Faso, Cape Verde, Gambia, Ghana, Guinea, Guinea-Bissau, Ivory Coast, Liberia, Mali, Mauritania, Niger, Nigeria, Senegal, Sierra Leone, Togo
EU	European Union	Austria, Belgium, Bulgaria, Czech Republic, Cyprus, Denmark, Estonia, Finland, France, Germany, Greece, Hungary, Ireland, Italy, Latvia, Lithuania, Luxembourg, Malta, Netherlands, Poland, Portugal, Romania, Slovakia, Slovenia, Spain, Sweden, United Kingdom
EFTA	European Free Trade Association	Iceland, Liechtenstein, Norway, Switzerland
GCC	Gulf Cooperation Council	Bahrain, Kuwait, Oman, Qatar, Saudi Arabia, United Arab Emirates
LAIA	Latin American Integration Association	Argentina, Bolivia, Brazil, Chile, Colombia, Cuba, Ecuador, Mexico, Paraguay, Peru, Uruguay, Venezuela
MERCOSUR	Southern Common Market	Argentina, Brazil, Paraguay, Uruguay, Venezuela (plus associate members Bolivia, Chile, Colombia, Ecuador, and Peru)
NAFTA	North American Free Trade Agreement	Canada, Mexico, United States
SAARC	South Asian Association for Regional Cooperation	Bangladesh, Bhutan, India, Maldives, Nepal, Pakistan, Sri Lanka
SACU	Southern African Customs Union	Botswana, Lesotho, Namibia, South Africa, Swaziland

SOURCES: **http://www.aseansec.org**; **http://www.apec.org**; **http://www.caricom.org**; **http://www.eurunion.org**; **http://www.nafta.org**.

Culture Clues   While negotiations in Southern Europe may take more than twice as long as in Northern Europe, the actual time spent on the business dimension is actually shorter. Germans, for example, can do without social chatter and want to get straight to the point.

WORLD VIEW

INTEGRATION AND SUSTAINABILITY

Economic integration will not make everyone happy, despite promises of great benefits from the free flow of people, goods, services, and money. Developed countries, such as the United States and Europe's wealthier nations, fear a hemorrhage of jobs as companies shift their operations to less prosperous regions with lower wages or fewer governmental controls.

Approximately 85 percent of the over-$350 billion in U.S.-Mexican trade moves on trucks. More than 4 million commercial vehicles enter the United States from Mexico each year at 25 border crossings in Texas, Arizona, New Mexico, and California. Currently, all but a fraction is limited to a narrow strip along the border where freight is transferred to American truckers for delivery to its final destination. Under NAFTA, cross-border controls on trucking were to be eliminated by the end of 1995, allowing commercial vehicles to move freely in four U.S. and six Mexican border states. But U.S. truckers, backed by the Teamsters Union, would have none of this, arguing that Mexican trucks were dangerous and exceeded weight limits. The union also worried that opening the border would depress wages, because it would allow U.S. trucking companies to team up with lower-cost counterparts in Mexico. In early 2001, the NAFTA Arbitration Panel ruled that Mexican trucks must be allowed to cross U.S. borders, and in December the Senate finally approved a measure that permitted Mexican truckers to haul cargo on U.S. roads as long as they are subject to strict safety and inspection rules. The Bush administration, initially opposed to the bill on the grounds that it singled out Mexico for tougher inspections and therefore violated NAFTA, withdrew its opposition after the September 11 terrorist attacks, accepting that safety standards on truck traffic, especially hazardous cargo, are a top priority. On the Mexican side, truckers are worried that if the border opens, U.S. firms will simply take over the trucking industry in Mexico. First trials of cross-border trucking were still waiting to start in 2008.

In Europe, politicians blame other member countries for the loss of investment opportunities and the jobs they represent. In France, firm labor laws protect wages and pensions and make redundancy decisions costly for employers. As a result, Italian-owned Moulinex-Brandt and British retailer Marks & Spencer recently decided to pull back operations. Moulinex-Brandt announced plans to close three factories, laying off 2,900 workers. Medef, a French employers' organization, insists that unless France reforms its legal and fiscal business environment, it will continue to lose jobs and wealth-creating enterprises to its competitors in Europe. France's three-year-old law reducing the work week to 35 hours from 39 does not help matters, either. Even France's own auto manufacturer, PSA Peugeot Citroën, has diverted jobs outside its home nation. Its workforce outside France has doubled to 68,000 over the last decade, while the domestic workforce has shrunk to 4,000. Nokia's decision to close down a major production facility for mobile devices in Bochum, Germany, and to move its manufacturing to more cost-competitive regions in Europe (such as Cluj in Romania) met with a hailstorm of protests from the German government to individual citizens.

SOURCES: "Nokia Closes Bochum, But Opens Cluj Factory," *Softpedia News*, January 15, 2008, available at **http://news.softpedia.com**; "U.S.-Mexico Trucking Program Still Waiting," *San Antonio Express-News*, May 2, 2007, pp. 1, 3; "Mexican Trucks May Get Full Access," *The Washington Post*, November 28, 2002, p. A4; Christopher Rhoads, "Clocking Out," *The Wall Street Journal*, August 8, 2002, p. A1; "Hogtied," *The Economist*, January 17, 2002, p. 35; Lyzette Alvarez, "Senate Votes to Let Mexican Trucks in U.S.," *The New York Times*, December 5, 2001; "Business Not As Usual," *The Economist*, April 26, 2001; Helen Dewar, "Battle on Mexican Trucking Heats Up," *The Washington Post*, July 25, 2001, p. A4.

TABLE 5.2 Membership of the European Union

1957	1973–1986	1995	2004		2007
France*	Great Britain (1973)	Austria*	Czech Republic	Latvia	Bulgaria
West Germany*	Ireland (1973)*	Finland*	Cyprus*	Lithuania	Romania
Italy*	Denmark (1973)	Sweden	Estonia	Malta*	
Belgium*	Greece (1981)*		Hungary	Poland	
Netherlands*	Spain (1986)*			Slovakia	
Luxembourg*	Portugal (1986)*			Slovenia*	
*Euro users					

SOURCES: **http://www.eurunion.org**

Quick Take *Joining the Club*

Turkey has aspired to join what is today's European Union since 1959 when it applied for associate membership, which it gained in 1963. Turkey signed a customs union agreement with the EU in 1995 and was officially recognized as a candidate for full membership in 1999. Negotiations were started in 2005, and the process is likely to take at least a decade to complete. Almost immediately thereafter, the EU froze negotiations on eight policy areas because of Turkey's refusal to open its ports and airports to vessels and aircraft from Cyprus. Overall, the membership bid has become the central controversy of the enlargement of the European Union.

Institutionally and commercially, Turkey is deeply integrated into Europe. For example, nearly 60 percent of its exports and over 50 percent of its imports are with the European Union members. Turkey's membership would bolster the EU's economy by $635 billion (ppp basis) and add a member that is part of the OECD and G-20. Arguments in favor of Turkey joining include the belief that this would bolster democratic institutions in Turkey and enable further improvements in human rights. Many fear that if Turkey is not granted membership in the EU, the winners will be the country's ultranationalists and that the West would lose an important ally.

The concerns are many as well. If Turkey joined the EU in 2015, it would become its most populous state within a decade due to strong population growth in the predominantly Muslim republic and low fertility rates in the European Union. As population size largely determines voting power in the EU, it would leapfrog Germany to become the state with the greatest political clout. Despite the fact that Europe already has over 15 million Muslims (3.5 million of whom are Turkish), critics have argued that Turkey is "in permanent contrast to Europe." Turkey is considerably poorer than EU states, with a per capita gross domestic product equal to a quarter the EU average. Many fear that more Turks would emigrate into European territories, which might result in tensions both on the labor side and on the level of society.

While many of the EU member states are in favor of membership, the mood among the general population is more negative, with nearly 60 percent of respondents being against and less than 30 percent in favor. A new cloud gathered over EU-Turkish relations in May 2007, when Nicolas Sarkozy, an opponent of Turkey's EU aspirations, was elected French president. Mr. Sarkozy's alternative proposal of a "Mediterranean Union" would combine various EU and non-EU countries around the Mediterranean Sea. "I want to say that Europe must give itself borders, that not all countries have a vocation to become members of Europe, beginning with Turkey which has no place inside the European Union," Mr. Sarkozy said.

SOURCE: "Turkey's EU Talks Inch Forward," *Financial Times*, December 20, 2007, p. 8; "The Slow Move Towards Accession," *Business Europe*, November 1-15, 2007, p. 8; "Don't Go Cold on Turkey," *The Wall Street Journal*, March 3, 2007, p. A8; "Turkey Has No Place Inside the European Union," *TurkishPress.com*, January 15, available at **http://www.turkishpress.com/news.asp?id=159133**; "The West's Eastern Front," *The Wall Street Journal*, November 28, 2006, p. A14.

EUROPEAN INTEGRATION

Development of the European Union

The first steps toward European integration were taken following the devastation of World War II, when a spirit of cooperation began to emerge across Europe. Established in 1948 to administer Marshall Plan aid from the United States, the Organization for European Economic Cooperation (OEEC) set the stage for more ambitious integration programs.

Over the following years several cooperative treaties and coalitions contributed to the eventual development of the European Union. Most notably, in 1957, the European Economic Community (EEC) was formally established by the **Treaty of Rome**. The document was (and is) quite ambitious. The cooperative spirit apparent throughout the treaty was based on the premise that the mobility of goods, services, labor, and capital—the "four freedoms"—was of paramount importance for the economic prosperity of the region. Founding members envisioned that the successful integration of the European economies would result in an economic power to rival that of the United States. Table 5.2 shows the founding members of the community in 1957 and members who have joined since, as well as those invited to join early in the 21st century.

Some countries were reluctant to embrace the ambitious integrative effort of the Treaty of Rome. In 1960, a looser, less integrated philosophy was endorsed with the formation of the European Free Trade Association (EFTA) by eight countries: United Kingdom, Norway, Denmark, Sweden, Austria, Finland, Portugal, and Switzerland. Barriers to trade among member countries were dismantled, although each country maintained its own policies with nonmember states. Since all but Norway, Switzerland, and newer members Iceland and Liechtenstein have joined or plan to join the EU, EFTA has lost much of its significance. Since 1994, the European Economic Area (EEA) agreement between the EU and three EFTA countries allows these EFTA countries to participate in the European Single Market without joining the EU. Switzerland is linked to the EU by Swiss-EU bilateral agreements, with a different content from that of the EEA agreement.

Another source of difficulty that intensified in the 1980s and continues today was the administration of the community's **common agricultural policy (CAP)**. Most industrialized countries, including the United States, Canada, and Japan, have adopted wide-scale government intervention and subsidization schemes for agriculture. In the case of the EU, however, these policies have been implemented on a community-wide, rather than national, level. The CAP includes: (1) a price-support system whereby EU agriculture officials intervene in the market to keep farm product prices within a specified range; (2) direct subsidies to farmers; and (3) rebates to farmers who export or agree to store farm products rather than sell them within the community. The implementation of these policies absorbs about two-thirds of the annual EU budget.

The CAP has caused problems both within the EU and in relationships with nonmembers. Within the EU, the richer, more industrialized countries resent the extensive subsidization of the more agrarian economies. Outside trading partners, especially the United States, have repeatedly charged the EU with unfair trade practices in agriculture.

TREATY OF ROME

The original agreement that established the foundation for the formation of the European Economic Community.

COMMON AGRICULTURAL POLICY (CAP)

An integrated system of subsidies and rebates applied to agricultural interests in the European Union.

Evolution of European Economic Community into European Union

By the mid-1980s, a sense of "Europessimism" permeated most discussions of European integration. Although the members remained committed in principle to the "four freedoms," literally hundreds of obstacles to the free movement of goods, services, people, and capital remained. For example, there were cumbersome border restrictions on trade in many goods, and although labor was theoretically mobile, the professional certifications granted in one country were often not recognized in others.

Growing dissatisfaction with the progress of integration, as well as threats of global competition from Japan and the United States, prompted the Europeans to take action. A policy paper published in 1985 (now known as the 1992 White Paper) exhaustively identified the

SINGLE EUROPEAN ACT

The legislative basis for the European integration.

Fast Facts

Is the euro in use anywhere in the Western Hemisphere?

The euro is in use in French Guyana, Guadaloupe, and Martinique, which are overseas departments of France.

MAASTRICHT TREATY

A treaty, agreed to in Maastricht, the Nether-lands, in 1991 but not signed until 1993, in which European community members agreed to a specific timetable and set of necessary conditions to create a single currency for the EU countries.

EUROPEAN UNION

The organization created on January 1, 1994, by the 12 member countries of the European community (now 27 members).

remaining barriers to the four freedoms and proposed means of dismantling them. It listed 282 specific measures designed to make the four freedoms a reality.

The implementation of the White Paper proposals was made possible through the 1987 **Single European Act**, which stated that "the community shall adopt measures with the aim of progressively establishing the internal market over a period expiring on 31 December 1992." The Single European Act envisaged a true common market where goods, people, and money could move between Germany and France with the same ease that they move between Wisconsin and Illinois.

Progress toward the goal of free movement of goods has been achieved largely due to the move from a "common standards approach" to a "mutual recognition approach." Under the common standards approach, EU members were forced to negotiate the specifications for literally thousands of products, often unsuccessfully. For example, because of differences in tastes, agreement was never reached on specifications for beer, sausage, or mayonnaise. Under the mutual recognition approach, the laborious quest for common standards is in most cases no longer necessary. Instead, as long as a product meets legal and specification requirements in one member country, it may be freely exported to any other, and customers serve as the final arbiters of success.

Less progress toward free movement of people in Europe has been made than toward free movement of goods. The primary difficulty is that EU members have been unable to agree on a common immigration policy. As long as this disagreement persists, travelers between countries must pass through border checkpoints. Some countries—notably Germany—have had relatively lax immigration policies, while others—especially those with higher unemploy-ment rates—favor strict controls. The member states have agreed to develop a common immigration policy at EU level by a coordinated approach which takes into account the economic and demographic situation of the EU. A second issue concerning the free move-ment of people is the acceptability of professional certifications across countries. In 1993, the largest EU member countries passed all of the professional worker directives. This means that workers' professional qualifications will be recognized throughout the EU, guaranteeing them equal treatment in terms of employment, working conditions, and social protection in the host country.

Attaining free movement of capital within the EU entailed several measures. First, it required that citizens be free to trade in EU currencies without restrictions. Second, the regulations governing banks and other financial institutions would be harmonized. In addition, mergers and acquisitions would be regulated by the EU rather than by national governments. Finally, securities would be freely tradable across countries. (The European Monetary System, its history, and future are discussed in detail in Chapter 8.)

A key aspect of free trade in services is the right to compete fairly to obtain government con-tracts. Under the 1992 guidelines, a government should not give preference to its own citizens in awarding government contracts. However, little progress has been made in this regard.

The 1991 **Maastricht Treaty**, ratified by all 12 then-member countries of the EC, created the **European Union (EU)**, starting January 1, 1994. The treaty called for a commitment to economic and monetary union and a move toward political union with common foreign and security policy.

Figure 5.2 summarizes the functions of the various bodies that make up the European Union.

Implications of the Integrated European Market

Perhaps the most important implication of the four freedoms for Europe is the economic growth that is expected to result. First, there will be growth resulting from the elimination of transaction costs associated with border patrols, customs procedures, and so forth. Second,

FIGURE 5.2   The Institutions of the European Union

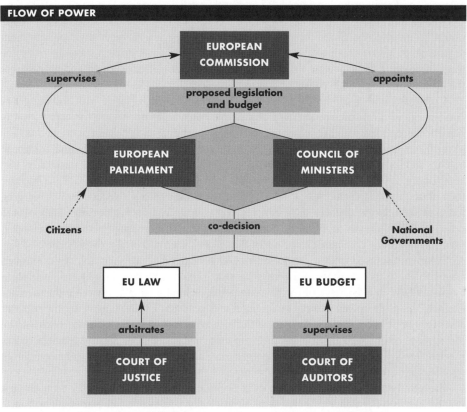

SOURCE: **http://news.bbc.co.uk/hi/english/static/in_depth/europe/2001/inside_europe/
eu_institutions/flow_chart.stm**; Web sites of the major institutions of the European Union can be found
at **http://www.europarl.europa.eu/addresses/institutions/websites.htm**.

economic growth will be spurred by the economies of scale achieved when production
facilities become more concentrated. Third, there will be gains from more intense competition
among EU companies. Firms that hold monopolies in one country will now be subject to
competition from firms in other EU countries. The introduction of the euro is expected to add
to the efficiencies, especially in terms of consolidation of firms across industries and across
countries. Furthermore, countries in Euroland will enjoy cheaper transaction costs and
reduced currency risks, and consumers and businesses will enjoy price transparency and
increased price-based competition.

Economic growth in Europe has important implications for firms within and outside the
EU. There will be substantial benefits for those firms already operating in Europe. Those firms
will gain because their operations in one country can now be freely expanded into others, and
their products may be freely sold across borders. In a border-free Europe, firms will have
access to a total of 493 million consumers. In addition, the free movement of capital will allow
the firms to sell securities, raise capital, and recruit labor throughout Europe.

For firms from nonmember countries, European integration presents various opportunities, depending on the firm's position within the EU. Well-established U.S.-based multinational marketers such as GE and Procter & Gamble are already taking advantage of the new
economies of scale. Rather than marketing on a country-by-country level, P&G has created

Fast Facts

What share of the world's total
foreign direct investment goes to
the European Union?

At 45 percent, the EU is the
world's largest recipient.

pan-regional business teams that are organized by product line but that are still able to recognize and respond to local needs.[5] Large-scale retailers, such as France's Carrefour and Germany's Aldi group, have created hypermarkets supplied by central warehouses with computerized inventories. Global brands like Heinz are expected to meet their procurement requirements. Many other multinationals are also developing pan-European strategies to exploit the still-emerging single market; that is, they are standardizing their products and processes to the greatest extent possible without compromising local input and implementation.

A company with a foothold in only one European market is faced with the danger of competitors who can use the strength of multiple markets. Furthermore, the elimination of barriers may do away with the company's competitive advantage. For example, more than half of the 45 major European food companies are in just one or two of the individual European markets and seriously lag behind broader-based U.S. and Swiss firms. Similarly, automakers PSA and Fiat are nowhere close to the cross-manufacturing presence of Ford and GM. To improve their presence, possible courses of action include expansion through acquisitions or mergers, formation of strategic alliances (for example, AT&T's joint venture with Spain's Telefónica to produce state of-the-art microchips), rationalization by concentrating only on business segments in which the company can be a pan-European leader, and finally, divestment.

Exporters also need to worry about maintaining their competitive position and continued access to the market. Companies with a physical presence may be in a better position to assess and to take advantage of the developments. Several financial services industries, for example, have set up call centers in Scotland and northern England, allowing them better access to the EU's consumers.[6] In some industries, marketers do not see a reason either to be in Europe at all or to change from exporting to more involved modes of entry. Machinery and machine tools, for example, are in great demand in Europe, and marketers in these companies say they have little reason to manufacture there.

The term **Fortress Europe** has been used to describe the fears of many U.S. firms about a unified Europe. The concern is that while Europe dismantles internal barriers, it will raise external ones, making access to the European market difficult for U.S. and other non-EU firms. In a move designed to protect European farmers, for example, the EU has occasionally banned the import of certain agricultural goods from the United States. Many U.S. firms are also concerned about the relatively strict domestic content rules recently passed by the EU. These rules require certain products sold in Europe to be manufactured with European inputs, leading to increased direct investment in Europe by U.S. firms.

FORTRESS EUROPE

Suspicion raised by trading partners of Western Europe who claim that the integration of the European Union may result in increased restrictions on trade and investment by outsiders.

4   LEARNING
OBJECTIVE

NORTH AMERICAN ECONOMIC INTEGRATION

Economic integration in North America has in recent years gained momentum. What started as a trading pact between two close and economically well-developed allies—the United States and Canada—has expanded to include Mexico, and long-term plans call for further additions. Unlike the EU, which has political integration as one of its goals, in North America the single purpose is economic integration.

U.S.–Canada Free Trade Agreement

After three failed tries in the 20th century, the United States and Canada signed a free trade agreement that went into effect January 1, 1989, creating a $5 trillion continental economy. Even before the agreement, however, the U.S. and Canada were already the world's largest trading partners, and there were relatively few trade barriers. Sectoral free trade agreements were already in existence; for example one for automotive products had lasted for over 20 years. The new arrangement eliminated duties selectively in three stages over the 1989–1999 period. For example, the first round eliminated a 3.9 percent tariff on U.S. computers shipped to Canada as well as 4.9 percent to 22 percent duties on whiskey, skates, furs, and unprocessed fish. Sensitive sectors such as textiles, steel, and agricultural products were not liberalized until the latter part of the transition period. Both countries see the free trade agreement as an important path to world competitiveness. Although there have been some dislocations due to production consolidation, the pact has created 750,000 jobs in the U.S. and 150,000 in Canada. It has also added as much as 1 percent in growth to both countries' economies. Trade between the U.S. and Canada exceeded $540 billion in 2006, with 79 percent of Canada's exports going to the United States.

Fast Facts

Except for Canada and Mexico, what country is physically closest to the United States?

Russia. In the Bering Strait, Russian and U.S. islands are only three miles apart.

North American Free Trade Agreement

Negotiations on a North American Free Trade Agreement (NAFTA) began in 1991 with the goal of creating the world's largest free market. The pact marked a bold departure: Never before had industrialized countries created such a massive free trade area with a developing country neighbor. In 2007, the free trade area includes over 450 million consumers with a total output of over $15.7 trillion.

Since Canada stands to gain very little from NAFTA (its trade with Mexico is 1 percent of its trade with the United States), issues arising from the agreement center on the gains and losses for the United States and Mexico. Proponents believe that the agreement will give U.S. firms access to a huge pool of relatively low-cost Mexican labor at a time when demographic trends indicate labor shortages in many parts of the United States. At the same time, many new jobs will be created in Mexico. The agreement will give firms in both countries access to millions of additional consumers, and the liberalized trade flows will result in faster economic growth in both countries. Overall, the corporate view toward NAFTA is overwhelmingly positive.

Opposition to NAFTA has risen from issues relating to labor, labor abuses, and the environment. At the outset, unions in particular worried about job loss to Mexico, given its lower wages and work standards. Some estimated that six million U.S. workers were vulnerable to job loss.

Trade between Canada, Mexico, and the United States has increased dramatically since NAFTA took effect, with total trade exceeding $883 billion in 2006.[7] Reforms have turned Mexico into an attractive market in its own right. Mexico's gross domestic product has been expanding by more than 3 percent every year since 1989, and exports to the United States have risen 20 percent per year to $198 billion in 2006. By institutionalizing the nation's turn to open markets, the free trade agreement has attracted considerable new foreign investment. The United States has benefited from Mexico's success. U.S. exports to Mexico are more than double those to Japan at $134 billion in 2006. While the surplus of $1.3 billion in 1994 has turned to a deficit of $64 billion in 2006, these imports have helped Mexico's growth and will, therefore, strengthen NAFTA in the long term. Furthermore, U.S. imports from Mexico have been shown to have much higher U.S. content than imports from other countries. At present, cooperation between Mexico and the United States is taking new forms beyond trade

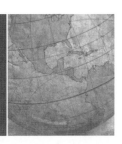

Culture Clues
Words can have different meanings or connotations in different parts of the world. The French word "char" means army tank in France and car in Quebec. The word "exciting" has different connotations in British English and in North American English. While North American executives talk about "exciting challenges" repeatedly, British executives use this word to describe only children's activities (children do exciting things in England, not executives).

SOURCE: Lionel Laroche, "Managing Cross-Cultural Differences in International Projects," *Engineering Dimensions*, November/December 1999, pp. 28-32.

and investment; for example, binational bodies have been established to tackle issues such as migration, border control, and drug trafficking.[8]

Among the U.S. industries that benefit are computer, auto, petrochemical, financial services, and the aerospace sector. Aerospace giants like Boeing, Honeywell, Airbus Industrie, and GE Aircraft Engines have recently made Mexico a center for both parts manufacture and assembly. Aerospace is now one of Mexico's largest industries, second only to electronics. That sector employs an estimated 10,000 workers and is currently worth $200 billion a year. That figure is expected to skyrocket in coming years, as U.S. corporations send more of their $35 billion business south.[9]

Gains and Losses

Free trade produces both winners and losers. Although opponents concede that NAFTA is likely to spur economic growth, they point out that this is not without cost to segments of the U.S. economy. Overall wages and employment for unskilled workers in the United States will fall because of Mexico's low-cost labor pool. U.S. companies have been moving operations to Mexico since the 1960s. The door was opened when Mexico liberalized export restrictions to allow for more so-called **maquiladoras**, plants that make goods and parts or process food for export back to the United States. The supply of labor was plentiful, the pay and benefits low, and the work regulations lax by U.S. standards. In the last two decades, maquiladoras evolved from low-end garment or small-assembly outfits to higher-end manufacturing of big-screen TVs, computers, and auto parts. The factories shipped half of Mexican exports, almost all of them to the United States. However, the NAFTA treaty required Mexico to strip maquiladoras of their duty-free status in 2001. Tariff breaks formerly given to all imported parts, supplies, equipment, and machinery used by foreign factories in Mexico now could apply only to inputs from Canada and Mexico. This effect was felt most by Asian operators because of their dependence of shipments from the Pacific (for example, 97 percent of the components for TVs assembled in Tijuana depended on imports from Asia). European companies felt less of an effect because of Mexico's free trade agreement with the EU, which eliminated tariffs gradually by the end of 2007.[10] Wages have also been rising, resulting in some low-end manufacturers of apparel and toys moving production to Asia. While the Mexican government is eager to attract maquiladora investment, it is also keen to move away from using cheap labor as the central element of competitiveness, Furthermore, many of the companies employing maquiladoras have also come under criticism for their wage practices.[11]

Despite fears of rapid job loss as companies sent business south of the border, recent studies have put job gain or loss at almost a washout. The good news is that free trade has created higher-skilled and better-paying jobs in the United States as a result of growth in exports. As a matter of fact, jobs in exporting firms tend to pay 10 to 15 percent more than the jobs they replace. Losers have been U.S. manufacturers of auto parts, furniture, and household glass; sugar, peanut, and citrus growers; and seafood and vegetable producers. The fact that job losses have been in more heavily unionized sectors has made these losses politically charged. In most cases, high Mexican shipping and inventory costs will continue to make it more efficient for many U.S. industries to serve their home market from U.S. plants.

NAFTA may be the first step toward a hemispheric bloc, but nobody expects it to happen any time soon. It took more than three years of tough bargaining to reach an agreement between the United States and Canada, two countries with parallel economic, industrial, and social systems. The challenges of expanding free trade throughout Latin America are significant. However, many U.S. companies fear that Latin Americans will move closer to the Europeans if free trade discussions do not progress. Both MERCOSUR and Mexico, for instance, have recently signed free trade agreements with the EU.[12] As a result of the stalled hemispheric free trade negotiations to achieve the Free Trade Area of the Americas (FTAA), the United States

MAQUILADORAS

Mexican border factories that make goods and parts or process food for export back to the United States. They benefit from lower labor costs.

Quick Take *Death by Sugar*

Escalating sugar prices recently led Kraft Foods to shift production of its Life Savers candy—a Michigan state icon for the last 35 years—to Quebec, Canada. The 600-employee plant closing is the latest casualty of U.S. agricultural tariffs and subsidies, blamed for causing sugar to cost twice and sometimes three times as much in the United States as it does in Canada and Mexico. The transfer will save Kraft an estimated $10 million a year in sugar costs alone. Import quotas, meant to protect American sugar growers from lower-priced competitors from overseas, have the unintended consequence of driving up prices for U.S. confectioners who are dependent on sugar for their main ingredient—Life Saver's colorful candies, for instance, are about 99 percent sugar.

Life Savers may be the tip of the iceberg. Chicago-based Brach Candy recently shuttered one of its factories, shedding 1,100 jobs, while heavy sugar users, like cereal makers Post and Kellogg's, are struggling to keep pace with high sugar costs. Ferrara Pan Candy Co., also based in Chicago but with two plants in Canada and one in Mexico, is not unusual in looking for growth beyond U.S. borders. While the success of NAFTA allows companies like Ferrara to shift operations, the irony is that its incentives to do so come from the very trade barriers put in place to protect U.S. industries from cross-border competition.

At the same time, the sugar industry study found that wages in U.S. candy factories were 27 times higher than Mexican wages and 20 percent higher than Canadian wages. Health care costs, tax rates, energy costs, and rent were also much cheaper in Mexico and Canada. On the other hand, wholesale sugar prices were nearly identical. The sugar industry alleges that candy companies that relocate hide those factors and use America's efficient sugar farmers as the scapegoat.

SOURCES: "Corporate Millionaires Likely to Spin Same Sob Story this Valentine's," *American Sugar Alliance*, February 8, 2006; "Sugar Lobby's Clout Threatens Economic Decay," *USA Today*, August 19, 2002, p. 14a; Tim Jones, "Life Savers Takes Business to Canada Over Sugar Costs," *The Chicago Tribune*, January 30, 2002, S1, pp. 1, 26.

---

has free trade arrangements with Chile, Colombia, and Panama. The Central America-Dominican Republic-United States Free Trade Agreement (CAFTA-DR) of 2005 includes seven signatories: the United States, Costa Rica, Dominican Republic, El Salvador, Guatemala, Honduras, and Nicaragua.

OTHER ECONOMIC ALLIANCES

Integration in Latin America

Before the signing of the U.S.-Canada Free Trade Agreement, all major trading bloc activity had taken place elsewhere in the Americas. However, none of the activity in Latin America has been hemispheric; i.e., Central America had its structures, the Caribbean nations had theirs, and South America had its own forms. However, for political and economic reasons, these attempts have never reached their full potential. In a dramatic transformation, these nations have sought free trade as a salvation from stagnation, inflation, and debt.

Southern Cone Trading Bloc—MERCOSUR

Mercado Comun Del Sur—or MERCOSUR—was created in 1991 and includes Brazil, Argentina, Paraguay, Uruguay, and Venezuela (since 2006). Bolivia, Chile, Colombia, Ecuador, and Peru have recently joined this South American trading bloc as associate members. MERCOSUR has three main objectives:

1. Establishment of a free-trade zone
2. Creation of a common external tariff system (i.e., a customs union)
3. Free movement of capital, labor, and services

In addition, future plans call for the harmonization of economic, fiscal, and trade policies. Venezuela's recent addition to the group has experts wondering if MERCOSUR will reorient itself as a political force.

It has been likened to the European Union, but with an area of 12 million sq km (4.6 million sq miles), it is four times as big. The bloc's combined market encompasses more than 250 million people and accounts for more than three-quarters of the economic activity on the continent. MERCOSUR is the world's fourth-largest trading bloc.

Of the five MERCOSUR countries, Brazil is the most advanced in manufacturing and technology. São Paulo is one of the world's major industrial cities and is home to the affiliates and subsidiaries of many foreign corporations. Even with its significant industrial base, vast interior areas of Brazil and their rich resources remain virtually untapped. Major infrastructure improvements are under way to permit these resources to be brought to market in a cost-efficient manner. Infrastructure and transportation improvements throughout member nations and in other parts of South America are an important outgrowth of MERCOSUR.

Following the MERCOSUR pact, trade among member nations increased, reaching $20 billion in 2000. However, the 2001 currency crisis in Argentina that threatened to devastate the country's economy put MERCOSUR under immense strain. Never strong, trade within the MERCOSUR trade bloc fell by 10 percent in 2001. Trade between Argentina and Brazil, the two largest members, took an immediate nosedive, as cash-strapped Argentine companies slashed imports and Brazilians, fearing nondelivery, placed orders elsewhere. Intra-MERCOSUR exports now account for only 13 percent of its members' total exports (intra-EU exports are 60 percent). Brazil's exports to Argentina, for example, its main partner in the MERCOSUR bloc, amount to only about 1 percent of its GDP.

The Europeans are MERCOSUR's biggest trading partners. Their trade annually exceeds $70 billion, compared to $57 billion in MERCOSUR–U.S. trade. (If U.S.-Venezuelan trade is added, annual trade reaches $102 billion.)[13] The EU and MERCOSUR plan to build a trans-atlantic free trade zone in the early part of the 21st century. Since 1995, when South America began to open up its markets, Europeans have won many of the top privatization deals. Spain's Telefónica de España spent $5 billion buying telephone companies in Brazil, Chile, Peru, and Argentina, where French Télécom and STET of Italy are active as well. In Brazil, seven of the ten largest private companies are European-owned, while just two are controlled by U.S. in-terests. Europeans dominate huge sectors in the economy, from automakers Volkswagen and Fiat to French supermarket chain Carrefour to Anglo-Dutch personal-care products group Gesy-Lever.[14]

Andean Common Market—ANCOM

The realization that if they do not unite they will become increasingly marginal in the global market spurred the Latin American countries of Bolivia, Colombia, Ecuador, Peru, and Venezuela to form the Andean Common Market (ANCOM) in 1991. When Venezuela joined MERCOSUR, it was required to resign from ANCOM, as Bolivia will have to do if it is admitted. This is because MERCOSUR's charter does not allow its member nations to have FTAs with nonmember nations. Bolivia, however, has said that it will not leave ANCOM. ANCOM and MERCOSUR leaders have discussed the possibility of allying to form a South American Community of Nations, modeled on the European Union, but those talks have not progressed quickly.

The potential gains from free trade among themselves that could be realized by the Andean Common Market countries was enhanced by expanded duty-free entry into the United States granted by Congress under the Andean Trade Preference Act (ATPA) in 1991. ATPA granted trade benefits to the Andean nations in exchange for antidrug efforts. The goal was to encourage alternatives to illegal coca cultivation and production in Bolivia, Colombia, Ecuador, and Peru by offering broader duty-free access to the U.S. market for legal crops and other commodities. While the production of illegal products has not waned, diversification has been successful in other respects. The agreement was renewed in 2002, allowing tax-free imports of textiles, wood products, leather, jewelry, wool fabric, and alpaca into the United States. The removal of tariffs represents savings of $300,000 a year to Andean nations, while protecting over 100,000 jobs.[15]

Central American Common Market—CACM

The Central American Common Market (CACM) was formed by the Treaty of Managua in 1960. Its members are Costa Rica, El Salvador, Guatemala, Honduras, and Nicaragua. The group anticipates the eventual liberalization of interregional trade and the establishment of a free-trade zone. The CACM has often been cited as a model integrative effort for other developing countries. By the end of the 1960s, the CACM had succeeded in eliminating restrictions on 80 percent of trade among members. A continuing source of difficulty, however, is that the benefits of integration have fallen disproportionately to the richer and more developed members.

Political difficulties in the area have also hampered progress. However, the member countries renewed their commitment to integration in 1990. A major change occurred in 2005 with the signing of the Central America-Dominican Republic-United States Free Trade Agreement. CAFTA-DR created the second-largest U.S. export market in Latin America, behind only Mexico, and the 13th-largest U.S. export market in the world. The United States exported $19.6 billion in goods to the five Central American countries and the Dominican Republic in 2006, more than all exports to Russia, India, and Indonesia combined. At the same time, U.S. imports amounted to $18.6 billion.

Caribbean Common Market—CARICOM

Integration efforts in the Caribbean have focused on the Caribbean Common Market formed in 1968. Its primary mandate is to provide a framework for regional political and economic integration. The following 14 nations make up the Caribbean community: Antigua and Barbuda, Bahamas, Barbados, Belize, Dominica, Grenada, Guyana, Jamaica, Montserrat, St. Kitts-Nevis, St. Lucia, St. Vincent and the Grenadines, Suriname, and Trinidad and Tobago.

Among CARICOM's objectives are the strengthening of the economic and trade regulations among member states, the expansion and integration of economic activities, and the achievement of a greater measure of economic independence for member states.

Before NAFTA, CARICOM members (excluding Suriname) benefited from the **Caribbean Basin Initiative (CBI)**, which, since 1983, extended trade preferences and granted access to the U.S. market. Under NAFTA, such preferences were lost, which means that the member countries have to cooperate more closely. Mexico and CACM have already started planning for a free trade agreement. In 2000, new legislation by the United States unilaterally extended NAFTA benefits to CBI countries to protect them from investment and trade diversion.[16]

CARIBBEAN BASIN INITIATIVE (CBI)

This agreement extended trade preferences to Caribbean countries and granted them special access to the markets of the United States.

INTEGRATION IN ASIA

The development of regional integration in Asia has been quite different from that in Europe and in the Americas. While European and North American arrangements have been driven by political will, market forces may compel politicians in Asia to move toward formal integration. In the meantime, however, Asian interest in regional integration is increasing for pragmatic reasons. First, European and American markets are significant for Asian producers, and some type of organization or bloc may be needed to maintain leverage and balance against the two other blocs. Second, given that much of the growth in trade for the nations in the region is from intra-Asian trade, having a common understanding and common policies will become necessary.

A future arrangement will most likely use the frame of the most-established arrangement in the region, the Association of Southeast Asian Nations (ASEAN).

Association of Southeast Asian Nations (ASEAN)

The Association of Southeast Asian Nations is comprised of ten member nations: Brunei, Cambodia, Indonesia, Laos, Malaysia, Myanmar, Philippines, Singapore, Thailand, and Vietnam. Under the auspices of the ASEAN Free Trade Agreement (AFTA), its objectives include reductions in tariffs to a maximum level of 5 percent among members as of 2003 and the creation of a customs union by 2010. Even a common currency has been proposed. Skepticism about the lofty targets has been raised about the group's ability to follow the example of the European Union given the widely divergent levels of economic development (e.g., Singapore vs. Laos) and the lack of democratic institutions (especially in Myanmar). ASEAN has also agreed to economic cooperation with China, Japan, and South Korea (the so-called ASEAN + 1 and ASEAN + 3 arrangements), as well as with India.

Broadening Asian economic cooperation has taken many forms. The Malaysians have pushed for the formation of the East Asia Economic Group (EAEG), which would add Hong Kong, Japan, South Korea, and Taiwan to the list. This proposal makes sense: Without Japan and the rapidly industrializing countries of the region such as South Korea and Taiwan, the effect of a free trade agreement is limited. In 1988, Australia proposed Asia Pacific Economic Cooperation (APEC) as an annual forum for 21 Pacific Rim countries to discuss the regional economy, cooperation, trade, and investment. The membership accounts for approximately 41 percent of the world's population, approximately 56 percent of world GDP, and about 49 percent of world trade. Originally, the model was not the European Union, with a central bureaucracy and harmonized policies, but the Organization of Economic Cooperation and Development (OECD), which is a center for research and high-level discussion. APEC has since established an ultimate goal of achieving regional free trade among its members by 2015 (or 2025 by some estimates).

World View: Full Speed Ahead into Asia explains how one U.S. automaker has succeeded in overcoming trade barriers in Asian markets.

Integration of the Indian Subcontinent

Economic integration has also taken place on the Indian subcontinent. In 1985, seven nations of the region (India, Pakistan, Bangladesh, Sri Lanka, Nepal, Bhutan, and the Maldives) launched the South Asian Association for Regional Cooperation (SAARC). Cooperation is limited to relatively noncontroversial areas, such as agriculture and regional development. Elements such as the formation of a common market have not been included.

WORLD VIEW

FULL SPEED AHEAD INTO ASIA

General Motors—and all the major car makers—are driving into Asia. From 2001 to 2010, vehicle sales in Asia are expected to grow by more than those of Europe and North America combined, making Asia the second-largest automotive market, with sales approaching $20 million per year. Despite the lure of the substantial market potential made possible by Asia's growing middle class, challenges include aggressive competition not only from foreign rivals but from local manufacturers, who benefit from barriers to free trade in the region. For example, in Indonesia, GM—the world's second-largest industrial company—faces competition from a local model, the Timor, which, due to government support in the form of lower duties on imported components, costs substantially less than GM's cheapest models. (Not surprisingly, before President Suharto's resignation, the company was run by one of his sons.)

To find its way around trade barriers and get an equal footing in Asia's emerging markets, GM has invested heavily to build up local manufacturing and distribution. The company's buildup in Asia started in 1990 with the establishment of a regional office in Hong Kong and representative offices in Bangkok, Jakarta, Kuala Lumpur, and Beijing.

In 1994, GM's Asia headquarters was moved from Detroit to Singapore. Singapore not only provides coordination and support, but allows GM to tailor manufacturing, sales, and distribution to local requirements. In Japan, GM now owns a 49 percent equity stake in Isuzu, while in China, the company established GM China as a separate entity. GM has two factories there and is planning a third. Recently, through a $100 million joint venture with Chinese state-owned car manufacturers, GM is making headway in the minivan sector, one of the fastest-growth segments of the Chinese auto industry. Another recent investment, this time a $251 million stake in ailing automaker Daewoo Motor Company, gives GM a foothold in South Korea, Asia's second-largest auto market. To highlight its presence in Asia, GM is investing $450 million in a regional manufacturing facility in Thailand's Rayong Province to build the specially designed and engineered Opel "Car for Asia" beginning early in the 21st century. In spite of the Asian economic crisis, which hit Thailand especially hard and forced the company to scale down its investments there, GM shows no signs of letting up on its drive into Asia.

To combat protectionism and further the cause of free trade, GM has developed a three-pronged strategy. The first approach focuses on executives working with government representatives from the United States, the EU, and Japan to dismantle what GM regards as the largest flaws.

The company uses its clout as a major investor, but it can also call on support from industries that follow it into a new market, such as component manufacturers. On the second level, GM works within existing frameworks to balance the effects of nationalistic policies. In countries such as Indonesia and Malaysia, it develops company-specific plans to preserve avenues of sales, even under challenging circumstances. Finally, GM is also pursuing its business strategy in Asia's free trade areas. Because it will be a long time before barriers are taken down in the Asia Pacific Economic Cooperation Forum (APEC), its immediate focus is on the ASEAN Free Trade Area (AFTA). GM is hopeful that the automotive sector will be a beneficiary of tariff reductions—provided that member governments can be persuaded that such cuts are in their best interests.

GM's moves to increase capacity and sales in Asia could help GM to fend off Toyota's challenge to GM's six-decade reign as the world's number-one car maker. For example, GM, through its joint ventures, sold 876,747 cars in China in 2006, compared with 276,774 vehicles for Toyota.

SOURCES: "GM Retrenches in Europe, Shifts Gaze East," *The Wall Street Journal*, April 18, 2007, p. A.4; Robyn Meredith, "Crazy Like a Fox," *Forbes*, July 8, 2002, p. 74; Peter Wonacott, "GM's Chinese Unit, Two Partners, Join Up to Make Minivehicles," *The Wall Street Journal*, June 4, 2002, p. D6; "U.S. Auto Makers Demonstrate Commitment to Thailand," U.S.–ASEAN Business Council press release, May 12, 1999, **http://www.us–asean.org**; see also: **http://www.gmbuypower.com** and **http://www.gmautoworld.com.tw**.

Integration in Africa

Africa's economic groupings range from currency unions among European nations and their former colonies to customs unions among neighboring states. In addition to wanting to liberalize trade among members, African countries want to gain better access to European and North American markets for farm and textile products.

International Groupings

OECD Organization for Economic Co-operation and Development
OPEC Organization of the Petroleum Exporting Countries
Commonwealth
OECD / Commonwealth

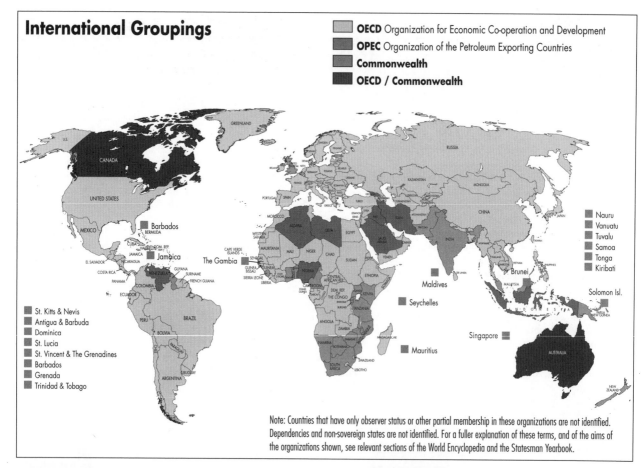

Note: Countries that have only observer status or other partial membership in these organizations are not identified. Dependencies and non-sovereign states are not identified. For a fuller explanation of these terms, and of the aims of the organizations shown, see relevant sections of the World Encyclopedia and the Statesman Yearbook.

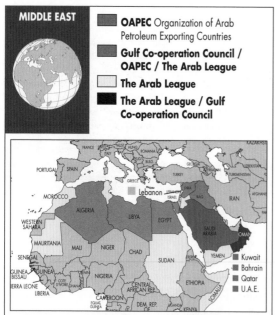

MIDDLE EAST

OAPEC Organization of Arab Petroleum Exporting Countries
Gulf Co-operation Council / OAPEC / The Arab League
The Arab League
The Arab League / Gulf Co-operation Council

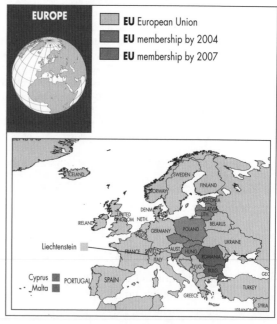

EUROPE

EU European Union
EU membership by 2004
EU membership by 2007

Sources: Based on Statesman Yearbook; *The European Union: A Guide for Americans*, 2000, **www.eurunion.org/infores/euguide/euguide.html**; "Afrabet Soup," *The Economist*, February 10, 2001, p. 77, **www.economist.com**

PACIFIC BASIN

AFTA ASEAN (Association of South East Asian Nations) Free Trade Area

AMERICAS

NAFTA North American Free Trade Agreement

ANCOM Andean Common Market

MERCOSUR Southern Common Market

CARICOM Caribbean Community and Common Market

CACM Central American Common Market

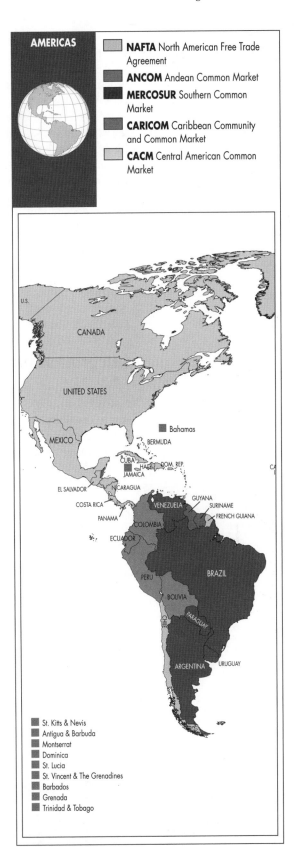

St. Kitts & Nevis
Antigua & Barbuda
Montserrat
Dominica
St. Lucia
St. Vincent & The Grenadines
Barbados
Grenada
Trinidad & Tobago

AFRICA

OAU *non-members of the* Organization for African Unity

Monetary area covering France's former colonies

SADC Southern African Development Community

COMESA Common Market for East and Southern Africa (formerly **PTA**)

ECOWAS Economic Community of West African States

Monetary area covering France's former colonies / **ECOWAS**

SADC / COMESA

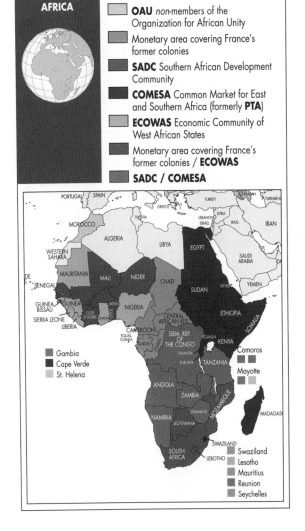

Gambia
Cape Verde
St. Helena

Swaziland
Lesotho
Mauritius
Reunion
Seychelles

Comoros

Mayotte

Fast Facts

Of the countries listed, which is the most dependent on the banana trade: Belize, Costa Rica, Guatemala, Honduras, Nicaragua, or St. Lucia?

St. Lucia. Over 60 percent of its exports, all of which go to the European Union, are in bananas.

Given that most of the countries are too small to negotiate with the other blocs, alliances have been the solution. In 1975, 16 West African nations attempted to create a mega-market large enough to interest investors from the industrialized world and reduce hardship through economic integration. The objective of the Economic Community of West African States (ECOWAS) was to form a customs union and eventually a common market. Although many of its objectives have not been reached, its combined population of 160 million represents the largest economic entity in sub-Saharan Africa. Other entities in Africa include the Common Market for Eastern and Southern Africa (COMESA), the Economic Community of Central African States (CEEAC), the Southern African Customs Union (SACU), the Southern African Development Community (SADC), and some smaller, less globally oriented blocs such as the Economic Community of the Great Lakes Countries, the Mano River Union, and the East African Community (EAC). Most member countries are part of more than one bloc (for example, Tanzania is a member in both the EAC and SADC). In 2002, African nations established the African Union (AU) for regional cooperation. Eventually plans call for a pan-African parliament, a court of justice, a central bank, and a shared currency.[17] The blocs, for the most part, have not been successful, due to the small membership and lack of economic infrastructure to produce goods to be traded inside the blocs. Moreover, some of the blocs have been relatively inactive for substantial periods of time while their members endure internal political turmoil or even warfare among one another.[18]

Integration in the Middle East

Countries in the Arab world have made some progress in economic integration. The Arab Maghreb Union ties together Algeria, Libya, Mauritania, Morocco, and Tunisia in northern Africa. The Gulf Cooperation Council (GCC) is one of the most powerful, economically speaking, of any trade groups. The per capita income of its six member states (Bahrain, Kuwait, Oman, Qatar, Saudi Arabia, and the United Arab Emirates) is in the 90th percentile in the world. The GCC was formed in 1980 mainly as a defensive measure, due to the perceived threat from Iran and Iraq. Its aim is to achieve free trade arrangements with the EU and EFTA as well as bilateral trade agreements with western European nations. A recent proposal among GCC members calls for the creation of a single currency—along the lines of the euro—for member nations by 2010. A strong regional currency may help the GCC become a viable trading bloc, able to compete in the new global economic order that has emerged under the WTO. Two key elements required to create a common currency are already under way: the dismantling of barriers to trade among member nations and the creation of a GCC member bank.[19]

Other Cooperative Trade Relationships

An important characteristic that distinguishes developing countries from industrialized countries is the nature of their export earnings. While industrialized countries depend heavily on the export of manufactured goods, technology, and services, developing nations rely chiefly on the export of primary products and raw materials, such as copper, iron ore, and agricultural

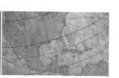

Culture Clues   One of the challenges in achieving economic integration in Asia is the resentment and suspicion felt toward the Japanese, due to their military occupation of countries such as China (in the 1930s) and Korea (1910–1945). The Japanese called their attempt to dominate the Asia-Pacific the "Co-Prosperity Sphere."

products. This distinction is important for several reasons. First, the level of price competition is higher among sellers of primary goods, because of the typically larger number of sellers and also because primary goods are homogeneous. This can be seen by comparing the sale of computers with, for example, copper. Only three of four countries are competitive forces in the computer market, whereas at least a dozen compete in the sale of copper.

Furthermore, while goods differentiation and therefore brand loyalty are likely to exist in the market for computers, buyers of copper are likely to purchase on the basis of price alone. A second distinguishing factor is that supply variability is greater in the market for primary goods because production often depends on uncontrollable factors such as weather. For these reasons, market prices of primary goods—and therefore developing country export earnings—are highly volatile. Responses to this problem have included cartels and commodity price agreements.

Cartels

A **cartel** is an association of producers of a particular good. While a cartel may consist of an association of private firms, our interest is in the cartels formed by nations. The objective of a cartel is to suppress the market forces affecting its good in order to gain greater control over sales revenues. A cartel may accomplish this objective in several ways. First, members may engage in price fixing. This entails an agreement by producers to sell at a certain price, eliminating price competition among sellers. Second, the cartel may allocate sales territories among its members, again suppressing competition. A third tactic calls for members to agree to restrict production, and therefore supplies, resulting in artificially higher prices.

The most widely known cartel is the Organization of Petroleum Exporting Countries (OPEC). It consists of 13 oil-producing and -exporting countries (Algeria, Angola, Ecuador, Indonesia, Iran, Iraq, Kuwait, Libya, Nigeria, Qatar, Saudi Arabia, United Arab Emirates, and Venezuela). OPEC became a significant force in the world economy in the 1970s. In 1973, the Arab members of OPEC were angered by U.S. support for Israel in the war in the Middle East. In response, the Arab members declared an embargo on the shipment of oil to the United States and quadrupled the price of oil—from approximately $3 to $12 per barrel. OPEC tactics included both price fixing and production quotas. Continued price increases brought the average price per barrel to nearly $35 by 1981.

OPEC, as any cartel, has had its challenges. First, not all oil-producing countries are members of OPEC. The current OPEC members account for about 40 percent of world oil production, and about two-thirds of the world's proven oil reserves. Most non-OPEC countries (e.g., United States, Norway, United Kingdom, Canada) have private oil sectors, and their governments have little control over production levels, which OPEC, on its part, controls for pricing stability. Secondly, the cohesiveness of members in a cartel may not always be complete. Sales have occurred at less than agreed-upon prices, and production quotas have been violated. A third challenge is balancing the market's tolerance for high prices (with the record of $112 per barrel in early 2008) and the need for oil revenues to support member countries' domestic spending programs. The low value of the dollar since 2002 has not helped; for example, OPEC's price floor of $80 in 2008 was closer to $58 if adjusted to the falling dollar.[20]

Commodity Price Agreements

International **commodity price agreements** involve both buyers and sellers with the joint objective of managing the price of a certain commodity. The free market is often allowed to determine the price of the commodity over a certain range. However, if demand and supply pressures cause the commodity's price to move outside that range, an elected or appointed manager will enter the market to buy or sell the commodity to bring the price back into the range. The manager controls the **buffer stock** of the commodity. If prices float downward, the

---

CARTEL

An association of producers of a particular good, consisting either of private firms or of nations, formed for the purpose of suppressing the market forces affecting prices.

COMMODITY PRICE AGREEMENT

An agreement involving both buyers and sellers to manage the price of a particular commodity, but often only when the price moves outside a predetermined range.

BUFFER STOCK

Stock of a commodity kept on hand to prevent a shortage in times of unexpectedly great demand; under international commodity and price agreements, the stock controlled by an elected or appointed manager for the purpose of managing the price of the commodity.

manager purchases the commodity and adds to the buffer stock. Under upward pressure, the manager sells the commodity from the buffer stock. This system is somewhat analogous to a managed exchange rate system, in which authorities buy and sell to influence exchange rates. International commodity agreements have been in effect for sugar, tin, rubber, cocoa, and coffee. The tremendous pressures exerted by declining demand, falling prices, over-production, and the conflicting interests of producers have destroyed commodity price agreements.

ECONOMIC INTEGRATION AND THE INTERNATIONAL MANAGER

Regional economic integration creates opportunities and challenges for the international manager. It affects, for instance, a company's entry mode by favoring direct investment, because one of the basic rationales for integration is to generate favorable conditions for local production and interregional trade. By design, larger markets are created with potentially more opportunity. Harmonization efforts may also result in standardized regulations, which can positively affect production and marketing efforts.

Before making decisions regarding integrating markets, the international manager must approach opportunities from four different perspectives: assessment of the effects of changes, development of long-term strategic planning, reorganization, and lobbying for favorable trade terms.

Effects of Change

Change in the competitive landscape resulting from moves toward integration can be dramatic, especially if scale opportunities can be exploited in relatively homogeneous demand conditions. This could be the case, for example, for industrial goods and consumer durables, such as cameras and watches, as well as for professional services. To assess opportunities, the international manager must take into consideration the varying degrees of change-readiness within the markets themselves. Consider, for example, that governments and other stakeholders, such as labor unions, may oppose the liberalization of competition, especially where national monopolies exist, such as in the airline, automobile, energy, or telecommunication industries. Once trade is deregulated, monopolies have to transform into competitive industries, often with favorable results for the home nation. Due to European free trade influences, the price of long-distance calls in Germany, for example, fell by 40 percent, forcing former monopoly, Deutsche Telekom, to streamline its operations and seek new business abroad. Similarly, by fostering a single market for capital, the euro is pushing Europe closer to a homogeneous market in goods and services, thereby exerting additional pressure on prices.[21]

Long-Term Strategic Planning

The international manager must develop a strategic response to the new environment to maintain a sustainable long-term competitive advantage. Those companies already present in an integrating market should fill in gaps in goods and market portfolios through acquisitions or alliances to create a regional or—better still—a global company. In industries such as automobiles, mobile telephony, and retailing, trading blocs in the 21st century may be dominated by two or three giants, leaving room only for niche players. Those with currently weak positions, or no presence at all, will have to create alliances with established firms for market entry and development. In the e-commerce sector for instance, the Argentine and Brazilian subsidiaries of Yahoo!, have recently created alliances with local automotive sites. As a result of efforts by Ford, General Motors, and Fiat to sell low-price vehicles over the Internet, online car sales have surged in Latin America, growing nearly 400 percent in a single year to an estimated

$504 million. Their experiences in selling cars over the Internet may, in the future, pave the way for automakers to conduct e-commerce in larger, more affluent global markets.[22]

Reorganization

Changes resulting from moves toward economic integration inevitably call for company reorganization. Structurally, authority will have to be more centralized so regional programs can be executed. Employees who understand the subtleties of consumer behavior across markets and are therefore able to evaluate the similarities and differences among cultures and markets become increasingly valuable. In developing systems for planning and implementing regional programs, the region-wide view will be essential, affecting, for instance, the selection of marketing communications and advertising messages. In Europe, the introduction of the euro has meant increased coordination in pricing as compared to the relative autonomy in price setting previously enjoyed by country organizations. Companies may move corporate or divisional headquarters from the domestic market to be closer to the customer or centers of innovation. Dow Chemical, for instance, has created global business divisions that are responsible for investment and market development. Procter & Gamble differentiates between high-income and low-income markets, allowing local management in richer countries greater responsibility for profits and the allocation of resources, while branding decisions remain at the global level. In Germany, due to intense competition from Henkel, the local team has more clout when it comes to marketing and branding, too. In poorer regions, such as China and Eastern Europe, country managers have power over sourcing, but P&G's global division makes decisions on production, sales, and branding.[23]

Lobbying

The international manager, as a change agent, must constantly seek ways to influence the competitive environment. For example, it was very important for the U.S. pharmaceutical industry to obtain tight patent protection as part of the NAFTA agreement, and substantial time and money was spent on lobbying both the executive and legislative branches of the U.S. government in the effort to meet its goal. Often, policymakers rely heavily on the knowledge and experience of the private sector in carrying out its own work. Influencing change will therefore mean providing policymakers with industry information, such as test results. Lobbying will usually have to take place at multiple levels simultaneously; within the EU, this means the European Commission in Brussels, the European Parliament in Strasbourg, or the national governments within the EU. Managers with substantial resources have established their own lobbying offices in Brussels, while smaller companies get their voices heard through joint offices or their industry associations.

Culture Clues   Culture does play a role in lobbying in Brussels vs. lobbying in Washington, D.C. One does not have to grapple with 20 different languages in Washington as you do in Brussels. Although English is increasingly imposing itself as the *lingua franca* in Brussels, significantly, many MEPs still value being approached in their native language. Internal political cultures are starkly different, too. While U.S.-style politics tend to be polarized around bipartisanship and highly adversarial, Brussels politics draw on a wider array of parties and specific national issues that are often deeply rooted in a country's governance culture (e.g: British laissez-faire vs. French command and control).

SOURCES: "EU and US Approaches to Lobbying," *Euractiv.com*, February 15, 2005.

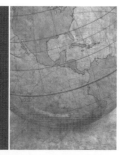

SUMMARY

Economic integration involves agreements among countries to establish links through the movements of goods, services, and factors of production across borders. These links may be weak or strong, depending on the level of integration.

 Levels of integration include the free trade area, customs union, common market, and full economic union.

 The benefits derived from economic integration include trade creation, economies of scale, improved terms of trade, the reduction of monopoly power, and improved cross-cultural communication.

The most significant drawback of economic integration is that it may work to the detriment of nonmembers by causing deteriorating terms of trade and trade diversion.

In addition, no guarantee exists that all members share the gains from integration. The biggest impediment to economic integration is nationalism, whereby nations resist the surrendering of national autonomy for the sake of cooperative agreements.

 The most successful example of economic integration is the European Union. The EU has succeeded in eliminating most barriers to the free flow of goods, services, and factors of production. In addition, the EU has established a common currency and central bank.

 In the Americas, NAFTA is paving the way for a hemispheric trade bloc through alliances with Canada and Latin America.

 A number of regional economic alliances exist in the Indian subcontinent, Africa, and Asia, but they have achieved only low levels of integration. Political difficulties, low levels of development, and problems with cohesiveness have impeded integrative progress among many developing countries. However, many nations in these areas are seeing economic integration as the only way to future prosperity.

International cartels and commodity price agreements represent attempts by producers of primary products to control sales revenues and export earnings. The former is an agreement by suppliers to fix prices, set production quotas, or allocate sales territories. Commodity price agreements involve an agreement to buy or sell a commodity to influence prices.

 Economic integration requires constant adjustment to the changes driven by the opening of markets. These adjustments include changes in the strategy to maintain competitive advantages as well as organizational modifications to implement these strategies.

KEY TERMS AND CONCEPTS

trading bloc	trade diversion	Fortress Europe
free trade area	internal economies of scale	maquiladoras
customs union	external economies of scale	Caribbean Basin Initiative
common market	Treaty of Rome	(CBI)
factors of production	common agricultural policy	cartel
factor mobility	(CAP)	commodity price agreement
economic union	Single European Act	buffer stock
political union	Maastricht Treaty	
trade creation	European Union	

REVIEW QUESTIONS

1. List the several types of trading blocs in existence around the world.
2. Describe the challenges facing a member country of a common market.
3. Define and give examples of trade creation and trade diversion.
4. Distinguish between external and internal economies of scale resulting from economic integration.
5. What are the main provisions of the Single European Act?
6. Summarize the trade agreements in effect in Latin America.
7. Describe the trading blocs of the Indian Subcontinent, Asia, Africa, and the Middle East. What particular problems do they encounter?
8. How might international managers best plan for increasing economic integration?

CRITICAL SKILL BUILDERS

1. Explain the difference between a free trade area and a customs union. Speculate why negotiations were held for a North American Free Trade Agreement rather than for a North American Common Market.

2. Are economic blocs (such as the EU and NAFTA) building blocks or stumbling blocks as far as worldwide free trade is concerned?

3. If regions of the world outside Europe and North America do not form their own trading blocs, they risk being marginalized in terms of world trade. Discuss.

4. In small groups, discuss the Western dependence on oil reserves in the Middle East from both perspectives. Present your arguments in favor of or against OPEC policies to the rest of the class.

5. Suppose that you work for a medium-sized manufacturing firm in the Midwest. Approximately 20 percent of your sales are to European customers. What threats and opportunities does your firm face as a result of an integrated European market?

ON THE WEB

1. Compare and contrast two different points of view on expanding trade by accessing the web site of The Business Roundtable, an industry coalition promoting increased trade to and from world markets (**www.brtable.org**), and the AFL-CIO, American Federation of Labor-Congress of Industrial Organizations (**www.aflcio.org**).

2. The euro will be either a source of competitive advantage or disadvantage for managers. Using "Euro case study: Siemens," available at **http://news.bbc.co.uk/hi/english/_events/the_launch_of_emu**, assess the validity of the two points of view.

ENDNOTES

1. "The Morning Brief: Free Trade Draws Even More Fire," *The Wall Street Journal*, October 4, 2007, online edition; "Politics & Economics: EU is Likely to Drop its Fight with France on Takeover Law; Commission, Aiming to Curb Economic Nationalism, is Outmaneuvered by Paris," *The Wall Street Journal*, May 25, 2006, p. A8; "Block That Trade Bloc," *U.S. News & World Report*, May 7, 2001, p. 38; Axel Krause, "EU Builds Political and Strategic Ties in Latin America," *Europe*, July–August 2001, pp. 12–14; *The World Factbook* available at **http://www.cia.gov**.
2. The discussion of economic integration is based on the pioneering work by Bela Balassa, *The Theory of Economic Integration* (Homewood, IL: Richard D. Irwin, 1961).
3. "U.S., EU Negotiators Meet over Steel Tariffs," *AP Worldstream*, March 19, 2002.
4. "Argentina Cries Foul as Choice Employers Beat a Path Next Door," *The Wall Street Journal*, May 2, 2000, pp. A1, A8.
5. Michael Goold, "From Baron to Hotelier," *The Economist*, May 11, 2002, p. 55.
6. "Where Have All the Foreigners Gone?" *The Economist*, October 13, 2001, p. 54.
7. For annual trade information, see **http://www.census.gov/foreign-trade/**.
8. "Fox and Bush, for Richer, for Poorer," *The Economist*, February 3, 2001, pp. 37–38.

9. Joel Millman, "Aerospace Suppliers Gravitate to Mexico," *The Wall Street Journal*, January 23, 2002, p. A17.

10. "The Decline of the Maquiladora," *BusinessWeek*, April 29, 2002, p. 59.

11. See, for example **www.crea-inc.org** and **www.maquilasolidarity.org**.

12. "Mexico, EU Sign Free-Trade Agreement," *The Wall Street Journal*, March 24, 2000, p. A15.

13. Congressional Research Service, *MERCOSUR: Evolution and Implications for U.S. Trade Policy*, Washington, D.C., January 5, 2007.

14. "Firms Rethink Hostility to Linking Trade, Labor Rights," *The Wall Street Journal*, February 2, 2001, p. A12; "EU Aims to Raise Global Stature with Ties to Asia, Latin America," *The Wall Street Journal*, June 28, 2000, p. A16.

15. Office of the United States Trade Representative, *Third Report to the Congress of the Operations of the Andean Trade Preferences Act as Amended*, Washington, D.C., April 30, 2007.

16. "Caribbean Parity Enters the Picture," *World Trade*, July 2000, p. 46.

17. "Try, Try Again," *The Economist*, July 11, 2002, p. 58.

18. "Afrabet Soup," *The Economist*, February 10, 2001, p. 77.

19. Josh Martin, "Gulf States to Adopt a Single Currency?" *Middle East*, May 2002, pp. 23–25.

20. Ayesha Daya, "OPEC May Cut Output to Defend $80 Oil," *Bloomberg.com*, February 8, 2008.

21. "Lean, Mean, European," *The Economist*, April 29, 2000, pp. 5–7.

22. Noah Elkin, "Online Auto Sales Rev Up in Latin America," *emarketer*, February 27, 2002, **http://www.emarketer.com**.

23. Michael Goold, "From Baron to Hotelier," *The Economist*, May 11, 2002, p. 55.

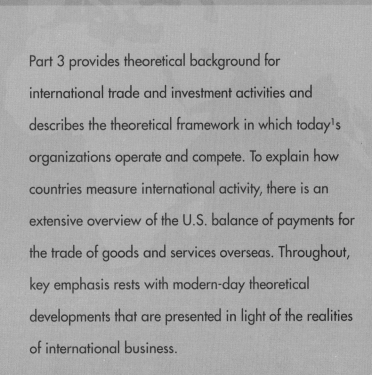

PART 3

GLOBAL TRADE AND INVESTMENT

Part 3 provides theoretical background for international trade and investment activities and describes the theoretical framework in which today¹s organizations operate and compete. To explain how countries measure international activity, there is an extensive overview of the U.S. balance of payments for the trade of goods and services overseas. Throughout, key emphasis rests with modern-day theoretical developments that are presented in light of the realities of international business.

CHAPTER 6

TRADE AND INVESTMENT THEORY

Mattel's Chinese Sourcing Crisis

Mattel discovered on July 30, 2007, that a number of its toys manufactured in China contained lead paint. The previous month had seen a series of recalls, rising political tensions between the United States and Chinese governments, and a suicide. But no company had been in China longer than Mattel; the original Barbie had been created there in 1959. Mattel had long known the risks associated with a toy product's value stream. These toys are based on a global supply chain that is highly sensitive to petrochemical (plastics) and labor input costs, environmental and human rights sensitivities to socially responsible and sustainable business practices, transportation and logistic disruptions, border crossings, cost and time to market—all of which add to risk.

Growing concerns and controversies over labor practices had led Mattel to establish its Global Manufacturing Principles in 1997, in which it established principles and practices for all companies and sites that manufacture Mattel products, either company-owned or licensed manufacturing. The Global Manufacturing Principles (GMP) were established to confirm the company's commitment to responsible manufacturing practices around the world. To support the GMP standards the company created the Mattel Independent Monitoring Council (MIMCO). Mattel was highly regarded as the first global consumer products company to apply the system to both its own facilities and core contractors on a worldwide basis. But the problems had still happened.

The crisis started in June when U.S. toy maker RC2 recalled 1.5 million Thomas the Tank Engine products made in Guangdong, the Chinese province adjacent to Hong Kong and long the center for contract manufacturing by Western firms. Mattel had then followed with a disturbing series of three product recalls in less than one month. The recalls were for toys manufactured by companies that Mattel had worked with and depended on for many years. The toys were found to contain high levels of lead paint, a chemical banned many years ago, but still secretly used by manufacturers around the globe in an effort to reduce costs (paint with lead often dries more quickly and with a glossier finish).

Chinese manufacturers were the source of 65 percent of Mattel's toys. Of those 65 percent, one-half were owned by Mattel and one-half manufactured for the company under licensed manufacturing agreements. Mattel still owned the factories that make the majority of its core products like Barbie and Hot Wheels. But for the other 50 percent of its products, it relied on a set of vendors. Regardless of who owned the actual manufacturing facility, many of the non-Mattel vendors had in turn outsourced many components and parts to other companies. All of the businesses in this complex supply chain were facing the same competitive cost pressures in China—rising wage rates, a shortage of skilled labor in coastal provinces, escalating material and commodity prices—some of which may have been the motivation for suppliers to cut corners and costs. It was therefore not clear that outsourced manufacturing was really the culprit in this case, or simply the fact that much of the manufacturing and material industries operating throughout China were relatively fragmented, newly developed, under heavy cost pressures, and generally unregulated.

The rising anxieties over Chinese products and their associated risks and returns in 2007 reflected a multitude of different political, economic, and business difficulties. The rapid growth of the Chinese economy was already well-known and well-documented: Approximately 5 percent of all manufactured goods in the world were now Chinese; 25 percent of all products sold in the United States had significant Chinese content; global commodity prices of oil, copper, molybdenum, steel, and other materials were seeing record levels as the rate of infrastructure and business development in China caused global shortages and market pressures. But the costs of such rapid economic development were only now starting to become painfully apparent.

The rate of manufacturing growth had far surpassed the ability of the Chinese government on all levels to manage the growth. Regulatory shortfalls—health, safety, and environmental—were now obvious. Although Mattel and other companies were now confessing their own guilt and accepting responsibility for managing their own product risks, the Chinese government was scurrying to close regulatory gaps and protect not only the export customers who were not protecting themselves, but trying to preserve the reputation of Chinese manufacturing and avoid increasing trade restrictions or barriers to their products in foreign markets.[1]

As You Read This Chapter

1. Consider the variety of factors that drive global supply chains and the resulting international trade transactions.
2. Whether it is lead paint on toys or defective sliding sides on baby cribs, whose responsibility is it to assure safety—the company, the country, or both?
3. As more and more of global business becomes dependent on international trade in products and services, many people believe that these pressures for ever-cheaper sourcing will lead to more and more similar controversies. What do you think?

The debates, the costs, the benefits, and the dilemmas of international trade have in many ways remained unchanged since the 13th century, when Marco Polo crossed the barren wastelands of Eurasia. At its heart, international trade is all about the gains—and the risks—to the firm and the country as a result of a seller from one country servicing the needs of a buyer in another country. If a Spanish firm wants to sell its product to the enormous market of mainland China, whether it produces at home and ships the product from Cadiz to Shanghai (international trade), or actually builds a factory in Shanghai (international investment), the goal is still the same: to sell a product for profit in a foreign market.

This chapter provides a directed path through centuries of thought on why and how trade and investment across borders occurs. Although theories and theorists come and go with time, a few basic questions have dominated this intellectual adventure:

• Why do countries trade?
• Do countries trade or do firms trade?

- Do the elements that give rise to the competitiveness of a firm, an industry, or a country as a whole arise from some inherent endowment of the country itself, or do they change with time and circumstance?
- Once identified, can these sources of competitiveness be manipulated or managed by firms or governments to the benefit of traders?

International trade is expected to improve the productivity of industry and the welfare of consumers. Let us learn how and why we still seek the exotic silks of the Far East.

 # THE AGE OF MERCANTILISM

AUTARKY

Self-sufficiency: a country that is not participating in international trade.

The evolution of trade into the form we see today reflects three events: the collapse of feudal society, the emergence of the mercantilist philosophy, and the life cycle of the colonial systems of the European nation-states. Feudal society was a state of **autarky**, a society that did not trade because all of its needs were met internally. The feudal estate was self-sufficient, although hardly "sufficient" in more modern terms, given the limits of providing entirely for oneself. Needs literally were only those of food and shelter, and all available human labor was devoted to the task of fulfilling those basic needs. As merchants began meeting in the marketplace, as travelers began exchanging goods from faraway places at the water's edge, the attractiveness of trade became evident.

In the centuries leading up to the Industrial Revolution, international commerce was largely conducted under the authority of governments. The goals of trade were, therefore, the goals of governments. As early as 1500, the benefits of trade were clearly established in Europe, as nation-states expanded their influence across the globe in the creation of colonial systems. To maintain and expand their control over these colonial possessions, the European nations needed fleets, armies, food, and all other resources the nations could muster. They needed wealth. Trade was therefore conducted to fill the governments' treasuries, at minimum expense to themselves but to the detriment of their captive trade partners. Although colonialism normally is associated with the exploitation of those captive societies, it went hand in hand with the evolving exchange of goods among the European countries themselves, **mercantilism**.

MERCANTILISM

Political and economic policy in the 17th and early 18th centuries aimed at increasing a nation's wealth and power by encouraging the export of goods in return for gold.

Mercantilism mixed exchange through trade with accumulation of wealth. Since government controlled the patterns of commerce, it identified strength with the accumulation of specie (gold and silver) and maintained a general policy of exports dominating imports. Trade across borders—exports—was considered preferable to domestic trade because exports would earn gold. Import duties, tariffs, subsidization of exports, and outright restriction on the importation of many goods were used to maximize the gains from exports over the costs of imports. Laws were passed making it illegal to take gold or silver out of the country, even if such specie was needed to purchase imports to produce their own goods for sale. This was one-way trade, the trade of greed and power.

The demise of mercantilism was inevitable given class structure and the distribution of society's product. As the Industrial Revolution introduced the benefits of mass production, lowering prices and increasing the supplies of goods to all, the exploitation of colonies and trading partners came to an end. However, governments still exercise considerable power and influence on the conduct of trade.

Why Countries Trade

The question of why countries trade has proved difficult to answer. Since the second half of the 18th century, academicians have tried to understand not only the motivations and benefits of international trade, but also why some countries grow more quickly and become wealthier than others through trade. Figure 6.1 provides an overview of the evolutionary path

Quick Take *Trading Salt*

In ancient Hebrew and Arabic, the words for *war* and *peace* derive from the words *salt* and *bread*. Such was the importance of salt that it is thought to have been the cause of the first war that mankind initiated. Salt was so important to the Romans that soldiers jealously guarded the salt fields of the Dead Sea in Palestine and controlled caravan routes that brought this precious commodity westward. From the Middle Ages, European demand for salt, used to cure cod and herring, was virtually limitless.

While the northern seas teemed with fish, salt—a southern commodity resulting from solar evaporation—was in short supply. It was considered so valuable that nations such as England built their foreign policies around the imperative of securing southern sea-salt supplies.

For centuries, salt was the critical ingredient in trading agricultural products overseas. Only salt had the ability to turn perishable foods into durable trade goods. To take a simple example, cheese could be easily exported to foreign markets, whereas milk could not. Today, the value of salt has declined, not because it is any less useful, but because there are abundant sources of supply. It is used for de-icing roads as well as in the creation of thousands of goods, including pharmaceuticals, textiles, and paper.

SOURCES: "A World Built on Pillars of Salt," Interview with author Mark Kurlansky, *Business Week Online*, January 24, 2002, **http://www.businessweek.com**; "Salt Made the World Go Round," **http://www.salt.org.il**, accessed January 3, 2003.

of trade theory since the fall of mercantilism. Although somewhat simplified, it shows the line of development of the major theories put forward over the past two centuries. It also serves as an early indication of the path of modern theory: the shifting of focus from the country to the firm, from cost of production to the market as a whole, and from the perfect to the imperfect.

ABSOLUTE ADVANTAGE AND THE DIVISION OF LABOR

Adam Smith is considered the father of economics. In *The Wealth of Nations* (1776), he attempted to explain the process by which markets and production actually operate in society. He introduced two concepts that are fundamental to trade theory: absolute advantage and the division of labor.

Production, the creation of a product for exchange, always requires the use of society's primary element of value, human labor. Smith noted that some countries, owing to the skills of their workers or the quality of their natural resources, could produce the same products as others with fewer labor-hours. He termed this efficiency **absolute advantage**.

Smith observed the production processes of the early stages of the Industrial Revolution in England and recognized the fundamental changes that were occurring. In previous states of society, a worker performed all stages of a production process, with resulting output that was little more than sufficient for the worker's own needs. The factories of the industrializing world were, however, separating the production process into distinct stages, each performed exclusively by one individual. This specialization increased the production of workers

2 LEARNING OBJECTIVE

ABSOLUTE ADVANTAGE

A country that is capable of producing a product with fewer labor hours.

FIGURE 6.1   The Evolution of Trade Theory

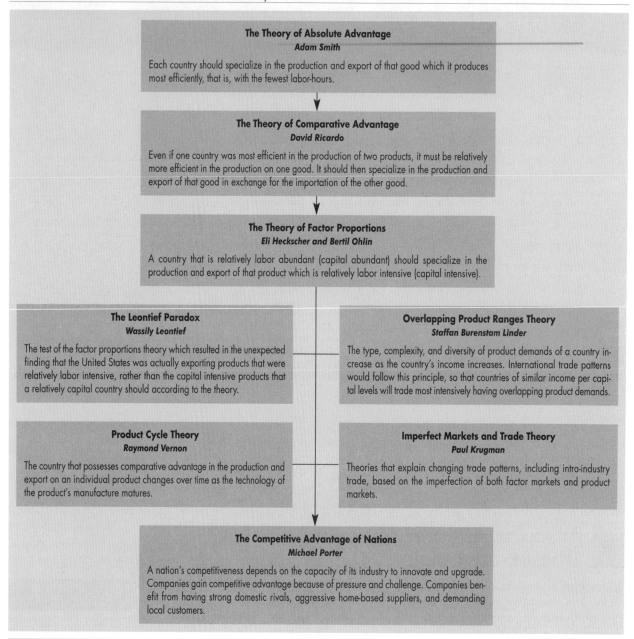

The Theory of Absolute Advantage
Adam Smith

Each country should specialize in the production and export of that good which it produces most efficiently, that is, with the fewest labor-hours.

The Theory of Comparative Advantage
David Ricardo

Even if one country was most efficient in the production of two products, it must be relatively more efficient in the production on one good. It should then specialize in the production and export of that good in exchange for the importation of the other good.

The Theory of Factor Proportions
Eli Heckscher and Bertil Ohlin

A country that is relatively labor abundant (capital abundant) should specialize in the production and export of that product which is relatively labor intensive (capital intensive).

The Leontief Paradox
Wassily Leontief

The test of the factor proportions theory which resulted in the unexpected finding that the United States was actually exporting products that were relatively labor intensive, rather than the capital intensive products that a relatively capital country should according to the theory.

Overlapping Product Ranges Theory
Staffan Burenstam Linder

The type, complexity, and diversity of product demands of a country increase as the country's income increases. International trade patterns would follow this principle, so that countries of similar income per capital levels will trade most intensively having overlapping product demands.

Product Cycle Theory
Raymond Vernon

The country that possesses comparative advantage in the production and export on an individual product changes over time as the technology of the product's manufacture matures.

Imperfect Markets and Trade Theory
Paul Krugman

Theories that explain changing trade patterns, including intra-industry trade, based on the imperfection of both factor markets and product markets.

The Competitive Advantage of Nations
Michael Porter

A nation's competitiveness depends on the capacity of its industry to innovate and upgrade. Companies gain competitive advantage because of pressure and challenge. Companies benefit from having strong domestic rivals, aggressive home-based suppliers, and demanding local customers.

DIVISION OF LABOR

The practice of subdividing a production process into stages that can then be performed by labor repeating the process, as on a production line.

and industries. Smith termed it the **division of labor**. Smith's analogy of a pin factory best encapsulates one of the most significant principles of the industrial age:

> To take an example, therefore, from a very trifling manufacture; but one in which the division of labour has been very often taken notice of, the trade of the pin maker; a workman not educated to this business ... could scarce, perhaps, with his utmost industry, make one pin in a day, and certainly could not make twenty. But in a way in which this business is now carried on, not only the whole

work is a peculiar trade, but it is divided in to a number of branches, of which the greater part are likewise peculiar trades. One man draws out the wire, another straights it, a third cuts it, a fourth points it, a fifth grinds it at the top for receiving the head; to make the head requires two or three distinct operations; to put it on is a peculiar business … I have seen a small manufactory of this kind where ten men only were employed, and where some of them consequently performed two or three distinct operations. But though they were very poor, and therefore but indifferently accommodated with the necessary machine, they could, when they exerted themselves, make among them about twelve pounds of pins in a day. There are in a pound upwards of four thousand pins of a middling size.[2]

Smith then extended his division of labor in the production process to a division of labor and specialized product across countries. Each country would specialize in a product for which it was uniquely suited. More would be produced for less. Thus, with each country specializing in products for which it possessed absolute advantage, countries could produce more in total and exchange products—trade—for goods that were cheaper in price than those produced at home.

Comparative Advantage

Although Smith's work was instrumental in the development of economic theories about trade and production, it did not answer some fundamental questions about trade. First, Smith's trade relied on a country possessing absolute advantage in production, but did not explain what gave rise to the production advantages. Second, if a country did not possess absolute advantage in any product, could it (or would it) trade?

David Ricardo, in *On the Principles of Political Economy and Taxation* (1819), took the basic ideas set down by Smith a few steps further. Ricardo noted that even if a country possessed absolute advantage in the production of two products, it still must be relatively more efficient than the other country in one good's production than the other. Ricardo termed this the **comparative advantage**. Each country would then possess comparative advantage in the production of one of the two products, and both countries would then benefit by specializing completely in one product and trading for the other.

COMPARATIVE ADVANTAGE

The ability to produce a good or service more cheaply, relative to other goods and services, than is possible in other countries.

A Numerical Example of Classical Trade

To fully understand the theories of absolute advantage and comparative advantage, consider the following example: Two countries, France and England, produce only two products, wheat and cloth (or beer and pizza, or guns and butter, and so forth). The relative efficiency of each country in the production of the two products is measured by comparing the number of labor-hours needed to produce one unit of each product. Table 6.1 provides an efficiency comparison of the two countries.

England is obviously more efficient in the production of wheat. Whereas it takes France four labor-hours to produce one unit of wheat, it takes England only two hours to produce the same unit of wheat. France takes twice as many labor-hours to produce the same output. England has absolute advantage in the production of wheat. France needs two labor-hours to produce a unit of cloth that it takes England four labor-hours to produce. England therefore requires two more labor-hours than France to produce the same unit of cloth. France has absolute advantage in the production of cloth. The two countries are exactly opposite in relative efficiency of production.

David Ricardo took the logic of absolute advantage in production one step further to explain how countries could exploit their own advantages and gain from international trade. Comparative advantage, according to Ricardo, was based on what was given up or traded off in producing one product instead of the other. In this example, England needs only two-fourths as

TABLE 6.1 Absolute Advantage and Comparative Advantage

COUNTRY	WHEAT	CLOTH
England	2*	4*
France	4*	2*

*Labor-hours per unit of output

England has absolute advantage in the production of wheat. It requires fewer labor-hours (2 being less than 4) for England to produce one unit of wheat.

France has absolute advantage in the production of cloth. It requires fewer labor-hours (2 being less than 4) for France to produce one unit of cloth.

England has comparative advantage in the production of wheat. If England produces one unit of wheat, it is forgoing the production of 2/4 (0.50) of a unit of cloth. If France produces one unit of wheat, it is forgoing the production of 4/2 (2.00) of a unit of cloth. England therefore has the lower opportunity cost of producing wheat.

France has comparative advantage in the production of cloth. If England produces one unit of cloth, it is forgoing the production of 4/2 (2.00) of a unit of wheat. If France produces one unit of cloth, it is forgoing the production of 2/4 (0.50) of a unit of wheat. France therefore has the lower opportunity cost of producing cloth.

many labor-hours to produce a unit of wheat as France, while France needs only two-fourths as many labor-hours to produce a unit of cloth. England therefore has comparative advantage in the production of wheat, while France has comparative advantage in the production of cloth. A country cannot possess comparative advantage in the production of both products, so each country has an economic role to play in international trade.

National Production Possibilities

PRODUCTION POSSIBILITIES FRONTIER

A theoretical method of representing the total productive capabilities of a nation used in the formulation of classical and modern trade theory.

If the total labor-hours available for production within a nation were devoted to the full production of either product, wheat or cloth, the **production possibilities frontiers** of each country can be constructed. Assuming both countries possess the same number of labor-hours, for example 100, the production possibilities frontiers for each country can be graphed, as in Figure 6.2.

If England devotes all labor-hours (100) to the production of wheat (which requires two labor-hours per unit produced), it can produce a maximum of 50 units of wheat. If England devotes all labor to the production of cloth instead, the same 100 labor-hours can produce a maximum of 25 units of cloth (100 labor-hours/4 hours per unit of cloth). If England did not trade with any other country, it could only consume the products that it produced itself. England would therefore probably produce and consume some combination of wheat and cloth such as point A in Figure 6.2 (15 units of cloth, 20 units of wheat). France's production possibilities frontier is constructed in the same way, with France producing and consuming at some point such as point D in Figure 6.2 (20 units of cloth, 15 units of wheat).

These frontiers depict what each country could produce in isolation—without trade. The slope of the production possibility frontier of a nation is a measure of how one product is traded off in production with the other (moving up the frontier, England is choosing to produce more wheat and less cloth). The slope of the frontier reflects the "trade-off" of producing one product over the other; the trade-offs represent prices, or **opportunity costs**. Opportunity cost is the forgone value of a factor of production in its next-best use. If England chooses to produce more units of wheat (in fact, produce only wheat), moving from point A

OPPORTUNITY COST

Cost incurred by a firm as a result of taking one action rather than another.

FIGURE 6.2   Production Possibility Frontiers, Specialization of Production, and the Benefits of Trade

England

1. Initially produces and consumes at point A.

2. England chooses to specialize in the production of wheat and shifts production from point A to point B.

3. England now exports the unwanted wheat (30 units) in exchange for imports of cloth (30 units) from France.

4. England is now consuming at point C, where it is consuming the same amount of wheat but 15 more units of cloth than at original point A.

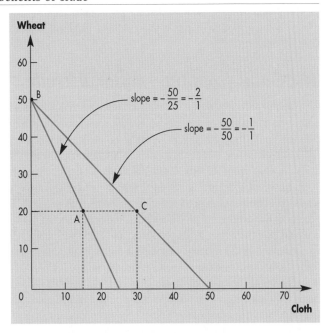

France

1. Initially produces and consumes at point D.

2. France chooses to specialize in the production of cloth and shifts production from point D to point E.

3. France now exports the unwanted cloth (30 units) in exchange for imports of wheat (30 units) from England.

4. France is now consuming at point F, where it is consuming the same amount of cloth but 15 more units of wheat than at original point D.

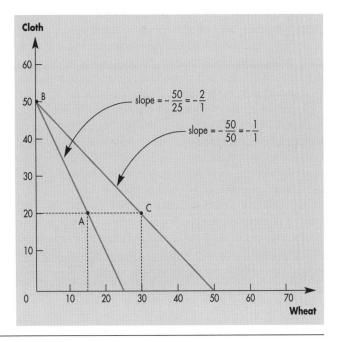

to point B along the production possibilities frontier, it is giving up producing cloth. The "cost" of the additional wheat is the loss of cloth. The slope of the production possibilities frontier is the ratio of product prices (opportunity costs). The slope of the production possibilities frontier for England is −50/25, or −2.00. The slope of the production possibilities frontier for France is flatter, −25/50, or −0.50.

The relative prices of products also provide an alternative way of seeing comparative advantage. The flatter slope of the French production possibilities frontier means that to produce more wheat (move up the frontier), France would have to give up the production of relatively more units of cloth than would England, with its steeper sloped production possibilities frontier.

The Gains from International Trade

Continuing with Figure 6.2, if England were originally not trading with France (the only other country), and it was producing at its own maximum possibilities (on the frontier and not inside the line), it would be producing at point A. Since it was not trading with another country, whatever it was producing, it must also be consuming. So England could be said to be consuming at point A, also. Therefore, without trade, you consume what you produce.

If, however, England recognized that it has comparative advantage in the production of wheat, it should move production from point A to point B. England should specialize completely in the product it produces best. It does not want to consume only wheat, however, so it would take the wheat it has produced and trade with France. For example, England may want to consume only 20 units of wheat, as it did at point A. It is now producing 50 units, and therefore has 30 units of wheat it can export to France. If England could export 30 units of wheat in exchange for imports of 30 units of cloth (a 1:1 ratio of prices), England would clearly be better off than before. The new consumption point would be point C, where it is consuming the same amount of wheat as point A, but is now consuming 30 units of cloth instead of just 15. More is better; England has benefited from international trade.

France, following the same principle of completely specializing in the product of its comparative production advantage, moves production from point D to point E, producing 50 units of cloth. If France now exported the unwanted cloth, for example 30 units, and exchanged the cloth with England for imports of 30 units of wheat (note that England's exports are France's imports), France too is better off as a result of international trade. Each country would do what it does best, exclusively, and then trade for the other product.

But at what prices will the two countries trade? Since each country's production possibilities frontier has a different slope (different relative product prices), the two countries can determine a set of prices between the two domestic prices. England's price ratio was –2:1, while France's domestic price was –1:2. Trading 30 units of wheat for 30 units of cloth is a price ratio of –1:1, a slope or set of prices between the two domestic price ratios. The dashed line in Figure 6.2 illustrates this set of trade prices.

Are both countries better off as a result of trade? Yes. The final step to understanding the benefits of classical trade theory is to note that the point where a country produces (point B for England and point E for France in Figure 6.2) and the point where it consumes are now different. This allows each country to consume beyond its own production possibilities frontier. Society's welfare, which is normally measured in its ability to consume more wheat, cloth, or any other goods or services, is increased through trade.

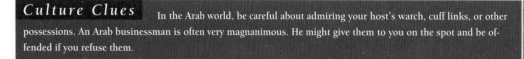

Culture Clues   In the Arab world, be careful about admiring your host's watch, cuff links, or other possessions. An Arab businessman is often very magnanimous. He might give them to you on the spot and be offended if you refuse them.

Current Account Balances as a Percentage of Gross Domestic Product

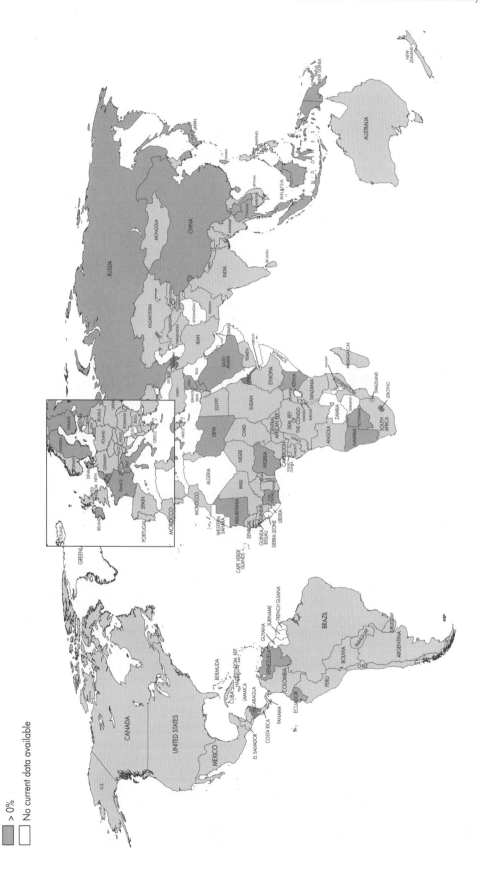

> -20%
0% to -20%
> 0%
No current data available

Source: 2001 *World Development Indicators*, The World Bank.

Applying Classical Trade Theory

Classical trade theory contributed much to the understanding of how production and trade operates in the world economy. Although, like all economic theories, they are often criticized for being unrealistic or out of date, the purpose of a theory is to simplify reality so that the basic elements of the logic can be seen. Several of these simplifications have continued to provide insight in understanding international business.

- Division of labor: Smith's explanation of how industrial societies can increase output using the same labor-hours as in pre-industrial society is fundamental to our thinking even today. Smith extended this specialization of the efforts of a worker to the specialization of a nation.
- Comparative advantage: Ricardo's extension of Smith's work explained for the first time how countries that seemingly had no obvious reason for trade could individually specialize in producing what they did best and trade for products they did not produce.
- Gains from trade: The theory of comparative advantage argued that nations could improve the welfare of their populations through international trade.

A nation could actually achieve consumption levels beyond what it could produce by itself. To this day this is one of the fundamental principles underlying the arguments for all countries to strive to expand and "free" world trade.

 # FACTOR PROPORTIONS TRADE THEORY

Trade theory changed drastically in the first half of the 20th century. Concepts developed by Swedish economist Eli Heckscher, and later expanded by his former student Bertil Ohlin, formed the theory of international trade that is still widely accepted today: factor proportions theory.

Factor Intensity in Production

..ıe Heckscher-Ohlin theory considered two factors of production, labor and capital. Technology determines the way they combine to form a good. Different goods required different proportions of the two factors of production.

Figure 6.3 illustrates what it means to describe a good by its factor proportions. The production of one unit of good X requires four units of labor and one unit of capital. At the same time, to produce one unit of good Y requires four units of labor and two units of capital. Good X therefore requires more units of labor per unit of capital (4 to 1) relative to Y (4 to 2). X is therefore classified as a relatively labor-intensive product, and Y is relatively capital intensive. These **factor intensities**, or **proportions**, are truly relative and are determined only on the basis of what product X requires relative to product Y and not to the specific numbers of labor to capital.

It is easy to see how the factor proportions of production differ substantially across goods. For example, the manufacturing of leather footwear is still a relatively labor-intensive process, even with the most sophisticated leather treatment and patterning machinery. Other goods, such as computer memory chips, however, although requiring some highly skilled labor, require massive quantities of capital for production. These large capital requirements include the enormous sums needed for research and development and the manufacturing facilities needed for clean production to ensure the extremely high quality demanded in the industry.

According to **factor proportions theory**, factor intensities depend on the state of technology—the current method of manufacturing a good. The theory assumed that the same technology of production would be used for the same goods in all countries. It is not,

FACTOR INTENSITIES/ FACTOR PROPORTIONS

The proportion of capital input to labor input used in the production of a good.

FACTOR PROPORTIONS THEORY

Systematic explanation of the source of comparative advantage.

WORLD VIEW

LOW-COST LABOR ACROSS SPACE AND TIME

Global corporations have long enjoyed the benefits of low-cost labor by manufacturing offshore. Now, a burgeoning export trade in business support and information technology services—sometimes referred to as India, Inc.—is transforming the economy of India, which offers an educated, English-speaking workforce at a fraction of first-world wages. NASSCOM, India's association of IT companies, predicts income of $17 billion by 2008 from the export of skilled labor. Aided by technological advances that provide seamless real-time connections with clients, service providers promise fast turnaround as well as low cost. GE Capital Services employs more than 5,000 white-collar workers at its international call center, while companies such as American Express and Swissair save between 40 and 50 percent by shipping data processing work electronically to India. Conseco plans to shift 2,000 white-collar jobs to India, a savings of $30 million a year, while Citigroup's e-Serve International, based in Mumbai, employs a further 2,000 people in such back-office tasks as processing letters of credit and money transfers. In health-related services, despite concerns that outsourcing risks the invasion of patient confidentiality, outsourcing of America's medical transcription services doubled by 2005 to $4 billion, outstripping capacity.

The demand for India's labor force goes far beyond administrative support. In the IT sector, for instance, India offers hundreds of software-development companies, with programming expertise in key languages such as C++, Cobol, and Java. India has about 445,000 IT workers, and its universities churned out enough new talent to grow the market to 625,000 by 2005. Software giant EDS has 17 offshore locations, of which the largest is in India.

By shipping application development work to lower-cost EDS employees overseas, the company is able to pass along cost savings to clients. Accenture recently won a $250 million software installation project for DuPont, possible only because 40 percent of development work would take place offshore in India and Spain.

Pushing even further upstream, companies like GE are increasing their research and development presence in India. At a new technology park near Bangalore, GE hopes to double its R&D capacity within a three-year period. One out of three of the center's employees is a PhD, giving GE a unique, relatively low-cost access to advanced scientists. In creative fields, too, India is pushing the envelope. In the film industry, Crest Communications, based in Mumbai, offers a $2 million state-of-the-art computer graphics studio, complete with highly trained special effects artists. Crest, which acquired Hollywood production company Rich Animation, the producer of such films as *Swan Princess*, claimed that it could make a film like *Toy Story 2* for half the American cost.

SOURCES: Paula Musich, "Outsourcing Looks Overseas," *eWeek*, March 25, 2002, p. 12; Larry Greenemeier, "Offshore Outsourcing Grows to Global Proportions," *Information Week*, February 11, 2002; "Back Office to the World," *The Economist*, May 5, 2001, p. 89.

FIGURE 6.3 Factor Proportions in Production

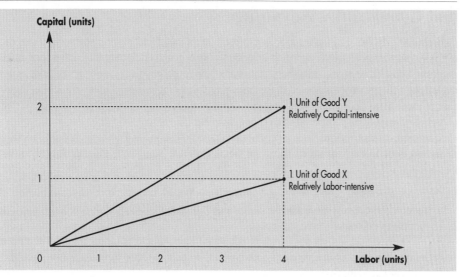

Quick Take *Ethical Capitalism*

Corporate social responsibility has great momentum. All the more reason to be aware of its limits.

How wonderful to think that you can make money and save the planet at the same time. "Doing well by doing good" has become a popular business mantra: The phrase conjures up a Panglossian best-of-all-possible-worlds, the idea that firms can be successful by acting in the broader interests of society as a whole even while they satisfy the narrow interests of shareholders. The noble sentiment will no doubt echo around the Swiss Alps next week as chief executives hobnob with political leaders at the World Economic Forum in Davos.

For these are high times for what is clunkingly called corporate social responsibility (CSR). No longer is it enough for annual reports to have a philanthropic paragraph about the charity committee; now companies put out long tracts full of claims about their fair trading and carbon neutralizing. One huge push for CSR has come from climate change: "Sustainability" is its most dynamic branch. Another has been the Internet, which helps activists scrutinize corporate behavior around the globe. But the biggest force is the presumption that a modern business needs to be, or at least appear to be, "good" to hang on to customers and recruit clever young people.

"Ethical Capitalism: How Good Should Your Business Be?" *The Economist* (print edition), January 17, 2008.

therefore, differences in the efficiency of production that will determine trade between countries as it did in classical theory. Classical theory implicitly assumed that technology or the productivity of labor is different across countries. Otherwise, there would be no logical explanation why one country requires more units of labor to produce a unit of output than another country. Factor proportions theory assumes no such productivity differences.

Factor Endowments, Factor Prices, and Comparative Advantage

If there is no difference in technology or productivity of factors across countries, what then determines comparative advantage in production and export? The answer is that factor prices determine cost differences. And these prices are determined by the endowments of labor and capital the country possesses. The theory assumes that labor and capital are immobile; factors cannot move across borders. Therefore, the country's endowment determines the relative costs of labor and capital as compared with other countries.

Using these assumptions, factor proportions theory states that a country should specialize in the production and export of those products that use intensively its relatively abundant factor.

- A country that is relatively labor-abundant should specialize in the production of relatively labor-intensive goods. It should then export those labor-intensive goods in exchange for capital-intensive goods.
- A country that is relatively capital-abundant should specialize in the production of relatively capital-intensive goods. It should then export those capital-intensive goods in exchange for labor-intensive goods.

The Leontief Paradox

One of the most famous tests of any economic or business theory occurred in 1950, when economist Wassily Leontief tested whether the factor proportions theory could be used to explain the types of goods the United States imported and exported.

Leontief's premise was based on a widely shared view that some countries, such as the United States, are endowed with large amounts of capital, while others were short on capital but have abundant labor resources. Thus, it was thought that the United States would be more efficient in producing capital-intensive products while importing labor-intensive goods from overseas.

Leontief first had to devise a method to determine the relative amounts of labor and capital in a good. His solution, known as **input-output analysis**, is a technique of decomposing a good into the values and quantities of the labor, capital, and other potential factors employed in the good's manufacture. Leontief then used this methodology to analyze the labor and capital content of all U.S. merchandise imports and exports. The hypothesis was relatively straightforward: U.S. exports should be relatively capital-intensive (use more units of capital relative to labor) than U.S. imports. The results were, however, a bit of a shock.

Leontief found that the products that U.S. firms exported were relatively more labor-intensive than imported products.[3] It seemed that if the factor proportions theory were true, the United States is a relatively labor-abundant country! Alternatively, the theory could be wrong. Neither interpretation of the results was acceptable to many in the field of international trade.

A variety of explanations and continuing studies have attempted to solve what has become known as the **Leontief Paradox**. At first, it was thought to have been simply a result of the specific year (1947) of the data. However, the same results were found with different years and data sets. Second, it was noted that Leontief did not really analyze the labor and capital contents of imports but rather the labor and capital contents of the domestic equivalents of these imports. It was possible that the United States was actually producing the products in a more capital-intensive fashion than were the countries from which it also imported the manufactured goods.[4] Finally, the debate turned to the need to distinguish different types of labor and capital. For example, several studies attempted to separate labor factors into skilled labor and unskilled labor. These studies have continued to show results more consistent with what the factor proportions theory would predict for country trade patterns.

Linder's Overlapping Product Ranges Theory

The difficulties in confirming the factor proportions theory led many in the 1960s and 1970s to search for new explanations of the determinants of trade between countries. The work of Staffan Burenstam Linder focused not on the production or supply side, but instead on the preferences of consumers—the demand side.

Linder argued that trade in manufactured goods was dictated not by cost concerns but rather by the similarity in product demands across countries. Linder's was a significant departure from previous theory and was based on two principles:

1. As per-capita income rises, the complexity and quality level of the products demanded by the country's residents also rises. The range of product sophistication demanded is largely determined by the country's level of income.
2. The businesses that produce a society's needs are more knowledgeable about their domestic market than foreign markets. A logical pattern is for firms to gain success and market share at home first, then expand to foreign markets that are similar in their demands or tastes.

INPUT-OUTPUT ANALYSIS

A method for estimating market activities and potential that measures the factor inflows into production and the resultant outflow of products.

LEONTIEF PARADOX

Wassily Leontief's studies indicated that the United States was a labor-abundant country, exporting labor-intensive products. This was a paradox because of the general belief that the United States was a capital-abundant country that should be exporting capital-intensive products.

This would mean that global trade in manufactured goods is influenced by similarity of demands. The countries that would see the most intensive trade are those with similar per-capita income levels, for they would possess a greater likelihood of overlapping product demands. For example, the United States and Canada have almost parallel sophistication ranges, implying a lot of common ground or overlapping product ranges for intensive international trade and competition. They are quite similar in their per-capita income levels. By contrast, Mexico and the United States or Mexico and Canada are not. Mexico has a significantly different product sophistication range as a result of a different per-capita income level.

The overlapping product ranges described by Linder would today be termed **market segments**. Not only was Linder's work instrumental in extending trade theory beyond cost considerations, but it also found a place in the field of international marketing.

MARKET SEGMENT

Overlapping ranges of trade targets with common ground and levels of sophistication.

3 LEARNING OBJECTIVE

PRODUCT CYCLE THEORY

A theory that views products as passing through four stages—introduction, growth, maturity, decline—during which the location of production moves from industrialized to lower-cost developing nations.

INTERNATIONAL INVESTMENT AND PRODUCT CYCLE THEORY

A very different path was taken by Raymond Vernon in 1966 concerning what is now termed **product cycle theory**. Diverging significantly from traditional approaches, Vernon focused on the product rather than on the country and the technology of its manufacture, or on its factor proportions. Most striking was the appreciation of the role of information: knowledge, and the costs and power that go hand in hand with knowledge. Vernon rejected the notion that knowledge is a universal free good and introduced it as an independent variable in the decision to trade or to invest.

Using many of the same basic tools and assumptions of factor proportions theory, Vernon added two technology-based premises to the factor-cost emphasis of existing theory:

1. Technical innovations leading to new and profitable products require large quantities of capital and highly skilled labor. These factors of production are predominantly available in highly industrialized, capital-intensive countries.
2. These same technical innovations, both the product itself and—more importantly—the methods for its manufacture, go through three stages of maturation as the product becomes increasingly commercialized. As the manufacturing process becomes more standardized and low-skill labor-intensive, the comparative advantage in its production and export shifts across countries.

Stages of the Product Cycle

Product cycle theory is both supply-side (cost of production) and demand-side (income levels of consumers) in its orientation. Each of these three stages that Vernon described combines differing elements of the others.

STAGE I: THE NEW PRODUCT Innovation requires highly skilled labor and large quantities of capital for research and development. The product will normally be most effectively designed and initially manufactured near the parent firm and therefore in a highly industrialized market, due to the need for proximity to information and the need for communication

Culture Clues   When in Russia, it's a good idea to have a large supply of business cards to hand out. They should be printed in Cyrillic, and the university degree of the Western businessperson should be included. During negotiations, be sure to hand out one to everyone present, in order not to overlook someone who might turn out to be important.

among the many different skilled-labor components required. In this development stage, the product is nonstandardized. The production process requires a high degree of flexibility (meaning continued use of highly skilled labor). Costs of production are therefore quite high.

STAGE II: THE MATURING PRODUCT As production expands, its process becomes increasingly standardized. The need for flexibility in design and manufacturing declines, and therefore the demand for highly skilled labor declines. The innovating country increases its sales to other countries. Competitors with slight variations develop, putting downward pressure on prices and profit margins. Production costs are an increasing concern.

As competitors increase, as well as their pressures on price, the innovating firm faces critical decisions on how to maintain market share. Vernon argues that the firm faces a critical decision at this stage: either to lose market share to foreign-based manufacturers using lower-cost labor or to invest abroad to maintain its market share by exploiting the comparative advantages of factor costs in other countries. This is one of the first theoretical explanations of how trade and investment become increasingly intertwined.

STAGE III: THE STANDARDIZED PRODUCT In this final stage, the product is completely standardized in its manufacture. Thus, with access to capital on world capital markets, the country of production is simply the one with the cheapest unskilled labor. Profit margins are thin, and competition is fierce. The product has largely run its course in terms of profitability for the innovating firm.

The country of comparative advantage has therefore shifted as the technology of the product's manufacture has matured. The same product shifts in its location of production. The country possessing the product during that stage enjoys the benefits of net trade surpluses. But such advantages are fleeting, according to Vernon. As knowledge and technology continually change, so does the country of that product's comparative advantage.

Trade Implications of the Product Cycle

Product cycle theory shows how specific products were first produced and exported from one country but, through product and competitive evolution, shifted their location of production and export to other countries over time. Figure 6.4 illustrates the trade patterns that Vernon visualized as resulting from the maturing stages of a specific product cycle. As the product and the market for the product mature and change, the countries of its production and export shift.

The product is initially designed and manufactured in the United States. In its early stages (from time t_0 to t_1), the United States is the only country producing and consuming the product. Production is highly capital-intensive and skilled-labor intensive. At time t_1 the United States begins exporting the product to Other Advanced Countries, as Vernon classified them. These countries possess the income to purchase the product in its still New Product Stage, in which it was relatively high-priced. These Other Advanced Countries also commence their own production at time t_1 but continue to be net importers. A few exports, however, do find their way to the Less Developed Countries at this time as well.

As the product moves into the second stage, the Maturing Product Stage, production capability expands rapidly in the Other Advanced Countries. Competitive variations begin to appear as the basic technology of the product becomes more widely known and the need for skilled labor in its production declines. These countries eventually also become net exporters of the product near the end of the stage (time t_3). At time t_2, the Less Developed Countries begin their own production, although they continue to be net importers. Meanwhile, the lower cost of production from these growing competitors turns the United States into a net importer

FIGURE 6.4   Trade Patterns and Product Cycle Theory

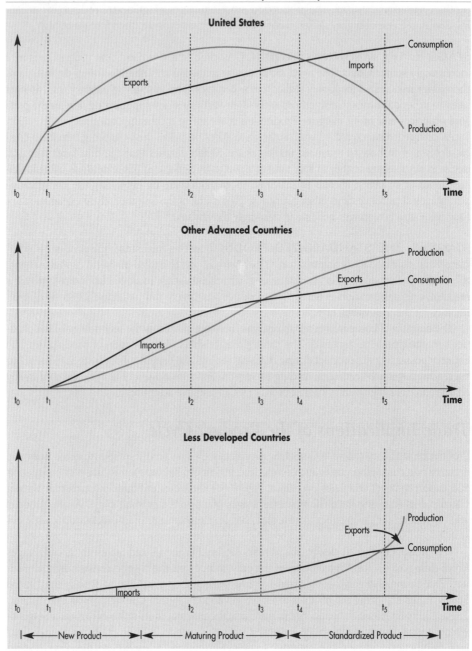

SOURCE: Raymond Vernon, "International Investment and International Trade in the Product Cycle," *Quarterly Journal of Economics* (May 1966): 199.

by time t_4. The competitive advantage for production and export is clearly shifting across countries at this time.

The third and final stage, the Standardized Product Stage, sees the comparative advantage of production and export now shifting to the Less Developed Countries. The product is now a relatively mass-produced product that can be made with increasingly less-skilled labor. The United States continues to reduce domestic production and increase imports. The Other Advanced Countries continue to produce and export, although exports peak as the Less Developed Countries expand production and become net exporters themselves. The product has run its course or life cycle in reaching time t_5.

A final point: Note that throughout this product cycle, the countries of production, consumption, export, and import are identified by their labor and capital levels, not firms. Vernon noted that it could very well be the same firms that are moving production from the United States to Other Advanced Countries to Less Developed Countries. The shifting location of production was instrumental in the changing patterns of trade but not necessarily in the loss of market share, profitability, or competitiveness of the firms. The country of comparative advantage could change.

Contributions of Product Cycle Theory

Although interesting in its own right for increasing emphasis on technology's impact on product costs, product cycle theory was most important because it explained international investment. Not only did the theory recognize the mobility of capital across countries (breaking the traditional assumption of factor immobility), it shifted the focus from the country to the product. This made it important to match the product by its maturity stage with its production location to examine competitiveness.

Product cycle theory has many limitations. It is obviously most appropriate for technology-based products that are likely to experience changes in production process as they mature. Other products, either resource-based (such as minerals and other commodities) or services (which employ capital but mostly in the form of human capital), are not so easily characterized by stages of maturity. And product cycle theory is most relevant to products that eventually fall victim to mass production and therefore cheap labor forces. But, all things considered, product cycle theory served to breach a wide gap between the trade theories of old and the intellectual challenges of a new, more globally competitive market in which capital, technology, information, and firms themselves were more mobile.

 # THE NEW TRADE THEORY

Global trade developments in the 1980s and 1990s led to much criticism of the existing theories of trade. Rapid growth in world trade, coupled with the sudden expansion of the U.S. merchandise trade deficit in the 1980s, forced academics and policymakers to take another look at the determinants of international trade.

Two new contributions to trade theory were met with great interest. Paul Krugman, along with several colleagues, developed a theory of how trade is altered when markets are not perfectly competitive or when production of specific products possesses economies of scale. A second and very influential development was the growing work of Michael Porter, who examined the competitiveness of industries on a global basis, rather than relying on country-specific factors to determine competitiveness.

Economies of Scale and Imperfect Competition

Paul Krugman's theoretical developments once again focused on cost of production and how cost and price drive international trade. Using theoretical developments from microeconomics and market structure analysis, Krugman focused on two types of economics of scale: internal economies of scale and external economies of scale.[5]

INTERNAL ECONOMIES OF SCALE

When the cost per unit of the product of a single firm continues to fall as the firm's size continues to increase.

ABANDONED PRODUCT RANGES

The outcome of a firm narrowing its range of products to obtain economies of scale, which provides opportunities for other firms to enter the markets for the abandoned products.

INTRA-INDUSTRY TRADE

The simultaneous export and import of the same good by a country. It is of interest, due to the traditional theory that a country will either export or import a good, but not do both at the same time.

PRODUCT DIFFERENTIATION

The effort to build unique differences or improvements into products.

INTERNAL ECONOMIES OF SCALE When the cost per unit of output depends on the size of an individual firm, the larger the firm, the greater the scale benefits and the lower the cost per unit. A firm possessing **internal economies of scale** could potentially monopolize an industry (creating an imperfect market), both domestically and internationally. If it produces more, lowering the cost per unit, it can lower the market price and sell more products, because it sets market prices.

The link between dominating a domestic industry and influencing international trade comes from taking this assumption of imperfect markets back to the original concept of comparative advantage. For this firm to expand sufficiently to enjoy its economies of scale, it must take resources away from other domestic industries. A country then sees the range of products in which it specializes narrowing, providing an opportunity for other countries to specialize in these so-called **abandoned product ranges**. Countries again search out and exploit comparative advantage.

A particularly powerful implication of internal economies of scale is that it provides an explanation of intra-industry trade. **Intra-industry trade** occurs when a country seemingly imports and exports the same product, an idea that is obviously inconsistent with any of the trade theories put forward in the past three centuries. According to Krugman, internal economies of scale may lead a firm to specialize in a narrow product line (to produce the volume necessary for economies-of-scale cost benefits); other firms in other countries may produce products that are similarly narrow, yet extremely similar: **product differentiation**. If consumers in either country wish to buy both products, they will be importing and exporting products that are, for all intents and purposes, the same.

EXTERNAL ECONOMIES OF SCALE When the cost per unit of output depends on the size of an industry, not the size of the individual firm, the industry of that country may produce goods at lower costs than the same industry that is smaller in other countries. A country can potentially dominate world markets in a particular product, not because it has one massive firm producing enormous quantities (for example, Boeing), but rather because it has many small firms that interact to create a large, competitive, critical mass (for example, semiconductors in Penang, Malaysia). No one firm need be all that large, but several small firms may create such a competitive industry in total that firms in other countries cannot compete.

Unlike internal economies of scale, external economies of scale may not necessarily lead to imperfect markets, but they may result in an industry maintaining its dominance in its field in world markets. This may explain why all industries do not necessarily always move to the country with the lowest-cost energy, resources, or labor. What gives rise to this critical mass of small firms and their interrelationships is a much more complex question. The work of Michael Porter provides a partial explanation of how these critical masses are sustained.

The Competitive Advantage of Nations

The focus of early trade theory was on the country or nation and its inherent, natural, or endowment characteristics that might give rise to increasing competitiveness. As trade theory evolved, it shifted its focus to the industry and product level, leaving the national-level competitiveness question somewhat behind. Recently, many have turned their attention to the question of how countries, governments, and even private industry can alter the conditions within a country to aid the competitiveness of its firms.

The leader in this area of research has been Michael Porter of Harvard. As he states,

National prosperity is created, not inherited. It does not grow out of a country's natural endowments, its labor pool, its interest rates, or its currency's values, as classical economics insists.

A nation's competitiveness depends on the capacity of its industry to innovate and upgrade. Companies gain advantage against the world's best competitors because of pressure and challenge.

They benefit from having strong domestic rivals, aggressive home-based suppliers, and demanding local customers.

In a world of increasingly global competition, nations have become more, not less, important. As the basis of competition has shifted more and more to the creation and assimilation of knowledge, the role of the nation has grown. Competitive advantage is created and sustained through a highly localized process. Differences in national values, culture, economic structures, institutions, and histories all contribute to competitive success. There are striking differences in the patterns of competitiveness in every country; no nation can or will be competitive in every or even most industries. Ultimately, nations succeed in particular industries because their home environment is most forward-looking, dynamic, and challenging.[6]

Porter argued that innovation is what drives and sustains competitiveness. A firm must avail itself of all dimensions of competition, which he categorized into four major components of "the diamond of national advantage."

1. *Factor conditions:* The appropriateness of the nation's factors of production to compete successfully in a specific industry. Porter notes that although these factor conditions are very important in the determination of trade, they are not the only source of competitiveness as suggested by the classical, or factor proportions, theories of trade. Most important for Porter is not the initial endowment, but the ability of a nation to continually create, upgrade, and deploy its factors (such as skilled labor).
2. *Demand conditions:* The degree of health and competition the firm must face in its original home market. Firms that can survive and flourish in highly competitive and demanding local markets are much more likely to gain a competitive edge. Porter notes that it is the character of the market, not its size, that is paramount in promoting the continual competitiveness of the firm. And Porter translates character as demanding customers.
3. *Related and supporting industries:* The competitiveness of all related industries and suppliers to the firm. A firm that is operating within a mass of related firms and industries gains and maintains advantages through close working relationships, proximity to suppliers, and timeliness of product and information flows. The constant and close interaction is successful if it occurs not only in terms of physical proximity, but also through the willingness of firms to work at it.
4. *Firm strategy, structure, and rivalry:* The conditions in the home nation that either hinder or aid in the firm's creation and sustaining of international competitiveness. Porter notes that no one managerial, ownership, or operational strategy is universally appropriate. It depends on the fit and flexibility of what works for that industry in that country at that time.

These four points, as illustrated in Figure 6.5, constitute what nations and firms must strive to "create and sustain through a highly localized process" to ensure their success.

FIGURE 6.5 Determinants of National Competitive Advantage: Porter's Diamond

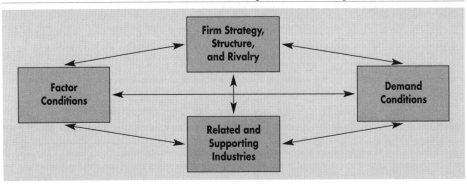

WORLD VIEW

THE PRICE OF OPEN MARKETS

Two weeks after the terrorist attacks on the World Trade Center and the Pentagon on September 11, 2001, U.S. trade representative Robert Zoellick made a profound statement about the importance of continuing to work toward open markets. Countering initial criticism that exploitation of third-world economies had inadvertently led to the attacks, Zoellick defended the role of free trade in world affairs:

> Erecting new barriers and closing old borders will not help the impoverished. It will not feed hundreds of millions struggling for subsistence. It will not liberate the persecuted. It will not improve the environment in developing countries or reverse the spread of AIDS. It will not help the railway orphans I visited in India. It will not improve the livelihoods of the union members I met in Latin American. It will not aid the committed Indonesians I visited who are trying to build a functioning, tolerant democracy in the largest Muslim nation in the world.

Mike Moore, director general of the World Trade Organization, also perceives the role of the international business community to be critical in raising standards of living worldwide. Responding to a growing disillusionment with the benefits of the globalization of business, he states, "Trade is a key engine for growth, but currently developing country products face obstacles in entering rich country markets. By opening these markets, we can help lift millions of people out of poverty."

Moore echoed Zoellick's call for action by the global business community against the severe poverty that has been considered a factor in the emergence of hotbeds of terrorism in places such as Afghanistan and Pakistan. The United Nations, the International Monetary Fund, the World Bank, and the World Trade Organization are working on a special campaign to help the 1.2 billion people in the world who live on less than $1 a day and the 2.6 billion who live on less than $2 per day. Further, hundreds of corporations have renewed their support of programs aimed at fighting tropical diseases and promoting literacy.

SOURCES: "What's Next for the Global Economy?" *Business Week Online*, February 11, 2002, **http://www.businessweek.com**; speech by Mike Moore, "Preparations for the Fourth WTO Ministerial Conference," Paris, October 9, 2001, **http://www.wto.org**.

Porter's emphasis on innovation as the source of competitiveness reflects an increased focus on the industry and product, more than we have seen in the past three decades. The acknowledgment that the nation is "more, not less, important" is to many eyes a welcome return to a positive role for government and even national-level private industry in encouraging international competitiveness. Factor conditions as a cost component, demand conditions as a motivator of firm actions, and competitiveness all combine to include the elements of classical, factor proportions, product cycle, and imperfect competition theories in a pragmatic approach to the challenges that the global markets of the 21st century present to the firms of today.

THEORY OF INTERNATIONAL INVESTMENT

5 LEARNING OBJECTIVE

Trade is the production of a good or service in one country and its sale to a buyer in another country. In fact, it is a firm (not a country) and a buyer (not a country) that are the subjects of trade, domestically or internationally. A firm is therefore attempting to access a market and its buyers. The producing firm wants to utilize its competitive advantage for growth and profit and can also reach this goal by international investment.

Although this sounds easy enough, consider any of the following potholes on the road to investment success, any of which may be avoided by producing within another country.

- Sales to some countries are difficult because of tariffs imposed on your good when it is entering. If you were producing within the country, your good would no longer be an import.

- Your good requires natural resources that are available only in certain areas of the world. It is therefore imperative that you have access to the natural resources. You can buy them from that country and bring them to your production process (import) or simply take the production to them.
- Competition is constantly pushing you to improve efficiency and decrease the costs of producing your good. You therefore may want to produce where it will be cheaper—cheaper capital, cheaper energy, cheaper natural resources, or cheaper labor. Many of these factors are still not mobile, and therefore you will go to them rather than bring them to you.

There are thousands of reasons why a firm may want to produce in another country, and not necessarily in the country that is cheapest for production or the country where the final good is sold.

The subject of international investment arises from one basic idea: the mobility of capital. Although many of the traditional trade theories assumed the immobility of the factors of production, it is the movement of capital that has allowed **foreign direct investments** across the globe. If there is a competitive advantage to be gained, capital can and will get there.

Nike's international success is a result of the company's efforts to connect the brand to consumers emotionally, culturally, and with local relevance. In June 2000, Nike joined "Global Compact," a UN project that supports human rights and environmental standards in business. Nike's involvement lends credence to the project, since its annual sales in Asia are more than $1.1 billion.

The Theory of Foreign Direct Investment

What motivates a firm to go beyond exporting or licensing? What benefits does the multinational firm expect to achieve by establishing a physical presence in other countries? These are the questions that the theory of foreign direct investment has sought to answer. As with trade theory, the questions have remained largely the same over time, while the answers have continued to change. With hundreds of countries, thousands of firms, and millions of products and services, there is no question that the answer to such an enormous question will likely get messy.

The following overview of investment theory has many similarities to the preceding discussion of international trade. The theme is a global business environment that attempts to satisfy increasingly sophisticated consumer demands, while the means of production, resources, skills, and technology needed become more complex and competitive.

Firms as Seekers

A firm that expands across borders may be seeking any of a number of specific sources of profit or opportunity.

1. *Seeking resources:* There is no question that much of the initial foreign direct investment of the 18th and 19th centuries was the result of firms seeking unique and valuable natural resources for their products. Whether it be the copper resources of Chile, the linseed oils of Indonesia, or the petroleum resources spanning the Middle East, firms establishing permanent presences around the world are seeking access to the resources at the core of their business.
2. *Seeking factor advantages:* The resources needed for production are often combined with other advantages that are inherent in the country of production. The same low-cost labor at the heart of classical trade theory provides incentives for firms to move production to countries possessing these factor advantages. As noted by Vernon's Product Cycle, the same

FOREIGN DIRECT INVESTMENT (FDI)

The establishment or expansion of operations of a firm in a foreign country. Like all investments, it assumes a transfer of capital.

Culture Clues   In Turkey, there is an expression that is equivalent to "buyer beware." *Kurtlu baklanin kor alicisi olur* literally means "The buyer of rotten beans is the blind man." When doing business in Turkey, it is your responsibility—not the seller's—to thoroughly check out the goods before you buy.

firms may move their own production to locations of factor advantages as the products and markets mature.

3. *Seeking knowledge:* Firms may attempt to acquire other firms in other countries for the technical or competitive skills they possess. Alternatively, companies may locate in and around centers of industrial enterprise unique to their specific industry, such as the footwear industry of Milan or the semiconductor industry of the Silicon Valley of California.

4. *Seeking security:* Firms continue to move internationally as they seek political stability or security. For example, Mexico has experienced a significant increase in foreign direct investment as a result of the tacit support of the United States, Canada, and Mexico itself, as reflected by the North American Free Trade Agreement.

5. *Seeking markets:* Not the least of the motivations, the ability to gain and maintain access to markets is of paramount importance to multinational firms. Whether following the principles of Linder, in which firms learn from their domestic market and use that information to go international, or the principles of Porter, which emphasize the character of the domestic market as dictating international competitiveness, foreign market access is necessary.

Firms As Exploiters of Imperfections

Much of the investment theory developed in the past three decades has focused on the efforts of multinational firms to exploit the imperfections in factor and product markets created by governments. The work of Hymer, Kindleberger, and Caves noted that many of the policies of governments create imperfections. These market imperfections cover the entire range of supply and demand of the market: trade policy (tariffs and quotas), tax policies and incentives, preferential purchasing arrangements established by governments themselves, and financial restrictions on the access of foreign firms to domestic capital markets.

1. *Imperfections in access:* Many of the world's developing countries have long sought to create domestic industry by restricting imports of competitive products in order to allow smaller, less-competitive domestic firms to grow and prosper—so-called **import substitution** policies. Multinational firms have sought to maintain their access to these markets by establishing their own productive presence within the country, effectively bypassing the tariff restriction.

2. *Imperfections in factor mobility:* Other multinational firms have exploited the same sources of comparative advantage identified throughout this chapter—the low-cost resources or factors often located in less-developed countries or countries with restrictions on the mobility of labor and capital. However, combining the mobility of capital with the immobility of low-cost labor has characterized much of the foreign direct investment seen throughout the developing world over the past 50 years.

3. *Imperfections in management:* The ability of multinational firms to successfully exploit or at least manage these imperfections still relies on their ability to gain an "advantage." Market advantages or powers are seen in international markets as in domestic markets: cost advantages, economies of scale and scope, product differentiation, managerial or marketing technique and knowledge, financial resources and strength. All these imperfections are the things of which competitive dreams are made. The multinational firm needs to find these in some form or another to justify the added complexities and costs of international investments.

Firms as Internalizers

The questions that have plagued the field of foreign direct investment are: Why can't all of the advantages and imperfections mentioned be achieved through management contracts or

IMPORT SUBSTITUTION

A policy for economic growth adopted by many developing countries that involves the systematic encouragement of domestic production of goods formerly imported.

Quick Take *Biopiracy*

Charges of biopiracy—the illegal use of one nation's natural resources for the economic gain of another—are often extreme and are therefore relatively easy to reconcile. The recent collection of blood samples from the Naga tribe in northeast India for genetic experiments, for example, is clearly a violation of human rights. But consider the following example: If a rare plant that grows only in the remote regions of an emerging nation has the potential to cure illnesses that plague the Western world, who should exploit it? Global pharmaceutical companies who have the money and means to develop medicines and deliver them expediently to patients who need them? Or should the people who live where the plant grows have the right to protect their natural resources from exploitation by outsiders?

In 2002, accusations of biopiracy were leveled by the tiny community of Kraho Indians, a community of 17 villages in northern Brazil, against the Federal University of São Paulo. Because a valuable plant grows on land legally demarcated for the Kraho by the Brazilian government, the Kraho claim that none but they have the right to extract samples or profit from their traditional knowledge of its beneficial medicinal qualities. For their part, Brazilian researchers worry that lack of cooperation between government and indigenous people could not only hold back Brazil's emerging biotech industry, but could mean the loss of discoveries that could benefit the entire planet.

SOURCES: Patrice M. Jones, "Biopiracy Opens Old Wounds in Brazil," *The Chicago Tribune*, August 30, 2002, p. 3; Vandana Schiva, "Biopiracy and the Poor," *World Watch*, July/August 2002, p. 25.

licensing agreements? Why is it necessary for the firm itself to establish a physical presence in the country? What pushes the multinational firm further down the investment decision tree?

The research of Buckley and Casson (1976) and Dunning (1977) has attempted to answer these questions by focusing on nontransferable sources of competitive advantage—proprietary information possessed by the firm and its people. Many advantages firms possess center around their hands-on knowledge of producing a good or providing a service. By establishing their own multinational operations, they can internalize the production, thus keeping confidential the information that is at the core of the firm's competitiveness. **Internalization** is preferable to the use of arms-length arrangements, such as management contracts or licensing agreements. They either do not allow the effective transmission of the knowledge or represent too serious a threat to the loss of the knowledge to allow the firm to successfully achieve the hoped-for benefits of international investment.

INTERNALIZATION

Occurs when a firm establishes its own multinational operation, keeping information that is at the core of its competitiveness within the firm.

Strategic Implications of Foreign Direct Investment

Consider a firm that wants to exploit its competitive advantage by accessing foreign markets as illustrated in the decision-sequence tree of Figure 6.6.

The first choice is whether to exploit the existing competitive advantage in new foreign markets or to concentrate its resources in the development of new competitive advantages in the domestic market. Although many firms may choose to do both as resources will allow, more and more firms are choosing to go international as at least part of their expansion strategies.

Second, should the firm produce at home and export to the foreign markets or produce abroad? The firm will choose the path that will allow it to access the resources and markets it needs to exploit its existing competitive advantage. But it will also consider two additional dimensions of each foreign investment decision: (1) the degree of control over assets, technology, information, and operations and (2) the magnitude of capital that the firm must risk. Each decision increases the firm's control at the cost of increased capital outlays.

After choosing to produce abroad, the firm must decide how. The distinctions among different kinds of foreign direct investment (branch 3 and downward in Figure 6.6), or licensing agreements to "greenfield" construction (building a new facility from the ground up), vary by degrees of ownership. The licensing management contract is by far the simplest and cheapest way to produce abroad. Another firm is licensed to produce the product, but with your firm's technology and know-how. The question is whether the reduced capital investment of simply licensing the product to another manufacturer is worth the risk of loss of control over the product and technology.

The firm that wants direct control over the foreign production process next determines the degree of equity control: to own the firm outright or as a joint investment with another firm. Trade-offs with joint ventures continue the debate over control of assets and other sources of the firm's original competitive advantage. Many countries try to ensure the continued growth of local firms and investors by requiring that foreign firms operate jointly with local firms.

FIGURE 6.6   The Direct Foreign Investment Decision Sequence

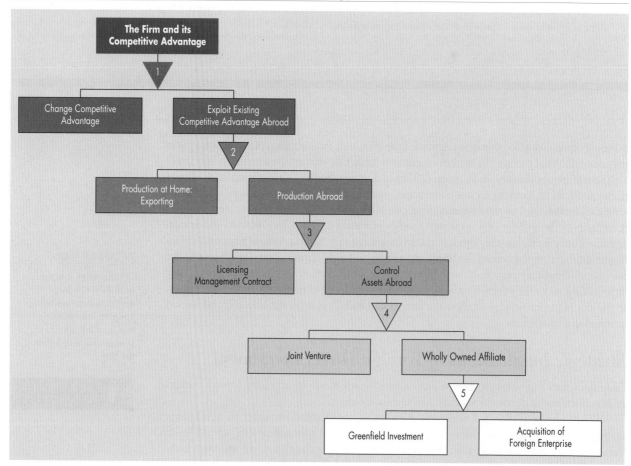

SOURCE: Adapted from Gunter Dufey and R. Mirus, "Foreign Direct Investment: Theory and Strategic Considernations" (University of Michigan, May 1985).

The final decision branch, between a greenfield investment and the purchase of an existing firm, is often a question of cost. A greenfield investment is the most expensive of all foreign investment alternatives. The acquisition of an existing firm is often lower in initial cost but may also contain a number of customizing and adjustment costs that are not apparent at the initial purchase. The purchase of a going concern may also have substantial benefits if the existing business possesses substantial customer and supplier relationships that can be used by the new owner in the pursuit of its own business.

SUMMARY

As world economies have grown and the magnitude of world trade has increased, the ideas that guided international trade and investment theory have similarly evolved to higher levels of sophistication. Trade theory informs the decisions that many firms face today, requiring them to directly move their capital, technology, and know-how to countries that possess unique factors of production or market advantages that will help them keep pace with market demands.

At its root, international trade assumes that trade will improve the quality of life for the consumers, both as individuals and as a nation. The rise of mercantilism saw trade evolve for the purposes of increasing wealth and power. Other theories emerged after mercantilism's failure to help explain the costs and benefits of trade.

The classical theories of Adam Smith and David Ricardo focused on the abilities of countries to produce goods more cheaply than other countries. The earliest production and trade theories saw labor as the major factor expense that went into any product. If a country could pay that labor less, and if that labor could produce more physically than labor in other countries, the country might obtain an absolute or comparative advantage in trade.

Subsequent theoretical development led to a more detailed understanding of production and its costs. Factors of production are now believed to include labor (skilled and unskilled), capital, natural resources, and other potentially significant commodities that are difficult to reproduce or replace, such as energy.

International trade is a complex combination of thousands of products, technologies, and firms that are constantly innovating to either keep up with or get ahead of competition. Modern trade theory looks beyond production cost to analyze how the demands of the marketplace alter who trades with whom and which firms survive domestically and internationally. The abilities of firms to adapt to foreign markets have required international trade theory to search out new and innovative approaches to what determines success and failure. Krugman's theory examined trade as altered when markets do not have parity, and Porter developed a theory about the competitiveness of industries on a global scale, rather than prior competitiveness determinants based primarily on country-specific factors.

International trade is defined by goods and services that are bought and sold between firms, not countries. While intertwined, international investment addresses more the idea of the movability of capital from a firm into the country itself.

 To understand what motivates firms to invest overseas, theorists have analyzed firms from multiple perspectives: firms as seekers, not only of aspects of competitiveness, such as new markets or cheaper resources, but of knowledge or technical expertise; firms as exploiters of imperfections created by government policies; and firms as internalizers, motivated to protect knowledge that is at the core of their competitiveness.

Once a firm makes a decision in favor of some form of foreign direct investment, the options range from the relatively simple, such as the decision to manufacture abroad or license other firms to do so, to the complex, including greenfield investment or acquisition of a foreign enterprise.

KEY TERMS AND CONCEPTS

autarky	factor intensities	abandoned product ranges
mercantilism	factor proportions theory	intra-industry trade
absolute advantage	input-output analysis	product differentiation
division of labor	Leontief Paradox	foreign direct investment
comparative advantage	market segment	import substitution
production possibilities frontier	product cycle theory	internalization
opportunity cost	internal economies of scale	

REVIEW QUESTIONS

1. Explain the relationship between absolute advantage and the division of labor.
2. According to the theory of comparative advantage, why is trade always possible between two countries, even when one is inefficient compared to the other?
3. What are the flaws inherent in factor intensity theory?
4. What, in your opinion, were the constructive impacts on trade theory resulting from· the empirical research of Wassily Leontief ?
5. Product cycle theory has always been a very "attractive" theory to many students. Why do you think that is?

6. Many trade theorists argue that the primary contribution of Michael Porter has been to repopularize old ideas in new, more applicable ways. To what degree do you think Porter's ideas are new or old?
7. How would you analyze the statement that "international investment is simply a modern extension of classical trade"?
8. Explain why firms are motivated to move beyond exporting or licensing to more complex forms of foreign direct investment.

CRITICAL SKILL BUILDERS

1. The factor proportions theory of international trade assumes that all countries produce the same product the same way. Would international competition cause or prevent this from happening? Discuss in small groups.
2. If the product cycle theory were accepted for the basis of policymaking, what should the U.S. government do to help its firms exploit the principles of the theory?
3. How can a crisis in Asia impact jobs and profits in Western nations? Give examples from recent world events. What obstacles and opportunities would such a crisis present?
4. We typically think of "commodities" as being relatively easy-to-manufacture goods with little product differentiation, such as paper, steel, or agricultural products. Consider the statement that Dell has made a commodity out of the personal computer. Research the company's competitive strategies, particularly its price-cutting policies. Do you think the PC is a commodity?
5. Research a small or mid-size business in your area that currently manufactures its product domestically and sells mainly within the domestic market. How might that company benefit from considering the decision-sequence tree illustrated in Figure 6.6? In groups, outline a foreign direct investment program for the company.

ON THE WEB

1. The differences across multinational firms are striking. Using a sample of firms such as those listed below, pull from their individual web pages the proportions of their incomes that are earned outside their country of incorporation. Also, consider the way in which international business is now conducted via the Internet. Several of these home pages allow the user to choose the language of the presentation viewed. Others, like DaimlerChrysler, report financial results in two different accounting frameworks, those used in Germany and the Generally Accepted Accounting Practices (GAAP) used in the United States.

Walt Disney	**http://www.disney.com**
Nestlé S.A.	**http://www.nestle.com**
Intel	**http://www.intel.com**
Mitsubishi Motors	**http://www.mitsubishi-motors.com**

2. There is no hotter topic in business today than corporate governance, the way in which firms are controlled by management and ownership across countries. Use the following sites to view recent research, current events, news items, and other information related to the relationships between a business and its stakeholders.

Corporate Governance Net	**http://www.corpgov.net**
Corporate Governance Research	**http://www.irrc.org**

3. International trade statistics between countries, as reported by each, often do not match. Go to **http://www.census.gov/foreign-trade** to view a study of trade statistics discrepancies between NAFTA member nations. Isolate reasons for the discrepancies and discuss their impact on trade between the United States, Canada, and Mexico.

ENDNOTES

1. Jeffrey E. Garten, "When Everything Is Made in China," *BusinessWeek*, June 17, 2002, p. 20; Bruce Einhorn, et al., "China and the WTO," *BusinessWeek*, October 22, 2001; "Korean Electronics Firms Relocating Their Overseas Plants," *Asia Pulse*, August 8, 2002.
2. Adam Smith, *An Inquiry into the Nature and Causes of the Wealth of Nations* (New York: E.P. Dutton, 1937), pp. 4–5.
3. In Leontief 's own words: "These figures show that an average million dollars' worth of our exports embodies considerably less capital and somewhat more labor than would be required to replace from domestic production an equivalent amount of our competitive imports. . . . The widely held opinion that—as compared with the rest of the world—the United States' economy is characterized by a relative surplus of capital and a relative shortage of labor proves to be wrong. As a matter of fact, the opposite is true." Wassily Leontief, "Domestic Production and Foreign Trade: The American Capital Position Re-Examined," *Proceedings of the American Philosophical Society*, 97, No. 4 (September 1953), p. 86.
4. If this were true, it would defy one of the basic assumptions of the factor proportions theory, that all products are manufactured with the same technology (and therefore the same proportions of labor and capital) across countries. However, continuing studies have found this to be quite possible in our imperfect world.
5. For a detailed description of these theories, see Elhanan Helpman and Paul Krugman, *Market Structure and Foreign Trade* (Cambridge: MIT Press, 1985).
6. Michael E. Porter, "The Competitive Advantage of Nations," Harvard Business Review (March–April 1990): pp. 73–74.

CHAPTER 7

China Joins the Club

In 2001, following 15 years of negotiations, China formally became a member of the World Trade Organization (WTO), signaling its commitment to establish clear and enforceable nondiscriminatory rules to conduct business within its own country and with other countries.

China's integration into the world economy has resulted in spectacular numbers, both in trade and in investment. China has been the fastest-growing economy in the past ten years, with annual real GDP growth averaging 10.8 percent. Its world trade quadrupled to $474 billion. In 2001, China retained its spot as the country with the largest trade imbalance with the United States, at $83 billion. While lowered trade barriers may permit more sales of foreign goods in China in the future, the rush by many European and American companies to establish plants in China for exporting goods may maintain China's trade imbalance with these trading partners. With Asian countries, however, China has been running a trade deficit since 2000 and will continue to be a source of demand as markets liberalize.

China received more foreign direct investment (FDI) in the 1990s than any country in the world except the United States. The inflows have amounted to more than $60 billion per year in the last five years, suggesting that China may emerge as Asia's hub for interregional demand for goods and services. Other countries, such as Japan, will have to focus on research and development, design, software, and high-precision manufactured goods.

Of economic significance is China's effort to stabilize its currency in the last five years. While its currency (*yuan renminbi*) is officially described as a managed float, it is effectively pegged to the U.S. dollar. China has thus been immune to the currency fluctuations that wreaked havoc among other emerging markets, such as Mexico, Indonesia, Russia, Brazil, and Argentina. However, China's increasing foreign exchange reserves, strong capital inflows, and current account surplus have put appreciating pressure on the currency, as have other Asian countries (especially Japan). With the trade liberalization that will result from China's membership in the WTO, the higher value of the *yuan* would aggravate the shock on domestic companies that compete with imports, as well as on exporters that have to compete in the global market, often on the basis of price. Chinese authorities have acknowledged the need for financial and currency liberalization, but the damaging impact of the rising currency in the short term will most likely keep the currency regime unchanged. This will naturally result in low currency risk for investors.

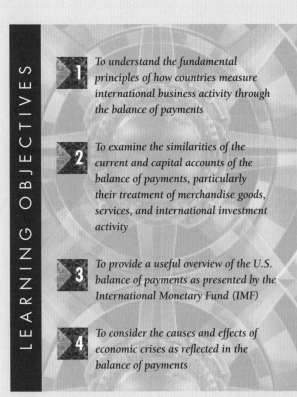

LEARNING OBJECTIVES

1 To understand the fundamental principles of how countries measure international business activity through the balance of payments

2 To examine the similarities of the current and capital accounts of the balance of payments, particularly their treatment of merchandise goods, services, and international investment activity

3 To provide a useful overview of the U.S. balance of payments as presented by the International Monetary Fund (IMF)

4 To consider the causes and effects of economic crises as reflected in the balance of payments

The Western world has had a commercial fascination with China for the last two thousand years. With WTO membership, China's economic stature will undoubtedly continue to grow. Increased investment will make China a global production base as global companies put their best practices to work in the largest emerging market in the world. As a result, the United States may lose more than 600,000 jobs and face a widening trade deficit with China, which may result in growing tensions between the two superpowers.[1]

As You Read This Chapter

1. Consider the significance of GDP as an economic indicator. Why should business people be aware of fluctuations in GDP at home and in the countries where they trade?
2. What are the effects of currency stability or instability?

International business transactions occur in many different forms over the course of each year. The measurement of all international economic transactions between the residents of a country and foreign residents is called the balance of payments.[2] Government policymakers need such measures of economic activity to evaluate the general competitiveness of domestic industry, to set exchange-rate or interest-rate policies or goals, and for many other purposes. Individuals and businesses use various BOP measures to gauge the growth and health of specific types of trade or financial transactions by country and regions of the world against the home country.

This chapter largely describes the various balance of payment accounts, their meanings, and their relationships, using the United States as the example. The chapter concludes with a discussion—and a number of examples—of how different countries with different policies or levels of economic development may differ markedly in their balance of payment accounts.

INTERNATIONAL TRANSACTIONS AND THE BALANCE OF PAYMENTS

International transactions take many forms. Each of the following examples is an international economic transaction that is counted and captured in the U.S. balance of payments.

LEARNING OBJECTIVE 1

- U.S. imports of Maserati sports cars, which are manufactured in Japan.
- A U.S.-based firm, Bechtel, is hired to manage the construction of a major water-treatment facility in the Middle East.
- The U.S. subsidiary of a French firm, Saint Gobain, pays profits (dividends) back to the parent firm in Paris.
- Auto giant Daimler-Benz, headquartered in Germany, merges with U.S. carmaker Chrysler.
- An American tourist purchases a hand-blown glass figurine in Venice, Italy.
- The U.S. government provides grant financing of military equipment for its NATO ally, Turkey.
- A Canadian dentist purchases a U.S. Treasury bill through an investment broker in Cleveland, Ohio.

These are just a small sample of the hundreds of thousands of international transactions that occur each year. The **balance of payments (BOP)** provides a systematic method for the classification of them all. There is one rule of thumb that will always aid in the understanding of BOP accounting: Watch the direction of the movement of money.

The balance of payments is composed of a number of subaccounts that are watched quite closely by groups as diverse as investors on Wall Street, farmers in Iowa, politicians on Capitol Hill, and board members across corporate America. These groups track and analyze the two major subaccounts, the **Current Account** and the **Financial Account**, on a continuing basis. Before describing these two subaccounts and the balance of payments as a whole, it is necessary to understand the rather unusual features of how balance of payments accounting is conducted.

Basics of BOP Accounting

There are three main elements to the process of measuring international economic activity:

1. Identifying what is and is not an international economic transaction
2. Understanding how the flow of goods, services, assets, and money creates debits and credits to the overall BOP
3. Understanding the bookkeeping procedures for BOP accounting

Identifying International Economic Transactions

Identifying international transactions is ordinarily not difficult. The export of merchandise, goods such as trucks, machinery, computers, telecommunications equipment, and so forth, is obviously an international transaction. Imports such as French wine, Japanese cameras, and German automobiles are also clearly international transactions. But this merchandise trade is only a portion of the thousands of different international transactions that occur in the United States or any other country each year.

Many other international transactions are not so obvious. All expenditures made by American tourists around the globe, for example, that are for goods or services (meals, hotel accommodations, and so forth) are recorded in the U.S. balance of payments as imports of travel services. The purchase of a U.S. Treasury bill by a foreign resident is an international financial transaction and is dutifully recorded in the U.S. balance of payments.

BOP as a Flow Statement

The BOP is often misunderstood because many people believe it to be a balance sheet, rather than a cash-flow statement. By recording all international transactions over a period of time, it tracks the continuing flow of purchases and payments between a country and all other countries. Unlike a firm's balance sheet, it does not add up the value of all assets and liabilities of a country.

There are two types of business transactions that dominate the balance of payments:

1. *Real assets:* The exchange of goods (automobiles, computers, watches, textiles) and services (banking services, consulting services, travel services) for other goods and services (barter) or for the more common type of payment, money.
2. *Financial assets:* The exchange of financial claims (stocks, bonds, loans, purchases or sales of companies) in exchange for other financial claims or money.

Although assets can be separated as to whether they are real or financial, it is often easier simply to think of all assets as being goods that can be bought and sold. An American tourist's

---

purchase of a handwoven rug in a shop in Bangkok is not all that different from a Wall Street banker buying a British government bond for investment purposes.

BOP Accounting: Double-Entry Bookkeeping

The balance of payments employs an accounting technique called **double-entry bookkeeping**. This is the age-old method of accounting in which every transaction produces a debit and a credit of the same amount. Simultaneously. It has to. A debit is created whenever an asset is increased, a liability is decreased, or an expense is increased. Similarly, a credit is created whenever an asset is decreased, a liability is increased, or an expense is decreased.

An example clarifies this process. A U.S. retail store imports from Japan $2 million worth of consumer electronics. A negative entry is made in the merchandise-import subcategory of the current account in the amount of $2 million. Simultaneously, a positive entry of the same $2 million is made in the financial account for the transfer of a $2 million bank account to the Japanese manufacturer. Obviously, the result of hundreds of thousands of such transactions and entries should theoretically result in a perfect balance.

That said, it is now a problem of application, and a problem it is. The measurement of all international transactions in and out of a country over a year is a daunting task. Mistakes, errors, and statistical discrepancies will occur. The primary problem is that although double-entry bookkeeping is employed in theory, the individual transactions are recorded independently. Current and financial account entries are recorded independent of one another, not together as double-entry bookkeeping would prescribe. It must then be recognized that there will be serious discrepancies between debits and credits and the possibility in total that the balance of payments may not balance!

The balance of payments consists of two primary subaccounts: the Current Account and the Financial/Capital Account.

BOP CURRENT ACCOUNT

The Current Account includes all international economic transactions with income or payment flows occurring within the year, the current period. The Current Account consists of four subcategories:

1. **Goods trade account:** This records the export and import of goods. Merchandise trade is the oldest and most traditional form of international economic activity. Although many countries depend on imports of many goods (as they should according to the theory of comparative advantage), they also normally work to preserve either a balance of goods trade or even a surplus.
2. **Services trade account:** This records the export and import of services. Some common international services are financial services provided by banks to foreign importers and exporters, travel services of airlines, and construction services of domestic firms in other countries. For the major industrial countries, this subaccount has shown the fastest growth in the past decade.
3. **Income account:** This category is predominantly current income associated with investments that were made in previous periods. If a U.S. firm created a subsidiary in South Korea

2 LEARNING OBJECTIVE

Culture Clues   The Japanese obsession with pleasing guests does not mean they form friendships quickly. *Naniwabushi* (to get on such close personal terms with someone that they will have to do you a favor) is standard Japanese operating procedure. Hence, accepting lavish gifts from a Japanese business acquaintance can lead to obligations that may later prove awkward, if not downright painful.

to produce metal parts in a previous year, the proportion of net income that is paid back to the parent company in the current year (the dividend) constitutes current investment income. Additionally, wages and salaries paid to nonresident workers are also included in this category.

4. **Current transfers account:** Transfers are the financial settlements associated with the change in ownership of real resources or financial items. Any transfer between countries that is one-way, a gift, or a grant, is termed a current transfer. A common example of a current transfer would be funds provided by the U.S. government to aid in the development of a less-developed nation.

All countries possess some amount of trade, most of which is merchandise. Many smaller and less-developed countries have little in the way of service trade, or items that fall under the income or transfers subaccounts.

The Current Account is typically dominated by the first component described—the export and import of merchandise. For this reason, the balance of trade (BOT), which is so widely quoted in the business press in most countries, refers specifically to the balance of exports and imports of goods trade only. For a larger industrialized country, however, the BOT is somewhat misleading because service trade is not included; it may be opposite in sign on net, and it may actually be fairly large as well.

Table 7.1 summarizes the U.S. Current Account and its components for 2002-2006. As illustrated, the U.S. goods trade balance has consistently been negative but has been partially offset by the continuing surplus in services trade.

Goods Trade

Figure 7.1 places the Current Account values of Table 7.1 in perspective over time by dividing the Current Account into its two major components: (1) goods trade, and (2) services trade and investment income. The first and most striking message is the magnitude of the goods trade deficit in the 2000s (a continuation of a position created in the early 90s). The

TABLE 7.1 The United States Current Account, 2002-2006 (billions of U.S. dollars)

	2002	2003	2004	2005	2006
Goods exports	685	717	811	898	1027
Goods imports	−1165	−1261	−1477	−1682	−1861
Goods trade balance (BOT)	−479	−544	−666	−783	−835
Services trade credits	289	299	346	385	419
Services trade debits	−227	−250	−292	−316	−343
Services trade balance	61	49	54	69	76
Income receipts	281	321	402	505	650
Income payments	−254	−275	−346	−457	−614
Income balance	28	45	56	48	37
Current transfers, credits	12	15	20	19	24
Current transfers, debits	−76	−86	−105	−107	−114
Net transfers	−64	−71	−84	−89	−90
Current Account Balance	−454	−520	−640	−755	−811

SOURCE: Derived from International Monetary Fund's *Balance of Payments Statistics Yearbook 2007*.

FIGURE 7.1   U.S. Balance on Goods Trade & Balance on Services & Income, 1993–2006

Balance on Goods   ■ Balance on Services & Income

Source: Data derived from the International Monetary Fund's *Balance of Payments Statistics Yearbook,* 2007, p. 1038.

balance on services and income, although not large in comparison to net goods trade, has generally run a surplus over the past two decades.

The deficits in the BOT of the past decade have been an area of considerable concern. Merchandise trade is the original core of international trade. It has three major components: manufactured goods, agriculture, and fuels. The manufacturing of goods was the basis of the Industrial Revolution and the focus of the theory of international trade described in the previous chapter. The U.S. goods trade deficit of the 1980s and 1990s was mainly caused by a decline in traditional manufacturing industries that have, over the past two centuries, employed many of America's workers. Declines in the net trade balance in areas such as steel, automobiles, automotive parts, textiles, shoe manufacturing, and others caused massive economic and social disruption. The problems of dealing with these shifting trade balances will be discussed in detail in the next chapter.

The most encouraging news for U.S. manufacturing trade is the growth of exports in recent years. A number of factors contributed to the growth in exports, such as the weaker dollar (which made U.S.-manufactured goods cheaper in relation to the currencies of other countries), more rapid economic growth in Europe, and a substantial increase in agricultural exports. Understanding merchandise import and export performance is much like understanding the market for any single product. The demand factors that drive both imports and exports are income, the economic growth rate of the buyer, and price (the price of the product in the eyes of the consumer after passing through an exchange rate). For example, U.S. merchandise imports reflect the income level and growth of American consumers and industry. As income rises, so does the demand for imports.

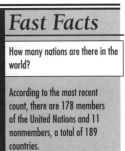

Fast Facts

How many nations are there in the world?

According to the most recent count, there are 178 members of the United Nations and 11 nonmembers, a total of 189 countries.

Exports follow the same principles but in the reversed position. U.S. merchandise exports depend not on the incomes of U.S. residents, but on the incomes of the buyers of U.S. products in all other countries around the world. When these economies are growing, the demand for U.S. products will also rise. However, the recent economic crises in Asia now raise questions regarding U.S. export growth in the immediate future.

The service component of the U.S. Current Account is one of mystery to many. As illustrated in both Table 7.1 and Figure 7.1, the United States has consistently achieved a surplus in services trade income. The major categories of services include travel and passenger fares, transportation services, expenditures by U.S. students abroad and foreign students pursuing studies in the United States, telecommunications services, and financial services.

BOP CAPITAL AND FINANCIAL ACCOUNT

The Capital and Financial Account of the balance of payments measures all international economic transactions of financial assets. It is divided into two major components, the Capital Account and the Financial Account.

- *The Capital Account.* The Capital Account is made up of transfers of financial assets and the acquisition and disposal of nonproduced/nonfinancial assets. The magnitude of capital transactions covered is of relatively minor amount and will be included in principle in all of the following discussions of the financial account.

Quick Take   *Individual Remittances in the Balance of Payments*

Over 150 million migrants sent an estimated $301 billion to their families in 162 developing countries in 2006, says the International Fund for Agricultural Development, a UN body. Remittances have been increasingly recognized as an effective means to alleviate poverty, particularly in rural areas where access to credit would otherwise be impossible. Although India and Mexico receive the most cash, at around $24.5 billion each, this represents less than 3 percent of GDP. By contrast, Guinea-Bissau relies heavily on its migrants' money, with remittances making up nearly half of GDP.

SOURCES: "Cash Back," *The Economist*, October 23, 2007.

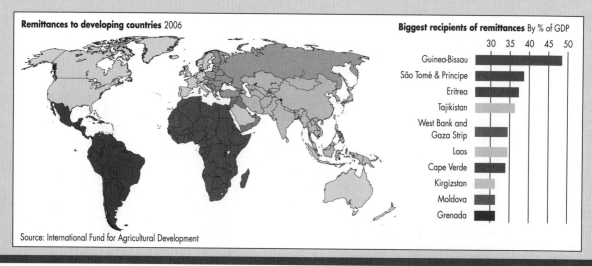

Remittances to developing countries 2006

Biggest recipients of remittances By % of GDP

Source: International Fund for Agricultural Development

- *The Financial Account.* The Financial Account consists of three components: direct investment, portfolio investment, and other asset investment. Financial assets can be classified in a number of different ways, including the length of the life of the asset (its maturity) and by the nature of the ownership (public or private). The Financial Account, however, uses a third way. It is classified by the degree of control over the assets or operations the claim represents: portfolio investment, where the investor has no control, or direct investment, where the investor exerts some explicit degree of control over the assets.

Table 7.2 shows the major subcategories of the U.S. Capital Account balance from 1997–2000, direct investment, portfolio investment, and other long-term and short-term capital.

1. **Direct investment account:** This is the net balance of capital dispersed out of and into the country for the purpose of exerting control over assets. For example, if a U.S. firm either builds a new automotive parts facility in another country or actually purchases a company in another country, this would fall under direct investment in the U.S. balance of payments accounts. When the capital flows out of the United States, it enters the balance of payments as a negative cash flow. If, however, foreign firms purchase firms in the United States, it is a capital inflow and enters the balance of payments positively. Whenever 10 percent or more of the voting shares in a U.S. company is held by foreign investors, the company is classified as the U.S. affiliate of a foreign company and a foreign direct investment. Similarly, if U.S. investors hold 10 percent or more of the control in a company outside the country, that company is considered the foreign affiliate of a U.S. company.

2. **Portfolio investment account:** This is net balance of capital that flows in and out of the country but does not reach the 10 percent ownership threshold of direct investment. If a U.S. resident purchases shares in a Japanese firm, but does not attain the 10 percent threshold, it is considered a portfolio investment (and in this case an outflow of capital). The purchase or sale of debt securities (like U.S. Treasury bills) across borders is also classified as portfolio investment because debt securities by definition do not provide the buyer with ownership or control.

DIRECT INVESTMENT ACCOUNT

An account in the BOP statement that records investments with an expected maturity of more than one year and an investor's ownership position of at least 10 percent.

PORTFOLIO INVESTMENT ACCOUNT

An account in the BOP statement that records investments in assets with an original maturity of more than one year and where an investor's ownership position is less than 10 percent.

TABLE 7.2 The United States Financial Account and Components, 2002-2006
(billions of U.S. dollars)

	2002	2003	2004	2005	2006
Direct Investment					
Direct investment abroad	−154	−150	−279	8	−235
Direct investment in the US	84	64	146	109	181
Net direct investment	−70	−86	−133	117	−55
Portfolio Investment					
Assets, net	−49	−123	−153	−203	−426
Liabilities, net	428	550	867	832	1017
Net portfolio investment	379	427	714	629	591
Other Investment					
Other investment assets	−88	−54	−475	−245	−396
Other investment liabilities	286	250	449	263	662
Net other investment	198	196	−27	18	265
Net Financial Account Balance	507	537	554	763	802

SOURCE: Derived from International Monetary Fund's *Balance of Payments Statistics Yearbook 2007.*

FIGURE 7.2   The United States Financial Account Components, 1993–2006

Billions of US dollars

[Chart showing three data series: Net Direct Investment, Net Portfolio Investment, and Net Other Investment, from 1993 to 2006, with values ranging from -200 to 800 billion US dollars]

Source: Data derived from the International Monetary Fund's *Balance of Payments Statistics Yearbook*, 2007, p. 1038.

3. **Other investment assets/liabilities:** This final category consists of various short-term and long-term trade credits, cross-border loans from all types of financial institutions, currency deposits and bank deposits, and other accounts receivable and payable related to cross-border trade.

Direct Investment

Figure 7.2 shows how the major subaccounts of the U.S. capital account, net direct investment, portfolio investment, and other investment have changed since 1993.

As seen in earlier chapters, foreign investment into any country raises two major concerns—control and profit. Most countries possess restrictions on what foreigners may own, largely based on the premise that domestic land, assets, and industry in general should be held by residents of the country. For example, until 1990 it was not possible for a foreign firm to own more than 20 percent of any company in Finland. This rule is the norm, rather than the exception. The United States has traditionally had few restrictions on what foreign residents or firms can own or control; most that remain today are related to national security concerns. As opposed to many of the traditional debates over whether international trade should be free or not, there is not the same consensus that international investment should necessarily be free.

The second major source of concern over foreign direct investment is who receives the profits from the enterprise. Foreign companies owning firms in the United States ultimately profit from the activities of the firms or, put another way, from the efforts of American workers. In spite of evidence that foreign firms typically reinvest most of their profits in the United States (in fact, at a higher rate than domestic firms), the debate on possible profit drains

Telecom's titan, AT&T Corporation, launched China's first foreign telecom venture with Telecom's Shanghai branch after seven years of negotiation.

WORLD VIEW

HOME-COUNTRY OWNERSHIP IN AFRICA

The manager of the state-owned Tanzanian Brewery used to spend his mornings dealing with a long line of people outside his office. Most carried notes that read along these lines: "I am having a funeral at my brother's house this weekend. Please ensure that there is an adequate supply of beer." The note would usually be signed by a government minister or other important official.

The Tanzanian Brewery was built to produce 1.3 million liters of beer a day, but produced only 400,000. It had a 25 percent share of the market but provided a bad-tasting product. A privatization drive by the Tanzanian government enabled South African Breweries to buy a 50 percent stake in the defunct state-run operation. By cutting jobs, building a new brewery, and improving the taste, South Africa grabbed 75 percent of the market. Today, the government retains almost 25 percent of ownership and receives 59 percent of cash value added, in the form of excise duties, value-added tax, customs duties, and dividends.

Tanzania has privatized more than half of its 250 companies, including cashew and tobacco farms, mines, and a cigarette factory. But the most difficult part is ahead. Companies that remain to be privatized include decrepit state-run utilities. Moreover, the government insists that these companies land largely in the hands of its citizens, who do not have the capital to invest in them.

In theory, the state has made strides to open up the country for business. In practice, investing in Tanzania is like riding a roller coaster. Frequent power failures and shoddy telephone networks demonstrate the country's lack of investment in its infrastructure. Both foreign and local business people complain about the labyrinth-like tax system. Permits and licenses arrive late or not at all, unless certain palms are greased.

Meanwhile, in the Republic of Mali, one of West Africa's poorest economies, an influx of foreign aid has helped farmers make the shift from government control into the private sector. The

Observatoire du Marché Agricole (OMA), armed with an $8.5 million grant from the U.S. Agency for International Development and other donors, set out to deregulate the Mali grain market, where fixed agricultural prices restricted farmers' access to buyers at the same time that people were dying from lack of food.

In a country with poor roads, nonexistent telecommunications, and a population that is 50 percent illiterate, the challenge was to disseminate information of grain availability and prices from village to village. The answer was a low-cost communications system that uses FM radio to send grain prices in 58 markets to regional offices. Radio stations then broadcast market reports, connecting farmers with remote communities and aid organizations in search of supplies. Not only has deregulation increased the bargaining power of grain farmers and made them more efficient, it has curbed starvation as low-cost surpluses are shifted to areas of shortages.

While not yet self-sufficient, OMA expects that it will soon be able to raise 10 percent of its operating costs by selling market data to commercial banks and selling advertising on its airwaves. Niger, Burkina Faso, and other nations are establishing their own systems around the Mali model, and it is a matter of time before farmers will be able to trade across national borders.

Clearly, privatization and deregulation are mechanisms for greater efficiency in emerging and undeveloped economies. Unfortunately, though, governments cannot simply wave a magic wand and make them a reality—a great deal of work remains to be done.

SOURCES: Silvia Sansoni, "Silicon Mali," February 4, 2002, **http://www.forbes.com**; "Risky Returns," *The Economist*, May 18, 2000, p. 85; South Africa Breweries, Annual Report 2000, **http://www.sabplc.com**; "Focus on East Africa," **http://sei2000.com/eastafrica2000**; Dar es Salaam, "Private Sector Beer is Best," *The Economist*, November 2, 1996, p. 46.

has continued. Regardless of the actual choices made, workers of any nation feel that the profits of their work should remain in the hands of their own citizens.

The choice of words used to describe foreign investment can also influence public opinion. If these massive capital inflows are described as "capital investments from all over the world showing their faith in the future of American industry," the net capital surplus is represented as decidedly positive. If, however, the net capital surplus is described as resulting in "the United States as the world's largest debtor nation," the negative connotation is obvious. Both are essentially spins on the economic principles at work. Capital, whether short-term or long-term, flows to where it believes it can earn the greatest return for the level of risk. Although in an accounting sense that is "international debt," when the majority of the capital inflow is in the form of direct investment and a long-term commitment to jobs, production, services, technological, and other competitive investments, the impact on the competitiveness of American industry (an industry located within the United States) is increased. The "net debtor" label is misleading in that it inappropriately invites comparison with large-debt crisis conditions suffered by many countries in the past, like Mexico and Brazil.

Portfolio Investment

Portfolio investment is capital invested in activities that are purely profit-motivated (return), rather than ones made in the prospect of controlling or managing the investment. Investments that are purchases of debit securities, bonds, interest-bearing bank accounts, and the like are only intended to earn a return. They provide no vote or control over the party issuing the debt. Purchases of debt issued by the U.S. government (U.S. Treasury bills, notes, and bonds) by foreign investors constitute net portfolio investment.

Returning to Figure 7.2, portfolio investment has shown a much more volatile behavior than net direct investment over the past decade. Many U.S. debt securities, such as U.S. Treasury securities and corporate bonds, were in high demand in the late 1980s, while surging emerging markets in both debt and equities caused a reversal in direction in the 1990s. The motivating forces for portfolio investment flows are always the same: return and risk. This theoretical fact, however, does not make them any more predictable.

Current and Financial Account Balance Relationships

Figure 7.3 illustrates the current and financial account balances for Japan, the U.S., and Germany over recent years. They are all presented on the same scale so that relative magnitudes

FIGURE 7.3   Current Account and Financial/Capital Account Balances, 1993–2006

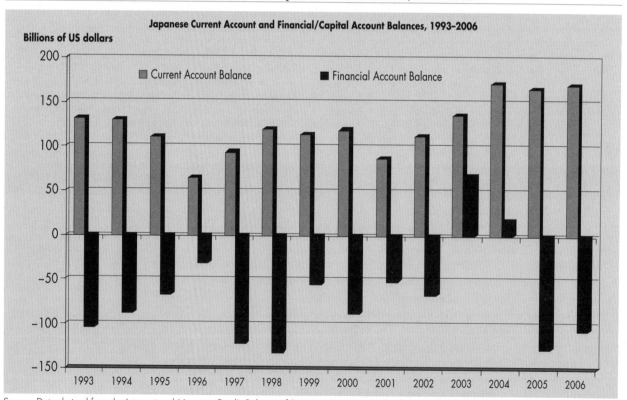

Source: Data derived from the International Monetary Fund's *Balance of Payments Statistics Yearbook*, 2007, p. 511.

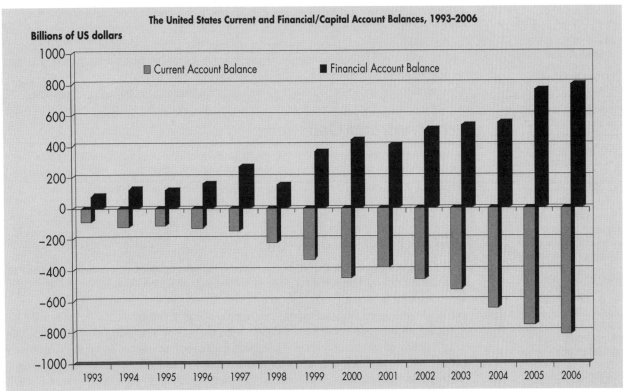

Source: Data derived from the International Monetary Fund's *Balance of Payments Statistics Yearbook*, 2007, p. 1038.

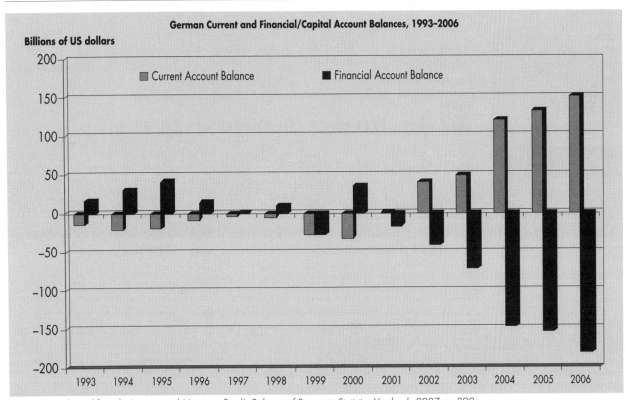

Source: Data derived from the International Monetary Fund's *Balance of Payments Statistics Yearbook*, 2007, p. 392.

NET ERRORS AND OMISSIONS ACCOUNT

Makes sure the BOP actually balances.

OFFICIAL RESERVES ACCOUNT

An account in the BOP statement that shows (1) the change in the amount of funds immediately available to a country for making international payments and (2) the borrowing and lending that has taken place between the monetary authorities of different countries either directly or through the IMF.

FIXED EXCHANGE RATE

The government of a country officially declares that its currency is convertible into a fixed amount of some other currency.

FLOATING EXCHANGE RATE

Under this system, the government possesses no responsibility to declare that its currency is convertible into a fixed amount of some other currency; this diminishes the role of official reserves.

are comparable across the three countries. What the figure shows is one of the basic economic and accounting relationships of the balance of payments: the inverse relationship between the Current and Financial accounts. This inverse relationship is not accidental. The methodology of the balance of payments—double-entry bookkeeping—requires that the current and financial accounts be offsetting. Countries experiencing large current account deficits "finance" these purchases through equally large surpluses in the financial account, and vice versa.

Net Errors and Omissions

As noted before, because Current Account and Financial Account entries are collected and recorded separately, errors or statistical discrepancies will occur. The **net errors and omissions account** (this is the title used by the International Monetary Fund) makes sure that the BOP actually balances.

Official Reserves Account

The **official reserves account** is the total currency and metallic reserves held by official monetary authorities within the country. These reserves are normally composed of the major currencies used in international trade and financial transactions (so-called "hard currencies" such as the U.S. dollar, German mark, and Japanese yen) and gold.

The significance of official reserves depends generally on whether the country is operating under a **fixed exchange rate** regime or a **floating exchange rate** system. If a country's currency is fixed, this means that the government of the country officially declares that the currency is convertible into a fixed amount of some other currency. For example, for many years the South Korean *won* was fixed to the U.S. dollar at 484 *won* equal to one U.S. dollar. It is the government's responsibility to maintain this fixed rate (also called parity rate). If for some reason there is an excess supply of Korean *won* on the currency market, to prevent the value of the *won* from falling, the South Korean government must support the *won*'s value by purchasing *won* on the open market (by spending its hard currency reserves, its official reserves) until the excess supply is eliminated. Under a floating rate system, the government possesses no such responsibility, and the role of official reserves is diminished.

 ## THE BALANCE OF PAYMENTS IN TOTAL

Table 7.3 provides the official balance of payments for the United States as presented by the International Monetary Fund (IMF), the multinational organization that collects these statistics for more than 160 different countries around the globe. It gives a comprehensive overview of how the individual accounts are combined to create some of the most useful summary measures for multinational business managers.

The Current Account (line A in Table 7.3), the Capital Account (line B), and the Financial Account (line C) combine to form the basic balance (Total, Groups A through C). This is one of the most frequently used summary measures of the BOP. It is used to describe the international economic activity of the nation as determined by market forces, not by government decisions (such as currency market intervention). The U.S. basic balance totaled a deficit of $13 billion in 2006. A second frequently used summary measure, the overall balance, also called the official settlements balance (Total of Groups A to D in Table 7.3), was at a deficit of $31 billion in 2006.

The meaning of the balance of payments has changed over the past 30 years. As long as most of the major industrial countries were still operating under fixed exchange rates, the interpretation of the BOP was relatively straightforward. A surplus in the BOP implied that the

Quick Take   *How Cooked Are China's Books?*

Even as China makes the heady transformation into an economic powerhouse, the rapidly shifting nature of its market system makes it nearly impossible to pin down the nation's GDP with any accuracy. While the central government reported gains of 7.3 percent in 2001, statistics gleaned from individual provinces put the figure a full two points higher. And though the official figure, created from sample surveys rather than hard-core statistical reports, may be suspect, so too are the growth rates reported at the provincial level. Unfortunately, there is a widespread tendency for local authorities to pump up their numbers for political gain. During a ten-month period, there were, for example, a staggering 62,000 offences against China's statistics laws.

Outside China, economists rate actual GDP lower than either report. Citing such factors as overly low inflation estimates and severe overvaluation of unsold goods produced by state-owned factories, a recent report by the University of Pittsburgh pins China's GDP at about half the official figure. The report considered such indicators as energy consumption, employment, and consumer prices in creating its estimates.

Even so, economists in Beijing defend the official figure, explaining that under-reporting in affluent provinces—a way of avoiding paying taxes to central government—makes up for other falsified figures.

SOURCE: "How Cooked Are the Books?" *The Economist*, March 14, 2002, p. 45.

---

demand for the country's currency exceeded the supply and that the government should then allow the currency value to increase (revalue) or to intervene and accumulate additional foreign currency reserves in the Official Reserves Account. This would occur as the government sold its own currency in exchange for other currencies, thus building up its stores of hard currencies. A deficit in the BOP implied an excess supply of the country's currency on world

Quick Take   *India Borrows Its Way Out of Trouble*

In October 2000, India hit on a not-so-novel idea to shield an economy made vulnerable by high international oil prices. The government floated a scheme for State Bank of India, the country's largest bank, to sell five-year foreign currency deposits to expatriate Indians to help tackle a worsening balance of payments situation. By October 2001, SBI, whose largest owner is the Indian Central Bank, had collected $5.5 billion from the sale of India Millennium Deposits (IMD).

India's oil import bill was also expected to double to about $18 billion. A widening trade deficit and a sell-off by foreign portfolio investors put the balance of payments in the red by about $1 billion in the quarter that ended June 2000, as compared with a surplus of $3.32 billion in the previous quarter. The rupee had lost around 6 percent of its value against the dollar.

SOURCES: "An Incredible Shrinking Government," *The Economist*, February 7, 2002, **http://www.economist.com**; Niharika Bisaria, "Going on a Millennium Hunt," October 18, 2001, **http://www. hometrade.com**; Kala Rao, "India Tries to Borrow Its Way Out of Trouble," *Euromoney*, London, November 2000.

TABLE 7.3 The United States Balance of Payments, Analytic Presentation, 1993-2006 (billions of US dollars)

	1993	1994	1995	1996	1997	1998	1999	2000	2001	2002	2003	2004	2005	2006
A. Current Account	**-82**	**-118**	**-110**	**-121**	**-140**	**-217**	**-324**	**-445**	**-377**	**-454**	**-520**	**-640**	**-755**	**-811**
Goods: exports fob	459	505	577	614	680	672	687	775	722	685	717	811	898	1027
Goods: imports fob	-589	-669	-749	-803	-877	-917	-1030	-1224	-1146	-1165	-1261	-1477	-1682	-1861
Balance on Goods	-131	-164	-172	-189	-196	-245	-343	-450	-424	-479	-544	-666	-783	-835
Services: credit	184	199	217	238	255	260	271	291	286	289	299	346	385	419
Services: debit	-122	-132	-142	-151	-166	-182	-189	-217	-219	-227	-250	-292	-316	-343
Balance on Goods and Services	-69	-97	-96	-102	-108	-167	-262	-376	-358	-418	-495	-612	-714	-759
Income: credit	134	165	212	226	261	259	285	353	291	281	321	402	505	650
Income: debit	-110	-149	-191	-205	-252	-265	-299	-368	-259	-254	-275	-346	-457	-614
Balance on Goods, Services, and Income	45	-80	-76	-81	-99	-173	-275	-391	-326	-390	-449	-556	-666	-722
Current transfers: credit	6	6	8	9	8	9	9	10	9	12	15	20	19	24
Current transfers: debit	-44	-45	-42	-49	-49	-54	-58	-64	-60	-76	-86	-105	-107	-114
B. Capital Account	**0**	**0**	**0**	**1**	**0**	**1**	**-4**	**1**	**-1**	**-1**	**-3**	**-2**	**-4**	**-4**
Capital account: credit	0	0	1	1	0	1	0	1	1	1	1	1	1	1
Capital account: debit	0	-1	0	0	0	0	-4	0	-2	-2	-4	-3	-5	-5
Total, Groups A Plus B	***-83***	***-119***	***-110***	***-120***	***-139***	***-217***	***-328***	***-444***	***-379***	***-455***	***-524***	***-643***	***-759***	***-815***
C. Financial Account	**83**	**125**	**123**	**165**	**273**	**152**	**368**	**444**	**408**	**507**	**537**	**554**	**763**	**802**
Direct investment	-33	-34	-41	-5	1	36	146	135	25	-70	-86	-133	117	-55
Direct investment abroad	-84	-80	-99	-92	-105	-143	-155	-152	-142	-154	-150	-279	8	-235
Direct investment in United States	51	46	58	87	106	178	301	288	167	84	64	146	109	181
Portfolio investment assets	-146	-60	-123	-150	-119	-136	-131	-125	-91	-49	-123	-153	-203	-426
Equity securities	-63	-48	-65	-83	-58	-101	-114	-100	-109	-17	-118	-85	-143	-139
Debt securities	-83	-12	-57	-67	-61	-35	-17	-25	18	-32	-5	-69	-61	-288
Portfolio investment liabilities	111	139	237	368	386	269	355	475	428	428	550	867	832	1017
Equity securities	21	1	17	11	68	42	112	194	121	54	34	62	89	149
Debt securities	90	139	221	357	318	227	242	281	307	374	516	806	743	869
Other investment assets	31	-41	-121	-179	-263	-74	-159	-303	-142	-88	-54	-475	-245	-396
Monetary authorities	0	0	0	0	0	0	0	0	0	0	0	0	0	
General government	0	0	-1	-1	0	0	3	-1	0	0	1	2	6	5
Banks	31	-4	-75	-92	-141	-36	-76	-138	-136	-38	-26	-353	-161	-297
Other sectors	1	-36	-45	-86	-122	-38	-86	-164	-9	-50	-29	-124	-90	-104
Other investment liabilities	120	120	170	132	268	57	158	262	188	286	250	449	263	662
Monetary authorities	68	10	47	57	-19	7	25	-7	35	72	17	15	19	13
General government	1	3	1	1	-3	-3	-1	-1	-2	0	-1	0	0	3
Banks	40	108	64	22	171	30	67	94	88	118	136	346	220	317
Other sectors	11	0	59	52	118	23	67	176	66	96	98	88	24	329
Total, Groups A Through C	***0***	***6***	***14***	***45***	***133***	***-65***	***40***	***0***	***29***	***51***	***14***	***-89***	***4***	***-13***
D. Net Errors and Omissions	**1**	**-11**	**-4**	**-52**	**-132**	**72**	**70**	**-68**	**-14**	**-42**	**-13**	**86**	**-18**	**-18**
Total, Groups A Through D	***1***	***-5***	***10***	***-7***	***1***	***7***	***110***	***-68***	***15***	***9***	***0***	***-3***	***-14***	***-31***
E. Reserves and Related Items	**-1**	**5**	**-10**	**7**	**-1**	**-7**	**9**	**0**	**-5**	**-4**	**2**	**3**	**14**	**2**

SOURCE: International Monetary Fund, *Balance of Payments Statistics Yearbook 2007*, p. 1038.
Note: Totals may not match original source due to rounding.

markets, and the government would then either devalue the currency or expend its official reserves to support its value. But the transition to floating exchange rate regimes in the 1970s (described in the following chapter) changed the focus from the total BOP to its various subaccounts like the Current and Financial Account balances. These are the indicators of economic activities and currency repercussions to come. The crises in Mexico (1994), Asia (1997), Turkey (2001), and Argentina and Venezuela (2002) highlight the continuing changes in the role of the balance of payments.

Quick Take: India Borrows Its Way Out of Trouble describes India's recent initiative to solve a worsening balance of trade by attracting the offshore capital held by its own residents.

THE BALANCE OF PAYMENTS AND ECONOMIC CRISES

International managers can use the sum of cross-border international economic activity—the balance of payments—to forecast economic conditions and, in some cases, the likelihood of economic crises. The mechanics of international economic crisis often follow a similar path of development:

4 LEARNING OBJECTIVE

1. A country that experiences rapidly expanding current account deficits will simultaneously build financial account surpluses (the inverse relationship noted previously in this chapter).
2. The capital that flows into a country, giving rise to the financial account surplus, acts as the "financing" for the growing merchandise/services deficits—the constituent components of the current account deficit.
3. Some event, whether it be a report, a speech, an action by a government or business inside or outside the country, raises the question of the country's economic stability. Investors of many kinds, portfolio and direct investors in the country, fearing economic problems in the near future, withdraw capital from the country rapidly to avoid any exposure to this risk. This is prudent for the individual but catastrophic for the whole if all individuals move similarly.
4. The rapid withdrawal of capital from the country, so-called "capital flight," results in the loss of the financial account surplus, creating a severe deficit in the country's overall balance of payments. This is typically accompanied by rapid currency depreciation (if a floating-rate currency) or currency devaluation (if a fixed-rate currency).

International debt and economic crises have occurred for as long as there has been international trade and commerce. And they will occur again. Each crisis has its own unique characteristics, but all follow the economic fundamentals described above. (The one additional factor that differentiates many of the crises is whether inflation is a component.) The recent Asian economic crisis was a devastating reminder of the tenuous nature of international economic relationships.

The Asian Crisis

The roots of the Asian currency crisis extended from a fundamental change in the economics of the region—the transition of many Asian nations from net exporters to net importers. Starting as early as 1990 in Thailand, the rapidly expanding economies of the Far East began importing more than they exported, requiring major net capital inflows to support their currencies. As long as the capital continued to flow in—for manufacturing plants, dam projects, infrastructure development, and even real estate speculation—the pegged exchange rates of the region could be maintained. When the investment capital inflows stopped, however, crisis was inevitable.

The most visible roots of the crisis were the excesses in capital flows into Thailand in 1996 and early 1997. With rapid economic growth and rising profits forming the backdrop, Thai firms, banks, and finance companies had ready access to capital on the international markets, finding cheap U.S. dollar loans offshore. Thai banks continued to raise capital internationally, extending credit to a variety of domestic investments and enterprises beyond the level that the Thai economy could support. Capital flows into the Thai market hit record rates, pouring into investments of all kinds, including manufacturing, real estate, and even equity market margin-lending. As the investment "bubble" expanded, some participants raised questions about the economy's ability to repay the rising debt. The *baht* came under sudden and severe pressure.

CURRENCY COLLAPSE The Thai government and central bank intervened in the foreign exchange markets both directly (using up precious hard-currency reserves) and indirectly (by raising interest rates to attempt to stop the continual outflow). The Thai investment markets ground to a halt, causing massive currency losses and bank failures. On July 2, 1997, the Thai Central Bank, which had been expending massive amounts of its limited foreign exchange reserves to defend the *baht*'s value, finally allowed the *baht* to float (or sink in this case). The *baht* fell 17 percent against the U.S. dollar and over 12 percent against the Japanese yen in a matter of hours. By November, the *baht* had fallen from *baht* 25/US$ to *baht* 40/US$, a fall of about 38 percent. Thailand was not alone in creating massive current account deficits in the period leading up to 1997. In fact, with the rather special exceptions of China and Singapore, all of East Asia—Indonesia, North and South Korea, Malaysia, and the Philippines—was in current-account deficit beginning in 1994.

Within days, a number of neighboring Asian nations, some with and some without characteristics similar to Thailand, came under speculative attack by currency traders and capital markets. The Philippine peso, the Malaysian *ringgit*, and the Indonesian *rupiah* all fell within months. In late October, Taiwan caught the markets off-balance with a surprise competitive devaluation of 15 percent. The Taiwanese devaluation seemed only to renew the momentum of the crisis. Although the Hong Kong dollar survived (at great expense to the central bank's foreign exchange reserves), the Korean *won* was not so lucky. In November the historically stable Korean *won* also fell victim, falling from *won* 900/US$ to more than *won* 1,100/US$. By the end of November the Korean government was in the process of negotiating a US$50 billion bailout of its financial sector with the IMF. The only currency that had not fallen besides the Hong Kong dollar was the Chinese *yuan renminbi*, which was not freely convertible. Although the *yuan renminbi* had not been devalued, there was rising speculation that the Chinese government would devalue it for competitive reasons.

CAUSES OF ECONOMIC CRISIS The Asian economic crisis—the crisis was more than just a currency collapse—had many roots besides the traditional balance of payments difficulties. The causes are different in each country, yet there are specific underlying similarities that allow for comparison: corporate socialism, corporate governance, and banking stability and management.

Corporate Socialism Although Western markets have long known the cold indifference of the free market, the countries of post–World War II Asia have known mostly the good. Because of the influence of government and politics in the business arena, even in the event of failure, governments would not allow firms to fail, workers to lose their jobs, or banks to close. When

WORLD VIEW

OFFICIAL FOREIGN EXCHANGE RESERVES: THE RISE OF CHINA

The rise of the Chinese economy has been accompanied by a rise in its current account surplus and, subsequently, its accumulation of foreign exchange reserves. As illustrated by Exhibit A, China's foreign exchange reserves quintupled between 2002 and 2006, from $200 billion to $1.0 trillion. There is no real precedent in global financial history for this build-up in foreign exchange reserves. These reserves allow the Chinese government to manage the value of the Chinese *yuan* (also referred to as the *renminbi*) and its impact on Chinese competitiveness in the world economy. The magnitude of these reserves will allow the Chinese government to maintain a relatively stable managed fixed rate of the *yuan* against other major currencies like the U.S. dollar as long as it chooses.

The sheer size and magnitude of China's official reserves (excluding gold) is illustrated by Exhibit B, which shows the 17 largest

countries in terms of their reserve holdings in 2007. China's reserves are roughly $200 billion larger than the second-largest country reserves, those of Japan. Note that only five countries even have reserves that exceed $200 billion. The United States, with roughly $65 billion in reserves, pales in comparison to the growing caches of the booming Asian economies.

Many suggestions have been made as to what China could do with its growing reserves. Most of the proposals—stockpiling oil or other commodities, for example—would only result in pushing up the price of these other critical global commodities, while not really stopping the accumulation of official reserves. The only real solution to this "problem," if it is a problem, is to reduce the Chinese current account surplus or allow the yuan to float to a stronger value. Both solutions, however, are not in line with China's current political plan.

EXHIBIT A China's Foreign Exchange Rates (billions of US$)

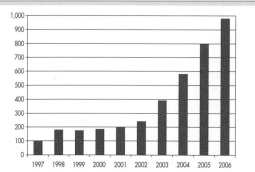

SOURCE: Thomson Datastream, FT research, *Financial Times*, Monday September 25, 2006. (2006 is estimate.)

EXHIBIT B Rising Reserves in Asia (billions of US$)

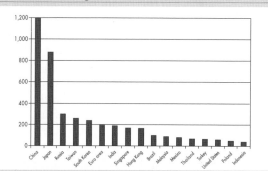

SOURCE: National statistics, Thomson Datastream, *The Economist*, May 29, 2007.

the problems reached the size seen in 1997, the business liability exceeded the capacities of governments to bail businesses out. Practices that had persisted for decades without challenge, such as lifetime employment, were now no longer sustainable. The result was a painful lesson in the harshness of the marketplace.

Corporate Governance An expression largely unused until the 1990s, corporate governance refers to the complex process of how a firm is managed and operated, to whom it is accountable, and how it reacts to changing business conditions. There is little doubt that many firms operating within the Far Eastern business environments mainly were controlled by either families or groups related to the governing party or body of the country. The interests

Culture Clues   When invited to the home of an Arab businessman for dinner, skip your previous meal so that you have a keen appetite. Proper appreciation of a meal is shown by eating large quantities.

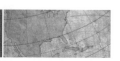

of stockholders and creditors were often secondary at best to the primary motivations of corporate management. Without the motivation to focus on "the bottom line," the bottom line deteriorated.

Banking Liquidity and Management Banking is one of the sectors that have fallen out of fashion in the past two decades. Bank regulatory structures and markets have been deregulated nearly without exception around the globe. The central role played by banks in the conduct of business, however, was largely ignored and underestimated.

As firms across Asia collapsed, as government coffers were emptied, as speculative investments made by the banks themselves failed, banks closed. Without banks, the "plumbing" of business conduct was shut down. Firms could not obtain the necessary working-capital financing they needed to manufacture their products or provide their services. This pivotal role of banking liquidity was the focus of the International Monetary Fund's bail-out efforts.

GLOBAL EFFECTS OF ECONOMIC CRISIS The Asian economic crisis had global impact. What started as a currency crisis quickly became a region-wide recession (or depression, depending on the definition).[3] The slowed economies of the region quickly caused major reductions in world demand for many products, especially commodities. World oil markets, copper markets, and agricultural products all saw severe price falls as demand fell. These price falls were immediately noticeable in declining earnings and growth prospects for other emerging economies.

The post-1997 period has been one of dramatic reversal for the countries of East Asia. Every nation within East Asia listed has run a current account surplus as a result of massive recession (imports fell voluntarily, as well as being restricted by governments), significant domestic currency devaluation (resulting in significantly lower purchasing power, meaning the countries could no longer afford to purchase imports), and rising exports (as currency devaluation made a country's merchandise relatively cheaper for countries in other parts of the world to purchase). Unfortunately, the adjustment period has been one of massive unemployment, social disruption, and economic reconstruction with high human cost.

SUMMARY

Global trade flows are captured in the balance of payments, the summary statement of all international transactions between one country and all other countries. Countries with different government policies toward international trade and investment, or different levels of economic development, differ in their balance of payments. The monitoring of the various subaccounts of a country's balance of payments activity is helpful to decision-makers and policymakers at all levels of government and industry in detecting the underlying trends and movements of fundamental economic forces driving a country's international economic activity.

The balance of payments is a flow statement, summarizing all the international transactions that occur across the geographic boundaries of the nation over a period of time, typically a year. Because of its use of double-entry bookkeeping, the BOP must always balance in theory, though in practice there are substantial imbalances as a result of statistical errors and misreporting of current account and capital account flows.

The first major subaccount of the BOP is the Current Account. It summarizes income and payment flows within the current year or current accounting period. It consists of four subcategories: goods trade, services trade, income, and current transfers.

The second major subaccount of the BOP is the Capital and Financial Account. The Capital Account is made up of transfers of financial assets and of nonproduced/ nonfinancial assets. The Financial Account consists of direct investment, portfolio investment, and other asset investment. Although most nations strive for current account surpluses, it is not clear that a balance on current or capital account, or a surplus on current account, is either sustainable or desirable.

Using statistics from more than 160 countries, the IMF created a comprehensive overview of some of the most useful measures utilized by multinational business managers. See Table 7.3.

International managers can use the BOP to forecast economic conditions and, in some cases, the likelihood of economic crises. The Asian currency crisis had its roots in traditional balance of payment difficulties. Other causes included failures in corporate socialism, corporate governance, and banking liquidity and management.

KEY TERMS AND CONCEPTS

Balance of payments (BOP)	services trade account	net errors and omissions
current account	income account	account
financial account	current transfer account	official reserves account
double-entry bookkeeping	direct investment account	fixed exchange rate
goods trade account	portfolio investment account	floating exchange rate

REVIEW QUESTIONS

1. Why must a country's balance of payments always be balanced in theory?
2. What is the difference between the merchandise trade balance (BOT) and the current account balance?
3. What is service trade?
4. What is the difference between the Current Account and the Capital Account?
5. While the United States "suffered" a current account deficit and a capital account surplus in the 1980s, what were the respective balances of Japan doing?
6. How do exchange-rate changes alter trade so that the trade balance actually improves when the domestic currency depreciates?
7. How have trade balances in Asia contributed to the cause of the current Asian crisis?
8. Summarize the effects of the Asian crisis on the global economy.

CRITICAL SKILL BUILDERS

1. Why is foreign direct investment so much more controversial than foreign portfolio investment? How did this relate to Mexico in the 1990s?
2. What does it mean for the United States to be one of the world's most-indebted countries? Should this be a concern for government policymakers?
3. In pairs or small groups, use your library's resources or the Internet to find an up-to-date balance of payments report for an emerging economy. Discuss any patterns you see that may be considered red flags for companies exporting to or investing in that nation. Present your findings to the rest of the class.
4. In groups, discuss the causes and effects of a currency crisis. Refer to recent events in Asia and South America.
5. How might businesses in a developing nation benefit or suffer from an ongoing economic crisis in a neighboring emergent economy? Discuss.

ON THE WEB

1. The IMF, the World Bank, and the United Nations are only a few of the major world organizations that track, report, and aid international economic and financial development. Using these web sites and others that may be linked to them, briefly summarize the economic outlook for the developed and emerging nations of the world. For example, the full text of Chapter 1 of the World Economic Outlook published annually by the World Bank is available through the IMF's Web page.

International Monetary Fund	**http://www.imf.org**
United Nations	**http://www.unsystem.org**
The World Bank	**http://www.worldbank.org**
Europa (EU) Homepage	**http://www.europa.eu.int**
Bank for International Settlements	**http://www.bis.org**

2. Current economic and financial statistics and commentaries are available via the IMF's web page under "What's New," "Fund Rates," and the "IMF Committee on Balance of Payments Statistics." For an in-depth examination of the IMF's ongoing initiative on the validity of these statistics, termed metadata, visit the IMF's Dissemination Standards Bulletin Board listed below.

International Monetary Fund	**http://www.imf.org**
IMF's Dissemination Standards Bulletin Board	**http://www.dsbb.imf.org**

3. Visit Moody's sovereign ceilings and foreign-currency ratings service site on the Web to evaluate what progress is being made in the nations of the Far East on recovering their perceived creditworthiness.

Moody's Sovereign Ceilings	**http://www.moodys.com**

ENDNOTES

1. "A Survey of China," The Economist, April 8, 2000, pp. 1–16; "Trade Gap Shrinks," MSNBC, February 21, 2002; Kenichi Ohmae, "Profits and Perils of China, Inc.," Strategy and Business, First Quarter, 2002, pp. 68–79; Chi Lo, "Will China Re-Value the Renminbi?" **http://www.financeasia.com**, accessed January 3, 2003; Chi Lo, "China's FDI Strength Is Good for Asia," **http://www.financeasia.com**, accessed January 3, 2003.
2. The official terminology used throughout this chapter, unless otherwise noted, is that of the International Monetary Fund (IMF). Since the IMF is the primary source of similar statistics for balance of payments and economic performance worldwide, it is more general than other terminology forms, such as that employed by the U.S. Department of Commerce.
3. The magnitude of the economic devastation in Asia is still largely unappreciated by Westerners. At a recent conference sponsored by the Milken Institute in Los Angeles, a speaker noted that the preoccupation with the economic problems of Indonesia was incomprehensible since "the total gross domestic product of Indonesia is roughly the size of North Carolina." The following speaker provided a rebuttal, noting that the last time he checked, "North Carolina did not have a population of 220 million people."

PART 4

GLOBAL FINANCE

Operating internationally requires managers to be aware of a highly complex environment that is constantly in flux. Part 4 explores the workings of the international monetary system and its influence on the conduct of business. By understanding international currency exchange — its guiding principles and its operations — it is possible to identify vital linkages between exchange rates and interest rates. Part 4 concludes with a strategic investigation of financial management, accounting, and taxation as they affect the conduct of business across borders.

CHAPTER 8

FOREIGN EXCHANGE AND GLOBAL FINANCIAL MARKETS

Iceland — A Small Country in a Global Capital Market

The last one or two years had been something of a shock to the Icelandic people. Long used to being ignored in the world, Iceland's economic situation and its interest rates — some of the highest in the world recently — had suddenly garnered much international attention.

Iceland's economy had been growing at record rates in recent years. Gross domestic product had grown at just over 8 percent in 2004, 6 percent in 2005, and was still above 4 percent at the end of 2006. While the average unemployment rate of the major economic powers was roughly 6 percent, Iceland's over-heating economy had only 3 percent unemployment. But accompanying rapid economic growth in a small economy, as happens frequently in economic history, inflation raises its ugly head. And of course the central bank reacts predictably: slowing money supply growth to try and control inflationary forces. The result is increasing interest rates.

These higher interest rates had a number of different impacts. First, Iceland was considered very stable and low-risk in the international marketplace. The Icelandic government had an investment-grade credit rating. So foreign investors, particularly the money market investors behind the carry trade made famous in Japan, found Icelandic money market interest rates very attractive. Capital from foreign investors, American and European, flowed into the big four Icelandic banks and money market accounts of all kinds to take advantage of these higher money market rates.

But the carry trade depends on exchange rates as well as interest rates. A foreign investor exchanging U.S. dollars or

Iceland's Interest & Exchange Rates Swing

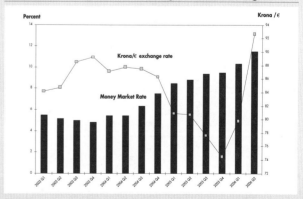

SOURCE: International Monetary Fund, *International Financial Statistics*, monthly.

euros for Icelandic krona, and then investing in the higher-yielding money market rates in Iceland, must feel relatively confident that the krona will not fall in value versus their currency by the time they need to bring the money back home. And they did. The krona had actually strengthened consistently against both the dollar and the euro in 2004 and 2005. By the end of 2005, the krona was stronger against both the dollar and the euro than it had been since 2000. But as the krona continued to strengthen against other major currencies, its export competitiveness declined. Iceland's current account, already in deficit, began to skyrocket in size. Iceland's current account deficit was 16 percent of its gross domestic product (GDP) at the end of 2005 and was expected to stay that high through the remainder of 2006. For comparison, other countries with current account deficits of note were only half that of Iceland's: New Zealand (8 percent), Hungary (7 percent), and even the United States (6 percent). Not only was Iceland's current account in deficit, but the size of its outstanding debt in total, accumulated over a number of years, was troublesome. Suddenly, in February 2006, things changed. Capital started flowing out of Iceland. The size of the country's current account deficit had become front-page news, and major

investors, including those in the carry trade, feared that the krona would fall, undermining their interest arbitrage gains. Foreign investors dumped krona at a record rate. Over the following two quarters, the Icelandic krona plummeted in value against the euro and the dollar, although money market interest rates were still high and attractive in relative terms. But investors were no longer convinced. Their fear of a falling krona had become a self-fulfilling prophecy. In the end, the speculators caused to happen exactly what they feared would happen: a weaker Icelandic krona.

As You Read This Chapter

1. Consider how the size of a country — its economy and its financial markets — may be influenced by a global financial environment in which capital can move across borders and currencies in enormous volume in mere seconds.
2. Think about how increasingly open economies, like Iceland's, support the growth of global business through open exchange of currency and capital.

Global financial markets serve as links between the financial markets of individual countries and as independent markets outside the jurisdiction of any one country. The market for currencies is at the heart of this international financial market. International trade and investment transactions are often denominated in a foreign currency, so the purchase of the currency precedes the purchase of goods, services, or assets.

This chapter begins by providing a detailed guide to the structure and functions of the foreign currency markets. It then explores the international financial markets and the securities markets that connect the financial markets of individual nations. All firms striving to attain or preserve competitiveness in the global arena must work with and within the frameworks of these markets, which operate independently of the jurisdiction or supervision of governmental authorities.

THE PURPOSE OF EXCHANGE RATES

If countries are to trade, they must be able to exchange currencies. To buy wheat or corn or DVD players, the buyer must first have the currency in which the product is sold. An American firm purchasing consumer electronic products manufactured in Japan must first exchange its U.S. dollars for Japanese yen, then purchase the products. The exchange of one country's currency for another should be a relatively simple transaction, but as we shall see, it's not.

1 LEARNING OBJECTIVE

What Is a Currency Worth?

At what rate should one currency be exchanged for another? For example, what should the exchange rate be between the U.S. dollar and the Japanese yen? The simplest answer is that the exchange rate should equalize purchasing power. For example, if the price of a movie ticket in the United States is $6, the "correct" exchange rate would be one that exchanges $6 for the amount of Japanese yen it would take to purchase a movie ticket in Japan. If ticket prices are ¥540 (¥ is a common symbol for the yen) in Japan, then the exchange rate that would equalize purchasing power would be:

$$\frac{¥540}{\$6} = \frac{¥90}{\$}$$

PURCHASING POWER PARITY (PPP)

A theory that the prices of tradable goods will tend to equalize across countries.

LAW OF ONE PRICE

The theory that the relative prices of any single good between countries, expressed in each country's currency, is representative of the proper or appropriate exchange rate value.

Therefore, if the exchange rate between the two currencies is ¥90/$, moviegoers can purchase tickets, regardless of which country they are in. This is the theory of **purchasing power parity (PPP)**, generally considered the definition of what exchange rates ideally should be. The purchasing power parity exchange rate is simply the rate that equalizes the price of the identical product or service in two different currencies:

Price in Japan = Exchange rate × Price in the U.S.

If the price of the same product in each currency is $P^¥$ and $P^\$$, and the spot exchange rate between the Japanese yen and the U.S. dollar is $S¥/\$$, the price in yen is simply the price in dollars multiplied by the spot exchange rate:

$$P^¥ = S^{¥/\$} \times P^\$$$

If this is rearranged (dividing both sides by $P^\$$), the spot exchange rate between the Japanese yen and the U.S. dollar is the ratio of the two product prices:

$$S^{¥/\$} = \frac{P^¥}{P^\$}$$

These prices could be the price of just one good or service, such as the movie ticket mentioned previously, or they could be price indices for each country that cover many different goods and services. Either form is an attempt to find comparable products in different countries (and currencies) in order to determine an exchange rate based on purchasing power parity. The question then is whether this logical approach to exchange rates actually works in practice.

The Law of One Price

The version of purchasing power parity that estimates the exchange rate between two currencies using just one good or service as a measure of the proper exchange for all goods and services is called the **Law of One Price**. To apply the theory to actual prices across countries, we need to select a product that is identical in quality and content in every country. To be truly theoretically correct, we would want such a product to be produced entirely domestically, so that there are no import factors in its construction.

Where would one find such a perfect product? McDonald's. Table 8.1 presents what *The Economist* magazine calls "the golden-arches standard." What McDonald's provides is a product that is essentially the same the world over and is produced and consumed entirely domestically.

The Big Mac Index compares the actual exchange rate with the exchange rate implied by the purchasing power parity measurement of comparing Big Mac prices across countries. For example, say the average price of a Big Mac in the U.S. on a given date is $3.41. On the same

Foreign exchange traders at banks can move millions of dollars, yen, or marks around the world with a few keystrokes on their networked computers. The deregulation of international capital flows contributes to faster, cheaper transactions in the currency markets.

TABLE 8.1 The Hamburger Standard

	BIG MAC PRICES		IMPLIED PPP† OF THE DOLLAR	ACTUAL DOLLAR EXCHANGE RATE JULY 2nd	UNDER(−) / OVER(+) VALUATION AGAINST THE DOLLAR, %
	IN LOCAL CURRENCY	IN DOLLARS			
United States‡	$3.41	3.41			
Argentina	Peso 8.25	2.67	2.42	3.09	−22
Australia	A$3.45	2.95	1.01	1.17	−14
Brazil	Real 6.90	3.61	2.02	1.91	+6
Britain	£1.99	4.01	1.71§	2.01§	+18
Canada	C$3.88	3.68	1.14	1.05	+8
Chile	Peso 1,565	2.97	459	527	−13
China	Yuan 11.0	1.45	3.23	7.60	−58
Czech Republic	Koruna 52.9	2.51	15.5	21.1	−27
Denmark	DKr 27.75	5.08	8.14	5.46	+49
Egypt	Pound 9.54	1.68	2.80	5.69	−51
Euro area**	€3.06	4.17	1.12††	1.36††	+22
Hong Kong	HK$12.0	1.54	3.52	7.82	−55
Hungary	Forint 600	3.33	176	180	−2
Indonesia	Rupiah 15,900	1.76	4,663	9,015	−48
Japan	¥280	2.29	82.1	122	−33
Malaysia	Ringgit 5.50	1.60	1.61	3.43	−53
Mexico	Peso 29.0	2.69	8.50	10.8	−21
New Zealand	NZ$4.60	3.59	1.35	1.28	+5
Peru	New Sol 9.50	3.00	2.79	3.17	−12
Philippines	Peso 85.0	1.85	24.9	45.9	−46
Poland	Zloty 6.90	2.51	2.02	2.75	−26
Russia	Rouble 52.0	2.03	15.2	25.6	−41
Singapore	S$3.95	2.59	1.16	1.52	−24
South Africa	Rand 15.5	2.22	4.55	6.97	−35
South Korea	Won 2,900	3.14	850	923	−8
Sweden	SKr33.0	4.86	9.68	6.79	+42
Switzerland	SFr6.30	5.20	1.85	1.21	+53
Taiwan	NT$75.0	2.29	22.0	32.8	−33
Thailand	Baht 62.0	1.80	18.2	34.5	−47
Turkey	Lire 4.75	3.66	1.39	1.30	+7
Venezuela	Bolivar 7,400	3.45	2,170	2,147	+1
Colombia	Peso 6,900	3.53	2,023	1,956	+3
Costa Rica	Colon 1,130	2.18	331	519	−36
Estonia	Kroon 30.0	2.61	8.80	11.5	−23
Iceland	Kronur 469	7.61	138	61.7	+123
Latvia	Lats 1.39	2.72	0.41	0.51	−20
Lithuania	Litas 6.60	2.61	1.94	2.53	−24
Norway	Kroner 40.0	6.88	11.7	5.81	+102
Pakistan	Rupee 140	2.32	41.1	60.4	−32
Pataguay	Guarani 10,500	2.04	3,079	5,145	−40
Saudi Arabia	Riyal 9.00	2.40	2.64	3.75	−30
Slovakia	Koruna 61.3	2.49	18.0	24.6	−27
Sri Lanka	Rupee 210	1.89	61.6	111	−45
UAE	Dirhams 10.0	2.72	2.93	3.67	−20
Ukraine	Hryvnia 9.25	1.84	2.71	5.03	−46
Uruguay	Peso 62.0	2.59	18.2	23.9	−24

†Purchasing-power parity: local price divided by price in United States; ‡Average of New York, Chicago, Atlanta and San Francisco §Dollars per pound; **Weighted average of prices in euro area; ††Dollars per euro

SOURCES: McDonald's; *The Economist*

date, the price of a Big Mac in Canada, in Canadian dollars, is C\$3.88. This then is used to calculate the PPP exchange rate as before:

$$\frac{\text{C\$3.88 per Big Mac}}{\text{\$3.41 per Big Mac}} = \text{C\$1.1378/\$}$$

The exchange rate between the Canadian dollar and the U.S. dollar should be C\$1.1378/\$, according to a PPP comparison of Big Mac prices. The actual exchange rate on the date of comparison was C\$1.05/\$. This means that each U.S. dollar was actually worth 1.05 Canadian dollars, when the index indicates that each U.S. dollar should have been worth 1.1378 Canadian dollars. Therefore, if one is to believe in the Big Mac index, the Canadian dollar was overvalued by 8 percent.

 # THE MARKET FOR CURRENCIES

FOREIGN CURRENCY EXCHANGE RATE

The price of any one country's currency in terms of another country's currency.

The price of any one country's currency in terms of another country's currency is called a **foreign currency exchange rate**. For example, the exchange rate between the U.S. dollar (\$ or USD) and the European euro (€ or EUR) may be "0.8622 dollars per euro," or simply abbreviated as \$0.8622/€. This is the same exchange rate as when stated "EUR1.00 = USD .8622." Because most international business activities require at least one of the two parties to first purchase the country's currency before purchasing any good, service, or asset, a proper understanding of exchange rates and exchange-rate markets is very important to the conduct of international business.

A word about currency symbols: As already noted, the letters USD and EUR are often used as the symbols for the U.S. dollar and the European Union's euro. These are the computer symbols (ISO-4217 codes). The field of international finance suffers, however, from a lack of agreement when it comes to currency abbreviations.

DIRECT EXCHANGE QUOTATION

A foreign exchange quotation that specifies the amount of home-country currency needed to purchase one unit of foreign currency.

This chapter uses the more common symbols used in the financial press — \$ and € in this case. As a practitioner of international finance, however, stay on your toes. Every market, every country, and every firm, may have its own set of symbols. For example, the symbol for the British pound sterling can be £ (the pound symbol), GBP (Great Britain pound), STG (British pound sterling), ST£ (pound sterling), or UKL (United Kingdom pound).

INDIRECT EXCHANGE QUOTATION

Foreign exchange quotation that specifies the units of foreign currency that could be purchased with one unit of the home currency.

Exchange-Rate Quotations and Terminology

The order in which the foreign exchange rate is stated is sometimes confusing to the uninitiated. For example, when the rate between the U.S. dollar and the European euro was stated as \$0.8622/€, a **direct exchange quotation** on the U.S. dollar was used. This is simultaneously an **indirect exchange quotation** on the European euro. The direct quote on any currency refers to the currency stated first; an indirect quotation refers to the subject currency that is stated second. Figure 8.1 illustrates both direct and indirect quotations for major world currencies, for Wednesday, January 30, 2008.

SPOT EXCHANGE RATES

Contracts that provide for two parties to exchange currencies, with delivery in two business days.

Most of the quotations listed in Figure 8.1 are **spot exchange rates**. A spot transaction is the exchange of currencies for immediate delivery. Although it is defined as immediate, in actual practice, settlement occurs two business days following the agreed-upon exchange. The other time-related quotations listed in Figure 8.1 are the forward exchange rates. **Forward exchange rates** are contracts that provide for two parties to exchange currencies on a future date at an agreed-upon exchange rate.

FORWARD EXCHANGE RATES

Contracts that provide for two parties to exchange currencies on a future date at an agreed-upon exchange rate.

Forwards are typically traded for the major volume currencies for maturities of one, three, and six months (from the present date). The forward, like the basic spot exchange, can be for any amount of currency. Forward contracts serve a variety of purposes, but their primary

WORLD VIEW

MALTA, TAXATION, AND THE EU

In the marinas of Malta there is much talk of gleaming new yachts snapped up by buyers with wads of cash and little interest in sailing. The Maltese lira will disappear in January 2008, when the tiny Mediterranean archipelago joins the euro area. Many Maltese have savings stashed under mattresses and are scared of attracting the taxman's attention if they go to the bank to convert them to euros. Several tax amnesties have yielded little in the way of deposits. Instead, Maltese seem to be rushing to spend their hidden lire on big-ticket items while they still can.

The government is hoping the euro will transport Malta's economy to a bright future based on services. The dwindling of Britain's military presence over the 1970s withered the island's old fortress economy. With great effort, the authorities lured some manufacturing, including textile factories, microchip plants, and presses that print banknotes. But textiles are drifting off to China and other parts of Asia, and chip foundries might follow, forcing Malta's manufacturers to move upmarket. Increasingly Maltese firms, such as makers of high-quality wooden furniture, are finding that their products are competitive around Europe. Bordeaux's newest posh hotel has doors made in Malta.

Malta is also discovering that in an increasingly virtual world, being an island is no longer an obstacle to providing services, especially in finance and computing. In the late 1980s the government tried building a typical offshore financial center, complete with tax sheltering and secrecy. But that got in the way of another Maltese aim: to join the European Union. So the country changed tack and aimed for integration into Europe, with a financial sector that passed all European tests for onshore probity.

One big effect of joining the EU was a surge in inward investment. Last year the flow was around 550m Maltese lire ($188m), more than 25 times the level ten years ago, according to Lawrence Gonzi, the prime minister. Foreigners are attracted chiefly by Malta's tax system, which allows income tax on dividends to be offset against corporate tax, reducing the effective tax rate on dividends from 35 percent to 5 percent. It also helps that accommodation and labor costs are between one-half and one-third those of rival hubs, such as Dublin and Luxembourg.

Most of the investment is going into financial services and one niche in particular: the in-house or "captive" insurance operations of big carmakers. BMW has moved its captive insurance unit from Dublin; Renault, PSA Peugeot Citroën, Volkswagen, Vodafone, and RWE have also set up shop in Valletta, Malta. These units, which are run by insurance-management firms such as Marsh & McLellan, are allowed to sell a range of other insurance products around the EU. There are also some 250 hedge funds based in Malta. The value of assets under their management has grown sevenfold to 7.5 billion ($10.6 billion) in the three years since EU accession.

Other industries are beginning to follow. Lufthansa, which already services its smaller planes at Malta's airport, plans to tend to its wide-body fleet there as well. The Maltese have created a special course for aircraft technicians at a local college to ensure a steady supply of qualified workers. About 20 pharmaceutical firms making generic drugs have also joined the herd of businesses streaming to Valletta, because a wrinkle in Maltese law allows them to do development work on copycat versions of patented drugs and so to be ready to market them in the EU when the patent expires.

But the most spectacular recent arrivals are investors from the United Arab Emirates seeking a European bridgehead. Dubai Holding, an investment firm that has attracted technology giants such as Microsoft, Hewlett-Packard, Cisco, and Oracle to a development called Internet City on the outskirts of Dubai, is spending more than $300m to set up a similar facility in Malta. "They wanted a one-stop shop for Europe," says Mr. Gonzi, "and they have undertaken to create 3,500 proper IT jobs." He is hoping this will attract other big names to Malta. Again, the local vocational college has promised to churn out suitably qualified workers. If only the bigger economies in Europe could move so nimbly in the face of globalization.

SOURCE: "Maltese Business: Virtual Bridges," *The Economist*, October 4, 2007.

purpose is to allow a firm to lock in a future rate of exchange. This is a valuable tool in a world of continually changing exchange rates.

The quotations listed will also occasionally indicate if the rate is applicable to business trade (the commercial rate) or for financial asset purchases or sales (the financial rate). Countries that have government regulations regarding the exchange of their currency may post official rates, while the markets operating outside their jurisdiction will list a floating rate. In this case, any exchange of currency that is not under the control of its government is interpreted as a better indication of the currency's true market value.

FIGURE 8.1   Exchange Rate and Cross Rate Tables

Currencies

January 29, 2008

U.S.-dollar foreign-exchange rates in late New York trading

Country/currency	Tues in US$	Tues per US$	US$ vs. YTD chg (%)	Country/currency	Tues in US$	Tues per US$	US$ vs. YTD chg (%)
Americas				**Europe**			
Argentina peso*	.3173	3.1516	0.1	Czech Rep. koruna**	.05681	17.603	−3.2
Brazil real	.5616	1.7806	unch	Denmark krone	.1982	5.0454	−1.2
Canada dollar	1.0006	.9994	0.6	Euro area euro	1.4773	.6769	−1.2
1-mos forward	.9998	1.0002	0.7	Hungary forint	.005731	174.49	0.7
3-mos forward	.9988	1.0012	0.8	Norway krone	.1842	5.4289	−0.1
6-mos forward	.9967	1.0033	1.0	Poland zloty	.4077	2.4528	−0.6
Chile peso	.002152	464.68	−6.7	Russia ruble‡	.04084	24.486	−0.3
Colombia peso	.0005133	1948.18	−3.5	Slovak Rep. koruna	.04383	22.815	−0.9
Ecuador US dollar	1	1	unch	Sweden krona	.1564	6.3939	−1.1
Mexico peso*	.0922	10.8507	−0.6	Switzerland franc	.9150	1.0929	−3.5
Peru new sol	.3410	2.933	−2.2	1-mos forward	.9156	1.0922	−3.4
Uruguay peso†	.04760	21.01	−2.5	3-mos forward	.9166	1.0910	−3.2
Venezuela b. fuerte	.466287	2.1446	unch	6-mos forward	.9175	1.0899	−3.0
				Turkey lira**	.8504	1.1758	0.7
Asia-Pacific				UK pound	1.9896	.5026	−0.1
				1-mos forward	1.9862	.5035	unch
Australian dollar	.8897	1.1240	−1.5	3-mos forward	1.9788	.5054	0.2
China yuan	.1390	7.1949	−1.5	6-mos forward	1.9669	.5084	0.5
Hong Kong dollar	.1281	7.8051	0.1				
India rupee	.02545	39.293	−0.3				
Indonesia rupiah	.0001073	9320	−0.7	**Middle East/Africa**			
Japan yen	.009339	107.08	−3.9				
1-mos forward	.009360	106.84	−3.8	Bahrain dinar	2.6582	.3762	0.1
3-mos forward	.009397	106.42	−3.6	Egypt pound*	.1796	5.5689	0.6
6-mos forward	.009446	105.86	−3.3	Israel shekel	.2741	3.6483	−5.4
Malaysia ringgit§	.3089	3.2373	−2.1	Jordan dinar	1.4104	.7090	unch
New Zealand dollar	.7781	1.2852	−1.5	Kuwait dinar	3.6623	.2731	−0.1
Pakistan rupee	.01597	62.617	1.6	Lebanon pound	.0006634	1507.39	−0.3
Phillippines peso	.0247	40.453	−1.9	Saudi Arabia riyal	.2667	3.7495	unch
Singapore dollar	.7031	1.4223	−1.3	South Africa rand	.1387	7.2098	5.3
South Korea won	.0010590	944.29	0.9	UAE dirham	.2723	3.6724	unch
Taiwan dollar	.03098	32.279	−0.5				
Thailand baht	.03200	31.250	4.0	SDR††	1.5905	.6287	−0.8

*Floating rate   †Financial   §Government rate   ‡Russian Central Bank rate   **Rebased as of Jan 1, 2005
††Special Drawing Rights (SDR); from the International Monetary Fund; based on exchange rates for U.S., British and Japanese currencies.
Note: Based on trading among banks of $1 million and more, as quoted at 4 p.m. ET by Reuters.

SOURCE: *Wall Street Journal*

Direct and Indirect Quotations

The *Wall Street Journal* quotations shown in Figure 8.1 list rates of exchange between major currencies, both in direct and indirect forms. The exchange rate for the Japanese yen (¥) versus the U.S. dollar in Figure 8.1 is ¥106.43/$. This is a direct quote on the Japanese yen and an indirect quote on the U.S. dollar. The inverse of this spot exchange rate for the same day is listed in the first column, the indirect quote on the U.S. dollar, $.009396/¥. The two forms of the exchange rate are of course equal, one being the inverse of the other:

$$\frac{1}{¥106.43/\$} = \$.009396/¥$$

EUROPEAN TERMS

Quoting a currency rate as a country's currency against the U.S. dollar (e.g., yen/U.S. dollars).

Fortunately, world currency markets do follow some conventions to minimize confusion. With only a few exceptions, most currencies are given in direct quotes versus the U.S. dollar (SF/$, Baht/$, Pesos/$), also known as **European terms**. The major exceptions are currencies at one time or another associated with the British Commonwealth, including the Australian dollar and now the European euro. These currencies, customarily quoted as U.S. dollars per pound sterling or U.S. dollars per Australian dollar, are known as **American terms**. Once again, it makes no real difference whether you quote U.S. dollars per Japanese yen or Japanese yen per U.S. dollar, as long as you know which is being used for the transaction.

Figure 8.2, the foreign currency quotations from The Financial Times of London, provides wider coverage of the world's currencies, including many of the lesser known and traded. These quotes are for December 31, 2007.

Cross Rates

Although it is common among exchange traders worldwide to quote currency values against the U.S. dollar, it is not necessary. Any currency's value can be stated in terms of any other currency. When the exchange rate of a currency is stated without using the U.S. dollar as a reference, it is referred to as a **cross rate**. For example, if the Japanese yen and European euro are both quoted versus the U.S. dollar, they would appear as ¥133.15/$ and $.8622/€. But if the ¥/€ cross rate is needed, it is simply a matter of multiplication:

$$¥133.15/\$ \times \$.8622/€ = ¥114.80/€$$

The yen-per-euro cross rate of 114.80 is the third leg of the triangle of currencies, which must be true if the first two exchange rates are known. If one of the exchange rates changes due to market forces, the others must adjust for the three exchange rates again to align. If they are out of alignment, it would be possible to make a profit simply by exchanging one currency for a second, the second for a third, and the third back to the first. This is known as **triangular arbitrage**. Besides the potential profitability of arbitrage that may occasionally occur, cross rates have become increasingly common in a world of rapidly expanding trade and investment.

Foreign Currency Market Structure

The market for foreign currencies is a worldwide market that is informal in structure. This means that it has no central place, pit, or floor (like the floor of the New York Stock Exchange) where the trading takes place. The "market" is actually the thousands of telecommunications links among financial institutions around the globe, and it is open 24 hours a day. Someone, somewhere, is nearly always open for business. As described in Quick Take: Online Global Currency Exchange, trading is also moving to the Internet.

Until recently there was little data on the actual volume of trading on world markets. Starting in 1986, the Bank for International Settlements (BIS) started surveying the activity of currency trading every three years. While the first three surveys reported astronomical growth in foreign currency trading, the most recent figures show a marked decline. In April 2001, average daily turnover was $1.2 trillion, a decrease of 19 percent from April 1998. In part, the fall-off can be explained by the growing role of electronic brokers, not represented in the survey. The introduction of the euro, which eliminated the need for foreign exchange transactions among 12 European currencies, also contributed. A more significant factor, however, may be a decrease in risk tolerance that has followed turbulence in the financial markets in recent years.[1]

AMERICAN TERMS

Quoting a currency rate as the U.S. dollar against another country's currency (e.g., U.S. dollars/yen).

CROSS RATES

Exchange rate quotations that do not include the U.S. dollar as one of the two currencies quoted.

TRIANGULAR ARBITRAGE

The exchange of one currency for a second currency, the second for a third, and the third for the first in order to make a profit.

Culture Clues   Always put money in an envelope before handing it to a Japanese person. This applies to business situations, as well as payments such as monthly rent. When giving a gift of money, buy a decorative money envelope in which to enclose the cash.

FIGURE 8.2   Guide to World Currencies

FT GUIDE TO WORLD CURRENCIES   www.ft.com/gtrs

The table reproduces the Financial Times "FT Guide to World Currencies" for Dec 31, listing for each country/currency its value and weekly change against £ STG, US $, EURO €, and Yen (¥ 100). The full grid of currencies (Afghanistan through Zimbabwe, plus SDR) and their exchange-rate columns is printed here.

SOURCE: *Financial Times of London*

LEARNING OBJECTIVE 2

EVOLUTION OF THE GLOBAL MONETARY SYSTEM

The mixed-fixed/floating exchange rate system operating today is only the latest stage of a continuing process of change. The systems that have preceded the present system varied between gold-based standards (the gold standard) and complex systems in which the U.S. dollar largely took the place of gold (the Bretton Woods Agreement). To understand why the dollar, the mark, and the yen are floating today, it is necessary to return to the (pardon the pun) golden oldies.

The Gold Standard

GOLD STANDARD

A standard for international currencies in which currency values were stated in terms of gold.

Although there is no recognized starting date, the **gold standard** as we understand it today began sometime in the 1880s and lasted up through the outbreak of World War I. The gold standard was premised on three basic ideas:

1. A system of fixed rates of exchange existed between participating countries.
2. "Money" issued by member countries had to be backed by reserves of gold.

3. Gold would act as an automatic adjustment, flowing in and out of countries and automatically altering the gold reserves of a country if imbalances in trade or investment did occur.

Under the gold standard, each country's currency would be set in value per ounce of gold. For example, the U.S. dollar was defined as $20.67 per ounce, while the British pound sterling was defined as £4.2474 per ounce. Once each currency was defined versus gold, the determination of the exchange rate between the two currencies (or any two currencies) was simple:

$$\frac{\$20.67/\text{ounce of gold}}{£4.2474/\text{ounce of gold}} = \$4.8665/£.$$

The use of gold as the pillar of the system was a result of historical tradition and not anything inherently unique to the gold metal itself. It was shiny, soft, rare, and generally acceptable for payment in all countries.

Interwar Years, 1919–1939

The 1920s and 1930s were a tumultuous period. The British pound sterling, the dominant currency prior to World War I, survived the war but was greatly weakened. The U.S. dollar returned to the gold standard in 1919, but gold convertibility was largely untested across countries throughout the 1920s, as world trade took a long time to recover from the destruction of the war. With the economic collapse and bank runs of the 1930s, the United States was forced, once again, to abandon gold convertibility.

The economic depression of the 1930s was worldwide. As countries came under increasingly desperate economic conditions, many (including the United States) resorted to isolationist policies and protectionism. World trade slowed to a trickle, and with it the general need for currency exchange. It was not until the latter stages of World War II that international trade and commerce once again demanded a system for currency convertibility and stability.

Quick Take *Online Global Currency Exchange*

Currenex is the first independent and open online global currency exchange, linking institutional buyers and sellers worldwide. Currenex's Internet-based service, FXtrades, provides banks, corporate treasury departments, institutional funds/asset managers, government agencies, international organizations, and central banks instant access to the $1 trillion daily globe foreign exchange market, through multiple price discovery mechanisms on an open, impartial exchange.

FXtrades is a real-time marketplace that provides secure and comprehensive FX trading from initiation and execution to settlement and reporting. As members in the Currenex exchange, CFOs, treasurers, and fund managers can approach currency transactions knowing that they are able to secure the most competitive bid while improving operational efficiencies, increasing productivity, and providing tight integration with back-office operations.

Currenex, founded in 1999, has major multinational members, including MasterCard International and Intel Corporation, as well as more than 25 global market-making banks, among them ABN Amro, Barclays Capital, and Merrill Lynch.

SOURCES: See **http://www.currenex.com**.

Quick Take *New EU Members and Adoption of the Euro*

These new members will not automatically adopt the euro as their currency. They will be allowed to adopt the euro only after they have met the criteria all euro members have had to meet from the very beginning: a high degree of price stability, sustainable government finances, a stable exchange rate, and convergence in long-term interest rates.

As illustrated, only Slovenia has adopted the euro in place of its traditional currency at the time this book went to press.

COUNTRY	CURRENCY	CURRENT EXCHANGE RATE REGIME	EXPECTED EURO ADOPTION
Bulgaria	lev	Pegged to the euro	2010
Cyprus	pound	Pegged to the euro	2008
Czech Republic	koruna	Free-floating; managed against the euro	2012
Estonia	kroon	Pegged to the euro	2010
Hungary	forint	Free-floating, but references the euro	2010-2012 (under debate)
Latvia			
Lithuania	lat	Pegged to the euro	2012 (earliest)
	litas	Pegged to the euro	2010
Malta	lira	Pegged to a basket of the €, $, and £	2008
Poland	zloty	Free-floating, but references the euro	2012 (tentative)
Romania	leu	Free-floating	2014
Slovakia	koruna	Free-floating, but references the euro	2009 (tentative)
Slovenia	euro	Slovenian tolar replaced by euro in 2007	2007

The Bretton Woods Agreement, 1944–1971

The governments of 44 of the Allied powers gathered together in Bretton Woods, New Hampshire, in 1944 to plan for the postwar international monetary system. The delegates labored long, and in the end, all parties agreed that a postwar system would be stable and sustainable only if it was able to provide sufficient liquidity to countries during periods of crisis. Any new system had to have facilities for the extension of credit for countries to defend their currency values.

BRETTON WOODS AGREEMENT

An agreement reached in 1944 among finance ministers of 45 Western nations to establish a system of fixed exchange rates.

After weeks of debate, the **Bretton Woods Agreement** was reached. The plan called for the following:

1. Fixed exchange rates between member countries, termed an "adjustable peg"
2. The establishment of a fund of gold and currencies available to members for stabilization of their respective currencies (the International Monetary Fund)
3. The establishment of a bank that would provide funding for long-term development projects (the World Bank)

Like the gold standard at the turn of the century, all participants were to establish par values of their currencies in terms of gold. Unlike the prior system, however, there was little, if any, convertibility of currencies to gold expected. Instead, convertibility was against the U.S. dollar ("as good as gold"). In fact, the only currency officially convertible to gold was the U.S.

FIGURE 8.3   The U.S. Dollar-British Pound Exchange Rate, 1948–2007

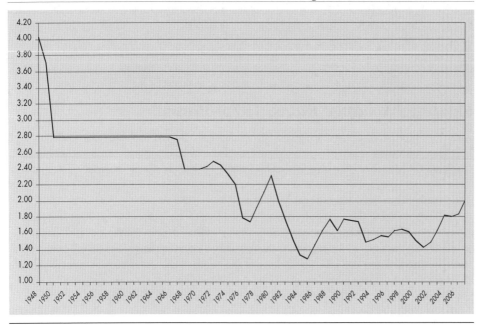

dollar (pegged at $35/ounce). This reliance on the value of the dollar and on the stability of the U.S. economy led to 25 years of relatively stable currency, followed by the system's eventual collapse.

One indicator of the success of the Bretton Woods system is the stability that it provided the major world currencies throughout the 1950s and 1960s (the long, flat line in Figure 8.3). The U.S. dollar–British pound exchange rate enjoyed its longest period of stability at this time, a balance it has certainly not achieved either before or since.

Times of Crisis, 1971–1973

On August 15, 1971, U.S. President Richard M. Nixon announced, "I have instructed [Treasury] Secretary [John B.] Connally to suspend temporarily the convertibility of the dollar into gold or other assets." With this simple statement, President Nixon effectively ended the fixed exchange rates established at Bretton Woods.

In the weeks and months following the August announcement, world currency markets devalued the dollar, although the United States had only ended gold convertibility and had not officially declared the dollar's value to be less. In late 1971, the Group of Ten finance ministers met at the Smithsonian Institution in Washington, D.C., to try to piece together a system to keep world markets operational. First, the dollar was officially devalued to $38/ounce of gold (as if anyone had access to gold convertibility). Secondly, all other major world currencies were revalued against the dollar (the dollar was relatively devalued), and all would now be allowed to vary from their fixed parity rates by plus/minus 2.25 percent (rather than the previous 1.00 percent).

Without convertibility of at least one of the member currencies to gold, the system was doomed from the start. Within weeks, currencies were surpassing their allowed deviation limits; revaluations were occurring more frequently; and the international monetary system no longer worked as a "system": It was chaos. Finally, world currency trading nearly ground to a halt in March 1973. The world's currency markets closed for two weeks. When they reopened, major currencies (particularly the U.S. dollar) were simply allowed to float in value. In January 1976, the Group of Ten once again met, this time in Jamaica, and the Jamaica Agreement officially recognized what the markets had known for years — the world's currencies were no longer fixed in value.

Floating Exchange Rates, 1973–Present

Since March of 1973, the world's major currencies have floated in value versus one another. This flotation poses many problems for the conduct of international trade and commerce, problems that are themselves the subject of entire courses of study (currency risk management for one). The inability of a country's government to control the value of its currency on world markets has been a harsh reality for most.

Throughout the 1970s, if a government wished to alter the current value of its currency, or even slow or alter a trending change in the currency's value, the government would simply buy or sell its own currency in the market, using its reserves of other major currencies. This process of **direct intervention** was effective as long as the depth of the government's reserve pockets kept up with the volume of trading on currency markets. For these countries — both then and now — the primary problem is maintaining adequate foreign exchange reserves.

By the 1980s, however, the world's currency markets were so large that the ability of a few governments (the United States, Japan, and Germany, for example) to move a market simply through direct intervention no longer existed. The major tool now left was for a government (at least when operating alone) to alter economic variables, such as interest rates — that is, to alter the motivations and expectations of market participants for capital movements and currency exchange. During periods of relatively low inflation (a critical assumption), a country that wishes to strengthen its currency versus others might raise domestic interest rates to attract capital from abroad. Although relatively effective in many cases, the downside of this policy is that it raises interest rates for domestic consumers and investors alike, possibly slowing the domestic economy. The result is that governments today must often choose between an external economic policy action (raising interest rates to strengthen the currency) and a domestic economic policy action (lowering interest rates to stimulate economic activity).

There is, however, one other method of currency-value management that has been selectively employed in the past 15 years: **coordinated intervention**. After the U.S. dollar had risen in value dramatically over the 1980-to-1985 period, the Group of Five, or G5 nations (France, Japan, West Germany, the United States, and the United Kingdom), met at the Plaza Hotel in New York in September 1985 and agreed to a set of goals and policies called the Plaza Agreement. These goals were to be accomplished through coordinated intervention among the central banks of the major nations. With the Bank of Japan (Japan), the Bundesbank (Germany), and the Federal Reserve (United States) all intervening in the currency markets simultaneously, they hoped to reach the combined level of strength needed to push the dollar's value down. Their actions were met with some success in that instance, but there have been few occasions since then of coordinated intervention.

INTERNATIONAL MONEY MARKETS

A financial market or money market is traditionally defined as a market for deposits, accounts, or securities that have maturities of one year or less. The international money markets, often termed the eurocurrency markets, constitute an enormous financial market that is, in many ways, free of the regulatory constraints of financial and government authorities.

DIRECT INTERVENTION

The process governments used in the 1970s if they wished to alter the current value of their currency. It was done by simply buying or selling their own currency in the market, using their reserves of other major currencies.

COORDINATED INTERVENTION

A currency-value management method whereby the central banks of the major nations simultaneously intervene in the currency markets, hoping to change a currency's value.

3 LEARNING OBJECTIVE

Eurocurrency Markets

A **eurocurrency** is any foreign currency-denominated deposit or account at a financial institution outside the country of the currency's issuance. For example, U.S. dollars that are held on account in a bank in London are termed **eurodollars**. Similarly, Japanese yen held on account in a Parisian financial institution are classified as euroyen. The euro prefix does not mean these currencies or accounts are only European, as Japanese yen on account in Singapore would also be classified as a eurocurrency.

Eurocurrency Interest Rates

What is the significance of these foreign currency-denominated accounts? Simply put, it is the purity of value that comes from no governmental interference or restrictions with their use. Eurocurrency accounts are not controlled or managed by governments (for example, the Bank of England has no control over eurodollar accounts); therefore, the financial institutions pay no deposit insurance, hold no reserve requirements, and normally are not subject to any interest rate restrictions with respect to such accounts. Eurocurrencies are one of the purest indicators of what these currencies should yield in terms of interest. Sample eurocurrency interest rates are shown in Table 8.2.

There are hundreds of different major interest rates around the globe, but the international financial markets focus on a very few, the **interbank interest rates**. Interbank rates charged by banks to banks in the major international financial centers, such as London, Frankfurt, Paris, New York, Tokyo, Singapore, and Hong Kong, are generally regarded as "the interest rate" in the respective market. The interest rate that is used most often in international loan agreements is the eurocurrency interest rate on U.S. dollars (eurodollars) in London between banks: the London interbank offer rate (LIBOR). Because it is a eurocurrency rate, it floats freely without regard to governmental restrictions on reserves or deposit insurance or any other regulation or restriction that would add expense to transactions using this capital. The interbank rates for other currencies in other markets are often named similarly: PIBOR (Paris interbank offer rate), MIBOR (Madrid interbank offer rate), HIBOR (either Hong Kong or Helsinki interbank offer rate), SIBOR (Singapore interbank offer rate). While LIBOR is the offer rate — the cost of funds "offered" to those acquiring a loan — the equivalent deposit rate in the **euromarkets** is LIBID, the London interbank bid rate, the rate of interest other banks can earn on eurocurrency deposits.

How do these international eurocurrency and interbank interest rates differ from domestic rates? Not by much. They generally move up and down in unison, by currency, but often differ by the percentage by which the restrictions alter the rates of interest in the domestic markets. For example, because the euromarkets have no restrictions, the spread between the offer rate and the bid rate (the loan rate and the deposit rate) is substantially smaller than in domestic markets. This means the loan rates in international markets are a bit lower than domestic market loan rates, and deposit rates are a bit higher in the international markets than in domestic markets.

However, this is only a big-player market. Only well-known international firms, financial or nonfinancial, have access to the quantities of capital necessary to operate in the euromarkets. But, as described in the following sections on international debt and equity markets, more and more firms are gaining access to the euromarkets to take advantage of deregulated capital flows.

EUROCURRENCY

A bank deposit in a currency other than the currency of the country where the bank is located; not confined to banks in Europe.

EURODOLLARS

U.S. dollars deposited in banks outside the United States; not confined to banks in Europe.

INTERBANK INTEREST RATES

The interest rate charged by banks to banks in the major international financial centers.

EUROMARKETS

Money and capital markets in which transactions are denominated in a currency other than that of the place of the transaction; not confined to Europe.

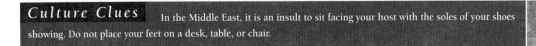

Culture Clues   In the Middle East, it is an insult to sit facing your host with the soles of your shoes showing. Do not place your feet on a desk, table, or chair.

TABLE 8.2 Exchange Rates and Eurocurrency Interest Rates

INTEREST RATE/EXCHANGE RATES	MATURITY	EURO-DOLLAR INTEREST RATES	EURO-POUND INTEREST RATES
	1 month	1.900%	3.850%
	3 months	1.920%	4.040%
	6 months	2.200%	4.260%
	12 months	2.500%	4.650%
Exchange rates:			
Spot rate	1 month		$1.4178/£
	3 months		$1.4104/£
	6 months		$1.4035/£
	12 months		$1.3887/£

Linking Eurocurrency Interest Rates and Exchange Rates

Eurocurrency interest rates also play a large role in the foreign exchange markets. They are, in fact, the interest rates used in the calculation of the forward rates noted earlier. Recall that a forward rate is a contract for a specific amount of currency to be exchanged for another currency at a future date, usually 30, 60, 90, 180, or even 360 days in the future. Forward rates are calculated from the spot rate in effect on the day the contract is written, along with the respective eurocurrency interest rates for the two currencies.

For example, to calculate the 90-day forward rate for the U.S. dollar–British pound cross rate, $1.4178/£ (as shown in Figure 8.1), the spot exchange rate is multiplied by the ratio of the two eurocurrency interest rates — the eurodollar and the europound rates. Note that it is important to adjust the interest rates for the actual period of time needed, 90 days (3 months) of a 360-day financial year:

$$\text{90-Day Forward Rate} = \text{Spot} \times \frac{1 + \left(i_{90}^{\$} \times \frac{90}{360} \right)}{1 + \left(i_{90}^{£} \times \frac{90}{360} \right)}$$

Now, plugging in the spot exchange rate of $1.4178/£ and the two 90-day (3-month) eurocurrency interest rates from Table 8.2 (1.920 percent for the dollar and 4.040 percent for the pound), the 90-day forward exchange rate is:

$$\text{90-Day Forward Rate} = \$1.4178/£ \times \frac{\left[1 + \left(.0192 \times \frac{90}{360}\right)\right]}{\left[1 + \left(.0404 \times \frac{90}{360}\right)\right]} = \$1.4104/£$$

SELLING FORWARD

A market transaction in which the seller promises to sell currency at a certain future date at a pre-specified price.

The forward rate of 1.4104/£ is a "weaker rate" for the British pound than the current spot rate. This is because one British pound will yield $1.4178 in the spot market, but only $1.4104 in the forward market (at 90 days). The British pound would be said to be "**selling forward at a discount**," while the dollar would be described as "selling forward at a premium" because its value is stronger at the 90-day forward rate.

The Locations of the World's International Financial Centers (IFCs) and International Offshore Financial Centers (IOFCs)

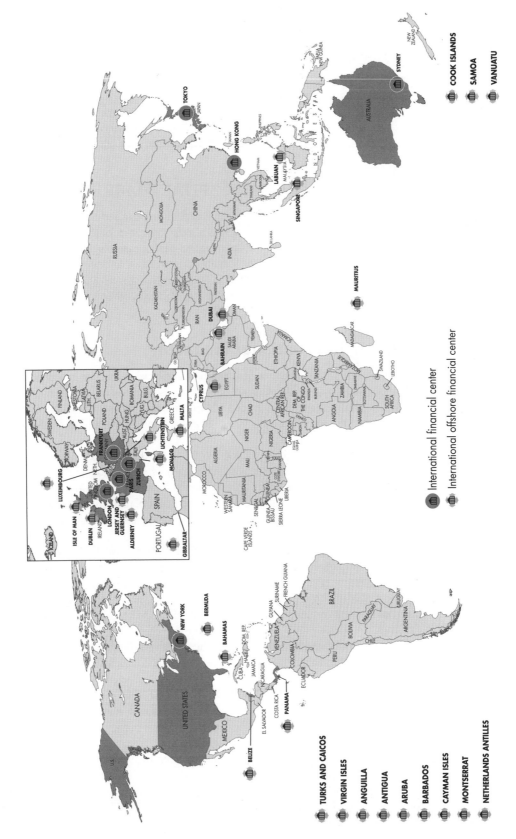

Note: *International Financial Centers (IFCs)* are the traditional centers of international financial activity, and normally include the conduct of both domestic and international financial transactions. *International Offshore Financial Centers (IOFCs)* are centers of offshore financial activities only (no interaction is allowed with the domestic financial or business community), and normally exist because of specific tax laws and provisions which encourage their establishment and allow them special treatment.

International financial center

International offshore financial center

Source: *Multinational Business Finance,* 7th Ed., Eiteman, Stonehill, and Moffett.

Why is this the case? The reason is that the 90-day eurocurrency interest rate on the U.S. dollar is lower than the corresponding eurocurrency interest rate on the British pound. If it were the other way around — if the U.S. dollar interest rate were higher than the British pound interest rate — the British pound would be selling forward at a premium. The forward exchange rates quoted in the markets, and used so frequently in international business, simply reflect the difference in interest rates between currencies.

Businesses frequently use forward exchange rate contracts to manage their exposure to currency risk. Corporations use many other financial instruments and techniques beyond forward contracts to manage currency risk, but forwards are still the mainstay of industry.

 # INTERNATIONAL CAPITAL MARKETS

4 LEARNING OBJECTIVE

Just as with money markets, international capital markets serve as links among the capital markets of individual countries, as well as a separate market of their own — the capital that flows into the euromarkets. In the international capital markets, firms can now raise capital, with debit or equity, with fixed or floating interest rates, in any of a dozen currencies, for maturities ranging from one month to 30 years. Although the international capital markets traditionally have been dominated by debt instruments, international equity markets have shown considerable growth in recent years.

Defining International Financing

The definition of what constitutes an international financial transaction is dependent on two fundamental characteristics: (1) whether the borrower is domestic or foreign, and (2) whether the borrower is raising capital denominated in the domestic currency or in a foreign currency. These two characteristics form four categories of financial transactions, as illustrated in Figure 8.4

CATEGORY 1: DOMESTIC BORROWER/DOMESTIC CURRENCY This is a traditional domestic financial-market activity. A borrower who is a resident within the country raises capital from domestic financial institutions denominated in local currency. All countries with basic market economies have their own domestic financial markets, some large and some quite small. This is still, by far, the most common type of financial transaction.

CATEGORY 2: FOREIGN BORROWER/DOMESTIC CURRENCY This is when a foreign borrower enters another country's financial market and raises capital denominated in the local currency. The international dimension of this transaction is based only on who the borrower is. Many borrowers, both public and private, increasingly go to the world's largest financial markets to raise capital for their enterprises. The ability of a foreign firm to raise capital in another country's financial market is sometimes limited by that government's restrictions on who can borrow, as well as the market's willingness to lend to foreign governments and companies that it may not know as well as domestic borrowers.

CATEGORY 3: DOMESTIC BORROWER/FOREIGN CURRENCY Many borrowers in today's international markets need capital denominated in a foreign currency. A domestic firm may actually issue a bond to raise capital in its local market where it is known quite well, but raise the capital in the form of a foreign currency.

This type of financial transaction occurs less often than the previous two types because it requires a local market in foreign currencies, a eurocurrency market. A number of countries, such as the United States, tightly restrict the amount and types of financial transactions in foreign currency. International financial centers, such as London and Zurich, have been the traditional centers of these types of transactions.

FIGURE 8.4   Categorizing International Financial Transactions:
Issuing Bonds in London

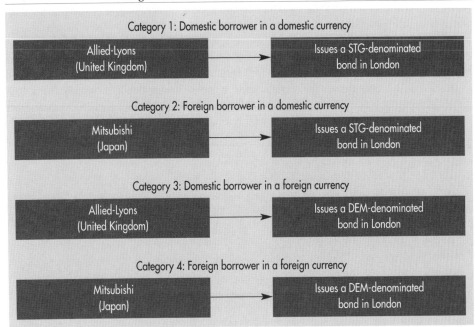

CATEGORY 4: FOREIGN BORROWER/FOREIGN CURRENCY This is the strictest form of the traditional eurocurrency financial transaction, a foreign firm borrowing foreign currency. Once again, this type of activity may be restricted as to which borrowers are allowed into a country's financial markets and which currencies are available. This type of financing dominates the activities of many banking institutions in the **offshore banking** market.

Using this classification system makes it possible to categorize any individual international financial transaction. For example, the distinction between an international bond and a eurobond is simply that of a Category 2 transaction (foreign borrower in a domestic currency market) and a Category 3 or 4 transaction (foreign currency denominated in a single local market or many markets).

OFFSHORE BANKING

The use of banks or bank branches located in low-tax countries, often Caribbean islands, to raise and hold capital for multinational operations.

 ## INTERNATIONAL BANKING AND BANK LENDING

Banks have existed in different forms and roles since the Middle Ages. Bank loans have provided nearly all of the debt capital needed by industry since the start of the Industrial Revolution. Even in this age, in which securitized debt instruments (bonds, notes, and other types of tradable paper) are growing as sources of capital for firms worldwide, banks still perform a critical role by providing capital for medium-sized and smaller firms, which dominate all economies.

Structure of International Banking

Similar to the direct foreign investment decision sequence discussed in Chapter 6, banks can expand their cross-border activities in a variety of ways. A bank that wants to conduct business with clients in other countries, but does not want to open a banking operation in that

CORRESPONDENT BANKS

Banks located in different countries and unrelated by ownership that have a reciprocal agreement to provide services to the other's customers.

country, can do so through correspondent banks or representative offices. A **correspondent bank** is a bank (unrelated by ownership) based in a foreign country. By the nature of its business, it has knowledge of the local market and access to clients, capital, and information, which a foreign bank does not.

A second way that banks may gain access to foreign markets without actually opening an overseas banking operation is through representative offices. A **representative office** is basically a sales office for a bank. It provides information regarding the financial services of the bank, but it cannot deliver the services itself: It cannot accept deposits or make loans. The foreign representative office of a U.S. bank will typically sell the bank's services to local firms that may need banking services for trade or other transactions in the United States.

WORLD VIEW

THE PETRODOLLAR PEG

America should worry more about fixed exchange rates in the Gulf than the gently rising Chinese yuan.

American politicians and businessmen view China's undervalued exchange rate and its huge current-account surplus as the main cause of America's vast deficit. Thus next week a high-powered delegation led by Henry Paulson, America's treasury secretary, will fly to Beijing to persuade China to take measures to reduce its surplus. But are they heading to the right place? At the global level, the biggest counterpart to America's deficit is the combined surpluses of the oil-exporting emerging economies. They are expected to run a total current-account surplus of some $500 billion this year, dwarfing China's likely surplus of $200 billion (see chart).

Counting only the Middle East oil exporters, the surplus has surged from $30 billion in 2002 to an estimated $280 billion this year. One reason why this gets much less attention than the smaller $160 billion increase in China is that only a fraction of it has gone

into official reserves, which are publicly reported. Most of it is stashed in government oil-stabilization or investment funds, such as the Abu Dhabi Investment Authority, which are much more secretive than the People's Bank of China — but which probably hold just as many dollar assets.

One big difference is that China is now allowing the yuan to rise against the dollar. The exchange rate is up by an annual rate of almost 7 percent since September. In contrast, the six members of the Gulf Co-operation Council, or GCC (Saudi Arabia, United Arab Emirates, Kuwait, Bahrain, Oman, and Qatar), which account for virtually all of the Middle East's surplus, still peg their currencies firmly to the dollar. This is partly in preparation for the GCC's plan to adopt a single currency by 2010. But the bizarre result is that over the past four years of soaring oil prices, their real trade-weighted exchange rates have fallen.

The Gulf economies are running an average current-account surplus of 30 percent of their GDP, well in excess of China's surplus of 8 percent. Oil exporters cannot spend their windfall overnight, and it makes sense for them to run a surplus when oil prices rise, as a buffer for when oil prices fall. Even so, one can have too much of a good thing. It might be best for the Gulf States as well as the world economy if they abandoned their dollar pegs and shifted to some sort of currency basket. A more flexible exchange-rate regime would allow them to regain control of their monetary policies and so cool down their overheating economies. By pegging their exchange rates to the dollar, they have had to adopt America's monetary policy, leaving real interest rates too low (often negative) for such fast-growing economies. Credit is growing too rapidly, inflation is rising and the prices of assets, especially property in places such as Dubai.

SOURCES: Abstracted from "The Petrodollar Peg," *The Economist,* December 7, 2006.

SURPLUS TO REQUIREMENTS Current-account surpluses

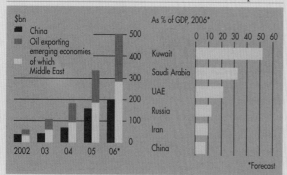

SOURCE: International Monetary Fund, *The economist.*

If a bank wants to conduct banking business within the foreign country, it may open a branch banking office, a banking affiliate, or even a wholly owned banking subsidiary. A branch office is an extension of the parent bank but is not independently financed or independently incorporated and therefore is commonly restricted in the types of banking activities that it may conduct.

INTERNATIONAL SECURITY MARKETS

Although banks continue to provide a large portion of the international financial needs of government and business, it is the international debt securities markets that have experienced the greatest growth in the past decade. The international security markets include bonds, equities, and private placements.

The International Bond Market

The **international bond** market provides the bulk of financing. The four categories of international debt financing discussed previously apply particularly to the international bond markets. Foreign borrowers have been using the large, well-developed capital markets of countries such as the United States and the United Kingdom for many years. These issues are classified generally as **foreign bonds**, as opposed to eurobonds. Each has gained its own pet name for foreign bonds issued in that market. For example, foreign bonds issued in the United States are called Yankee bonds; in the United Kingdom, Bulldogs; in the Netherlands, Rembrandt bonds; and in Japan, Samurai bonds. When bonds are issued by foreign borrowers in these markets, they are subject to the same restrictions that apply to all domestic borrowers. If a Japanese firm issues a bond in the United States, it still must comply with all rules of the U.S. Securities and Exchange Commission, including the one that requires bonds to be dollar-denominated.

Bonds that fall into Categories 3 and 4 are termed **eurobonds**. The primary characteristic of these instruments is that they are denominated in a currency other than that of the country where they are sold. For example, many U.S. firms may issue euroyen bonds on world markets. These bonds are sold in international financial centers, such as London or Frankfurt, but they are denominated in Japanese yen. Because these eurobonds are scattered about the global markets, most are a type of bond known as a **bearer bond**. A bearer bond is owned officially by whomever is holding it, with no master registration list being held by government authorities, who might then track who is earning interest income from bond investments.[2] Bearer bonds have a series of small coupons that border the bond itself. On an annual basis, one of the coupons is cut or "clipped" from the bond and taken to a banking institution that is one of the listed paying agents. The bank will pay the holder of the coupon the interest payment due; usually, no official records of payment are kept.

INTERNATIONAL EQUITY MARKETS

Firms are financed with both debt and equity. Although the debt markets have been the center of activity in the international financial markets over the past three decades, there are signs that international equity capital is becoming more popular.

Again, using the same categories of international financial activities, the Category 2 transaction of a foreign borrower in a domestic market in local currency is the predominant

---

REPRESENTATIVE OFFICE

An office of an international bank established in a foreign country to serve the bank's customers in the area in an advisory capacity; it does not take deposits or make loans.

INTERNATIONAL BOND

A bond issued in domestic capital markets by foreign borrowers (foreign bonds) or issued in the eurocurrency markets in currency different from that of the home currency of the borrower (eurobonds).

FOREIGN BOND

Bonds issued by a foreign corporation or government for sale in a country different from its home country, and denominated in the currency of the country in which it is issued.

EUROBOND

A bond that is denominated in a currency other than the currency of the country in which the bond is sold.

BEARER BOND

A bond owned officially by whoever is holding it.

5 | LEARNING OBJECTIVE

international equity activity. Foreign firms often issue new shares in foreign markets and list their stock on major stock exchanges, such as those in New York, Tokyo, or London. The purpose of foreign issues and listings is to expand the investor base in the hope of gaining access to capital markets in which the demand for shares of equity ownership is strong.

A foreign firm that wants to list its shares on an exchange in the United States does so through **American Depository Receipts (ADRs)**. These are the receipts to bank accounts that hold shares of the foreign firm's stock in that firm's country. The equities are actually in a foreign currency, so by holding them in a bank account and listing the receipt on the account on the American exchange, the shares can be revalued in dollars and redivided so that the price per share is more typical of that of the U.S. equity markets ($20 to $60 per share frequently being the desired range).

There was considerable growth in the 1990s in the euro-equity markets. A euro-equity issue is the simultaneous sale of a firm's shares in several different countries, with or without listing the shares on an exchange in that country. The sales take place through investment banks. Once issued, most euro equities are listed at least on the Stock Exchange Automated Quotation System (SEAQ), the computer-screen quoting system of the International Stock Exchange (ISE) in London.

Gaining Access to Global Financial Markets

Although the global markets are large and growing, this does not mean they are for everyone. For many years, only the largest of the world's multinational firms could enter another country's capital markets and find acceptance. The reasons are lack of information and unknown reputation.

Financial markets are by definition risk-averse. This means they are very reluctant to make loans to or buy debt issued by firms that they know little about. Therefore, the ability to gain access to the international markets is dependent on a firm's reputation, its ability to educate the markets about what it does, how successful it has been, and its patience. The firm must, in the end, be willing to expend the resources and effort required to build a credit reputation in the international markets. If successful, the firm may enjoy the benefits of new, larger, and more diversified sources of the capital it needs.

The individual firm, whether a chili-dog stand serving the international tastes of office workers at the United Nations Plaza or a major multinational firm such as McDonald's or Honda of Japan, is affected by the workings of the international financial markets. Although the owner of the chili-dog stand probably has more important and immediate problems to deal with, it is clear that firms such as Honda see the movements in these markets as critically important to their long-term competitiveness.

AMERICAN DEPOSITORY RECEIPTS (ADRS)

Receipts to bank account that holds shares of a foreign firm's stock in that firm's country.

Fast Facts

What is the U.S. Mint?

The U.S. Mint, founded in 1792, makes all U.S. coins. It also safeguards the Treasury Department's store of gold and silver at Fort Knox, Kentucky.

SUMMARY

This chapter has explored the operations of world currency markets and their influence on the conduct of international business. It is estimated that more than $1 trillion worth of currencies changes hands daily, and the majority of it is in one of the world's three major floating currencies: U.S. dollars, euros, or Japanese yen.

The purpose of exchange-rate systems is to provide a free and liquid market for the world's currencies while ensuring some degree of stability and predictability to currency values.

The theory of purchasing power parity (PPP) defines what exchange rates ideally should be by equalizing the price of an identical product or service in two different currencies.

Currency quotations on the world's stock markets include both spot rates and forward rates of exchange. Cross rates allow for indirect quotations from any currency into any other currency.

The world's currency markets have experienced rapid growth in recent years, followed by a brief period of decline during global recession.

The global monetary system has seen periods of success and failure as exchange rates, once fixed to the value of gold, became fixed to the value of the dollar, then evolved into the floating exchange system that prevails today.

Eurocurrencies allow for the easy transfer of funds around the world without interference or restrictions imposed by governments. For this reason, eurocurrency interest rates float freely and are not subject to frequent transaction expenses.

There are four ways to categorize international financing, depending on whether the borrower is domestic or foreign and whether the capital raised is in a domestic or foreign currency.

The international securities market includes bonds, equities, and private placements. International bond markets provide most business financing. Equity markets allow foreign firms to expand their investor base by listing their stocks on major foreign exchanges.

KEY TERMS AND CONCEPTS

purchasing power parity (PPP)	triangular arbitrage	offshore banking
Law of One Price	gold standard	correspondent bank
foreign currency exchange rate	Bretton Woods Agreement	representative office
direct exchange quotation	direct intervention	international bond
indirect exchange quotation	coordinated intervention	foreign bond
spot exchange rates	eurocurrency	eurobond
forward exchange rates	eurodollars	bearer bond
European terms	interbank interest rate	American Depository Receipts
American terms	euromarkets	(ADRs)
cross rates	selling forward	

REVIEW QUESTIONS

1. Why are exchange rates necessary?
2. Distinguish between spot and forward currency.
3. Why was it so important that the U.S. dollar be convertible to gold for the Bretton Woods system to operate efficiently?
4. Why did the major world currencies move from a fixed to a floating exchange rate system in the 1970s? Are fixed exchange rates preferable to floating exchange rates?

5. What is a eurocurrency? What is a eurocurrency interest rate? Is it different from LIBOR?
6. Summarize the four ways of categorizing international capital markets.
7. What is the difference between an international bond and a eurobond?
8. Explain why it is sometimes difficult for firms to gain access to global financial markets.

CRITICAL SKILL BUILDERS

1. Your company imports Christmas decorations from Korea. In March, you receive a quote from a new manufacturer who will supply 50,000 glass Christmas-tree ornaments for a total of 100,000 Korean *won*. The *won* currently trades at 2.20 won to the dollar, but your banker advises you that its value is likely to fall by as much as 15 percent by the time you take delivery of the ornaments in September. To gain the best possible price, what are your options?

2. Consider how the debt crises in recent decades are linked to exchange rates. Discuss.

3. For each situation described below, discuss which rate (bid or offer) would apply.

   a. A Pakistani importer wishes to convert rupees to U.S. dollars to pay for a shipment. His bank is quoting R/$ R48.51–48.61.

   b. Assume that in the example above the required U.S. dollar payment is $75,000. How many rupees would be required?

   c. An exporting firm in Singapore has just received payment in U.S. dollars and wants to convert it to Singapore dollars. The bank is quoting S$/$ 1.8366–1.8375.

   d. A Japanese manufacturing firm must make a payment in U.S. dollars. The bank has made its quotation in American terms as follows: $/¥ .009430–.009436.

4. What is the difference between debt financing and equity financing? Discuss situations in which a company expanding overseas may need both.

5. Why have international financial markets grown so rapidly in the past decade? Is this rate of growth likely to continue? What changes do you see in the international financial markets in the coming decade? Consider the influences of both developed and emerging economies.

ON THE WEB

1. Although major currencies, such as the U.S. dollar and the Japanese yen, dominate the headlines, there are nearly as many currencies as countries in the world. Many of these currencies are traded in extremely thin and highly regulated markets, making their convertibility suspect. Finding quotations for these currencies is sometimes very difficult. Using the Web page listed below, see how many African currency quotes you can find. See Emerging Markets at **http://www.emgmkts.com**.

2. Visit **http://www.nyse.com/international/**. Review the activities of the New York Stock Exchange that relate to the expansion of emerging markets, such as China. What are the benefits of listing on the NYSE for companies in developing economies? How is a non-U.S. company treated differently from a U.S. company?

3. What is the difference between the European Central Bank and the European Investment Bank? Visit their Web sites at **http://www.ecb.int** and **http://www.eib.eu.int** to review the role and objectives of each. Why is each bank an essential resource for companies operating in Europe?

ENDNOTES

1. "Central Bank Survey of Foreign Exchange and Derivatives Market Activity in 2001," Bank for International Settlements press release, March 18, 2002.
2. Bearer bonds were issued by the U.S. government up until the early 1980s, when they were discontinued. Even though they were called bearer bonds, a list of bond registration numbers was still kept and recorded in order to tax investors holding the bearer instruments.

CHAPTER 9

GLOBAL FINANCIAL MANAGEMENT

Porsche and Stakeholder Capitalism

"Yes, of course we have heard of shareholder value. But that does not change the fact that we put customers first, then workers, then business partners, suppliers, and dealers, and then shareholders."

Dr. Wendelin Wiedeking, CEO, Porsche,
Die Zeit, April 17, 2005

LEARNING OBJECTIVES

1 To understand how value is measured and how capital is managed across the multiple units of firms

2 To understand how international business and investments are funded and how their cash flow is managed

3 To understand the three primary currency exposures that confront the multinational firm

4 To understand how accounting practices differ across countries and how these differences may alter the competitiveness of firms in international markets

5 To understand the problems faced by many U.S.-based multinational firms that experience taxation liabilities at home and in foreign countries

6 To examine the mechanics of financing import-export operations

Porsche had always been different. Statements by Porsche leadership, like the one above, always made many analysts nervous about the company's attitude toward shareholders. The company was a paradox. Porsche's attitudes and activities were like that of a family-owned firm, but it had succeeded in creating substantial shareholder value for more than a decade. Porsche's CEO, Dr. Wendelin Wiedeking, had been credited with clarity of purpose and sureness of execution. Porsche's management had created confusion in the marketplace as to which value proposition Porsche presented. Was Porsche continuing to develop an organizational focus on *shareholder value*, or was it returning to its more traditional German roots of *German cronyism*? Simply put, was Porsche's leadership pursuing family objectives at the expense of the shareholder?

Although Porsche was traded on the Frankfurt Stock Exchange (and associated German exchanges), control of the company remained firmly in the hands of the founding families, the Porsche and Piëch families. Porsche had two classes of shares, *ordinary* and *preference*. The two families held all 8.75 million *ordinary shares*—the shares that held all voting rights. The second class of share, *preference shares*, participated only in profits. All 8.75 million preference shares were publicly traded. Approximately 50 percent of all preference shares were held by large institutional investors in the United States, Germany, and the United Kingdom; 14 percent were held by the Porsche and Piëch families; and 36 percent were held by small private investors. As noted by the Chief Financial Officer, Holger Härter, "As long as the two families hold on to their stock portfolios, there won't be any external influence on company-related decisions. I have no doubt that the families will hang on to their shares."

Porsche was somewhat infamous for its independent thought and occasional stubbornness when it came to disclosure and compliance with reporting requirements—the prerequisites of being publicly traded. In 2002 the company had chosen not to list on the New York Stock Exchange after the passage of the Sarbanes-Oxley Act. The company pointed to the specific requirement of Sarbanes-Oxley that senior management sign off on the financial results of the company personally as inconsistent with German law (which it largely was) and illogical for management to accept. Management had also long been critical of the practice of quarterly reporting and had, in fact, been removed from the Frankfurt exchange's stock index in September 2002 because of its refusal to report quarterly financial results.

But, after all was said and done, the company had just reported record profits for the tenth consecutive year. Returns were so good and had grown so steadily that the company had paid out a special dividend of €14 per share in 2002, in addition to increasing the size of the regular dividend. There was a continuing concern that management came first. In the words of one analyst, "… we think there is the potential risk that management may not rate shareholders' interests very highly." The compensation packages of Porsche's senior management team were nearly exclusively focused on current-year profitability (83 percent of executive board compensation was performance-related pay), with no management incentives or stock option awards related to the company's share price. But the share price had continued to climb year after year, so regardless of their concerns, the analysts could not complain. Shareholders and family members alike were making money.

As You Read This Chapter

1. Should stockholders distinguish between a company's ability to generate results for stockholders versus its willingness to do so?
2. Consider the financial objective: Is pursuing the interests of Porsche's controlling families different from maximizing the returns to its public share owners?

MAXIMIZATION OF SHAREHOLDER VALUE

The ultimate goal of the management of a multinational firm to increase the value of the shareholder's investment as much as possible.

What does the management of any firm operating outside national borders attempt to achieve? The **maximization of shareholder value** is, of course, the ultimate goal, and given the good graces of the marketplace, that is indeed what is eventually achieved. But internally, within the virtual walls of the firm, what exactly is management trying to maximize or minimize in pursuit of this goal? This chapter first discusses how the global firm trades off complex goals in order to preserve and create shareholder value and how the financial management activities of the firm differ from domestic management. The chapter then provides an overview of the major differences between accounting practices and corporate taxation philosophies among major industrial countries. Although the average business manager cannot be expected to have a detailed understanding of these topics, familiarity aids in understanding why "certain things are done certain ways" in international business.

 ## GLOBAL FINANCIAL GOALS

 The multinational firm, because it is a conglomeration of many firms operating in a multitude of economic environments, must determine for itself the proper balance among three primary financial objectives:

1. Maximization of consolidated, after-tax income
2. Minimization of the firm's effective global tax burden
3. Correct positioning of the firm's income, cash flows, and available funds

These goals are frequently contradictory, in that the pursuit of one goal may result in a less-desirable outcome for another. Management must make decisions about the proper trade-offs among goals and their effects in the future (which is why people—not computers—are employed as managers).

International Capital Budgeting

Any investment, whether it is the purchase of stock, the acquisition of real estate, or the construction of a manufacturing facility in another country, is financially justified if the present value of expected cash inflows is greater than the present value of expected cash outflows—in other words, if it has a positive **net present value (NPV)**. The construction of a capital budget is the process of projecting the net operating cash flows of the potential investment to determine if it is indeed a good investment.

Capital Budget Components and Decision Criteria

Capital budgets are only as good as the accuracy of the cost and revenue assumptions on which they are based. Adequately anticipating all of the incremental expenses that the individual project imposes on the firm is critical to a proper analysis. A capital budget is composed of three primary cash flow components:

1. **Capital outlays:** Initial expenses and capital outlays are normally the largest net cash outflow occurring over the life of an investment. Because they occur up front, they have a substantial impact on the net present value of the project.
2. **Operating cash flows:** These are the net cash flows the project is expected to yield, once production is under way. The primary positive net cash flows of the project are realized in this stage; net operating cash flows will determine the success or failure of the investment.
3. **Terminal cash flows:** These represent the salvage value or resale value of the project at its end. The terminal value will include whatever working capital balances can be recaptured, once the project is no longer in operation (at least by this owner).

The financial decision criterion for an individual investment is whether the net present value of the project is positive or negative. The net cash flows in the future are discounted by the average cost of capital for the firm (the average of debt and equity costs). The purpose of discounting is to capture the fact that the firm has acquired investment capital at a cost (interest). The same capital could have been used for other projects or other investments. It is therefore necessary to discount the future cash flows to account for this forgone income of the capital, or opportunity cost. If the NPV is positive, then the project is an acceptable investment. If the project's NPV is negative, then the cash flows expected to result from the investment are insufficient to provide an acceptable rate of return, and the project should be rejected.

A Proposed Project Evaluation

The capital budget for a manufacturing plant in Singapore serves as a basic example. Coyote, a U.S. manufacturer of household consumer products, is considering the construction of a plant in Singapore in 2004. It would cost S$1,660,000 to build and would be ready for operation on January 1, 2005. Coyote would operate the plant for three years and then sell it to the Singapore government.

To analyze the proposed investment, Coyote must estimate annual sales revenues, production costs, overhead expenses, depreciation allowances for the new plant and equipment, and the Singapore tax liability on corporate income. The estimation of all net operating cash flows is very important to the analysis of the project. Often the entire acceptability of a foreign investment may depend on the sales forecast for the foreign project.

But Coyote needs U.S. dollars, not Singapore dollars. The only way the stockholders would be willing to undertake the investment is if it would be profitable in terms of their own currency, the U.S. dollar. This is the primary theoretical distinction between a domestic capital budget and a multinational capital budget. The evaluation of the project in the viewpoint of

NET PRESENT VALUE (NPV)

The sum of the present values of all cash inflows and outflows from an investment project discounted at the cost of capital.

CAPITAL BUDGET

The financial evaluation of a proposed investment to determine whether the expected returns are sufficient to justify the investment expenses.

CAPITAL OUTLAYS

Upfront costs and expenses of a proposed investment.

OPERATING CASH FLOWS

Cash flows arising from the firm's everyday business activities.

TERMINAL CASH FLOWS

Salvage value or resale value of the project at its termination.

the parent company will focus on whatever cash flows, either operational or financial, will find their way back to the parent firm in U.S. dollars.

Coyote must therefore forecast the movement of the Singapore dollar (S$) over the four-year period. The spot rate on January 1, 2004, is S$1.6600/US$. Coyote concludes that the rate of inflation will be roughly 5 percent higher per year in Singapore than in the United States. If the theory of purchasing power parity holds, as described in Chapter 8, it should take roughly 5 percent more Singapore dollars to buy a U.S. dollar per year. Using this assumption, Coyote forecasts the exchange rate from 2004 to 2007.

After considerable study and analysis, Coyote estimates that the net cash flows of the Singapore project, in Singapore dollars, would be those on line 1 in Table 9.1. Line 2 lists the expected exchange rate between Singapore dollars and U.S. dollars over the four-year period, assuming it takes 5 percent more Singapore dollars per U.S. dollar each year (the Singapore dollar is therefore expected to depreciate versus the U.S. dollar). Combining the net cash flow forecast in Singapore dollars with the expected exchange rates, Coyote can now calculate the net cash flow per year in U.S. dollars. Coyote notes that although the initial expense is sizable, S$1,660,000 or US$1,000,000, the project produces positive net cash flows in its very first year of operations (2005) of US$172,117, and remains positive every year thereafter.

Coyote estimates that the cost to the company of capital, both debt and equity combined, is about 16 percent per year. Using this as the rate of discount, the discount factor for each of the future years can be calculated. Finally, the net cash flow in U.S. dollars multiplied by the present value factor yields the present values of each net cash flow. The net present value of the Singapore project is a negative US$107,919; Coyote may now decide not to proceed with the project, because it is financially too risky.

Risks in International Investments

How is the Coyote capital budget different from a similar project constructed in Bangor, Maine? It is riskier, at least from the standpoint of cross-border risk. The higher risk of an international investment arises from the different countries—their laws, regulations, potential for interference with the normal operations of the investment project, and, obviously, currencies, all of which are unique to international investment.

The risk of international investment is considered greater because the proposed investment will be within the jurisdiction of a different government. Governments have the ability to pass

TABLE 9.1 Multinational Capital Budget: Singapore Manufacturing Facility

LINE #	DESCRIPTION	2004	2005	2006	2007
1	Net cash flow in S$	(1,660,000)	300,000	600,000	1,500,000
2	Exchange rate, S$/US$	1.66	1.743	1.8302	1.9217
3	Net cash flow in US$	(1,000,000)	172,117	327,833	780,559
4	Present value factor	1.0000	0.8621	0.7432	0.6407
5	Present value in US$	(1,000,000)	148,377	243,633	500,071
6	Net present value in US$	(107,919)			
7	Net present value in S$	5,505			

Notes:
a. The spot exchange rate of S$1.6600/US$ is assumed to change by 5 percent per year, 1.6600 x 1.05 = 1.7430.
b. The present value factor assumes a weighted average cost of capital, the discount rate, of 16 percent. The present value factor then is found using the standard formula of $1/(1 + 16)^t$, where t is the number of years in the future (1, 2, or 3).

new laws, including the potential nationalization of the entire project. The typical problems that may arise from operating in a different country are changes in foreign tax laws, restrictions placed on when or how much in profits may be repatriated to the parent company, and other types of restrictions that hinder the free movement of merchandise and capital among the proposed project, the parent company, and any other country relevant to its material inputs or sales.

The other major distinction between a domestic investment and a foreign investment is that the perspective of the parent company and the project are no longer the same. The two perspectives differ because the parent values only cash flows it derives from the project. So, for example, in Table 9.1 the project generates sufficient net cash flows in Singapore dollars that the project is acceptable from the project's viewpoint, but not from the parent's viewpoint. Assuming the same 16 percent discount rate, the NPV in Singapore dollars is 1S$5,505, while the NPV to the U.S. parent is 2US$107,919, as noted previously. But what if the exchange rate were not to change at all, remaining fixed for the 2004–2007 period? The NPV would then be positive from both viewpoints (the project NPV remains at 1S$5,505; the parent's NPV is now US$3,316). Or what if the Singapore government were to restrict the payment of dividends back to the U.S. parent firm or somehow prohibit the subsidiary from exchanging Singapore dollars for U.S. dollars (capital controls)? Without cash flows in U.S. dollars, the parent would have no way of justifying the investment. And all of this could occur while the project itself is sufficiently profitable when measured in local currency. This split between project and parent viewpoints is a critical difference in international investment analysis.

CAPITAL STRUCTURE: INTERNATIONAL DIMENSIONS

2 LEARNING OBJECTIVE

The way a firm is funded is referred to as its capital structure. Capital is needed to open a factory, build an amusement park, or even start a hot-dog stand. If capital is provided by owners of the firm, it is called equity. If capital is obtained by borrowing from others, such as commercial banking institutions, it is termed debt. Debt must be repaid, with interest, over some specified schedule. Equity capital, however, is kept in the firm.

Any firm's ability to grow and expand is dependent on its ability to acquire additional capital as it grows. The net profits generated over previous periods may be valuable but are rarely enough to provide needed capital expansion. Firms therefore need access to capital markets, both debt and equity. Chapter 8 provided an overview of the major debt and equity markets available internationally, but it is important to remember that the firm must have access to the markets to enjoy their fruits.

The Capital Structure of Foreign Subsidiaries

The choice of what proportions of debt and equity to use in international investments is usually dictated by either the **debt-equity structure** of the parent or the debt-equity structure of competitive firms in the host country. The parent firm sees equity investment as capital at risk; therefore, it would usually prefer to provide as little equity capital as possible. Although funding the foreign subsidiary primarily with debt would still put the parent's capital at risk, debt service provides a strict schedule for cash flow repatriation to the lender. Equity capital's return—dividends from profits—depends on managerial discretion.

The sources of debt, listed in Table 9.2, are not always available, since many countries have relatively small capital markets. The parent firm is then often forced to provide not only the equity but also a large proportion of the debt to its foreign subsidiaries.

DEBT-EQUITY STRUCTURE

A firm's combination of capital obtained by borrowing from others, such as banks (debts), and capital provided by owners (equity).

Inflation Rates and Interest Rates around the World

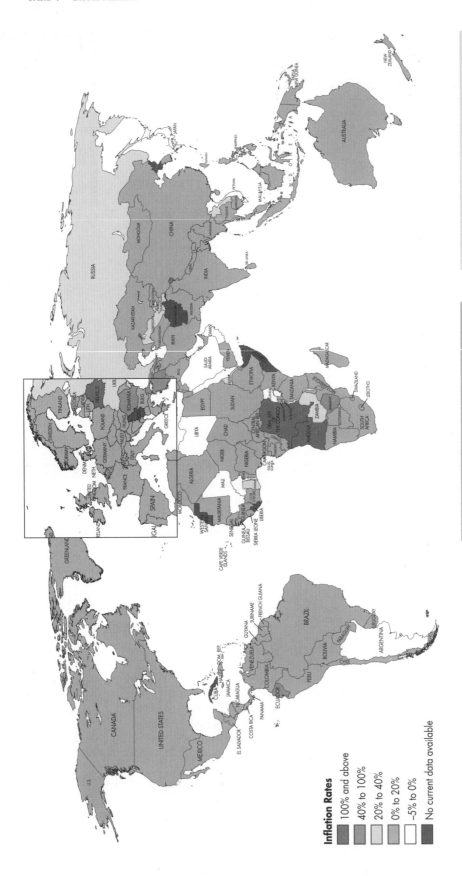

Inflation Rates

- 100% and above
- 40% to 100%
- 20% to 40%
- 0% to 20%
- –5% to 0%
- No current data available

Highest Inflation Rates

Dem. Rep. of Congo	555.7	Burundi	31.9
Angola	325.0	Moldova	31.3
Belarus	169.0	Malawi	29.6
Ecuador	96.2	Ukraine	28.2
Zimbabwe	55.9	Laos	27.1
Turkey	54.9	Uzbekistan	25.4
Romania	45.7	Ghana	25.0
Tajikistan	34.0		

Highest Lending Rates

Dem. Rep. of Congo	119.2	Belarus	45.6
Angola	74.9	Zambia	35.1
Ecuador	58.6	Russia	34.3
Kyrgystan	55.4	Armenia	33.4
Zimbabwe	50.0	Mongolia	32.2
Ukraine	49.5	Moldova	30.1
Malawi	48.2	Bolivia	30.0
Uruguay	47.9		

Sources: *2001 World Development Indicators,* The World Bank; International Monetary Fund, **www.imf.org/external/ pubs/ft/weo/2001/01/data/**

International Working Capital and Cash Flow Management

Working capital management is the financing of short-term or current assets, but the term is used here to describe all short-term financing and financial management of the firm. Even a small multinational firm will have a number of different cash flows moving throughout its system at one time. The maintenance of proper liquidity, the monitoring of payments, and the acquisition of additional capital when needed—all of these require a great degree of organization and planning in international operations.

WORKING CAPITAL MANAGEMENT

The management of a firm's current assets (cash, accounts receivable, inventories) and current liabilities (accounts payable, short-term debt).

Operating Cash Flows and Financing Cash Flows

Firms possess both operating cash flows and financing cash flows. Operating cash flows arise from the everyday business activities of the firm, such as paying for materials or resources (accounts payable) or receiving payments for items sold (accounts receivable) or licenses granted. **Financing cash flows** arise from the funding activities of the firm. The servicing of existing funding sources, interest on existing debt, and dividend payments to shareholders constitute potentially large and frequent cash flows. Periodic additions to debt or equity through new bank loans, new bond issuances, or supplemental stock sales may also add to the volume of financing cash flows in the multinational firm.

FINANCING CASH FLOWS

The cash flows arising from the firm's funding activities.

Cash Flow Management

The structure of the firm dictates how cash flows and financial resources can be managed. The trend in the past decade has been toward the increasing centralization of most financial and treasury operations. The centralized treasury often is responsible for both funding operations and cash flow management. It may enjoy significant economies of scale, offering more services and expertise to the various units of the firm worldwide than the individual units themselves could support. However, regardless of whether the firm follows a centralized or decentralized approach, there are a number of operating structures that help the multinational firm manage its cash flows.

NETTING Netting, or cash flow coordination between units, can occur between each subsidiary and the parent, and between the subsidiaries themselves. Coordination simply requires some planning and budgeting of interfirm cash flows in order that two-way flows are netted against one another. Netting is particularly helpful if the two-way flow is in two different currencies, as each would otherwise suffer currency exchange charges for intrafirm transfers.

NETTING

Cash flow coordination between a corporation's global units so that only one smaller cash transfer must be made.

TABLE 9.2 Financing Alternatives for Foreign Affilliates

FOREIGN AFFILIATE CAN RAISE EQUITY CAPITAL:	FOREIGN AFFILIATE CAN RAISE DEBT CAPITAL:
1. From the parent	1. From the parent
2. From a joint-venture partner in the parent's country, a joint-venture partner in the host country, or a share issue in the host country	2. From a bank loan or bond issue in the host country or the parent firm's home country
3. From a third-country market such as a share issue in the Euro-equity market	3. From a third-country bank loan, bond issue, Euro-syndicated credit, or Euro-bond issue

CASH POOLING   A large firm with a number of units operating both within an individual country and across countries may be able to economize on the amount of firm assets needed in cash if one central pool is used for **cash pooling**. With one pool of capital and up-to-date information on the cash flows in and out of the various units, the firm spends much less in terms of forgone interest on cash balances, which are held in safekeeping against unforeseen cash flow shortfalls.

CASH POOLING

Used by multinational firms to centralize individual units' cash flows, resulting in less spending or fore-gone interest on unnecessary cash balances.

LEADS AND LAGS   The timing of payments between units of a multinational is somewhat adjustable. Again, this allows the management of payments between a parent firm and its subsidiaries to be much more flexible, allowing the firm not only to position cash flows where they are needed most, but also to help manage currency risk. A foreign subsidiary that is expecting its local currency to fall in value relative to the U.S. dollar may try to speed up, or **lead**, its payments to the parent firm. Similarly, if the local currency is expected to rise versus the dollar, the subsidiary may want to wait, or **lag**, payments until exchange rates are more favorable.

LEADS

Paying a debt early to take advantage of exchange rates.

LAGS

Paying a debt late to take advantage of exchange rates.

RE-INVOICING   Multinational firms with a variety of manufacturing and distribution subsidiaries scattered over a number of countries within a region may often find it more economical to have one office or subsidiary taking ownership of all invoices and payments between units. The subsidiary literally buys from one unit and sells to a second unit, thereby taking ownership of the goods and **re-invoicing** the sale to the next unit. Once ownership is taken, the sale/purchase can be redenominated in a different currency, netted against other payments, hedged against specific currency exposures, or repriced in accordance with potential tax benefits of the re-invoicing center's host country.

RE-INVOICING

The policy of buying goods from one unit, selling them to a second unit, and re-invoicing the sale to the next unit, to take advantage of favorable exchange rates.

INTERNAL BANKS   Some multinational firms have found that their financial resources and needs are becoming either too large or too sophisticated for the financial services that are available in many of their local subsidiary markets. One solution to this has been the establishment of an **internal bank** within the firm. The internal bank actually buys and sells payables and receivables from the various units, which frees the units of the firm from struggling for continual working-capital financing and lets them focus on their primary business activities.

INTERNAL BANK

A multinational firm's financial management tool that actually acts as a bank to coordinate finances among its units.

COMBINING METHODS   All of these structures and management techniques are often combined in different ways to fit the needs of the individual multinational firm. Some techniques are encouraged or prohibited by laws and regulations (for example, many countries limit the ability to lead and lag payments), depending on the host-country's government and stage of capital market liberalization. Multinational cash flow management requires flexibility in thinking—artistry in some cases—as much as technique on the part of managers.

 FOREIGN EXCHANGE EXPOSURE

3 LEARNING OBJECTIVE

Companies today know the risks of international operations. They are aware of the substantial risks to balance sheet values and annual earnings that interest rates and exchange rates may inflict on any firm at any time. Financial managers, international treasurers, and financial officers of all kinds are expected to protect the firm from such risks. Firms have, in varying

Culture Clues   In Saudi Arabia, the system of hospitality is based on mutuality. An invitation must be returned; an equal gift must be offered in return. The offer of hospitality to visit an Arab's home must be accepted. Today, you may be the guest, but tomorrow you must play the host.

degrees, three types of foreign currency exposure: transaction exposure, economic exposure, and translation exposure.

Managing Transaction Exposure

Only two conditions are necessary for a **transaction exposure** to exist: (1) a cash flow that is denominated in a foreign currency, and (2) the cash flow that will occur at a future date. For example, a U.S. firm that exports products to France will receive a guaranteed (by contract) payment in French francs in the future. Any contract, agreement, purchase, or sale that is denominated in a foreign currency that will be settled in the future constitutes a transaction exposure.

The risk of a transaction exposure is that the exchange rate might change—for better or worse—between the present date and the settlement date. Suppose that an American firm signs a contract to purchase heavy rolled-steel pipe from a South Korean producer for 21,000,000 Korean *won*. The payment is due in 30 days upon delivery. The 30-day account payable, so typical of international trade and commerce, is a transaction exposure for the U.S. firm. If the spot exchange rate on the date the contract is signed is *Won* 700/$, the U.S. firm would expect to pay:

$$\frac{Won\ 21{,}000{,}000}{Won\ 700/\$} \quad = \quad \$30{,}000$$

But the firm is not assured of what the exchange rate will be in 30 days. If the spot rate at the end of 30 days is *Won* 720/$, the U.S. firm would actually pay less. The payment would then be $29,167. If, however, the exchange rate changed in the opposite direction, for example to *Won* 650/$, the payment could just as easily increase to $32,308.

Management of transaction exposures usually is accomplished by hedging. **Natural hedging** is the term used to describe how a firm might arrange to have foreign currency cash flows coming in and going out at roughly the same times and same amounts. The exposure is managed simply by matching offsetting foreign currency cash flows. For example, a Canadian firm that generates a significant portion of its total sales in U.S. dollars may acquire U.S. dollar debt. The U.S. dollar earnings from sales could then be used to service that debt. In this way, regardless of whether the C$/US$ exchange rate goes up or down, the firm would be naturally hedged against the movement. If the U.S. dollar went up in value against the Canadian dollar, the U.S. dollars needed for debt service would be generated automatically by export sales to the United States. U.S. dollar inflows would match U.S. dollar cash outflows.

Contractual hedging occurs when a firm uses financial contracts to hedge the transaction exposure. The most common foreign currency contractual hedge is the forward contract, as explained in Chapter 8, although other financial instruments and derivatives, such as currency futures and options, are also used. Forward contracts allow the firm to be assured a fixed rate of exchange between the desired two currencies at the precise future date. The forward contract would also be for the exact amount of the exposure.

Managing Economic Exposure

Economic exposure, also called operating exposure, is the change in the value of a firm arising from unexpected changes in exchange rates. Economic exposure emphasizes that there is a limit to a firm's ability to predict either cash flows or exchange rate changes in the medium to long term. All firms, either directly or indirectly, have economic exposure—even domestic concerns. A barber in Ottumwa, Iowa, seemingly isolated from exchange rate chaos, nevertheless is affected when the dollar rises or falls. If U.S. products become increasingly expensive to foreign buyers, American manufacturers, such as John Deere in Iowa, are forced to cut back production and lay off workers, and businesses of all types decline—even the business of barbers.

TRANSACTION EXPOSURE

The potential for losses or gains when a firm is engaged in a transaction denominated in a foreign currency.

NATURAL HEDGING

The structuring of a firm's operations so that cash flows by currency, inflows against outflows, are matched.

CONTRACTUAL HEDGING

A multinational firm's use of contracts to minimize its transaction exposure.

ECONOMIC EXPOSURE

The potential for long-term effects on a firm's value as the result of changing currency values.

WORLD VIEW

SHAREHOLDER WEALTH OR STAKEHOLDER CAPITALISM?

Which will generate greater global competitiveness: *shareholder wealth maximization* or the more traditional model of *stakeholder capitalism*?

SHAREHOLDER WEALTH MAXIMIZATION

The Anglo-American markets—the United States and United Kingdom primarily—have followed the philosophy that a firm's objective should be *shareholder wealth maximization*. More specifically, the firm should strive to maximize the return to shareholders, as measured by the sum of capital gains and dividends. This philosophy is based on the assumption that stock markets are efficient. This means that the share price is always correct, as it quickly incorporates all new information about expectations of return and risk in share prices. Share prices, in turn, are deemed the best allocators of capital in the macroeconomy.

Agency theory is the study of how shareholders can motivate management to accept the prescriptions of shareholder wealth. For example, liberal use of stock options should encourage management to think like shareholders. If, however, management deviates too far from shareholder objectives, the company's board of directors is responsible for replacing the managers. In cases where the board is too weak or ingrown to take this action, the discipline of the equity markets could do it through a takeover. This discipline is made possible by the one-share, one-vote rule that exists in most Anglo-American markets.

STAKEHOLDER CAPITALISM

In the non-Anglo-American markets, particularly Continental Europe, controlling shareholders also strive to maximize long-term returns to equity. However, they are more constrained by powerful other stakeholders like creditors, labor unions, governments, and communities. In particular, labor unions are often much more powerful than in the Anglo-American markets. Governments often intervene more in the marketplace to protect important stakeholder groups, such as local communities, the environment, and employment. Banks and other financial institutions often have cross-memberships on corporate boards and as a result are frequently quite influential. This model has been labeled *stakeholder capitalism*.

Stakeholder capitalism does not assume that equity markets are either efficient or inefficient. It does not really matter because the firm's financial goals are not exclusively shareholder-oriented since they are constrained by the other stakeholders. In any case, stakeholder capitalism assumes that long-term "loyal" shareholders, typically controlling shareholders, should influence corporate strategy rather than the transient portfolio investor.

Although both philosophies have their strengths and weaknesses, two trends in recent years have led to an increasing focus on shareholder wealth. First, as more of the non Anglo-American markets have increasingly privatized their industries, the shareholder wealth focus is seemingly needed to attract international capital from outside investors, many of whom are from other countries. Second, and still quite controversial, many analysts believe that shareholder-based multinationals are increasingly dominating their global industry segments.

The impacts of economic exposure are as diverse as are firms in their international structure. Take the case of a U.S. corporation with a successful British subsidiary. The British subsidiary manufactures and then distributes the firm's products in Great Britain, Germany, and France. The profits of the British subsidiary are paid out annually to the American parent corporation. What would be the impact on the profitability of the British subsidiary and the entire U.S. firm if the British pound suddenly fell in value against all other major currencies?

If the British firm had been facing competition in Germany, France, and its own home market from firms in those other two continental countries, it would instantly become more competitive. If the British pound is cheaper, so are the products sold internationally by British-

---

Culture Clues   When you don't talk business can be as important as when you do. In Britain, for instance, as soon as the day is done, so is business. Nothing will turn your hosts off faster than continuing shoptalk in the pub or over dinner.

based firms. The British subsidiary of the American firm would, in all likelihood, see rising profits from increased sales.

But what of the value of the British subsidiary to the U.S. parent corporations? The same fall in the British pound that allowed the British subsidiary to gain profits would also result in substantially fewer U.S. dollars when the British pound earnings are converted at the end of the year. It seems that it is nearly impossible to win in this situation. Actually, from the perspective of economic exposure management, the fact that the firm's total value—subsidiary and parent together—is roughly a wash as a result of the exchange rate change is desirable. Sound financial management assumes that a firm will profit and bear risk in its line of business, not in the process of settling payments on business already completed.

Management of economic exposure means being prepared for the unexpected. A firm such as Hewlett-Packard (HP), which is highly dependent on its ability to remain cost-competitive in markets both at home and abroad, may choose to take actions now that would allow it to passively withstand any sudden unexpected rise of the dollar. This could be accomplished through diversification: diversification of operations and diversification of financing.

Diversification of operations would allow the firm to be desensitized to the impacts of any one pair of exchange rate changes. For example, a multinational firm, such as Hewlett-Packard, may produce the same product in manufacturing facilities in Singapore, the United States, Puerto Rico, and Europe. If a sudden and prolonged rise in the dollar made production in the United States prohibitively expensive, HP already is positioned to shift production to a relatively cheaper currency environment.

Although firms rarely diversify production location for the sole purpose of currency diversification, there is a substantial additional benefit from such global expansion.

Diversification of financing serves to hedge economic exposure much in the same way as it did with transaction exposures. A firm with debt denominated in many different currencies is sensitive to many different interest rates. If one country or currency experiences rapidly rising inflation rates and interest rates, a firm with diversified debt will not be subject to the full impact of such movements. Purely domestic firms, however, are actually somewhat captive to the local conditions and are unable to ride out such interest-rate storms as easily.

Managing Translation Exposure

Translation exposure, or accounting exposure, results from the conversion or translation of foreign-currency-denominated financial statements of foreign subsidiaries and affiliates into the home currency of the parent firm. This is necessary to prepare consolidated financial statements for all firms, as country law requires. The purpose is to have all operations, worldwide, stated in the same currency terms for comparison purposes. Management often uses the translated statements to judge the performance of foreign affiliates and their personnel on the same currency terms as the parent firm itself.

However, a problem often arises from the translation of balance sheets in foreign currencies into the domestic currency. Which assets and liabilities are to be translated at current exchange rates (at the current balance sheet date) versus historical rates (those in effect on the date of the initial investment)? Or should all assets and liabilities be translated at the same rate? The answer is somewhere in between, and the process of translation is dictated by financial accounting standards.

At present in the United States, the proper method for translating foreign financial statements is given in Financial Accounting Standards Board statement No. 52 (FASB 52). If a foreign subsidiary is operating in a functional foreign currency environment, most assets, liabilities, and income statement items of foreign affiliates are translated using current exchange rates (the exchange rate in effect on the balance sheet date). For this reason, it is often referred to as the current-rate method.

TRANSLATION EXPOSURE

The potential effect on a firm's financial statements of a change in currency values.

WORLD VIEW

TO HEDGE OR NOT TO HEDGE?

With the U.S. dollar on a downswing, particularly against the euro, U.S. exporters see a way to sell more products, because their prices seem lower to foreign customers. But if currencies fluctuate before delivery and payment, with the dollar climbing back up, those same customers can be in for a nasty surprise. To offset the currency risk, large banks offer "hedging services," locking in the amount of dollars companies will receive for the sales they expect in a given period, whether it's a matter of weeks or months. Imagine, for instance, that a U.S. company sells $5 million in machine parts to a customer in Germany. At the time of the sale, the dollar is equal to the euro. By the time the goods are delivered, the dollar has strengthened against the euro. The German customer pays €5 million as promised, but that's now only worth $4.5 million. In this case, the bank takes a $500,000 hit. (Of course, in the meantime, the bank has exchanged currencies on a daily basis to offset its risk.)

With 75 percent of its operating profits generated overseas, Coca-Cola, like most multinationals, engages in hedging to protect itself from currency fluctuations. As in the simpler example above, large companies hedge their foreign earnings by buying options for future delivery at a guaranteed currency exchange rate. Yet in most cases, since there is no bank involved, the outcome can be unpredictable. In 2000, Coca-Cola gained $87 million through hedging. The company was particularly successful in Europe, where the euro

plunged more than 20 cents on the dollar in the first ten months of the year. Currency valuation slashed earnings at McDonald's by 5 percent, while Coca-Cola managed to hedge away its exposure. The following year, however, the company lost $12 million because of hedging. Analysts anticipated further losses in 2002 as the global economic downturn continued. Coca-Cola's difficulties present an opportunity for rival PepsiCo. With only 20 percent of profits coming from international markets, PepsiCo is relatively safe from currency fluctuations.

Should investors, then, take corporations to task for failing to hedge successfully? Hedging is too much akin to gambling for the answer to be "yes." By buying forward contracts, swaps, or options to get fixed rates, a company is making a bet that a currency will move either up or down. Few could predict the euro's rapid fall—or its steady climb back up to almost dollar parity in the summer of 2002.

SOURCES: Betsy Schiffman, "Still Want to Teach the World to Sing?" *Forbes*, January 16, 2002, **http://www.forbes.com**; Debra Sparks, "Business Won't Hedge the Euro Away," *BusinessWeek*, December 4, 2000; Dylan Rivera, "Hedging Offers Way for Companies to Keep Profits from Disappearing," *The Oregonian*, July 16, 2002.

Translation exposure under FASB 52 results in no cash flow impacts under normal circumstances. Although consolidated accounting does result in CTA translation losses or gains on the parent's consolidated balance sheet, the accounting entries are not ordinarily realized. Unless liquidation or sale of the subsidiary is anticipated, neither the subsidiary nor the parent firm should expend real resources on the management of an accounting convention.

INTERNATIONAL ACCOUNTING

Accounting standards and practices are, in many ways, no different in their origins from any other legislative or regulatory statutes. Laws reflect the people, places, and events of their time. Most accounting practices and laws are linked to the objectives of the parties who will use the financial information, including investors, lenders, and governments.

The fact that accounting principles differ across countries is not, by itself, a problem. However, since the accounting and taxation structures of countries are influenced by lenders, investors, and government policymakers, difficulties arise. Two firms, for instance, with identical structures, products, and strategies but based in different countries can look entirely different on paper, depending upon the accounting standards applied. In extreme cases, one may seem profitable while the other is clearly operating at a loss. Global **accounting diversity** can lead to any of the following: (1) poor or improper business decision-making; (2) difficulties in raising capital in different or foreign markets; and (3) difficulty in monitoring competitive factors across firms, industries, and nations.

Worldwide Accounting Standards

The International Accounting Standards Committee (IASC), with representatives from nine countries worldwide, seeks to create a single set of high-quality, understandable, and enforceable accounting standards. The standards would allow for transparent and comparable information in general-purpose financial statements across all countries worldwide. At present, governments limit access to capital to those companies that comply with local accounting practices; international standards would facilitate the raising of capital across borders.

U.S. corporations and accounting firms have long resisted the move toward international accounting standards (IAS), insisting that no standards are as rigorous as their own Generally Accepted Accounting Principles (GAAP). However, the Enron debacle and the bust-up of the Big Five accounting group, Andersen, that resulted from it, gave supporters of international standards an unexpected boost. The energy trader and its auditors allegedly colluded to hide off-balance-sheet transactions from investors, disguising the real financial performance of the company. Under IAS, Enron's accounting irregularities would have been spotted.[1]

ACCOUNTING DIVERSITY

The range of differences in national accounting practices.

Fast Facts

In what developed nation is housing a nontaxable perk of the job?

In Japan. Employees typically receive a housing allowance, which is not taxable. Some companies guarantee low-cost loans for the construction of housing. Larger Japanese corporations often provide executive housing, as well as dormitory-style accommodations for unmarried factory workers.

Quick Take *Zimbabwe's Disposable Currency*

Once one of the most prosperous countries in Africa, Zimbabwe seems to be nearing economic collapse.

What does it feel like to hold a few million dollars in your hands? If you're in Zimbabwe, and your wages are in Zimbabwean dollars, not very good. With hyperinflation running at 4,500 percent on an annual basis, all this cash is worth less than $100. Once one of the most prosperous countries in Africa, Zimbabwe seems to be nearing economic collapse. Unemployment is estimated at 80 percent. Electricity has been rationed to just four hours a day. A loaf of bread costs 44,000 Zimbabwean dollars, about 18 cents at black-market exchange rates—or $176 at the official rate.

To earn public support ahead of elections scheduled for March, President Robert Mugabe, who has been in power since 1980, imposed price controls in late June, which have been largely ignored. He also proposed legislation to transfer

51 percent of foreign-owned firms to local ownership and establish a government fund to help citizens buy stock in public companies.

The government would be able to reject any mergers, acquisitions, or new investments in which indigenous Zimbabweans do not hold a majority stake. To many it is an echo of Mugabe's seizure of thousands of white-owned farms, mostly without compensation, in what he called a redistribution of land to poor blacks. Instead, choice farms were handed to government officials, and food production plummeted, leading to a humanitarian crisis. Along with their shrinking buying power, Zimbabweans now have the lowest life expectancy in the world: It has dropped under Mugabe from 60 to 37 for men and from 65 to 34 for women.

SOURCE: "Zimbabwe's Disposable Currency," *Fortune*, August 6, 2007.

Preferred Items for Export in Countrtrade Transactions

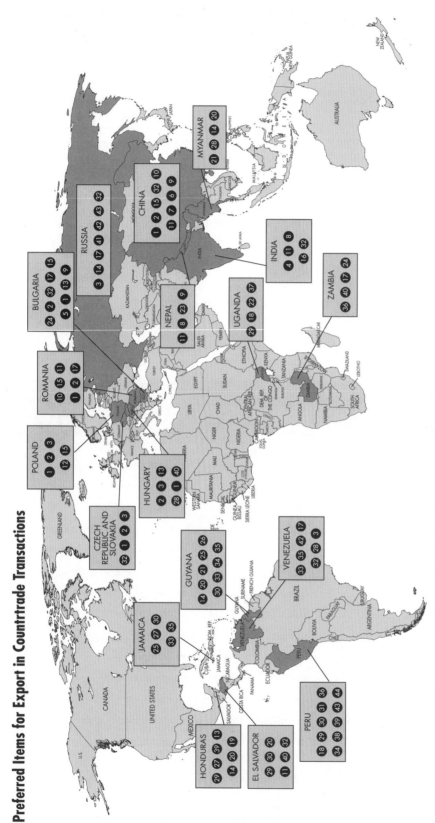

Preferred Items for Export in Countertrade Transactions

1 Industrial machinery
2 Equipment
3 Manufactured goods
4 Engineering goods
5 Plastic products
6 Sporting goods
7 Toys
8 Hides, skins & leather
9 Clothing
10 Footwear
11 Textiles
12 Animals
13 Foodstuffs
14 Timber & wood products
15 Minerals
16 Gems & jewelry
17 Metals
18 Fish meal
19 Lobster
20 Shrimp
21 Rice
22 Tea
23 Grain
24 Tobacco
25 Rum
26 Molasses
27 Fruits & vegetables
28 Agriculture
29 Coffee
30 Sugar
31 Cotton
32 Chemicals & allied products
33 Bauxite
34 Gold
35 Alumina
36 Copper
37 Iron ore
38 Lead
39 Zinc
40 Electricity
41 Natural gas
42 Petroleum
43 Petroleum products
44 Crude oil

Source: *The World Factbook 2000*

Principal Accounting Differences across Countries

There are several ways to classify and group national accounting systems and practices. Figure 9.1 illustrates one such classification. Here, accounting systems are first subdivided into micro-based (characteristics of the firms and industries) and macro-uniform (following fundamental government or economic factors per country). The micro-based national accounting systems are then broken down into those that follow a theoretical principle or pragmatic concerns. The latter category includes the national accounting systems of countries as diverse as the United States, Canada, Japan, the United Kingdom, and Mexico.

Table 9.3 provides an overview of nine major areas of significant differences in accounting practices across countries. There are, of course, many more hundreds of differences, but the nine serve to highlight some of the fundamental philosophical differences. Accounting differences are real and persistent, and there are still substantial questions of competitive advantages and informational deficiencies that may result from these continuing differences across countries.

 ## INTERNATIONAL TAXATION

Governments, alone, have the power to tax. Each government wants to tax all companies within its jurisdiction without placing burdens on domestic or foreign companies that would restrain trade. Each country states its jurisdictional approach formally in the tax treaties that

5 LEARNING OBJECTIVE

FIGURE 9.1 Nobes Classification of National Accounting Systems

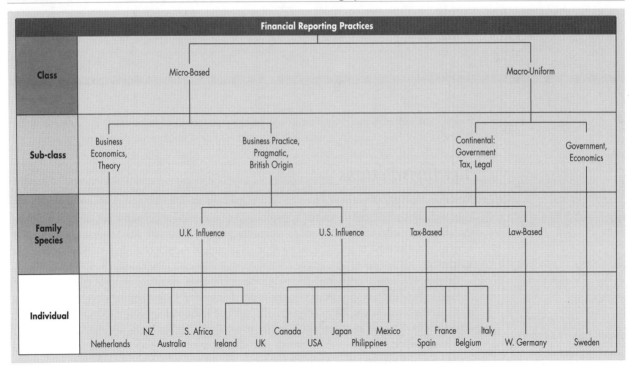

SOURCE: C. W. Nobes, "International Classification of Accounting Systems," unpublished paper, April 1980. Table C, as cited in *International Accounting*, 2d ed., Frederick D.S. Choi and gerhard G. Mueller (Upper Saddle River, NJ: Prentice-Hall, 1992, p. 34.

Quick Take *How Green Is My Balance Sheet?*

When it comes to environmental accounting, many companies have yet to come clean. Those that publish "green accounts" usually offer a few charts (printed, of course, on recycled and unbleached paper) showing trends in their output of waste. But the gases and gunk are measured in kilos or tonnes, not pounds or dollars, and few companies convert data into figures that can appear in financial accounts.

The task is easier in the United States than elsewhere, if only because U.S. accounting rules force companies to include detailed data on known environmental liabilities. But in Europe information is much more patchy. However, thanks to an awards program initiated by Britain's Association of Chartered & Certified Accountants, with entries from 14 accountancy bodies across the continent, some firms, such as Shell International, ScottishPower, and Thorn EMI, now publish figures on environmental liabilities.

Environmental accounting might be more popular in Europe if companies had a blueprint to follow. While guidelines exist for reporting a firm's energy consumption and

impact on the environment, none tell bean-counters how to translate this into monetary values. A few have tried. One is BSO/ Origin, a Dutch information technology firm started with 10 million guilders by entrepreneur Eckart Wintzen more than 25 years ago. The company created a method for applying financial values to natural resources used and environmental damage incurred. If environmental costs total 3.7 million guilders ($2 million) for the year, the company subtracts 450,000 guilders of "environmental expenditure" to arrive at $3.3 million guilders of "net value extracted." When Wintzen merged BSO/Origin with Phillips in 1996, it had 10,000 employees in 25 countries. He now leads Ex'tent, a management and investment company specializing in socially and environmentally responsible enterprises.

SOURCES: Sarah Perrin, "Good Citizen, Good Business," *Accounting & Business*, Association of Chartered & Certified Accountants, **http://www.accaglobal.com**; **http://www.silentplanet.com**, accessed January 3, 2003; abstracted in part from "How Green Is My Balance Sheet?" *The Economist*, September 3, 1994, p. 75.

---

it signs with other countries. One of the primary purposes of tax treaties is to establish the boundaries of each country's jurisdiction to prevent double taxation of international income.

Tax Jurisdictions

Nations usually follow one of two basic approaches to international taxation: a residential approach, or a territorial or source approach. The residential approach taxes the international income of residents without regard to where the income is earned. The territorial approach to transnational income taxes all parties within its territorial jurisdiction, regardless of country of residency.

In practice, most countries must combine the two approaches and tax foreign and domestic firms equally. For example, the United States and Japan both apply the residential approach to their own resident corporations and the territorial approach to income earned by nonresidents. Other countries, such as Germany, apply the territorial approach to dividends paid to domestic firms from their foreign subsidiaries; such dividends are assumed to be taxed abroad and are exempt from further taxation.

Within the territorial jurisdiction of tax authorities, a foreign corporation is typically defined as any business that earns income within the host country's borders but is incor-

TABLE 9.3 Summary of Principal Accounting Differences around the World

ACCOUNTING PRINCIPLE	UNITED STATES	JAPAN	UNITED KINGDOM	FRANCE	GERMANY	NETHERLANDS	SWITZERLAND	CANADA	ITALY	BRAZIL
1. Capitalization of R&D costs	Not allowed	Allowed in certain cases	Allowed in certain cases	Allowed in certain cases	Not allowed	Allowed in certain cases	Allowed in certain cases	Allowed in certain cases	Allowed in certain cases	Allowed in certain cases
2. Fixed asset revaluations stated at amount in excess of cost	Not allowed	Not allowed	Allowed	Allowed	Not allowed	Allowed in certain cases	Not allowed	Not allowed	Allowed in certain cases	Allowed
3. Inventory valuation using LIFO	Allowed	Allowed	Allowed but rarely done	Not allowed	Allowed in certain cases	Allowed	Allowed	Allowed	Allowed	Allowed but rarely done
4. Finance leases capitalized	Required	Allowed in certain cases	Required	Not allowed	Allowed in certain cases	Required	Allowed	Required	Not allowed	Not allowed
5. Pension expense accrued during period of service	Required	Allowed	Required	Allowed	Required	Required	Allowed	Required	Allowed	Allowed
6. Book and tax timing differences on balance sheet as deferred tax	Required	Allowed in certain cases	Allowed	Allowed in certain cases	Allowed but rarely done	Required	Allowed	Allowed	Allowed but rarely done	Allowed
7. Current rate method of currency translation	Required	Allowed in certain cases	Required	Allowed	Allowed	Required	Required	Allowed in certain cases	Required	Required
8. Pooling method used for mergers	Required in certain cases	Allowed in certain cases	Allowed in certain cases	Not allowed	Allowed in certain cases	Allowed but rarely done	Allowed but rarely done	Allowed but rarely done	Not allowed	Allowed but rarely done
9. Equity method used for 20—50% ownership	Required	Required	Required	Allowed in certain cases	Allowed	Required	Required	Required	Allowed	Required

SOURCE: Adapted from "A Summary of Accounting Principle Differences Around the World," Phillip R. Peller and Frank J. Schwitter, 1991, p. 4.3.

porated under the laws of another country. The foreign corporation usually must surpass some minimum level of activity (gross income) before the host country assumes primary tax jurisdiction. However, if the foreign corporation owns income-producing assets or a permanent establishment, the threshold is automatically surpassed.

Tax Types

DIRECT TAXES

Taxes applied directly to income.

INDIRECT TAXES

Taxes applied to non-income items, such as value-added taxes, excise taxes, tariffs, and so on.

VALUE-ADDED TAX (VAT)

A tax on the value added at each stage of the production and distribution process; a tax assessed in most European countries and also common among Latin American countries.

Taxes are generally classified as direct and indirect. **Direct taxes** are calculated on the actual income of an individual or a firm. **Indirect taxes**, such as sales taxes, severance taxes, tariffs, and value-added taxes, are applied to purchase prices, material costs, quantities of natural resources mined, and so forth. Although most countries still rely on income taxes as the primary method of raising revenue, tax structures vary widely.

Value-added tax (VAT) is the primary revenue source for the European Union. A value-added tax is applied to the amount of product value added by the production process. The tax is calculated as a percentage of the product price, less the cost of materials and inputs used in its manufacture, which have been taxed previously. Through this process, tax revenues are collected literally on the value added by that specific stage of the production process. Under the existing General Agreement on Tariffs and Trade (GATT), the legal framework under which international trade operates, value-added taxes may be levied on imports into a country or group of countries (such as the European Union) in order to treat foreign producers entering the domestic markets on a par with firms within the country paying VAT. Similarly, VAT may be refunded on export sales or sales to tourists who purchase products for consumption outside the country or community.

Quick Take   *Transfer Pricing or Tax Evasion?*

The fact that fully 60 percent of world trade takes place within multinational corporations has led to renewed interest in the movement of money between far-flung subsidiaries. Where associated businesses are located in different countries, a practice known as transfer pricing is key to determining how much profit is taxable in each. Assume, for instance, that a profitable German computer manufacturer buys microchips from its own Korean subsidiary. The amount paid—the transfer price—determines the amount of profit the Korean unit reports and how much it pays in local taxes. If the goods are sold at below-market prices, the Korean sister company, while part of a profitable multinational, may show a loss and so pay less to the Korean government in taxes. Clearly, this leads to trade distortions and opens the door to tax evasion. In one case, for example, Nippon Roche K.K. allegedly failed to declare taxable income totaling ¥14 billion over a three-year period. The company was accused of manipulating prices of raw materials for cancer drugs and other medicine purchased from its Swiss sister company. In a settlement between Japanese and Swiss tax authorities, Switzerland paid a sum of some ¥5.5 billion to compensate for the amount of undeclared income transferred to the parent firm to avoid double taxation. As electronic commerce across borders continues to rise, the issue of transfer pricing is likely to attract increased attention in the future.

SOURCES: John Neighbour, "Transfer Pricing: Keeping It at Arm's Length," *OECD Observer* (Paris), January, 2002, pp. 29–30; David Hardesty, *E-Commerce Tax News*, February 3, 2002, **http://www.ecommercetax.com**; "Transfer Pricing for Electronic Commerce," "Swiss Unit Faces Hefty Penalty for Tax Evasion," *Japan Times*, November 10, 1996.

FINANCING IMPORT/EXPORT OPERATIONS

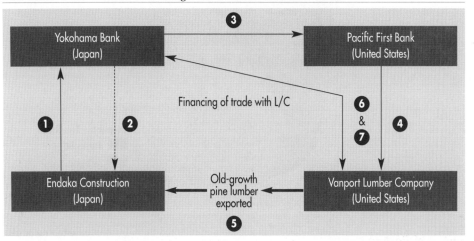

Unlike most domestic business, international business often occurs between two parties that do not know each other well and may be physically separated from each other by thousands of miles. Yet, in order to conduct business, a large degree of financial trust must exist. An order from a foreign buyer may, for instance, constitute a degree of credit risk (the risk of not being repaid) that the producer (the exporter) cannot afford to take. Other factors that tend to intensify this problem include the increased lag times necessary for international shipments and the potential risks of payments in different currencies. For this reason, arrangements that provide guarantees for exports are important to countries and companies wanting to expand international activities. This can be accomplished through a sequence of documents surrounding the **letter of credit (L/C)**.

Trade Financing Using a Letter of Credit

A lumber manufacturer in the Pacific Northwest, Vanport, receives a large order from a Japanese construction company, Endaka, for a shipment of old-growth pine lumber. Vanport has not worked with Endaka before and therefore seeks some assurance that payment will actually be made. Vanport ordinarily does not require any assurance of the buyer's ability to pay (sometimes a small down payment or deposit is made as a sign of good faith), but an international sale of this size is too large a risk. If Endaka could not or would not pay, the cost of returning the lumber products to the United States would be prohibitive. Figure 9.2 illustrates the following sequence of events that will complete the transaction.

1. Endaka Construction (Japan) requests a letter of credit (L/C) to be issued by its bank, Yokohama Bank.
2. Yokohama Bank determines whether Endaka is financially sound and capable of making the payments as required. This is a very important step, because Yokohama Bank simply wants to guarantee the payment, not make the payment.
3. Yokohama Bank, once satisfied with Endaka's application, issues the L/C to a representative in the United States or to the exporter's bank, Pacific First Bank (US). The L/C guarantees payment for the merchandise if the goods are shipped as stipulated in the accompanying

LEARNING OBJECTIVE 6

LETTER OF CREDIT (L/C)

Undertaking by a bank to make payment to a seller upon completion of a set of agreed-on conditions.

Fast Facts

What is the Bermuda Triangle?

The Bermuda Triangle, or Devil's Triangle, is an area located off the southeastern Atlantic coast of the United States noted for a high incidence of unexplained losses of ships, small boats, and aircraft. The apexes of the triangle are generally accepted to be Bermuda, Miami, Florida, and San Juan, Puerto Rico.

FIGURE 9.2   Trade Financing with a Letter of Credit (L/C)

Corporate Tax Rates around the World

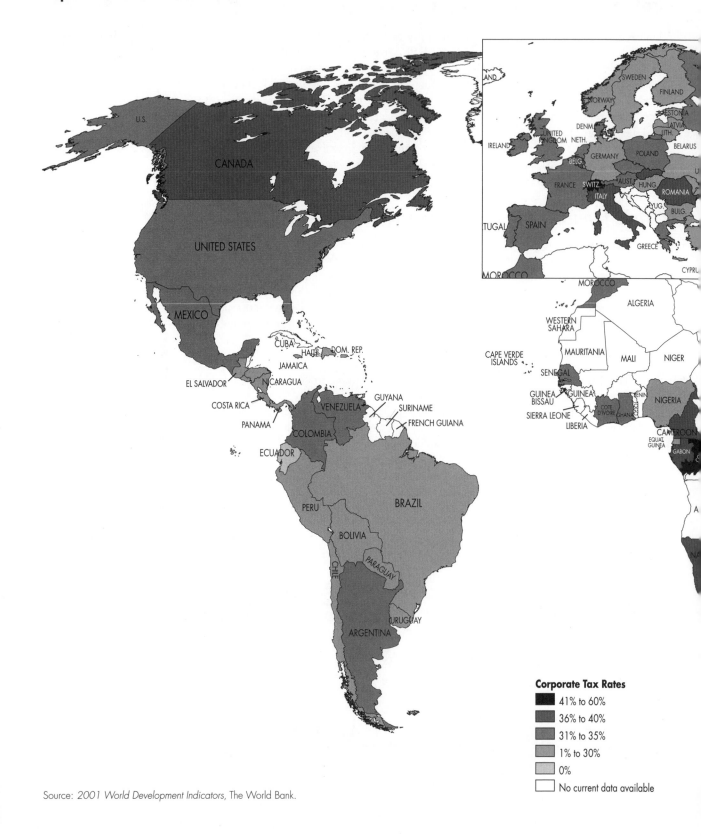

Corporate Tax Rates

- 41% to 60%
- 36% to 40%
- 31% to 35%
- 1% to 30%
- 0%
- No current data available

Source: *2001 World Development Indicators*, The World Bank.

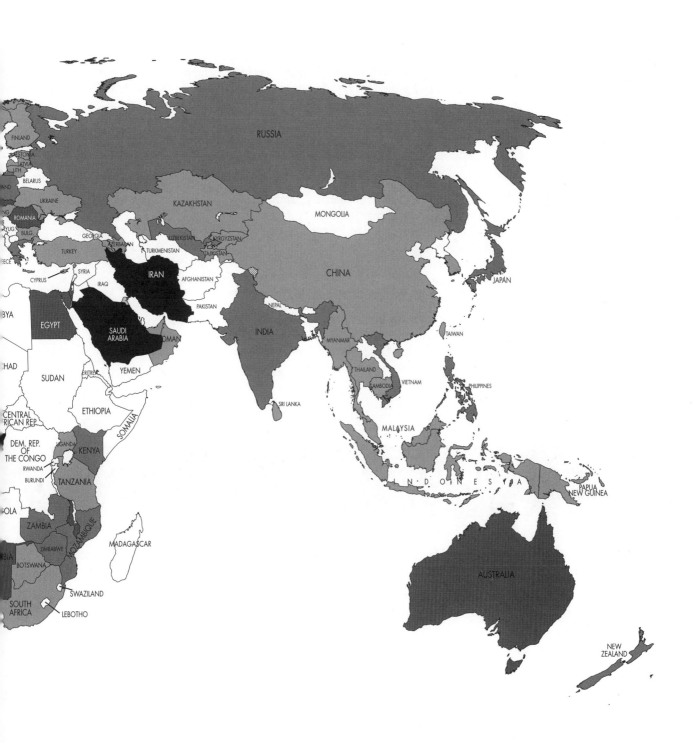

documents. Customary documents include the commercial invoice, a customs clearance and invoice, the packing list, a certification of insurance, and a bill of lading.

4. The exporter's bank, Pacific First, assures Vanport that payment will be made, after evaluating the letter of credit. At this point, the credit standing of Yokohama Bank has been substituted for the credit standing of the importer itself, Endaka Construction.

5. When the lumber order is ready, it is loaded onboard the shipper (called a common carrier). When the exporter signs a contract with a shipper, the signed contract, or the **bill of lading**, serves as the receipt that the common carrier has received the goods.

6. Vanport draws a draft against Yokohama Bank for payment. The draft is the document used in international trade to effect payment and explicitly requests payment for the merchandise, which is now shown to be shipped and insured, consistent with all requirements of the previously issued L/C. (If the draft is issued to the bank issuing the L/C, Yokohama Bank, it is termed a **bank draft**. If the draft is issued against the importer, Endaka Construction, it is a **trade draft**.) The draft, L/C, and other appropriate documents are presented to Pacific First Bank for payment.

7. If Pacific First has confirmed the letter of credit from Yokohama Bank, it will immediately pay Vanport for the lumber and then collect from the issuing bank, Yokohama. If Pacific First has not confirmed the letter of credit, it only passes the documents to Yokohama Bank for payment (to Vanport). The confirmed, as opposed to unconfirmed, letter of credit obviously speeds up payment to the exporter.

If the trade relationship continues over time, both parties will gain faith and confidence in the other. With this strengthening of financial trust, the trade financing relationship will loosen. Sustained buyer-seller relations across borders eventually end up operating on an open account basis similar to domestic commerce.

BILL OF LADING

A contract between an exporter and a carrier indicating that the carrier has accepted responsibility for the goods and will provide transportation in return for payment.

BANK DRAFT

A financial withdrawal document drawn against a bank.

TRADE DRAFT

A financial withdrawal document drawn against a company.

SUMMARY

All traditional functional areas of financial management are affected by the internationalization of the firm. Capital budgeting, firm financing, capital structure, working capital, and cash flow management, as well as all traditional accounting and taxation functions, are made more difficult by business activities that cross borders and oceans, not to mention currencies and markets.

Capital budgeting allows firms to predict the likely profitability of projects before any foreign investment is made. Due to currency fluctuations, a project that appears profitable to a local subsidiary may not seem so to the parent company. The choice among various cash flow management methods depends on the host-country government and stage of capital market liberalization.

In addition to the traditional areas of financial management, international financial management must deal with the three types of currency exposure: (1) transaction exposure, (2) economic exposure, and (3) translation exposure. Each presents serious choices regarding its exposure analysis and its degree of willingness to manage the inherent risks.

Accounting practices differ substantially across countries. The efforts of a number of inter-national associates and agencies in the past two decades have, however, led to increasing cooperation and agreement among national accounting authorities. Real accounting differences remain, and many of these differences still contribute to the advantaged com-petitive position of some countries' firms over international competitors.

International taxation is a subject close to the pocketbook of every multinational firm. Although the tax policies of most countries are theoretically designed to not change or influence financial and business decision-making by firms, they often do.

The letter of credit provides a system of guarantees for companies engaging in import-export trade, reducing the risk of nonpayment for goods and services delivered in cross-border transactions.

KEY TERMS AND CONCEPTS

maximization of shareholder value	netting	translation exposure
net present value (NPV)	cash pooling	accounting diversity
capital budget	leads	direct taxes
capital outlays	lags	indirect taxes
operating cash flows	re-invoicing	value-added tax (VAT)
terminal cash flows	internal bank	letter of credit
debt-equity structure	transaction exposure	bill of lading
working capital management	natural hedging	bank draft
financing cash flows	contractual hedging	trade draft
	economic exposure	

REVIEW QUESTIONS

1. Why is it important to identify the cash flows of a foreign investment from the perspective of the parent firm rather than from just the project?
2. How would the capital structure of a purely domestic firm differ from that of a firm with multiple international subsidiaries?
3. Which type of firm do you believe is more "naturally hedged" against exchange-rate exposure, the purely domestic firm (the barber) or the multinational firm (subsidiaries all over the world)?
4. What is the nature of the purported benefit that accounting principles provide British firms over American firms in the competition for mergers and acquisitions?

5. Why do you think foreign subsidiaries in which U.S. corporations hold more than 50 percent voting power are classified and treated differently for U.S. tax purposes?
6. Why do the U.S. tax authorities want U.S. corporations to charge their foreign subsidiaries for general and admin-istrative services? What does this mean for the creation of excess foreign tax credits by U.S. corporations with foreign operations?
7. What is value-added tax and what benefits or drawbacks does it entail for European companies?
8. How can an exporter of goods or services protect itself against nonpayment? Describe the process.

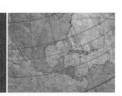

Culture Clues   In India, "yes" often means "maybe." An Indian who hesitates to say "no" may be trying to convey a willingness to try a task that may be unrealistic and that will likely never get done. When conducting business in India, particularly with employees, it is important to create a safe and comfortable work environment, where it is okay to say no, and it's also okay to make mistakes without fear of repercussions.

CRITICAL SKILL BUILDERS

1. As a manufacturer and marketer of hard candies, your company has decided to relocate its operations to Mexico, where the costs of raw materials—i.e., sugar—and labor will increase efficiency. At the same time, your company plans to develop new markets in South America and China. What aspects of capital structure and risk exposure must be taken into consideration?

2. In small groups, discuss this potential dilemma: "High political risk requires companies to seek a quick payback on their investments. Striving for a quick payback, however, exposes firms to charges of exploitation and results in increased political risk."

3. Do you think all firms, in all economic environments, should operate under the same set of accounting principles? Name two major indications that progress is being made toward standardizing accounting principles across countries.

4. After you hand your passport to the immigration officer in country X, he misplaces it. A small "donation" would certainly help him find it again. Should you give him the money? Is this a business expense to be charged to your company? Should it be tax-deductible?

5. As a company expands into the global business arena and establishes wholly owned subsidiaries abroad, new financial challenges appear. These include managing cash flow across international borders and financing the subsidiary using international security markets. Subsidiaries abroad also require a new perspective on such issues as accounting practices and taxation. Create a brief financial plan of action for a company making its first moves in foreign markets.

ON THE WEB

1. Using the following major periodicals as starting points, find a current example of a firm with a substantial operating exposure problem. To aid in your search, you might focus on businesses having major operations in countries with recent currency crises, either through devaluation or major home-currency appreciation. Sources are *Financial Times* at **http://www.ft.com**; *The Economist* at **http://www.economist.com**; and *The Wall Street Journal* at **http://www.wsj.com**.

2. In the World Trade Organization's Agreement on Government Procurement, how are off-sets defined and what stance is taken toward them (refer to the government procurement page on the web site **http://www.wto.org**)?

3. The Financial Accounting Standards Board (FASB) promulgates standard practices for the reporting of financial results by U.S. companies. However, it also often leads the way in the development of new practices and emerging issues around the world. One such major issue today is the valuation and reporting of financial derivatives and derivative agreements by firms. Use the FASB's web site (**http://raw.rutgers.edu/raw/fasb/**) and sites for major accounting firms and other interest groups around the world to see current proposed accounting standards and reactions to them. Another useful site is the Treasury Management Association at **http://www.tma.org**.

ENDNOTES

1. "Europe's Bean Counters Are Sneering," *BusinessWeek*, January 28, 2002; Jonathan Weil, "Accounting Board Is Formed to Create One Set of Standards for Use Worldwide," *The Wall Street Journal*, January 26, 2001; see also **http://www.iasc.org.uk**.

PART 5

GLOBAL OPERATIONS

To operate successfully abroad, firms must first understand not only the environmental factors that lead them to seek new markets overseas, but their own motivations for doing so. They must then prepare for their market entry by developing a realistic and achievable global entry or expansion strategy. Over time, expansion can occur through foreign direct investment and can lead to the formation of the multi-national corporation. In Part 5, we will explore how firms move into global markets and the marketing, promotion, distribution, and management strategies that lead to their long-term success or failure.

CHAPTER 10

EXPORTING AND GLOBAL EXPANSION

Apples Go International

What are apples from the state of Virginia doing in Cuba? Well, for one thing, they're making a profit. The Virginia Apple Growers Association (VAGA) decided to take its products, 11 different varieties of apples, overseas. To do so, the Association created an export trading company (ETC) called the Virginia Apple Trading Company (VATC). By sharing the costs of finding clients, marketing their products abroad, and shipping and transportation, an international presence became possible for Virginia apple growers. Furthermore, because of U.S. ETC antitrust legislation, participating growers can act jointly to set export prices and share product and market information, enabling them to act more like a large company than many small ones. VAGA eventually awarded the management contract for the ETC to GIC Group, a U.S. agribusiness consulting and investment advisory firm.

Today, Virginia growers ship apples and processed apple products such as applesauce and apple juice to more than 20 countries and regions including: Central America, Caribbean, Cuba, Mexico, Brazil, Russia, Scandinavia, United Kingdom, and India. In the state of Virginia, apple growing is a very important economic activity. Apple orchards cover over 18,000 acres of the landscape, and apple growers contribute an estimated $235 million to the economy. The United States produces about 250 million bushels of apples annually—that's enough for almost one bushel for every person! (1 bushel = approximately 42 pounds). However, the average American consumer eats only about 19 pounds of fresh apples, 4 pounds of canned apples, and 1.7 gallons of apple juice. This excess capacity is an obvious motivation for going international.

However, for a small private business, going international is a daunting task. Therefore, for these apple growers, an ETC arrangement became not only practical, but necessary. Although there are relatively few export trading companies in the United States, their services have enabled thousands of small and medium-sized business to tap the potential of the international marketplace.

SOURCES: GIC Group, **http://www.gicgroup.com/Management_Services/ETC/vatc.asp**, accessed February 17, 2008; Virginia Department of Agriculture and Consumer Services, Richmond, VA, **http://www.vdacs.virginia.gov/international/vatc-english.html**, accessed April 19, 2006; "Apple Facts." Vermont Apples. **http://www.vermontapples.org/facts.html**, accessed February 17, 2008.

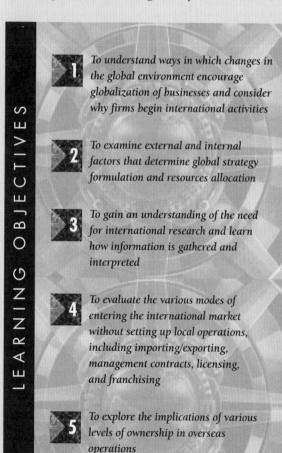

LEARNING OBJECTIVES

1 To understand ways in which changes in the global environment encourage globalization of businesses and consider why firms begin international activities

2 To examine external and internal factors that determine global strategy formulation and resources allocation

3 To gain an understanding of the need for international research and learn how information is gathered and interpreted

4 To evaluate the various modes of entering the international market without setting up local operations, including importing/exporting, management contracts, licensing, and franchising

5 To explore the implications of various levels of ownership in overseas operations

As You Read This Chapter

1. How can a producer from a high-cost country (e.g. U.S.) compete in a low-cost nation such as Cuba?
2. What can governments do to encourage smaller firms to expand their operations abroad?

Rapid transformation of the world marketplace forces companies large and small to look outward from their domestic markets not only for future growth, but for survival. This chapter begins by exploring the motivations that drive companies to enter new markets, leading them to formulate global strategies that take advantage of underlying market, cost, competitive, and environmental factors—a knowledge that is gained by thorough international business research. The chapter then shows the various options open to companies that are preparing to begin or expand their international activities. Even though new markets are constantly emerging, firms cannot simply jump into the international marketplace and expect to be successful. They must recognize and adjust to needs and opportunities abroad; have quality, in-demand products; understand their customers; and do their homework.

This chapter begins by providing a detailed guide to the structure and functions of the foreign currency markets. It then explores the international financial markets and the securities markets that connect the financial markets of individual nations. All firms striving to attain or preserve competitiveness in the global arena must work with and within the frameworks of these markets, which operate independently of the jurisdiction or supervision of governmental authorities.

GLOBALIZATION DRIVERS

Several external and internal factors drive the development of a global marketplace. These can be divided into market, cost, environmental, and competitive factors.

1. *Market factors:* Similarities in demand conditions across multiple countries encourage the development of single global strategies. For example, in markets as far-flung as North America, Europe, and the Far East, there are consumer groups that share similar educational backgrounds, income levels, lifestyles, use of leisure time, and aspirations. Approximately 600 million in number, these consumers can in many ways be treated as a single market with the same spending habits.[1] Global distribution channels, as well as advances in technology, also serve to ease the process of conducting business on a global scale.

2. *Cost factors:* Avoiding cost inefficiencies and duplication of effort are two of the most powerful globalization drivers. Often, single-country populations are simply not large enough for a firm to achieve meaningful economies of scale. In pharmaceuticals, for instance, the cost of developing a new blockbuster drug can exceed $1.7 billion. Only a global market can offset the risks of escalating R&D cost.[2] The same is true in the consumer goods sector, where a new brand launch from P&G or Unilever can cost up to $100 million. Quick Take: Mininationals Leap into Global Markets describes how small companies are able to operate globally from a handful of manufacturing bases, allowing them to swiftly seize new markets.

3. *Environmental factors:* As explored in Chapter 3, the falling of government and fiscal barriers to trade has facilitated the globalization of markets and the activities of companies within them. Rapid technological advances also contribute to the process. Newly emerg-

ing markets, in particular, benefit from technological advances that allow them to leapfrog over stages of economic development.

4. *Competitive factors:* Global strategies are often necessary to prevent competitors from gaining undue advantage, not only overseas but in the home market. If a competitor manufactures on a global scale and therefore achieves global economies of scale, it can undercut prices in the home market. When McAfee lowered its prices to lure customers from its competitors, Symantec, the world's largest security software developer, responded in kind by dropping prices on like products by as much as 70 percent. Similarly, global strategies can be used to thwart the growth potential of competitors. Caterpillar faced mounting global competition from Komatsu but found that strengthening its products and operations was not enough to meet the challenge. Although Japan was a small part of the world market, as a secure home base (no serious competitors), it generated 80 percent of Komatsu's cash flow. To put a check on its major global competitor's market share and cash flow, Caterpillar formed a joint venture with Mitsubishi to serve the electric truck market in Japan.[3]

 # A COMPREHENSIVE VIEW OF INTERNATIONAL EXPANSION

The central driver of internationalization is the level of managerial commitment to overseas expansion. Commitment grows gradually from an awareness of the potential of foreign markets and eventually leads to the company embracing international business as a strategic imperative. Management commitment triggers various international business activities, ranging from indirect exporting and importing to direct involvement in the global market. Eventually, the firm may expand further through measures such as strategic alliances, joint ventures, or foreign direct investment.

All of the processes and decisions involved in developing the commitment to go international are linked to one another. A comprehensive view of these links is presented schematically in Figure 10.1.

FIGURE 10.1   A Comprehensive Model of International Market Entry and Development

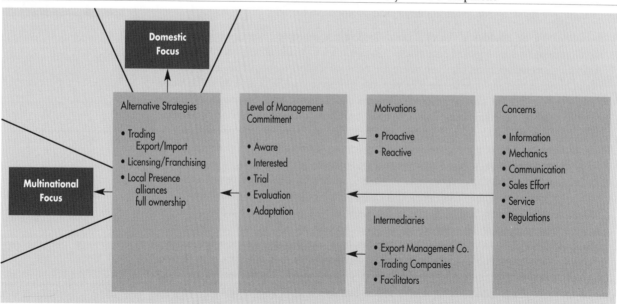

Quick Take *Mininationals Leap into Global Markets*

Only a short time ago, Cheryl Schaefer Alves was creating and selling handbags out of her home. Today her company, Sunny Hawaii, is wholesaling handbags to more than 4,000 accounts around the globe. Though the fashion handbag and accessories market has become more crowded in recent times, Alves says that her company has been able to stay on top of fast-moving fashion trends with its "tropically inspired" handbags. By moving her manufacturing process to China, she has cut costs and increased profitability.

Sunny Hawaii is a prime example of the small to medium-sized firms that are reinventing the global corporation. Termed *mininationals*, their success proves that sheer size is no longer a buffer against competition, especially in markets that demand specialized products. Electronic process technology allows mininationals to compete on price and quality—often with greater flexibility than larger rivals. In today's open trading regions, they are able to serve the world from a handful of manufacturing bases. Less red tape means they can move swiftly in seizing new markets.

The lessons learned from these new-generation global players are to: (1) keep focused on being a leader in a market niche; (2) stay lean to save on costs and accelerate decision-making; (3) take ideas and technologies international—to and from wherever they can be found; (4) take advantage of employees, regardless of nationality, to globalize thinking; and (5) solve customers' problems by creating customized solutions.

SOURCES: Frank Meyer, "How Can Small Agencies Land the Big Fish," February 19, 2008; "Small firm goes global by staying focused" *Pacific Business News*, March 3, 2006.

Why Go Global?

The four globalization drivers described so far explain why globalization has emerged as a business strategy. Table 10.1 summarizes the major reasons that prompt small and mid-size firms to make their first moves into overseas markets. These are divided into proactive motivations, or why companies *want* to go global, and reactive motivations, or why they *have* to do so.

PROACTIVE MOTIVATIONS Profits are the major proactive motivation. In order to increase profits, companies may either look to increase sales volume by selling into new markets or to reduce costs by producing overseas. However, the expectation of higher profits may not

TABLE 10.1 Motivations for International Business

PROACTIVE	REACTIVE
Profit advantage	Competitive pressures
Unique products	Overproduction
Technological advantage	Declining domestic sales
Exclusive information	Excess capacity
Tax benefit	Saturated domestic markets
Economies of scale	Proximity to customers and ports

occur right away. Particularly in start-up operations, the cost of setting up often reduces initial profitability. Even with thorough planning, unexpected influences—such as shifts in exchange rates, for example—can change the profit picture substantially.

Unique products or technological advantage are another major stimulus, assuming, of course, that the product is in demand in foreign markets and is not available from competitors. The firm must consider, too, how long any unique product advantage will last. The fast pace of technology, the creativity of competitors, and the lack of adequate international patent protection all shorten product life spans in foreign markets.

Special knowledge about foreign customers or market situations may be another proactive stimulus. It is usually short-term, since competitors quickly catch up with the information advantage.

Tax benefits also motivate overseas sales. If government uses preferential tax treatment to encourage exports, firms either are able to compete by offering low prices in foreign markets or to accumulate higher profits.

A final proactive motivation involves economies of scale. International activities may enable a firm to increase output and therefore rise more rapidly on the learning curve. Increased production for international markets can help reduce the cost of production for domestic sales and make the firm more competitive at home, too.

REACTIVE MOTIVATIONS Reactive motivations influence firms to seek out new markets due to change or pressures in the domestic economy. Competitive pressures are one example. A company may fear losing domestic market share to competing firms that have benefited from economies of scale gained through international business activities. Further, it may fear losing foreign markets permanently by literally missing the boat when competitors expand overseas.

Overproduction is another reactive motivation. During downturns in the domestic business cycle, foreign markets can provide an ideal outlet for excess inventories. A mistake some firms make is to withdraw from foreign markets once domestic demand bounces back. International customers may prove "once bitten, twice shy"—they are not interested in temporary or sporadic business relationships.

Declining domestic sales, whether measured in sales volume or market share, are a key motivator. A product at the end of its domestic life cycle may find new markets overseas. High-tech products outmoded by the latest innovation are a good example. Some hospitals, for instance, may be much better off acquiring lower-cost, "just-dated" MRI equipment than waiting until they have funding for the latest state-of-the-art technologies.

Excess capacity is a powerful motivator. If equipment is not fully utilized, firms may see expansion abroad as an ideal way to achieve broader distribution of fixed costs. Alternatively, if all fixed costs are assigned to domestic production, the firm can—at least in the short term—penetrate foreign markets with a pricing scheme that focuses mainly on variable cost. In the longer term, however, such pricing may lead to charges of dumping.

The reactive motivation of a saturated domestic market has similar results to that of declining domestic sales. Again, firms in this situation can use the international market to prolong the life of their goods and even of their organization.

A final reactive motivation is proximity to customers and ports. A firm located near a border may sell into the neighboring country without even thinking of itself as international.

STRATEGIC PLANNING FOR GLOBAL EXPANSION

2 LEARNING OBJECTIVE

Taking advantage of the global marketplace requires long-term planning. Figure 10.2 summarizes the stages decision-makers go through when formulating a global strategy. The planning process starts with a complete assessment of the business. While a later section in this chapter explores the critical role of research in selecting markets and launching products in those selected, this section provides an overview of the self-assessment process a firm must undergo before developing global entry or expansion strategies. In practice, analysis focuses on three areas: (1) level of management commitment, (2) internal organizational factors, and (3) market and competition.

Management Commitment

The issue of **managerial commitment** is a critical one because foreign market penetration requires a vast amount of market development activity, sensitivity toward foreign environments, research, and innovation. All of this takes time, resources, and expertise. To nurture commitment, it is important to involve all levels of management early on in the international planning process and to impress on all players that the effort will succeed only if the entire firm is behind it.

The first step in developing commitment is to become aware of international business opportunities. Management must then determine the degree and timing of the firm's internationalization. For instance, a German corporation that expands its operation to neighboring countries Austria, Switzerland, or Belgium is less international than one that launches operations in Japan and Brazil. Further, a company that enters markets selectively is less international than one that attempts to enter multiple global markets from the outset. With regard to timing, immediate market entry might be a priority because clients are waiting for the product or because competitors are moving in on the same market. A successful global strategy hinges on management agreement and support regarding both degree and timing of international activities.

MANAGERIAL COMMITMENT

The desire and drive on the part of management to act on an idea and to support it in the long run.

FIGURE 10.2   Global Strategy Formulation

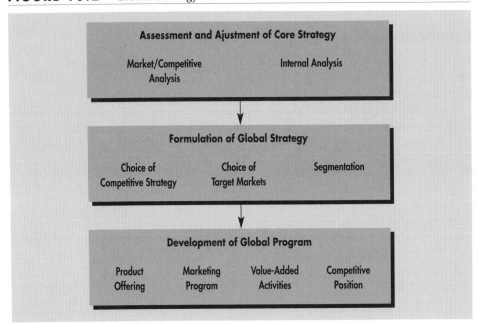

The authors appreciate the contributions of Robert M. Grant in the preparation of this figure.

Company-wide international orientation does not develop overnight, but rather needs time to grow. It is a matter of learning, of acquiring experiential knowledge. A firm must learn about foreign markets and institutions, but also about its own internal resources in order to know what it is capable of when exposed to new and unfamiliar conditions. Planning and execution of an export venture must be incorporated into the firm's strategic management process, which become increasingly crucial as markets around the world become more linked and more competitive.

Internal Organizational Factors

A thorough assessment of internal organizational resources is a critical early step in determining a company's capacity for establishing and sustaining competitive advantage within global markets. Expansion may require a prolonged period of financial investment before returns are realized. In terms of human resources, expansion requires experienced and culturally wise managers, often in short supply. In many cases, commitment to expand internationally means depriving other areas of the organization of valuable resources. When Starbucks made the decision to focus on the global coffee industry, it increased its emphasis on coffee quality and cut back on peripheral products like baked goods and sandwiches.[4]

Market and Competition Analysis

Market and competition analysis usually starts with an overview of different regions, then further splits into analysis by country. Regional groupings are particularly helpful if they help identify similarities in demographic and behavioral traits. For example, dividing Europe into northern, central, and southern regions provides for easier analysis than treating it as a single market. An important consideration is that data may be more readily available if existing structures and frameworks are used.[5] In general, as a later section on international business research explains more fully, factors to consider when analyzing markets and competition include market size, growth potential, the number and type of competitors, government regulations, and economic and political activity.

Competitive Strategy Formulation

COST LEADERSHIP STRATEGY

A pricing tactic where a company offers an identical product or service at a lower cost than the competition.

DIFFERENTIATION STRATEGY

Takes advantage of the company's real or perceived uniqueness on elements such as design or after-sales service.

FOCUS STRATEGY

A deliberate concentration on a single industry segment.

The firm has three general choices of strategies: (1) cost leadership, (2) differentiation, and (3) focus.[6] Any one of these can be pursued on a global or regional basis, or the firm may decide to mix and match strategies as a function of market or product dimensions.

In pursuing **cost leadership strategy**, the company offers an identical product or service at a lower cost than competition. This often means investment in scale economies and strict control of costs, such as overhead, research and development, and logistics. A **differentiation strategy**, whether it is industry-wide or focused on a single segment, takes advantage of the product's real or perceived uniqueness on elements such as design or after-sales service. Starbucks brand, for example, is a standout among Japan's coffee-shop culture, largely due to brand and taste, but also because of the spacious and smoke-free store environment. Differentiation strategies do not, however, ignore the critical importance of containing costs or offering competitive prices. Ikea, for instance, built a clear positioning and unique brand image around products aimed at "young people of all ages"—low price for quality goods was central to Ikea's appeal.

Through a **focus strategy**, a firm concentrates on a single industry segment, like Starbucks in the example above. A focus strategy may be oriented toward either low cost or differentiation.

Most global companies combine high differentiation with cost containment to enter markets or expand their market shares. As discussed further in Chapter 12, flexible manufacturing systems, standard components, and tight supply chains allow companies to customize an increasing amount of their production, while at the same time saving on costs. Global activities permit the exploitation of scale economies not only in production but also in marketing activities.

INTERNATIONAL BUSINESS RESEARCH

The single most important cause for failure in international business is insufficient preparation and information. Failure to comprehend cultural disparities, failure to remember that customers differ from country to country, and failure to investigate whether or not a market exists prior to entry has made international business a high-risk activity.[7] International business research is instrumental to international business success because it permits the firm to take into account different environments, attitudes, and market conditions.

Why Conduct Research?

Many firms do little research before they enter a foreign market. Often, decisions concerning entry and expansion or selection of distributors are made after a cursory, subjective assessment. Research is all too often far less rigorous, less formal, and less quantitative than for domestic activities.

The reasons are many and begin with a lack of sensitivity to differences in culture, consumer tastes, and market demands. Further, many firms—perhaps in an effort to close their eyes to potential difficulties—are unwilling to accept that a country's labor rules, distribution systems, availability of media, or advertising regulations may be entirely different from those in the home market. Often, a lack of familiarity with national and international data sources, the perceived expense of data collection (despite the growing number of low-cost Internet sources), and an inability to apply data obtained, explain why firms neglect research. In many cases, research is overlooked simply because firms tend to build their international business activities gradually, often based on unsolicited orders. Over time, experience is used as a substitute for organized research.

Despite such reservations, research is as (or more) important globally than it is domestically. It not only shines a spotlight on new opportunities, but it exposes risk. It is vital in strategy development, as it is the means of identifying all the requirements of market entry, penetration, and expansion. On a continuing basis, research provides the feedback needed to fine-tune business activities, anticipate future events, and prepare for change.

Pre-Entry Research

Figure 10.3 provides a summary of the various stages through which companies research and assess the potential of export markets. The research process begins with a cursory analysis of general variables of a country, including total and per capita gross national product (GNP), mortality rates, and population figures. These factors enable the researcher to determine whether corporate objectives might be met in the market. For example, high-priced consumer products might not succeed in China, as their price may be equal to the customer's annual salary, customer benefits may be minimal, and the government is likely to prohibit their importation. A preliminary screening helps reduce the number of markets to be considered to a manageable number.

The next step is to amass information on promising country markets, including rate of growth, governmental or other restrictions, and demand trends within the targeted industry. Although precise data on individual products may not be obtainable, general product or

FIGURE 10.3   A Sequential Process of Researching Foreign Market Potentials

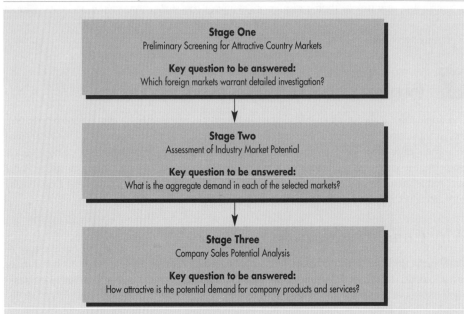

Stage One
Preliminary Screening for Attractive Country Markets

Key question to be answered:
Which foreign markets warrant detailed investigation?

Stage Two
Assessment of Industry Market Potential

Key question to be answered:
What is the aggregate demand in each of the selected markets?

Stage Three
Company Sales Potential Analysis

Key question to be answered:
How attractive is the potential demand for company products and services?

SOURCE: S. Tamer Cavusgil, "Guidelines for Export Market Research," *Business Horizons* 28 (November–December 1985): 29. Copyright 1985 by the Foundation for the School of Business at Indiana University. Reprinted by permission.

service category information usually is. While this overview is still cursory, it serves to quickly evaluate markets and further reduce their number.

Next, it's time to select appropriate markets for in-depth evaluation. The focus is now on opportunities for a specific type of service, product, or brand, and research includes an assessment as to whether demand already exists or can be stimulated. Aggregate industry data alone may not suffice. For example, the demand for sports equipment should not be confused with the market potential for a specific new brand. The research should identify demand and supply patterns and evaluate any regulations and standards. This final stage also requires a competitive assessment, matching markets to corporate strengths and providing an analysis of the best potential for specific offerings.

Market Expansion Research

After initial market entry, research plays a critical role in global success. It allows firms to amass detailed information for possible business expansion. It also allows them to monitor the political climate so that the firm successfully can maintain its international operation. Research data enables international managers to evaluate new business partners or assess the impact of a technological breakthrough on future operations. The better defined the research objective is, the better the researcher will be able to determine information requirements and thus conserve the time and financial resources of the firm.

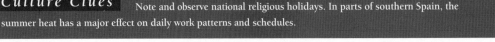

Culture Clues   Note and observe national religious holidays. In parts of southern Spain, the summer heat has a major effect on daily work patterns and schedules.

CONDUCTING SECONDARY RESEARCH *

Table 10.2 demonstrates that firms require both macro data, related to countries and trade, and micro data, which is specific to the firm's activities. Both kinds of information are available through **secondary research**—that is, the use of data already collected by some other organization, such as governments, international institutions, service organizations, trade associations, directories, and other firms.

SECONDARY RESEARCH

The collection and analysis of data originally collected to serve another purpose rather than the specific objectives of the firm.

Government Sources

Governments typically collect information on such macro issues as population trends, general trade flows among countries, and world agriculture production. They are also good sources of micro information, including data on specific industries, their growth prospects, and the extent and direction to which they are traded. While information is often offered only in the local language, the fact that much of the data is numerical aids in the translation task. Embassies and consulates, as well as government-sponsored web sites or fee-based data libraries, are good places to start. The user should be cautioned, however, that the printed information is often dated and that the industry categories used abroad may not be compatible with industry categories used at home.

International Organizations

The *Statistical Yearbook* produced by the United Nations (UN) contains international trade data on products and provides information on exports and imports by country.

Because of the time needed for worldwide data collection, the information is often quite dated. Other more specialized sources include:

- UN Conference on Trade and Development (**http://www.unctad.org**): issues surrounding developing nations, such as debt and market access
- World Bank (**http://www.worldbank.org**): publishes the World Atlas, with general data on population, growth trends, and GNP figures; region- or country-specific economic data
- World Trade Organization (**http://www.wto.org**) and Organization for Economic Cooperation and Development (**http://www.oecd.org**): publishes quarterly and annual trade data on member countries
- International Monetary Fund (**http://www.imf.org**): publishes summary economic data and occasional staff papers that evaluate region- or country-specific issues in depth

TABLE 10.2 Critical International Information

MACRO DATA	MICRO DATA
• Tariff information	• Local laws and regulations
• U.S. export/import data	• Size of market
• Nontariff measures	• Local standards and specifications
• Foreign export/import data	• Distribution system
• Data on government trade policy	• Competitive activity

SOURCE: Michael R. Czinkota, "International Information Needs for U.S. Competitiveness," *Business Horizons* 34, 6 (November–December 1991): 86–91.

Electronic Information Services

International online computer database services, numbering in the thousands, are an excellent and not-too-expensive source of information external to the firm, such as exchange rates, international news, and import restrictions. Several databases offer product- and market-specific data, gleaned from systematic searches through a wide range of periodicals, reports, and books in different languages. Many of the main news agencies make market-specific information available through online databases. Some, like the Economist Intelligence Unit (**http://www.eiu.com**) provide extensive data on companies in given countries and the products they buy and sell.

Online databases are easier than ever to access and can provide valuable insights. For example, the U.S. Department of Commerce offers Global Business Opportunities (GLOBUS), which provides daily trade leads and international procurement opportunities. In addition the National Trade Data Bank (NTDB) provides access to Country Commercial Guides and Market Research reports.[8]

In spite of the ease of access to up-to-the-minute data via the Internet, it must be remembered that search engines cover only a portion of international sources and are heavily biased toward English-language publications. As a result, a researcher who relies solely on electronic information may lose out on valuable input.[9]

SERVICE ORGANIZATIONS A wide variety of service organizations located around the world offer data, including banks, accounting firms, freight forwarders, airlines, international trade consultants, research firms, and publishing houses. Frequently, they are able to provide information on business practices, legislative or regulatory requirements, and political stability, as well as trade and financial data.

TRADE ASSOCIATIONS World trade clubs and domestic and international chambers of commerce provide good information on trade flows and trends in local markets. Industry associations often collect a wide variety of data from members that are then published in aggregate form.

DIRECTORIES AND NEWSLETTERS Local, national, and international directories primarily serve to identify firms and to provide brief background data, such as the name of the CEO, the level of capitalization of the firm, contact information, and product descriptions. A host of newsletters discuss specific international business issues, such as international trade finance, legislative activities, countertrade, international payment flows, and customs news. They usually cater to niche audiences but offer important information in specific areas.

Interpreting Secondary Data

Once secondary data have been obtained, the next task is to convert them into useful, task-specific information. Secondary data should be evaluated regarding the quality of the source, recency, and relevance to the task at hand. Clearly, because the information was collected without the current research requirements in mind, there may well be difficulties in coverage, categorization, and comparability. For example, market penetration of digital recorders may be useful only as a proxy variable for the potential demand for DVD players. Similarly, in an industrial setting, information about plans for new port facilities may be useful in determining future container requirements.

Interpretation of data also requires a level of creative thinking. A researcher for a shipping company, for instance, may need to interpret from data about a new port facility the potential demand for shipping containers. This requires creative inferences, and such creativity brings risks. Therefore, once interpretation and analysis have taken place, it is necessary to cross-check the results with other possible sources of information or with experts.

 # CONDUCTING PRIMARY RESEARCH

Even though secondary data are useful to the researcher, on many occasions **primary research** is necessary as well. Several worldwide research firms offer primary as well as secondary research services. Typically, primary research is necessary to obtain specific answers to specific questions:

- How much does the typical Spaniard spend on entertainment?
- What is the sales potential for our measuring equipment in India?
- What effect will our new engine have on our green consumers in Germany?
- What service standards do e-commerce customers expect in Japan?

The researcher must have a clear idea of what the population under study should be and where it is located before deciding on the country or region to investigate. It may not, for example, be necessary to conduct research across an entire country if the objective is to distribute into urban areas. In other cases, if the product will penetrate nationwide, differing economic, geographic, or behavioral factors may require multiple-region research. One firm, for instance, conducted its research only in large Indonesian cities during the height of tourism season, but projected the results to the entire population. Based on the results, the company set up large production and distribution facilities to meet the expected demand, but realized only limited sales to city tourists.[10]

Determining Research Techniques

Once the type of data sought is determined, the researcher must choose a research technique. As in domestic research, several types of research are available. Each provides different levels of objectivity or subjectivity, and each has its own unique strengths and weaknesses. When the required information is **qualitative** in nature, allowing for an understanding of given situations, behavioral patterns, or underlying dimensions of consumer choices, the best research techniques are personal interviews, focus groups, and observation. When **quantitative** results are required with statistical validity, surveys and experimentation are the most appropriate research instruments.

Interviews

Personal interviews with knowledgeable people can be of great value. Individual bias, however, can slant the findings, so the intent should be to obtain not a wide variety of data, but rather in-depth information. When specific answers are sought to very narrow questions, interviews can be particularly useful.

Focus Groups

In typical **focus group research**, a group of seven to ten knowledgeable people is gathered together for a limited period of time (two to four hours) to thoroughly discuss a specific topic. Focus groups are a highly efficient means of rapidly accumulating a substantial amount of information. Because of the interaction among participants, hidden issues are sometimes

PRIMARY RESEARCH

The collection and analysis of data for a specific research purpose through interviews, focus groups, surveys, observation, or experimentation.

QUALITATIVE INFORMATION

Data that have been analyzed to provide a better understanding, description, or prediction of given situations, behavioral patterns, or underlying dimensions.

QUANTITATIVE INFORMATION

Data amassed in numerical order to search for statistical significance or trends.

PERSONAL INTERVIEWS

Face-to-face research method, the objective of which is to obtain in-depth information from a knowledgeable individual.

FOCUS GROUP RESEARCH

A research method in which representatives of a proposed target audience contribute to market research by participating in an unstructured discussion.

raised that are difficult to detect through personal interviews. The skill of the group leader in stimulating discussion is crucial to the success of a focus group. Focus groups do not provide statistically significant data, but rather information about perceptions, emotions, and attitudinal factors.

When planning international research using focus groups, the researcher must be aware of the importance of language and culture in the interaction process. Even before the session begins, special preparation may be necessary. For instance, in some countries, offering a fee is sufficient motivation for participants to open up in discussion. In other countries, it may be necessary to host a luncheon or dinner for the group so that members get to know each other and are willing to interact.

Once the session is under way, it's important to remember that not all societies encourage frank and open exchange and disagreement among individuals. Status consciousness may mean that the opinion of one participant is reflected by all others. Disagreement may be seen as impolite, or certain topics may be taboo. Unless a native focus group leader is used, it also is possible to completely misread the interactions among group participants and to miss out on nuances and constraints participants feel when making comments in a group setting.

Observation

OBSERVATION RESEARCH

A research method in which the subject's activity and behavior are watched.

Observation research requires the researcher to play the role of a nonparticipating observer of activity and behavior. In an international setting, observation can be extremely useful in shedding light on practices not previously encountered or understood. For example, Toyota sent a group of its engineers and designers to southern California to observe how women get into and operate cars. They found that women with long fingernails have trouble opening doors and operating various knobs on the dashboard. Toyota was then able to redesign some of its automobile exteriors and interiors, producing more desirable cars.[11]

Survey Research

SURVEY RESEARCH

A research method involving the use of questionnaires delivered in person, by mail, telephone, or online to obtain statistically valid, quantifiable research information.

Survey research is useful in quantifying concepts. Surveys are usually conducted via questionnaires administered personally, by mail, or by telephone. Use of the survey technique presupposes that the population under study is accessible and able to comprehend and respond to questions posed. For mail surveys, a major precondition is the feasibility of using the postal system, which is not a given in all countries. Similarly, telephone or web-based surveys may be inappropriate if telephone ownership or Internet access is rare. In such instances, even if the researcher randomized the calls, the results would be highly biased.

Because surveys deal with people who, in an international setting, display major differences in culture, preference, education, and attitude, to mention just a few factors, the use of the survey technique must be carefully examined. For example, in some regions of the world, recipients of letters may be illiterate. Others may be very literate, but totally unaccustomed to standard research-scaling techniques. Figure 10.4 provides an example of a rating scale

FIGURE 10.4   The Funny Faces Scale[12]

Very Happy   Happy   Not Happy But   Unhappy   Very Unhappy
                                   Also Not Unhappy

WORLD VIEW

EXCELLENCE IN INTERNATIONAL RESEARCH

The Church of Jesus Christ of Latter-day Saints, commonly known as the Mormon Church, was organized by Joseph Smith in 1830 in New York. It has grown into an organization with 12 million members and congregations throughout the world and is currently increasing at an average rate of about 1 million new members every three years. It generates close to $6 billion in annual income from its non-church-related businesses and enterprises and has $30 billion in assets. One of its key growth strategies is to send many of its members abroad as missionaries. Therefore, the church has thousands of young and experienced travelers, returning with foreign language skills and intercultural understanding. Indeed Utah, where the Mormon population is highly concentrated, has speakers fluent in 90 percent of the world's written languages, and 30 percent of its U.S.-born adult males speak a second language. Due to its large and globally educated workforce, Utah is successfully attracting businesses such as Intel, eBay, American Express, and Goldman Sachs.

Young Mormon followers, 19 to 22 years of age, are expected to go on a mission abroad for 18 to 24 months. There are currently approximately 60,000 full-time missionaries serving in more than 330 mission districts around the world. Most missionaries learn new languages during their brief stay at the missionary training centers, where about 50 different languages are taught, and become fully proficient during their stay abroad. In any country in which they are located, missionaries go door to door, promoting their religion and indirectly developing their sales skills. Young individuals are completely immersed in the host culture, live among local families, and therefore have a personal understanding of the people of the country. Individuals with such extensive experience abroad can be great resources to their companies as sources of global knowledge. Their personal insight into local cultures can help enlighten employers about marketing abroad.

CEOs in Utah note the diverse foreign language experience, high ethics, and family-oriented attitudes of the Mormon workforce as significant factors in the success of their businesses. Employers look for individuals who are not only well rounded but have a specific area of expertise. Having a workforce that knows foreign languages and has the experience of living abroad adds to a company's ability to research international markets.

SOURCES: "Utah CEOs Cite Cost Advantages, Ethics and Local Workforce as Top Reasons to Locate Companies Here," *PR Newswire US*, November 3, 2005; Earl Fry, Wallace McCarlie, Derek Wride, and Stacey Sears, "Mapping Globalization along the Wasatch Front," Pacific Council on International Policy, **http://www.pacificcouncil.org**, accessed February 19, 2008; Eric Johnson, "Get The Fire: Young Mormon Missionaries Abroad," Mormonism Research Ministry, **www.mrm.org**, accessed February 22, 2008.

developed by researchers to work with a diverse population with relatively little education. In its use, however, it was found that the same scale aroused negative reactions among better-educated respondents, who considered the scale childish and insulting to their intelligence. Sometimes, recipients of a survey may be reluctant to respond in writing, particularly when sensitive questions are asked. In some nations, for instance, information about income, even when requested in categorical form, is considered highly proprietary; in others, the purchasing behavior of individuals is not readily divulged.[13]

Experimentation

Experimental techniques determine the effect of an intervening variable and help establish precise cause-and-effect relationships. However, **experimentation** is difficult to implement in international research. The researcher faces the daunting task of designing an experiment in which most variables are held constant or are comparable across cultures. For example, an experiment to determine a causal effect within the distribution system of one country may be very difficult to transfer to another country because the distribution system may be quite different. For this reason, experimental techniques are only rarely used, even though their potential value to the international researcher is recognized.

EXPERIMENTATION

A research method capable of determining the effects of a variable on a situation.

Ongoing Research

As stated earlier, many firms gradually build on their international activities without conducting any purposeful market-entry or expansion research. No matter what its stage of internationalization, however, any firm can benefit from creating what is known as an **information system** for collecting and centralizing timely, accurate, and accessible information on specific markets or on specific international activities. One type of information system that is particularly useful for international managers is the **export complaint system**, which allows customers to contact the original supplier abroad in order to inquire about products, make suggestions, or present complaints. Firms are finding that about 5 percent of customers abroad are dissatisfied with the product. By establishing direct contact via e-mail, a toll-free telephone number, or a web site, firms do not need to rely on the filtered feedback from channel intermediaries and can learn directly about product failures, channel problems, or other causes of customer dissatisfaction. The development of such an export complaint system requires substantial resources, intensive planning, and a high degree of cultural sensitivity. Customers abroad must be informed about how to complain, and their cost of complaining must be minimized—for example, by offering an interactive web site. The response to complaints must also be tailored to the culture of the complainant. Very important is the firm's ability to aggregate and analyze complaints and to make use of them internally. Complaints are often the symptom for underlying structural problems of a product or a process. If used properly, an export complaint system can become a rich source of information for product improvement and innovation.

To build an information system, corporations use one or a combination of three mechanisms to obtain data: environmental scanning, Delphi studies, and scenario analyses.

1. *Environmental scanning*—Valuable for long-term strategic planning, **environmental scanning** involves the ongoing search and collection of political, social, and economic issues internationally. Data collected may also include information on changes or anticipated changes in the attitudes of public institutions and private citizens.
2. *Delphi studies*—To enrich the information obtained from factual data, corporations and governments frequently use creative and highly qualitative data-gathering methods. One approach is through **Delphi studies**. These studies are particularly useful in the international environment because they allow for the aggregation of information from experts who most likely cannot come together physically. Typically, Delphi studies are carried out with groups of about 30 well-chosen participants who possess expertise in an area of concern, such as future developments of the international trade environment. The participants are asked to identify major issues and to rank their statements on each according to importance. The aggregated information and comments are sent to all participants, who are then able to agree or disagree with the various rank orders and the comments. This allows statements to be challenged. In another round, the participants respond to the challenges. Several rounds of challenges and responses result in a reasonably coherent consensus. Increasingly conducted through the Internet, Delphi studies are able to bridge large distances and therefore make experts quite accessible at a reasonable cost. When carried out on a regular basis, they can provide crucial augmentation of the factual data. For example, a large portion of Chapter 14 is based on an extensive Delphi study carried out by the authors.
3. *Scenario analysis*—One approach to **scenario analysis** involves the development of a series of plausible scenarios that are constructed from trends observed in the environment. Another method consists of formally reviewing assumptions built into existing business plans and positions. Subsequently, some of these key assumptions, such as economic growth rates, import penetration, speed of international transportation, and political stability, can be varied. By projecting variations for medium- to long-term periods, com-

---

INFORMATION SYSTEM

Can provide the decision-maker with basic data for most ongoing decisions.

EXPORT COMPLAINT SYSTEMS

Allow customers to contact the original supplier of a product in order to inquire about products, make suggestions, or present complaints.

ENVIRONMENTAL SCANNING

Obtaining ongoing data about a country.

DELPHI STUDIES

A research tool using a group of participants with expertise in the area of concern to predict and rank major future developments.

SCENARIO ANALYSIS

The identification of crucial variables and the analysis of the effects of their variations on business conditions.

pletely new environmental conditions can emerge. The conditions can then be analyzed for their potential domestic and international impact on corporate strategy. For scenarios to be useful, management must analyze and respond to them by formulating contingency plans. Such planning will broaden horizons and may prepare managers for unexpected situations. Through the anticipation of possible problems, managers hone their response capability and in turn shorten response times to actual problems.

Target Country Selection

The choice of countries into which to expand depends on the firm's competitive strategy and the extent of market entry desired. The selection also involves decisions relating to market attractiveness, current company position, and allocation of resources. The basic alternatives are concentration on a small number of markets and **diversification**, which is characterized by growth in a relatively large number of markets.

DIVERSIFICATION

A market expansion policy characterized by growth in a relatively large number of markets or market segments.

In many cases, the choice of market is spurred by success in markets with similar demographics or with similar competitive environments. European PC makers, such as Germany's Maxdata and Britain's Tiny are both taking aim at the U.S. market based on the premise that if they can compete with the big multinationals (Dell, Compaq, Hewlett-Packard, and Gateway) at home, there is no reason why they cannot be competitive in North America as well.[14] In other cases, market selection is motivated by the larger industry context. Korean automaker, Hyundai, for example, plans to greatly enlarge its presence in two of the world's largest markets. By increasing production by 60 percent in both India and China, Hyundai hopes to increase market share and break into the industry's top five by 2011.[15]

Target Market Segmentation

Effective **market segmentation** recognizes that groups within markets differ sufficiently to warrant individual approaches. It allows global companies to take advantage of the benefits of standardization (such as economies of scale and consistency in positioning) while addressing the unique needs and expectations of specific target groups. The best example of a segment that spans country markets is the teen segment, which is converging as a result of common tastes in sports and music fueled by computer literacy, travels abroad, and, in many countries, financial independence. Today's satellite TV and global network concepts such as MTV not only help create the segment, but provide global companies access to the teen audience around the world.[16]

MARKET SEGMENTATION

Grouping of consumers based on common characteristics such as demographics, lifestyles, and so on.

The greatest challenge for the global company is the choice of an appropriate basis for segmentation. The objective is to arrive at groupings that are not only substantial enough to merit the segmentation effort (for example, there are nearly 210 million teenagers in the industrialized world, who spend $195 billion yearly), but who are also reachable by the marketing effort, since advertising on MTV delivers an audience that consists largely of teens.[17]

The possible bases for segmentation are summarized in Figure 10.5. Managers have traditionally used a combination of them.

An alternative approach to environmental segmentation is to group together markets that reflect a high degree of homogeneity with respect to marketing mix variables: product, price, distribution, and promotion.

Culture Clues   Western managers in China joint ventures should take advantage of their positions, as representatives of a prestigious entity, to store up capital with local decision-makers through *quanxi*, or relationships. These are a potent instrument in protecting one's interests. In fact, they are more powerful than written documents, which are seen as a necessary ritual when dealing with Westerners.

FIGURE 10.5   Bases for Global Market Segmentation

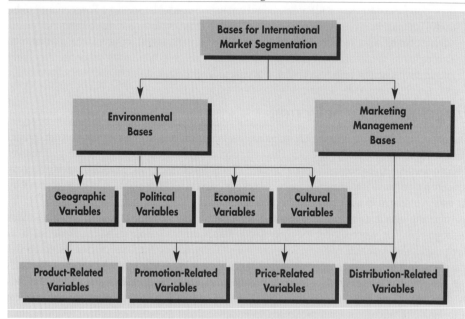

SOURCE: Imad B. Baalbaki and Naresh K. Malhotra, "Marketing Management Bases for International Market Segmentation: An Alternate Look at the Standardization/Customization Debate," *International Marketing Review* 10, 1 (1993): 19–44.

Global Program Development

Once target countries and segments have been identified, the firm must determine the parameters of its global program. This involves four key decisions:

1. *Degree of standardization in the product offering:* While globalization involves some level of standardization in order to achieve economies of scale, different markets still demand some product customization. The need for localization varies by product and intended consumer segment. Fashion products can either focus on uniqueness or develop an appeal to sameness. Information technology products are susceptible to power requirements, keyboard configurations (e.g., Europe alone may require 20 different keyboards), instruction-manual language, and warning labels compliant with local regulations.

2. *Marketing program:* Nowhere is the need for the local touch as critical as in the execution of the marketing program. While uniformity is important for strategic elements (for example, positioning), most firms take care to localize necessary tactical elements of the marketing program, such as distribution. This approach has been called **glocalization**. For example, Unilever achieved great success with a fabric softener that used common positioning, advertising theme, and symbolism (a teddy bear) but differing brand names (e.g. Snuggle, Cajoline, Kuschelweich, Mimosin, and Yumos) and bottle sizes.[18]

3. *Value-adding activities:* Globalization strives for cost reductions by pooling production or other activities or exploiting factor costs or capabilities. Rather than duplicating activities, a firm concentrates them in a single location. Many global companies, for instance, establish R&D centers to serve multiple markets from one or more central bases. In the telecommunications sector, Nokia's 20,000 research and development people work in 12 different countries, including China, Finland, Germany, Hungary, and China. The company has also

GLOCALIZATION

A term coined to describe the networked global organization approach to an organizational structure.

entered into development agreements with operators such as France Telecom and Vodafone to bring innovations to market more efficiently.[19]

The quest for cost savings and improved transportation and transfer methods has allowed some marketers to concentrate customer service activities rather than having them present in all country markets. For example, Sony used to have repair centers in all the Scandinavian countries and Finland; today all service and maintenance activities are performed in a regional center in Stockholm, Sweden.

4. *Competitive strategy:* Firms need to defend their competitive position, not only in new markets but at home. When Fuji began cutting into its U.S. market share, Kodak responded by increasing its own penetration in Japan and created a new subsidiary to deal strictly with that market. Kodak solicited the support of the U.S. government to gain better access to Japanese distribution systems that the company insisted were unfairly blocked. **Cross-subsidization**—the use of resources accumulated in one part of the world to fight a competitive battle in another—is a powerful global competitive strategy. The telecom industry in Asia, for example, has been characterized by state monopoly with heavy cross-subsidization of tariffs to meet universal service and social priorities.[20]

GLOBAL MARKET ENTRY STRATEGIES

CROSS-SUBSIDIZATION

The use of resources accumulated in one part of the world to fight a competitive battle in another.

Once a company has made a commitment to global expansion, formulated its global strategy, and researched potential new markets, there are still many fundamental decisions to be made. The most critical is to decide among several methods of entry. Typical entry strategies are exporting and importing, licensing, and franchising, all of which allow access to markets without direct investment or ownership. More extensive methods of developing foreign markets include expansion through alliances and joint ventures, as well as foreign direct investment.

Exporting and Importing

Firms can be involved in exporting and importing either indirectly or directly. Indirect involvement means that the firm participates through an intermediary and does not deal with foreign customers or firms. Direct involvement means that the firm works with and develops a relationship with foreign customers, suppliers, or markets. In both cases, goods and services either go abroad or come to the domestic market from abroad, and goods may have to be adapted to suit the targeted market. However, the less direct its involvement, the less likely the firm is to build its knowledge and experience of how to do business abroad, hampering further expansion.

Firms that export or import directly have the opportunity to learn more quickly the competitive advantages of their products and can therefore expand more rapidly. Direct exporting or importing affords them better control over international activities, and they are able to forge relationships with trading partners, leading to further international growth and success. Of course, there are hurdles, including the difficulty of identifying and targeting foreign suppliers and/or customers and finding the right marketing channels space, all of which can be costly and time-consuming. Some firms overcome such barriers through the use of "storeless" distribution networks, such as mail-order catalogs or e-commerce. In Japan, for example, the complexity of traditional distribution systems, high retail rental rates, and crowded shelves have led many firms to launch new products via direct marketing and the Internet.[21]

As a firm and its managers gather experience with exporting, they move through different levels of commitment, ranging from awareness, interest, trial, evaluation, and, finally, adaptation of an international outlook as part of corporate strategy. Of course, not all firms progress with equal speed. Some will do so very rapidly, perhaps encouraged by success with an e-commerce approach, and move on to other forms of international involvement, such as foreign direct investment. Others may withdraw from exporting, due to disappointing experiences or as part of a strategic resource allocation decision.[22]

INTERNATIONAL INTERMEDIARIES Both direct and indirect importers and exporters frequently make use of intermediaries that can assist with troublesome yet important details, such as documentation, financing, and transportation. Intermediaries also can identify foreign suppliers and customers and help the firm with long- or short-term market penetration efforts. Together with export facilitators, intermediaries can bring the global market to the domestic firm's doorstep and help overcome financial and time constraints. Figure 10.6 shows the range of expertise they offer. Major types of international intermediaries are export management companies and trading companies.

EXPORT MANAGEMENT COMPANIES Firms that represent others for a commission or that work as distributors performing specific international business services are known as **export management companies (EMCs)**. Most EMCs focus on a particular geographic area where their expertise enables them to offer specialized services. EMCs have two primary forms of operation: They perform services as agents, or they take title to goods and operate internationally on their own account.

When working as an **international agent**, the EMC is primarily responsible for developing foreign business and sales strategies and establishing contacts abroad. Because the EMC does not share in profits, it depends heavily on high sales volumes, on which it is paid commissions. An EMC may therefore be tempted to take on as many products and as many clients as possible to obtain high sales volumes. As a result, the EMC may spread itself too thin and may be unable to adequately represent all the clients and products it carries.

When operating as an **international distributor**, the EMC purchases products from the domestic firm, takes title, and assumes the trading risk. Selling in its own name, it has the

EXPORT MANAGEMENT COMPANIES (EMCS)

Domestic firms that specialize in performing international business services as commission representatives or as distributors.

INTERNATIONAL AGENT

A representative or intermediary for the firm that works to develop business and sales strategies and that develops contacts.

INTERNATIONAL DISTRIBUTOR

A representative or intermediary for the firm that purchases products from the firm, takes title, and assumes the selling risk.

FIGURE 10.6   Multiple Roles of International Intermediaries

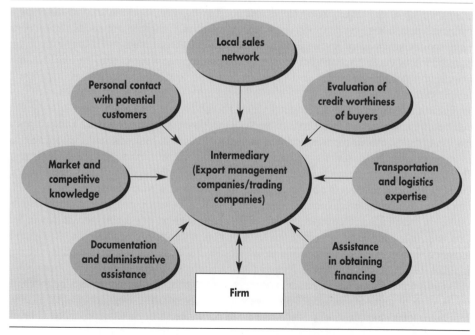

opportunity to reap greater profits than when acting as an agent. The potential for greater profit is appropriate, because the EMC has drastically reduced the risk for the domestic firm while increasing its own risk. The burden of the merchandise acquired provides a major motivation to complete an international sale successfully. The domestic firm selling to the EMC is in the comfortable position of having sold its merchandise and received its money without having to deal with the complexities of the international market. On the other hand, it is less likely to gather much international business expertise.

In addition to its compensation, an EMC may require the firm to pay market development expenses, including, for example, the cost of product samples, promotional activities such as trade show attendance or trade advertising, or even costs associated with contacting customers. Sometimes this takes the form of an annual retainer, while in other cases, direct expenses are passed along to the firm.

For an EMC relationship to work, both parties must fully recognize the delegation of responsibilities, the costs associated with those activities, and the need for information sharing, cooperation, and mutual reliance. As technology continues to ease the conduct of business across borders, EMCs must ensure that they deliver true value-added services that make them a critical link to foreign markets. Their market knowledge, resources, and expertise with export processes must, for example, lower their client export-related transaction costs or otherwise provide efficiencies or levels of market penetration that clients are not able to achieve on their own.

TRADING COMPANIES Another major intermediary is the **trading company**, which has its origins in early Europe. There, traders were awarded exclusive trading rights and protection by naval forces in exchange for tax payments. Today the most famous trading companies are the *sogoshosha* of Japan, which act as intermediaries for about one-third of the country's exports and two-fifths of its imports. They play a unique role in world commerce by importing, exporting, countertrading, investing, and manufacturing. Their vast size allows them to benefit from economies of scale and earn high rates of return, even though their profit margins are less than 2 percent. World View: Survival of the Fittest describes the changing roles of trading companies as they struggle to keep up with changes in the global business environment.

For many decades, trading companies were considered a Japan-specific phenomenon that could operate successfully as intermediaries only within the Japanese culture. In the last few decades, however, countries as diverse as Korea, Brazil, and Turkey have established their own trading companies that handle large portions of national exports. Their success, however, is in good measure due to special and preferential government incentives, rather than market forces alone. This makes them vulnerable to changes in government policies.

In 1982, legislation designed to improve the export performance of small and mid-size firms facilitated the creation of U.S. **export trading companies (ETCs)**.

Antitrust laws were relaxed to permit companies to band together in joint export efforts, thus sharing the costs of international market penetration. Further, banks were allowed to participate in trading companies, providing better access to capital and therefore permitting more trading transactions and easier receipt of title to goods. The trading company concept offers a one-stop shopping center for both the firm and its foreign customers. The firm can be assured that all international functions will be performed efficiently by the trading company, and, at the same time, the foreign customer will have to deal with few individual firms.

Although ETCs seem to offer major benefits to U.S. firms wishing to penetrate international markets, they have not been used very extensively. By 2008, only 93 individual ETCs were certified by the U.S. Department of Commerce. Yet these certificates covered more than 5,000 firms, mainly because various trade associations had applied for certification for all of their members.[23]

TRADING COMPANY

A company, such as the *sogoshosha* of Japan, that acts as an intermediary for multiple companies in such areas as import-export, countertrade, investing, and manufacturing.

EXPORT TRADING COMPANY (ETC)

The result of 1982 legislation to improve the export performance of small and medium-sized firms, ETCs allow businesses to band together to export or offer export services. Additionally, the law permits bank participation in trading companies and relaxes antitrust provisions.

WORLD VIEW

SURVIVAL OF THE FITTEST

Mitsubishi Corp's recent winning of four new big oil projects in Libya might lead some to ask: What is a Japanese trading company doing bidding on an oilfield project? For most of Japan's postwar-era *sogoshosha*, like Mitsubishi, made their reputations as suppliers.

For one hundred years, Japan's trading companies steered the economy through new and unexplored waters. After World War II, they were essential intermediaries between Japanese manufacturers and overseas markets, serving as a conduit through multinational export and import regulations. As venture capital firms, they ushered in many of the speculative investments that fueled Japan's growth in the 1980s.

In the 1990s, a massive downturn in the Japanese economy threatened to destroy the big trading companies that spurred postwar prosperity, but after bearing the brunt of the country's 15-year economic slump, these big trading companies are back. Rather than

just selling goods or mediating deals, however, the trading companies are now acting as investors. They are buying up assets and exploration rights and even striving for complete control over major projects.

The scale of this transformation became clear only recently, when Japan's five leading trading companies announced record earnings for FY2007. Mitsubishi, Japan's strongest trading company, for example, increased its net profit by 92 percent over FY2006. And oil is only a fraction of the story. The company received much of its growth from metals and coal. Some 28 percent of Mitsubishi's profit came from its Australian coking-coal subsidiary.

SOURCES: "The Non-Performing Country," *The Economist*, February 14, 2002; "Back in the Black: Japan's once-powerful trading firms have revived, thanks to the commodities boom," *Newsweek*, October 16, 2007.

International Licensing

LICENSING

A method through which one firm allows another to produce or package its product or use its intellectual property in exchange for compensation.

Licensing can be an extremely effective way to achieve penetration in international markets, either as a sole export strategy or in conjunction with other international activities. Under a licensing agreement, one firm permits another to use its intellectual property for compensation designated as **royalty**. The property licensed might include patents, trademarks, copyrights, technology, technical know-how, or specific business skills.

Licensing has intuitive appeal to many would-be international managers. As an entry strategy, it requires neither capital investment nor detailed involvement with foreign customers. By generating royalty income, licensing provides an opportunity to exploit research and development already conducted. After initial costs, the licensor can reap benefits until the end of the license contract period. Licensing also reduces the risk of expropriation because the licensee is a local company that can provide leverage against government action.

Licensing may help to avoid host-country regulations applicable to equity ventures. Licensing also may provide a means by which foreign markets can be tested without major involvement of capital or management time. Similarly, licensing can be used as a strategy to pre-empt a market before the entry of competition, especially if the licensor's resources permit full-scale involvement only in selected markets.

A special form of licensing, **trademark licensing**, permits the names or logos of designers, sports teams, or movie stars to appear on a multitude of products including clothing, games, gifts, and novelties. Licensors can make millions of dollars with little effort, while licensees can produce a brand or product that consumers will recognize immediately.

Licensing is not without disadvantages. It leaves most international marketing functions to the licensee. As a result, the licensor gains only limited expertise. Moreover, the initial toehold in the foreign market may not be a foot in the door. In exchange for the royalty, the licensor

ROYALTY

The compensation paid by one firm to another under a licensing agreement.

TRADEMARK LICENSING

The licensing of instantly recognizable logos, names, or images for use on unrelated products such as gifts, toys, or clothing.

may create its own competitor not only in the markets for which the agreement was made but also in third markets.

Licensing has come under criticism from supranational organizations, such as the United Nations Conference on Trade and Development (UNCTAD). It has been alleged that licensing lets multinational corporations (MNCs) capitalize on older technology. Such technology, however, may be in the best interest of the recipient. Guinness Brewery, for example, in order to produce Guinness Stout in Nigeria, licensed equipment that was used in Ireland at the turn of the 20th century. This equipment had additional economic life in Nigeria because it presented a good fit with local needs.[24]

Franchising is one way to expand into international markets. An example is this Starbucks franchise in Beijing.

International Franchising

Franchising is the granting of the right by a parent company to another independent entity to do business in a prescribed manner. The right can take the form of selling the franchisor's products, using its name, production, and marketing techniques or its general business approach. The major forms of franchising are manufacturer-retailer systems (such as car dealerships), manufacturer-wholesaler systems (such as soft-drink companies), and service-firm retailer systems (such as lodging services and fast-food outlets). Typically, to be successful in international franchising, the firm must be able to offer unique products or unique selling propositions. A franchise must offer a high degree of standardization in order to provide instant recognition.

From a franchisee's viewpoint, buying into a franchise reduces risk by implementing a proven concept. From a governmental perspective, franchises are favored because they require little outflow of foreign exchange, and the bulk of the profits—as well as jobs—remain in the country.

FRANCHISING

A form of licensing that allows a distributor or retailer exclusive rights to sell a product or service in a specified area.

GLOBAL MARKET DEVELOPMENT STRATEGIES

The world is too large and the competition too strong for even the largest companies to do everything independently. The convergence of technologies and the integration of markets increase not just the costs but the risks of manufacturing and marketing goods on a global scale. Partly as a reaction to increased risk and partly to better exploit opportunities, multinational corporations often join forces to achieve global goals. Strategic alliances with suppliers, customers, companies in other industries, and even competitors help to control both the costs and the risks of conducting business at the international level.

5 LEARNING OBJECTIVE

Strategic Alliances

A **strategic alliance** (or partnership) is an informal or formal arrangement between two or more companies that match complementary strengths to achieve common business objectives. It is something more than the traditional customer-vendor relationship but something less than an outright acquisition. Alliances can take a variety of forms ranging from informal cooperation to joint ownership of worldwide operations.

STRATEGIC ALLIANCES

A term for collaboration among firms, often similar to joint ventures, but not necessarily involving joint capital investment.

Culture Clues   In India, senior colleagues are obeyed and respected. In meetings, only the most senior participant might speak, but that does not mean that others in the room agree with what is said. They may maintain silence, without contradicting the speaker, out of respect for seniority. Westernized Indians, however, can be quite direct and assertive and appreciate being treated in the same manner.

Quick Take *International Television Programming*

American television programming and adaptations of American shows have historically dominated the world market. The growth of television and the number of channels created a worldwide demand for programming. Many countries licensed American television shows in the 1980s and '90s in addition to creating local content. For example, the soap opera *Santa Barbara* ran for over ten years in Russia, until 2002, even though NBC had cancelled the show in the United States in 1992.

However, television has not been spared from globalization. Today, domestic stations have become more experienced in creating their own programming, and audiences demand shows more reflective of their own cultural preferences. What do the American TV shows *American Idol*, *The Office*, *Who Wants To Be a Millionaire*, and *Whose Line is it Anyway* have in common? All of them are adaptations of popular British shows. Shows created outside of the United States are increasingly being licensed for a worldwide television market. While the concept is the same, it is important to provide for local content

adaptations. In India, *Who Wants to be a Millionaire* is hosted by a Bollywood legend; in Russia the "Ask the Audience Life-Line" is not very helpful, as the studio audience tries to give the wrong answers to contestants.

Licensing television shows and movies creates the potential for a tremendous growth in revenue. The costs of exporting a television show vary. Some shows, like *Epitafios*, are no-cost product extension into new markets. In contrast, *Who Wants to be a Millionaire* is licensed, and entire local versions of the shows are created, usually by local companies with royalties going back to the parent company. In most instances, costs such as advertising and translation are the responsibility of the licensee, thus contributing to a higher profit margin for the licensor.

SOURCES: *Who Wants to be a Millionaire* homepage, **http://abc.go. com/primetime/millionaire/abouttheshow/facts.html**, accessed January 30, 2006; Anthony Faiola, "We're Playing Their Toons," *The Washington Post*, December 6, 2004, p. C01; Edward Jay Epstein, "Hollywood's Profits, Demystified," *Slate.com*, August 8, 2005, **http://www.slate.com/id/2124078/fr**, accessed February 17, 2008.

Alliances can range from information cooperation in the market development area to joint ownership of worldwide operations. For Example, Texas Instruments has reported agreements with companies such as IBM, Hyundai, Fujitsu, Alcatel, and L. M. Ericsson, using such terms as "joint development agreement," "cooperative technical effort," "joint program for development," "alternative sourcing agreement," and "design/ exchange agreement for cooperative product development and exchange of technical data."[25]

Market development is one reason for the growth in such alliances. In Japan, Motorola is sharing chip designs and manufacturing facilities with Toshiba to gain greater access to the Japanese market. Another focus is spreading the cost and risk inherent in production and development efforts. Texas Instruments and Hitachi have teamed up to develop the next generation of memory chips.[26] The costs of developing new jet engines are so vast that they force aerospace companies into collaboration; one such consortium was formed by United Technologies' Pratt & Whitney division, Britain's Rolls-Royce, Motoren-und-Turbinen Union from Germany, Fiat of Italy, and Japanese Aero Engines.[27] Some alliances are also formed to block or co-opt competitors. For example, Caterpillar formed a heavy equipment joint venture with Mitsubishi in Japan to strike back at its main global rival, Komatsu, in its home market.

Informal Alliances

In informal cooperative deals, partners work together without a binding agreement. Typically, partners who are not direct competitors in each other's markets may exchange information on new products, processes, or technologies. They may even exchange personnel for limited periods of time. Informal arrangements often exist among small to mid-size companies, where collaboration benefits both parties.

Contractual Agreements

Through contractual agreements, alliance partners join forces for joint R&D, marketing, production, licensing, cross-licensing, or cross-marketing activities. To gain a stronghold in China's potentially vast auto market, Toyota recently formed a contractual agreement with China's largest automaker, First Automotive (FAW), to build large-scale production of a wide range of models. Toyota, which will have no equity stake, will provide management expertise, technology, marketing assistance, and cash, while FAW will provide workers, factories, and equipment.[28] Firms also can have a reciprocal arrangement whereby each partner provides the other access to its market. The New York Yankees and Manchester United, for instance, sell each other's licensed products and develop joint sponsorship programs. International airlines share hubs, coordinate schedules, and simplify ticketing. Alliances such as Star (joining airlines such as United and Lufthansa), Oneworld (British Airways and American Airlines), and Sky Team (Delta and Air France) provide worldwide coverage for their customers in both the travel and shipping communities.

International licensing is another area where contractual agreements are common. For example, television networks like ABC and NBC, as described in Quick Take: International Television Programming, use contract licensing to import popular television programs.

Management Contracts

In countries where governments insist on complete or majority ownership of firms, **management contracts** are a viable option for foreign expansion. Here, a firm sells its expertise and builds a market presence without either the risks or benefits of ownership. In time, local managers are trained to take over operations. Management contracts have clear benefits for the client or client government, who gain access to skills, resources, and support services that would be difficult and costly to build up locally. Consider, for example, the benefits available to hotels managed by the Sheraton Corporation, which include instant access to Sheraton's worldwide reservation system. Management contracts also offer distinct advantages to the supplier. They lower the risk of participating in an international venture while providing the opportunity to gain expertise in new markets. They also allow firms to leverage existing skills and resources commercially.

One specialized form of management contract is the **turnkey operation**, whereby the client acquires a complete international system, together with skills sufficient to operate and maintain it. Companies like AES, for example, are part of a consortium that builds electric power facilities around the world, operates them, and, in some cases, even owns parts of them.

Equity Participation

Multinational corporations that seek a measure of control in companies that are strategically important to them frequently acquire minority ownership. Ease of market entry is another attraction of equity participation and explains why Ford, Mercedes-Benz, and BMW are all pursuing opportunities in China.[29]

MANAGEMENT CONTRACTS

The firm sells its expertise in running a company while avoiding the risks or benefits of ownership.

TURNKEY OPERATION

A specialized form of management contract between a customer and an organization to provide a complete operational system together with the skills needed for unassisted maintenance and operation.

Joint Ventures

A **joint venture** is the long-term participation of two or more companies in an enterprise in which each party contributes assets, has some equity, and shares risk. The reasons for establishing a joint venture can be divided into three groups: (1) government suasion or legislation; (2) one partner's needs for other partners' skills; and (3) one partner's needs for other partners' attributes or assets.

The key to a joint venture is the sharing of a common business objective, which makes the arrangement more than a customer-vendor relationship but less than an outright acquisition. The partners' rationales for entering into the arrangement may vary. An example is New United Motor Manufacturing, Inc. (NUMMI), a joint venture between Toyota and GM. Toyota needed direct access to the U.S. market, while GM benefited from the technology, management expertise, and quality standards of its Japanese partner.[30]

Joint ventures are valuable when the pooling of resources results in a better outcome for each partner than if each were to conduct its activities individually. This is particularly true when each partner has a specialized advantage in areas that benefit the venture. For example, a firm may have new technology yet lack sufficient capital to carry out foreign direct investment on its own. Through a joint venture, market penetration is achieved more easily. Similarly, one partner may have a distribution system already in place, which leads to high-volume sales of the other partner's product in a shorter period of time. Another key benefit of joint ventures is the ability of foreign firms to minimize the risks involved in investing and operating in emerging, potentially unstable economies.

In some markets, joint ventures may be the only means through which a firm can operate profitably at all. Import restrictions or tariff barriers, for instance, are often avoided through joint-venture relationships with domestic companies. India restricts equity participation in local operations by foreigners to 40 percent, so joint ventures are a viable alternative for international firms who wish to operate there. Recently, several Western firms have used joint ventures to gain access to markets in eastern and central Europe. In markets like these, joint ventures can ease relationships between foreign firms and local governments or such organizations as trade unions. Negotiations for certifications or licenses are often easier, simply because authorities may not perceive themselves as dealing with a foreign firm. Access to local capital markets, too, may be possible. In some cases, joint ventures even make foreign companies eligible for tax incentives, grants, or government support.

Despite their many advantages, joint ventures all too frequently fall short of expectations and/or are disbanded. The reasons typically include conflicts of interest or differences in management styles, problems with disclosure of sensitive information, or disagreement over how profits are to be shared.

Consortia

A new drug, computer, or telecommunications switch can cost more than $1 billion to develop and bring to market. To combat the high costs and risks of research and development, research **consortia** have emerged in the United States, Japan, and Europe. Since the passage of the Joint Research and Development Act of 1984 (which allows both domestic and foreign firms to participate in joint basic research efforts without the fear of antitrust action), well over 100 consortia have been registered in the United States. These consortia pool their resources for research into technologies ranging from artificial intelligence and electric car batteries to semiconductor manufacturing.

The European Union has several megaprojects to develop new technologies, under the names BRITE, COMET, ESPRIT, EUREKA, RACE, and SOKRATES. Japanese consortia have worked on producing the world's highest-capacity memory chip and other advanced computer technologies. On the manufacturing side, the formation of Airbus Industries secured European production of commercial jets. The consortium, now backed by the European Aeronautic Defense and Space Company (EADS), which emerged from the link-up of the German Daimler-Benz Aerospace AG, the French Aerospatiale Matra, and CASA of Spain has become a prime global competitor.[31]

Elements of Successful Alliances

Table 10.3 summarizes what it takes for interfirm alliances of any kind to be beneficial for each partner. Strategic alliances operate in a dynamic business environment and must therefore adjust to changing market conditions. The agreement between partners should provide for changes in the original concept so that the venture can flourish and grow. The trick is to have a prior understanding as to which party will take care of which pains and problems so that a common goal is reached.

Full Ownership

For some firms, the decision to invest overseas is, initially at least, considered only in the context of 100 percent ownership. Ethnocentricity may explain this bias—management may believe that no outside entity should have an impact on corporate decision-making. Starbucks, for example, limits its global expansion strategies to licenses, joint ventures, and company operations, believing that local ownership in the form of franchising will dilute the Starbucks brand. Quick Take: Starbucks Teas Up in Japan demonstrates that the company's success hinges on its ability to recreate the entire Starbucks experience outside the United States.

In order to make a rational decision about the degree of ownership, management must evaluate the extent to which total control is critical to the success of international marketing activities. While full ownership may be desirable, it may not be a prerequisite for success. In other cases, the corporate culture may be such that full ownership is essential. If strong interdependencies between headquarters and local operations factor into the firm's success, perhaps nothing short of total coordination achieved through ownership will guarantee acceptable performance.

As explained in Chapter 3, however, the current international environment is hostile to full ownership by multinational firms. Indeed, government actions through legal restrictions

TABLE 10.3 Key Provisions of Successful Interfirm Alliances

1. Clear definitions of the interfirm relationship, its objectives, and its duration
2. Agreement on ownership, control, and management
3. Agreement on protection of sensitive or proprietary information
4. Policies on financial structure, including allocation of costs and profits
5. Clarity on taxation and fiscal obligations
6. Guidelines on employment, training, and skills transfer
7. Agreement on government assistance, if any
8. Plans for transfer of technology
9. Marketing and distribution arrangements
10. Environmental protection and ethics policies
11. Clear guidelines for record keeping and inspection
12. Mechanism for the settlement of disputes
13. Mechanism for dissolution of relationship

Quick Take *Environment And Sustainability*

Starbucks Teas Up In Japan

For decades, Japan's neighborhood *kisaten* were the place to be when it came to coffee. In a nation of tea drinkers, young people who once sipped coffee from tiny cups in smoky, dimly lit shops now flock to Starbucks for double espressos and giant lattes. The Seattle-based company recently opened its 722th store in Japan. Initially drawn to Japan by its large market, consumers' high disposable income, and affinity for Western brands, the coffee giant further enticed customers by tailoring some of its drinks to fit the tastes of the Japanese customer; stepping away from its standard indulgently sweet menu, Starbucks added a number of green tea beverages, which are now available at stores around the globe.

The company's strategy of maintaining its identity and its environmental leadership posture suits Japanese consumers well. According to Martin Coles, president of Starbucks International, "It's very easy to get swept up in this desire to localize a brand. The Japanese consumer is probably one of the most discerning consumers in the world. But if anything, they want the same experience that they've had in Los Angeles, Hawaii, Europe, or wherever."

Because Starbucks does no advertising in Japan, its success is even more dazzling. With its comfy couches and its American rock or hip-hop music, the chain has quickly become a household name—as well as the number-one-ranked chain in Japan's restaurant sector. Unlike its competitors, the chain is not a franchise—Starbucks currently uses three business structures in international markets: licenses, joint ventures, and company-owned operations.

Ownership allows the company to protect its brand and duplicate those aspects of it that set Starbucks apart from the other coffee house chains. It also permits easier and quicker introduction of environmentally responsive policies. For example, Starbucks is now using recycled content for hot beverage cups, which is estimated to lower the dependence on tree fiber by more than five million pounds annually. The firm is also committed to reduce its environmental footprint through preservation in places where coffee is grown and by recycling coffee grounds into nutrient-rich soil.

SOURCES: **http://www.starbucks.co.jp/en/**, accessed February 17, 2008. "Starbucks' green tea success with Japanese consumers leads to worldwide popularity," Japan External Trade Organization, April 2006, **www.jetro.org**, accessed February 17, 2008. "Starbucks Corporation," McGraw-Hill Higher Education, **http://www.mhhe.com/business/management/thompson/11e/case/starbucks-2.html**, accessed February 17, 2008; "environmental affairs" **www.starbucks.com**, accessed February 29, 2008.

or discriminatory policies lessen the attraction of ownership. The Venezuelan government, for example, recently made moves to nationalize the country's telecommunications and electric industries. Many companies in both industries are owned, in part, by foreign firms.[32] Volatility in the political or economic environment also makes full ownership a risky proposition. In many countries, the choice is either to abide by existing restraints and accept a reduction in control or to lose the opportunity to operate there at all.

SUMMARY

Firms do not become experienced in international business overnight, but rather progress gradually through an internationalization process.

The convergence of several factors—market, cost, environmental, and competitive—has led to the globalization of business, presenting new opportunities and challenges.

Motivations to expand overseas are either proactive (initiated by aggressive management) or reactive (defensive responses to environmental changes or pressures).

Thorough strategic planning allows firms to increase their chances of success overseas. It involves external and internal analysis, target country selection and segmentation, and global program development.

Constraints of time, resources, and expertise are the major inhibitors to international research. Nevertheless, firms need to carry out secondary and often primary research in order to explore foreign market opportunities and challenges successfully. To provide ongoing information to management, an information system is also essential.

The most frequently used entry strategies include importing/exporting, often with the aid of international intermediaries or facilitators, and licensing and franchising. None of these methods require ownership or foreign direct investment in target markets.

Interfirm alliances, including management contracts, joint ventures, and consortia, allow firms a presence in foreign markets while minimizing costs and risks. Full ownership, while allowing total control, is a risky proposition, especially in politically unstable economies.

KEY TERMS AND CONCEPTS

managerial commitment	information system	trading company
cost leadership strategy	export complaint systems	export trading company (ETC)
differentiation strategy	environmental scanning	licensing
focus strategy	Delphi studies	royalty
secondary research	scenario analysis	trademark licensing
primary research	diversification	franchising
qualitative information	market segmentation	strategic alliances
quantitative information	glocalization	management contract
personal interviews	cross-subsidization	turnkey operation
focus group research	export management companies	joint venture
observation research	(EMCs)	consortiium/consortia
survey research	international agent	
experimentation	international distributor	

REVIEW QUESTIONS

1. Summarize the four sets of factors driving globalization.
2. Explain the stages involved in formulating a global strategy. Are these processes sequential or concurrent?
3. Describe the positive and negative impacts of international expansion on domestic business activities.
4. What are the major differences between domestic and international research?
5. Discuss the possible shortcomings of secondary data. When is primary data necessary?
6. What is the purpose of export intermediaries? How can an intermediary avoid circumvention by a client or customer?
7. "Licensing is really not a form of international involvement because it requires no substantial additional effort on the part of the licensor." Comment.
8. Why is full ownership of a foreign operation a less-than-desirable goal?

CRITICAL SKILL BUILDERS

1. Globalization is not only an imperative for survival and future growth, it is the inevitable consequence of business expansion. Prepare your arguments for and against this statement, then debate the topic in teams.
2. Select a small to mid-size business in your area. Analyze ways in which the company currently operates in the international arena. Then create a blueprint for cost-effective, profitable expansion.
3. You are employed by National Engineering, a firm that designs subways. Because you have had a course in international business, your boss asks you to spend the next week exploring international possibilities for the company. How will you go about this task?
4. The rate of expropriation has been ten times greater for a joint venture with the host government than for a 100 percent U.S.-owned subsidiary. Is this contrary to logic?
5. Comment on the observation that "a joint venture may be a combination of Leonardo da Vinci's brain and Carl Lewis' legs; one wants to fly, the other insists on running."

ON THE WEB

1. Prepare a one-page memo to a foreign company introducing your product or service. Include a contact listing of ten businesses in foreign countries looking to import your particular product. Include the company name, address, and other contact information, along with special requirements of the company you note from its posting of an offer to buy. Cite the sources from which you prepared your list. Look at: **http://www.tradematch.co/uk** or **http://www.mnileads.com**.

2. Show macro, aggregate changes in international markets by listing the total value of three commodities exported from your country to five other countries for the last four years. For each of the countries, provide a one-paragraph statement in which you identify positive or negative trends. Give your opinion on whether or not these trends are relevant or reflect the reality of today's international business environment. What are the dangers of relying on perceived trends? Use Internet sources provided in the chapter and others of your finding to conduct research on products from your hometown or region.

3. Bestfoods is one of the largest food companies in the world with operations in more than 60 countries and products sold in 110 countries in the world. Based on the brand information given on its web site (**http://www.bestfoods.com**), what benefits does a company derive from having a global presence? How is the acquisition by Unilever likely to affect the company's future?

ENDNOTES

1. Kenichi Ohmae, Triad Power—*The Coming Shape of Global Competition* (New York: Free Press, 1985), pp. 22-27.
2. "Drug development cost hit $1.7 billion," **www.in-PharmaTechnologist.com**, accessed January 29, 2008.
3. Rochelle Garner, "McAfee Margins Under Siege by Symantec, Microsoft," *Bloomberg*, December 3, 2007; Carole Vaporean, "Caterpillar to offer electric mining truck in 2008, *Reuters*, March 28, 2007.
4. David Goldman, "Starbucks puts the brakes on new stores," *CNNMoney.com*, January 30, 2008, **http://money.cnn.com**.
5. George S. Yip, *Total Global Strategy II* (Upper Saddle River, NJ: Prentice Hall, 2002).
6. Michael Porter, Competitive Advantage (New York: The Free Press, 1987), chapter 1.
7. David A. Ricks, *Blunders in International Business*, 4th ed. (Hoboken, NJ: Wiley, 2006).
8. "National Trade Data Bank," **www.Stat-USA.gov**, accessed February 29, 2008.
9. Michael R. Czinkota, "International Information Cross-Fertilization in Marketing: An Empirical Assessment," *European Journal of Marketing* 34, November 12, 2000, pp. 1305–1314.
10. Ricks, *Blunders in International Business*.
11. Michael R. Czinkota and Masaaki Kotabe, "Product Development the Japanese Way," in M. Czinkota and M. Kotabe, *Trends in International Business: Critical Perspectives* (Oxford: Blackwell Publishers, 1998), pp. 153–158.
12. C. K. Corder, "Problems and Pitfalls in Conducting Marketing Research in Africa," Marketing Expansion in a Shrinking World, ed. Betsy Gelb. *Proceedings of American Marketing Association Business Conference* (Chicago: AMA, 1978), pp. 86–90.
13. Ibid.
14. Richard Tomlinson, "Europe's New Computer Game," *Fortune*, February 21, 2000, pp. 219–224.
15. "Hyundai and Kia aim to increase sales of new cars in 2008," *International Herald Tribune*, January 2, 2008.
16. "Think Local," *The Economist*, April 13, 2002.
17. **www.overpopulation.org**, "Family I, Teens & Tween," *News and Observer*, January 28, 2008.
18. Pascal Cagni, "Think Global, Act European," *Developments in Strategy and Business*, August 30, 2004, **http://www.strategy-business.com/export/export.php?article_id=4510703**, accessed February 8, 2008.
19. Global Markets and Marketing, **http://mhhe.com/business/marketing/etzel 12e/graphics/etze112mark/common/etze103.pdf**, accessed February 17, 2008.
20. **http://www.nokia.com/A402785** , accessed February 17, 2008.
21. **www.Sony.com**, accessed February 19, 2008.
22. Nigel Mukherrjee. *Telecommunications International*. Norwood: June 2005. Vol. 39, Iss. 6; p. S20.
23. Michael R. Czinkota and Masaaki Kotabe, "Entering the Japanese Market: A Reassessment of Foreign Firms' Entry and Distribution Strategies," *Industrial Marketing Management*, 29 (2000), pp. 483–491.
24. Pieter Pauwels and Paul Matthyssens, "A Strategy Process Perspective on Export Withdrawal," *Journal of International Marketing* 7, 4 (1999): pp. 10–37.
25. Sepia Thomson, Office of Export Trading Company Affairs, U.S. Department of Commerce, Washington, D.C., February 22, 2008.
26. Texas Instruments' homepage, **http://www.ti.com**, accessed February 22, 2008.
27. **www.unctad.org**, accessed February 19, 2008.
28. "Competition through cooperation," *Monash Business Review*, vol. 3, no. 3, November, 2007, **http://publications.epress.monash.edu/doi/abs/10.2104/mbr07041?journalCode=mbr**, accessed February 19, 2008.
29. Keith Bradsher, "Toyota and Chinese Carmaker in Venture," *The New York Times*, August 30, 2002, p. 1.
30. Ibid.
31. **www.eads.com**, accessed February 10, 2008.
32. Simon Ramero, "Chaves Moves to Nationalize Two Industries," *The New York Times*, January 9, 2007.

And Now for the Next 1 Billion Consumers

During the first 50 years of the info-tech era, more than 1 billion people have come to use computers, the vast majority in the developed markets of Europe, North America, and Australasia. Those markets have become increasingly saturated and do not provide the needed growth. Computer sales are expected to increase a mere 6 percent per year between 2005 and 2008. The next billion consumers have to be found in the emerging markets of the 21st century: China, India, Russia, South Africa, and Brazil. Sales in info-tech in these markets are expected to increase by 11 percent per year over the next five

years, fueled mostly by the burgeoning ranks of millions of middle-class consumers. These newly wealthy consumers are showing preferences for fashionable brands as well as for features every bit as sophisticated as those demanded by their developed-country counterparts.

The challenges of succeeding in the emerging markets are forcing the established global players to come up with innovative new approaches. Some of the areas requiring fundamental rethinking include the following:

- *Design.* Solutions have to be simpler and more durable. TVS Electronics, an Indian printer manufacturer, is producing devices for India's 1.2 million small shops. They are an all-in-one computer, cash register, and inventory-management system. They can be operated with icons, because many of the clerks are illiterate. They have to be robust to withstand the elements such as heat and dust.
- *Innovation.* Marketers have to innovate for the peculiarities of emerging markets. Electricity may often be unavailable and unreliable. Hewlett-Packard adjusted to this by designing a small solar panel to charge digital printers for itinerant photographers in India. In South Africa, HP is working with a solar fabric that is cheaper and less fragile.
- *Business Development.* Old strategies may have to be adjusted. IBM figures that it can do well in China only by supplying technology to local companies. It developed a low-cost, $12 microprocessor and a simple network computer for China's Culturecom, which is selling computers and Internet access services in the country's rural areas.
- *Competition.* Companies such as Cisco, Dell, and Microsoft dominate global markets. However, many new challengers are using their low costs and intimate knowledge of local or similar emerging markets to expand their businesses. Chinese network systems

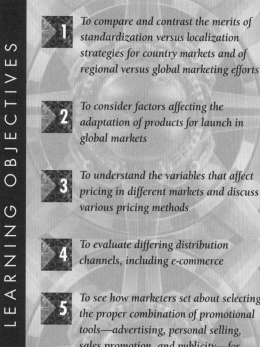

1 *To compare and contrast the merits of standardization versus localization strategies for country markets and of regional versus global marketing efforts*

2 *To consider factors affecting the adaptation of products for launch in global markets*

3 *To understand the variables that affect pricing in different markets and discuss various pricing methods*

4 *To evaluate differing distribution channels, including e-commerce*

5 *To see how marketers set about selecting the proper combination of promotional tools—advertising, personal selling, sales promotion, and publicity—for targeted global markets*

company Huawei can charge 50 percent less than Cisco and has made sales in markets in Africa and Europe.

- *Pricing.* Pressure on prices can lead to innovative solutions on financing. Poland needed to modernize its driver's licensing system but could not afford it. Hewlett-Packard agreed to install Poland's new computer system in exchange for a cut of the fees drivers pay each time they get new licenses or renew old ones.

While the first billion customers may have created a sector with annual revenues of more than $1 trillion, sales for the second billion will not reach the same level. Lower prices in these markets may put pressure on prices everywhere. However, staying out of these markets is not an option. Some companies have actually started taking resources, people, and projects away from established markets (such as Western Europe) and shifting them to less-mature markets.[1]

As You Read This Chapter

1. In what ways will companies have to make two types of adjustments: those they have to and those they better accommodate?
2. Why does a company need not only to develop marketing programs for individual markets but also to coordinate these programs across regions, even the entire world?

The task of marketing is to plan and execute programs that will ensure a long-term competitive advantage for the company. This task has two integral parts: (1) the determining of specific target markets and (2) marketing management, which consists of manipulating marketing-mix elements to best satisfy the needs of the individual target markets. Chapter 10 has already covered target-marketing selection as an aspect of international business research. Here we focus on the adjustment of marketing strategy for global operations.

 ## STANDARDIZATION VS. ADAPTATION FOR GLOBAL MARKETS

Once target markets have been selected, global marketing begins in earnest. An important first step is a thorough assessment of the marketing mix for the product to be introduced into new markets. A key question in international marketing concerns the extent to which the elements of the marketing mix—product, price, place, and distribution—should be standardized to ease their production and their introduction into new markets.

To determine what modifications in the marketing mix are needed or warranted, there are three basic options:

1. Make no special provisions for the global marketplace but, rather, identify potential target markets and then choose products that can easily be marketed with little or no modification (the **standardization approach**).
2. Adapt to local conditions in each and every target market (the **multidomestic approach**).
3. Incorporate differences into a regional or global strategy that will allow for local differences in implementation (the **globalization approach**).

STANDARDIZATION APPROACH

Policy of making minimal or no changes to the marketing mix for the global marketplace.

MULTIDOMESTIC APPROACH

Policy of adapting the marketing mix to suit each country entered.

GLOBALIZATION APPROACH

Creation of a regionally or globally similar marketing-mix strategy.

In today's environment, standardization usually means cross-national strategies, rather than a policy of viewing foreign markets as secondary and therefore not important enough to adapt products for them. Ideally, the international marketer should "think globally and act locally," focusing on neither extreme—that is, neither full standardization nor full localization. Global thinking requires flexibility in exploiting good ideas and products on a worldwide basis, regardless of their origin. For example Yum! Brands' restaurants approach the Chinese market in this way. While the Kentucky Fried Chicken menu features its signature "Original Recipe" fried chicken, it also creates products that appeal to local tastes such as the Spicy Dragon Twister, Pi Dan Congee (rice porridge), Fu Yung, Vegetable Soup, and Egg Tart (signature dessert). Pizza Hut restaurants display upscale decor to satisfy their customers' preference for "five-star service and atmosphere at a three-star price." The casual dining atmosphere is centered around an extensive menu that covers soup, salads, appetizers, and a range of pizzas such as Seafood Catch (seafood mix, crab sticks, green pepper, pineapple) and The Hot One (chili pepper, onion, tomato, beef, spicy chicken). Even with the success of KFC and Pizza Hut in China, the company is not resting on its laurels. Yum! China is testing East Dawning, the company's first Chinese quick-service restaurant brand to provide affordable, great-tasting, authentic quick-service Chinese food to the Chinese consumer.[2] Factors that encourage standardization or adaptation are summarized in Table 11.1.

Even when marketing programs are based on highly standardized ideas and strategies, they depend on three sets of variables: (1) the market(s) targeted; (2) the product and its characteristics; and (3) company characteristics, including factors such as resources and policy.

Questions of adaptation have no easy answers. Marketers in many firms rely on decision-support systems to aid in program adaptation, while others consider every situation independently. All goods must, of course, conform to environmental conditions over which the marketer has no control. Further, the international marketer may use adaptation to enhance its competitiveness in the marketplace.

PRODUCT STRATEGIES

2 LEARNING OBJECTIVE

Goods or services form the core of the firm's international operations. Its success depends on how well goods satisfy needs and wants and how well they are differentiated from those of the competition. This section focuses on product and product-line adaptation to foreign markets, as well as product counterfeiting as a current problem facing international marketers.

Factors affecting product adaptation to foreign market conditions are summarized in Figure 11.1. The changes vary from minor ones, such as translation of a user's manual, to major ones, such as a more economical version of the product. Many of the factors have an impact on product selection as well as product adaptation for a given market.

TABLE 11.1 Standardization Versus Adaptation

FACTORS ENCOURAGING STANDARDIZATION	FACTORS ENCOURAGING ADAPTATION
• Economies in product R & D	• Differing use conditions
• Economies of scale in production	• Government and regulatory influences
• Economies in marketing	• Differing buyer behavior patterns
• Control of marketing programs	• Local initiative and motivation in implementation
• "Shrinking" of the world marketplace	• Adherence to the marketing concept

FIGURE 11.1   Factors Affecting Product Adaptation Decisions

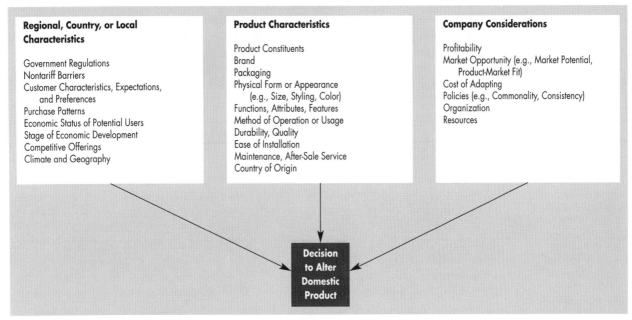

Regional, Country, or Local Characteristics

Government Regulations
Nontariff Barriers
Customer Characteristics, Expectations, and Preferences
Purchase Patterns
Economic Status of Potential Users
Stage of Economic Development
Competitive Offerings
Climate and Geography

Product Characteristics

Product Constituents
Brand
Packaging
Physical Form or Appearance (e.g., Size, Styling, Color)
Functions, Attributes, Features
Method of Operation or Usage
Durability, Quality
Ease of Installation
Maintenance, After-Sale Service
Country of Origin

Company Considerations

Profitability
Market Opportunity (e.g., Market Potential, Product-Market Fit)
Cost of Adapting
Policies (e.g., Commonality, Consistency)
Organization
Resources

Decision to Alter Domestic Product

Sources: Adapted from V. Yorio, *Adapting Products for Export* (New York: The Conference Board, 1983), p. 7.

Regional, Country, or Local Characteristics

Typically, the market environment mandates the majority of product modifications. However, the most stringent requirements often result from government regulations. Some may serve no purpose other than political ones (such as protection of domestic industry or response to political pressures). Because of the sovereignty of nations, individual firms must comply, but they can influence the situation either by lobbying directly or through industry associations to have the issue raised during trade negotiations.

As covered in more detail in Chapter 4, nontariff barriers include product standards, testing or approval procedures, subsidies for local products, and bureaucratic red tape. Government regulations may be spelled out, but firms need to be ever vigilant for changes and exceptions. The member countries of the European Economic Area are imposing standards in more than 10,000 product categories, ranging from toys to tractor seats. While in the past, companies such as Murray Manufacturing have had to change their products to comply with multiple-country standards in Europe (in Murray's case, connected to noise levels of its lawnmowers), they will be able to produce one European product in the future. Overall, U.S. producers may be forced to improve product quality because some rules require adoption of an overall system approved by the International Standards Organization (ISO). By 2007, a total of 897,866 ISO 9000 certificates (relating to product and process quality) and 129,199 ISO 14000 certificates (relating to environmental management) had been issued in 157 countries worldwide.[3]

Product decisions made by marketers of consumer products are especially affected by local behavior, tastes, attitudes, and traditions—all reflecting the marketer's need to gain the customer's approval. A knowledge of cultural and psychological differences may be the key to success. For example, Brazilians rarely eat breakfast, or they eat it at home; therefore,

The developing and industrialized world meet at a crossroad in Vietnam. New trade agreements have opened the Vietnamese market to U.S. service providers.

Dunkin' Donuts markets doughnuts as snacks, as dessert, and for parties. To further appeal to Brazilians, doughnuts are made with local fruit fillings such as papaya and guava. In China, Seagram, the makers of such high-end brands as Chivas Regal and Absolut, offers a low-price, locally produced whiskey named 30% High. The drink targets young men who can't afford pricey spirits but want an alternative to *baijiu*, a throat-burning distilled spirit drunk by their parents. Believing that young Chinese men drink as part of a bonding ritual with their friends, the advertising for 30% High reflects a spirit of camaraderie—young men sharing good times. With its sophisticated but affordable image, the new drink hopes to tap into a growing market.[4]

Often no concrete product changes are needed, only a change in the product's positioning. **Positioning** is the perception by consumers of the firm's brand in relation to competitors' brands—that is, the mental image that a brand, or the company as a whole, evokes. Coca-Cola took a risk in marketing Diet Coke in Japan because the population is not overweight by Western standards. Further, Japanese women do not like to drink anything clearly labeled as a diet product. The company changed the name to Coke Light and subtly shifted the promotional theme from "weight loss" to "figure maintenance."

The monitoring of competitors' product features is crucial, both for determining what has to be done to meet and beat them as well as for product-adaptation decisions. Competitive offerings may provide a baseline against which resources can be measured—for example, they may help to determine what it takes to reach a critical market share in a given competitive situation. American Hospital Supply, a Chicago-based producer of medical equipment, adjusts its product in a pre-emptive way by making products that are hard to duplicate. As a result, the firm increased sales and earnings in Japan about 40 percent a year over a ten-year period.

Management must take into account the stage of economic development and buying power of the market. For example, Nestlé was able to double the sales of their Bono cookies in Brazil after shrinking the package from 200 grams to 140 grams with a commensurate price decrease.[5] As a country's economy advances, buyers are in a better position to buy and to demand more sophisticated products and product versions. On the other hand, the situation in some developing markets may require backward innovation; that is, the market may require a drastically simplified version of the firm's product because of lack of purchasing power or of usage conditions. Economic conditions may shift rapidly, thus warranting change in the product or the product line. During the Asian currency crisis, McDonald's replaced French fries with rice in its Indonesian restaurants, due to cost considerations.

Product Characteristics

Product characteristics are the inherent features of the product offering, whether actual or perceived. The inherent characteristics of products, and the benefits they provide to consumers in the various markets in which they are marketed, make certain products good candidates for standardization—and others not.

The international marketer has to make sure that products do not contain ingredients that might violate legal requirements or religious or social customs. DEP Corporation, a Los Angeles manufacturer of hair and skin products, takes particular pains to make sure that no Japan-bound products contain formaldehyde, an ingredient commonly used in the United States, but illegal in Japan. Where religion or custom determines consumption, ingredients may have to be replaced for the product to be acceptable. In Islamic countries, for example, vegetable shortening has to be substituted for animal fats. In deference to Hindu and Muslim beliefs, McDonald's Maharaja Mac is made with mutton in India.

Packaging is an area where firms generally do make modifications. Due to the longer time that products spend in channels of distribution, international companies, especially those marketing food products, have used more expensive packaging materials and/or more

---

POSITIONING

The perception by consumers of a firm's product in relation to competitors' products.

Fast Facts

What are the five most valuable global brands in the world?

According to the annual review by *BusinessWeek* and Interbrand, the top five are Coca-Cola, Microsoft, IBM, General Electric, and Nokia. The 2007 brand value of Coca-Cola was $65.3 billion.

Quick Take *Russia's New Capitalism*

Economic transformation has revitalized the streets of Moscow, where open markets and the removal of trade barriers are helping create a bustling international city.

Moscow's newly affluent middle class enjoys fine dining and shops for furniture at Ikea. According to Ikea, the figure in Russia is $85 per store visit —exactly the same as in affluent Sweden. Unprecedented spending on improving the city's aging infrastructure, diverse job opportunities, and world-class retailing are all signs that living standards are on the rise.

Moscow is the poster-child city of Russia's recovery. In 2006, economic growth reached a respectable 6.7 percent, inflation was held in check, and the national currency remained steady. A miracle of post-Cold War stability, the government is making headway with much-needed reforms. A boom in Russia's oil industry and foreign investments in the private sector spurs further economic growth, making Russia the tenth-largest economy in the world. The media industry—the gateway to Russia's huge market of 141 million consumers—has become a hot ticket. NTV, the nation's largest independent TV network, has attracted the attention of global media moguls such as Rupert Murdoch's News Corporation, Vivendi, and Bertelsmann.

SOURCES: Lilia Shevtsova, "Think Again: Vladimir Putin," *Foreign Policy*, January/February 2008, pp. 34-40; "Russia's booming economy," *Economist Intelligence Unit Briefing*, June 18, 2007, p. 1; IKEA: How the Swedish Retailer Became a Global Cult Brand," *BusinessWeek*, November 14, 2005, pp. 34-46; Paul Klebnikov, "Intrigue, Arrest Warrants, Sex Scandals—Russia's TV Networks Are in the Play Again," February 4, 2002, **http://www.forbes.com**; Peter Baker, "Step Out into the New Moscow," *The Washington Post*, July 11, 2001.

---

expensive transportation modes for export shipments. Food processors have solved the problem by using airtight, reclosable containers that seal out moisture and other contaminants. Increasingly, environmental concerns are having an impact on packaging decisions. First, governments want to reduce packaging waste by encouraging marketers to adopt the four environmentally correct Rs: redesign, reduce, reuse, and recycle. Uganda, for instance, raised tariffs on polythene used in packaging from 10 percent to a prohibitive 50 percent. Medical products are exempted from the tariff.[6] Second, many markets have sizable segments of consumers who are concerned enough about protecting the environment to change their consumption patterns, which has resulted in product modifications, such as the introduction of recyclable yogurt containers from marketers such as Dany and Danone in Europe.

The promotional aspect of packaging relates primarily to labeling. The major adjustments concern legally required dual-language labeling, as in Canada (French and English), Belgium (French and Flemish), and Finland (Finnish and Swedish). Other governmental requirements include more informative labeling of products for consumer protection and education. Inadequate identification, failure to use the required languages, or inadequate or incorrect descriptions printed on the labels may all cause problems.

Brand names convey the image of the good or service. Offhand, brands may seem to be one of the most easily standardized items in the product offering. However, the establishment of worldwide brands is difficult; how can a marketer establish world brands when the firm sells 800 products in more than 200 countries, most of them under different names? This is the situation of Gillette. A typical example is Silkience hair conditioner, which is sold as Soyance in France, Sientel in Italy, and Silkience in Germany. Standardizing the name to reap promotional benefits is difficult because names have become established in each market, and the action would lead to objections from local managers or even government. In response, marketers have standardized all other possible elements of brand aesthetics, such as color, symbols, and packaging. However, global brands are perceived to be more value-added for the consumer, either through better quality (as a function of worldwide acceptance) or by enhancing the consumer's self-perception as being cosmopolitan, sophisticated, and modern.[7]

When a product that is sold internationally requires repairs, parts, or service, the problems of obtaining, training, and holding a sophisticated engineering or repair staff are not easy to solve. If the product breaks down and the repair arrangements are not up to standard, the product image will suffer. In some cases, products abroad may not even be used for their intended purpose and thus may require not only modifications in product configuration but also in service frequency. For instance, snowplows exported from the United States are used to remove sand from driveways in Saudi Arabia.

The country of origin of a product, typically communicated by the phrase "made in (country)," has considerable influence on quality perceptions. The perception of products manufactured in certain countries is affected by a built-in positive or negative assumption about quality. The international marketer must take steps to overcome, or at least neutralize, biases. The issue is especially important to developing countries that need to increase exports and for importers who source products from countries different from where they are sold. Consider, for instance, the case of a California-based company that has begun exporting Japanese-style lunch boxes—*bento*—into Japan. The boxes are made in the United States from organically grown California rice, which is one-third of the cost of Japanese rice. While rice imports face duties of nearly 500 percent, the boxes are categorized as processed food and escape the hefty tariffs. Japanese farmers responded with outrage that a foreign-based company—actually a subsidiary of a larger Japanese concern—is able to sell a dish traditionally made with Japanese rice at a time when the agricultural sector is forced to cut production in line with decreased demand.[8]

Company Considerations

Company policy will often determine the presence and degree of adaptation. Discussions of product adaptation often end with the question, "Is it worth it?" The answer depends on the company's ability to control costs, to correctly estimate market potential, and, finally, to secure profitability. The decision to adapt should be preceded by a thorough analysis of the market. Formal market research with primary data collection and/or testing is warranted. From the financial standpoint, some companies have specific return-on-investment levels (for example, 25 percent) to be satisfied before adaptation. Others let the requirement vary as a function of the market considered and also the time in the market—that is, profitability may be initially compromised for proper market entry.

Most companies aim for consistency in their market efforts. This means that all products must fit in terms of quality, price, and user perceptions. Consistency may be difficult to attain, for example, in the area of warranties. Warranties can be uniform only if use conditions do not vary drastically and if the company is able to deliver equally on its promise anywhere it has a presence.

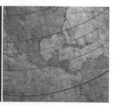

Culture Clues   Global brands compete on emotion, catering to aspirations that cut across cultural differences. Global brands may cater to consumers' needs to feel cosmopolitan, something that local brands cannot deliver. Global brands may also convey that their user has reached a certain status both professionally and personally. This type of recognition represents both perception and reality, enabling brands to establish credibility in markets. As one consumer put it: "Local brands are who I am, global brands are who I want to become."

Product Line Management

International marketers' product lines consist of local, regional, and global brands. In a given market, an exporter's product line, typically shorter than its domestic offerings, concentrates on the most profitable products. Product lines may vary dramatically from one market to another, depending on the extent of the firm's operations. Some firms at first cater only to a particular market segment, then eventually expand to cover an entire market. For example, Japanese auto manufacturers moved into the highly profitable luxury-car segment after establishing a strong position in the world small-car segment.

Carefully crafted brand portfolios allow companies to serve defined parts of specific markets. At Whirlpool, the Whirlpool brand is used as the global brand to serve the broad middle-market segment, while regional and local brands cover others. Throughout Europe the Bauknecht brand is targeted at the upper end of customers seeking a reputable German brand. Ignis and Laden are positioned as price-value brands, Ignis Europe-wide, Laden in France. This approach applies to Whirlpool's other markets as well: In Latin America, Consul is the major regional brand.[9]

The domestic market is not the only source of new-product ideas for the international marketer, nor is it the only place where they are developed. Some products may be developed elsewhere for worldwide consumption because of an advantage in skills. Colgate-Palmolive has set up centers of excellence around the world; in hair care, they are located in Paris and Bangkok. Ford Europe was assigned the task to develop the Ford Focus, which was then introduced to North America a year later.

Product Counterfeiting

About $200-$250 billion in domestic and export sales is estimated to be lost by U.S. companies annually because of product counterfeiting and trademark patent infringement of consumer and industrial products.[10] The hardest hit are software, entertainment, and pharmaceutical sectors. Counterfeit goods are any goods bearing an unauthorized representation of a trademark, patented invention, or copyrighted work that is legally protected in the country where it is marketed.

The practice of product counterfeiting has spread to high technology and services from the traditionally counterfeited products: high-visibility, strong brand name consumer goods. In addition, management has to worry about whether raw materials and components purchased for production of counterfeit products that copycat their brand names are up to par.[11]

In today's environment, firms are taking more aggressive steps to protect themselves. Victimized firms are not only losing sales but also goodwill, in the longer term, if customers, believing they are getting the real product, unknowingly end up with a copy of inferior quality. In addition to the normal measures of registering trademarks and copyrights, firms are taking steps in product development to prevent the copying of trademarked goods. New authentication materials in labeling, for example, are virtually impossible to duplicate.

PRICING STRATEGIES

Pricing is the only element in the marketing mix that is revenue-generating; all of the others are costs. It should therefore be used as an active instrument of strategy in the major areas of marketing decision-making. Pricing in the international environment is more complicated than in the domestic market, however, because of such factors as government influence, different currencies, and additional costs. International pricing situations can be divided into four general categories: export pricing, foreign market pricing, price coordination, and intra-company, or transfer, pricing.

3 LEARNING OBJECTIVE

Income Distribution: A Factor in Evaluating Market Potential

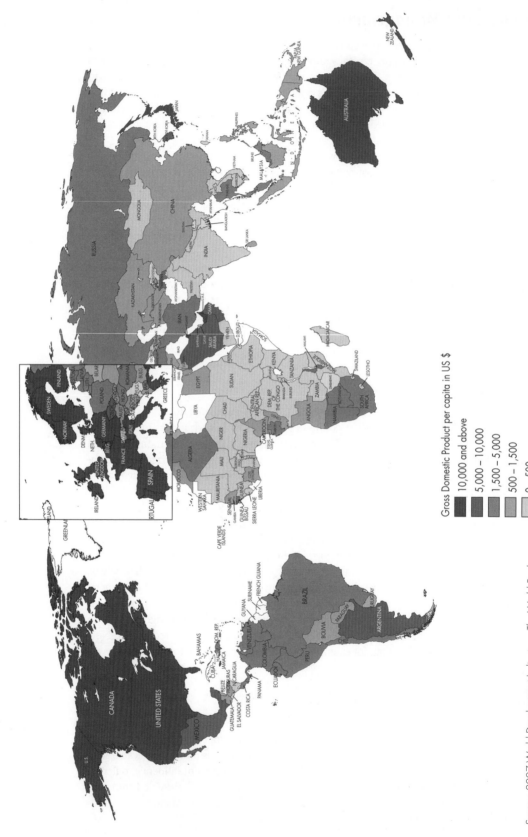

Gross Domestic Product per capita in US $

- 10,000 and above
- 5,000 – 10,000
- 1,500 – 5,000
- 500 – 1,500
- 0 – 500
- No current data available

Source: 2007 World Development Indicators, The World Bank, available at **http://www.worldbank.org/data/**

Export Pricing

Three general price-setting strategies in international marketing are: a standard worldwide price; dual pricing, which differentiates between domestic and export prices; and market-differentiated pricing. The first two are cost-oriented pricing methods that are relatively simple to establish, are easy to understand, and cover all of the necessary costs. **Standard worldwide pricing** is based on average unit costs of fixed, variable, and export-related costs. In **dual pricing**, domestic and export prices are differentiated, and two approaches are available: cost-plus and the marginal cost. The **cost-plus method** involves the actual costs, that is, a full allocation of domestic and foreign costs to the product. Although this type of pricing ensures margins, the final price may put the product beyond the reach of the customer. As a result, some exporters resort to flexible cost-plus strategy, wherein discounts are provided when necessary as a result of customer type, intensity of competition, or size of order. The **marginal cost method** considers the direct costs of producing and selling for export as the floor beneath which prices cannot be set. Fixed costs for plants, R&D, domestic overhead, and domestic marketing are disregarded. An exporter can thus lower export prices to be competitive in markets that otherwise might have been considered beyond access.

Market-differentiated pricing is the most complex of the three methods. Based on customer demand, it is, however, more consistent with the marketing concept. This method also allows consideration of competitive forces in setting export price. The major problem is the exporter's perennial dilemma: lack of information. Therefore, in most cases, marginal costs provide a basis for competitive comparisons, on which the export price is set.

Drivers of Export Prices

In preparing a quotation, the exporter must be careful to take into account unique export-related costs and, if possible, include them. They are in addition to the normal costs shared with the domestic side. They include:

1. The cost incurred in modifying the good for foreign markets.
2. Operational costs associated with export activities. Examples are personnel, market research, additional shipping and insurance costs, communications costs with foreign customers, and overseas promotional costs.
3. Costs incurred in entering foreign markets. These include tariffs and taxes, risks associated with a buyer in a different market (mainly commercial credit risks and political risks), and dealing in other than the exporter's domestic currency—that is, foreign exchange risk.

The combined effect of both clear-cut and hidden costs results in export prices far in excess of domestic prices. This is called **price escalation**. Dollar-based prices may also become expensive to local buyers in the case of currency devaluation. For example, during the Asian currency turmoil, many companies in Indonesia, Malaysia, South Korea, and Thailand scaled down their buying. The exporter has many alternatives under these circumstances, such as stretching out payment terms, cutting prices, or bringing scaled-down, more affordable products to the affected markets. Inexpensive imports often trigger accusations of dumping, a topic covered in Chapter 4, which can lead to international price wars.

Many multinationals have diversified their production bases partly to help them insulate their operations from long-term currency fluctuations. But for companies that have specialized their production by region, this may not work. Terex Corporation, one of the world's largest producers of construction equipment, makes mini-excavators in Europe and has found selling them in the United States to be a challenge due to the 30 percent slide of the dollar against the euro since 2002. Meanwhile, the company's factory in the United States that makes aerial platforms has had to double its personnel due to surging overseas demand.[12]

STANDARD WORLDWIDE PRICING

A price-setting strategy based on average unit costs of fixed, variable, and export-related costs.

DUAL PRICING

A price-setting strategy in which the export price differs from the domestic price.

COST-PLUS METHOD

A pricing policy in which there is a full allocation of foreign and domestic costs to the product.

MARGINAL COST METHOD

This method considers the direct costs of producing and selling goods for export as the floor beneath which prices cannot be set.

MARKET-DIFFERENTIATED PRICING

A price-setting strategy based on market-specific demand rather than cost.

PRICE ESCALATION

The increase in export prices due to additional marketing costs related specifically to exports.

Foreign Market Pricing

Pricing within the individual markets in which the firm operates is determined by: (1) corporate objectives, (2) costs, (3) customer behavior and market conditions, (4) market structure, and (5) environmental constraints. All of these factors vary from country to country, and pricing policies of the multinational corporation must vary as well. Despite arguments in favor of uniform pricing in multinational markets, price discrimination is an essential characteristic of the pricing policies of firms conducting business in differing markets.

Calls for price coordination have increased, especially after the introduction of the euro across 12 member nations of the European Union. The single currency made prices completely transparent for all buyers. Quick Take: Driving Down Prices across Europe illustrates the problem.

Significant price gaps from country to country led to the emergence of **gray marketing**. The term refers to brand-name imports that enter a country legally but outside regular, authorized distribution channels. The gray market is fueled by companies that sell goods in foreign markets at prices that are far lower than prices charged to, for example, U.S. distributors, and by one strong currency, such as the dollar or the yen. The gray market activity is estimated to be $20 billion per year, and includes cars, watches, cameras, and even baby powder. This phenomenon not only harms the company financially but also may harm its reputation,

GRAY MARKETING

The marketing of authentic, legally trademarked goods through unauthorized channels.

Q T Quick Take *Driving Down Prices across Europe*

The launch of a single currency taught car buyers the true meaning of pricing transparency. For years, identical cars cost 20 percent more in Germany and Austria than they did, for example, in Greece. It was not unusual for British consumers to take a train to Belgium if they needed a new car. Differences in local taxes and legally required features only partly explain the huge price disparity. The real cause lies in a dated exemption to Europe's antitrust laws, meant to protect local manufacturers from competition from low-priced imported vehicles. The exemption allows carmakers to sell exclusively through selected dealerships, each with its own sales territory. Dealerships, which are often manufacturer-owned, not only block out imports but are able to legally fix prices within their exclusive territories, usually based on what the market will bear. New regulations proposed by the EU aim to drive down prices across Europe by removing dealer exclusivity. Further, dealers will be able to sell outside their territories, opening up competition. While the auto industry is challenging the

changes, one company, at least, sees the value of offering a single price across Europe. BMW recently announced a single basic sticker price in euros for its new 7-series. The company plans to extend its pricing model across other brands.

Some argue that price differences can be maintained across Europe through product differentiation. Simpler products could be sold in less prosperous regions, whereas the more involved ones might go to markets that can afford them. At the minimum, prices will need to be coordinated to shield the company from the gray market challenge.

SOURCES: Mahmut Parlar and Kevin Weng, "Coordinating Pricing and Production Decisions in the Presence of Price Competition," *European Journal of Operational Research* 170 (number 1, 2006): pp. 211-236; EU Proposals to Overhaul Car Sales in Europe Come Under Immediate Fire in Biggest Market, Germany," *AP Worldstream*, February 5, 2002; "BMW to Charge the Same Basic Price for New 7-Series Throughout Europe," *AP Worldstream*, January 3, 2002; "Driving a Hard Bargain," *The Economist*, January 26, 2002, p. 55; "Car Prices Across Europe," *BBC News*, February 11, 2002, **http://www.bbc.co.uk**.

because authorized distributors often refuse to honor warranties on items bought through the gray market. In Asia, the mobile handset category is one of the hardest hit by gray markets. Ever since cell phone firms unlocked the International Mobile Equipment Identity (IMEI) code from their handsets to allow any models to use their services, manufacturers have suffered. Handsets smuggled into Thailand by unauthorized dealers are capturing customers who otherwise would have purchased from Nokia or Siemens. As part of its strategy to tackle gray markets, Nokia forged a deal with Blisstel, one of the nation's leading handset retailers. Under the deal, Blisstel can no longer import Nokia handsets from unauthorized sources but must buy them direct from Nokia Thailand or its dealers.[13]

Transfer Pricing

Transfer pricing, or intracompany pricing, is the pricing of sales to members of the corporate family. The overall competitive and financial position of the firm forms the basis of any pricing policy. In this, transfer pricing plays a key role. Intracorporate sales can easily change consolidated global results because they often are one of the most important ongoing decision areas in a company.

Doing business overseas requires coping with complexities of environmental peculiarities, the effect of which can be alleviated by manipulating transfer prices. Factors that call for adjustments include taxes, import duties, inflationary tendencies, unstable governments, and other regulations. For example, high transfer prices on goods shipped to a subsidiary and low transfer prices on goods imported from it will result in minimizing the tax liability of a subsidiary operating in a country with a high income tax. Tax liability thus results not only from the absolute tax rate but also from differences in how income is computed. On the other hand, a higher transfer price may have an effect on the import duty to be paid.

As a general rule, the best approach for the company is to follow the **arm's length principle** whereby it prices internally as it would price to a third, unrelated party. This principle is preferred by most governments and recommended by the OECD to streamline tax liabilities and to enhance transparency.

TRANSFER PRICE

The pricing of products as sold by a firm to its own subsidiaries and affiliates.

ARM'S LENGTH PRINCIPLE

A basis for intracompany transfer pricing; the price that an unrelated party would have paid for the same transaction.

 ## DISTRIBUTION STRATEGIES

Channels of distribution provide the essential links that connect producers and customers. The channel decision is the most long-term of marketing-mix decisions, in that it cannot be readily changed. In addition, it involves relinquishing some of the control the firm has over the marketing of its products. These two factors make choosing the right channel structure a crucial decision.

4 LEARNING OBJECTIVE

Channel Design

The term **channel design** refers to the length and width of the channel employed. Channel design is determined by factors that can be summarized as the 11 Cs, detailed below. While there are no standard answers to channel design, the international marketer can use the 11 Cs as a checklist to determine the proper approach to reach target audiences before selecting channel members to fill the roles.

1. *Customers.* The demographic and psychographic characteristics of targeted customers form the basis for channel-design decisions. Answers to questions such as what customers need as well as why, when, and how they buy are used to determine channel selection. Customer characteristics may cause one product to be distributed through two different

CHANNEL DESIGN

The length and width of the distribution channel.

types of channels. All sales of Caterpillar's earthmoving equipment are handled by independent dealers, except for sales to many governments, which are direct.

2. *Culture.* The marketer must analyze existing channel structures or the distribution culture of a market. For example, the general complexity of the Japanese distribution system is a major reason foreign companies fail to penetrate the market. Foreign legislation affecting distributors and agents is an essential part of distribution culture. For example, legislation may require foreign companies to be represented only by firms that are 100 percent locally owned or may ban some forms of distribution (such as direct distribution) altogether.

3. *Competitors.* Often, channels utilized by the competition may make up the only distribution system that is accepted both by the trade and by consumers. In this case, the international marketer's task is to use the existing structure more effectively and efficiently, as Wal-Mart has been able to do in Europe. An alternate strategy is to use a totally different distribution approach to create competitive advantage, as Ikea has been able to do with its use of supermarketing concepts in furniture retail.

4. *Company objectives.* Sometimes, management goals may conflict with the best possible channel design. Fast-food chains, for instance, typically rush into newly opened markets, as in Asia and Latin America. The company objective is to establish mass sales as soon as possible by opening numerous restaurants in the busiest sections of several cities. Unfortunately, channel control has proven to be quite difficult because of the sheer number of openings over a relatively short period of time.

5. *Character.* The type or character of the good influences channel design. Generally, the more specialized, expensive, bulky, or perishable the product and the more it may require after-sale service, the more likely the channel is to be relatively short. Staple items, such as soap, tend to have longer channels, while services have short channels.

6. *Capital.* Often, capital—or the firm's financial strength—determines the type of channel and the basis on which channel relationships will be built. The stronger the firm's finances, the more able it is to establish channels it either owns or controls. Intermediaries' requirements for beginning inventories, selling on a consignment basis, preferential loans, and need for training will all have an impact on the type of approach chosen.

7. *Cost.* Closely related to capital is cost—that is, the expenditure incurred in maintaining a channel once it is established. Costs will naturally vary over the life cycle of the relationship, as well as over the life cycle of the product marketed.

8. *Coverage.* The term *coverage* describes both the number of areas in which the marketer's products are represented and the quality of that representation. Coverage, therefore, is two-dimensional in that both horizontal and vertical coverage need to be considered in channel design.

9. *Control.* The use of intermediaries will automatically lead to loss of some control over the marketing of the firm's products. The looser the relationship is between the marketer and the intermediaries, the less control can be exerted. The longer the channel, the more difficult it becomes for the marketer to have a final say over pricing, promotion, and the types of outlets in which the product will be made available.

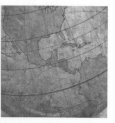

Culture Clues   Many market observers believed that small retail players in Latin America would be swept away by the sector's consolidation and the rapid entry of new hypermarkets and supermarkets. That had been the case in the U.S. and Europe, where small retailers have retained only 10 to 20 percent of the consumer packaged-goods market as large retailers have grown. So far, this has not occurred in Latin America. Small-scale independent supermarkets and traditional stores together still account for between 45 and 61 percent of consumer-goods retailing in Latin American countries.

10. *Continuity*. Nurturing continuity rests heavily on the marketer because foreign distributors may have a more short-term view of the relationship. For example, Japanese wholesalers believe that it is important for manufacturers to follow up initial success with continuous improvement of the product. If such improvements are not forthcoming, competitors are likely to enter the market with similar, but lower-priced products, and the wholesalers of the imported product will turn to Japanese suppliers.

11. *Communication*. Proper communication helps convey the marketer's goals to the distributors, it solves conflict situations, and it aids in the overall marketing of the product. Communication is a two-way process that does not permit the marketer to dictate to intermediaries. In addition, distributors can be important marketing-communications partners through cooperative promotional programs.

SELECTION AND SCREENING OF INTERMEDIARIES Once the basic design of the channel has been determined, the international marketer must begin a search to fill the defined roles with the best available candidates. Choices will have to be made within the framework of the company's overall philosophy on distributors versus agents, as well as whether the company will use an indirect or direct approach to foreign markets.

As noted in Chapter 10, various sources exist to assist the marketer in locating intermediary candidates. One of the easiest and most economical ways is to use the service of governmental agencies. The U.S. Department of Commerce has various services that can assist firms in identifying suitable representatives abroad; some have been designed specifically for that purpose. A number of private sources are also available to the international marketer. Trade directories, such as those by Dun & Bradstreet, usually list foreign representatives geographically and by product classification. Telephone directories, especially the yellow-page sections or editions, can provide distributor lists. Although not detailed, the listings will give addresses and an indication of the products sold. The firm can solicit the support of some of its facilitating agencies, such as banks, advertising agencies, shipping lines, and airlines. The marketer can take an even more direct approach by buying advertising space to solicit representation. The advertisements typically indicate the type of support the marketer will be able to give to its distributor.

Intermediaries can be screened on their performance and professionalism. An intermediary's performance can be evaluated on the basis of financial standing and sales, as well as the likely fit it would provide in terms of its existing product lines and coverage. Professionalism can be assessed through reputation and overall standing in the business community.

MANAGING THE CHANNEL RELATIONSHIP A channel relationship can be likened to a marriage in that it brings together two independent entities that have shared goals. For the relationship to work, each party has to be open about its expectations and openly communicate changes perceived in the other's behavior that might be contrary to the agreement. A framework for managing channel relationships is provided in Table 11.2.

The complicating factors that separate the two parties fall into three categories: ownership, geographic and cultural distance, and different rules of law. Rather than lament their existence, both parties must take strong action to remedy them. Often, the first major step is for both parties to acknowledge that differences exist.

It is clear that distributors play their most important role in the initial stages of a company's presence in a new market. Over time, the company itself will absorb the needed market-specific assets and establish its own integrated distribution system. One study found that the few distributors who managed to continue as representatives for multinationals over the long term were located in markets not considered strategic or possessed assets that the multinational could not replicate.[14] An example of the latter category is the Saudi Arabian market, where distributors with connections to the royal family are critically important.

TABLE 11.2 Managing Relations with Overseas Distributors

HIGH EXPORT PERFORMANCE INHIBITORS ⟶	BRING ⟶	REMEDY LIES IN
Separate ownership	• Divided loyalties • Seller-buyer atmosphere • Unclear future intentions	Offering good incentives, helpful support schemes, discussing plans frankly, and interacting in a mutually beneficial way
Geographic and cultural separation	• Communication blocks • Negative attitudes toward foreigners • Physical distribution strains	Making judicious use of two-way visits, establishing a well-managed communication program
Different rules of law	• Vertical trading restrictions • Dismissal difficulties	Complying fully with the law, drafting a strong distributor agreement

SOURCE: Philip J. Rosson, "Source Factors in Manufacture—Overseas Distributor Relationships in International Marketing," in *International Marketing Management*, ed. Erdener Kaynak (New York: Praeger, 1984), p. 95.

E-COMMERCE AS A DISTRIBUTION CHANNEL Increasingly, various marketing constituents are seeing the web as more than a communication tool and also as a builder of interactive relationships and as a device to sell products and services.[15] As shown in Table 11.3, e-commerce, the ability to offer goods and services over the Web—both business to consumer (B2C) and business to business (B2B)— is expected to reach significant compound annual growth rates in the next few years around the world. While the United States is the largest player in e-commerce, the non-U.S. portion is expected to grow substantially with the expansion of e-commerce markets in Asia in particular. Total e-commerce spending is expected to rise from $6.3 trillion in 2007 to $13.6 trillion in 2012. The biggest engine of growth for B2B e-commerce is expected to be global transactions. Other forms of e-business will expand as well. The value of European online marketing, including e-mail, search, and display advertising, is expected to double from around €7.5 billion in 2006 to more than €16 billion in 2012, 18 percent of total media budgets.[16]

Firms entering the e-commerce arena do not have to do so on their own. Hub sites (also known as virtual malls or digital intermediaries) bring together buyers, sellers, distributors, and transaction-payment processors in one single marketplace, making convenience the key attraction. Entities such as Priceline.com (**http://www.priceline.com**), eBay (**http://www. ebay.com**), Shoplet (**http://www.shoplet.com**), Quadrem (**http://www.quadrem.com**), and ECnet (**http://www.ecnet.com**) are leading the way.

As soon as a company offers Internet access, it must be prepared to provide 24-hour order-taking and customer service, have the regulatory and customs-handling expertise to deliver internationally, and have an in-depth understanding of marketing environments for the further development of the business relationship. The instantaneous interactivity users experience leads them to expect expedient delivery of answers and products ordered. In fact, a survey pointed to customer service response times as a significant factor in future decisions to purchase from a particular site.[17] Many people living outside of the United States who buy online expect U.S.-type customer service. However, in many cases they may find that the company's e-readiness does not extend to international markets.

The challenges faced in terms of response and delivery capabilities can be overcome through outsourcing services or by building international distribution networks. Air express carriers such as DHL, FedEx, and UPS offer full-service packages that leverage their own Internet infrastructure with customs clearance and e-mail shipment notification. If a company needs help in order fulfillment and customer support, logistics centers offer warehousing and

Services as a Portion of Gross Domestic Product

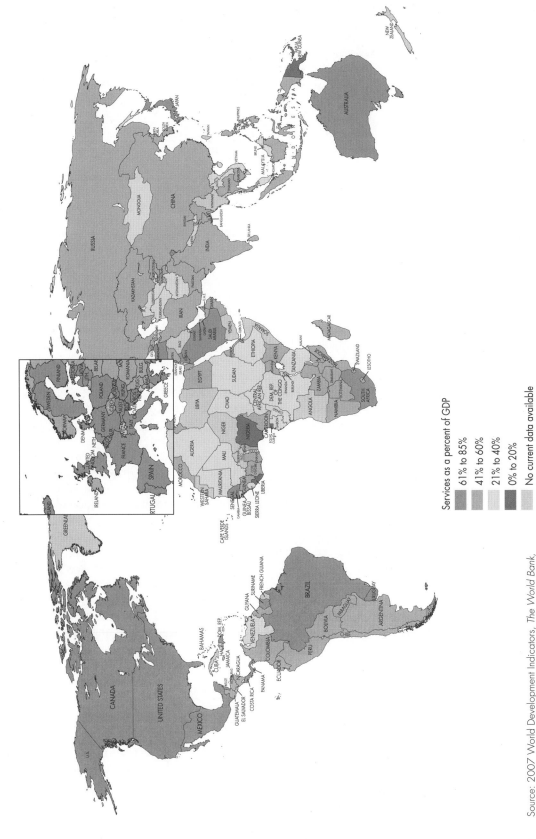

Source: 2007 World Development Indicators, *The World Bank*,
available at **http://www.worldbank.org/data/**

Services as a percent of GDP

61% to 85%

41% to 60%

21% to 40%

0% to 20%

No current data available

TABLE 11.3 Worldwide E-Commerce Revenue by Region (in $billions)

REGION	2007	2012	CAGR (IN %)
Worldwide	6,311	13,649	18.0
United States	2,400	4,689	15.9
Western Europe	2,186	3,788	13.2
Japan	501	1,500	24.4
Asia-Pacific	839	2,289	23.8
Rest of the World	383	1,390	29.8
Share of B2B (in %)	89.9	90.8	

SOURCE: IDC's Internet Consumer Market Model, version 11.2; **http://www.idc.com**.

inventory management services as well as same-day delivery from in-country stocks. DHL, for example, has eight express logistics centers and 287 strategic parts centers worldwide, with key centers in Bahrain for the Middle East, Brussels for Europe, and Singapore for Asia-Pacific. Some companies elect to build their own international distribution networks. Both QVC, a televised shopping service, and Amazon.com, an online retailer of books and consumer goods, have distribution centers in Great Britain and Germany to take advantage of the European Internet audience and to fulfill more quickly and cheaply the orders generated by their web sites.

Transactions and the information they provide about the buyer allow for greater customization and for service by region, by market, or even by individual customer. One of the largest online sellers, Dell Computer, has created Premier Pages for its corporate customers. Premier Pages is linked to the customer's intranet, allowing approved employees to configure PCs, pay for them, and track their delivery status. It also provides access to instant technical support and Dell sales representatives. Presently, there are 5,000 companies with this service, and $5 million of Dell PCs are ordered every day.[18]

Another difficulty related to using the Internet as a worldwide channel is the risk of government intervention. AOL's joint venture to open up the Chinese market, for instance, raised awkward issues. The company was asked what it would do if the Chinese government demanded names, e-mails, or other records relating to political dissidents.[19] The Japanese government has considered requiring sellers of used goods to obtain licenses, which could prevent companies like eBay or Yahoo! from offering online auction sites in the Japanese market.[20] Government regulations also affect the product itself. Virtual Vineyards has to worry about country-specific alcohol regulations, while software makers such as Softwareland.com have to comply with U.S. software export regulations. Taxes are another controversial issue. No real consensus exists on the taxes due for products sold online, especially in the case of cross-border transactions. While the United States and the EU do not want to impose new taxes on sales through the Internet, there is no uniformity in the international taxation of transactions.[21]

PROMOTIONAL STRATEGIES

The international marketer must choose a proper combination of the various promotional tools—advertising, personal selling, sales promotion, and publicity—to create images among the intended target audience. The choice will depend on the target audience, company objectives, the product or service marketed, the resources available for the endeavor, and the availability of promotional tools in a particular market. Increasingly, the focus is not a product or service but the company's image.

Quick Take *Buying Cars on the Web*

While U.S. drivers must go through dealers to buy a new car, in Taiwan, all it takes is a PC and a mouse. General Motors already sells one in ten vehicles through the Internet and aims to increase its penetration level to a third of all sales in coming years.

The lack of an established dealership system makes emerging markets, especially in Asia and Latin America, ideal for selling on the web. The Internet makes it possible to offer a customized, built-to-order program for every customer, as well as to keep costs down. Ford is experimenting with its Internet ideas in markets such as the Philippines, where it has set up an e-commerce system that links consumers, dealers, the manufacturer, and suppliers to create a seamless e-business ordering system.

In addition to being able to buy cars online, Taiwanese customers can make service appointments through the GM web site. The company will come to the owner's house or office, pick up the car, and return it within hours or overnight after completing the service. Although the United States has the greatest potential for online buying due to the large e-ready customer base, channel culture in terms of entrenched dealers determined to maintain their position prevents GM from realizing it. As a result, GM and Ford are focusing more on the supplier side of their e-operations.

SOURCES: "Car Makers Rev Up to New E-Commerce Initiatives," *Network World*, September 2, 2002, pp. 1, 16; "Follow-Through," *Forbes*, December 24, 2001, p. 48; "GM Tests E-Commerce Plans in Emerging Markets," *The Wall Street Journal*, October 25, 1999, p. B6.

Advertising

The key decision-making areas in advertising are: (1) media strategy, (2) creative strategy, and (3) organization of the promotional program.

MEDIA STRATEGY **Media strategy** is applied to the selection of media vehicles and the development of a media schedule. Media spending varies dramatically around the around the world as seen in Table 11.4. The United States continues to dominate with over $170 billion in expenditure, but China is expected to become the fourth-largest and Russia the sixth-largest advertising markets by 2010. The mature U.S. market anticipates slower growth in the future,

MEDIA STRATEGY

Strategy applied to the selection of media vehicles and the development of a media schedule.

TABLE 11.4 Global Advertising Expenditure By Region

	2006	2010
North America	182.6	207.5
Western Europe	102.4	123.9
Asia-Pacific	88.9	116.6
Central/Eastern Europe	23.8	43.2
Latin America	20.6	26.8
Africa/Middle East	13.7	24.9
World	432.1	542.8

SOURCE: ZenithOptimedia, "Global Ad Spending to Accelerate in 2008 Despite Credit Squeeze," December 3, 2007, available at **www.zenithoptimedia.com**.

but the Asian markets in particular are expected to witness robust growth with the run-up to the Beijing Olympics in 2008. The top five corporate advertisers in 2007 were Procter & Gamble ($8.52 billion), Unilever ($4.54), General Motors ($3.30), L'Oreal ($3.12), and Toyota ($3.10).[22]

In terms of media, television is the most-used medium at $160 billion in 2006, followed by newspapers ($123), magazines ($53) and the Internet ($27). The Internet will nearly double its share of global advertising spending between 2006 and 2010 at the expense of other media. Internet spending is expected to grow to $61 billion by 2010, overtaking radio in 2008 and magazines in 2010 with 11.5 percent of the total pie. In some markets, such as Northern Europe, Internet spending is going to be more than 20 percent of all advertising spending.[23]

GLOBAL MEDIA

Media vehicles that have target audiences on at least three continents and have a central buying office for placements.

Global media vehicles have been developed that have target audiences on at least three continents and for which the media buying takes place through a centralized office. These media have traditionally been publications that, in addition to the worldwide edition, have provided advertisers the option of using regional editions. For example, *Time* provides 133 editions, enabling advertising to reach a particular country, a continent, or the world. Other global publications include *The International Herald Tribune*, *The Wall Street Journal*, and *National Geographic*. The Internet provides the international marketer with an additional global medium. Web exposure is often achieved through cooperation with Internet service providers.

In broadcast media, panregional radio stations have been joined in Europe by television as a result of satellite technology. More than half of the households in Europe have access to additional television broadcasts, either through cable or direct satellite, and television is no longer restricted by national boundaries. As a result, marketers need to make sure that advertising works not only within markets but across countries as well. The launch of StarTV, featured in the ad in Figure 11.2, has increased the use of regional advertising in Asia.

Media regulations vary. Some regulations include limits on the amount of time available for advertisements; in Italy, for example, the state channels allow a maximum of 12 percent of advertising per hour and 4 percent over a week, and commercial stations allow 18 percent per hour and 15 percent per week. Furthermore, the leading Italian stations do not guarantee audience delivery when spots are bought. Strict separation between programs and commercials is almost a universal requirement, preventing U.S.-style sponsored programs. Restrictions on items, such as comparative claims and gender stereotypes are prevalent; for example, Germany prohibits the use of superlatives such as "best."

CREATIVE STRATEGY

Development of the content of a promotional message such as an advertisement, publicity release, sales promotion activity, or Web-based promotion.

CREATIVE STRATEGY Developing the promotional message is referred to as **creative strategy**. The marketer must determine what the consumer is really buying—that is, the consumer's motivations. They will vary, depending on:

1. The diffusion of the product, service, or concept into the market. For example, to penetrate Third World markets with online advertising is difficult when few potential customers have access to computers.
2. The criteria on which the consumer will evaluate the product. For example, in traditional societies, the time-saving qualities of a product may not be the best ones to feature, as Campbell Soup learned in Italy, Brazil, and Poland, where preparers felt inadequate if they did not make soups from scratch.

Culture Clues   Product placement in TV shows, movies, games, or web sites has grown to a $4.4 billion business according to PQ Media. The basic drivers of this phenomenon are the success of reality shows and the more-empowered consumer who can skip traditional ads with the touch of a button. In addition, governments (e.g., the European Union) have relaxed their restrictions on product placement. In some markets, product placement may be an effective method of attracting attention due to constraints on traditional media.

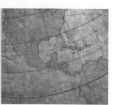

FIGURE 11.2   Broadcast Media in Asia

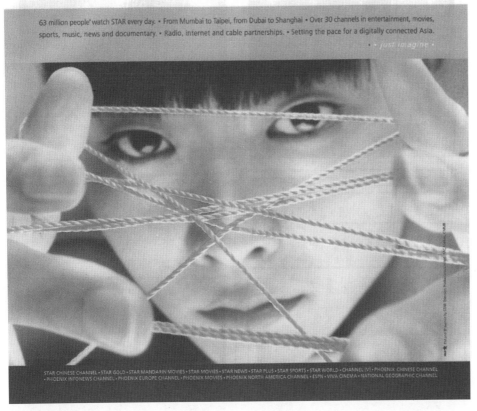

Across Asia, we capture
the imagination of millions

63 million people' watch STAR every day. • From Mumbai to Taipei, from Dubai to Shanghai • Over 30 channels in entertainment, movies, sports, music, news and documentary. • Radio, internet and cable partnerships. • Setting the pace for a digitally connected Asia.

• • *just imagine* •

STAR CHINESE CHANNEL • STAR GOLD • STAR MANDARIN MOVIES • STAR MOVIES • STAR NEWS • STAR PLUS • STAR SPORTS • STAR WORLD • CHANNEL [V] • PHOENIX CHINESE CHANNEL • PHOENIX INFONEWS CHANNEL • PHOENIX EUROPE CHANNEL • PHOENIX MOVIES • PHOENIX NORTH AMERICA CHANNEL • ESPN • VIVA CINEMA • NATIONAL GEOGRAPHIC CHANNEL

SOURCE: StarTV

3. The product's positioning. For example, Parker Pen's upscale image around the world may not be profitable enough in a market that is more or less a commodity business. The solution is to create an image for a commodity product and make the public pay for it—for example, the U.S. positioning of Perrier is as a premium mineral water.

The ideal situation in developing message strategy is to have a world brand—a product that is manufactured, packaged, and positioned the same around the world. However, a number of factors will force companies to abandon identical campaigns in favor of recognizable campaigns. The factors are culture, of which language is the main manifestation, economic development, and lifestyles. Consider, for example, the campaign for Marriott International presented in Figure 11.3. While the ads share common graphic elements, two distinct approaches are evident. The top set of advertisements from the United States and Saudi Arabia are an example of a relatively standard approach, given the similarity in target audiences (i.e., the business traveler) and in the competitive conditions in the markets. The second set features ads for Latin America and German-speaking Europe. While the Latin advertisement stresses comfort, the German version focuses on results. While most of

FIGURE 11.3   Global Advertising Campaign Approaches

Courtesy Marriott International, **http://www.marriott.com**.

CORPORATE IMAGE
ADVERTISING

Umbrella marketing
communications to make
the company as a whole
be correctly understood
and seen more positively.

Marriott's ads translate the theme ("When you're comfortable you can do anything") to suit the local culture, the German version uses English-language wording.

An increasing number of companies are engaging in **corporate image advertising** in support of their more traditional tactical product-specific and local advertising efforts. Especially for multi-divisional companies, an umbrella campaign may help either in boosting the lesser-known product lines or in making the company itself better understood or perceived more positively. Companies may announce repositioning strategies through image campaigns to both external and internal constituents. GE's campaign, branded Ecomagination, is a company-wide initiative to push environmentally friendly products. The plan is to double company revenues from eco-safe products to $20 billion by 2010. To go beyond the campaign, each of GE's 11 business units are to come up with at least five big ideas capable of generating $100 million of revenue within the next three to five years.[24]

Many multinational corporations are staffed and equipped to perform the full range of promotional activities. In most cases, however, they rely on the outside expertise of advertising agencies and other promotions-related companies, such as media-buying companies and specialty marketing firms. In a study of 40 multinational marketers, 32.5 percent are using a single agency worldwide, 20 percent are using two, 5 percent are using three, 10 percent are using four, and 32.5 percent are using more than four agencies. Of the marketers using only one or two agencies, McCann-Erickson was the most popular with 17 percent of the companies.[25] Local agencies will survive, however, because of governmental regulations. In Peru, for example, a law mandates that any commercial aired on Peruvian television must be 100 percent nationally produced. Local agencies tend to forge ties with foreign ad agencies for better coverage and customer service, and thus become part of the general globalization effort. Marketers are choosing specialized interactive shops over full-service agencies for Internet advertising. However, a major weakness with the interactive agencies is their lack of international experience.

Personal Selling

Although advertising is often equated with the promotional effort, in many cases promotional efforts consist of **personal selling**. In the early stages of internationalization, exporters rely heavily on personal contact. The marketing of industrial goods, especially of high-priced items, requires strong personal selling efforts. In some cases, personal selling may be truly international; for example, Boeing or Northrop Grumman salespeople engage in sales efforts around the world. However, in most cases, personal selling takes place at the local level. The best interests of any company in the industrial area lie in establishing a solid base of dealerships staffed by local people. Personal selling efforts can be developed in the same fashion as advertising. For the multinational company, the primary goal again is the enhancement and standardization of personal selling efforts, especially if the product offering is standardized.

PERSONAL SELLING

Marketing efforts focusing on one-on-one efforts with customers.

Sales Promotion

Sales promotion has been used as the catchall term for promotion that is not advertising, personal selling, or publicity. Sales promotion directed at consumers involves such activities as couponing, sampling, premiums, consumer education and demonstration activities, cents-off packages, point-of-purchase materials, and direct mail.

The success in Latin America of Tang, General Foods' pre-sweetened powdered juice substitute, is for the most part traceable to successful sales promotion efforts.

One promotion involved trading Tang pouches for free popsicles from Kibon (General Foods' Brazilian subsidiary). Kibon also placed coupons for free groceries in Tang pouches. In Puerto Rico, General Foods ran Tang sweepstakes. In Argentina, in-store sampling featured Tang poured from Tang pitchers by girls in orange Tang dresses. Decorative Tang pitchers were a hit throughout Latin America.

For sales promotion to work, the campaigns planned by manufacturers or their agencies have to gain the support of the local retailer population. As an example, retailers must redeem coupons presented by consumers and forward them to the manufacturer or to the company

WORLD VIEW

SOCIAL PROGRAMS AND SUSTAINABILITY

The goal of One Laptop Per Child is to place laptops costing only $100 each in the hands of 150 million school children in developing countries. The premise is that computers would spur children to learn and explore outside of a classroom and to share discoveries with their families. At the national level, these laptops would improve both public education and the economy in the long term.

To achieve the $100 price, the laptop will be a stripped-down product, usable for basic word-processing, Internet access, and e-mail. It will have no hard drive, but instead will use flash memory similar to that used in digital cameras. The processor is planned to run at 500MHz. Though spartan, the design is ingenious: Each laptop will include a Wi-Fi radio transmitter designed to knit machines into a wireless hub so they can share a connection and pass it on from one computer to another. In addition to the standard power cord, the computer will also be equipped with an electricity-generating crank. The swiveling eight-inch screen is the biggest challenge in terms of cost. To keep the price down, the screen will run in two modes, with a high-resolution monochrome mode for word-processing and a lower-resolution color mode for Internet use. The first versions will be powered by an AMD microprocessor and use an open-source Linux-based operating system provided by Red Hat. All of the systems have to be quite robust given the high heat, dust, and moisture conditions in targeted markets.

The laptop will be sold at $100 to governments in countries such as Brazil, Egypt, Nigeria, and Thailand and to the general public

for $200. Even at $100 apiece, it is not certain that developing countries can afford the $15 billion to supply 150 million laptops.

At the corporate level, responses vary. AMD, on the one hand, is "absolutely committed" to the project, and it fits with its initiative to bring the Internet and computing access to half the world by 2015. It expects the project to be a business for AMD, not just philanthropy. On the other hand, Intel argues that the product's limited programs will not satisfy users. Dell has proposed that it is not feasible to manufacture a $100 computer to meet the company's high standards. The company's argument is that any computer should prepare students for the applications they will be using after they get out of school. Microsoft is supportive of the program but would like the computer to use Microsoft's software rather than the open-source alternatives currently proposed. Analysts have suggested that if the final choice is not Microsoft software, the company will launch its own laptop for the developing markets.

SOURCES: "Intel to Chip in with Low-Cost Rural PC," *Knight Ridder News Service*, January 11, 2006, p. 1; "Intel Claims $100 Laptop Will Not Appeal," *Telecomworldwire*, December 12, 2005, p. 1; "I'd Like to Teach the World to Type," *Fortune*, November 28, 2005, pp. 63-64; "The $100 Laptop Moves Closer to Reality," *The Washington Post*, November 14, 2005, pp. B1, B2. See also **www.redhat.com/magazine/014dec05/features/olpc/**.

---

handling the promotion. A. C. Nielsen tried to introduce cents-off coupons in Chile and ran into trouble with the nation's supermarket union, which notified its members that it opposed the project and recommended that coupons not be accepted. The main complaint was that an intermediary, such as Nielsen, would unnecessarily raise costs and thus the prices to be charged to consumers. Also, some critics felt that coupons would limit individual negotiations, because Chileans often bargain for their purchases.

Sales promotion directed at intermediaries, also known as trade promotion, includes activities such as trade shows and exhibits, trade discounts, and cooperative advertising. For example, attendance at an appropriate trade show is one of the best ways to make contacts with government officials and decision-makers, work with present intermediaries, or attract new ones.

Public Relations

Public relations is the marketing communications function charged with executing programs to earn public understanding and acceptance, which means both internal and external communication. Internal communication is important, especially in multinational companies, to create an appropriate corporate culture. External campaigns can be achieved through the use

---

Fast Facts

What is the world's largest trade show?

CeBIT is the world's largest trade fair, showcasing digital IT and telecommunications solutions for home and work environments. CeBIT offers an international platform for comparing notes on current industry trends, networking, and product presentations. Deutsche Messe AG has organized CeBIT in Hanover each spring since 1986.

of corporate symbols, corporate advertising, customer relations programs, the generation of publicity, as well as getting a company's view to the public via the Internet. Some material on the firm is produced for special audiences to assist in personal selling.

A significant part of public relations activity focuses on portraying multinational corporations as good citizens of their host markets. IBM's policy of good corporate citizenship means accepting responsibility as a participant in community and national affairs and striving to be among the most admired companies in host countries. In Thailand, for example, IBM provides equipment and personnel to universities and donates money to the nation's wildlife fund and environmental protection agency. The World View on the previous page highlights one of the leading social programs of the 21st century.

Public relations activity includes anticipating and countering criticism. The criticisms range from general ones against all multinational corporations to specific complaints. These complaints may be based on a market, for example, or a company's presence in a country with objectionable labor standards. CalPERS, the giant California pension fund, for example, recently announced its intention to pull out of investments in four emerging markets: Indonesia, Malaysia, the Philippines, and Thailand.[26] Complaints may concern a product or the way in which it is promoted.

Consider, for example, Nestlé's promotion of infant formula in developing countries where infant mortality is unacceptably high. The complaint may also center on the company's conduct in a given situation for example, Andersen's shredding of accounting records from the scandal-plagued Enron.

SUMMARY

The task of the international marketer is to seek new opportunities in the world marketplace and satisfy emerging needs through creative management of the firm's products, pricing, distribution, and promotional policies. By its very nature, marketing is the most sensitive of business functions to environmental effects and influences.

A critical decision in international marketing concerns the degree to which the overall marketing program should be standardized or localized. The ideal is to standardize as much as possible without compromising the basic task of marketing: satisfying the needs and wants of the target market.

Products may need to be adapted in order to suit a variety of regional environment characteristics. This includes both changes to the product itself and to its packaging.

Several issues affect the pricing of products for export markets, including the cost of the export operation, market conditions, and environmental constraints. Companies with multinational subsidiaries must also determine transfer prices for goods moved between sister companies.

4   Each foreign market offers its own mix of distribution channels, including e-commerce channels, which must be evaluated in terms of the company's objectives and competitive strategy.

5   The international marketer must choose a proper combination of the various promotional tools—advertising, personal selling, sales promotion, and publicity—to create the desired brand image within its target markets.

KEY TERMS AND CONCEPTS

standardization approach	marginal cost method	media strategy
multidomestic approach	market-differentiated pricing	global media
globalization approach	price escalation	creative strategy
positioning	gray marketing	corporate image advertising
standard worldwide pricing	transfer price	personal selling
dual pricing	arm's length principle	
cost-plus method	channel design	

REVIEW QUESTIONS

1. Is globalization ever a serious possibility, or is the regional approach the closest the international marketer can ever hope to get to standardization?
2. Name some of the factors to consider when adapting a product for global launch.
3. What steps can companies take to protect their products from counterfeiting?
4. Explain ways in which export pricing differs from domestic pricing.

5. What is transfer pricing?
6. How effective is e-commerce as a global distribution channel? For what types of goods or services is it best suited?
7. Is it realistic to expect that personal selling can be achieved consistently on a global scale?
8. Can a single global advertising campaign ever suit all nations in which a product is sold? Explain why or why not.

CRITICAL SKILL BUILDERS

1. A mid-size technology company in your area has created a great new product that allows for seamless, instantaneous, and secure data transfer via mobile handsets. Should the company attempt a global product launch or enter new markets country by country? Explain the reasons for your recommendation.
2. How can a company determine whether adaptation of a product to suit multiple markets is worth the investment?
3. Do you think it's fair that marketers selling on the Internet are able to avoid sales taxes? Why or why not?

4. As international manager at a global firm, you are asked to find and hire effective intermediaries to carry your range of specialized products into Asia. You quickly find that all the best intermediaries are already under contract to competitors. What are your options?
5. In small groups, research the topic of gray markets and find examples in several industry sectors. Then debate the arguments for and against gray marketing.

ON THE WEB

1. The software industry is the hardest hit by piracy. Using the web site of the Business Software Alliance (**http://www.bsa.org**), assess how this problem is being tackled.

2. The FIFA World Cup is, in effect, a marketing platform from which a company can create awareness, enhance its image, and foster goodwill. FIFA offers sponsors a multitude of ways to promote themselves and their products in conjunction with the FIFA World Cup as well as other FIFA events. Using FIFA's web site (**www.fifa.com**), assess the different ways a sponsor can benefit from this association.

ENDNOTES

1. "As Its Brands Lag at Home, Unilever Makes a Risky Bet," *The Wall Street Journal*, March 22, 2007, pp. A1, A12; Tarun Khanna, Krishna Palepu, and Jayant Sinha, "Strategies that Fit Emerging Markets," *Harvard Business Review* 83 (June 2005): pp. 63-76; and "Tech's Future," *BusinessWeek*, September 27, 2004, pp. 82-89.

2. "Taking a Bite Out of China, *Nation's Restaurant News*, October 15, 2007, pp. S20-22.

3. ISO Survey, 2006, available at **http://www.iso.ch**.

4. Normandy Madden, "Seagram Targets China's Drinkers," *Ad Age Global*, June 2001, p. 10.

5. "Marketers Pursue the Shallow-Pocketed," *The Wall Street Journal*, January 26, 2007, p. B3.

6. "Uganda Increases Tax on Polythene Bags to Protect Environment," Xinhau News Agency, August 31, 2002.

7. Johny K. Johansson and Ilkka A. Ronkainen, "The Esteem of Global Brands," *Journal of Brand Management* 12 (number 5, 2005): pp. 339-354; Johny K. Johansson and Ilkka A. Ronkainen, "Are Global Brands the Right Choice for Your Company?" *Marketing Management*, March/April, 2004, pp. 53-56.

8. Kathryn Tolbert, "Rice Farmers Want American-Made Box Lunches Taken Off the National Menu," *The Washington Post*, August 6, 2001, p. A10.

9. Ilkka A. Ronkainen and Ivan Menezes, "Implementing Global Marketing Strategy: An Interview with Whirlpool Corporation," *International Marketing Review* 13 (number 3, 1996): pp. 56-63.

10. International Anti-Counterfeiting Coalition, **http://www.iacc.org**.

11. For worldwide piracy information, see **http://www.iipa.com**.

12. "Dollar Lifts Exporters, Blunting Housing Bust," *The Wall Street Journal*, October 1, 2007, pp. A1, A19.

13. Sirivish Toomgum, "Nokia Signs Up Partners to Curb 'Gray' Sales," *Nation* (Thailand), August 16, 2002.

14. David Arnold, "Seven Rules of International Distribution," *The Mirage of Global Markets* (Upper Saddle River, NJ; Prentice-Hall, 2003), pp. 149-150.

15. **http://www.idc.com**.

16. "European Online Marketing Tops €16 Billion In 2012," *Forrester Research*, July 12, 2007, available at **http://www.forrester.com**.

17. "Yes, I Would Like Some Help, Thank You," *Marketing News*, February 18, 2002, p. 3.

18. Eryn Brown, "Nine Ways to Win on the Web," *Fortune*, May 24, 1999, pp. 112–125; see also **http://premier.dell.com**.

19. Steven Mufson and John Pomfret, "You've Got Dissidents?" *The Washington Post*, August 29, 2001, pp. A1, A13.

20. John Markoff, "Auction Sites in Japan Fear Move to Limit Online Sales," *The New York Times*, February 6, 2002, p. C5.

21. Christia Victor and Wen-Jang Jih, "Fair or Not? The Taxation of E-Commerce," *Information Systems Management* 23 (number 1, 2006): pp. 68-73.

22. *AdAge's 21st Annual Global Marketers*, November 19, 2007, p. 4.

23. ZenithOptimedia, "Global Ad Spending to Accelerate in 2008 Despite Credit Squeeze," December 3, 2007, available at **www.zenithoptimedia.com**.

24. Jonah Bloom, "GE: The Marketing Giant Lights Up with Imagination," *Creativity*, October 2005, p. 63; and Matthew Creamer, "GE Sets Aside Big Bucks to Show Off Some Green," *Advertising Age*, May 9, 2005, p. 7.

25. "U.S. Multinationals," *Advertising Age International*, June 1999, p. 39.

26. "Calpers' Asian Retreat Is a Victory for Ethics," *Financial Times*, February 22, 2002, **http://www.ft.com**.

GLOBAL SUPPLY CHAIN

Tracking the International Shipment

Radio Frequency Identification (RFID) technology permits new levels of cost savings, efficiency, and business intelligence. The technology attaches small electronic tags to products. Transmitters or readers of the tags at several locations then are able to track the products. These tags can signal market demand and allow for real-time production and delivery.

Companies like Ikea, FedEx, Fujitsu, and Wal-Mart have been RFID technology's main proponents. By some estimates, Wal-Mart could save $8.35 billion each year using

RFID! This large figure contains the savings from reduced stock-outs, theft, and inventory, as well as lower labor costs.

RFID technology can alter the supply-chain-management process in any organization that produces, moves, or sells physical goods. Hospitals, for instance, would be able to place tags on all patients, thus knowing their exact location and all their medical information.

The technology is already used by Nestlé Corporation. Nestlé manufactures its candy bars through a complex process that involves storing the confectionaries on trays throughout the production period. For quality control purposes it is crucial that these trays undergo constant cleaning. Serious quality problems could arise if a few trays miss their scheduled cleaning sessions. Escort Memory Systems offered Nestlé a solution involving adhesive tags. The tags are attached to Nestlé's trays until the end of the production cycle. At the beginning of the process, as the trays are first filled, information about weight and time is recorded on the tags. When the trays pass through Nestlé's scales, the actual weight is compared with the desired weight to reduce overfills. As this information is instantly linked to Nestlé's system by RFID readers, it is possible to track the locations of trays at all times. Len Woods, Senior Control System Supervisor, commented, "If problems arise we are notified, enabling us to take remedial action well before any quality control issues arise."

SOURCES: "Escort Memory Systems Provides Material Handling Solution at Nestlé," courtesy of Escort Memory Systems, **http://www.ems-rifd.com/pr/nestlepr.html**, accessed February 23, 2008; Ayman Abouseif, "How RFID can help optimize supply chain management," **www.ameinfo.com**, posted on February 22, 2008; "Radio Silence," *The Economist*, June 7, 2007; Edmund W. Schuster, Stuart J. Allen, David L. Brock, *Global RFID*, Springer, Heidelberg 2007.

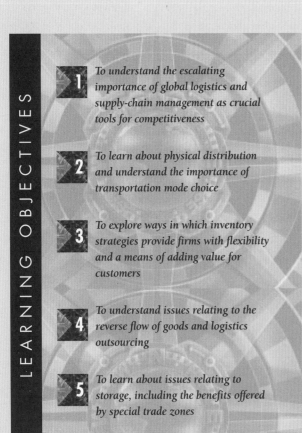

LEARNING OBJECTIVES

1 *To understand the escalating importance of global logistics and supply-chain management as crucial tools for competitiveness*

2 *To learn about physical distribution and understand the importance of transportation mode choice*

3 *To explore ways in which inventory strategies provide firms with flexibility and a means of adding value for customers*

4 *To understand issues relating to the reverse flow of goods and logistics outsourcing*

5 *To learn about issues relating to storage, including the benefits offered by special trade zones*

For the international firm, customer locations and sourcing opportunities are widely dispersed. The firm can attain a strategically advantageous position only if it is able to successfully manage complex international networks known as the **supply chain**, which consists of its vendors, suppliers, other third parties, and its customers. Neglect of links within and outside the firm not only brings higher costs but also the risk of eventual noncompetitiveness, because of diminished market share, more expensive supplies, or lower profits.

GLOBAL LOGISTICS

Global logistics is the design and management of a system that controls the flow of materials into, through, and out of the international corporation. It encompasses the total movement concept by covering the entire range of operations concerned with the movement of goods, including, therefore, both exports and imports simultaneously. An overview of the international supply chain is shown in Figure 12.1.

There are two major phases in the movement of materials. The first is **materials management**, or the timely movement of raw materials, parts, and supplies into and through the firm. The second is **physical distribution**, which involves the movement of the firm's finished product to its customers. In both phases, movement is seen within the context of the entire process. Stationary periods (storage and inventory) are therefore included. The basic goal of logistics management is the effective coordination of both phases and their various components to result in maximum cost effectiveness while maintaining service goals and requirements.

There are three key concepts to business logistics: (1) the systems concept, (2) the total-cost concept, and (3) the trade-off concept. The **systems concept** is based on the notion that materials-flow activities within and outside the firm are so extensive and complex that they can be considered only in the context of their interaction. Instead of each corporate function, supplier, and customer operating with the goal of individual optimization, the systems concept stipulates that some components may have to work suboptimally to maximize the benefits of the system as a whole. The intent of the systems concept is to provide the firm, its suppliers, and its customers, both domestic and foreign, with the benefits of synergism expected from the coordinated application of size.

A logical outgrowth of the systems concept is the development of the **total-cost concept**. To evaluate and optimize logistical activities, cost is used as a basis for measurement. The purpose of the total-cost concept is to minimize the firm's overall logistics cost by implementing the systems concept appropriately.

The third logistics concept, the **trade-off concept**, recognizes the links within logistics systems that result from the interaction of their components. For example, locating a warehouse

---

SUPPLY CHAIN

A complex global network created by a firm to connect its vendors, suppliers, other third parties, and its customers in order to achieve greater cost efficiencies and to enhance competitiveness.

1   LEARNING OBJECTIVE

MATERIALS MANAGEMENT

The timely movement of raw materials, parts, and supplies into and through the firm.

PHYSICAL DISTRIBUTION

The movement of finished products from suppliers to customers.

SYSTEMS CONCEPT

A concept of logistics based on the notion that materials-flow activities are so complex that they can be considered only in the context of their interaction.

TOTAL-COST CONCEPT

A decision concept that identifies and links expenditures in order to evaluate and optimize logistical activities.

TRADE-OFF CONCEPT

A decision concept that recognizes interactions within the decision system.

FIGURE 12.1   The International Supply Chain

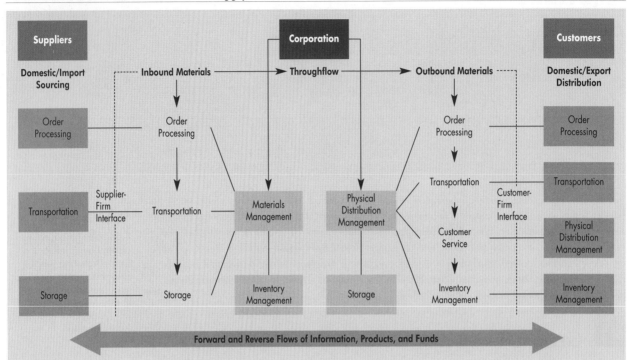

near the customer may reduce the cost of transportation. However, additional costs are associated with new warehouses. Similarly, a reduction of inventories will save money but may increase the need for costly emergency shipments. Managers can maximize performance of logistics systems only by formulating decisions based on the recognition and analysis of such trade-offs.

Supply-Chain Management

SUPPLY-CHAIN MANAGEMENT

Connecting the value-adding activities of a company's supply side with its demand side.

The integration of these three concepts has resulted in the new paradigm of **supply-chain management**, which encompasses the planning and management of all activities involved in sourcing and procurement, conversion, and logistics. It also includes coordination and collaboration with channel partners, which can be suppliers, intermediaries, third-party service providers, and customers. In essence, supply-chain management integrates supply and demand management within and across companies.[1]

Advances in information technology have been crucial to progress in supply-chain management. Consider the example of Gestamp (Spain's leading supplier of metal components for car manufacturers), which used electronic data interchange technology to integrate inbound and outbound logistics between suppliers and customers. The company reports increased manufacturing productivity, reduced investment needs, increased efficiency of the billing process, and led to a lower rate of logistic errors across the supply process after implementing a supply-chain-management system.[2]

JUST-IN-TIME INVENTORY SYSTEMS

Materials scheduled to arrive precisely when they are needed on a production line; minimizes storage requirements.

A cohesive and effective supply chain is at the core of **just-in-time inventory systems**, which are crucial to maintaining manufacturing costs at globally competitive levels. Within Siemens AG's Medical Solutions Group, for instance, a tightly controlled supply chain optimizes order management, scheduling, materials logistics, assembly, testing, shipping, and installation, allowing the firm a seamless process to deliver critical medical equipment to customers worldwide. Efficient supply-chain design can increase customer satisfaction, save money, reduce delivery lead times, and eliminate waste.

While there are limitations to the amount of time or cost that can be saved in the physical shipping of goods across oceans or land masses, supply-chain management is a powerful tool in speeding up the many other processes related to the sourcing of materials and the delivery of goods to ultimate customers.

New Dimensions of Global Logistics

In domestic operations, logistics decisions are guided by the experience of the manager, possible industry comparisons, an intimate knowledge of trends, and discovered heuristics—or rules of thumb. The logistics manager in the global firm, on the other hand, frequently has to depend on educated guesses to determine the steps required to obtain a desired service level. Variations in locale mean variations in environment. Lack of familiarity with such variations leads to uncertainty in the decision-making process. By applying decision rules based only on the environment encountered at home, the firm will be unable to adapt well to new circumstances, and the result will be inadequate profit performance. The long-term survival of international activities depends on an understanding of the differences inherent in the international logistics field.

GLOBAL TRANSPORTATION ISSUES

Transportation determines how and when goods will be received. The transportation issue can be divided into three components: infrastructure, the availability of modes, and the choice of modes among the given alternatives.

Transportation Infrastructure

In industrialized countries, firms can count on an established transportation network. Around the globe, however, major variations in infrastructure will be encountered. Some countries may have excellent inbound and outbound transportation systems but weak internal transportation links. This is particularly true in former colonies, where the original transportation systems were designed to maximize the extractive potential of the countries. In such instances, shipping to the market may be easy, but distribution within the market may be difficult and time-consuming. Infrastructure problems also exist in countries whose transportation networks were established between major ports and cities in past centuries. The areas lying outside the networks typically encounter problems in bringing their goods to market.

With the easing of barriers around the world, new trade opportunities await successful internationalists. Yet access to suppliers and customers is often fraught with difficulties. The firm's **logistics platform**, determined by a location's ease and convenience of market reach under favorable cost circumstances, is a key component of its competitive position. Since different countries and regions offer alternative logistics platforms, the firm must recognize that infrastructure issues are an important component of target market selection.

In some countries, for example, railroads may be an excellent transportation mode, far surpassing the performance of trucking, while in others rail freight is a gamble at best. If the

2   LEARNING OBJECTIVE

LOGISTICS PLATFORM

Vital to a firm's competitive position, it is determined by a location's ease and convenience of market reach under favorable cost circumstances.

Culture Clues   Green or white packaging will be unsuccessful in many Asian countries, where these colors connote either disease or mourning.

product is amenable to pipeline transportation, it pays to investigate any future routing of pipelines before committing to a particular location. Transportation of cargo from the place of manufacture to seaports or airports is another essential consideration. Mistakes can prove costly. Consider the case of the food-processing firm that built a pineapple cannery at the delta of a river in Mexico. Since the pineapple plantation was located upstream, the plan was to float the ripe fruit down to the cannery on barges. To the firm's dismay, however, come harvest time, the river current was far too strong for barge traffic. Since no other feasible alternative method of transportation existed, the plant was closed, and the new equipment was sold for a fraction of its original cost.[3]

Frequency of transportation is another important issue, and extreme variations exist. For example, a particular port may not be visited by a ship for weeks, or even months. Sometimes only small carriers, which are unable to move large equipment, will serve a given location.

Business strategist Michael Porter underlines the importance of infrastructure as a determinant of national competitive advantage, highlighting the capability of governmental efforts to influence this critical issue.[4] For that reason, infrastructure is a critical issue for any governments seeking to attract new industries or retain existing firms.

Quick Take   *Changing Logistics in China*

China is a developing country when it comes to logistics, but one that is opening up to foreigners and expanding rapidly. China's economic health largely depends on trade. The expansion of trade signals a need for increased improvements in transportation and logistics. The vice-minister of the National Development and Reform Commission, Ou Xinqian, stated that China's logistics industry will soon be transformed from its current "initial" state to a more "well-developed" one.

The Chinese government is pouring money into the process and encourages investors to do the same. The growing improvement in China's logistics is not only attracting local companies but the big international corporations as well.

DHL, UPS, and FedEx are looking to China as a place of increased revenue. Foreign companies are having a good impact on local logistics providers (currently there are more than 18,000 registered in China) by forcing local firms to compete and therefore offer global quality standards. Options such as temperature-controlled warehouses and outsourced parts distribution are increasingly standard.

China's logistics expense is 21 percent of its GDP while it is only half that in developed countries. Much of this can be attributed to poor means of transportation, namely inadequate roads and railways. A second drawback is corruption, as most of the transactions are handled by several middlemen who often demand something extra in order to speed up the transaction. This problem became highly visible when the former deputy director of Beijing's transport department was convicted for bribery and embezzlement. Yet many international companies look at China as a place with opportunity for growth, development, and—most important—revenue.

SOURCES: Helen Atkinson, "China's New Logistics Choices," *Journal of Commerce*, May 9, 2005; "Logistics Industry Moving Forward," *China Daily*, May 19, 2005; Jamie Bolton, Andrew Sleigh, "China Logistics: The infrastructure imperative," *Logistics Management*, July 1, 2007; Wu Qiong, "China 2007 trade surplus hits new record," *China View*, January 11, 2008, **www.chinaview.cn**, accessed February 17, 2008.

Availability of Modes

Global business frequently requires transportation of cargo via ocean or airfreight, two modes that most domestic corporations rarely use. In addition, combinations such as **land bridges** or **sea bridges** may permit the transfer of freight among various modes of transportation, resulting in **intermodal movements**. The international logistics manager must understand the specific properties of the different modes to be able to use them intelligently.

Ocean Shipping

Water transportation is a key mode for international freight movement. Three types of vessels operating in ocean shipping can be distinguished by their service: liner service, bulk service, and tramp or charter service. **Liner service** offers regularly scheduled passage on established routes. **Bulk service** mainly provides contractual services for individual voyages or for prolonged periods of time. **Tramp service** is available for irregular routes and is scheduled only on demand.

In addition to the services offered by ocean carriers, the type of cargo a vessel can carry is also important. The most common types are conventional (break-bulk) cargo vessels, container ships, and roll-on-roll-off vessels. Conventional cargo vessels are useful for oversized and unusual cargoes but may be less efficient in their port operations. Container ships carry standardized containers that greatly facilitate the loading and unloading of cargo and intermodal transfers. As a result, the time the ship has to spend in port is reduced, as are port charges. **Roll-on-roll-off (RORO)** vessels are essentially oceangoing ferries. Trucks can drive onto built-in ramps and roll off at the destination. Another vessel similar to the RORO vessel is the **lighter aboard ship (LASH) vessel**. LASH vessels consist of barges stored on the ship and lowered at the point of destination. The individual barges can then operate on inland waterways, a feature that is particularly useful in shallow water.

The availability of a certain type of vessel, however, does not automatically mean that it can be used. The greatest constraint in international ocean shipping is the lack of ports and port services. For example, modern container ships cannot serve some ports because the local equipment cannot handle the resulting traffic. The problem is often found in developing countries, where local authorities lack the funds to develop facilities. In some instances, nations may purposely limit the development of ports to impede the inflow of imports. Increasingly, however, governments have begun to recognize the importance of an appropriate port facility structure and are developing such facilities in spite of the large investments necessary.

Air Shipping

Airfreight is available to and from most countries. This includes the developing world, where it is often a matter of national prestige to operate a national airline. The tremendous growth in international airfreight is shown in Figure 12.2. The volume of airfreight in relation to the total volume of shipping in international business remains quite small. Yet 40 percent of the world's manufactured exports by value travel by air.[5] Clearly, high-value items are more likely to be shipped by air, particularly if they have a high density—that is, a high weight-to-volume ratio.

Airlines make major efforts to increase the volume of airfreight by developing better and more efficient ground facilities, introducing airfreight containers, and marketing a wide variety of special services to shippers. In addition, some airfreight companies have specialized and become partners in the international logistics effort.

From the shipper's perspective, the products involved must be appropriate for air shipment, in terms of their size and weight. In addition, the market situation for any given

LAND BRIDGE

Transfer of ocean freight among various modes of land-based transportation.

SEA BRIDGE

The transfer of freight among various modes of ocean freight.

INTERMODAL MOVEMENTS

The transfer of freight from one type of transportation to another.

LINER SERVICE

Ocean shipping characterized by regularly scheduled passage on established routes.

BULK SERVICE

Ocean shipping provided on contract, either for individual voyages or for prolonged periods of time.

TRAMP SERVICE

Ocean shipping via irregular routes, scheduled only on demand.

ROLL-ON-ROLL-OFF (RORO)

Transportation vessels built to accommodate trucks that can drive on in one port and drive off at their destinations.

LIGHTER ABOARD SHIP (LASH) VESSEL

Barge stored on a ship and lowered at the point of destination to operate on inland waterways.

FIGURE 12.2   International Airfreight, 1960-2025, A Forecast

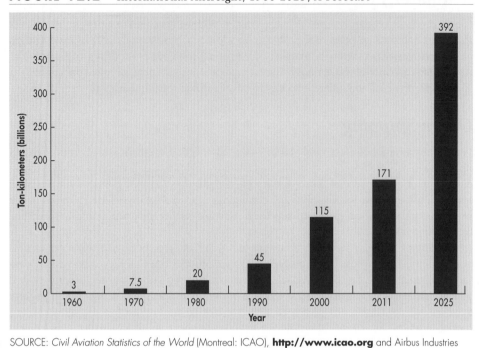

SOURCE: *Civil Aviation Statistics of the World* (Montreal: ICAO), **http://www.icao.org** and Airbus Industries Global Market Forecast, 2006-2025, **http://www.airbus.com**, accessed February 28, 2008.

UPS, the world's largest package distribution company, transports more than 3.1 billion parcels and documents annually. To transport packages most efficiently, UPS has developed an elaborate network of "hubs" or central sorting facilities located throughout the world.

TRANSIT TIME

The period between departure and arrival of a shipment.

product must be evaluated. Airfreight may be needed if a product is perishable or if, for other reasons, it requires a short transit time. The level of customer service needs and expectations can also play a decisive role. For example, the shipment of an industrial product that is vital to the ongoing operations of a customer may be much more urgent than the shipment of packaged consumer products.

Selecting a Mode of Transport

The international logistics manager must make the appropriate selection from the available modes of transportation. The decision will be heavily influenced by the needs of the firm and its customers. The manager must consider the performance of each mode on four dimensions: transit time, predictability, cost, and on-economic factors. A useful overview of different modes of transportation and their comparative strengths is provided in Table 12.1.

TRANSIT TIME   The period between departure and arrival of the carrier varies significantly between ocean freight and airfreight. For example, the 45-day **transit time** of an ocean shipment can be reduced to 24 hours if the firm chooses airfreight. The length of transit time can have a major impact on the overall operations of the firm. As an example, a short transit time may reduce or even eliminate the need for an overseas depot. Also, inventories can be significantly reduced if they are replenished frequently. As a result, capital can be freed up and used to finance other corporate opportunities. Transit time can also play a major role in emergency situations. For example, if the shipper is about to miss an important delivery date because of production delays, a shipment normally made by ocean freight can be made by air.

Perishable products require shorter transit times. Transporting them rapidly prolongs the shelf life in the foreign market. Air delivery may be the only way to enter foreign markets

TABLE 12.1 Evaluating Transportation Choices

	MODE OF TRANSPORTATION				
CHARACTERISTICS OF MODE	AIR	PIPELINE	HIGHWAY	RAIL	WATER
Speed (1 = fastest)	1	4	2	3	5
Cost (1 = highest)	1	4	3	4	5
Loss and Damage (1 = least)	3	1	4	5	2
Frequency[1] (1 = best)	3	1	2	4	5
Dependability (1 = best)	5	1	2	3	4
Capacity[2] (1 = best)	4	5	3	2	1
Availablity (1 = best)	3	5	1	2	4

[1]Frequency: number of times mode is available during a given time period.
[2]Capacity: ability of mode to handle large or heavy goods.

SOURCE: Ronald H. Ballou, Business Logistics and Supply Chain Management, 5th ed., p. 143. Copyright © 2004. Reprinted by permission of Pearson Education, Inc., Upper Saddle River, NJ.

successfully with products that have a short life span. International sales of cut flowers have reached their current volume only as a result of airfreight.

Quick Take *Environment and Sustainability*

Organic Food Has a Carbon Footprint

Organic or not, carbon emissions are a major problem with food shipping. Mangoes, green peppers, and bananas are examples of products where the organic version needs to travel farther to get to market. Many of the benefits of buying organic food items are offset by the carbon emissions released to get them to the buyer. Those companies that want to be considered green need to look at ways of mitigating the effects of their carbon emissions.

ShipGreen, Greenworld LLC has started to apply the concept of carbon offsets to the shipping industry. Using the unique weight, distance, and transportation mode of a shipment, ShipGreen is able to determine the amount of carbon dioxide emissions it produced and presents customers with several options for offsetting the impact of their shipment, such as reforestation and solar or wind power projects that prevent or remove carbon dioxide.

Currently, the majority of ShipGreen's customers are e-commerce companies that want to adopt a greener approach. By incorporating ShipGreen programs into their web sites, e-commerce companies can provide their customers with the option of adding a fee to their order. The proceeds are then used to buy carbon credits for projects certified according to the Kyoto protocol by a third party. The credits are calculated using an algorithm developed at the University of California, Berkeley, which not only takes into account tailpipe emissions, but also energy used and emissions from making the fuels, manufacturing the vehicles, and constructing and operating the infrastructure for transportation.

SOURCES: Danny Bradbury, "Cutting the carbon footprint: plain sailing?" *BusinessGreen*, February 25, 2008; Greenworld LLC web site, **http://www.greenworldorganics.com**, accessed February 26, 2008.

At all times, the logistics manager must understand the interactions between different components of the logistics process and their effect on transit times. Unless a smooth flow throughout the entire supply chain can be assured, bottlenecks will deny any benefits from specific improvements. For example, some consumer retailers have tried to offer instant gratification to their customers by providing custom services – such as body scanning for clothes measurements – and immediately transmitting the data electronically to suppliers. Even though the custom clothes are being worked on right away, it may take weeks to get the finished item to the customer.

PREDICTABILITY Providers of both ocean freight and airfreight service wrestle with the issue of reliability. Both modes are subject to the vagaries of nature, which may impose delays. Yet, because reliability is a relative measure, the delay of one day for airfreight tends to be seen as much more severe and "unreliable" than the same delay for ocean freight. However, delays tend to be shorter in absolute time for air shipments. As a result, arrival time via air is more predictable. This attribute has a major influence on corporate strategy. For example, because of the higher **predictability** of airfreight, inventory safety stock can be kept at lower levels. Greater predictability can also serve as a useful sales tool, because it permits more precise delivery promises to customers. If inadequate port facilities exist, airfreight may again be the better alternative. Unloading operations for oceangoing vessels are more cumbersome and time-consuming than for planes. Finally, merchandise shipped via air is likely to suffer less loss and damage from exposure of the cargo to movement. Therefore, once the merchandise arrives, it is more likely to be ready for immediate delivery—a fact that also enhances predictability.

An important aspect of predictability is the capability of a shipper to track goods at any point during the shipment. **Tracking** becomes particularly important as corporations increasingly obtain products from and send them to multiple locations around the world. Being able to coordinate the smooth flow of a multitude of interdependent shipments can make a vast difference in a corporation's performance. Tracking allows the shipper to check on the functioning of the supply chain and to take remedial action if problems occur. Cargo can also be redirected if sudden demand surges so require. However, such an enhanced corporate response to the predictability issue is possible only if the shipper and the carrier develop an appropriate information system that is easily accessible to the user.

COST International transportation services are usually priced on the basis of cost of the service provided and value of the service to the shipper. Due to the high value of the products shipped by air, airfreight is often priced according to the value of the service. In this instance, of course, price becomes a function of market demand and the monopolistic power of the carrier.

The manager must decide whether the clearly higher cost of airfreight can be justified. In part, this will depend on the cargo's properties. The physical density and the value of the cargo will affect the decision. Bulky products may be too expensive to ship by air, whereas very compact products may be more appropriate for airfreight transportation. High-priced items can absorb transportation costs more easily than low-priced goods, because the cost of transportation as a percentage of total product cost will be lower. As a result, sending diamonds by airfreight is easier to justify than sending coal. Alternatively, a shipper can decide to mix modes of transportation in order to reduce overall cost and time delays. For example, part of the shipment route can be covered by air, while another portion can be covered by truck or ship.

Most important, however, are the supply-chain considerations of the firm. The manager must determine how important it is for merchandise to arrive on time. This means factoring in all corporate, supplier, and customer activities that are affected by the modal choice and exploring the full implications of each alternative. Hot fashions, for instance, obviously need

PREDICTABILITY

The degree of likelihood that a shipment will arrive on time and in good condition.

TRACKING

The capability of a shipper to determine the location of goods at any point during the shipment.

WORLD VIEW

GLOBAL SMALL BUSINESS: CARRIERS TO THE RESCUE!

When running a small or medium-sized international enterprise (SME), it is difficult to have all required resources at hand. Yet SMEs need much information in order to become strong competitors in today's market. A variety of shipping carriers offer customized supply-chain management assistance to small businesses, since companies often spend more than 10 percent of their revenue just to manage their supply chain.

For a small business it is important to focus on its core competencies, reduce costs, and improve customer service. Most of the inner workings behind supply-chain management can be outsourced to a third party. FedEx offers its business clients resources and technology necessary to move products all the way through the supply chain and back if necessary. That way FedEx touches on return management, which, in an era of shopping on the web, takes on growing importance.

The DHL Small Business Resource Center allows SMEs to communicate with one another online. This permits business owners to share their knowledge and tips about logistics. DHL has also created an online database containing peer-to-peer knowledge, reference-guided articles, and special offers, all targeted toward SMEs.

UPS has also created a branch for small businesses where it offers improved and less time-consuming shipping technology, visibility of the supply-chain process (so a business can get paid more quickly by the end consumer), and dependability of the UPS Brown brand. With each of the three major global carriers offering outsourcing services to small businesses, it becomes easier for firms to take the international leap.

SOURCES: "DHL Helps Small Businesses Respond to Key Growth Challenges," *Business Wire*, August 1, 2005; **http://www.fedex.com**, accessed February 17, 2008; **http://www.ups.com**, accessed February 17, 2008.

very timely delivery. In some cases, a firm may want to use airfreight as a new tool for aggressive market expansion. In others, airfreight may be considered a good way to begin operations in new markets without making sizable investments into warehouses and distribution centers.

NON-ECONOMIC FACTORS The transportation sector, nationally and internationally, both benefits and suffers from government involvement. Even though transportation carriers are one prime target in the sweep of privatization around the globe, many carriers are still owned, or are heavily subsidized, by governments. As a result, governmental pressure is exerted on shippers to use national carriers, even if more economical alternatives exist. Such **preferential policies** are most often enforced when government cargo is being transported. Restrictions are not limited to developing countries. For example, the U.S. federal government requires that all travelers on government business use national flag carriers when available.

For balance of payments reasons, international quota systems of transportation have been proposed. The United Nations Conference on Trade and Development (UNCTAD), for example, has recommended that 40 percent of the traffic between two nations be allocated to vessels of the exporting country, 40 percent to vessels of the importing country, and 20 percent to third-country vessels. However, stiff international competition among carriers and

PREFERENTIAL POLICIES

Government policies that favor certain (usually domestic) firms: for example, the use of national carriers for the transport of government freight, even when more economical alternatives exist.

Culture Clues   The Chinese believe that certain days of the year are more auspicious than others. Some business people will even insist on consulting the stars or waiting for a lucky day before dispatching or receiving goods.

the price sensitivity of customers frequently render such proposals ineffective, particularly for trade between industrialized countries.

Although many justifications are possible for such national policies, ranging from prestige to national security, they distort the economic choices of the international corporation. Yet these policies are a reflection of the international environment within which the firm must operate. Proper adaptation is necessary.

Export Documentation

A firm must deal with numerous forms and documents when exporting to ensure that all goods meet local and foreign laws and regulations.

A bill of lading is a contract between the exporter and the carrier indicating that the carrier has accepted responsibility for the goods and will provide transportation in return for payment. The bill of lading can also be used as a receipt and to prove ownership of the merchandise. There are two types of bills, negotiable and non-negotiable. **Straight bills of lading** are non-negotiable and are typically used in prepaid transactions. The goods are delivered to a specific individual or company. **Shipper's order** bills of lading are negotiable; they can be bought, sold, or traded while the goods are still in transit and are used for letter-of-credit transactions. The customer usually needs the original or a copy of the bill of lading as proof of ownership to take possession of the goods.

A **commercial invoice** is a bill for the goods stating basic information about the transaction, including a description of the merchandise, total cost of the goods sold, addresses of the shipper and seller, and delivery and payment terms. The buyer needs the invoice to prove ownership and to arrange payment. Some governments use the commercial invoice to assess customs duties.

A variety of other export documents may be required. Some of the more common ones are summarized in Table 12.2.

Terms of Shipment and Sale

The responsibilities of the buyer and the seller should be spelled out as they relate to what is and what is not included in the price quotation and when ownership of goods passes from seller to buyer. **Incoterms** are the internationally accepted standard definitions for terms of sale set by the International Chamber of Commerce (ICC). The Incoterms 2000 went into effect on January 1, 2000, with significant revisions to better reflect changing transportation technologies and the increased use of electronic communications.[6] Although the same terms may be used in domestic transactions, they gain new meaning in the global arena. The terms are grouped into four categories; (1) the "E"-terms, whereby the seller makes the goods available to the buyer only at the seller's own premises; (2) the "F"-terms, whereby the seller is called upon to deliver the goods to a carrier appointed by the buyer; (3) the "C"- terms, whereby the seller has to contract for carriage, but without assuming the risk of loss or damage to the goods or additional costs after the dispatch; and finally (4) the "D"-terms, whereby the seller has to bear all costs and risks to bring the goods to the destination determined by the buyer. The most common of the Incoterms used in international marketing are summarized in Figure 12.3.

Prices quoted **ex-works (EXW)** apply only at the point of origin, and the seller agrees to place the goods at the disposal of the buyer at the specified place on the specified date or within the fixed period. All other charges are for the account of the buyer.

One of the new Incoterms is **free carrier (FCA)**, which replaces a variety of FOB terms for all modes of transportation, except vessel. FCA (a named inland point) applies only at a designated inland shipping point. The seller is responsible for loading goods into the means

---

STRAIGHT BILL OF LADING

A non-negotiable bill of lading usually used in prepaid transactions in which the transported goods involved are delivered to a specific individual or company.

SHIPPER'S ORDER

A negotiable bill of lading that can be bought, sold, or traded while the subject goods are still in transit and that is used for letter of credit transactions.

COMMERCIAL INVOICE

A bill for transported goods that describes the merchandise and its total cost and lists the addresses of the shipper and seller and delivery and payment terms.

INCOTERMS

International Commerce Terms. Widely accepted terms used in quoting export prices.

EX-WORKS (EXW)

Price quotes that apply only at the point of origin; the seller agrees to place the goods at the disposal of the buyer at the specified place on a specified date or within a fixed period.

FREE CARRIER (FCA)

Applies only at a designated inland shipping point. Seller is responsible for loading goods into the means of transportation; buyer is responsible for all subsequent expenses.

TABLE 12.2 Summary of Common Export Documents

DOCUMENT	ISSUED BY	GENERAL PURPOSE
Pro forma invoice	Seller	Quotation to buyer; used to obtain import license and letter-of-credit financing
Sales contract	Seller or buyer	Confirms all details of transaction
Export license	U.S. government	Required by U.S. law
Carrier's receipt	Truck or rail carrier	Acknowledgment that carrier has accepted cargo for transportation to pier or airport
Dock/warehouse receipt	Pier or warehouse	Acknowledgment that cargo has been received
Ocean bill of lading/ airway bill	Steamship company or airline	Contract between shipper and shipping company for transport of cargo
Insurance certificate	Insurance company	Evidence that cargo is insured against stated risks
Inspection certificate	Inspection company	Confirms to financing bank and buyer that cargo meets specifications set forth in sales contract and/or letter of credit
Packing lists	Seller	Required by shipping company and foreign customs
Commercial invoice	Seller	Actual invoice for goods
Consular invoice	Foreign government	Used to control imports and identify goods
Certificate of origin	U.S. Chamber of Commerce	Required by foreign government
Shipper's export declaration	Seller	Required by U.S. government to control exports and compile trade statistics

FREE ALONGSIDE SHIP (FAS)

Exporter quotes a price for the goods alongside a vessel at a port. Seller handles cost of unloading and wharfage; loading, ocean transportation, and insurance are left to buyer.

FREE ON BOARD (FOB)

FOB is the term used when the ownership/liability of goods passes from the seller to the buyer at the time the goods cross the shipping point to be delivered.

COST AND FREIGHT (CFR)

Seller quotes a price for the goods, including the cost of transportation to the named port of debarkation. Cost and choice of insurance are left to the buyer.

COST, INSURANCE, AND FREIGHT (CIF)

Seller quotes a price including insurance, all transportation, and miscellaneous charges to the point of debarkation from the vessel or aircraft.

CARRIAGE PAID TO (CPT)

The price quoted by an exporter for shipments not involving waterway transport, not including insurance.

CARRIAGE AND INSURANCE PAID TO (CIP)

The price quoted by an exporter for shipments not involving waterway transport, including insurance.

DELIVERY DUTY PAID (DDP)

Seller delivers the goods, with import duties paid, including inland transportation from import point to the buyer's premises.

DELIVERY DUTY UNPAID (DDU)

Only the destination customs duty and taxes are paid by the consignee.

of transportation; the buyer is responsible for all subsequent expenses. If a port of exportation is named, the costs of transporting the goods to the named port are included in the price.

Free alongside ship (FAS) at a named U.S. port of export means that the exporter quotes a price for the goods, including charges for delivery of the goods, alongside a vessel at the port. The seller handles the cost of unloading and wharfage; loading, ocean transportation, and insurance are left to the buyer.

Free on board (FOB) applies only to vessel shipments. The seller quotes a price covering all expenses up to, and including, delivery of goods on an overseas vessel provided by or for the buyer.

Under **cost and freight (CFR)** to a named overseas port of import, the seller quotes a price for the goods, including the cost of transportation to the named port of debarkation. The cost of insurance and the choice of insurer are left to the buyer.

With **cost, insurance, and freight (CIF)** to a named overseas port of import, the seller quotes a price that includes insurance, all transportation, and miscellaneous charges to the point of debarkation from the vessel. With non-waterway transport, the terms are **carriage paid to (CPT)** or **carriage and insurance paid to (CIP)**.

With **delivery duty paid (DDP)**, the seller delivers the goods, with import duties paid, including inland transportation from import point to the buyer's premises.

With **delivery duty unpaid (DDU)**, the buyer pays only the destination customs duty and taxes. Ex-works signifies the maximum obligation for the buyer; delivery duty paid puts the maximum burden on the seller.

Careful determination and clear understanding of terms used, and their acceptance by the parties involved, are vital in order to avoid subsequent misunderstandings and disputes, not

FIGURE 12.3   Selected Trade Terms

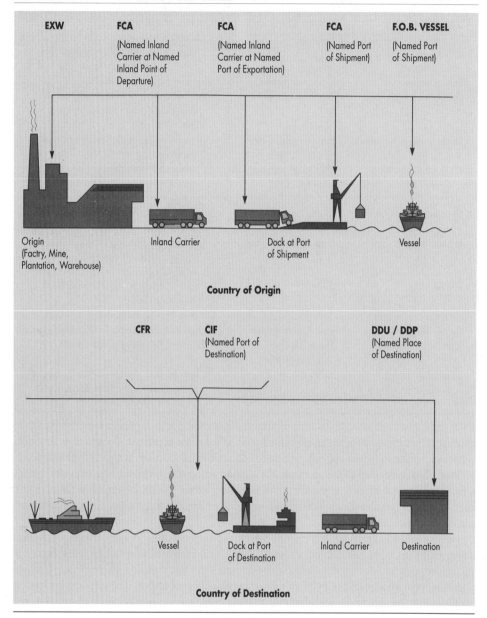

only between the parties but also within the marketer's own organization. These terms are also powerful competitive tools. The exporter should therefore learn what importers usually prefer in the particular market and what the specific transaction may require. An inexperienced importer may be discouraged from further action by a quote, such as an ex-plant from Jessup, Maryland, whereas CIF Helsinki will enable the Finnish importer to handle the remaining costs, because they are incurred in a familiar environment.

GLOBAL INVENTORY ISSUES

Inventories tie up a major portion of corporate funds. Capital used for inventory is not available for other corporate opportunities. Annual **inventory carrying costs** (the expense of maintaining inventories), though heavily influenced by the cost of capital and industry-specific conditions, can account for 25 percent or more of the value of the inventories themselves.[7] In addition, just-in-time inventory policies, which minimize the volume of inventory by making it available only when it is needed, are increasingly required by multinational manufacturers and distributors engaging in supply-chain management. They choose suppliers on the basis of their delivery and inventory performance and their ability to integrate themselves into the supply chain. Proper inventory management may therefore become a determining variable in obtaining a sale.

The purpose of establishing inventory systems—to maintain product movement in the delivery pipeline and to have a cushion to absorb demand fluctuations—is the same for domestic and global operations. The international environment, however, includes unique factors, such as currency exchange rates, greater distances, and duties. At the same time, international operations provide the corporation with an opportunity to explore alternatives not available in a domestic setting, such as new sourcing or location alternatives. In global operations, the firm can make use of currency fluctuation by placing varying degrees of emphasis on inventory operations, depending on the stability of the currency of a specific country. Entire operations can be shifted to different nations to take advantage of new opportunities. International inventory management can therefore be much more flexible in its response to environmental changes.

In deciding the level of inventory to be maintained, the international manager must consider three factors: (1) the order cycle time, (2) desired customer service levels, and (3) use of inventories as a strategic tool.

Order Cycle Time

The total time that passes between the placement of an order and the receipt of the merchandise is referred to as **order cycle time**. Two dimensions are of major importance to inventory management: the length of the total order cycle and its consistency. In international business, the order cycle is frequently longer than in domestic business. It comprises the time involved in order transmission, order filling, packing and preparation for shipment, and transportation. Order transmission time varies greatly internationally, depending on the method of communication. Supply-chain-driven firms use **electronic data interchange (EDI)** rather than facsimile, telex, telephone, or mail.

EDI is the direct transfer of information technology between computers of trading partners. The usual paperwork the partners send each other, such as purchase orders and confirmations, bills of lading, invoices, and shipment notices, are formatted into standard messages and transmitted via a direct-link network or a third-party network. EDI can save a large part of the processing and administrative costs associated with traditional ways of exchanging information.

The order-filling time may also increase, because lack of familiarity with a foreign market makes the anticipation of new orders more difficult. Packing and shipment preparation require more detailed attention. Finally, of course, transportation time increases with the distances involved. Larger inventories may have to be maintained both domestically and internationally to bridge the time gaps.

Consistency, the second dimension of order cycle time, is also more difficult to maintain in international business. Depending on the choice of transportation mode, delivery times

INVENTORY CARRYING COSTS

The expense of maintaining goods in storage.

ORDER CYCLE TIME

The total time that passes between the placement of an order and the receipt of the merchandise.

ELECTRONIC DATA INTERCHANGE (EDI)

The direct transfer of information technology between computers of trading partners.

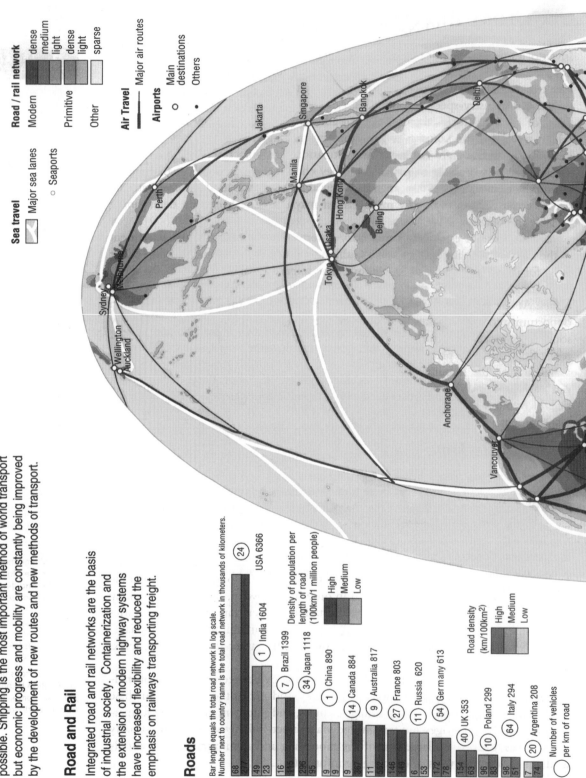

Trade and Travel Networks

Civilization depends on trade for growth and travel makes this possible. Shipping is the most important method of world transport but economic progress and mobility are constantly being improved by the development of new routes and new methods of transport.

Road and Rail

Integrated road and rail networks are the basis of industrial society. Containerization and the extension of modern highway systems have increased flexibility and reduced the emphasis on railways transporting freight.

Roads

Bar length equals the total road network in log scale.
Number next to country name is the total road network in thousands of kilometers.

(24) USA 6366

(1) India 1604

(7) Brazil 1399

(34) Japan 1118

(1) China 890

(14) Canada 884

(9) Australia 817

(27) France 803

(11) Russia 620

(54) Germany 613

(40) UK 353

(10) Poland 299

(64) Italy 294

(20) Argentina 208

◯ Number of vehicles per km of road

Density of population per length of road
(100km/1 million people)
- High
- Medium
- Low

Road density (km/100km²)
- High
- Medium
- Low

Legend

Sea travel
- Major sea lanes
- ○ Seaports

Road / rail network
- Modern: dense / medium / light
- Primitive: dense / light
- Other: sparse

Air Travel
- Major air routes

Airports
- ○ Main destinations
- • Others

Labels on map: Jakarta, Singapore, Bangkok, Delhi, Perth, Manila, Hong Kong, Beijing, Tokyo, Osaka, Melbourne, Sydney, Wellington, Auckland, Anchorage, Vancouver

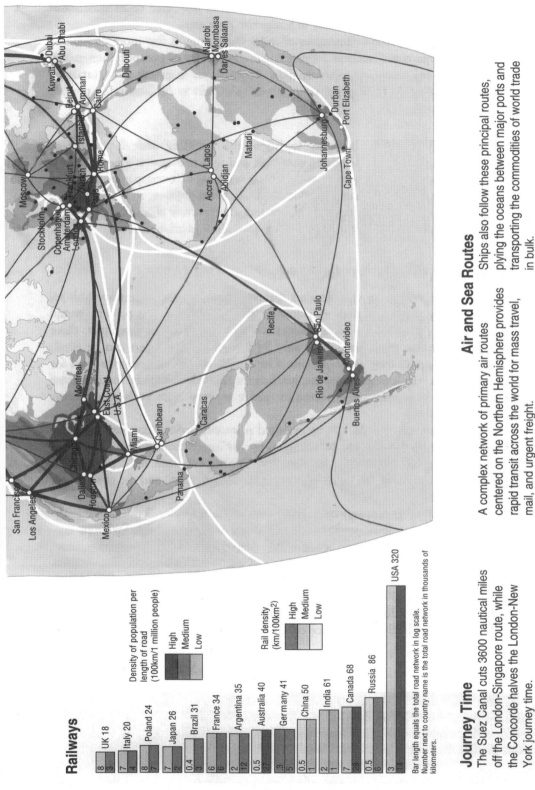

Railways

UK	8 / 3
Italy	7 / 4
Poland	8 / 7
Japan	7 / 2
Brazil	0.4 / 3
France	6 / 6
Argentina	2 / 12
Australia	0.5 / 27
Germany	3 / 5
China	0.5 / 1
India	2 / 1
Canada	7 / 28
Russia	0.5 / 6
USA	3 / 14

Density of population per length of road (100km/1 million people)
High
Medium
Low

Rail density (km/100km²)
High
Medium
Low

Bar length equals the total road network in log scale.
Number next to country name is the total road network in thousands of kilometers.

Journey Time

The Suez Canal cuts 3600 nautical miles off the London-Singapore route, while the Concorde halves the London-New York journey time.

Air and Sea Routes

A complex network of primary air routes centered on the Northern Hemisphere provides rapid transit across the world for mass travel, mail, and urgent freight.

Ships also follow these principal routes, plying the oceans between major ports and transporting the commodities of world trade in bulk.

Sail (via Cape) 164 days

Steam (via Cape) 43 days

Steam (via Suez) 28 days

Supertanker (via Cape) 28 days

Diesel (via Suez) 15 days

Singapore — London — New York

Concorde 3½ hours

Jet 7 hours

Propeller 12 hours

First Flight 4½ days

Source: Bartholomew.

may vary considerably from shipment to shipment. The variation requires the maintenance of larger safety stocks to be able to fill demand in periods when delays occur.

REVERSE LOGISTICS **Reverse logistics**—the handling and disposition of returned products and use of related materials and information—is an important way for firms to improve customer service and increase revenue. With the growth of direct-to-customer Internet sales, the reverse supply chain has exploded, amounting to over $100 billion per year – greater than the GDP of two-thirds of the world's countries! Industries facing the highest return volume are magazine/book publishing (50 percent), catalog retailers (18 to 35 percent), and greeting card companies (20 to 30 percent).[8] Just the disposal of returned merchandise can result in major headaches and costs.

CUSTOMER SERVICE LEVELS The level of customer service denotes the responsiveness that inventory policies permit for any given situation. A customer service level of 100 percent would be defined as the ability to fill all orders within a set time—for example, three days. If, within the same three days, only 70 percent of the orders can be filled, the customer service level is 70 percent. The choice of customer service level for the firm has a major impact on the inventories needed. In highly industrialized nations, firms frequently are expected to adhere to very high levels of customer service.

Yet service levels should not be oriented primarily around cost or customary domestic standards. Rather, the level chosen for use internationally should be based on expectations encountered in each market. The expectations depend on past performance, product desirability, customer sophistication, and the competitive status of the firm.

Because high customer service levels are costly, the goal should not be the highest customer service level possible, but rather an acceptable level. Different customers have different priorities. Some will be prepared to pay a premium for speed, some may put a higher value on flexibility, and another group may see low cost as the most important issue. If, for example, foreign customers expect to receive their merchandise within 30 days, for the international corporation to promise delivery within 10 or 15 days does not make sense. Indeed, such delivery may result in storage problems and will likely reduce price competitiveness.

Inventory as a Strategic Tool

The international corporation can use inventories as a strategic tool in dealing with currency valuation changes or to hedge against inflation. By increasing inventories before an imminent devaluation of a currency, instead of holding cash, the corporation may reduce its exposure to devaluation losses. Similarly, in the case of high inflation, large inventories can provide an important inflation hedge. In such circumstances, the international inventory manager must balance the cost of maintaining high levels of inventories with the benefits that might be accrued from hedging against inflation or devaluation. Many countries, for example, charge a property tax on stored goods. If the increase in tax payments outweighs the hedging benefits to the corporation, it would be unwise to increase inventories before a devaluation.

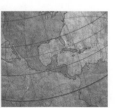

Culture Clues   The Japanese term *kyouzon*, *kyouei* roughly translates to "coexistence and mutual prosperity." When applied to business, it means that organizations must band together to help one another survive, especially in times of crisis. Japanese business partnerships are often based on a profound belief in mutual prosperity—no one should get rich at the expense of their customers or suppliers. Perhaps this is the earliest form of supply-chain management.

WORLD VIEW

WHEN THERE IS MORE TO A NAME

Products in Asia often carry brand names that are translated from their original names. They are either direct translations (which result in a different-sounding but same-meaning name in the local language) or phonetic (which result in the same sound but usually a different meaning). Given the globalization of markets, marketers not only need to decide whether to translate their brand names but also must consider the form, content, style, and image of such translations.

In Europe and the Americas, brand names such as Budweiser, Canon, and Coca-Cola have no meaning in themselves, and few are even aware of the origins of the name. But to Chinese-speaking consumers, brand names include an additional meaning. Budweiser means "hundreds of power and influence," Canon stands for "perfect capability" and Coca-Cola means "tasty and happy."

Chinese and Western consumers share similar standards when it comes to evaluating brand names. Both appreciate a brand name that is catchy, memorable, and distinct and that says something indicative of the product. But because of cultural and linguistic

factors, Chinese consumers expect more in terms of how names are spelled, written, and styled and whether they are considered lucky. In a study of Fortune 500 companies in China, the vast majority of marketers were found to localize their brand names using, for the most part, transliteration. Following this insight, when Frito-Lay introduced Cheetos in the Chinese market, it did so under a phonetically similar Chinese name that translates as "Many Surprises."

SOURCES: Nader Tavassoli and Jin K. Han "Auditory and Visual Brand Identifiers in Chinese and English," *Journal of International Marketing* 10 (no. 2, 2002): pp. 13-28; F.C. Hong, Anthony Pecotich, and Clifford J. Schultz, "Brand Name Translation Language Constraints, Product Attributes and Consumer Perceptions in East and Southeast Asia," *Journal of International Marketing* 10 (no. 2, 2002): pp. 29-45; Fuming Jiang, and Bruce W. Stening, *The Chinese Business Environment.* (Cheltenham, U.K. and Northampton, MA: Edward Elgar, 2007).

GLOBAL PACKAGING ISSUES

The responsibility for appropriate packaging rests with the shipper of goods. The shipper must therefore ensure that the goods are prepared appropriately for international shipping. Packaging is instrumental in getting the merchandise to the ultimate destination in a safe, maintainable, and presentable condition. Packaging that is adequate for domestic shipping may be inadequate for international transportation, because the shipment will be subject to the motions of the vessel on which it is carried. Added stress in international shipping also arises from the transfer of goods among different modes of transportation. Figure 12.4 provides examples of some sources of stress in intermodal movement that are most frequently found in international transportation.

4 LEARNING OBJECTIVE

Packaging decisions must take into account differences in environmental conditions—for example, climate. When the ultimate destination is very humid or particularly cold, special provisions must be made to prevent damage to the product. The task becomes even more challenging when one considers that, in the course of long-distance transportation, dramatic changes in climate can take place. Still famous is the case of a firm in Taiwan that shipped drinking glasses to the Middle East. The company used wooden crates and padded the glasses with hay. Most of the glasses, however, were broken by the time they reached their destination. As the crates traveled into the drier Middle East, the moisture content of the hay dropped. By the time the crates were delivered, the thin straw offered almost no protection.[9]

The weight of packaging must also be considered, particularly when airfreight is used, as the cost of shipping is often based on weight. At the same time, packaging material must be sufficiently strong to permit stacking in international transportation.

Another consideration is that, in some countries, duties are assessed according to the gross weight of shipments, which includes the weight of packaging. Obviously, the heavier the packaging, the higher the duty will be.

The shipper must pay sufficient attention to instructions provided by the customer for packaging. For example, requests by the customer that the weight of any one package should not exceed a certain limit or that specific package dimensions should be adhered to, usually are made for a reason. Often they reflect limitations in transportation or handling facilities at the point of destination.

Although the packaging of a product is often used as a form of display abroad, international packaging can rarely serve the dual purpose of protection and display. Therefore, double packaging may be necessary. The display package is for future use at the point of destination; another package surrounds it for protective purposes.

One solution to the packaging problem in international logistics has been the development of intermodal containers—large metal boxes that fit on trucks, ships, railroad cars, and airplanes and ease the frequent transfer of goods in international shipments. Developed in different forms for both sea and air transportation, containers also offer better utilization of carrier space because of standardization of size. The shipper, therefore, may benefit from lower transportation rates. In addition, containers can offer greater safety from pilferage and damage.

Container traffic is heavily dependent on the existence of appropriate handling facilities, both domestically and internationally. In addition, the quality of inland transportation must be considered. If transportation for containers is not available and the merchandise must be unloaded, the expected cost reductions may not materialize.

In some countries, rules for the handling of containers may be designed to maintain employment. For example, U.S. union rules obligate shippers to withhold containers from firms that do not employ members of the International Longshoremen's Association for the loading or unloading of containers within a 50-mile radius of Atlantic or Gulf ports. Such restrictions can result in an onerous cost burden.

In summary, close attention must be paid to international packaging. The customer who orders and pays for the merchandise expects it to arrive on time and in good condition. Even with replacements and insurance, the customer will not be satisfied if there are delays. Dissatisfaction will usually translate directly into lost sales.

FIGURE 12.4   Stresses in Intermodal Movement

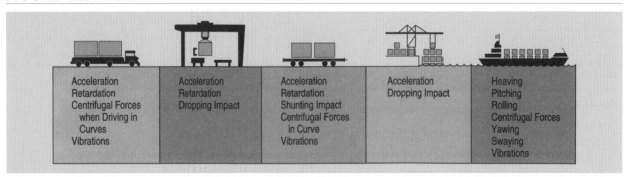

Note: Each transportation mode exerts a different set of stresses and strains on containerized cargoes. The most commonly overlooked are those associated with ocean transport.

SOURCE: David Greenfield, "Perfect Packing for Export," from *Handling and Shipping Management*, September 1980 (Cleveland, Ohio: Penton Publishing), p. 47. Reprinted by permission.

GLOBAL STORAGE ISSUES

Although international logistics is discussed as a movement or flow of goods, a stationary period is involved when merchandise becomes inventory stored in warehouses. Heated arguments can arise within a firm over the need for and utility of warehousing merchandise internationally. On the one hand, customers expect quick responses to orders and rapid delivery. Accommodating the customer's expectations would require locating many distribution centers around the world. On the other hand, warehouse space is expensive. In addition, the larger volume of inventory increases the inventory carrying cost. Fewer warehouses allow for consolidation of transportation and therefore lower transportation rates to the warehouse. However, if the warehouses are located far from customers, the cost of outgoing transportation increases. The international logistician must consider the trade-offs between service and cost to the supply chain in order to determine the appropriate levels of warehousing.

Storage Facilities

The **storage location decision** addresses how many distribution centers to have and where to locate them. The availability of facilities abroad will differ from the domestic situation. For example, while public storage is widely available in some countries, such facilities may be scarce or entirely lacking in others. Also, the standards and quality of facilities can vary widely. As a result, the storage decision of the firm is often accompanied by the need for large-scale, long-term investments. Despite the high cost, international storage facilities should be established if they support the overall logistics effort. In many markets, adequate storage facilities are imperative to satisfy customer demands and to compete successfully. For

STORAGE LOCATION DECISION

A decision concerning the number of facilities to establish and where they should be situated.

 # Quick Take *Keep It Green!*

From the outside, the intermodal steel container may not appear to be a very exciting piece of transportation equipment, but inside, some of them incorporate advanced technology that maintains the condition and value of the cargo. Such is the case of Maersk Sealand's "Fresh Mist" humidity-controlled refrigerated containers, designed to prevent dehydration of fresh produce during long ocean voyages. It does this by maintaining the moisture inside a refrigerated container at optimal levels, which keeps the produce fresh longer. The fresh produce arrives heavier and better looking, with a longer shelf life that commands a higher price in overseas markets.

Inside the container, sophisticated microprocessor technology atomizes water into minute particles and injects them into the air stream—maintaining optimal humidity levels without damage to the product packaging. In addition to including advanced technology in its shipping containers Maersk Line has also made efforts to use environmentally friendly resources when possible. Recently, it announced that it now has more than 10,000 containers made with bamboo flooring. According to Maersk Line, bamboo is a quick-growing grass that can be harvested every three to four years, and thereby it constitutes an environmental friendly alternative to the traditional wooden floorboards.

SOURCE: **http://www.maerskline.com**, accessed February 24, 2008.

example, because the establishment of a warehouse connotes a visible presence, a firm can convince local distributors and customers of its commitment to remain in the market for the long term.

Once the decision is made to use storage facilities abroad, the warehouse conditions must be carefully analyzed. As an example, in some countries warehouses have low ceilings. Packaging developed for the high stacking of products is therefore unnecessary or even counterproductive. In other countries, automated warehousing is available. Proper bar coding of products and the use of package dimensions acceptable to the warehousing system are basic requirements. In contrast, in warehouses that are still stocked manually, weight limitations will be of major concern. And if no forklift trucks are available, palletized delivery is of little use.

To optimize the logistics system, the logistician should analyze international product sales and then rank products according to warehousing needs. Products that are most sensitive to delivery time might be classified as "A" products. "A" products would be stocked in all distribution centers, and safety stock levels would be kept high. Alternatively, the storage of products can be more selective, if quick delivery by air can be guaranteed. Products for which immediate delivery is not urgent could be classified as "B" products. They would be stored only at selected distribution centers around the world. Finally, "C" products, for which there is little demand, would be·stocked only at headquarters. Should an urgent need for delivery arise, airfreight could again assure rapid shipment. Classifying products enables the international logistician to substantially reduce total international warehousing requirements and still maintain acceptable service levels.

Special Trade Zones

FOREIGN TRADE ZONES

Special areas where foreign goods may be held or processed without incurring duties and taxes.

Areas where foreign goods may be held or processed and then re-exported without incurring duties are called **foreign trade zones**. The zones can be found at major ports of entry and also at inland locations near major production facilities. For example, Kansas City, Missouri, has one of the largest U.S. foreign trade zones.

The existence of trade zones can be quite useful to the international firm. For example, in some countries, the benefits derived from lower labor costs may be offset by high duties and tariffs. As a result, location of manufacturing and storage facilities in these countries may prove uneconomical. Foreign trade zones are designed to exclude the impact of duties from the location decision. This is done by exempting merchandise in the foreign trade zone from duty payment. The international firm can therefore import merchandise; store it in the foreign trade zone; and process, alter, test, or demonstrate it—all without paying duties. If the merchandise is subsequently shipped abroad (that is, re-exported), no duty payments are ever due. Duty payments become due only if the merchandise is shipped into the country from the foreign trade zone.

Trade zones can also be useful as trans-shipment points to reduce logistics cost and redesign marketing approaches. For example, Audiovox was shipping small quantities of car alarms from a Taiwanese contract manufacturer directly to distributors in Chile. The shipments were costly, and the marketing strategy of requiring high minimum orders stopped distributors from buying. The firm resolved the dilemma by using a Miami trade zone to ship the alarms from Taiwan and consolidate the goods with other shipments to Chile. The savings in freight costs allowed the Chilean distributors to order whatever quantity they wanted and allowed the company to quote lower prices. As a result, sales improved markedly.[10]

All parties to the arrangement benefit from foreign trade zones. The government maintaining the trade zone achieves increased employment and investment. The firm using the trade zone obtains a spearhead in the foreign market without incurring all of the costs customarily associated with such an activity. As a result, goods can be reassembled, and large shipments can be broken down into smaller units. Also, goods can be repackaged when packaging weight becomes part of the duty assessment. Finally, goods can be given domestic "made-in" status if assembled in the foreign trade zone. Thus, duties may be payable only on the imported materials and component parts, rather than on the labor that is used to finish the product.

In addition to foreign trade zones, governments also have established export processing zones and special economic areas. **Export processing zones** usually provide tax- and duty-free treatment for production facilities whose output is destined abroad. The maquiladoras of Mexico, described in Chapter 5, are one example of a program that permits firms to take advantage of sharp differentials in labor costs. Firms can carry out the labor-intensive part of their operations in Mexico, while sourcing raw materials or component parts from other nations.

One country that has used trade zones very successfully for its own economic development is China. Through the creation of **special economic zones**, in which there are no tariffs, substantial tax incentives, and low prices for land and labor, the government has attracted many foreign investors, bringing in billions of dollars. The investors have brought new equipment, technology, and managerial know-how and have increased local economic prosperity.

For the logistician, the decision whether to use such zones mainly is framed by the overall benefit for the supply-chain system. Clearly, additional transport and retransport are required, warehousing facilities need to be constructed, and material handling frequency will increase. However, the costs may well be balanced by the preferential government treatment or by lower labor costs.

EXPORT PROCESSING ZONES

Special areas that provide tax- and duty-free treatment for production facilities whose output is destined abroad.

SPECIAL ECONOMIC ZONES

Special tariff-free areas where there are substantial tax incentives and low prices for land and labor to which the government hopes to attract foreign direct investment.

SUMMARY

As competitiveness becomes increasingly dependent on efficiency, global logistics and supply-chain management gain major importance. The supply chain is concerned with the flow of materials into, through, and out of the international corporation and therefore includes supplier and customer relationships, as well as materials management and physical distribution.

The logistician must recognize the total systems demands on the firm, its suppliers, and customers to develop trade-offs between various logistics components. By taking a supply-chain perspective, the manager can develop logistics systems that are supplier- and customer-focused and highly efficient. Implementation of such a system requires close collaboration between all members of the supply chain.

International logistics differs from domestic activities in that it deals with greater distances, new variables, and greater complexity because of national differences. One major factor to consider is transportation. The international manager needs to understand transportation infrastructures in other countries and the various modes of transportation. The choice among these modes will depend on the customer's demands and the firm's transit time, predictability, and cost requirements. In addition, non-economic factors, such as government regulations, weigh heavily in this decision.

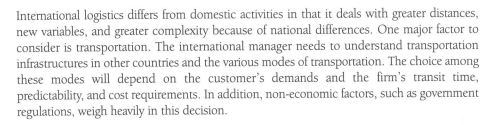

Inventory management is another major consideration. Inventories abroad are expensive to maintain, yet they are often crucial for international success. The logistician must evaluate requirements for order cycle times and customer service levels to develop a global inventory policy that can also serve as a strategic management tool.

 Global packaging is important because it ensures arrival of the merchandise at the ultimate destination in safe condition. In developing packaging, environmental conditions, such as climate and handling conditions, must be considered.

 The logistics manager must also deal with international storage issues and determine where to locate inventories. International warehouse space will have to be leased or purchased, and decisions will have to be made about utilizing foreign trade zones.

KEY TERMS AND CONCEPTS

supply chain	lighter aboard ship (LASH)	carriage paid to (CPT)
materials management	vessel	carriage and insurance paid to (CIP)
physical distribution	transit time	
systems concept	predictability	delivery duty paid (DDP)
total-cost concept	tracking	delivery duty unpaid (DDU)
trade-off concept	preferential policies	inventory carrying costs
supply-chain management	straight bill of lading	order cycle time
just-in-time inventory systems	shipper's order	electronic data interchange (EDI)
logistics platform	commercial invoice	
land bridge	incoterms	reverse logistics
sea bridge	ex-works (EXW)	storage location decision
intermodal movements	free carrier (FCA)	foreign trade zones
liner service	free alongside ship (FAS)	export processing zones
bulk service	free on board (FOB)	special economic zones
tramp service	cost and freight (CFR)	
roll-on-roll-off (RORO)	cost, insurance, and freight (CIF)	

REVIEW QUESTIONS

1. Explain the key aspects of supply-chain management.
2. In what ways does international transportation differ from domestic transportation?
3. Contrast the use of ocean shipping and airfreight.
4. Explain the meaning and impact of transit time in international logistics.
5. How and why do governments interfere in "rational" freight-carrier selection?
6. How can an international firm reduce its order cycle time?
7. What aspects of packaging influence the transportation decision?
8. What are special trade zones and how do they benefit global companies?

CRITICAL SKILL BUILDERS

1. Why should customer service levels differ internationally? For example, is it ethical to offer a lower customer service level in developing countries than in industrialized countries? Discuss in a debate format.
2. Choose a small or mid-size business in your area or one that you research on the Internet. Discuss ways in which the company may benefit by improving its supply chain. What recommendations would you make?

3. You work for a restaurant chain close to the Mexican border that receives requests for deliveries into Mexico. What steps can you take to fulfill those orders? What issues arise that do not also pertain to domestic sales?

4. You work for a company that makes educational toys and sells mainly to teachers but also directly to parents. In early September, you learn that, due to a pending longshoreman's strike in Los Angeles, your shipment, due to leave Singapore next month, is likely to be delayed. What steps can you take to cut down on your losses during one of your main selling seasons, the run-up to Christmas? Create a crisis action plan for the business.

ON THE WEB

1. What types of information are available to the exporter on the Transport Web? Go to **http://www.transportweb.com**, and give examples of transportation links that an exporter would find helpful and explain why.

2. Use an online database to select a freight forwarder. (Refer to **http://www.freightnet.com** or **http://www.forwarders.com**, directories of freight forwarders.)

3. When you first set up your web site featuring a designer line of specialty pens and stationery, you did not expect to receive orders from abroad. But from time to time, you receive orders from Europe, Australia, Canada, and Japan that you would like to fill. Create a plan for delivery of your products via airfreight. Check the web sites for UPS, FedEx, and Airborne Express to compare rates and find out more about making small, occasional shipments abroad. See **http://www.fedex.com**; **http://www.ups.com**; **http://www.airborne.com**.

ENDNOTES

1. Council of Supply Chain Management Professionals, **http://www.cscmp.org/website/aboutcscmp/ definitions/definitions.asp**, accessed February 14, 2008.

2. Accenture Global, **http://www.accenture.com.global/service/by_subject/supply_chain_mgmt/ client_successes/enhancedmanagement.htm**, accessed February 23, 2008.

3. David A. Ricks, *Blunders in International Business*, 3rd ed. (Malden, MA: Blackwell Publishing, Incorporated, 1999), p. 20.

4. Michael E. Porter, *The Competitive Advantage of Nations* (New York: The Free Press, 1990).

5. **www.iata.org**, accessed February 23, 2008.

6. International Chambers of Commerce, Incoterms 2000 (Paris: ICC Publishing, 2000).

7. Dennis Lord, "The Real Cost of Carrying Inventory," **http://www.imsconsulting.ca/article.php?name= highcost**, accessed April 24, 2008.

8. "Reverse Logistics: superior performance through focused resources commitments to information technology," **www.sciencedirect.com**, accessed February 23, 2008.

9. David A. Ricks, *Blunders in International Business*, 4th ed. (Malden, MA: Blackwell Publishing, Incorporated, 2006), p. 29.

10. Marita von Oldenborgh, "Power Logistics," *International Business*, October 1994, pp. 32–34.

CHAPTER 13

MANAGING GLOBALLY

Procter & Gamble: The New Global Organization

Globalization is at the heart of Procter & Gamble's corporate restructuring, code-named Organization 2005. Organization 2005 recognizes that there is a big difference between selling products in 140 countries around the world and truly planning and managing lines of business on a global basis. There are five key elements to the changes:

1. *Global business units.* P&G moved from business units driven by geography to three business units (Beauty, Global Health and Wellbeing, and Household Care) based on product lines. This drives innovation by centering strategy and profit responsibility globally on brands rather than on geographics.
2. *Market development organizations.* The company established seven MDO regions that tailor global programs to local markets and develop marketing strategies to build P&G's entire business, based on superior local-consumer and customer knowledge.
3. *Global business services.* GBS brings together business activities such as accounting, human resource systems, order management, and information technology into a single global organization, to provide these services to all P&G business units at best-in-class quality, cost, and speed. They are located in the Americas (San Jose, Costa Rica); Europe (Newcastle, UK); the Middle East; Africa; and Asia (Manila, Philippines).
4. *Corporate functions.* P&G has redefined the role of corporate staff. Most have moved into new business units, with the remaining staff refocused on developing cutting-edge new knowledge and serving corporate needs. In addition, 54 "change agents" have been assigned to work across the seven MDOs to lead cultural and business change by helping teams work together more effectively through greater use of information technology (IT), in particular, real-time collaboration tools.
5. *Culture.* Changes to P&G's culture should create an environment that produces bolder, mind-stretching goals and plans; bigger innovations; and greater speed. For example, the reward system has been redesigned to better link executive compensation with new business goals and results.

A good example of the increased use of collaborative technology is a product called Swiffer, a dust sweeper with disposable cloths electrostatically charged to attract dust and dirt. Swiffer represents collaboration among multiple P&G product groups, including paper and chemicals. The product

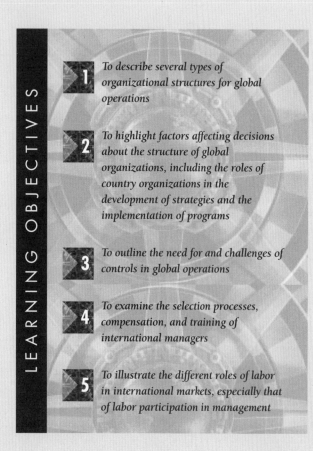

LEARNING OBJECTIVES

1 To describe several types of organizational structures for global operations

2 To highlight factors affecting decisions about the structure of global organizations, including the roles of country organizations in the development of strategies and the implementation of programs

3 To outline the need for and challenges of controls in global operations

4 To examine the selection processes, compensation, and training of international managers

5 To illustrate the different roles of labor in international markets, especially that of labor participation in management

took just 18 months from test market to global availability. In the past, this might have taken years, because management in each region was responsible for the product's launch in his or her geography. Collaborative technologies, including chat rooms on the company's intranet, are transforming the company's conservative culture to one that encourages employees to be candid, test boundaries, and take chances.

Not all has gone well with the planned changes, however. The biggest oversight was the level of personal upheaval that changes would demand of employees. More than half of P&G's executives are in new jobs. Physical transfers were significant as well; for example, about 1,000 people were moved to Geneva from around Europe and another 200 to Singapore from different Asian locations. Furthermore, the changed reporting structures raised concerns. Food and beverages managers, who are mostly in Cincinnati, Ohio, report to a president in Caracas, Venezuela, while everyone

in laundry and household cleaners reports to Brussels in Belgium. Personnel transferred from MDOs suddenly had no brands to manage and had to think across borders. The change from a U.S.-centric company to a globally thinking one was a substantial demand for personnel in a short period of time; the timetable of the process has subsequently been re-evaluated.[1]

As You Read This Chapter

1. How well does P&G's new structure meet the needs of a global organization? Does it serve as a model for all firms that plan to go global?
2. Consider the opportunities and drawbacks of major organizational upheavals. Is the change really necessary?

As companies evolve from purely domestic to multinational, their organizational structure and control systems must change to reflect new strategies. With growth comes diversity, in terms of products and services, geographic markets, and people in the company itself, creating a new set of challenges for the company. Two critical issues are basic to all of these challenges: (1) developing the type of organization that provides the best possible framework for developing worldwide strategies, while at the same time maintaining flexibility with respect to individual markets and operations; and (2) determining the type and degree of control to be exercised from headquarters to maximize effectiveness. Organizational structures, an organization's ability to implement strategies and control systems, have to be adjusted as market conditions change, as seen in the chapter's opening vignette.

This chapter focuses on the advantages and disadvantages of various organizational structures and their control systems, as well as their appropriateness at different stages of globalization. The chapter goes on to explain the complexities of selecting, compensating, and managing a globally dispersed workforce. The overall objective is to understand the intraorganizational relationships critical to a firm's attempt to optimize its competitiveness on a global scale.

ORGANIZATIONAL STRUCTURE

The basic functions of an organization are to provide: (1) a route and locus of decision-making and coordination and (2) a system for reporting and communications. Authority and communication networks are typically depicted in the organizational chart.

LEARNING OBJECTIVE

The basic configurations of global organizations correspond to those of purely domestic ones; the greater the degree of internalization, the more complex the structures can become. The types of structures that companies use to manage foreign activities can be divided into three categories, as shown in Table 13.1.

TABLE 13.1 How an Organization's Structure Changes as It Becomes More Involved in
Global Business Activities

DEGREE OF COMPANY GLOBALIZATION	UNIT TYPICALLY RESPONSIBLE	TYPICAL TITLE OF UNIT MANAGER
1. Occasional export order	Domestic sales department	Domestic sales manager
2. Increasing volume of foreign sales	Newly-formed unit—export sales department	Manager/director—export sales
3. Major corporate effort to extend reach into foreign markets	International division (may involve some joint ventures or direct foreign investment)	Vice president
4. Total corporate commitment to conduct operations on a global basis	Wholly owned foreign subsidiaries; joint ventures, and/or other forms of interfirm cooperation	Senior vice president

Stage 1—Little or No Formal Organization

In the early stages of global involvement, domestic operations assume responsibility for
international activities. Transactions are conducted on a case-by-case basis, either by the
resident expert or with the help of facilitating agents, such as freight forwarders. As demand
from the international marketplace grows and interest within the firm expands, the organizational structure will reflect it. As shown in Figure 13.1, an export department appears as a
separate entity. Organizationally, the department may be a subset of marketing (alternative b
in Figure 13.1) or may have equal ranking with the various functional departments
(alternative a). The choice will depend on the importance the firm assigns to overseas
activities. Because establishing the export department is the first real step toward internationalization, it should be a full-fledged marketing function and should not be limited to sales.

The more the firm becomes involved in foreign markets, the more quickly the export
department structure will become obsolete. For example, the firm may undertake joint ventures
or direct foreign investment, which require those involved to have functional experience. The
firm therefore typically establishes an international division.

FIGURE 13.1   The Export Department Structure

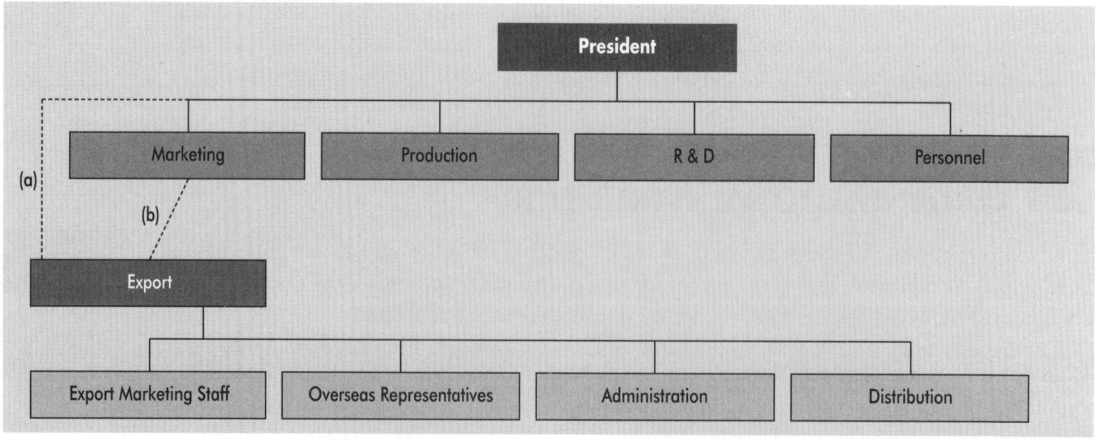

Stage 2—The International Division

The international division centralizes all of the responsibility for global activities, as illustrated in Figure 13.2. The approach aims to eliminate a possible bias against global operations that may exist if domestic divisions are allowed to serve international customers independently. The international division concentrates international expertise, information flows concerning foreign market opportunities, and authority over international activities. However, manufacturing and other related functions remain with the domestic divisions to take advantage of economies of scale.

To avoid putting the international division at a disadvantage in competing for products, personnel, and corporate services, coordination between domestic and global operations is necessary. Coordination can be achieved through a joint staff or by requiring domestic and international divisions to interact in strategic planning.

Companies may outgrow their international divisions as their sales outside of the domestic market grow in significance, diversity, and complexity. European companies have traditionally used international divisions far less than their U.S. counterparts, because of the relatively small size of their domestic markets. Philips, Nestlé, or Nokia, for example, would never have grown to their current prominence by relying on their home markets alone. Globalization of markets and the narrowing ratio between domestic and international sales make international divisions increasingly less appropriate.

Stage 3—The Global Organization

Global structures have grown out of competitive necessity. In many industries, competition is on a global basis, with a result that companies must have a high degree of reactive capability.

TYPES OF GLOBAL STRUCTURES Six basic types of global structures are available:

1. Global product structure, in which product divisions are responsible for all manufacture and marketing worldwide
2. Global area structure, in which geographic divisions are responsible for all manufacture and marketing in their respective areas

> ## Fast Facts
>
> **What are the most livable cities in the world for expatriates?**
>
> A 2007 study from Mercer, a leading human resources consulting firm, listed Switzerland's main commercial and cultural center, Zurich, as the best of 215 cities considered globally, followed by Geneva, Vancouver, and Vienna. In the Asia-Pacific region, Auckland, New Zealand (5), led the pack, while Sydney (9) cracked the top 10. Meanwhile, in North America, Canadian cities such as Toronto and Ottawa fared better than U.S. ones, of which Honolulu (27) performed best. The hardest of the hardship postings: Brazzaville, the capital city of the Republic of the Congo (214), and Baghdad (215).

FIGURE 13.2   The International Division Structure

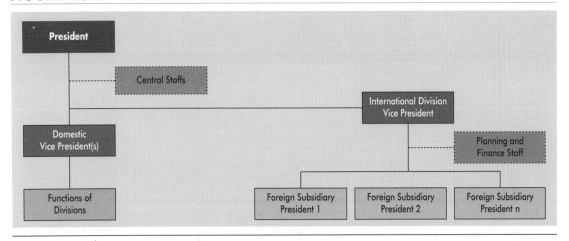

3. Global functional structure, in which functional areas (such as production, marketing, finance, and personnel) are responsible for the worldwide operations of their own functional area
4. Global customer structure, in which operations are structured based on distinct worldwide customer groups
5. Mixed—or hybrid—structure, which may combine the other alternatives
6. Matrix structure, in which operations have reporting responsibility to more than one group (typically, product, functions, or area)

GLOBAL PRODUCT STRUCTURE

An organizational structure in which product divisions are responsible for all global activity.

Global Product Structure A **global product structure** gives worldwide responsibility to strategic business units for the marketing of their product lines, as shown in Figure 13.3. Most consumer-product firms use some form of this approach, mainly because of the diversity of their offerings. One of the major benefits is improved cost efficiency through centralization of manufacturing facilities. This is crucial in industries in which competitive position is determined by world market share, which in turn is often determined by the degree to which manufacturing is rationalized. Adaptation to this approach may cause problems, because it is usually accompanied by consolidation of operations and plant closings. Black & Decker rationalized many of its operations in its worldwide competitive effort against Makita, the Japanese power-tool manufacturer. In a similar move, Ford merged its large and culturally distinct European and North American auto operations by vehicle platform type to make more efficient use of its engineering and product development resources against global rivals.[2]

Other benefits of the product structure are the ability to balance the functional inputs needed for a product and the ability to react quickly to product-specific problems in the marketplace. Product-specific attention is important, because products vary in terms of the adaptation they need for different foreign markets. A product structure means that even

Quick Take *Beyond Organizational Structures*

Royal Philips Electronics of the Netherlands is one of the world's biggest electronics companies, as well as the largest in Europe, with 128,100 employees in more than 60 countries and sales in 2006 of $34 billion. In the past 60 years, it has gone through major phases of changes in its organizational structure.

In the last years, changes have been made that are not necessarily evident in organization charts. For example, a chief marketing officer has been appointed to help counter criticism of technology and new-product bias at the expense of customer orientation. Under an initiative called "One Philips," the company has introduced a number of low-key changes. Employees are encouraged to work on cross-cultural and cross-functional teams. New awards have been instituted

for employees who have created value for the company by collaborating with others outside of their immediate units. Transfers across geographic entities as well as product units are expected as an explicit requirement for advancement. Top executives at Philips have argued that up to 80 percent of the desired changes will come about through readjustment of attitudes, the rest from using appropriate incentives, most of them not directly monetary. To accelerate these changes, Philips brought together its top 1,000 managers for a series of workshops designed to find ways to cut through organizational barriers.

SOURCE: "The Matrix Master," *The Economist*, January 21, 2006, 4; See also **www.philips.com**.

FIGURE 13.3   The Global Product Structure

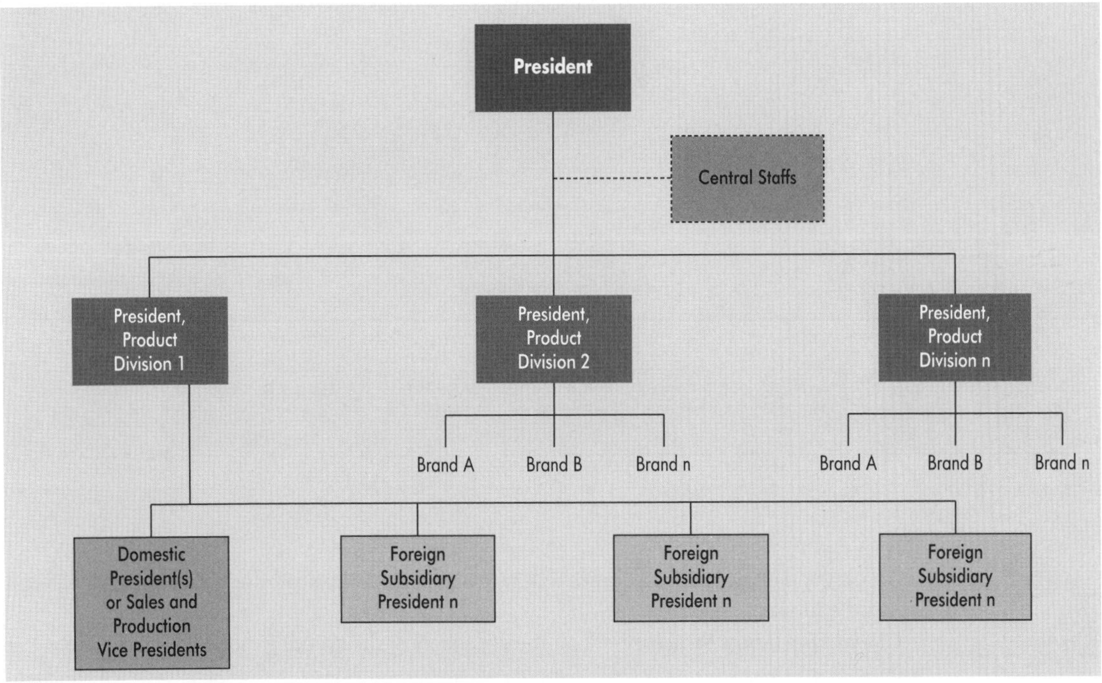

smaller brands receive individual attention. All in all, the product approach is ideally suited to the development of a global strategic focus in response to global competition.

At the same time, the product structure fragments global expertise within the firm, because a central pool of international experience no longer exists. The structure assumes that managers will have adequate regional experience or advice to allow them to make balanced decisions. Coordination of activities among the various product groups operating in the same markets is crucial to avoid unnecessary duplication of basic tasks. For some of these tasks, such as market research, special staff functions may be created and then filled by the product divisions when needed. If they lack an appreciation for the global dimension, product managers may focus their attention only on the larger markets or only on the domestic markets and fail to take the broader, long-term view.

Global Area Structure   Firms that adopt a **global area structure**, as illustrated in Figure 13.4, are organized on the basis of geographical regions; for example, operations may be divided into those dealing with North America, the Far East, Latin America, and Europe. Central staffs are responsible for providing coordination and support for worldwide planning and control activities.

Integration of trade zones has increased the attractiveness of area structures. For example, with the integration of European markets, many multinational corporations relocated their European headquarters to Brussels, where the EU is based. Similarly, especially since NAFTA, a U.S. headquarters is often the power center for the Americas. Cultural similarity also favors the establishment of an area structure. In some cases, historical connections between countries lead companies to choose this type of structure, combining, for example, Europe with the Middle East and Africa.

The area approach follows the marketing concept most closely because it allows for concentrated attention on individual areas and markets. If market conditions vary dramatically with respect to product acceptance and operating conditions, an area structure is appropriate.

GLOBAL AREA STRUCTURE

An organizational structure in which geographic divisions are responsible for all global activity.

FIGURE 13.4   The Global Area Structure

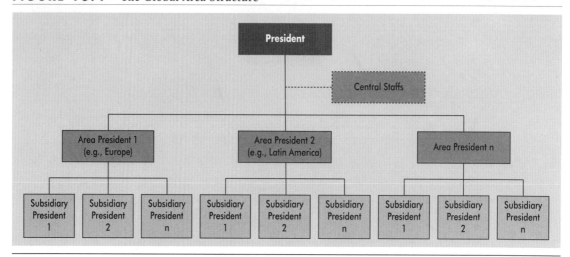

GLOBAL FUNCTIONAL STRUCTURE

An organizational structure in which departments are formed on the basis of functional areas, such as production, marketing, and finance.

PROCESS STRUCTURE

A variation of the functional structure in which departments are formed on the basis of production processes.

GLOBAL CUSTOMER STRUCTURE

An organizational structure in which divisions are formed on the basis of customer groups.

MIXED STRUCTURE

An organizational structure that combines two or more organizational dimensions; for example, products, areas, or functions.

It is also a good choice for companies that have relatively narrow product lines with similar end uses and end users.

Global Functional Structure Of all the approaches, the **global functional structure** is the simplest from the administrative viewpoint because it emphasizes the basic tasks of the firm, such as manufacturing, sales, and research and development. The approach, illustrated in Figure 13.5, works best when both products and customers are relatively few and similar in nature. Coordination is typically the key problem, which is why many companies create staff functions to interact between the functional areas.

A variation of the functional approach is one that uses processes as a basis for structure. The **process structure** is common in the energy and mining industries, where one corporate entity may be in charge of exploration worldwide and another may be responsible for the actual mining operations.

Global Customer Structure Firms may also organize their operations using the **global customer structure**, especially if the customer groups they serve are dramatically different— for example, consumers, businesses, and governments. Catering to such diverse groups may require concentrating specialists in particular divisions. The product may be the same, but the buying processes of the various customer groups may differ. Governmental buying, for example, is characterized by bidding, in which price plays a larger role than when businesses are the buyers.

Mixed Structure A **mixed structure**—or hybrid structure—combines two or more organizational dimensions simultaneously. It permits adequate attention to product, area, or functional needs, as needed. A mixed structure may only be the result of a transitional period after a merger or an acquisition, or it may come about because of unique market characteristics or product line. It may also provide a useful structure before the implementation of a worldwide matrix structure, which will be discussed next.

Naturally, organizational structures are never as clear-cut and simple as presented here. Whatever the basic format may be, product, functional, and area inputs are needed. Alternatives could include an initial product structure that would subsequently have regional groupings or an initial regional structure with subsequent product groupings. However, in the long term, coordination and control across such structures can become tedious.

Matrix Structure In order to facilitate planning for, organizing, and controlling interdependent businesses, critical resources, strategies, and geographic regions, many multi-

FIGURE 13.5   The Global Functional Structure

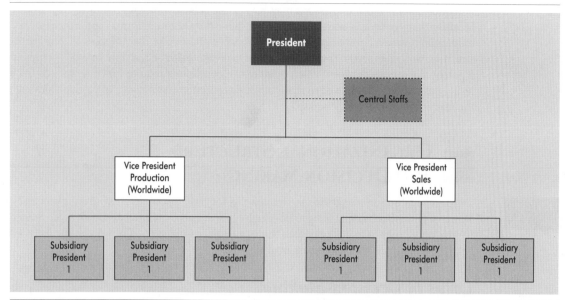

nationals have adopted the **matrix structure**. Organizational matrices integrate the various approaches already discussed. Philips, for example, has seven product divisions (which are then divided into 60 product groups) that manufacture products for continent-wide regions, rather than individual markets. Philips has three general types of country organizations. In "key" markets, such as the United States, France, and Japan, product divisions manage their own marketing, as well as manufacturing. In "local business" countries, such as Nigeria and Peru, the organizations function as importers from product divisions, and if manufacturing occurs, it is purely for the local market. In "large" markets, such as Brazil, Spain, and Taiwan, a hybrid arrangement is used, depending on the size of the company and economic situation. The product divisions and the national subsidiaries interact in a matrix-like configuration, with the product divisions responsible for the globalization dimension and the national sub-sidiaries responsible for local representation and coordination of common areas of interest, such as recruiting.

Matrices vary in terms of their number of dimensions. For example, Dow Chemical's three-dimensional matrix consists of five geographic areas, three major functions (marketing, manufacturing, and research), and more than 70 products. The matrix approach helps cut through enormous organizational complexities by ensuring cooperation among business managers, functional managers, and strategy managers.

A significant problem with a matrix structure arises from the fact that every management unit may have a multidimensional reporting relationship, which may cross functional, regional, or operational lines. Because of the dual, or even multiple, reporting channels, conflicts are

MATRIX STRUCTURE

An organizational structure that uses functional and divisional structures simultaneously.

Culture Clues   As new markets emerge, they may be first be delegated to an established country organization for guidance with the ultimate objective of having them be equal partners with others in the organization. When Estonia regained its independence and started its transformation to a market economy, many companies assigned their country organization in Finland the responsibility of the Estonian unit's development. In Latvia's case, the Swedish country organization got the job. Since then, the development of new markets such as the "Stans" (e.g., Tajikistan and Uzbekistan) has been delegated to country organizations in Russia and Turkey.

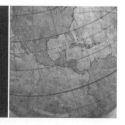

likely to erupt. Furthermore, complex issues are forced into a two-dimensional decision framework, and even minor issues may have to be solved through committee discussion. Ideally, managers should solve the problems themselves through formal and informal communication; however, physical and cultural distance often make that impossible. The matrix structure, with its inherent complexity, may actually increase the reaction time of a company, a potentially serious problem when competitive conditions require quick responses. As a result, the authority has started to shift, in many organizations, from area to product, although the matrix still may officially be used.

ORGANIZATIONAL STRUCTURE AND DECISION-MAKING

2 LEARNING OBJECTIVE

Organizational structures provide the frameworks for carrying out decision-making processes. However, for that decision-making to be effective, a series of organizational initiatives are needed to develop strategy to its full potential, that is, to ensure implementation of strategy decisions both at the national level and across markets.

Locus of Decision-Making

Organizational structures, by themselves, do not indicate where the authority for decision-making and control rests within the organization, nor do they reveal the level of coordination between units. If subsidiaries are granted a high degree of autonomy, the decision-making system at work is called **decentralization**. In decentralized systems, controls are relatively loose and simple, and the flows between headquarters and subsidiaries are mainly financial; that is, each subsidiary operates as a profit center. On the other hand, if controls are tight and the strategic decision-making is concentrated at headquarters, the decision-making system is described as **centralization**. Typically, firms are neither completely centralized nor decentralized; for example, some functions—such as finance—lend themselves to more centralized decision-making; others—such as promotional decisions—do so far less. Research and development in organizations is typically centralized, especially in cases of basic research work. Some companies have added R&D functions on a regional or local basis, partly because of governmental pressures.

The advantage of allowing maximum flexibility at the country-market level is that subsidiary management knows its market and can react to changes more quickly. Problems of motivation and acceptance are avoided when decision-makers are also the implementers of the strategy. On the other hand, many multinationals faced with global competitive threats and opportunities have adopted global strategy formulation, which, by definition, requires a higher degree of centralization. What has emerged as a result can be called **coordinated decentralization**. This means that overall corporate strategy is provided from headquarters, while subsidiaries are free to implement it within the range agreed upon in consultation between headquarters and the subsidiaries.

Factors Affecting Structure and Decision-Making

The organizational structure and locus of decision-making in a multinational corporation are determined by a number of factors, such as: (1) its degree of involvement in international operations, (2) the products the firm markets, (3) the size and importance of the firm's markets, and (4) the human resource capability of the firm.

The effect of the degree of involvement on structure and decision-making was discussed previously. With low degrees of involvement, subsidiaries can enjoy high degrees of autonomy,

DECENTRALIZATION

The granting of a high degree of autonomy to subsidiaries.

CENTRALIZATION

The concentrating of control and strategic decision-making at headquarters.

COORDINATED DECENTRALIZATION

The provision of an overall corporate strategy by headquarters, while granting subsidiaries the freedom to implement their own corporate strategies within established ranges.

WORLD VIEW

KNOWLEDGE ACROSS BOUNDARIES

There are three broad approaches to knowledge management. One is to create a system where all information goes to everybody, which is hugely inefficient; the second tells people what others think they need to know, which may not match their real needs; and the third enables them to find for themselves whatever they want to know. Spurred by competitive pressures, global knowledge networks enable multinationals to share information and best practices across geographically dispersed units and time zones. Corporations save millions of dollars each year as a result of the up-to-the-minute knowledge transfer and feedback that such networks allow. In addition, the bonds that develop between employees in locations scattered around the globe are instrumental in achieving global objectives.

Whether the goal is customer loyalty, increased production efficiency, or retention of skilled employees, a knowledge-sharing network focused on improvement of operational practices worldwide helps multinationals meet the challenge of building a cohesive, global, corporate culture.

Ford Motor Company has established 25 "communities of practice" organized around functions. For example, painters in every assembly plant around the world belong to the same community of practice. If local employees find a better way of conducting any of the 60-plus steps involved in painting, a template for that improvement is disseminated to all plants, where the process can be replicated. In the last five years, Ford has discovered a total of 8,000 better ways of doing business through its Best Practices Replication Plan, saving more than $886 million in operating efficiencies.

Eureka, a knowledge-sharing system at Xerox, saves the company between $25 million and $125 million a year, depending on how the numbers are tallied. The system connects service technicians around the world, who provide information and, more importantly, feedback intended to improve Xerox's electronic product documentation.

Eureka has evolved into an easy-access, problem-solving database, with more than 30,000 tips submitted by technicians in every country in which Xerox operates. The success of Eureka inspired Xerox to create knowledge-sharing systems to benefit other operational functions: Focus 500 allows the companies' top 500 executives to share information on their interactions with customers and industry partners; Project Library details costs, resources, and cycle times of more than 2,000 projects, a vital resource in improving Six Sigma quality in project management; and PROFIT allows salespeople to submit hot selling tips—with cash incentives for doing so.

A recent merger between energy giants Texaco and Chevron represented an opportunity to integrate global knowledge networks. Active in nearly 180 countries, ChevronTexaco expects to leverage its knowledge systems into millions of dollars in cost savings. The company's information technology-enabled infrastructure allows scientists across the globe to work in virtual teams. More than 50,000 employees share platforms for every business process and communication, allowing real-time interactions among global workforces.

SOURCES: "Thinking for a Living," *The Economist*, January 21, 2006, pp. 9-12; Louise Lee, "The Other Instant Powerhouse in Energy Trading," *BusinessWeek*, November 26, 2001; Kristine Ellis, "Sharing Best Practices Globally," *Training*, July 2001; **http://www.chevrontexaco.com**.

---

as long as they meet their profit targets. The firm's country of origin and political history can affect their degree of involvement in global operations. For example, Swiss-based Nestlé, with only 3 to 4 percent of its sales from its small domestic market, has traditionally had a highly decentralized organization. Increasingly, companies do not want constituents to think they are from anywhere in particular or want to be perceived as having a home base in each of the markets where they operate. For example, Lenovo's main corporate functions are divided between Beijing, Singapore, and Raleigh, North Carolina.[3]

The type and variety of products marketed affects organizational decisions. Companies that market consumer products typically have product organizations with high degrees of decentralization, allowing for maximum local flexibility. On the other hand, companies that market technologically sophisticated products—such as GE, which markets turbines—display centralized organizations with worldwide product responsibilities. Even within matrix organizations, one of the dimensions may be granted more say in decisions; for example, at Dow Chemical, geographical managers have been granted more authority than other managers.

Size of markets matters too. For many firms, going global has meant transferring world headquarters of important business units abroad. European pharmaceuticals giant Novartis, for example, moved its research hub from Switzerland to the United States, the world's largest and most lucrative pharmaceuticals market. In recent years, several other major drug manufacturers have made similar strategic decisions, including Aventis (from France) and Pharmacia (from Sweden).[4]

The human factor in any organization is critical. Managers at both headquarters and the country organizations must bridge the physical and cultural distances separating them. If country organizations have competent managers who rarely need to consult headquarters about their challenges, they may be granted high degrees of autonomy. In the case of global organizations, local management must understand overall corporate goals, in that decisions that meet the long-term objectives may not be optimal for the individual local market.

Global Networks

No international structure is perfect, and many have challenged the wisdom of even looking for an ideal structure. Instead, they have recommended attention to new processes that would, within a given structure, help to develop new perspectives and attitudes that reflect and respond to the complex, opposing demands of global integration and local responsiveness.[5] The question thus changes from which structural alternative is best to how the different perspectives of various corporate entities can better be taken into account when making decisions. In structural terms, nothing may change. As a matter of fact, Philips has not changed its basic matrix structure, yet major changes have occurred in internal relations. The basic change was from a decentralized federation model to a networked global organization, the effects of which are depicted in Figure 13.6. The term "glocal" has been coined to describe this approach.[6]

Companies that have adopted the glocal approach have incorporated the following three dimensions into their organizations: (1) the development and communication of a clear corporate vision, (2) the effective management of human resource tools to broaden individual perspectives and develop identification with corporate goals, and (3) the integration of individual thinking and activities into the broad corporate agenda.[7] The first dimension relates to a clear and consistent long-term corporate mission that guides individuals wherever they work in the organization. Examples of this are Johnson & Johnson's corporate credo of customer focus and NEC's C&C (computers and communications). The second relates both to the development of global managers who can find opportunities in spite of environmental challenges, as well as creation of a global perspective among country managers. The third dimension relates to the development of a cooperative mind-set among country organizations to ensure effective implementation of global strategies. Managers may believe that global strategies are intrusions on their operations if they do not have an understanding of the corporate vision, have not contributed to the global corporate agenda, or are not given direct responsibility for its implementation. Defensive, territorial attitudes can lead to the emergence of the **not-invented-here syndrome**, that is, country organizations objecting to or rejecting an otherwise sound strategy.

The network avoids the problems of effort duplication, inefficiency, and resistance to ideas developed elsewhere by giving subsidiaries the latitude, encouragement, and tools to pursue local business development within the framework of the global strategy. Headquarters considers each unit a source of ideas, skills, capabilities, and knowledge that can be utilized for the benefit of the entire organization. This means that subsidiaries must be upgraded from

NOT-INVENTED-HERE SYNDROME

A defensive, territorial attitude that, if held by managers, can frustrate effective implementation of global strategies.

FIGURE 13.6   The Global Functional Structure

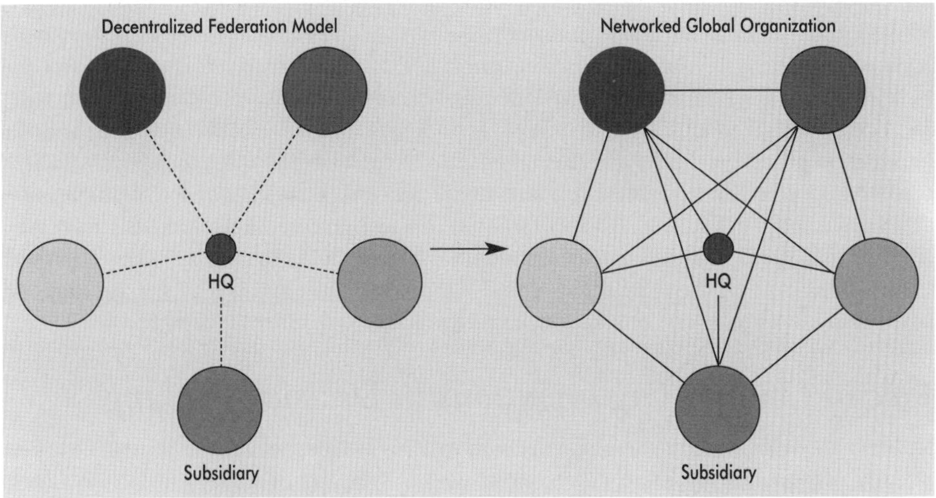

SOURCE: Thomas Gross, Ernie Turner, and Lars Cederholm, "Building Teams for Global Operations," *Management Review*, June 1987 (New York: American Management Association), p. 34.

mere implementers and adaptors to contributors and partners in the development and execution of worldwide strategies. Efficient plants may be converted into international production centers, innovative R&D units that are centers of excellence (and thus role models), and leading subsidiary groups given the leadership role in developing new strategies for the entire corporation.

Promoting Internal Cooperation

The global business entity in today's environment can be successful only if it is able to move intellectual capital within the organization; that is, to take ideas and move them around faster and faster.

One of the tools is teaching. For example, Jack Welch, former CEO of GE, coined the term "boundarylessness" to mean that people are allowed to act without regard to status or functional loyalty and can look for better ideas from anywhere. Top leadership of GE spend considerable time at their training centers interacting with up-and-comers from all over the company. Each training class is given a real, current company problem to solve, and the reports can be career makers (or breakers). When GE launched a massive effort to embrace e-commerce, many managers found that they knew little about the Internet. Following a London-based manager's idea to have an Internet mentor, GE now encourages all managers to work with such a mentor during training for a period of time each week.[8]

Another method to promote internal cooperation for global strategy implementation is the use of global teams or councils. In the case of a new product, an international team of managers may be assembled to develop strategy. Both Procter & Gamble and Henkel have successfully introduced pan-European brands using a strategy that was developed by European teams. On a broader and longer-term basis, companies use councils to share best practices— for example, ideas that may have saved money or time or a process that is more efficient than an existing one.

The term "network" also implies two-way communications between headquarters and subsidiaries and between subsidiaries themselves. While this communication can take the form of newsletters or regular and periodic meetings of appropriate personnel, new technologies are allowing businesses to link far-flung entities and eliminate the traditional barriers of time and distance. **Intranets** integrate a company's information assets into a single accessible system using Internet-based technologies, such as e-mail, news groups, and the web. In effect, the formation of **virtual teams** becomes a reality. The benefits of intranet are: (1) increased productivity so that there is no longer a time lag between an idea and the information needed to assess and implement it; (2) enhanced knowledge capital, which is constantly updated and upgraded; (3) facilitated teamwork, enabling online communication at insignificant expense; and (4) incorporation of best practice at a moment's notice by allowing managers and functional-area personnel to make to-the-minute decisions anywhere in the world. As all these examples show, the networked approach is not a structural adaptation but a procedural one, calling for a change in management mentality.

Role of Country Organizations in Decision-Making

Rather than making them a part of the decision-making process, headquarters quite often sees country organizations as merely the coordinators or adapters of strategy in local markets. Furthermore, they often view all country organizations as the same, despite their unique characteristics, or even their levels of sales. This view severely limits utilization of the firm's resources and deprives country managers of the opportunity to exercise creativity.

The role that a particular country organization can play naturally depends on that market's overall strategic importance, as well as its organizational competence. The role of a **strategic leader** can be played by a highly competent national subsidiary located in a strategically critical market. A strategic leader serves as a partner to headquarters in developing and implementing strategy. For example, strategic leader markets may have products designed specifically to cater to their needs. Nissan's Z-cars have been traditionally designated for the U.S. market, starting with the 240Z in the 1970s to the latest 350Z introduced in 2002. Design work for the Z-cars takes place in La Jolla, California.[9]

A **contributor** is a country organization with a distinctive competence, such as product development. Increasingly, country organizations are the source of new products. These range from IBM's breakthrough in superconductivity research, generated in its Zurich lab, to low-end innovations, such as Procter & Gamble's liquid Tide, made with a fabric-softening compound developed in Europe. Similarly, country organizations may be designated as worldwide centers of excellence for a particular product category, such as ABB Strömberg in Finland for its electric drives, for which it is a recognized world leader. For products or technologies with multiple applications, leadership may be divided among different country operations. For example, DuPont's global brand manager for Lycra delegates responsibility for each different application of the product to managers in a country where the application is strongest, for example, Brazil for swimwear and France for fashion.[10] **Implementers** provide the critical mass for the global effort. These country organizations may exist in smaller, less-developed countries in which there is less corporate commitment for market development. Although most entities are given this role, it should not be slighted, because the implementers provide the opportunity to capture economies of scale and scope that are the basis of a global strategy.

Culture Clues Virtual team members find it difficult to prevent the workplace from intruding on private life. Managers feel that they are stretching their workdays in order to have meetings in other time zones. However, managers who can navigate these challenges are rewarded with being able to work with the highest and most motivated professionals.

Depending on the role of the country organization, its relationship with headquarters will vary, from loose control, based mostly on support, to tighter control to ensure that strategies get implemented appropriately. Yet, in each of these cases, it is imperative that country organizations have enough operating independence to cater to local needs and to provide motivation to country managers. Further, country organizations are a principal means by which global companies can tap into new opportunities in markets around the world.

CONTROLS

Within an organization, controls serve as an integrating mechanism. They are designed to reduce uncertainty, increase predictability, and ensure that behaviors originating in separate parts of the organization are compatible and in support of common organizational goals despite physical, cultural, and temporal distances.

Types of Controls

Table 13.2 provides a brief overview of the types of control and their objectives. Control can be viewed in two ways: the control of output and the control of behavior. **Output controls** include balance sheets, sales data, production data, product-line growth, and performance reviews of personnel. All these make output easy to measure and compare. **Behavioral controls** require the exertion of influence over behavior after—or, ideally, before—it leads to action. Behavioral controls are qualitative rather than quantitative and can be achieved through the preparation of manuals on such topics as sales techniques, to be made available to subsidiary personnel, or through efforts to fit new employees into the corporate culture. Corporations rarely use one pure control mechanism. Rather, most use both quantitative and qualitative measures, placing different levels of emphasis on different types of performance measures and on how they are derived.

OUTPUT CONTROLS

Organizational controls, such as balance sheets, sales data, production data, product-line growth, and performance reviews of personnel.

BEHAVIORAL CONTROLS

Organizational controls that involve influencing how activities are conducted.

Bureaucratic/Formalized Control

The elements of a bureaucratic/formalized control system are: (1) an international budget and planning system, (2) the functional reporting system, and (3) policy manuals used to direct functional performance.

Budgets refers to shorter-term guidelines regarding investment, cash, and personnel policies, while *plans* refers to formalized plans with more than a one-year horizon. The budget and planning process is the major control instrument in headquarters-subsidiary relationships. It has four main purposes: (1) allocation of funds among subsidiaries; (2) planning and

TABLE 13.2 Comparison of Bureaucratic and Cultural Control Mechanisms

| | TYPE OF CONTROL | |
OBJECT OF CONTROL	PURE BUREAUCRATIC/ FORMALIZED CONTROL	PURE CULTURAL CONTROL
Output	Formal performance reports	Shared norms of performance
Behavior	Company policies, manuals	Shared philosophy of management

SOURCE: B.R. Baliga and Alfred M. Jaeger, "Multinational Corporations: Control Systems and Delegation Issues," *Journal of International Business Studies* 15 (Fall 1984): pp. 25–40.

coordination of global production capacity and supplies; (3) evaluation of subsidiary performance; and (4) communication and information exchange among subsidiaries, product organizations, and corporate headquarters.

Functional reports are another control instrument used by headquarters in managing subsidiary relations. These vary in number, complexity, and frequency. Typically, the structure and elements of the reports are highly standardized, to allow for consolidation at the headquarters level. Since the frequency of reports required from subsidiaries is likely to increase because of globalization, it is essential that subsidiaries see the rationale for the often-time-consuming exercise. Two approaches, used in tandem, can facilitate the process: participation and feedback.

On the behavioral front, headquarters may want to guide the way in which subsidiaries make decisions and implement agreed-upon strategies. U.S.-based multinationals tend to be far more formalized than their Japanese and European counterparts, with a heavy reliance on policy manuals for all major functions. Manuals cover such topics as recruitment, training, motivation, and dismissal policies.

Cultural Control

An alternative to bureaucratic control is seen in the organization that emphasizes corporate values and culture, with evaluations based on the extent to which an individual or entity fits in with the norms. Cultural controls require an extensive socialization process to which informal, personal interaction is central. Substantial resources have to be spent to train the individual to share the corporate culture, or "the way things are done at the company." To build common vision and values, managers spend a substantial share of their first months at Matsushita in what the company calls "cultural and spiritual training." Although more prevalent in Japanese organizations, many Western entities have similar programs, such as Philips' "organization cohesion training" and Unilever's "indoctrination."

In selecting home-country nationals and, to some extent, third-country nationals, global companies are exercising cultural control. The assumption is that the managers have already internalized the norms and values of the company, and they tend to run a country organization with a more global view. In some cases, the use of headquarters personnel to ensure uniformity in decision-making may be advisable; for example, Volvo uses a home-country national for the position of chief financial officer. Expatriates are used in subsidiaries, not only for control purposes but also to effect change processes.

Management training programs for overseas managers, as well as time spent at headquarters, will indoctrinate individuals to the company's ways of doing things. Similarly, formal visits by headquarters teams (for example, for a strategy audit) or informal visits (perhaps to launch a new product) will enhance the feeling of belonging to the same corporate family. Furthermore, to generate global buy-in, annual bonus schemes have shifted away from the performance of the employee's individual unit and towards the company as a whole. This sends a signal that the company wants people to work together. At Toyota and IBM, most of the bonus is linked to the performance of the business as a whole in a region, and only a small part is based on individual performance. At BP, individual performance assessments exclude the effects of oil prices and exchange rates because they are outside the employee's control.[11]

MANAGING GLOBAL MANAGERS

The importance of the quality of the workforce—from executive level down to the factory floor—cannot be overemphasized, regardless of the stage of globalization. While in the early stages, the focus is typically on understanding cultural differences, as firms become more

Quick Take *Corporate Acculturation*

Toyota has 580 different companies with 299,300 employees around the world and 51 factories outside of Japan, and it sells nearly 9 million cars in more than 170 countries. What holds these operations together and makes them part of a cohesive entity is a strong corporate culture.

The "Toyota Way" has five distinct elements: (1) *Kaizen*, the process of continuous improvement that has Toyota employees coming back to work each day determined to perform better than the day before; (2) *Genchi genbustu*, which expects fact-based consensus-building on defining challenges; (3) *Kakushin*, which focuses on radical innovation in terms of technologies and models; (4) *Challenge* to get employees to see challenges not as something undesirable but as way to help reach improvements; (5) *Teamwork* to sharing knowledge with others in the team and to putting the company's interests before those of the individual; and (6) *Respect* for other people, not just as people but for their skills and special knowledge.

Ultimately, employees reach a point of "emotional fortitude," where their behavior is consistent with the organization's objectives. In the West, where individualism is at a higher level, it is more difficult for employees to absorb this.

SOURCES: Thomas A. Stewart and Anand P. Raman, "Lessons from Toyota's Long Drive," *Harvard Business Review* 85 (July/August 2007): 74-82; "Inculcating Culture," *The Economist*, January 21, 2006, p. 11; see also **http://www.toyota.co.jp/en/index_company.html**.

global, they move toward integrating country-to-country differences within the overall corporate culture.

Early Stages of Globalization

As noted earlier, in the early stages, the marketing or sales manager of the firm is usually responsible for initiating export activities. As foreign sales increase, an export manager will be appointed and given the responsibility for handling export documentation, developing and maintaining customers, interacting with the firm's intermediaries, and planning for overall market expansion.

Typically, firms will hire an experienced export manager from outside the firm, rather than promote an inexperienced candidate from within. The reason is that knowledge of the product or industry is less important than international experience. In the early stages, a highly entrepreneurial spirit with a heavy dose of trader mentality is required.

Advanced Stages of Globalization

As the firm progresses from exporting to an international division to foreign direct involvement, human resources planning activities will initially focus on need vis-à-vis various markets and functions. Existing personnel can be assessed and plans made to recruit, select, and train employees for positions that cannot be filled internally. The four major categories of overseas assignments are: (1) CEO, to oversee and direct the entire operation; (2) functional head, to establish and maintain departments and ensure their proper performance; (3) trouble-shooters, who are utilized for their special expertise in analyzing, and thereby preventing or solving particular problems; and (4) white- or blue-collar workers. Many technology companies have had to respond to shortages in skilled employees by globalized recruitment using web sites or by hiring headhunters in places such as China and India. For example, of the 120 different nationalities working at Nokia, 45 percent are represented in senior management as coming from a non-Finnish ethnicity.[12]

One of the major sources of competitive advantage for global corporations is their ability to attract talent from around the world. As shown in Figure 13.7, corporations need systematic management-development systems, with the objective of creating and carefully allocating management personnel. Increasingly, plans call for international experience as a prerequisite for advancement.

In global corporations, there is no such thing as a universal global manager, but rather a network of global specialists, in four general groups of managers that have to work together. Global business (product) managers have the task to further the company's global-scale efficiency and competitiveness. Country managers have to be sensitive and responsive to local market needs and demands but, at the same time, be aware of global implications. Functional managers have to make sure that the corporation's capabilities in technical, manufacturing, marketing, human resource, and financial expertise are linked and can benefit from one another. Corporate executives at headquarters have to manage interactions among the three groups of managers, as well as identify and develop the talent to fill the positions.

Global companies should show clear career paths for managers assigned overseas and develop the systems and the organization for promotion. This approach serves to eliminate many of the perceived problems and thus motivates managers to seek out foreign assignments. Furthermore, when jobs open up, the company can quickly determine who is able and willing to take them. Foreign assignments can occur at various stages of the manager's tenure. In the early stages, assignments may be short term, such as a membership in an international task force or six to 12 months at headquarters in a staff function. Later, an individual may serve as a business-unit manager overseas. Many companies use cross-postings to other countries or across product lines to further an individual's acculturation to the corporation. A period in a head office department or a subsidiary will not only provide an understanding of different national cultures and attitudes but also improve an individual's "know-who" and therefore establish unity and a common sense of purpose, necessary for the proper implementation of global programs.

Jeffrey Bezos, founder and CEO of online retailer Amazon.com, with Japanese home-country manager Junichi Hasegawa.

© AFP/GETTY IMAGES

FIGURE 13.7   International Management Development

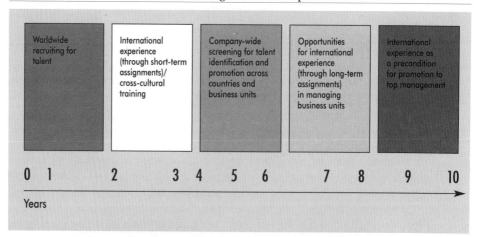

SOURCE: Adapted from Ingo Theuerkauf, "Reshaping the Global Organization," *McKinsey Quarterly*, No. 3, 1991, p. 104; and Paul Evans, Vladimir Pucik, and Jean-Louis Barsoux, *The Global Challenge: Frameworks for International Human Resource Management* (New York: McGraw-Hill/Irwin), 2002, Ch. 2–4.

Interfirm Cooperative Ventures

Global competition is forging new cooperative ties between firms from different countries, thereby adding a new management challenge. Although many of the reasons cited for these alliances (described in Chapter 10) are competitive and strategic, the human resource function is critical to their implementation. As a matter of fact, one of the basic reasons so many ventures fail relates to human resource management—the failure of managers from venture partners to work together effectively.

While the ingredients for success differ with the type of cooperative venture, there are two basic elements. First, a successful interfirm relationship requires the assignment and motivation of people in appropriate ways so that the venture can fulfill its strategic objectives. This requires particular attention to such issues as job skills and compatibility of communication and other work styles. For example, some cooperative ventures have failed because one of the partners assigned relatively weak management resources to the venture or because managers found themselves with conflicting loyalties to the parent organization and the cooperative venture organization. Second, the venture requires strategic management of the human resources function—that is, the appropriate use of managerial capabilities, not only in the cooperative venture but in other later contexts, possibly back in the parent organization. An individual manager needs to see that an assignment in a cooperative venture is part of his or her overall career development.

Selecting Managers for Overseas Assignments

The traits that have been suggested as necessary for the global manager cover a broad range, as summarized in Table 13.3. Their relative importance may vary dramatically, of course, depending on the firm's situation, as well as where the choice is being made.

COMPETENCE FACTORS An expatriate manager usually has far more responsibility than a manager in a comparable domestic position and must be far more self-sufficient in making decisions, conducting daily business, and leading others. However, regardless of management skills, a new environment still requires the ability to adapt the skills to local conditions. For this reason, cultural knowledge and language ability are important selection criteria.

ADAPTABILITY FACTORS The manager's own motivation, to a great extent, determines the viability of an overseas assignment and consequently its success. Adaptability means a positive and flexible attitude toward change. The manager assigned overseas must progress from factual knowledge of a culture to interpretive cultural knowledge, trying as much as possible

TABLE 13.3 Criteria for Selecting Managers for Overseas Assignment

COMPETENCE	ADAPTABILITY	PERSONAL CHARACTERISTICS
Technical knowledge	Interest in overseas work	Age – *you cannot do this*
Leadership ability	Relational abilities	Education
Experience, past performance	Cultural empathy	Sex
Area expertise	Appreciation of new	Health
Language	management styles	Marital status
	Appreciation of environmental	Social acceptability
	constraints	
	Adaptability of family	

to become part of the new scene, which may be quite different from the one at home. Since a foreign assignment often puts strains on the manager's family, the adaptability criterion extends to the family, too.

PERSONAL CHARACTERISTICS Despite all of the efforts made by global companies to recruit the best people available, demographics still play a role in the selection process. Because of the level of experience typically needed, many foreign assignments go to managers in their mid-30s or older. Normally, companies do not recruit candidates from graduating classes for immediate assignment overseas. They want their international people first to become experienced and familiar with the corporate culture, and this can best be done at the head-quarters location.

Companies like Bayer have taken positive steps to propel women managers into global careers. Bayer's initiative takes the form of a program that embraces diversity awareness training, multiple mentoring programs, career development and international delegate programs, employee networks, and succession planning. As part of the company's Delegate Career Development Program, women and minority candidates are given overseas assignments of two to three years' duration.[13]

Health conditions and marital status also factor into the selection decision. Such characteristics as background, religion, race, and sex usually become critical only in extreme cases in which a host environment would clearly reject a candidate based on one or more of these variables. The Arab boycott of the state of Israel, for example, puts constraints on the use of managers of Jewish and Arab origin. Women cannot negotiate contracts in many Middle Eastern countries. This would hold true even if the woman were president of the company.

ADAPTABILITY SCREENING AND ORIENTATION Because of the cost of transferring a manager abroad and the high attrition rates associated with foreign assignments, many firms go beyond standard selection procedures and use **adaptability screening** as an integral part of the process. Screening usually involves in-depth interviews with the candidate and the family from various perspectives. Selected candidates—and often their spouses—then participate in an orientation program on internal and external aspects of the assignment. If the company is still in the export stage, the emphasis is on interpersonal skills and local culture. With expatriates, the focus will be on both training and interacting with host-country nationals. Actual methods vary from area studies to sensitivity training, subjects covered in Chapter 2. That chapter also covers aspects of culture shock that influence the success or failure of selected managers.

ADAPTABILITY SCREENING

A selection procedure that usually involves interviewing both the candidate and his or her family members for an overseas assignment to determine how well they are likely to adapt to another culture.

Compensating Global Managers

A firm's expatriate compensation program has to be effective in: (1) providing an incentive to leave the home country on a foreign assignment, (2) maintaining a given standard of living, (3) taking into consideration career and family needs, and (4) facilitating re-entry into the home country. To achieve these objectives, firms pay a high premium, beyond base salaries, to induce managers to accept overseas assignments. The costs to the firm are 2 to 2.5 times the cost of

Quick Take *Staffing Creatively*

Companies are sending more people abroad than ever before, but they are trying to keep down the costs of doing so. The traditional business-class expatriate, usually male and Western, is steadily being replaced by an economy version who may well come from any country in the organization. Companies are trying hard to reduce their reliance on the traditional sort of expatriates, not only because firms want to avoid the expense of sending people abroad, but companies are also increasingly aware that having locals in top jobs can be a boon in foreign markets. Many expatriates are charged with finding their replacements as quickly as they can. Promising local candidates are often sent to head office to learn the ropes before returning with the prospect of taking over an expatriate's job. Increasingly, employees from developing countries are being sent to developed ones rather than the other way around. Well-educated Indians, Chinese, Brazilians or Mexicans, often with degrees from foreign universities, are perfect candidates for many European or American firms that want them to gain experience in the head office before they take on greater responsibility in their home markets. Tetra-Pak is a case in point. It used to send an army of expatriates, once all Swedes, to open and manage its factories around the world. Now it is encouraging more local executives to step up into important roles. One way it is doing this is to build up talent and experience in local clusters. This involves frequent transfers of employees within certain regions, such as Latin America and Southeast Asia. The best performers are groomed to make bigger geographic moves.

Given the importance of families in making expatriate decisions, some employers are offering new types of foreign posting. More people are being sent on short-term, "commuter" assignments where they do not need to uproot their families. The commuting trend is particularly common in Europe: A banker from Vienna, for instance, may spend Monday to Friday working in Dresden and then fly home at the weekend. In some cases, where the locations are not that far from each other, a daily commute may be feasible.

SOURCES: David G. Collings, Hugh Scullion, Michael J. Morley, "Changing Patterns of Global Staffing in the Multinational Enterprise: Challenges to the Conventional Expatriate Assignment and Emerging Alternatives," *Journal of World Business*, 42 (number 2, 2007): pp. 198-214; "Travelling More Lightly—Staffing Globalization," *The Economist*, June 24, 2006, pp. 99-101.

maintaining a manager in a comparable position at home. Corporate cost-cutting has been eroding some of the benefits packages of the past years. The falling dollar and changes in the U.S. tax code have also reduced the amount of disposable income. The average package given to a family of four moving from the United States to Tokyo in 1994 was 3.6 times the executive's base salary; in 2007, the same package would be 1.8 times the base.[14]

Compensation can be divided into two general categories: (1) base salary and salary-related allowances, and (2) non-salary-related allowances. Although incentives to leave home are justifiable in both categories, they create administrative complications for the personnel department in tying them to packages at home and elsewhere. As the number of transfers increases, firms develop general policies for compensating the manager rather than negotiate individually on every aspect of the arrangement.

BASE SALARY

Salary, not including special payments such as allowances, paid during overseas assignments.

COST-OF-LIVING ALLOWANCE (COLA)

An allowance paid during an assignment overseas to enable the employee to maintain the same standard of living as at home.

FOREIGN SERVICE PREMIUM

A financial incentive to accept an assignment overseas, usually paid as a percentage of the base salary.

HARDSHIP ALLOWANCE

An allowance paid during an assignment to an overseas area that requires major adaptation.

HOUSING ALLOWANCE

An allowance paid during an assignment overseas to provide appropriate living quarters.

TAX-EQUALIZATION PLAN

Reimbursement by the company when an employee in an overseas assignment pays taxes at a higher rate than at home.

EDUCATION ALLOWANCE

Reimbursement by company for dependent educational expenses incurred while a parent is assigned overseas.

Base salary, as with domestic positions, depends on qualifications and responsibilities. To ensure the manager maintains the same standard of living experienced at home, most compensation packages include **cost-of-living allowances (COLA)**, described in World View: How Far Will Your Salary Go?

Some firms offer a **foreign service premium**, which is, in effect, a bribe to encourage a manager to leave familiar conditions and adapt to new surroundings. Usually, it is calculated as a percentage range of 10 to 25 percent of base salary. In addition, **hardship allowances** compensate managers for relocating to difficult environments, such as countries that are politically or economically unstable or where the living conditions are unhealthy. For example, hardship premiums vary from 20 percent (Moscow) to 30 percent (Vladivostok).

Since housing costs and related expenses are typically the largest expenditure in the expatriate manager's budget, firms usually provide a **housing allowance** commensurate with the manager's salary level and position.

One of the major determinants of the manager's lifestyle abroad is taxes. A U.S. manager earning $100,000 in Canada would pay nearly $40,000 in taxes—in excess of $10,000 more than in the United States. For this reason, 90 percent of U.S. multinational corporations have **tax-equalization plans**. When a manager's overseas taxes are higher than at home, the firm will make up the difference. However, in countries with a lower rate of taxation, the company simply keeps the difference. The firm's rationalization is that it does not make any sense for the manager in Hong Kong to make more money than the person who happened to land in Singapore. Tax equalization is usually handled by accounting firms that make the needed calculations and prepare the proper forms. Managers can exclude a portion of their expatriate salary from U.S. tax; for 2006, the amount was $82,400, but income above that is subject to high effective taxes. The amount expatriates can exclude or deduct for housing costs has been limited in the last few years.[15]

Non-Salary-Related Allowances

Other types of allowances are made available to ease the transition into the period of service abroad. Typical allowances during the transition stage include: (1) a relocation allowance to compensate for moving expenses; (2) a mobility allowance as an incentive to managers to go overseas, usually paid in a lump sum and as a substitute for the foreign service premium; (3) allowances related to housing, such as home sale or rental protection, shipment and storage of household goods, or provision of household furnishings in overseas locations; (4) automobile protection that covers possible losses on the sale of a car (or cars) at transfer and having to buy a car overseas, usually at a higher cost; (5) travel expenses, using economy-class transportation, except for long flights (for example, from Washington to Taipei); and (6) temporary living expenses, which may become substantial if housing is not immediately available. Also, companies are increasingly providing support to make up for income lost by the accompanying spouse.

Education for children is one of the major concerns of expatriate families. In many cases, children may attend private schools, perhaps even in a different country. Firms will typically reimburse for such expenses in the form of an **education allowance**. In the case of college education, firms reimburse for one round-trip airfare every year, leaving tuition expenses to the family.

Finally, firms provide support for medical expenses, and especially for medical services at a level comparable to the expatriate's home country. Other health-related allowances are in place to allow the expatriate to periodically leave the challenging location for rest and relaxation. Some expatriates in Mexico City get $300 to $500 per family member each month to cover a getaway from the pollution of the city.[16]

Labor Union Membership as a Percentage of Total Employees

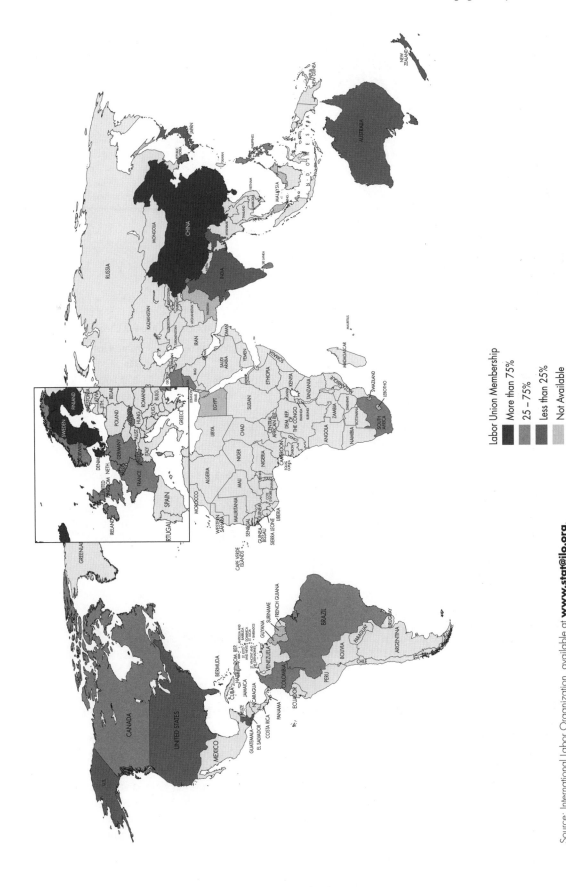

Labor Union Membership

- More than 75%
- 25 – 75%
- Less than 25%
- Not Available

Source: International Labor Organization, available at **www.stat@ilo.org**.

WORLD VIEW

HOW FAR WILL YOUR SALARY GO?

Living cost comparisons for Americans residing in foreign areas are developed four times a year by the U.S. Department of State Allowances staff. For each post, two measures are computed: (1) a government index to establish post allowances for U.S. government employees, and (2) a local index for use by private organizations. The government index takes into consideration prices of goods imported to posts and price advantages available only to U.S. government employees.

The local index is used by many business firms and private organizations to determine the cost-of-living allowance for their American employees assigned abroad. Local index measures for 12 key cities around the world are shown in the table below. Maximum housing allowances, calculated separately, are also given.

The reports are issued four times annually under the title *U.S. Department of State Indexes of Living Costs Abroad, Quarters Allowances, and Hardship Differentials.*

HOW FAR WILL YOUR SALARY GO?

LOCATION	COST OF LIVING INDEX[a] (WASHINGTON, DC = 100		MAXIMUM ANNUAL HOUSING ALLOWANCE		
	SURVEY DATE	INDEX	EFFECTIVE DATE	FAMILY OF 2	FAMILY OF 3-4
Buenos Aires, Argentina	Jan. 2005	81	NA	NA	NA
Canberra, Australia	Jul, 2006	126	Dec. 2006	$23,300.00	$25,630.00
Brussels, Belgium	Jul. 2005	162	Oct. 2005	$45,600.00	$50,160.00
Rio de Janeiro, Brazil	Nov. 2005	110	NA	NA	NA
Paris, France	Mar. 2005	189	Dec. 2005	$79,300.00	$87,230.00
Frankfurt, Germany	Jan. 2006	150	Dec. 2005	$41,200.00	$45,320.00
Hong Kong	Sep. 2005	159	NA	NA	NA
Tokyo, Japan	Jan. 2006	177	Jan. 2003	$83,500.00	$91,850.00
Mexico City	Jun. 2006	118	Jun. 1995	$37,500.00	$41,250.00
The Hague, Netherlands	Mar. 2006	118	May 2006	$54,900.00	$60,390.00
Geneva, Switzerland	Mar. 2006	177	Sep. 2006	$70,300.00	$77,330.00
London, UK	Oct. 2006	183	May 2006	$72,100.00	$79,310.00

[a] Excluding housing and education.
NA = Not available.

SOURCE: http://www.state.gov.

MANAGING THE GLOBAL WORKFORCE

5 LEARNING OBJECTIVE

None of the firm's objectives can be realized without a labor force, which can become one of the firm's major assets or one of its major problems, depending on the relationship that is established. Because of local patterns and legislation, headquarters' role in shaping the relations is mainly advisory, limited to setting the overall tone for the interaction. However, many of the practices adopted in one market or region may easily come under discussion in another, making it necessary for multinational corporations to set general policies concerning labor relations. Often multinational corporations have been instrumental in bringing about changes in the overall work environment in a country. And as decisions are made where to locate and how to streamline operations, education and training become important criteria for both countries and companies.

Labor strategy can be viewed from three perspectives: (1) the participation of labor in the affairs of the firm, especially as it affects performance and well-being; (2) the role and impact of unions in the relationship; and (3) specific human resource policies, in terms of recruitment, training, and compensation.

Labor Participation in Management

Over the past quarter-century, many changes have occurred in the traditional labor-management relationship as a result of dramatic changes in the economic environment and the actions of both firms and the labor force. The role of the worker is changing both at the level of the job performed and in terms of participation in the decision-making process. To enhance workers' role in decision-making, various techniques have emerged: self-management, codetermination, minority board membership, and works councils. In striving for improvements in the quality of work life, programs that have been initiated include flextime, quality circles, and work-flow reorganization. Furthermore, employee ownership has moved into the mainstream.

Labor Participation in Decision-Making

The degree to which workers around the world can participate in corporate decision-making varies considerably. Rights of information, consultation, and codetermination develop on three levels:

1. The shop-floor level, or direct involvement: for example, the right to be consulted in advance concerning transfers.
2. The management level, or through representative bodies: for example, works-council participation in setting new policies or changing existing ones.
3. The board level: for example, labor membership on the board of directors.

In some countries, employees are represented on the supervisory boards to facilitate communication between management and labor, thereby giving labor a clearer picture of the financial limits of management and providing management with a new awareness of labor's point of view. The process is called **codetermination**. In Germany, companies have a two-tiered management system with a supervisory board and the board of managers, which actually runs the firm. The supervisory board is legally responsible for the managing board. In some countries, labor has **minority participation**. In the Netherlands, for example, works councils can nominate (not appoint) board members and can veto the appointment of new members appointed by others. In other countries, such as the United States, codetermination has been opposed by unions as an undesirable means of cooperation, especially when management-labor relations are confrontational.

A tradition in labor relations, especially in Britain, is **works councils**. They provide labor a voice in corporate decision-making through a representative body, which may consist entirely of workers or of a combination of managers and workers. The councils participate in decisions on overall working conditions, training, transfers, work allocation, and compensation. In some countries, such as Finland and Belgium, workers' rights to direct involvement, especially as it involves their positions, are quite strong. The European Union's works council directive requires over 1,000 multinational companies, both European and non-European, to negotiate works-council agreements. The agreements provide for at least one meeting per year for improving dialogue between workers and management.[17]

CODETERMINATION

A management approach in which employees are represented on supervisory boards to facilitate communication and collaboration between management and labor.

MINORITY PARTICIPATION

Participation by a group having fewer than the number of votes necessary for control.

WORKS COUNCILS

Councils that provide labor a say in corporate decision-making through a representative body that may consist entirely of workers, or of a combination of managers and workers.

Britain, Finland, and Belgium are unique in providing such involvement. In many countries and regions, workers have few, if any, of these rights. The result is long-term potential for labor strife in those countries and possible negative publicity elsewhere. Over a ten-year period, from 1989 to 1998, the most working days lost occurred in Iceland, followed by Spain, Greece, Canada, Turkey, and Italy. In 1998, the most strike-prone country was Denmark, where workers sought a sixth week of paid holiday through strikes.[18]

In addition to labor groups and the media, investors and shareholders also are scrutinizing multinationals' track records on labor practices. As a result, a company investing in foreign countries should hold to global rather than local standards of safety, health, and fair pay. Companies subcontracting work to local or joint-venture factories need to evaluate industrial relations throughout the system, not only to avoid lost production due to disruptions, such as strikes, but to ensure that no exploitation exists. Companies like Nike and Reebok, for example, require subcontractors to sign agreements saying they will abide by minimum-wage standards. While companies have been long opposed to linking free trade to labor standards, the business community is rethinking its strategy, mainly to get trade negotiations moving.[19]

The Role of Labor Unions

The role of labor unions varies from country to country, often because of local traditions in management-labor relations. The variations include the extent of union power in negotiations and the activities of unions in general. In Europe, especially in the northern European countries, collective bargaining takes place between an employers' association and an umbrella organization of unions, on either a national or a regional basis, thereby establishing the conditions for an entire industry. On the other end of the spectrum, negotiations in Japan are on the company level, and the role of larger-scale unions is usually consultative. Another striking difference emerges in terms of the objectives of unions and the means by which they attempt to attain them. In the United Kingdom, for example, union activity tends to be politically motivated and identified with political ideology. In the United States, the emphasis has always been on improving workers' overall quality of life. In China, the objective of the All China Federation of Trade Unions, the only legal union umbrella group, is to build a harmonious society.[20]

Investment decisions can also be guided by union considerations. For example, of the more than 30 automobile plants in the United States owned by foreign companies, none have been organized by the United Auto Workers. Foreign car makers have located plants in Southern states where the UAW has little presence and where right-to-work laws prevent unions from forcing employees to join and pay dues. In Northern states, they have mostly chosen locations in rural areas away from UAW strongholds.[21]

Human Resource Policies

The objectives of a human resource policy pertaining to workers are the same as for management: to anticipate the demand for various skills and to have in place programs that will ensure the availability of employees when needed. For workers, however, the firm faces the problem on a larger scale and, in most cases, does not have an expatriate alternative. This means that, among other things, when technology is transferred for a plant, it has to be adapted to the local workforce.

Although most countries have legislation and restrictions concerning the hiring of expatriates, many of them—for example, some of the EU countries and some oil-rich Middle Eastern countries—have offset labor shortages by importing large numbers of workers from countries such as Turkey and Jordan. The EU, by design, allows free movement of labor. However, a mixture of backgrounds in the available labor pool can put a strain on personnel

Quick Take *Faster, Cheaper Abroad*

With the advent of high-speed modems and low-cost satellite and fiber-optic communications, service workers in foreign countries can sometimes deliver faster results than their domestic counterparts. During the high-tech boom of the late 1990s, corporations looked to overseas outsourcing to compensate for an acute shortage of information-technology professionals at home. Computer-related tasks shifted to such countries as India, Ireland, and the Philippines, where wages are a fraction of U.S. salaries. Today, close to half of all Fortune 500 companies used offshore programmers, a figure that has doubled over a three-year period. Nearly a third of Microsoft's 34,000 employees work abroad in countries from England to Israel to China. Much-smaller firms are also going overseas for skilled help. One firm has Israeli programmers at work in Israel or in the United States, and an entertainment firm in Newport Beach, California, uses Russian programmers to develop its Internet site. Unable to pay the $90,000 starting salary for U.S. programmers, the company found highly skilled Russian programmers eager to earn $18,000 annually in Russia.

Most leading companies are turning toward a model of innovation that employs global networks of partners. These can include U.S. chipmakers, Taiwanese engineers, Indian software developers, and Chinese factories. Depending on their capabilities and needs, many companies can profitably outsource almost any elements in the innovation chain from basic research to testing and even to new-product introduction. Given the complexities of present-day technologies, no one company can master it all. Outsourcing some development makes sense so the company's own engineers can focus on next-generation technologies. Outsourcing is about the flexibility to put resources in the right places at the right time.

SOURCES: Nitin Nohria, "Feed R&D – or Farm it Out," *Harvard Business Review* 83(July/August 2005): pp. 17-27; "Outsourcing Innovation," *BusinessWeek*, March 21, 2005, pp. 84-90; Barbara Rose, "High-Tech Jobs Flow to Foreign Workers," *The Chicago Tribune*, February 10, 2002, p. 1; "Fishermen on the Net," *The Economist*, November 8, 2001, p. 69; Marc Ballon, "U.S. High-Tech Jobs Going Abroad," *The Los Angeles Times*, April 24, 2000, p. C1.

development. As an example, the firm may incur considerable expense to provide language training to employees. In Sweden, a certain minimum amount of language training must be provided for all "guest workers" at the firm's expense.

Bringing a local labor force to the level of competency desired by the firm may also call for changes. As an example, managers at Honda's plant in Ohio encountered a number of problems: Labor costs were originally 50 percent higher and productivity 10 percent lower than in Japan. Automobiles produced there cost $500 more than the same models made in Japan and then delivered to the United States. Before Honda began U.S. production of the Accord, it flew 200 workers representing all areas of the factory to Japan to learn to build Hondas the Sayama way and then to teach their co-workers the skills.

Compensation of the workforce is a controversial issue. Payroll expenses must be controlled for the firm to remain competitive; on the other hand, the firm must attract appropriate numbers of the type of workers it needs. The compensation packages of U.S.-based multinational companies have come under criticism, especially when compensation is lower in developing countries than it is domestically—even if that is higher than the local average. Comparisons of compensation packages are difficult because of differences in the packages that are shaped by culture, legislation, collective bargaining, taxation, and individual characteristics of the job.

SUMMARY

This chapter discussed the structures and control mechanisms needed to operate in the international business field. The elements define relationships between the entities of the firm and provide the channels through which the relationships develop.

 International firms can choose from a variety of organizational structures, ranging from a domestic organization that handles ad hoc export orders to a full-fledged global organization. The choice will depend heavily on the degree of internationalization of the firm, the diversity of international activities, and the relative importance of product, area, function, and customer variables in the process.

 A determining factor of organizational structure is the degree to which headquarters wants to decide important issues concerning the whole corporation and the individual subsidiaries.

 While it is important to grant autonomy to country organizations so that they can be responsive to local market needs, it is of equal importance to ensure close cooperation among units to optimize corporate effectiveness. Control can be exercised through bureaucratic means, which emphasize formal reporting, or less formal ways, in which corporate culture plays a pivotal role.

 Issues relating to the selection, screening, and compensation of global managers relate to the level of globalization. The more globalized the firm becomes, the greater the care and expense that goes into the process.

 Increasingly, workers worldwide are taking an active role in the decision-making of a firm and in issues related to their own welfare. Various programs are causing dramatic organizational change, not only by enhancing the position of workers but by increasing the productivity of the workforce as well.

KEY TERMS AND CONCEPTS

global product structure	not-invented-here syndrome	cost-of-living allowance
global area structure	intranet	(COLA)
global functional structure	virtual team	foreign service premium
process structure	strategic leader	hardship allowance
global customer structure	contributor	housing allowance
mixed structure	implementer	tax equalization plan
matrix structure	output controls	education allowance
decentralization	behavioral controls	codetermination
centralization	adaptability screening	minority participation
coordinated decentralization	base salary	works councils

REVIEW QUESTIONS

1. Firms differ, often substantially, in their organizational structures, even within the same industry. What accounts for the differences in their approaches?
2. Discuss the benefits gained by adopting a matrix form of organizational structure.
3. What changes in the firm and/or in the environment might cause a firm to abandon the functional approach?
4. Outline the problems associated with altering a corporation's structure to improve its global effectiveness.
5. Is there more to the not-invented-here syndrome than simply hurt feelings on the part of those who believe they are being dictated to by headquarters?

6. One of the most efficient means of control is self-control. What type of program would you prepare for an incoming employee?
7. What additional benefit is brought into the expatriate selection and training process by adaptability screening?
8. What are the general policies that the multinational corporation should follow in dealing (or choosing not to deal) with a local labor union?

CRITICAL SKILL BUILDERS

1. "Implementers are the most important country organizations in terms of buy-in for a global strategy." Comment.
2. Select a business in your area that already has some export-import activities within its operation. How is the firm currently structured? What recommendations would you recommend if the firm plans on future global expansion into multiple new markets?
3. Comment on this statement by Lee Iacocca: "If a guy wants to be a chief executive 25 or 50 years from now, he will have to be well-rounded. There will be no more of 'Is he a good lawyer, is he a good marketing guy, is he a good finance guy?' His education and his experience will make him a total entrepreneur in a world that has really turned into one huge market. He better speak Japanese or German, he better understand the history of both of those countries and how they got to where they are, and he better know their economics pretty cold."
4. A manager with a current base salary of $100,000 is being assigned to Lagos, Nigeria. Assuming that you are that manager, develop a compensation and benefits package for yourself in terms of both salary-related and non-salary-related items.
5. What accounts for the success of Japanese companies with both American unions and the more ferocious British unions? In terms of the changes that have come about, are there winners or losers among management and workers? Could both have gained?

ON THE WEB

1. Internal cooperation in terms of best-practices transfer, for example, is a key objective for global organizations. Using the web site of Lotus (**http://www-306.ibm.com/software/lotus/**) and their section on case studies, outline how companies have used Lotus Notes and Domino8 to facilitate the interactive sharing of information.

2. Using the web site of Monster, the world's leading career network, **http://career-advice.monster.com/get-the-job/work-abroad/home.aspx**, establish what are the unique challenges of careers in cities outside of one's home country.

ENDNOTES

1. *Procter & Gamble 2007 Annual Report*, 22; "It Was a No-Brainer," *Fortune*, February 21, 2005, pp. 96-102; "P&G Profits by Paradox," *Advertising Age*, February 24, 2004, pp. 18-19, 31; Sonoo Singh, "P&G Opens Up Its Doors and Its Ears," *Marketing Week*, February 13, 2003, p. 21; Jack Neff, "Does P&G Still Matter?" *Advertising Age*, September 25, 2000, pp. 48–56; "Rallying the Troops at P&G," *The Wall Street Journal*, August 31, 2000, pp.. B1, B4.
2. Michael J. Mol, *Ford Mondeo: A Model T World Car?* (Hershey, PA: Idea Group Publishing, 2002), pp. 1-21.

3. "Why Multiple Headquarters Multiply," *The Wall Street Journal*, November 19, 2007, pp. B1, B3.

4. Vaness Furhmans and Rachel Zimmerman, "Novartis to Move Global Lab to U.S.," *The Wall Street Journal*, May 7, 2002, p. A3.

5. Christopher Bartlett, "MNCs: Get off the Reorganization Merry-Go-Round," *Harvard Business Review* 60, March/April 1983, pp. 138–146.

6. Thomas Gross, Ernie Turner, and Lars Cederholm, "Building Teams for Global Operations," *Management Review*, June 1987, pp. 32–36.

7. Christopher A. Bartlett and Sumantra Ghoshal, "Matrix Management: Not a Structure, a Frame of Mind," *Harvard Business Review* 68, July/August 1990, pp. 138–145.

8. "GE Mentoring Program Turns Underlings into Teachers of the Web," *The Wall Street Journal*, February 15, 2000, pp. B1, B16.

9. "The Zen of Nissan," *BusinessWeek*, July 22, 2002, pp. 46-49; and "Rebirth of the Z," *Time*, January 15, 2001, pp. 42-44.

10. David A. Aaker and Erich Joachimsthaler, "The Lure of Global Branding," *Harvard Business Review* 77, November/December, 1999, pp. 137–144.

11. Thinking for a Living," *The Economist*, January 21, 2006, pp. 9-12.

12. **http://www.nokia.com/A4433643**.

13. "Bayer Awarded Top Honor for Initiative Preparing Women for Global Leadership," *Health & Medicine Week*, May 6, 2002, p. 7.

14. Karen E. Thuemer, "Asia Adds Up," *Global Business*, June 2000, pp. 51–55.

15. "U.S. Softens Tax Increase for Some Expats," *The Wall Street Journal*, February 26, 2007, p. A2.

16. "Expat Life Gets Less Cushy," *The Wall Street Journal*, October 26, 2007, pp. W1, W10.

17. "EU Works Councils Get Underway," *Crossborder Monitor*, October 16, 1996, p. 4.

18. "Labour Disputes," *The Economist*, April 22, 2000, p. 96.

19. "Firms Rethink Hostility to Linking Trade, Labor Rights," *The Wall Street Journal*, February 2, 2001, p. A12.

20. "China Union Expands at McDonald's," *The Wall Street Journal*, April 7-8, 2007, p. A3.

21. "Honda and UAW Clash Over New Factory Jobs," *The Wall Street Journal*, October 10, 2007, pp. A1, A19.

PART 6

All global businesses face constantly changing world economic conditions. This is not a new situation or one to be feared, because change provides the opportunity for new market positions to emerge and for managerial talent to improve the competitive position of the firm. Recognizing change and adapting creatively to new situations are the most important tasks of the global executives, as Part 6 will show.

A Global Currency?

"Euros only," blare the headlines. Supermodel Gisele Bündchen supposedly accepts payment only in euros. Robert Chu, owner of East Village Wines in New York, tells reporters that many people come into his store wanting to pay in euros—and he is happy to accept them. European tourists increasingly come to the United States for extended shopping sprees—the low dollar value means huge discounts compared to their home markets. Some stores, like Billy's Antique & Props on East Houston Street in Manhattan, even have signs in the window that read "Euros Only."

Of course, all these reported signs of the dollar's demise have to be taken with a grain of salt. Chu explains that money is money, and we'll take it and just do the exchange. Billy Leroy clarifies that his sign is really just meant to grab attention. Actually, the store will accept British pounds, Canadian dollars, and U.S. dollars as well.

Nonetheless, these developments do highlight that the world continues to become more global. First, merchandise crossed borders, then people did. Now, increasingly the origin of currencies does not matter. We know about currency exchange—prices are listed in major newspapers or on the web—so why not facilitate transactions and accept them, as long as they are issued by reputable countries?

SOURCES: Angela Moore, " NYC Stores Begin Accepting Euro," Reuters, February 8, 2008; Robin Shulman, "New York Merchants Embrace Euro," *The Washington Post*, February 25, 2008, p. A3.

LEARNING OBJECTIVES

1 To understand trends in the political environment that change the shape of global competition

2 To learn how changes in the global financial environment affect firms both internationally and domestically

3 To appreciate how the ever-accelerating pace of technology drives change

4 To learn how governments can trigger changes that affect trade relations

5 To consider how firms must prepare to shift their products, pricing, distribution, and communications strategies to keep pace with global change

6 To learn about different career opportunities in global business

As You Read This Chapter

1. Discuss the many concerns that CEOs face in a global marketplace.

In today's complex business environment, changes are occurring more frequently and more rapidly, and they have a more severe impact than ever before. Due to growing real-time access to knowledge about customers, suppliers, and competitors, the global business environment is increasingly characterized by high speed bordering on instantaneity.[1] As a consequence, the past has lost much of its value as a predictor of the future. What occurs today may not only be altered in short order but be completely overturned or reversed. For example, political stability in a country can be disrupted over the course of just a few months. A major, sudden decline in world stock markets leaves corporations, investors, and consumers with strong feelings of uncertainty. Currency declines result in an entirely new business climate for global suppliers and their customers and can have quite unexpected effects, as the opening vignette showed.

This chapter will discuss possible future developments in the global business environment, highlight the implications of the changes for international business management, and offer suggestions for a creative response to the changes. The chapter also will explore the meaning of strategic changes as they relate to career choice and career path alternatives in global business.

THE GLOBAL BUSINESS ENVIRONMENT

This section analyzes the global business environment by looking at political, financial, societal, and technological conditions of change and providing a glimpse of possible future developments, as envisioned by an international panel of experts.[2]

1   LEARNING OBJECTIVE

The Political Environment

The global political environment is undergoing a substantial transformation characterized by the reshaping of existing political blocs, the formation of new groupings, and the breakup of old coalitions.

Planned versus Market Economies

The second half of the last century was shaped by political, economic, and military competition between the United States and the Soviet Union, which resulted in the creation of two virtually separate economic systems. This key adversarial posture has now largely disappeared, with market-based economic thinking emerging as the front-runner. Virtually all of the former centrally planned economies are undergoing a transition with the goal of becoming market-oriented.

Global business has made important contributions to this transition process. Trade and investment have offered the populace in these nations a new perspective, new choices, new jobs, and new alternatives for marketing their products and services. At the same time, the bringing together of two separate economic and business systems has resulted in new and sometimes devastating competition, a loss of government-ordained trade relationships, and substantial dislocations and pain during the adjustment process.

Many business activities will be subject to regional economic and political instability, increasing the risk of international business partners. To encourage progress toward the institution of market-based economies, it will be important to develop institutions and processes internally, to assure domestic and foreign investors of protection from public and private corruption and respect for property rights and contractual arrangements.

The North-South Relationship

The distinction between developed and less developed countries (LDCs) is unlikely to change. The ongoing disparity between developed and developing nations is likely to be based, in part, on continuing debt burdens and problems with satisfying basic needs. As a result, political uncertainty may well result in increased polarization between the haves and have-nots, with growing potential for political and economic conflict. Demands for political solutions to economic problems are likely to increase. According to the United Nations, 2.6 billion people live on less than $2 per day.[3]

The developing countries of Africa continue as a relatively "cool" region for global business purposes. Political instability and the resulting inability of many African firms to be consistent trading partners are the key reasons for such a pessimistic view. In light of global competition for investment capital, these drawbacks are instrumental in holding both investment and trade down to a trickle. Corporations are unlikely to address this starvation for funds. Periodic surges in the social conscience of industrialized nations may result in targeted investments by governments, multilateral institutions, and nongovernmental organizations (NGOs), but these funds are likely to be insufficient for a transformation of the economic future of the region. Debt forgiveness for heavily burdened nations has helped clean the slate of past mistakes. Special provisions for these nations to have easier access to developed country markets will make a marginal difference in export performance. Most important, however, is internal reform and the benchmarking of production, so that competitive products and services can be offered. It would appear unlikely that government assistance alone can overcome market reluctance. An emphasis on education, training, and the development of a supportive infrastructure is crucial, because that is where the investments and jobs go.[4] It is not enough to expect a rising tide to raise all boats. There must also be significant effort expended to ensure the seaworthiness of the boat, the functioning of its sails, and the capability of its crew. Market-oriented performance will be critical to success in the longer run.

ENVIRONMENTAL PROTECTION

Actions taken by governments to ensure survival of natural resources.

The issue of **environmental protection** will also be a major force shaping the relationship between the developed and the developing world. In light of the need and desire for economic growth, however, industrializing nations may strongly disagree as to what approaches to take. Of key concern will be the answer to the question: Who pays? For example, simply placing large areas of land out of bounds for development will be difficult for nations that intend to pursue all options for further economic progress to accept. Corporations, in turn, are likely to be more involved in protective measures if they are aware of their constituents' expectations and the repercussions of not meeting them. Corporations recognize that by being environmentally responsible, a company can build trust and improve its image—therefore becoming more competitive. For example, it was early in the 1990s that the first annual corporate environmental report was published; now well over 2,000 companies publish such reports.[5]

In light of divergent trends, three possible scenarios emerge. One scenario is that of continued global cooperation. The developed countries could relinquish part of their economic power to less developed ones, thus contributing actively to their economic growth through a sharing of resources and technology. Although such cross-subsidization will be useful and necessary for the development of LDCs, it may reduce the rate of growth of the standard of living in the more developed countries. It would, however, increase trade flows between developed and less developed countries and precipitate the emergence of new international business opportunities.

A second scenario is that of confrontation. Because of an unwillingness to share resources and technology sufficiently (or excessively, depending on the point of view), the developing and the developed areas of the world may become increasingly hostile toward one another. As a result, the volume of international business, both by mandate of governments and by choice of the private sector, could be severely reduced.

A third scenario is that of **isolationism**. Although there may be some cooperation between developing and developed nations, both groups, in order to achieve their domestic and international goals, may choose to remain economically isolated. This alternative may be particularly attractive if each region believes that it faces unique problems and therefore must seek its own solutions.

ISOLATIONISM

A policy that minimizes the economic integration between nations.

Emerging Markets

Much of the growth of the global economy will be fueled by the emerging markets of the Asia-Pacific region, particularly China and India. For the industrialized nations, this development will offer a significant opportunity for exports and investment, but it will also diminish, in the longer term, the basis for their status and influence in the world economy. While the nations in the region are likely to collaborate, they are not expected to form a bloc of the same type as the European Union or NAFTA. Rather, their relationship is likely to be defined in terms of trade and investment flows (e.g., Japan) and social contacts (e.g., the Chinese business community).

China's rapid emergence is particularly significant. Companies already present in China and those willing to make major investments there are likely to be the main beneficiaries of growth. Long-term commitment, willingness to transfer technology, and an ability to partner either with local firms through joint ventures or with overseas Chinese-run firms are considered crucial for success. The strategic impact of Chinese trade participation is also likely to change. China is likely to assume a much higher profile in its trading activities. For example, rather than be the supplier of goods that are marketed internationally by others under a Japanese or U.S. label, Chinese firms will increasingly develop their own brand names and fight for their own name recognition, customer loyalty, and market share.[6]

Among the other promising emerging markets are Korea and India. Korea could emerge as a participant in worldwide competition, while India is considered more important for the size of its potential market. Korean firms must still improve their ability to adopt a global mind-set. Some experts are also concerned about the chaebols' status as Korea becomes democratized. In addition, the possible impact of the reunification of the Korean peninsula on the country's globalization efforts must be taken into account.

With the considerable liberalization that took place in India, many expect it to offer major international marketing opportunities because of its size, its significant natural wealth, and its large, highly educated middle class. While many experts believe that political conflict (both domestic and regional), nationalism, and class structure may temper the ability of Indian companies to emerge as a worldwide competitive force, there is strong agreement that India's disproportionately large and specialized workforce in engineering and computer sciences makes the nation a power to be reckoned with.

Overall, the growth potential of these emerging economies may be threatened by uncertainty in terms of international relations and domestic policies, as well as social and political dimensions, particularly those pertaining to income distribution. Concerns also exist about infrastructural inadequacies, both physical—such as transportation—and societal—such as legal systems. The consensus of experts is, however, that growth in these countries will be significant.

The Effects of Population Shifts

The population discrepancy between the less developed nations and the industrialized countries will continue to increase. In the industrialized world, a population increase will become a national priority, given the fact that in many countries, particularly in Western Europe, the population is shrinking. The shrinkage may lead to labor shortages, and major

**POPULATION
STABILIZATION**

An attempt to control rapid increases in a nation's inhabitants.

societal difficulties may result when fewer workers have to provide for a growing elderly population.[7]

In the developing world, **population stabilization** will continue to be one of the major challenges of governmental policy. In spite of well-intentioned economic planning, continued rapid increases in population will make it more difficult to ensure that the pace of economic development exceeds population growth. If the standard of living of a nation is determined by dividing the GNP by its population, any increase in the denominator will require equal increases in the numerator to maintain the standard of living. With an annual increase in the world population of 100 million people, the task is daunting. It becomes even more complex when one considers that within countries with high population increases, large migration flows take place from rural to urban areas. As a result, by the end of this decade, most of the world's ten largest metropolitan areas will be in the developing world.[8] Within those areas, a large youth cohort may reach adulthood too quickly for the government to adapt. Problems are likely to emerge if society is unable to fulfill basic needs such as employment, housing, and education for large groups.[9]

FINANCIAL ENVIRONMENT

2 LEARNING OBJECTIVE

Debt constraints and low commodity prices create slow growth prospects for many developing countries. They will be forced to reduce their levels of imports and to exert more pressure on industrialized nations to open up their markets. Even if the markets are opened, however, demand for most primary products will be far lower than supply. Ensuing competition for market share will therefore continue to depress prices.

Developed nations have a strong incentive to help the debtor nations. The incentive consists of national security concerns and the market opportunities that economically healthy developing countries can offer. As a result, industrialized nations may very well find that funds transfers to debtor nations, accompanied by debt-relief measures such as debt forgiveness, are necessary to achieve economic stimulation at home.

The dollar will remain one of the major international currencies, with little probability of gold returning to its former status in the near future. However, some international transaction volume, in both trade and finance, is increasingly likely to be denominated in non-dollar terms, particularly using the euro. The system of floating currencies will likely continue, with occasional attempts by nations to manage exchange-rate relationships or at least reduce the volatility of swings in currency values. Yet, given the vast flows of financial resources across borders, it would appear that market forces, rather than government action, will be the key determinant of a currency's value. Therefore, factors such as investor trust, economic conditions, earnings perceptions, and political stability are likely to have a much greater effect on the international value of currencies than domestic monetary and fiscal experimentation.

Given the close links among financial markets, shocks in one market will quickly translate into rapid shifts in others and could easily overpower the financial resources of individual governments. Even if governments should decide to pursue closely coordinated fiscal and monetary policies, they are unlikely to be able to negate long-term market effects in response to changes in economic fundamentals.

Culture Clues   In China, business appointments need to be made in advance. The more important the person, the more lead time required. The Chinese do not like to conduct business over the telephone and generally do not take cold calls. Punctuality is considered a sign of courtesy, but arriving up to 10 or 15 minutes late is acceptable. Lateness does, however, require an apology.

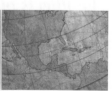

A looming concern in the international financial environment will be the **international debt load** of the United States. Both domestically and internationally, the nation is incurring debt that would have been inconceivable only a few decades ago.

In 1985, the United States became a net negative investor, internationally. The nation entered the new century with an international debt burden of more than $2 trillion. This debt level makes the United States the largest debtor nation in the world, owing more to other nations than all the developing nations combined. Others argue against an unsustainable scenario, believing that there are special mitigating circumstances that let the U.S. tolerate this burden, such as the fact that most of the debts are denominated in U.S. dollars and that, even at such a large debt volume, U.S. debt-service requirements are only a relatively small portion of GNP.[10] Yet this accumulation of foreign debt may very well introduce entirely new dimensions into the international business relationships of individuals and nations. Once debt has reached a certain level, the creditor, as well as the debtor, is hostage to the loans. The U.S. current account deficit has nearly doubled since 2000, increasing from $417 billion in 2000 to $708 billion in 2007.[11] The cumulative, net U.S. international debt reached $2.5 trillion in 2006. Interestingly, on average, foreign investors tended to accept lower rates of return on their investments in the U.S. than American investors generate from their foreign holdings. This discrepancy is due partially to the fact that a large percentage of U.S. debt is held by foreign governments in the form of low-yielding government debt.[12]

However, borrowing from abroad can lead to greater susceptibility to international market fluctuations and other associated risks. Federal Reserve chairman Ben Bernanke has stated that the U.S. current account deficit is certainly not sustainable at its current level.[13] The primary reason for concern is that a rapid capital outflow from the United States, similar to a bank run on a global scale, could lead to a serious financial crisis or "hard landing" for the U.S. economy. If central banks and sovereign wealth funds in the Middle East and Asia were to dispose of their huge dollar reserves because of fear of capital losses from dollar depreciation, the results for the American currency and economy could be very difficult. The dollar has been weakening for a while. From 2002 to 2007, it lost a quarter of its value against a broad range of currencies. Furthermore, outflows of U.S. private investment have increased rapidly in recent years, from $500 billion in 2005 to $1 trillion in 2006 and $1.8 trillion in the first half of 2007. These outflows could compromise the ability of the U.S. to borrow in order to finance its trade deficit.

Since foreign creditors expect a return on their investment, a substantial portion of future U.S. international trade activity will have to be devoted to generating sufficient funds for such repayment. For example, at an assumed interest rate or rate of return of 10 percent, the international U.S. debt level—without any growth—would require the annual payment of $320 billion, which amounts to almost 45 percent of current U.S. exports. Therefore, it seems highly likely that global business will become a greater priority than it is today and will serve as a source of major economic growth for U.S. firms.

To some degree, foreign holders of dollars may also choose to convert their financial holdings into real property and investments in the United States. This could result in an entirely new pluralism in U.S. society. It will become increasingly difficult and, perhaps, even unnecessary to distinguish between domestic and foreign products—as is already the case with Hondas made in Ohio. Senators and members of Congress, governors, municipalities, and unions will gradually be faced with conflicting concerns in trying to develop a national consensus on international trade and investment. National security issues may also be raised as major industries become majority-owned by foreign firms.

Industrialized countries are likely to attempt to narrow the domestic gap between savings and investments through fiscal policies. Without concurrent restrictions on international capital flows, such policies are likely to meet with only limited success. Lending institutions can be expected to become more conservative in their financing, a move that may hit smaller

INTERNATIONAL DEBT LOAD

Total accumulated, negative net investment position of a nation.

firms and developing countries the hardest. At the same time, the entire financial sector is likely to face continuous integration, ongoing bank acquisitions, and a reduction in financial intermediaries. Large customers will be able to assert their independence by the increasing ability to present their financial needs globally and directly to financial markets and obtain better access to financial products and providers.

A Changing Growth Perspective

There may well be a reconsideration of the economic growth construct, particularly regarding growth expectations. We have come to the point where mere stability and constancy is seen as wrong and as indicative of "falling behind." Imagine an executive telling his shareholders that he wants his company's sales to remain stable — most analysts would probably run him over on their way to other firms. But isn't stability in itself worthwhile and good? What ever happened to catching one's breath?

We're all familiar with the phrase "getting ready (or saving) for a rainy day." There is no implication that temporary setbacks are fatal. Rather, there is implied an acceptance, forged from experience with Mother Nature, that there are seasons, and that life has its ups and downs.

Even eagles occasionally descend to lower heights so that they can catch an updraft and soar again. There is nothing to be ashamed of if resources have to be rearranged and if one accepts that not everything is linear. It may well emerge that growth, particularly on a global level, is increasingly seen in the context of the angles on a protractor: Growth does not always have to take place at all degrees, on all levels, and simultaneously, because there are many different areas to grow.

TECHNOLOGICAL ENVIRONMENT

The Internet

The concept of the global village is commonly accepted today and indicates the importance of communication. Worldwide, the estimated number of people online in December 2007 was 1.32 billion, an almost threefold increase since 2000. Asia has the highest number of Internet users, with 510 million (38.7 percent). There is a persistent digital gap around the world, with Africa accounting for only 3.4 percent of Internet users, despite the fact that it accounts for 14.2 percent of the world's population. However, as Figure 14.1 shows, the gap is closing. The number of Internet users in Africa has grown 900 percent over the past seven years. Both the private and public sector make heavy use of the Internet and expand into new activities. Almost all business conducted by the cabinet of the Slovenian government, for example, is on the Web. The country's 15 cabinet members receive government business over a secure system, allowing politicians to discuss and vote on issues online.[14]

For both consumer services and business-to-business relations, the Internet is democratizing global business. It has made it easier for new global retail brands—like Amazon.com and CDnow—to emerge. The Internet is also helping specialists like Australia's high-sensitivity hearing-aids manufacturer, Cochlear, to reach target customers around the world without having to invest in a distribution network in each country. The ability to reach a worldwide audience economically via the Internet spells success for niche marketers, who could never make money by just servicing their niches in the domestic market. The Internet also allows customers, especially those in emerging markets, to access global brands at more competitive prices than those offered by exclusive national distributors.

Starting a new business will be much easier, allowing a far greater number of suppliers to enter a market. Small and medium-sized enterprises, as well as large multinational corporations,

FIGURE 14.1   Internet Users in the World Growth Between 2000 and 2007

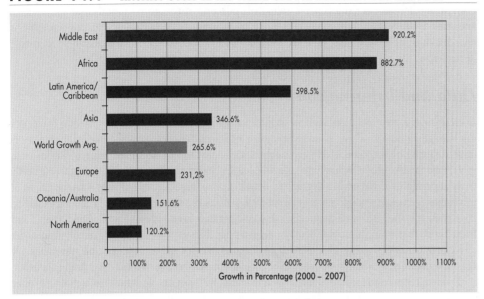

Note: Total World Internet Users estimate is 1,319,872,109 for year-end 2007.
Copyright © 2008, Miniwatts Marketing Group, **www.internetworldstats.com**

will now be full participants in the global marketplace. Businesses in developing countries can now overcome many of the obstacles of infrastructure and transport that limited their economic potential in the past. The global services economy will be a knowledge-based economy, and its most precious resource will be information and ideas. Unlike the classical factors of production—land, labor, and capital—information and knowledge are not bound to any region or country but are almost infinitely mobile and infinitely capable of expansion. This wide availability, of course, also brings new risks to firms. For example, one complaint can easily be developed into millions of complaints by using the Internet. Also of great impact on product marketing and customer feedback is the increasingly popular blogosphere—a new world of online journalism, where everyone with a computer is a potential critic or advertising target. Business is attempting to adapt to this new medium, as exemplified by a Korean venture called OhmyNews. It combines articles from 50 staff journalists with reports sent by e-mail or text-message from thousands of citizen reporters. OhmyNews says it has been profitable for a year and a half and expects revenues of $10 million for 2008. The greater reach also makes firms subject to much more scrutiny and customer response on a global scale. Overall, as World View: Direct from the Web explains, technological advances offer companies, large and small, exciting new opportunities to conduct business on a global scale.

High technology will also be one of the more volatile and controversial areas of economic activity internationally. Developments in biotechnology are already transforming agriculture, medicine, and chemistry. Genetically engineered foods, patient-specific pharmaceuticals, gene therapy, and even genetically engineered organs are on the horizon. Innovations such as these will change what we eat, how we treat illness, and how we evolve as a civilization.[15] However, skepticism about such technological innovations is rampant. In many instances, people are opposed to such changes for religious or cultural reasons or simply because they do not want to be exposed to such "artificial" products. Achieving agreement on what constitutes safe products and procedures, of defining the border between what is natural and what is not, will constitute one of the great areas of debate in the years to come. This is evident in the continuing debate over the relative safety of milk and meat from cloned animals.[16] Firms and their managers must remain keenly aware of popular perceptions and misperceptions and of changing government policies and politics in order to remain successful participants in markets.

Data and Information

Even though a greater diversification of information sources may typically provide for better knowledge evolution, there is an expectation of fewer data sources offering an increasingly large quantity of data, be it due to mergers, cost cutting, or a limited user willingness to pay. Such development is likely to affect accuracy and reliability—making data use heavily trust-dependent. To a growing degree, data users may demand more insights into the origin of information in order to gauge its believability. Just as butchers increasingly are expected to label the meat they sell with its precise origins (obtained from Farmer Joseph Smolensk, 5 km from here), information providers may need to offer data locale and source of origin in order to achieve trustworthiness. Under such conditions, the locality of data can be systematically used to enhance credibility—for example, through increased use of local debt-rating agencies.

Due to more transparent sourcing, firms and individuals will be less willing to offer information. Nebulous laws and restrictions may be increasing the threat of lawsuits. Also, the gains from free information, that have greatly helped businesses and individuals in the last decade, are likely to shrink.

There may be a tendency toward "organic" data—unaltered by manipulation or interpretation. Another alternative may be "comparative" data sets, which, on an ongoing basis, provide multi-source perspectives. In addition, quantitative data are likely to increasingly be combined with qualitative information, resulting in a diagnostic perspective that permits for a helicoptered perspective while holding the hand of the patient. Once data pass the trust threshold, they can then be used in a much more aggressive and insightful way, going far beyond the traditional retrospective use of statistics to look at history, toward making trends and prognoses for the future.

Advancements of information technology and convergence of new technologies will increasingly allow any new equipment to be more sophisticated and able to perform more functions with high performance at low cost. Even though companies will be willing to adopt these new technologies faster than ever before, doing so will only provide a competitive edge if it is not done at the expense of ease of use and customer friendliness. While youth markets will be quick to use new capabilities, more mature buyers will be reluctant to invest in products that require a high degree of additional learning. Excelling in technology alone has no intrinsic value. It is the application of technology to satisfy human needs and values, at a profit, that counts.

GLOBAL TRADE RELATIONS AND GOVERNMENT POLICY

4 LEARNING OBJECTIVE

In spite of the World Trade Organization (WTO), ongoing major imbalances in trade flows will tempt nations to apply their own national trade remedies, particularly in the anti-dumping field. Even though WTO rules permit a retaliation against unfair trade practices, such actions would only result in an ever-increasing spiral of adverse trade relations.

A key question will be whether nations are willing to abrogate some of their sovereignty, even during difficult economic times. An affirmative answer will strengthen the multilateral trade system and enhance the flow of trade. However, if key trading nations resort to the

WORLD VIEW

DIRECT FROM THE WEB

Can't find a U.S.-made snowboard at your local department store in Japan? Try the new mall on the Internet. A Portland, Oregon, firm is creating what could be described as a Japanese cybermall, an on-line shopping service that enables U.S. manufacturers and retailers to advertise and sell their products directly to consumers—in Japanese. The Japanese Internet service also teaches customers in Japan how to order products and services directly from the United States.

By setting up shop in local language cybermalls, U.S. firms can target potential customers around the globe without the costly headaches that often scare them away from the international marketplace. TKAI has provided Japan-specific e-business, web site development, online marketing, strategic consulting, and research services since 1995 to more than 40 clients, including Amazon.com, British Telecom, Outpost.com, JCPenney, Nokia, and PeopleSoft. In 2000, TKAI joined Ion Global, creating a worldwide business-consulting network spanning ten countries.

In August 2007, Ion Global was acquired by Aegis Group plc, the London-listed media communications and market research group and became part of Isobar—Aegis' global digital agency network. Aegis is a colossal marketing communications group, with revenues of more than 1 billion pounds.

TKAI's electronic service, called DIYer (for Do-It-Yourself Importer), averages 1,000 unique users per day. More than 5,000 people subscribe to its e-newsletter, according to owner Tim Clark. "We're helping companies enter the Japanese market, companies that want to take a crack without paying for major magazine ads or huge marketing campaigns," he said. The service is for companies "interested in dealing directly with customers in Japan," through catalog sales, for example.

Here's how it works: A U.S. manufacturer or retailer pays TKAI a fee for a display on the Import Center site. The fee varies according to the size and complexity of the display, but runs $350 and up. TKAI, whose staff includes fluent Japanese speakers, translates the copy into Japanese.

The web site is an information resource for Japanese customers who want to buy products or services "without going through middlemen or trading companies," according to Clark. Access is free of charge in Japan.

DIYer is not an e-commerce site, however. It provides information about products featured on overseas e-commerce sites that have received positive feedback from Japanese consumers. Japanese consumers visit the site to learn about featured products and for help with composing English e-mail, interpreting sizes and units of measurement, and understanding different shipping methods.

Mickey Kerbel, president of Xtreme Inc., which makes snowboards, said he paid $345 for a one-year listing with TKAI and has sold about $2,000 worth of merchandise in only a couple of months since going online. The site provides a low-cost way to gain access to some of the world's most affluent customers, according to Tim Clark. Internet use in the Asia-Pacific region is catching up to that of the United States. As of February 2002, Japan had close to 50 million users. "We're happy with the service and the list-building it has helped us with in the Japan market," said Mike Delph, management information systems manager at U.S. Cavalry, a Kentucky retailer of outdoor equipment and survival gear.

He said he's amassed a large list of names through electronic mail. "We've had more responses from the [Import Center] than we have on our own English language site," said a system administrator for Blue Tech, a computer products retailer based in La Jolla, California.

SOURCES: **http://www.nau.com**, accessed March 14, 2002; "Corporate Fact Sheet," TKAI web site, accessed April 25, 2001, **http://www.tkai.com**; telephone interview with Tim Clark, June 25, 1999; "CDC Corporation Signs Agreement to Sell Ion Global to Aegis Group," **http://www.ionglobal.com/news_2007_07.asp**, August 2007; accessed February 25, 2008.

development of insidious nontariff barriers, unilateral actions, and bilateral negotiations, protectionism will increase on a global scale, and the volume of international trade is likely to decline. The danger is real, and it is here that international business academics are, or should be, the guardians who separate fact from fiction in international trade policy discussions. Qualified not by weight of office but by expertise, international business experts are the indirect guarantors of and guides toward free and open markets. Without their input and impact, public apathy and ignorance may well result in missteps in trade policy.[17]

The efforts of governments to achieve self-sufficiency in economic sectors, particularly in agriculture and heavy industries, have ensured the creation of long-term, worldwide over-supply of some commodities and products, many of which, historically, had been traded widely. As a result, after some period of intense market-share competition aided by subsidies and governmental support, a gradual and painful restructuring of these economic sectors will have to take place. This will be particularly true for agricultural cash crops, such as wheat, corn, and dairy products, and industrial products, such as steel, chemicals, and automobiles.

Government Policy

International trade activity now affects domestic policy more than ever. For example, trade flows can cause major structural shifts in employment. Links between industries spread these effects throughout the economy. Fewer domestically produced automobiles will affect the activities of the steel industry. Shifts in the sourcing of textiles will affect the cotton industry. Global productivity gains and competitive pressures will force many industries to restructure their activities. In such circumstances, industries are likely to ask their governments to help in their restructuring efforts. Often, such assistance includes a built-in tendency toward protectionist action.

Restructuring is not necessarily negative. For example, since 1900, U.S. farm employment has dropped from more than 40 percent of the population to less than 3 percent.[18] Yet today, the farm industry feeds more than 304 million people in the United States and still produces large surpluses.[19] A restructuring of industries can greatly increase productivity and provide the opportunity for resource reallocation to emerging sectors of an economy.

Governments cannot be expected, for the sake of the theoretical ideal of "free trade," to sit back and watch the effects of deindustrialization on their countries. The most that can be expected is that they will permit an open-market orientation subject to the needs of domestic policy. Even an open-market orientation will be maintained only if governments can provide reasonable assurances to their own firms and citizens that the openness applies to foreign markets as well. Therefore, unfair trade practices, such as governmental subsidization, dumping, and industrial targeting, will be examined more closely, and retaliation for such activities is likely to be swift and harsh.

TRIGGER MECHANISMS

Specific acts or stimuli that set off reactions.

Increasingly, governments will need to coordinate policies that affect the international business environment. The development of international indexes and **trigger mechanisms**, which precipitate government action at predetermined intervention points, will be a useful step in that direction. Yet, for them to be effective, governments will need to muster the political fortitude to implement the policies necessary for cooperation. For example, international monetary cooperation will work in the long term only if domestic fiscal policies are responsive to the achievement of the coordinated goals.

At the same time as the need for collaboration among governments grows, it will become more difficult to achieve a consensus. As the aftermath of September 11, 2001, is brought to the fore, economic security and national security are often seen as competing with each other, rather than as complementary dimensions of national welfare that can operate in parallel and, to some degree, even be traded off against one another. Unless a new key common sense of purpose can be found by governments, collaborative approaches and long-term alliances will become increasingly difficult.

Governmental policymakers must take into account the international repercussions of domestic legislation. For example, in imposing a special surcharge tax on the chemical industry, designed to provide for the cleanup of toxic waste products, they need to consider

Culture Clues   In India, confusion often arises because of the reluctance of people to say "no." There is a general belief in the Indian culture that telling someone "no" is just too unkind. People will go to great extremes to avoid saying "no," even to a simple request. For example, if you ask someone for directions, whether they know the way or not, they do not want to disappoint you and may send you off in the wrong direction entirely!

Quick Take *Data Privacy*

Societies around the world are increasingly sensitive to issues of data privacy, and the concern has grown exponentially as a result of e-business. Readily accessible databases may contain information that is valuable to marketers but considered privileged by individuals. One recent EU directive aims to ensure free flow of data among member states, but it also demands high standards of data privacy. The directive further required member states to block transmission of data to non-EU countries whose domestic legislation did not provide acceptable levels of privacy protection. This provision makes it difficult for e-commerce businesses to operate as effectively in Europe as they can, for instance, in the United States. There are key differences between the European and the U.S. perspectives on data privacy. In order to avoid a costly conflict between the United States and the EU, a compromise position was negotiated in 2000. The United States agreed to set up a "safe harbor"—in essence, a list maintained by the Department of Commerce of companies that voluntarily adopt EU-style safeguards of their customers' private information. Companies on the list will receive unrestricted EU data flow. This inducement appears to have caught on. The list's 12 companies in early 2001 had grown to about 1,400 by early 2008. This turnaround could be attributed to several factors: a quest for promised Department of Commerce benefits, concern over a backlash from EU partners, or simply a desire to demonstrate to consumers and employees that the privacy of their information is valued in an age of rampant identity theft and fraud.

SOURCES: "Privacy: Safe Harbor Is a Lonely Harbor," *National Journal's Technology Daily*, January 5, 2001; "Data Privacy Deal," *The Journal of Commerce*, March 28, 2000; Charles A. Prescott, "The New International Marketing Challenge: Privacy," *Target Marketing* 22, no. 4, 1999, p. 28; Department of Commerce Safe Harbor List **http://web.ita.doc.gov/safeharbor/shlist.nsf/webPages/safe+harbor+list?OpenDocument&Start=1389** accessed February 25, 2008.

its repercussions on the international competitiveness of the chemical industry. Similarly, current laws, such as antitrust legislation, need to be reviewed if the laws hinder the global competitiveness of domestic firms.

Environment, Conservation, and Sustainability

China will demonstrate a lack of concern toward the environment, even though environmental problems will have a major effect on its ability to compete as a global manufacturing center. Medical, environmental, and other social costs will dramatically reduce the advantages of firms to manufacture in China—therefore leading to a move of FDI to other locations, including the U.S. and Europe.

One consequence of China's and India's rapid growth will be an ongoing depletion of natural resources. Aspirations for economic progress and better lifestyles will cause shortages in natural resources. In consequence, the sourcing and controlling of important raw materials will be a key strategic issue, often leading to preferential bilateral agreements, perhaps even in contradiction to multilateral arrangements. Governments will attempt to put more land into grain production and also use tools such as subsidies and price controls. Scarcity will also drive up the price of consumer alcohol. Protection of materials within society from theft will become a key issue (e.g. cutting electrical wires to steal copper). Recycling and recovery will grow as vital business opportunities. Farming will become highly attractive and profitable again, as fuel production from food accelerates.

The global shortage of potable water will be rediscovered as a key issue and a key constraint on global advancement and wellbeing. There will be much higher government investments in desalination and reverse osmosis technologies and more emphasis on water conservation.

In light of public concern about climate change, there will be growing preference for energy-saving technologies and a reduction and limit to energy use. A stream of scientific and non-scientific proof will be offered for global warming, with any unusual natural phenomenon being blamed for global warming. Public impressions and perceptions will lead to changes in living patterns—for example the population of arid and hot climate areas may well shift due to water shortages and possible limits to the use of air conditioning technology. Such effects will occur even if it becomes generally accepted that global warming is only slightly dependent on human activities—given the overriding argument of: What can it hurt?

Africa may well emerge in offering the most opportunities for green investments and the accumulation of carbon credits. However, as the transfer of resources resulting from carbon trading grows, such trading will become, in the eyes of governments, non-sustainable and therefore prohibitive. It is more likely that there will be an increase in international agreements (both multilateral and bilateral) that set a framework for corporations, promotion and subsidies for technologies, and products that protect the environment. Rich countries will give more importance to this concern, and most internationally operating companies will take this concern seriously. Key sectors for industry creation and expansion will focus on the protection of public health; the need for sustainability; the conservation of energy, water and natural resources; the growth of bio-technology, genomics, and nanotechnology; and the creation and promotion of eco products, services, and processes. For example, sustainable water recycling technologies will spawn new industries. Governments will adopt and encourage more advanced pollution control policies, particularly for heavy metals and engineered (non-naturally occurring) substances.

Terrorism

Terrorism has precipitated many major shifts in international business practices. In many ways, it has made the world a smaller place, confronted with events that occur at greater speed. There are clear expectations that terrorism is an ongoing phenomenon that will have to be confronted. Combating terrorism is a fact of life and history, resulting in a continuous job for push back, which has to be done multilaterally, without second thoughts or trade-offs. Counter-terrorism will be dangerous, and it will be important to maintain the will of the people and of governments to oppose the terrorists. There are Janus-like repercussions from the frailty of corporate and human memories.

Over time, impressions shift. During the days following a terrorist event, for example, there is typically the feeling of "but for some good fortune, it could have been me."

This feeling may eventually change to "this was an aberration and cannot happen to me," leading to an underestimation of danger and, often, insufficient policy measures.[20] However, there also needs to be a strong focus on the root causes of terrorism. Dimensions to be considered are policies toward immigrants, the sometimes-dividing role taken on by advocates of specific religions, cultures, regions, or races. Ways to address them can be education, improved nourishment, and the ability to control one's own destiny.[21]

There is major global ambivalence about which approaches to take to mitigate terrorism. Some believe very strongly that materialism and "having something to lose" are key dimensions in providing important values for those who see themselves as excluded from the benefits of globalization. Others, however, suggest a prime role for spirituality, empathy for, and understanding of cultural differences. Perhaps value combined with valuation will be the future direction.

There will also be a growing emphasis on national interests accompanied by limited readiness for multilateral solutions. It will be a key task for governments to diffuse such desires rather than accede to popular demands. Only with the collaboration of parties in conflict can one avoid local and regional protectionism, the emergence of de-globalization, and the spiraling reduction of the quality of life. The greatest imperative will be to develop and maintain the power to achieve and sustain peace.

Consumers appear willing to change their consumption habits if necessary for security needs. In response to cultural diversity and cross-border cultural conflicts, many may abrogate from earlier preferences, giving the impact of country of origin a totally new meaning. Corporations are likely to revive ethnocentric and polycentric policies and use export activities, much more than foreign direct investment, as the dominant form of international business relations. They will either pull out from those countries that are lacking law and order, or service them only at a very high-risk premium. Other specific international business responses to terrorism can be found in four key areas: customer management, production management, logistics, and people management.[22]

CUSTOMER MANAGEMENT Rather than just selling wherever possible, firms now focus more on where to sell, what to sell, and to whom to sell. Managers are developing a new appreciation for the type and degree of risk exposure in certain regions of the world. Leading risk factors include the policies of home and host governments, exchange-rate fluctuations, and economic turmoil.

More firms are developing trade portfolios that allocate effort and limits in different regions of the world. These portfolios are intended to achieve two goals: (1) to limit dependence on any region or customer in order to reduce a firm's exposure to conflict or unexpected interruptions; and (2) to systematically develop markets to balance existing exposure, to diversify a firm's risk, and to offer a fallback position.

There is now also a greater scrutiny of the alternative opportunities presented by foreign direct investment (FDI) and exporting. FDI demonstrates the long-term nature of a firm's objectives and makes use of local advantages. It also facilitates collaboration and reduces the firm's exposure to the vagaries of border-crossing transactions. At the same time, FDI renders the firm vulnerable to the effects of government policies and any divergence between home and host country. Some firms are looking beyond the strict economic dimensions of foreign direct investment. They use it to signal full confidence in an area or a partner, thus demonstrating commitment. Such a focus on relationship may well alter some of the approaches used by government agencies in charge of encouraging foreign direct investment inflow.

Exporting, in turn, permits a broader and quicker coverage of world markets with the ability to respond to changes. Risks are lower, but costs tend to be higher because of trans-shipment and transaction expenses. Even though an export orientation is seen to be less risky, many firms are not as aggressive as they used to be in seeking new business or new accounts. A desire to deal with old, established customers, with "people who we know and with whom we have developed a feeling of trust" has emerged, perhaps leading to a redevelopment of high-context relations around the world. An export approach appears to be the preferred method of new market entry these days. It may remain the principal tool of international expansion for firms new to the global market or those highly concerned about international risk.

Closely associated with an export strategy are increasing concerns about export controls on the corporate level. Ironically, this increase in self-examination occurs during a time when better linkages and cooperation between governments have made it possible to ease the levels of technology that can be traded internationally. Corporations have become more sensitive to the possibility of diversion or misuse of their exports and don't want to be accused of aiding and abetting an enemy. As a result, there is more intensive scrutiny of orders received, of customers who have placed these orders, and of product-use evaluation before an order is shipped.

PRODUCT MANAGEMENT Members of the supply chain now make it an imperative to identify and manage their dependence on international inputs. Industrial customers, in particular, are often seen as pushing for U.S.-based sourcing. A domestic source simply provides a greater feeling of comfort. As one executive said, "When we tell our customers their goods will be produced in West Virginia or Kentucky, they feel so much better than when we inform them about the shipments coming from Argentina, Greece, or Venezuela. They're worried about interruptions or other problems."

Some firms also report a new meaning associated with the "made-in" dimension in country-of-origin labeling. In the past, this dimension was viewed as enhancing products, such as perfumes made in France or cars made in Germany. Lately, the "made-in" dimension of some countries may create an exclusionary context by making both industrial customers and consumers reject products from specific regions. As a result, negative effects may result from geographic proximity to terrorists, as has been claimed by some for textile imports from Pakistan.

LOGISTICS MANAGEMENT The international pipeline has slowed down, but the structure of the pipeline and the scrutiny given to the materials going through the pipeline have become important.

Firms that had developed elaborate just-in-time delivery systems for their international supplies have been exposed to increased security measures that have reduced the speed of international transactions. These firms and their service providers continue to be affected by increased security measures. Firms are also focusing more on internal security and need to demonstrate externally how much more security-oriented they have become. In many instances, government authorities require evidence of threat-reduction efforts to speed shipments along. Also, insurance companies have increased their premiums substantially for firms that are exposed to increased risk.

In the past, cargo security measures concentrated on reducing theft and pilferage from a shipment. Increasingly, additional measures concentrate on possible undesirable accompaniments to incoming shipments. With this new approach, international cargo security starts well before the shipping even begins. One result of these changes—perhaps unintended—is a better description of shipment content and a more precise assessment of duties and other shipping fees.

Carriers with sophisticated hub-and-spoke systems have discovered that trans-shipments between the different spokes may add to delays because of the time needed to rescrutinize packages. While larger "clean areas" within ports may help reduce this problem, a redesign of distribution systems may lead to fewer hubs and more direct connections.

Firms with a just-in-time (JIT) system are also using alternative management strategies, such as shifting international shipments from air to sea. More dramatically, some firms are replacing international shipments with domestic ones, in which truck transport would replace transborder movement altogether and eliminate the use of vulnerable ports.

PEOPLE MANAGEMENT The heightened degree of scrutiny also extends to the employees of corporations. Without necessarily differentiating based on the country of origin of applicants for employment, firms now take a much closer look at credentials and claims of past achievements and activities. Some U.S. firms—even though globally oriented—are becoming more cautious in their practices for hiring foreign nationals. Accepting the

WORLD VIEW

WHEN EXPATRIATES RETURN HOME

When governments change policies, when restrictions are lifted, or when new opportunities emerge, expatriates may decide to come home. For example, when Syria's president Bashar al-Assad introduced new economic liberalization policies, investment projects increased by 250 percent, mainly due to expatriates investing their money and expertise in the country.

China is planning to reverse past brain drain by luring back Chinese students who have studied abroad. It used to be that students went abroad (typically to the United States), found employment there, and stayed on. However, due to support measures introduced by the Chinese government and due to different regulations, many expatriate former students have returned to China. If the government wants someone to encourage somebody to return home, it provides start-up funds for a new company or money for housing and cars. Particularly in the medical research field, the availability of resources, such as embryonic stem cells, and the permission to carry out exploratory research is attractive to leading scientists.

Other nations are also thinking about implementing attractive repatriation measures. For example, the German government is increasingly searching for ways to bring back university researchers who have left the country. Research progress is seen as very instrumental to the competitiveness of a nation. Therefore, there is a large effort under way to bring researchers back home.

One emerging policy issue concerns the security effects of such labor mobility. For example, in order to work in government laboratories, such as Los Alamos in the United States, a researcher must have U.S. citizenship. This requirement is designed to protect highly classified information and limit its dissemination to potential adversaries. But what about the researcher who has become a citizen but leaves a few years or even decades later? How can secrets be kept?

SOURCES: Julien Barnes-Dacy, "Syrian Expatriates Return Home in Hopes of New Wealth," *The Christian Science Monitor*, December 27, 2007; "Many Expatriate Scientists find Reasons to Return to China," *The Washington Post*, February 20, 2008, p. D5.

reality that controlling an individual's access to information is much more difficult once that person is inside the organization, these firms appear to have decided not even to consider for employment nationals from highly controversial countries. The World View on the return of expatriates discusses some of the problems associated with employment and the protection of information.

THE FUTURE OF GLOBAL BUSINESS MANAGEMENT

Global change results in an increased risk, yet participation in the global marketplace remains the only way to achieve long-term success. International markets are a source of high profits, as a quick look at a list of multinational firms shows. International activities also help cushion the firm from fall-offs in domestic demand that may result from adverse domestic conditions. For this reason, global participation may be crucial to the very survival of the firm. International markets also provide firms with foreign experience that helps them compete more successfully with foreign competitors in the domestic market.

5 LEARNING OBJECTIVE

Reputation Management

Firms appreciate the fact that public perceptions drive actions by consumers, governments, and competitors and thus make an effort to consider the effects of corporate actions on the public's view of the enterprise—both in the short as well as the long term.

Reforming The Global Corporation

Corporations are likely to face increasing pressures from a wide variety of stakeholders, including governments, unions, media, and the public at large. These grow increasingly more intense in light of a corporate migration from a Western-style organization to multi-polar structures, accompanied by a shift from a West-North to an East-South orientation. Accountability and transparency will be the basis for key developments.

Accounting systems will recognize and develop procedures for calculating the value of and the change of intangible corporate assets, so that they can increasingly be used to drive corporate capitalization and performance. Such assets will gradually become the prime measure of corporations and will have key influence on predicted future cash flows and stock prices. Value investors will recognize that the building of intangible assets is a multi-year, multifaceted endeavor. Consequently, buy-and-hold strategies will become more dominant and quarter-to-quarter performances will become less important in the investing decision.

Corporate responsibility will be interpreted to include broad-based activity and profit sharing. Low capital manufacturing facilities will be expected around the world. Stakeholders will demand greater involvement and, for better or for worse, will play a major role in the image building of the corporation. Since lapses in ethics or social responsibility will have a major negative impact on brand equity, strong corporations will increasingly be indicated with strong corporate social responsibility (CSR) programs and strong corporate ethical conduct.

There will be a backlash against excessive executive remuneration—not only from regulators but also from shareholders and inside managers and employees. Executive compensation will again be determined in comparison to average pay levels—which may well lead to pay raises for those at lower levels.

Emerging markets will increasingly account for larger portions of corporate profits and sales, particularly in light of their representation of more than two-thirds of the total consumer base. Corporations will be expected to provide improved product access and help overcome difficulties in logistics and infrastructures. For many products, the development strategies will need to shift from utmost sophistication to increased affordability.

Corruption is increasingly seen as a significant detractor from global welfare and local economic development. Its consequences are roads that are shoddily built, structures that collapse, clinics with equipment that is purchased too expensively or unable to do the job necessary. In all such circumstances, vast public expenditures do not achieve their envisioned use.

Typical side payments are between 10 to 15 percent of all major public expenditures, with much higher levels of misrouting in the developing world. "It is human nature to lubricate relationships with gratuity" is often said. More diversion is attributed to high-context cultures (e.g. Latin America, Latin Europe, Asia) and less to low-context ones (e.g. U.S. Nordic, Germanic). Yet the social acceptance of corruption is a big danger because it protects the elite from domestic scrutiny and control. Therefore, the ongoing impact of the U.S. Foreign Corrupt Practices Act (FCPA) and of OECD discussions will seen as instrumental in reducing or at least containing such misappropriations. However, more multilateral actions are necessary to ensure the enforcement of measures against corruptors.

Global Product Policy

Worldwide introduction of products will occur much more rapidly in the future. Already, global product life cycles have accelerated substantially. Whereas product introduction could previously be spread out over several years, firms now must prepare for product life cycles that can be measured in months or even weeks. As a result, firms must design products and plan even their domestic marketing strategies with the global product cycle in mind.

Early incorporation of the global dimension into product planning, however, does not point toward increased standardization. On the contrary, companies will have to be ready to deliver more mass customization. Customers are no longer satisfied with simply having a product: They want it to precisely meet their needs and preferences. **Mass customization** requires working with existing product technology, often in modular form, to create specific product bundles for a particular customer, resulting in tailor-made jeans or a customized car.

As global manufacturing becomes increasingly the norm for many firms, manufacturing technologies are moving around the world at an extraordinarily fast pace. As emerging nations race to catch up, their knowledge and ability to duplicate technologies means that all global companies must be constantly innovative in order to stay ahead. The ability to develop consistent comparative advantage is particularly important, because emerging country competitors are likely to have access to large and increasingly skilled labor pools at labor rates much lower than in Europe, Japan, or the United States.

An increase will occur in the trend toward strategic alliances that enable firms to take risks that they could not afford to take alone, facilitate technological advancement, and ensure continued international market access. These partners do not need to be large to make a major contribution. Depending on the type of product, even small firms can serve as coordinating subcontractors and collaborate in product and service development, production, and distribution.

MASS CUSTOMIZATION

Taking mass-produced product components and combining them in a variety of ways to result in a specific product for a particular customer.

Global Pricing

Global price competition will become increasingly heated. As their distribution spreads throughout the world, many products will take on commodity characteristics. Even complex products are fast becoming commodities. With commodities, small price differentials per unit may become crucial. However, since many new products and technologies will address completely new needs, forward pricing—which distributes development expenses over the planned or anticipated volume of sales—will become increasingly difficult and controversial as demand levels are impossible to predict with any kind of accuracy.

For consumer products, price competition will be substantial. Because of the increased dissemination of technology, the firm that introduces a product will no longer be able to justify higher prices for long; domestically produced products will soon be of similar quality. As a result, exchange-rate movements may play more significant roles in maintaining the competitiveness of the international firm. Firms can be expected to prevail on their government to manage the country's currency to maintain a favorable exchange rate. Technology also allows much closer interaction on pricing between producer and customer. The success of electronic commerce providers, such as eBay (**http://www.ebay.com**), demonstrates how auctioning and bidding, alone or in competition with others, offers new perspectives on the global price mechanism.

Through subsidization, targeting, government contracts, or other hidden forms of support, nations will attempt to stimulate their international competitiveness. Because of the price sensitivity of many products, the international manager will be forced to identify such unfair practices quickly, communicate them to his or her government, and insist on either similar benefits or on rapid government action to create an internationally level playing field.

At the same time, many firms will work hard to reduce the price sensitivity of their customers. By developing relationships with their markets, rather than just carrying out transactions, other dimensions—such as loyalty, consistency, the cost of shifting suppliers, and responsiveness to client needs—may become much more important than price.

Distribution Strategies

Innovative distribution approaches will determine new ways of serving markets. For example, television, through QVC, has already created a shopping mall used by more than 179 million customers.[23] The use of the Internet offers new distribution alternatives. Self-sustaining, consumer-distributor relationships may emerge through, say, refrigerators that report directly to grocery store computers that they are running low on supplies and require a home delivery billed to the customer's account.

The link to distribution systems will also be crucial to global firms in the business-to-business sector. As large retailers use sophisticated inventory tracking and reordering systems, only the firms able to interact with such systems will remain eligible suppliers. Therefore, firms need to create their own distribution systems that are able to respond to just-in-time (JIT) and direct-order entry requirements around the globe.

More sophisticated distribution systems will, at the same time, introduce new uncertainties and fragilities into corporate planning. For example, the development of just-in-time delivery systems makes firms more efficient yet, on an international basis, also exposes them to more risk through distribution interruptions. Therefore, a strike in a faraway country may be newly significant for a company that depends on the timely delivery of supplies.

Globally, there will be a greater emphasis on the markets offered by "second-tier cities," which are large cities not yet in the political or economic spotlight—particularly in Russia, China, and India. Firms will need to expand their distribution and market entry strategies to these large cities, thus creating new regional hubs. There must also be collaboration with the public sector to encourage infrastructural investments in these regions, which, in turn will increase their political and economic importance.

Global Communications

The advances made in international communications will also have a profound impact on international management. Entire industries are becoming more footloose in their operations; that is, they are less tied to their current location in their interaction with markets. Most affected by communications advances will be members of the services sector. International outsourcing of services makes it possible for corporations to center entire functions, like customer service, in countries where labor costs are low.

For manufacturers, intranet and Internet networks allow for instant sharing of massive amounts of data, documentation, and product images and specifications in globally dispersed locations. This opens opportunities not only for faster-paced research but for vastly improved supplier-manufacturer relationships.

Cost of Business Travel to International Cities

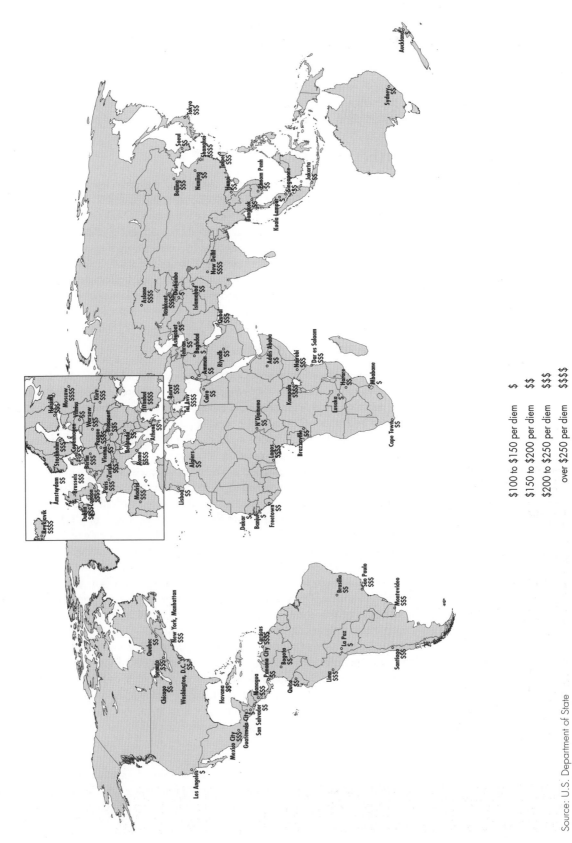

$100 to $150 per diem $
$150 to $200 per diem $$
$200 to $250 per diem $$$
over $250 per diem $$$$

Source: U.S. Department of State

CAREERS IN GLOBAL BUSINESS

As you have learned in this book, a career in global business is more than jet-set travel between New Delhi, Tokyo, Frankfurt, and New York. It is hard work and requires knowledge and expertise. As this final section will show, there are numerous ways to prepare yourself—and the rewards are substantial.

Further Training

Further study (for example, enrolling in a graduate business school program in global business) is always a good option. You can study either at home or abroad.

According to the Institute of International Education, 224,000 U.S. students studied abroad for academic credit in 2005/06 – an increase of 8.5 percent over the prior year's figures. In just the last decade, study abroad increased by 150 percent, up from fewer than 90,000 students in 1995/96. At the same time, business and management are the most popular fields of study for the 583,000 international students at American universities.[24] To supplement your studies, several organizations offer programs to assist students interested in studying abroad or in gathering foreign work experience.[25]

Employment Experience

For those ready to enter or rejoin the "real world" of global business, several opportunities await. One career option is to seek employment with a large multinational corporation. These firms constantly search for personnel to help them in their international operations.

Many multinational firms, while seeking specialized knowledge such as languages, expect employees to be firmly grounded in the practice and management of business. Rarely, if ever, will a firm hire a new employee at the starting level and immediately place him or her in a position of global responsibility. As explained in Chapter 13, job placements abroad are costly, and firms usually want a new employee to become thoroughly familiar with the company's internal operations before considering transfer to a global position. Once you do get a chance to travel, data like that presented in Table 14.1 will be invaluable. The chart evaluates cities around the globe, ranking them in terms of quality of life, according to 39 factors. They include political stability, personal freedom, air pollution, and the quality of health care, schools, restaurants, and theaters.

An alternative to working for a large multinational firm is to take a job with a small or medium-sized firm. Often, such firms have only recently developed a global outlook, and the new employee will arrive on the "ground floor." Initial involvement will normally be in the export field—evaluating potential foreign customers, preparing quotes, and dealing with activities such as shipping and transportation. With a very limited budget, the export manager will only occasionally visit international markets to discuss business strategies with distributors abroad. Most of the work will be done by mail, by fax, by e-mail, or by telephone. The hours are often long because of the need, for example, to reach a contact during business hours in Hong Kong. Yet the possibilities for implementing creative business transactions are virtually limitless. It is also gratifying and often rewarding that one's successful contribution will be visible directly through the firm's growing export volume.

Alternatively, international work in a small firm may involve importing—that is, finding low-cost sources that can be substituted for domestically sourced products. Decisions often must be based on limited information, and the manager is faced with many uncertainties. Often, things do not work out as planned. Shipments are delayed, letters of credit are canceled,

TABLE 14.1 Mercer Human Resource Consulting Worldwide
Quality of Living Survey 2007 (Top 25)

RANK 2007	CITY	COUNTRY	INDEX 2007
1	ZURICH	Switzerland	108.1
2	GENEVA	Switzerland	108.0
3	VANCOUVER	Canada	107.7
3	VIENNA	Austria	107.7
5	AUCKLAND	New Zealand	107.3
5	DUSSELDORF	Germany	107.3
7	FRANKFURT	Germany	107.1
8	MUNICH	Germany	106.9
9	BERN	Switzerland	106.5
9	SYDNEY	Australia	106.5
11	COPENHAGEN	Denmark	106.2
12	WELLINGTON	New Zealand	105.8
13	AMSTERDAM	The Netherlands	105.7
14	BRUSSELS	Belgium	105.6
15	TORONTO	Canada	105.4
16	BERLIN	Germany	105.2
17	MELBOURNE	Australia	105.0
18	LUXEMBOURG	Luxembourg	104.8
18	OTTAWA	Canada	104.8
20	STOCKHOLM	Sweden	104.7
21	PERTH	Australia	104.5
22	MONTREAL	Canada	104.3
23	NURNBERG	Germany	104.2
24	CALGARY	Canada	103.6
24	HAMBURG	Germany	103.6

SOURCE: William M. Mercer Consulting.
http://www.mercer.com/referencecontent.jhtml?idContent=1128060

and products almost never arrive in exactly the form and shape anticipated. Yet the problems are always new and offer an ongoing challenge.

As a training ground for international activities, there probably is no better starting place than a small or medium-sized firm. Later on, the person with some experience may find work with a trading or export management company, resolving other people's problems and concentrating almost exclusively on the international arena.

Self-Employment

A third alternative is to hang up a consultant's shingle or to establish a trading firm. Many companies are in need of help for their international business efforts and are prepared to part with a portion of their profits in order to receive it. Yet it requires in-depth knowledge and broad experience to make a major contribution from the outside or to successfully run a trading firm.

Specialized services that might be offered by a consultant include global market research, international strategic planning, or—particularly desirable—beginning-to-end assistance for

WORLD VIEW

GLOBAL EXPERIENCE LEADS TO THE TOP

E.V. Goings, president of Tupperware, took part in a total immersion program in Spanish—his third language—but he hardly stands out on his company's executive committee. The eight other members of the group speak two to four languages each, and all can boast of international work experience.

International exposure has long been trumpeted as essential for middle managers in multinationals, but these days, even chief executives are going global. To keep up with the growing importance of foreign markets, more companies are requiring candidates for top management positions to have strong international résumés. Victor J. Menezes, a native of Puna, India, has worked for Citigroup since 1972—in Hong Kong, China, Brussels, Latin America, and Africa. He is now chairman and CEO of Citibank, North America. During a trip to a recent acquisition in Poland, Menezes met with executives: several Poles, three Indians, an Englishman, an Argentinian, a Belgian, an Irishman, and a Chinese-Singaporean—and no Americans.

Executives who climbed the corporate ladder in the past typically ran successively bigger operations of a single product line or specialized in one discipline, like finance. Leaving the United States for an overseas post was often perceived as dangerous, taking executives far from the center of power. Today, however, international experience is often a top priority for executive headhunters. There is a strong positive relationship between international experience and the likelihood of being selected CEO. International experience early in one's career seems to encourage professional advancement: Over 40 percent of the CEOs in the S&P 100 report international experience, up from 4 percent in 1990.

"It sends the most powerful signal you can send [to employees] if the CEO has international experience or has been selected for that reason," says Jean-Pierre Rosso, chairman of CNH Global. Paolo Monferina, CEO at CNH, previously headed up Latin American operations at Fiatallis in Brazil and served as vice president of Fiat Geotech in London.

Combining high-profile roles abroad and at home seems to be the formula for success for many top management candidates. Other types of foreign exposure can also offer executives the opportunity for great upward mobility. Expertise in the bigger and more challenging emerging markets, such as Brazil, China, and India, can often pave the way to success.

A key reason why Andrea Jung was elected chairman and chief executive officer of Avon Products was that she had served the firm as president and COO (chief operating officer) of global marketing and later as chairman, with operating responsibility for all of Avon's global units.

SOURCES: Del Jones, "USA Plucks CEOs from All Across the World," *USA Today*, October 2, 2001; Paul Beckett, "To Fuel Its Growth, Citigroup Depends on Menezes' Work in Emerging Markets," *The Wall Street Journal*, February 21, 2001, p. C1; **http://www.avon.com**; **http://www.cnh.com**; Peter Magnusson and David Boggs, "International Experience and CEO selection: An empirical study," *Journal of International Management*, Issue 1, March 2006, pp. 107-125; J. Warner, Route to the top, *Chief Executive* 205 (2005), pp. 20–25 (Jan/Feb); "Elizabeth Smith Appointed President, Avon Products, Inc.," Avon Products Inc. press release, New York, September 11, 2007; Available at **http://www.avoncompany.com/investor/businessnews/index.html**; Retrieved March 10, 2008.

---

international entry or international negotiations. For an international business expert, the hourly billable rate typically is as high as $400 for principals and $150 for staff. Whenever international travel is required, overseas activities are often billed at the daily rate of $2,000 plus expenses. Even at such high rates, solid groundwork must be completed before all the overhead is paid. The advantage of this career option is the opportunity to become a true international entrepreneur. Consultants and those who conduct their own export-import or foreign direct-investment activities work at a higher degree of risk than those who are not self-employed, but they have an opportunity for higher rewards.[26]

SUMMARY

This final chapter has provided an overview of the environmental changes facing global managers and alternative managerial responses to the changes. Global business is a complex and difficult activity, yet it affords many opportunities and challenges.

Shifts in the political environment will affect the conduct of business among and between the world's trading regions. Continued growth of emerging markets will add to already intense competition.

Technology, including the Internet, will continue to drive change at an accelerated pace. While technology presents opportunities for innovation, it may also allow developing nations to catch up quickly with developed world competitors.

While global trade negotiations under the World Trade Organizations will continue, governments will balance their needs for trade with the best interests of their citizens.

Firms must respond to change through their global strategy development, product policies, pricing policies, distribution strategies, and communications.

There are multiple options for students desiring a career in global business, including further study.

There are multiple options for employment in large and small business and self-employment as a global consultant.

KEY TERMS AND CONCEPTS

environmental protection	population stabilization	trigger mechanisms
isolationism	international debt load	mass customization

REVIEW QUESTIONS

1. In what ways are trends in the global political environment likely to affect global trade in coming years?
2. For many developing countries, debt repayment and trade are closely linked. What does protectionism mean to them?
3. Should one worry about the fact that the United States is a debtor nation?
4. What is likely to happen to commodity prices in the future?
5. How would our lives and our society change if imports were banned?
6. How can you expand your experiential knowledge of global business?

CRITICAL SKILL BUILDERS

1. What is the danger in oversimplifying the globalization approach? Would you agree with the following statement? "If you want to succeed globally, you better believe that if something is working in a big way in one market, it will work in all markets."

2. Outline the basic reasons why a company does not necessarily have to be large and have years of experience to succeed in the global marketplace. Is this likely to change in future years?

3. Since crisis situations are more likely to occur in international locations than at home, it's better to manufacture at home during periods of global recession or political unrest. Prepare your arguments and debate in class.

4. Create a résumé and cover letter presenting yourself to a multinational company of your choosing for consideration for an entry level position. Make sure that you research the global activities of the company first and tailor your letter accordingly.

5. "You learn more, faster, and better at a multinational corporation than at a mid-sized company that is active in only one or two markets." Is this necessarily the case? Discuss your job preferences, both in the short term and in terms of career development.

ON THE WEB

1. What are the top ten trading partners for the United States? Use the U.S. Foreign Trade Highlights tables on the Department of Commerce's International Trade Administration site, **http://www.trade.gov**. Summarize the ways in which these trade relationships are likely to change in the future.

2. Using the site Living Abroad (**http://www.livingabroad.com**), research several international schools that may interest you. What are the most interesting links to other web sites concerning international issues? Why are you particularly interested in them?

3. Use a search portal to gain a competitive advantage. Examples: Google Trends and Yahoo Buzz, which provide real-time snapshots of consumer interests; Google reader, an RSS reader that can be mined for useful data; Google Analytics and Yahoo Site Explorer, which show consumer traffic at company web sites.

4. The site **http://www.overseasjobs.com** provides valuable information for those interested in jobs overseas. What skills do international employers seem to value most? Peruse the job listings and find several jobs that you might be interested in. Also take a look at the profiles of several international companies that you might be interested in working for. What characteristics do the international firms listed here possess?

ENDNOTES

1. William Lazer and Eric H. Shaw, "Global Marketing Management: At the Dawn of the New Millennium," *Journal of International Marketing*, 8, 1, 2000, pp. 65–77.

2. The information presented here is based largely on an original Delphi study by Michael Czinkota and Ilkka A. Ronkainen, using an international panel of experts, The Georgetown 2008 Delphi Study, Georgetown University, 2008.

3. Human Development Report 2007/2008: Fighting Climate Change, UN Development Program, **www.UNDP.org**, accessed March 6, 2008, p. 251.

4. "Bringing the Poor Online," *The Economist*, Feb. 22, 2008.

5. "Corporate Disclosure Resources," Washington University, **http://faculty.washington.edu/krumme/projects/disclosure/disclosurewebs.html**, accessed February 15, 2008.

6. "Shifting the Balance: Chinese and Indian Capitalism," *The Economist*, Jan. 24, 2008.

7. *Environmental Change and Security Program Report*, Issue 12, 2006-2007, The Woodrow Wilson International Center for Scholars, Washington DC, 2007, p. 95.

8. "Urban Population, Development and Environment Dynamics," Committee for International Cooperation in National Research in Demography, Paris, 2007, pp. 19 -23.

9. Richard P. Cincotta and Jack A. Goldstone, The Security Demographic, Assessing the Evidence, *Environmental Change and Security Program Report*, Issue 12, 2006-2007, The Woodrow Wilson International Center for Scholars, Washington D.C., 2007, p. 77.

10. Catherine L. Mann, "Is the U.S. Trade Deficit Still Sustainable?" Institute for International Economics, Washington, D.C., March 1, 2001; "The Dollar and the World Economy," *The Economist*, December 19, 2007.

11. U.S. Census Bureau, press release of March 11, 2008, **www.census.gov**, accessed March 11, 2008.

12. Robert E. Scott, "Despite Improving U.S. Current Account Deficits, Risk of Financial Crisis May Be Growing," Economic Policy Institute, September 17, 2007.

13. Chairman Ben S. Bernanke, Bundesbank Lecture, Berlin, Germany, September 11, 2007, **http://www.federalreserve.gov/newsevents/speech/bernanke20070911a.htm**; (accessed February 14, 2008).

14. **http://www.internetworldstats.com/stats7.htm**. Accessed Feb. 2, 2008.

15. Stephen Baker and Heather Green, "Social Media Will Change Your Business," *BusinessWeek*, February 20, 2008.

16. Andrea Thompson, "Cloned Milk and Meat: What's the Beef?" MSNBC, January 9, 2008.

17. Michael R. Czinkota, "The Policy Gap in International Marketing," *Journal of International Marketing*, 8, 1, 2000, pp. 99–111.

18. Labour Force Statistics, 1986–2006, Paris, OECD, 2007.

19. U.S. Census Bureau Population Clock, **http://www.census.gov/population/www/popclockus.html**; accessed March 11, 2008.

20. Peter W. Liesch, John Steen, Gary A. Knight, Michael R. Czinkota, "Internationally Managing in the Face of Terrorism-Induced Uncertainty," *21st Century Management: A Reference Handbook*, Charles Wankel, Ed. Thousand Oaks, CA: Sage Publications, 2008, pp. 200-208.

21. Michael R. Czinkota and Ilkka A. Ronkainen, *The 2008 Georgetown Delphi Study*, Georgetown University, Washington D.C., 2008.

22. Michael R. Czinkota, "From Bowling Alone to Standing Together," *Marketing Management*, April 2002.

23. QVC corporate website, **http://www.qvc.com/qic/qvcapp.aspx/app.html/params.file.|cp|mainhqfact, html/left.html.file.|nav|navhqabout,html/walk.html.|nav|navhqwel,html**, accessed March 8, 2008.

24. William M. Mercer Consulting, **http://www.mercer.com/referencecontent.jhtml?idContent=1128060**; retrieved Feb. 28, 2008.

25. "American Students Studying Abroad at Record Levels: Up 8.5%," Press Release by the Institute for International Education, November 12, 2007; available **http://opendoors.iienetwork.org/?p=113744**; accessed February 18, 2008.

26. The following sites are a good starting point for finding more information: **http://www.iiepassport.org**, **http://www.studyabroad.com**, **http://www.overseasjobs.com**; **http://www.egide.asso.fr**.

GLOSSARY

Abandoned product ranges—The outcome of a firm narrowing its range of products to obtain economies of scale, which provides opportunities for other firms to enter the markets for the abandoned products.

Absolute advantage—A country that is capable of producing a product with fewer labor hours.

Accounting diversity—The range of differences in national accounting practices.

Acculturation—The process of adjusting and adapting to a specific culture other than one's own.

Adaptability screening—A selection procedure that usually involves interviewing both the candidate and his or her family members for an overseas assignment to determine how well they are likely to adapt to another culture.

American Depository Receipts (ADRs)—Receipts to bank account that holds shares of a foreign firm's stock in that firm's country.

American terms—Quoting a currency rate as the U.S. dollar against another country's currency (e.g., U.S. dollars/yen).

Anti-dumping law—Legislation that allows the imposition of tariffs on foreign imports, designed to help domestic industries injured by unfair competition from abroad in cases where imported products are sold at less than fair market value.

Antitrust laws—Laws that prohibit monopolies, restraint of trade, and conspiracies to inhibit competition.

Arbitration—The procedure for settling a dispute in which an objective third party hears both sides and makes a decision; a procedure for resolving conflict in the international business arena through the use of intermediaries such as representatives of chambers of commerce, trade associations, or third country institutions.

Area briefings—Training programs that provide factual preparation prior to an overseas assignment.

Arm's length principle—A basis for intracompany transfer pricing; the price that an unrelated party would have paid for the same transaction.

Attitudes—Evaluation of alternatives based on values.

Autarky—Self-sufficiency: a country that is not participating in international trade.

Backtranslation—The retranslation of text to the original language by a different person from the one who made the first translation. Useful to find translation errors.

Balance of payments (BOP)—A statement of all transactions between one country and the rest of the world during a given period; a record of flows of goods, services, and investments across borders.

Bank draft—A financial withdrawal document drawn against a bank.

Base salary—Salary, not including special payments such as allowances, paid during overseas assignments.

Bearer bond—A bond owned officially by whoever is holding it.

Behavioral controls—Organizational controls that involve influencing how activities are conducted.

Bilateral agreement—Agreement or treaty between two nations focusing only on their interests.

Bill of lading—A contract between an exporter and a carrier indicating that the carrier has accepted responsibility for the goods and will provide transportation in return for payment.

Boycott—An organized effort to refrain from conducting business with a particular seller of goods or services; used in the international arena for political or economic reasons.

Bretton Woods Agreement—An agreement reached in 1944 among finance ministers of 45 Western nations to establish a system of fixed exchange rates.

Buffer stock—Stock of a commodity kept on hand to prevent a shortage in times of unexpectedly great demand; under international commodity and price agreements, the stock controlled by an elected or appointed manager for the purpose of managing the price of the commodity.

Bulk service—Ocean shipping provided on contract, either for individual voyages or for prolonged periods of time.

Capital budget—The financial evaluation of a proposed investment to determine whether the expected returns are sufficient to justify the investment expenses.

Capital flight—The flow of private funds abroad, because investors believe that the return on investment or the safety of capital is not sufficiently ensured in their own countries.

Capital outlays—Upfront costs and expenses of a proposed investment.

Caribbean Basin Initiative (CBI)—This agreement extended trade preferences to Caribbean countries and granted them special access to the markets of the United States.

Cartel—An association of producers of a particular good, consisting either of private firms or of nations, formed for the purpose of suppressing the market forces affecting prices.

Cash pooling—Used by multinational firms to centralize individual units' cash flows, resulting in less spending or foregone interest on unnecessary cash balances.

Centralization—The concentrating of control and strategic decision-making at headquarters.

Change agent— An institution or person who facilitates change in a firm or in a host country.

Channel design—The length and width of the distribution channel.

Code law—Law based on a comprehensive set of written statutes.

Codetermination—A management approach in which employees are represented on supervisory boards to facilitate communication and collaboration between management and labor.

Commercial invoice—A bill for transported goods that describes the merchandise and its total cost and lists the addresses of the shipper and seller and delivery and payment terms.

Commercial Service—A department of the U.S. Department of Commerce that gathers information and assists business executives in business abroad (see **http://www.usatrade.gov**).

Committee on Foreign Investments in the United States (CFIUS)—A federal committee, chaired by the U.S. Treasury, with the responsibility to review major foreign investments to determine whether national security or related concerns are at stake.

Commodity price agreement—An agreement involving both buyers and sellers to manage the price of a particular commodity, but often only when the price moves outside a predetermined range.

Common agricultural policy (CAP)—An integrated system of subsidies and rebates applied to agricultural interests in the European Union.

Common law—Law based on tradition and depending less on written statutes and codes than on precedent and custom—used in the United States.

Common market—a group of countries that agree to remove all barriers to trade among members, to establish a common trade policy with respect to nonmembers, and also to allow mobility for factors of production—labor, capital, and technology.

Comparative advantage—The ability to produce a good or service more cheaply, relative to other goods and services, than is possible in other countries.

Composition of trade—The ratio of primary commodities to manufactured goods and services in a country's trade.

Confiscation—The forceful government seizure of a company without compensation for the assets seized.

Consortium/consortia—A partnership among multiple companies in the same industry, usually with the aim of conducting costly research and development work. The costs—and the results—are shared among participating companies.

Contractual hedging—A multinational firm's use of contracts to minimize its transaction exposure.

Contributor—A national subsidiary with a distinctive competence, such as product development.

Coordinated decentralization—The provision of an overall corporate strategy by headquarters, while granting subsidiaries the freedom to implement their own corporate strategies within established ranges.

Coordinated intervention—A currency-value management method whereby the central banks of the major nations simultaneously intervene in the currency markets, hoping to change a currency's value.

Corporate image advertising—Umbrella marketing communications to make the company as a whole be correctly understood and seen more positively.

Correspondent banks—Banks located in different countries and unrelated by ownership that have a reciprocal agreement to provide services to each other's customers.

Cost and freight (CFR)—Seller quotes a price for the goods, including the cost of transportation to the named port of debarkation. Cost and choice of insurance are left to the buyer.

Cost, insurance, and freight (CIF)—Seller quotes a price including insurance, all transportation, and miscellaneous charges to the point of debarkation from the vessel or aircraft.

Carriage paid to (CPT)—The price quoted by an exporter for shipments not involving waterway transport, not including insurance.

Carriage and insurance paid to (CIP)—The price quoted by an exporter for shipments not involving waterway transport, including insurance.

Delivery duty paid (DDP)—Seller delivers the goods, with import duties paid, including inland transportation from import point to the buyer's premises.

Delivery duty unpaid (DDU)—Only the destination customs duty and taxes are paid by the consignee.

Inventory carrying costs—The expense of maintaining goods in storage.

Cost leadership strategy—A pricing tactic where a company offers an identical product or service at a lower cost than the competition.

Cost-of-living allowance (COLA)—An allowance paid during an assignment overseas to enable the employee to maintain the same standard of living as at home.

Cost-plus method—A pricing policy in which there is a full allocation of foreign and domestic costs to the product.

Creative strategy—Development of the content of a promotional message such as an advertisement, publicity release, sales promotion activity, or Web-based promotion.

Critical commodities list—A U.S. Department of Commerce file containing information about products that are either particularly sensitive to national security or controlled for other purposes.

Cross rates—Exchange rate quotations which do not include the U.S. dollar as one of the two currencies quoted.

Cross-subsidization—The use of resources accumulated in one part of the world to fight a competitive battle in another.

Cultural assimilator—Training program in which trainees for overseas assignments must respond to scenarios of specific situations in a particular country.

Cultural convergence—Increasing similarity among cultures accelerated by technological advances.

Culture shock—Pronounced reactions to the psychological disorientation that most people feel when they move for an extended period of time into a markedly different culture.

Culture—An integrated system of learned behavior patterns that are characteristic of the members of any given society.

Currency flows—The flow of currency from nation to nation, which in turn determines exchange rates.

Current account—An account in the BOP statement that records the results of transactions involving merchandise, services, and unilateral transfers between countries.

Current transfer account—A current account on the balance of payments statement that records gifts from the residents of one country to the residents of another.

Customs union—Collaboration among trading countries in which members dismantle barriers to trade in goods and services and also establish a common trade policy with respect to nonmembers.

Debt-equity structure—A firm's combination of capital obtained by borrowing from others, such as banks (debts), and capital provided by owners (equity).

Decentralization—The granting of a high degree of autonomy to subsidiaries.

Deemed export—Addresses people rather than products where knowledge transfer could lead to a breach of export restrictions.

Delphi Studies—A research tool using a group of participants with expertise in the area of concern to predict and rank major future developments.

Differentiation strategy—Takes advantage of the company's real or perceived uniqueness on elements such as design or after-sales service.

Direct exchange quotation—A foreign exchange quotation that specifies the amount of home country currency needed to purchase one unit of foreign currency.

Direct intervention—The process governments used in the 1970s if they wished to alter the current value of their currency. It was done by simply buying or selling their own currency in the market, using their reserves of other major currencies.

Direct investment account—An account in the BOP statement that records investments with an expected maturity of more than one year and an investor's ownership position of at least 10 percent.

Direct taxes—Taxes applied directly to income.

Diversification—A market expansion policy characterized by growth in a relatively large number of markets or market segments.

Division of Labor—The practice of sub-dividing a production process into stages which then can be performed by labor repeating the process, as on a production line.

Domestic policy—Public policy concerned with national issues but that may have direct or indirect bearing on foreign trade and investment.

Domestication—Government demand for partial transfer of ownership and management responsibility from a foreign company to local entities, with or without compensation.

Double-entry bookkeeping—A method of accounting in which every transaction produces both a debit and a credit of the same amount.

Dual pricing—A price-setting strategy in which the export price differs from the domestic price.

Dual-use item—Good or service that is useful for both military and civilian purposes.

Economic exposure—The potential for long-term effects on a firm's value as the result of changing currency values.

Economic infrastructure—The transportation, energy, and communication systems in a country.

Economic union—A union among trading countries that has the characteristics of a common market and also harmonizes monetary policies, taxation, and government spending and uses a common currency.

Education allowance—Reimbursement by company for dependent educational expenses incurred while a parent is assigned overseas.

Electronic data interchange—The direct transfer of information technology between computers of trading partners.

Embargo—A governmental action, usually prohibiting trade entirely, for a decidedly adversarial or political rather than economic purpose.

Environmental protection—Actions taken by governments to ensure survival of natural resources.

Environmental scanning—Obtaining ongoing data about a country.

Ethnocentrism—The regarding of one's own culture as superior to others'.

Eurobond—A bond that is denominated in a currency other than the currency of the country in which the bond is sold.

Eurocurrency—A bank deposit in a currency other than the currency of the country where the bank is located; not confined to banks in Europe.

Eurodollars—U.S. dollars deposited in banks outside the United States; not confined to banks in Europe.

Euromarkets—Money and capital markets in which transactions are denominated in a currency other than that of the place of the transaction; not confined to Europe.

European terms—Quoting a currency rate as a country's currency against the U.S. dollar (e.g., yen/U.S. dollars).

European Union—The organization created on January 1, 1994, by the 12 member countries of the European community (now 27 members).

Exchange controls—Controls on the movement of capital in and out of a country, sometimes imposed when the country faces a shortage of foreign currency.

Experiential knowledge—Acquisition of cultural competence through personal involvement.

Experimentation—A research method capable of determining the effects of a variable on a situation.

Export complaint systems—Allow customers to contact the original supplier of a product in order to inquire about products, make suggestions, or present complaints.

Export license—A license obtainable from the U.S. Department of Commerce Bureau of Industry and Security, which is responsible for administering the Export Administration Act.

Export management companies (EMCS)—Domestic firms that specialize in performing international business services as commission representatives or as distributors.

Export processing zones—Special areas that provide tax- and duty-free treatment for production facilities whose output is destined abroad.

Export trading company (ETC)—The result of 1982 legislation to improve the export performance of small and medium-sized firms, ETCs allow businesses to band together to export or offer export services. Additionally, the law permits bank participation in trading companies and relaxes antitrust provisions.

Export-control system—A system designed to deny or at least delay the acquisition of strategically important goods to adversaries; in the U.S., based on the Export Administration Act and the Munitions Control Act.

Expropriation—The government takeover of a company with compensation frequently at a level lower than the investment value of the company's assets.

External economies of scale—Lower production costs resulting from the interaction of many firms.

Ex-works (EXW)—Price quotes that apply only at the point of origin; the seller agrees to place the goods at the disposal of the buyer at the specified place on a specified date or within a fixed period.

Factor Intensities/ Factor Proportions—The proportion of capital input to labor input used in the production of a good.

Factor mobility—The ability to freely move factors of production across borders, as among common market countries.

Factor proportions theory—Systematic explanation of the source of comparative advantage.

Factors of production—All inputs into the production process, including capital, labor, land, and technology.

Fast track authority—Increased presidential powers over trade, whereby the U.S. Congress can either approve or disapprove proposed trade agreements, but not amend or change them.

Field experience—Experience acquired in actual rather than laboratory settings; training that exposes a corporate manager to a cultural environment.

Financial account—An account in the BOP statement that records transactions involving borrowing, lending, and investing across borders.

Financial incentives—Monetary offers intended to motivate; special funding designed to attract foreign direct investors that may take the form of land or building, loans, or loan guarantees.

Financial infrastructure—Facilitating financial agencies in a country; for example, banks.

Financing cash flows—The cash flows arising from the firm's funding activities.

Fiscal incentives—Incentives used to attract foreign direct investment that provide specific tax measures to attract the investor.

Fixed exchange rate—The government of a country officially declares that its currency is convertible into a fixed amount of some other currency.

Floating exchange rate—Under this system, the government possesses no responsibility to declare that its currency is convertible into a fixed amount of some other currency; this diminishes the role of official reserves.

Focus group research—A research method in which representatives of a proposed target audience contribute to market research by participating in an unstructured discussion.

Focus strategy—A deliberate concentration on a single industry segment.

Foreign bond—Bonds issued by a foreign corporation or government for sale in a country different from its home country, and denominated in the currency of the country in which it is issued.

Foreign currency exchange rate—The price of any one country's currency in terms of another country's currency.

Foreign direct investment (FDI)—The establishment or expansion of operations of a firm in a foreign country. Like all investments, it assumes a transfer of capital.

Foreign policy—The area of public policy concerned with relationships with other countries.

Foreign service premium—A financial incentive to accept an assignment overseas, usually paid as a percentage of the base salary.

Foreign trade zones—Special areas where foreign goods may be held or processed without incurring duties and taxes.

Fortress Europe—Suspicion raised by trading partners of Western Europe who claim that the integration of the European Union may result in increased restrictions on trade and investment by outsiders.

Forward exchange rates—Contracts that provide for two parties to exchange currencies on a future date at an agreed-upon exchange rate.

Franchising—A form of licensing that allows a distributor or retailer exclusive rights to sell a product or service in a specified area.

Free alongside ship (FAS)—Exporter quotes a price for the goods alongside a vessel at a port. Seller handles cost of unloading and wharfage; loading, ocean transportation, and insurance are left to buyer.

Free carrier (FCA)—Applies only at a designated inland shipping point. Seller is responsible for loading goods into the means of transportation; buyer is responsible for all subsequent expenses.

Free on board (FOB)—FOB is the term used when the ownership/liability of goods passes from the seller to the buyer at the time the goods cross the shipping point to be delivered.

Free Trade Area of the Americas (FTAA)—A hemispheric trade zone covering all of the Americas. Organizers hoped it would have been operational by 2005 but political changes in Latin America have put it on hold.

Free trade area—An area in which all barriers to trade among member countries are removed, although sometimes only for certain goods or services.

General Agreement On Tariffs And Trade (GATT)—An international code of tariffs and trade rules signed by 23 nations in 1947; headquartered in Geneva, Switzerland; 144 members currently; now part of the World Trade Organization.

General Agreement on Trade in Services (GATS)—A legally enforceable pact among GATT participants that covers trade and investments in the services sector.

Global area structure—An organizational structure in which geographic divisions are responsible for all global activity.

Global customer structure—An organizational structure in which divisions are formed on the basis of customer groups.

Global functional structure—An organizational structure in which departments are formed on the basis of functional areas, such as production, marketing, and finance.

Global media—Media vehicles that have target audiences on at least three continents and have a central buying office for placements.

Global product structure—An organizational structure in which product divisions are responsible for all global activity.

Globalization approach—Creation of a regionally or globally similar marketing-mix strategy.

Globalization— Awareness, understanding, and response to global developments and linkages.

Glocalization—A term coined to describe the networked global organization approach to an organizational structure.

Gold standard—A standard for international currencies in which currency values were stated in terms of gold.

Goods trade account—An account of the BOP statement that records funds used for merchandise imports and funds obtained from merchandise exports.

Gray marketing—The marketing of authentic, legally trademarked goods through unauthorized channels.

Gross domestic product (GDP)—Total monetary value of goods produced and services provided by a country over a one-year period.

Hardship allowance—An allowance paid during an assignment to an overseas area that requires major adaptation.

High-context culture—Culture in which behavioral and environmental nuances are an important means of conveying information.

Housing allowance—An allowance paid during an assignment overseas to provide appropriate living quarters.

Implementer—The typical subsidiary role, which involves implementing a strategy that originates with headquarters.

Import Substitution—A policy for economic growth adopted by many developing countries that involves the systematic encouragement of domestic production of goods formerly imported.

Import-Export Trade—The sale and purchase of tangible goods and services to and from another country.

Income account—An account of the BOP statement that records current income associated with investments that were made in previous periods.

Incoterms—International Commerce Terms. Widely accepted terms used in quoting export prices.

Indirect Exchange Quotation—Foreign exchange quotation that specifies the units of foreign currency that could be purchased with one unit of the home currency.

Indirect Taxes—Taxes applied to nonincome items, such as value-added taxes, excise taxes, tariffs, and so on.

Information system—Can provide the decision-maker with basic data for most ongoing decisions.

Input-Output Analysis—A method for estimating market activities and potential that measures the factor inflows into production and the resultant outflow of products.

Intellectual property rights (IPR)—Legal right resulting from industrial, scientific, literary, or artistic activity.

Interbank Interest Rates—The interest rate charged by banks to banks in the major international financial centers.

Intermodal movements—The transfer of freight from one type of transportation to another.

Internal Bank—A multinational firm's financial management tool that actually acts as a bank to coordinate finances among its units.

Internal economies of scale—Lower production costs resulting from greater production within one firm for an enlarged market.

Internal Economies of Scale—When the cost per unit of the product of a single firm continues to fall as the firm's size continues to increase.

Internalization—Occurs when a firm establishes its own multinational operation, keeping information that is at the core of its competitiveness within the firm.

International agent—A representative or intermediary for the firm that works to develop business and sales strategies and that develops contacts.

International bond—A bond issued in domestic capital markets by foreign borrowers (foreign bonds) or issued in the eurocurrency markets in currency different from that of the home currency of the borrower (eurobonds).

International debt load—Total accumulated, negative net investment position of a nation.

International distributor—A representative or intermediary for the firm that purchases products from the firm, takes title, and assumes the selling risk.

International law—The body of rules governing relationships between sovereign states; also certain treaties and agreements respected by a number of countries.

International Monetary Fund (IMF)—A specialized agency of the United Nations established in 1944. An international financial institution for dealing with Balance of Payment problems; the first international monetary authority with at least some degree of power over national authorities (see **http://www.imf.org**).

Intra-Industry Trade—The simultaneous export and import of the same good by a country. It is of interest, due to the traditional theory that a country will either export or import a good, but not do both at the same time.

Intranet—A process that integrates a company's information assets into a single accessible system using Internet-based technologies, such as e-mail, news groups, and the web.

Isolationism—A policy that minimizes the economic integration between nations.

Joint venture—Formal participation of two or more companies in an enterprise to achieve a common goal.

Just-in-time inventory systems—Materials scheduled to arrive precisely when they are needed on a production line; minimizes storage requirements.

Lags—Paying a debt late to take advantage of exchange rates.

Land bridge—Transfer of ocean freight among various modes of land-based transportation.

Law of one price—The theory that the relative prices of any single good between countries, expressed in each country's currency, is representative of the proper or appropriate exchange rate value.

Leads—Paying a debt early to take advantage of exchange rates.

Leontief Paradox—Wassily Leontief's studies indicated that the United States was a laborabundant country, exporting labor-intensive products. This was a paradox because of the general belief that the United States was a capital-abundant country that should be exporting capital-intensive products.

Letter of Credit (L/C)—Undertaking by a bank to make payment to a seller upon completion of a set of agreed-on conditions.

Licensing—A method through which one firm allows another to produce or package its product or use its intellectual property in exchange for compensation.

Lighter aboard ship (LASH) vessel—Barge stored on a ship and lowered at the point of destination to operate on inland waterways.

Liner service—Ocean shipping characterized by regularly scheduled passage on established routes.

Lobbyists—Well-connected individuals or firms that can provide access to policymakers and legislators to communicate new and pertinent information.

Local content regulation—Regulation to gain control over foreign investment by ensuring that a large share of the product is locally produced or a larger share of the profit is retained in the country.

Logistics platform—Vital to a firm's competitive position, it is determined by a location's ease and convenience of market reach under favorable cost circumstances.

Low-context culture—Culture in which most information is conveyed explicitly rather than through behavioral and environmental nuances.

Maastricht Treaty—A treaty, agreed to in Maastricht, the Netherlands, in 1991 but not signed until 1993, in which European community members agreed to a specific timetable and set of necessary conditions to create a single currency for the EU countries.

Macroeconomic Level—Level at which trading relationships affect individual markets.

Management contracts—The firm sells its expertise in running a company while avoiding the risks or benefits of ownership.

Managerial commitment—The desire and drive on the part of management to act on an idea and to support it in the long run.

Maquiladoras—Mexican border factories that make goods and parts or process food for export back to the United States. They benefit from lower labor costs.

Marginal cost method—This method considers the direct costs of producing and selling goods for export as the floor beneath which prices cannot be set.

Market segmentation—Grouping of consumers based on common characteristics such as demographics, lifestyles, and so on.

Market segment—Overlapping ranges of trade targets with common ground and levels of sophistication.

Market-differentiated pricing—A price-setting strategy based on market-specific demand rather than cost.

Marketing infrastructure—Facilitating marketing agencies in a country; for example, market research firms, channel members.

Mass customization—Taking mass-produced product components and combining them in a variety of ways to result in a specific product for a particular customer.

Materials management—The timely movement of raw materials, parts, and supplies into and through the firm.

Matrix structure—An organizational structure that uses functional and divisional structures simultaneously.

Maximization of shareholder value—The ultimate goal of the management of a multinational firm to increase the value of the shareholder's investment as much as possible.

Media strategy—Strategy applied to the selection of media vehicles and the development of a media schedule.

Mercantilism—Political and economic policy in the seventeenth and early eighteenth centuries aimed at increasing a nation's wealth and power by encouraging the export of goods in return for gold.

Microeconomic Level—Level of business concerns that affect an individual firm or industry.

Minority participation—Participation by a group having fewer than the number of votes necessary for control.

Mixed Aid Credits—Credits at rates composed partially of commercial interest rates and partially of highly subsidized developmental aid interest rates.

Mixed structure—An organizational structure that combines two or more organizational dimensions; for example, products, areas, or functions.

Most favored nation (MFN)—A term describing a GATT clause that calls for member countries to grant other member countries the same most favorable treatment they accord any country concerning imports and exports, now also known as *normal trade relations*.

Multidomestic approach—Policy of adapting the marketing mix to suit each country entered.

Multilateral agreement—Trade agreement or treaty among more than two parties; the intricate relationships among trading countries.

Multinational Corporations—Companies that invest in countries around the globe.

National Sovereignty—The supreme right of nations to determine national policies; freedom from external control.

Natural Hedging—The structuring of a firm's operations so that cash flows by currency, inflows against outflows, are matched.

Net errors and omissions account—Makes sure the BOP actually balances.

Net present value (NPV)—The sum of the present values of all cash inflows and outflows from an investment project discounted at the cost of capital.

Netting—Cash flow coordination between a corporation's global units so that only one smaller cash transfer must be made.

Nonfinancial Incentives—Nonmonetary offers designed to attract foreign direct investors that may take the form of guaranteed government purchases, special protection from competition, or improved infrastructure facilities.

Nontariff Barriers—Barriers to trade, other than tariffs. Examples include buy-domestic campaigns, preferential treatment for domestic bidders, and restrictions on market entry of foreign products, such as involved inspection procedures.

Not-invented-here syndrome—A defensive, territorial attitude that, if held by managers, can frustrate effective implementation of global strategies.

Observation research—A research method in which the subject's activity and behavior are watched.

Official reserves account—An account in the BOP statement that shows (1) the change in the amount of funds immediately available to a country for making international payments and (2) the borrowing and lending that has taken place between the monetary authorities of different countries either directly or through the IMF.

Offshore banking—The use of banks or bank branches located in low-tax countries, often Caribbean islands, to raise and hold capital for multinational operations.

Operating cash flows—Cash flows arising from the firm's every-day business activities.

Operating risk—The danger of interference by governments or other groups in one's corporate operations abroad.

Opportunity cost—Cost incurred by a firm as a result of taking one action rather than another.

Order cycle time—The total time that passes between the placement of an order and the receipt of the merchandise.

Output controls—Organizational controls, such as balance sheets, sales data, production data, product-line growth, and performance reviews of personnel.

Ownership risk—The risk inherent in maintaining ownership of property.

Personal interviews—Face-to-face research method, the objective of which is to obtain in-depth information from a knowledgeable individual.

Personal selling—Marketing efforts focusing on one-on-one efforts with customers.

Physical distribution—The movement of finished products from suppliers to customers.

Political risk—The risk of loss by an international corporation of assets, earning power, or managerial control as a result of political actions by the host country.

Political union—A group of countries that have common foreign policy and security policy and that share judicial cooperation.

Population stabilization—An attempt to control rapid increases in a nation's inhabitants.

Portfolio investment account—An account in the BOP statement that records investments in assets with an original maturity of more than one year and where an investor's ownership position is less than 10 percent.

Positioning—The perception by consumers of a firm's product in relation to competitors' products.

Predictability—The degree of likelihood that a shipment will arrive on time and in good condition.

Preferential policies—Government policies that favor certain (usually domestic) firms: for example, the use of national carriers for the transport of government freight, even when more economical alternatives exist.

Price control—Government regulation of the prices of goods and services; control of the prices of imported goods or services as a result of domestic political pressures.

Price escalation—The increase in export prices due to additional marketing costs related specifically to exports.

Primary research—The collection and analysis of data for a specific research purpose through interviews, focus groups, surveys, observation, or experimentation.

Process structure—A variation of the functional structure in which departments are formed on the basis of production processes.

Product cycle theory—A theory that views products as passing through four stages—introduction, growth, maturity, decline—during which the location of production moves from industrialized to lower-cost developing nations.

Product differentiation—The effort to build unique differences or improvements into products.

Production possibilities frontier—A theoretical method of representing the total productive capabilities of a nation used in the formulation of classical and modern trade theory.

Punitive tariff—A tax on an imported good or service intended to punish a trading partner.

Purchasing power parity (PPP)—A theory that the prices of tradable goods will tend to equalize across countries.

Qualitative information—Data that have been analyzed to provide a better understanding, description, or prediction of given situations, behavioral patterns, or underlying dimensions.

Quality of life—The standard of living combined with environmental and cultural factors; it determines the level of well-being of individuals.

Quantitative information—Data amassed in numerical order to search for statistical significance or trends.

Quotas—Legal restrictions on the import quantity of particular goods, imposed by governments as barriers to trade.

Reference group—A group, such as the family, co-workers, and professional and trade associations, that provides the values and attitudes that influence and shape behavior, including consumer behavior.

Re-invoicing—The policy of buying goods from one unit, selling them to a second unit, and reinvoicing the sale to the next unit, to take advantage of favorable exchange rates.

Representative office—An office of an international bank established in a foreign country to serve the bank's customers in the area in an advisory capacity; it does not take deposits or make loans.

Reverse logistics—A system responding to environmental concerns that ensures a firm can retrieve a product from the market for subsequent use, recycling, or disposal.

Roll-on-roll-off (RORO)—Transportation vessels built to accommodate trucks that can drive on in one port and drive off at their destinations.

Royalty—The compensation paid by one firm to another under a licensing agreement.

Sanction—A governmental action, usually consisting of a specific coercive trade measure, which distorts the free flow of trade for an adversarial or political purpose rather than an economic one.

Scenario analysis—The identification of crucial variables and the analysis of the effects of their variations on business conditions.

Sea bridge—The transfer of freight among various modes of ocean freight.

Secondary research—The collection and analysis of data originally collected to serve another purpose rather than the specific objectives of the firm.

Self-reference criterion—The unconscious reference to one's own cultural values.

Selling forward—A market transaction in which the seller promises to sell currency at a certain future date at a prespecified price.

Sensitivity training—Human relations training that focuses on personal and interpersonal interactions; training that focuses on enhancing an expatriate's flexibility in situations quite different from those at home.

Services trade account—An account of the BOP that records the international exchange of personal or professional services, such as financial and banking services, construction, and tourism.

Shipper's order—A negotiable bill of lading that can be bought, sold, or traded while the subject goods are still in transit and that is used for letter of credit transactions.

Single European Act—The legislative basis for the European integration.

Social infrastructure—The housing, health, educational, and other social systems in a country.

Social stratification—The division of a particular population into classes.

Special economic zones—Special tariff-free areas where there are substantial tax incentives and low prices for land and labor to which the government hopes to attract foreign direct investment.

Spot exchange rates—Contracts that provide for two parties to exchange currencies, with delivery in two business days.

Standard of living—The level of material affluence of a group or nation, measured as a composite of quantities and qualities of goods.

Standard worldwide pricing—A price-setting strategy based on average unit costs of fixed, variable, and export-related costs.

Standardization approach—Policy of making minimal or no changes to the marketing mix for the global marketplace.

Storage location decision—A decision concerning the number of facilities to establish and where they should be situated.

Straight bill of lading—A non-negotiable bill of lading usually used in prepaid transactions in which the transported goods involved are delivered to a specific individual or company.

Strategic alliances—A term for collaboration among firms, often similar to joint ventures, but not necessarily involving joint capital investment.

Strategic leader—A highly competent subsidiary located in a strategically critical market.

Supply chain—A complex global network created by a firm to connect its vendors, suppliers, other third parties, and its customers in order to achieve greater cost efficiencies and to enhance competitiveness.

Supply-chain management—Connecting the value-adding activities of a company's supply side with its demand side.

Survey research—A research method involving the use of questionnaires delivered in person, by mail, telephone, or online to obtain statistically valid, quantifiable research information.

Systems concept—A concept of logistics based on the notion that materials-flow activities are so complex that they can be considered only in the context of their interaction.

Tariffs—Taxes on imported goods and services, instituted by governments as a means to raise revenue and as barriers to trade.

Tax policy—A means by which countries may control foreign investors.

Tax-equalization plan—Reimbursement by the company when an employee in an overseas assignment pays taxes at a higher rate than at home.

Technology transfer—The transfer of systematic knowledge for the manufacture of a product, the application of a process, or the rendering of a service.

Terminal cash flows—Salvage value or resale value of the project at its termination.

Total-cost concept—A decision concept that identifies and links expenditures in order to evaluate and optimize logistical activities.

Tracking—The capability of a shipper to determine the location of goods at any point during the shipment.

Trade creation—A benefit of economic integration; the benefit to a particular country when a group of countries trades a product freely among themselves but maintains common barriers to trade with nonmembers.

Trade diversion—A cost of economic integration; the cost to a particular country when a group of countries trades a product freely among themselves but maintains common barriers to trade with nonmembers.

Trade draft—A financial withdrawal document drawn against a company.

Trademark licensing—The licensing of instantly recognizable logos, names, or images for use on unrelated products such as gifts, toys, or clothing.

Trade-off concept—A decision concept that recognizes interactions within the decision system.

Trading bloc—Formed by agreements among countries to establish links through movement of goods, services, capital, and labor across borders.

Trading company—A company, such as the *sogoshosha* of Japan, that acts as an intermediary for multiple companies in such areas as import-export, countertrade, investing, and manufacturing.

Tramp service—Ocean shipping via irregular routes, scheduled only on demand.

Transaction Exposure—The potential for losses or gains when a firm is engaged in a transaction denominated in a foreign currency.

Transfer price—The pricing of products as sold by a firm to its own subsidiaries and affiliates.

Transfer risk—The danger of having one's ability to transfer profits or products in and out of a country inhibited by governmental rules and regulations.

Transit time—The period between departure and arrival of a shipment.

Translation exposure—The potential effect on a firm's financial statements of a change in currency values.

Treaty of Rome—The original agreement that established the foundation for the formation of the European Economic Community.

Triangular arbitrage—The exchange of one currency for a second currency, the second for a third, and the third for the first in order to make a profit.

Trigger mechanisms—Specific acts or stimuli that set off reactions.

Turnkey operation—A specialized form of management contract between a customer and an organization to provide a complete operational system together with the skills needed for unassisted maintenance and operation.

Value-Added Tax (VAT)—A tax on the value added at each stage of the production and distribution process; a tax assessed in most European countries and also common among Latin American countries.

Values—Shared beliefs or group norms internalized by individuals.

Virtual team—A team of people who are based at various locations around the world and communicate through intranet and other electronic means to achieve a common goal.

Voluntary Restraint Agreements—Trade-restraint agreements resulting in self-imposed restrictions that are used to manage or distort trade flows, but do not violate existing international trade rules.

Working capital management—The management of a firm's current assets (cash, accounts receivable, inventories) and current liabilities (accounts payable, short-term debt).

Works councils—Councils that provide labor a say in corporate decision-making through a representative body that may consist entirely of workers, or of a combination of managers and workers.

World Bank—An international financial institution created to facilitate trade (see **http://www.worldbank.org**).

World Trade Organization (WTO)—The institution that supplanted GATT in 1995 to administer international trade and investment accords (see **http://www.wto.org**).

NAME INDEX

SUBJECT INDEX